M

ISBN 2-930066-39-3

© Euroconfidentiel s.a.

B.P. 54 - B-1332 GENVAL

TEL. : (+32 2) 652 02 84 - FAX : (+32 2) 653 01 80

RCN : 64561 - TVA : BE-439 362 785

ACCESS
TO EUROPEAN UNION

law, economics, policies

by Nicholas MOUSSIS

Graduate in law and economics
Doctor of international economic relations (Ph. D.)
Adviser at the European Commission

1997

7th revised edition

YOUR SOURCE OF EU INFORMATION

PRINTING HISTORY :

First published by EDIT-EUR (Euroconfidentiel s.a.) in 1991 under the title "*Access to Europe*, guide to Community Policies"

Second edition in 1992 (same title)

Third edition in 1993 (same title)

Fourth edition in 1994 under the title "*Access to European Union*, institutions and policies"

Fifth edition in 1995 (same title)

Sixth edition in 1996 under the title "*Access to European Union*, law, economics, policies

Seventh edition in 1997 (same title)

Foreword

To aspire to cover all Community policies in a single book is a challenge that would discourage most authors! And yet, Nicholas Moussis' work "Access to European Union", contains, year after year, a compact, clear and precise view of European policies. The responsibilities of the author as European official guarantee the reliability and quality of information in this book, which makes a useful contribution to the effort of making Europe better known to its citizens.

A study by the French Conseil d'Etat at the beginning of the 1990s showed that half of the law currently in force was of European origin, and that this proportion rose to 66% for new standards alone. These figures show the involvement of Europe in the legal and administrative life of Member States.

Since 1952, Community output seems to have expanded constantly, a phenomenon which is usually described - revealingly - as the "construction" of Europe: architects and masons busying themselves around an edifice, while onlookers must wait until it is completed before they can appreciate its quality. All are laying the stones of a cathedral, the design and majesty of which will only be fully appreciated by our successors. Building Europe undeniably takes time. If on the human scale and in the eyes of its most fervent supporters the process appears to be hopelessly slow, in the eyes of the historians it is surprisingly rapid. After all, what is forty years of living amicably together compared with 1 500 years of rivalries and wars on our continent?

Certainly, we cannot immediately break with such a long past. Solidarity among Europeans is not yet fully assured; it is still in the process of being created. This is the secret of the European alchemy initiated by the founding fathers: the "great work" is achieved in stages by a series of advances described in Access to Europe.

An excellent illustration of these advances is provided by simply listing the chapter headings of this book: customs union, common market, regional development, social progress, taxation, competition, environment, industry, research, energy, transports, agriculture, fisheries, audiovisual, culture, consumer policy, citizenship, development aid, common commercial policy, external relations... This list sums up admirably the success of our joint adventure, which, through an accumulation of victories, has finally written one of the finest pages of European history.

On this page of history economic and monetary union will certainly have a prominent place: the euro will make Europe more of a practical reality than it has ever been. In addition, it will bring many benefits to its citizens.

The euro is good for the citizen, business and the international monetary system. It is also one of the necessary components for creating a European framework for reducing unemployment.

1. The euro will make life easier for citizens and reduce costs for enterprises.

At present it is impossible to compare selling prices in the European single market without making complex calculations involving exchange rates, transfer costs and commissions for changing currencies. Tomorrow all prices will be in euros, as will everybody's pay slip. Consumers will gain, since they will find choices easier to make. It will also be easier to take advantage of the positive effects of competition within the European single market.

Citizens will also stop losing money in the form of commission for changing currencies, particularly when they are investing abroad. A recent study shows that if someone were to leave Brussels with 10 000 francs in his pocket to visit the other 14 countries in the Union and changed his money in each country he passed through, he would come back with only 5 000 francs. He would have lost half of his money, without having bought anything!

The euro will also reduce costs to businesses. It will do away with a large part of the fees for transactions, which represents a saving of up to ECU 30 thousand million per year, i.e. half a percentage point of the GDP for Europe, not to mention, the reduction in charges for transactions to provide cover against the risks of exchange rate fluctuations.

But there is also a further major advantage. Take the example of a German firm, with customers in Italy, Spain and Great Britain who pay in their own currency. Between August 1992 and August 1995 the Italian lira fell by 32% against the DM, the Spanish peseta fell by 25% and the pound sterling by 20%. Not only did the firm become less competitive compared with the firms in those three countries, but also its income collapsed in DM terms. The euro will enable all European firms to invoice in the same currency as their costs are expressed. Their efforts to be competitive will be rewarded by increased profits, since these no longer risk being wiped out by simple monetary fluctuations, which of their nature are beyond control.

2. The euro will contribute to greater stability in the international monetary system.

Europe alone produces one third of the world's wealth. It is the biggest commercial power in respect of both goods and services. Although it is an economic giant, it does not even exist in monetary terms, unlike the United States, which produces only 20% of the world's wealth, but whose currency - the dollar - is used for settlements in 40% of international transactions. While for American firms the world is - in a way - a vast domestic market, where exchange rate risks are small, since they can invoice in their own currency, there is a very real danger for European firms which trade in dollars. For example, between 1980 and 1995, i.e. in fifteen years, the value of the dollar doubled in terms of DM, but subsequently it fell by two-thirds. By becoming an international currency, based on strong and healthy economies, the euro will contribute to greater stability in the international monetary system.

3. The euro will contribute to creating a favourable environment for employment.

One out of ten potentially active Europeans is out of work. Unemployment affects 18.5 million people in Europe, i.e. twice the population of a country like Belgium. This figure is horrifying. Of course, the main responsibility for remedying this problem lies with the Member States. However, in opting for monetary union Europe is also laying the foundations for stronger job creation.

– *The euro will make firms more competitive and more profitable, thus enabling them to create more jobs.*

– *The euro will put an end to erratic variations in currencies. The monetary fluctuations which affected European currencies in 1995 resulted overall, in two years, by a drop of two points in growth, and they cost Europe approximately 1.5 million jobs.*

– *Lastly, the euro will release household savings. At present, more than half of this money is used for financing government deficits. Reducing government deficits in Europe would release ECU 60 thousand million per year, which could be more usefully employed in financing investment and supporting consumption. Putting government finances on a healthier footing will also provide Europe and European firms with low interest rates, which would help investment, growth and therefore employment.*

However, the euro must not be seen as an end in itself. It is both a tool to help Europeans to overcome their difficulties and a major step along the path to increasingly close union between the Member States.

Yves-Thibault de Silguy
Member of the European Commission

PREFACE TO THE SEVENTH EDITION

Documentation research for the annual updating of this book was closed at the end of July 1996 and covers the events, problems and achievements which were landmarks in the activities of the Community up to this date. The reference period of this work is consequently the previous academic year, which matches well with the Community year, since the month of August is traditionally the summer recess in the process of European integration, during which the Parliament and the Council stop working and the Commission only deals with current and urgent business.

*During this reference period, the European Union began a deep reflection on its future with the 1996 **Intergovernmental Conference** (IGC), which was prepared by Community institutions and other bodies in 1995 and was opened on 29 March 1996. The discussion on the revision of the Treaty on the EU hardly three years after its entering into force shows the vitality and the dynamism of European construction which, as we see in the **introduction** of this work, is a process without end. The IGC should prepare the Union for subsequent enlargement, which means giving thought to the functioning of the institutions, their composition, their working methods and their decision-making mechanisms. While strengthening the peace and prosperity that European construction guarantees since nearly fifty years, it should also prepare the European Union to take a protagonist's place in the world scene at the beginning of the twenty-first century.*

*However, at the beginning of 1996, the "mad cow" disease (BSE) has shown another side of the **customs union**. As, in normal times, it allows the free movement of goods, in case of an animal or plant disease, it multiplies the risk of contagion in all the union. The crisis, which has led to the collapse of the beef market, has nevertheless shown the utility of the Community phytosanitary and veterinary legislations, of common organs, like the Standing Veterinary Committee of the Union, and of common market support measures, like the cover by the EAGGF of the major part of the cost of destruction of contaminated animals.*

*As was underlined by the Madrid European Council in December 1995, the proper functioning of the **single market** is a fundamental element of a dynamic economy and thus of job creation. Efforts to ensure consolidation of the single market are now centred on the transposal of the Community's directives into national law and on non-legislative activity, such as the trans-European networks, whose development is a key component of the EU's strategy for growth, competitiveness and employment. Significant progress was made in the fields of industrial and intellectual property as well as that of financial services.*

The Madrid European Council unequivocally confirmed that the third stage of **economic and monetary union** *will begin on 1 January 1999 in full compliance with the convergence criteria, timing, protocols and procedures established by the Treaty on the EU. It also adopted the scenario for the single currency, which it called the Euro. It thus decided that phase C of the EMU, which will mark the completion of the process of introducing the single currency to all means of payment, should begin no later than 1 January 2002. What is even more revealing of the determination of the great majority of the Member States to pass to the final phase of the EMU is their effort to consolidate their budgetary position according to the Maastricht criteria, in spite of the social discontent that this effort often generates in the short term.*

In order to satisfy the criterion of curbing public deficits, the less wealthy countries must apply very strict budgetary disciplines, whereas they need, at the same time, to pursue and even increase public investments in order to close the prosperity gap with the other Member States. The **Community regional policy** *helps the less prosperous Member States elude this contradiction. Thus, 1995 show the beginning of the financing of programmes arising from the Community support frameworks and the single programming documents approved the previous year, financing which should contribute to economic and social cohesion.*

Reaffirming the priority status of job creation and **social progress**, *the Madrid European Council welcomed the momentum which had built up under the strategy mapped in Essen, taking the form more especially of Member States' multiannual employment programmes. Education and vocational training, which are vital tools for combating unemployment and boosting competitiveness, underwent an important evolution, notably with the adoption of the Socrates and "Youth for Europe" programmes as well as the implementation of the Leonardo da Vinci programme, which has already been the source of significant progress in vocational training.*

Consolidation and greater account of **environment policy** *in other Community policies and activities, diversification of the instruments used beyond the legislative approach and stronger emphasis on information and awareness-raising among the public were the main points to emerge from the review of the Community's fifth action programme on the environment. The Union also played a decisive role in the international defence of the environment, notably in controls of transfrontier shipments and disposal of hazardous waste, biological diversity and substances that deplete the ozone layer.*

The competitiveness of European industry improved as a result of a more favourable climate but also, above all, under the combined effect of the efforts made, on the one hand, by economic operators on restructuring, investment and productivity and, on the other, by public authorities in creating an environment favouring industrial activity, facilitating structural change and ensuring that the markets operate smoothly. Concerning more particularly **enterprise policy**, *the Commission continued to implement the integrated programme in favour of small and medium enterprises (newly defined) and the craft sector through a series of* *schemes aimed at improving the environment of SMEs and supporting their expansion.*

*The period under consideration saw a new departure in **research** and technological development (R&TD). The main points of the new strategy were the tighter coordination of the European research efforts and a sharper focusing of Community R&TD activities on problems of society. In the pursuit of the latter objective the Commission set up six task forces with the job of making the Union more competitive and producing results of immediate relevance to the citizens.*

*In the **energy** sector, the Commission presented a White Paper in which it proposes the principal lines of action for gradual convergence of the national policies around common objectives, notably the promotion of energy efficiency and the reduction of CO_2 emissions. The Commission also conducted a review of Community energy legislation with a view to simplifying it and removing every provision which could create a barrier to economic competitiveness or job creation.*

*Consolidation of the single market in **transport** continued, notably concerning rail transport and inland waterways. Substantial progress was made as regards the integration and interoperability of the trans-European transport networks, in particular for the trans-European high-speed rail system and for safety improvement in shipping and inland transport. The Commission adopted an action programme laying down the guidelines for a common approach to transport for the period 1995 to 2000.*

*In the sector of **agriculture**, the reform of the common agricultural policy has started bearing fruits: production has been brought under control, internal cereal consumption has increased, public stocks have gone down, the level of farm incomes overall has improved and the use of fertilizers and plant-health products has been reduced. However, the European farm world was shaken in 1996 by the mad cow disease (BSE) in the United Kingdom. Exceptional support measures for the beef market in this country as well as in France, Belgium and the Netherlands have not prevented the collapse of the beef market almost everywhere in Europe, as a result of the fears of the consumers for the effects of contaminated meat on their health.*

*In the **fisheries** sector several important regulations were adopted as part of the implementation of the new instruments of the common fisheries policy establishing the criteria, procedures, management and control measures applicable to the management and regulation of fishing effort. At international level, the Community concluded in the framework of various international organizations agreements for the conservation and management of straddling stocks and for dispute-settlement procedures.*

*The Commission took great trouble to answer questions from the **citizens**, clarify what was at stake and what was to be gained from European integration in terms of everyday life. In application of the principle "Doing less but doing it better", it endeavoured to reduce the number of proposals and improve the transparency of Community law. In the audiovisual sector, a Directive established the Community*

*regulatory framework for advanced television services, including digital televi-
sion; but the Directive on the free provision of audiovisual services became subject
to controversy concerning in particular the broadcasters obligation to reserve a
majority proportion of their transmission time for European works. However, the
new MEDIA programme helps professionals in the audiovisual industry to exploit
the European dimension of the market. In the cultural sector attention was paid
to copyright and related rights in the information society. Concerning citizens in
their role as consumers, the new three-year action plan (1996-1998) reflects the
fact that consumer activity impinges on the daily life of all citizens of the European
Union and endeavours to anticipate the changes generated by technological
developments and the opening up of markets. A new Directive aims at the
development of the information society, while guaranteeing individuals a high
level of protection with regard to the processing of personal data. Finally in the
field of justice and home affairs, major developments concern the adoption of the
Act drawing up the Europol Convention, which establishes a European police, and
of Decisions establishing the right to diplomatic protection, which entitles every
citizen of the Union to protection by the diplomatic or consular authorities of any
Member State in third countries.*

The role of the **European Union in the World** *experienced important developments. Concerning aid to development, the period under consideration saw the
mid-term review of Lomé IV aiming at strengthening the political and institutional facets of the Convention, defining the development of trade as the engine of
ACP-EC cooperation and streamlining implementation of financial and technical
cooperation. In the field of the common commercial policy, major developments
concern the common rules for imports of certain textile products from third
countries, which were adapted to the Agreement on textiles and clothing of the
World Trade Organization, and anti-dumping and anti-subsidy measures in
shipbuilding, which were based on the OECD Shipbuilding Agreement. Most
important new elements, however, concern the external relations of the Union.
Thus, the Madrid European Council adopted a timetable and a preparation
strategy for the next enlargement of the Union to Cyprus, Malta and the associated
countries of Central and Eastern Europe, including the Baltic States. The Union
also strengthened its links with several regions in the world. It consolidated its
relations with the independent States of the former Soviet Union, thanks to
negotiation of a new generation of partnership and cooperation agreements and
the intensification of the political dialogue. It has tightened its links with its
Mediterranean partners, thanks to the new Mediterranean policy which was
inaugurated at the Euro-Mediterranean Conference in Barcelona in November
1995. It has solemnly launched a new Asian strategy, in March 1996, at the
Euro-Asia summit, which brought together the Heads of State or Government of
the European Union, of the seven ASEAN member countries, of China, Japan and
South Korea. Last but not least, the EU strengthened its partnership with Latin
America, thanks to the signing of an interregional framework agreement for
economic and trade cooperation with Mercosur and to the renewal of the San José
dialogue with Central America. On the other hand, the relations between the EU
and the United States have been clouded because of the extra-territoriality of
certain American measures against Cuba, Iran and Libya, taken by the American*

Congress despite the adoption, in December 1995, of a new transatlantic agenda, which aims at organizing the cooperation between the two parties.

The free and easy manner of the United States vis-à-vis the European States and the relatively minor role played by the European Union at the peace process in the Middle East and former Yugoslavia throw into relief the deficit of the Union in the field of common foreign and security policy. Nevertheless, as seen in the **European perspectives***, the European Union, which is already a commercial superpower and which will become a monetary superpower thanks to the single currency, may also become a political superpower. This depends, on the one hand, on the results of the 1996 Intergovernmental Conference and, on the other, on the conclusions that the Member States will draw from that conference on their possibilities of creating a European federation.*

I should like to thank my colleagues at the European Commission who helped me with the research necessary for the preparation of this work. Obviously, I am solely responsible for the opinions expressed and the interpretations made of Community provisions and reference documents, particularly the very numerous documents of the European Commission.

N. M.
Brussels, November 1996.

SUMMARY

CONTENTS

INTRODUCTION

The purpose of this book is to examine a unique experiment in human history: the economic integration of different nations. That experiment now covers almost half a century, which is a very short time in the history of nations, but it allows a prospective view. The experiment is unique by virtue of its objective of establishing the basis for an increasingly closer union between European peoples. It is also unique because of its institutions, which have no equal in other international organizations. Lastly, it is unique on account of its achievements: never in human history have different nations cooperated so closely with one another, implemented so many common policies or, in such a short space of time, harmonized ways of life and economic situations which differed so greatly at the outset.

This book aspires to provide the reader with an overall view and the perspective necessary for understanding the complex organization which the European Union is. Indeed, it is virtually impossible to understand the functioning of a particular mechanism or of a specific body without having a comprehensive view of the organization and some knowledge of its historical development.

This publication aspires to being a practical manual for **any student of European integration**, whether academic student of the economic integration of Europe, jurist interested in Community law, which is ceaselessly growing and modified, economist wishing to acquire the latest information on European economic policies, historian wanting to understand the recent history of the continent or businessman seeking to understand the mechanisms of the large market in which he operates. It is therefore an interdisciplinary, pragmatic approach which is somewhat distinct from the precise lines of each of its constituent disciplines.

More specifically, this book examines the policies led by the European Union in all fields. Some of these policies are regarded as horizontal, as their effects extend to the entire Community economy (regional, competition, etc.). Others are sectoral policies, as they concern certain sectors of economic activity (industry, transport, etc.). Some are "common policies" (agriculture, fisheries, foreign trade), as they take the place of the essential aspects of national policies. Most, however, are "Community policies" which support and supplement national policies. Some Community policies tend, as they develop, to become common policies.

Although the book aspires to cover the activities of the Union in all fields and to follow their development in time, it is of necessity compact. It focuses on the main objectives, means, problems and attainments of each policy. Should the reader require more details in respect of any one area of Community activity, however, he/she is advised to consult the selected bibliography at the end of each chapter and especially the official texts of Community acts, referred to in the footnotes, as published in the **Official Journal of the European Communities (OJ)**. This book is also based on Commission publications, and in particular the monthly **Bulletin of the European Union** and the annual **General report** on the Activities of the European Union.

European integration

The beauty of the European edifice which has been under construction since the middle of the twentieth century lies in its originality and simplicity. The method of construction chosen, namely **the voluntary integration of different nations**, had never before been tested in human history. And yet it is most simple. It involves, by means of instruments voluntarily adopted by all, the gradual creation of imperceptible, but innumerable, links between the nations taking part in the experiment. Simple and flexible as it is, inasmuch as it can adjust its tempo to the peaks and troughs of the international economic situation, economic integration can nevertheless come about only between willing and democratically governed nations. For that reason, all attempts at integrating different nations by authoritarian methods have already failed in the past and are doomed to failure in the future. That is why European integration could only be achieved between nations free of all tyranny.

The simplicity of the method of construction ensures **the solidity of the Community edifice**. The links already created between the nations taking part in its construction are so solid that they cannot now be loosened. They can only be broken, but at enormous cost to the nation concerned, which would yet again be isolated. The Community edifice cannot, therefore, but grow larger in the future; wider through the accession of such other European countries as will accept its constraints, and taller by virtue of the construction of new storeys which are more advanced stages of integration.

Simplicity and originality also characterize the architectural plans for construction, as represented by the Community Treaties, and the building materials, as represented by the secondary legislation under the Treaties. Naturally, in common with all Man's works, European integration experiences day-to-day problems, consisting in particular of the difficulty of taking decisions in as large and diversified a family as the Union of Fifteen and of the difficulty of financing the operation. We shall examine these various problems in this section of the chapter, with the second section being given over to the players, the builders of the European edifice.

Method of integration

To get an idea of the post war period, the young people of today who have not experienced the Europe of hatred, the Europe at war, the Europe in ruins, should imagine a village devastated by a fratricidal war, with the houses more or less razed, with wild men trying to fill the breaches, barricading doors and windows to save their belongings from their enemy brothers. They open those doors only to let in goods they need in exchange for some surplus goods they produce. They watch each other from the windows and on occasion talk to each other, but without venturing forth to visit their neighbours for fear that they will squabble again and renew the hostilities. They produce some goods, to the best of their ability, in their narrow houses and handkerchief gardens. They are all wretched, because they believe that their neighbours have more goods, and of better quality, than they, which they cannot purchase. They therefore live in envy and fear of one another.

Ultimately, a wise man from the village comes out on to his balcony, calls for the others' attention, and makes a very simple speech to them. Instead of continuing to live in misery and anguish like this, instead of preparing for a war, instead of barricading themselves in their ruined houses, the wise man invites them to build a large communal house in which to live in peace, work together and trade their products at will. By saving their energies in this way, by giving each other a helping hand and by placing all their tools and know-how at the disposal of all, they will become prosperous, strong and, above all, friends.

Some tell him that it's too good to be true. Yes, he says, but there is a snag in all that, a sine qua non, namely that the bricks for the communal house must come from their own houses. Each brick they place in the new building, while slightly increasing their rights in respect of it, will enlarge the breach in their little ancestral home and will somewhat restrain their ownership of (that is to say **sovereignty** over) the latter. The quicker they resolve to give bricks for the new building, the sooner it will be completed to house them, whereas henceforth their houses will be open to visits and trade. Some call the wise man a fool and continue to barricade themselves in their houses. Others hesitate, saying that they first want to see the new building before they can believe that it can accommodate them as well. Others suggest an alternative which, without necessitating a new building and therefore the transfer of bricks from their beloved properties, will enable them to open their doors and trade their wares. Very few are those who believe the wise man's words straight away, countersign his architectural plan on the spot and immediately begin bringing their bricks to build the communal house.

The method of construction of the European edifice is as simple as the method of constructing a building. The common laws (regulations, directives,...) are superimposed on and strengthen one another as a result of the common action of the builders (European institutions). They thus form floors (stages of the European integration) and compartments on each floor (common policies). The individual homes of the partners are modified in line with the progress of the common building. One day they will all be unified under the same roof of the European edifice.

The common project is quite sound. In fact, just as it is difficult to remove a brick from the respective national houses to provide it for the construction of Europe, so is it also difficult to withdraw a brick from the latter once it has become a regulation or decision immediately applicable in the law of the Member States or a directive obliging States to adjust their national laws in order to attain the objectives towards which it is directed[1]. Those bricks which have been transferred, sometimes so laboriously, from the national houses to the communal house are quickly forgotten once they have been cemented on to the latter. They can scarcely be seen, just as it is difficult to make out from a distance a brick which is part of a large building. And yet these bricks, which we are spotlighting one by one in the chapters of this book, fashion Community and national policies which govern the Member States' economic activity and influence the day-to-day lives and occupations of the citizens of those States; hence the importance of being able to distinguish them and to know the function each one has to perform in the construction of Europe.

The countries which decided to join forces to build the communal house of the European Community and those which joined the venture at a later date have acknowledged that they had sufficient common interests to join up and entrust the management of these to common institutions. As said by Jean Monnet, adviser to the "wise man" Robert Schuman, union between individuals or communities is not natural; it can only be the result of an intellectual process... having as a starting point the observation of the need for change. Its driving force must be common interests between individuals or communities.

Integration stages

Europe is constructed brick by brick and storey by storey. The storeys are the stages of economic integration. Once completed, they are clearly distinguishable, but it is possible that, in the course of the building, part of the higher storey may be under construction while the lower storey is not yet finished. This is done because certain objectives of the previous stage can be attained only if the objectives of a more advanced integration stage are pursued at the same time. This sometimes gives a degree of imbalance to the Community edifice, but induces the protagonists to accelerate the tempo of construction in order to finish those parts of the building that they had initially left incomplete owing to the difficulties encountered or, on occasion, to lesser interest in view of structural or economic priorities.

---

1   On the basis of the case law of the Court of Justice, a transfer of competence in favour of the Community is total and definitive. See, for instance, the judgment of 5 May 1981, Commission v United Kingdom, ECR 1981, p. 1073.

At the outset, especially in a post-war period like that of the '50s, States erect high protection barriers against foreign trade and therefore against international competition. These may be customs barriers (tariffs, quotas and measures having equivalent effect), fiscal barriers (higher levels of taxation for goods largely manufactured outside the country), administrative barriers (complicated bureaucratic procedures for imports) or other, more subtle, barriers serving, nonetheless, in one way or another, to discourage or even prohibit imports.

Totalitarian regimes apart, such a protectionist system cannot last for long. It leads to great dissatisfaction on the part of consumers, whose choice is very restricted, and on the part of the most dynamic and least protected economic operators, who find their field of activity limited by the barriers. Both parties urge their government to reduce external protection. The latter can do so in two, not mutually exclusive ways: either within a framework of bilateral or multilateral cooperation, an imperfect solution from the economic point of view, but preferred by the United Kingdom, because it does not necessitate loss of national sovereignty; or in the framework of economic integration, a radical solution, preferred notably by France, implying the transfer of national sovereignty to common institutions.

In an international organization for **cooperation** such as the Organization for Economic Cooperation and Development (OECD) or the Council of Europe, the Member States undertake to cooperate with their partners in certain areas which are defined in advance, without in any way giving up their national sovereignty. On the other hand, in an organization for **economic integration** such as the ECSC or the EEC the Member States state their willingness to waive part of their national sovereignty to a supranational community or, in other words, to a common sovereignty.

A model of intergovernmental cooperation is the creation of a **free trade area**. In such an area, member countries abolish import duties and other customs barriers to the free movement of products manufactured in the territory of their partners. However, each country retains its own external tariff and its customs policy vis-à-vis third countries. It also retains entirely its national sovereignty.

By contrast, in a **customs union**, which is the first stage of economic integration, free movement concerns not only products manufactured in the territory of their partners, but all products, irrespective of origin, situated in the territory of the member countries. Furthermore, the latter lose their customs autonomy and apply a common external customs tariff to third countries. In order to manage the common customs tariff, the members of a customs union must have a common commercial policy. There is therefore, already at this stage, an important surrender of national sovereignty.

At the end of the subsequent stage, that of the **common market**, all goods and services can be offered on the same conditions as on an internal market, by virtue on the one hand of the pre-existent customs union and on the other of the gradual approximation of national economic policies. In addition to the free movement of goods, during this stage steps must be taken to ensure the free movement of employed persons, freedom of establishment of undertakings and self-employed persons, freedom to provide services and the free movement of capital. Moreover, in order that the large internal market may function efficiently, either common (agriculture, fisheries...) or Community (taxation, competition...) support policies - and, therefore, further surrender of national sovereignty - are necessary.

Even such an advanced stage of economic integration does not, however, entirely resemble a genuine single market, as currency fluctuations and the exchange risk can create further barriers to trade, and restrict the interpenetration of the financial markets and the establishment of undertakings in places where the production factors appear to be most propitious for their activities. One is therefore obliged, if the optimal conditions for production are to be created in a common market, to progress to the next stage of economic integration, viz. **economic and monetary union**. This implies a common monetary policy directed towards the creation of a common currency and the close coordination of economic policies with a view to achieving convergence and thereby leading to the approximation of the short-term, structural economic conditions of the countries and regions party to the union.

Before that integration stage is even wholly completed the Member States will have developed so many economic and political links between themselves that they will feel the need to approximate their non-economic policies as well: internal and judicial affairs policy, in order to protect efficiently their external borders against smugglers as well as arms and drugs traffickers; and foreign policy, so that the economic giant they have created has a voice commensurate with its size in the international organization of nations. One would thus have reached the stage of **political integration**, which can develop further towards an ever-closer cultural and social integration of peoples formerly divided by frontiers. In fact, European integration is an on-going process.

Birth and growth of the Community

In his historic declaration of 9 May 1950, **Robert Schuman**, Minister for Foreign Affairs of France, stated that "Europe will not be made all at once, or according to a single plan. It will be built through concrete achievements which first create a **de facto solidarity**." Schuman thus opted for the functional method of European integration rather than for the constitutional method, which would be based on the constitution of a federation. That meant that the European States, which had just regained their national sovereignty following the Second World War, did not need to give it up immediately and in its entirety for the benefit of a federal European State. They merely needed to renounce the dogma of the indivisibility of sovereignty and therefore certain parts of sovereignty in certain clearly defined areas. In return they would gain the right of inspection of those affairs of their partners which were placed under common management and would to that extent enlarge their own sovereignty. It was therefore a question of progressively reducing the existing contradiction between European integration and national independence.

In his declaration of 1950, Robert Schuman proposed the creation of a common market in two important economic sectors which had until then been used for military purposes, namely the coal and steel sectors: it would be a matter of integrating Germany economically and politically into a European Coal and Steel Community with France and other willing countries. He advocated some transfer of sovereignty to an independent High Authority which would exercise the powers previously held by the States in those sectors and the decisions of which would bind those States. That was to say that the cooperation of the Member States in those sectors should be completely different from that already existing within the traditional international organizations.

In addition to the Coal and Steel Community, Robert Schuman envisaged the creation of a common market for all products, on a scale comparable to that of the United States, in which the conditions would be fulfilled for rapid and regular economic expansion through economies of scale, better division of labour and the improved use of new production techniques. Even beyond economic integration, he envisaged political integration, by means of the merging of the essential economic interests of the European countries, through the creation in stages of a "European Federation". But that was to be achieved gradually through concrete achievements or, to use the building image, by means of brick upon brick to make up the Community edifice.

Although the appeal from the French Minister for Foreign Affairs was addressed to all European countries, only five - Germany, Italy, Belgium, the Netherlands and Luxembourg - gave a favourable reply. Therefore, only six States signed the Treaty establishing the **European Coal and Steel Community (ECSC)** in Paris on 18 April 1951. The "little Europe of Six" began its construction from 25 July 1952, date of entry into force of the ECSC Treaty. The United Kingdom, on the other hand, wanted a European free trade area to be set up which did not involve any waiving of national sovereignty. Customs duties would, of course, be abolished between member countries, but the latter would remain autonomous with regard to commercial policy vis-à-vis third countries. Denmark, Norway, Iceland, Austria, Portugal and Switzerland supported that argument.

The Six of the ECSC were, however, won over by enthusiasm for their adventure, for which there was no historical precedent. On 24 October 1950 the French Minister for Defence, Mr. Pleven, made a declaration to the National Assembly similar to that by R. Schuman. Against a backcloth of the Korean War and worsening tension between East and West, he proposed, as a solution to the problem of German rearmament, the creation of a European army answerable to the political institutions of the united Europe. How many Europeans still remember that surprising proposal was immediately accepted by the Governments of the Six and led to the signing in Paris of the Treaty establishing the **European Defense Community**? That undertaking was somewhat at variance with R. Schuman's idea of progressing little by little, as defence, like foreign policy, was logically amongst the last aspects of the construction of Europe.

What would have become of that Community if the French National Assembly had not refused, on 31 August 1954, to ratify the Treaty establishing it on the grounds that it regarded the abandonment of a national army as a serious infringement of French sovereignty? Probably that Community, along with the **European Political Community**, the draft of which was adopted on 10 March 1953 by the ad hoc Assembly set up by the ECSC Member States, would have proved to be premature as long as the de facto solidarity which Robert

Schuman and his adviser Jean Monnet considered necessary for the advent of European political union was missing.

On the other hand, the functioning of the common market in coal and steel showed that economic integration was possible and worthwhile and that it should extend to all products. Thus, the Ministers for Foreign Affairs of the Six, meeting in Messina from 1 to 3 June 1955, discussed the possibility of creating a common market embracing all products and a separate Community for nuclear energy. They instructed a committee of experts, chaired by the Belgian Minister for Foreign Affairs, Paul-Henri Spaak, to prepare a report on the matter. The committee presented its report on 21 April 1956, and its conclusions were approved by the Intergovernmental Conference in Venice on 29 May 1956. The Ministers for Foreign Affairs then decided to initiate negotiations between the six countries with a view to creating a **European Economic Community (EEC)** and a **European Atomic Energy Community (EAEC)**. Only ten months later, the 25 March 1957, a record time considering the subject-matter, the Six were able to sign, on the Capitol hill in Rome, the Treaties establishing the two new Communities.

Fresh British attempts at creating a vast European free trade area between the European Economic Community and the other Member States of the OECD failed during the autumn of 1958 owing to intractable differences of opinion between France and the United Kingdom. The riposte came in 1959 with the creation of the "little" **European Free Trade Association (EFTA)**, to which the United Kingdom, Norway, Sweden, Denmark, Austria, Portugal, Iceland and Switzerland acceded, with Finland being associated with it at a later date.

Having been impressed, however, by the early successes of the European Community, it was not long before the British Government was meditating on its refusal to play an active part in the work of European unification. It was aware that the United Kingdom could not maintain its political influence if it played a preponderant role only in the Commonwealth. Nor could EFTA, the objectives of which were economic - as opposed to the European Community, which also had political aims - allow it to impose its influence. So in August 1961 the United Kingdom submitted an initial official application to become a full member of the European Community. That example was followed by two other EFTA member countries, namely Denmark and Norway, and also by Ireland.

Accession of those countries initially met with the opposition of the President of the French Republic, General de Gaulle, who, being extremely mistrustful of the United Kingdom's application for accession, declared, right in the middle of the negotiations in 1963, that he wished to discontinue them. The second British application for accession, in 1967, with which Ireland, Denmark and Norway were yet again associated, was not examined for much time owing to France's misgivings. The issue of the accession of those countries could not be resolved until, following General de Gaulle's resignation in April 1969, the Conference of Heads of State and of Government held that same year in the Hague. After laborious negotiations, the Treaties of Accession were finally signed on 22 January 1972. The **accession of the United Kingdom, Ireland and Denmark** took effect from 1 January 1973, following favourable referenda (Ireland and Denmark) and ratification by the national parliaments. Only Norway's accession was prevented, after 53.49% of the Norwegian population opposed accession to the European Community in a referendum.

During the accession negotiations with the United Kingdom, Ireland, Denmark and Norway, one question had arisen: what would become of the other EFTA member countries (Sweden, Switzerland, Austria, Portugal, Finland and Iceland), some of which did not wish to join the European Community on the grounds of neutrality and one of which, Portugal, could not be accepted for accession as it was a dictatorship? A solution was ultimately found, in July 1972, with the conclusion of Free Trade Agreements between the European Community and the various EFTA member countries. Following its aborted accession, Norway was also incorporated into the free trade area thus created.

Once democracy was restored in Greece, Portugal and Spain, those countries submitted applications for accession to the European Community, in 1975 in Greece's case and in 1977 in the other two cases. **Greece** acceded to the Community on 1 January 1981, and **Spain and Portugal** on 1 January 1986.

With the signature of the Single European Act, in June 1987, the Twelve decided to complete their internal market on 31 December 1992. One year before that date, in December 1991, they decided in Maastricht to superpose on the single market an economic and monetary union, a judicial and internal affairs policy and a common foreign and security policy, thus transforming the European Community into a **European Union**.

Since the 1st January 1995, the Europe of Twelve became the Europe of Fifteen, with the **accession of Austria, Finland and Sweden**, the people of Norway having again voted against membership of the Union by a majority of 52.8%.

The case of withdrawal of a Community Member State has never occurred and is difficult to imagine. However, even though it is not specifically provided for in the Treaty, it is certainly possible, under conditions to be negotiated between the outgoing State and the others. The example of Greenland, although partial and special, bears witness to that. Greenland had been integrated into the EC in 1973 by virtue of its links with Denmark. The small population of Greenland was, however, most distrustful in particular of the Community's fisheries policy, as fishing was the island's main economic activity. Having voted by a small majority in a referendum to withdraw from the Community, the Danish Government and the EC agreed, in February 1984, to allow Greenland to leave the Community as from 1 February 1985 and to grant it the status of overseas territory associated with the EC. A similar solution could be found, if a Member State of the European Union decided to withdraw from it. It could, for example, find itself in the **European Economic Space**, which brings together, since the 1 January 1994, the Member States of the European Union with the Member States of the EFTA, minus Switzerland.

In the next three chapters we shall see the result of the events which enabled the Community, on the basis of customs union, to build a common market brick by brick and to draw up plans for its economic and monetary union. The European construction can, and one day certainly will, accommodate other European countries, notably those of Central and Eastern Europe, which were separated from it until the end of the '80s by an impassable wall, but which, following the demolition of the latter, see it as a strong, functional refuge. The European Union has already declared its intention to welcome these countries, as well as Cyprus and Malta; but, before it can do so, it must solve its institutional problems, which become more and more acute after each new enlargement. This issue will be expanded upon at the end of this book. It has to be emphasized here that any State wishing to accede to the Community has to be prepared to adopt, and be capable of adopting, during a given transition period, all the Community law which constitutes the various policies examined in this work. It must also be aware that those policies, through the bonds of solidarity which they create, weave much closer links between Member States than the European Treaties which are briefly examined in the following section.

The European Treaties

We shall not linger over the basic Treaties of the Communities, as we shall examine their objectives and main clauses in the later chapters, in particular in the section devoted to the legal framework for each Community policy. Here, we shall simply review those basic Treaties and the Treaties which have been adopted to revise some of their provisions and to lay the foundations of the subsequent stages of the European construction.

As we saw above, the first European Treaty, the one establishing the **European Coal and Steel Community (ECSC)**, was signed in Paris on 18 April 1951 and entered into force on 25 July 1952. Its main objective was to eliminate the various barriers to trade and to create a common market in which coal and steel products from the Member States could move freely in order to meet the needs of all Community inhabitants, without discrimination on grounds of nationality. Capital and workers in both sectors should also circulate freely. In order that all this could be achieved, the Treaty laid down certain rules on investment and financial aid, on production and prices, agreements and concentrations and on transport and Community institutions, including a High Authority and a special Council (of Ministers), the decisions of which would be binding on all Member States. Ambitious despite its restricted scope, the ECSC Treaty introduced a European Assembly and a European Court of Justice. The two sectors covered by the ECSC Treaty, namely coal and steel, are dealt with respectively in the chapter on energy and that on industry. When the ECSC Treaty expires in the year 2002, the specific rules covering these two sectors will gradually be incorporated into the EEC Treaty.

The Treaty establishing the **European Atomic Energy Community (EAEC,** but more commonly known as **Euratom)** was signed in Rome on 25 March 1957 and came into force on 1 January 1958. Its aim was to create a common market for nuclear materials and equipment, establish common nuclear legislation, introduce a common system for supplies of fissile materials, introduce a system for supervising the peaceful use of nuclear energy and common standards for safety and for health and safety protection of the population and workers against ionizing radiation. The key element in this Treaty was, however, a joint research programme, implemented in a Joint Research Centre, which was to make technology progress and stimulate nuclear production in Europe. Although it was very much in the limelight at the time of its establishment, Euratom has experienced many ups and downs as a result both of disillusionment as regards the economic prospects for nuclear energy and of the ambition of some Member States first to develop their own nuclear industry, and not purely for civil purposes. We shall discuss those problems in the chapters on research and on energy.

Signed at the same time as the Euratom Treaty on the Capitol hill in Rome on 25 March 1957, the Treaty establishing the **European Economic Community (EEC)** was likewise brought into force on 1 January 1958. Although the "Treaties of Rome" (EEC and EAEC) are sometimes referred to, the "Treaty of Rome" is obviously the EEC Treaty. By virtue of its nature and scope, that Treaty dominated the other European Treaties (until such time as it was itself capped by the Maastricht Treaty). Whilst the first two are specific, detailed and rigid "law treaties", the EEC Treaty is a "framework treaty". Apart from its "automatic" provisions relating to the attainment of customs union, it confines itself to setting out certain objectives and to giving pointers as to the general guidelines for policies to be pursued in some areas of economic activity. For the rest, it affords the Community institutions the possibility, gradually to introduce, with the unanimous agreement of the Member States, common or Community policies which they deem essential in order to attain the general objectives set forth in its preamble and in Articles 2 and 3.

The essential task which the Treaty of Rome assigns to the Community institutions is the creation of a common market between the Member States. That involves: (a) the achievement of a customs union entailing, on the one hand, the abolition of customs duties, import quotas and other barriers to trade between Member States and, on the other hand, the introduction of a Common Customs Tariff (CCT) vis-à-vis third countries[1], and (b) the implementation, inter alia through the harmonization of national policies, of four basic freedoms: freedom of movement of goods, of course, but also freedom of movement of workers, freedom of establishment and freedom to provide services and, finally, freedom of capital movements[2].

Although in the preamble to the Treaty the Member States declared that they were determined to lay the foundations of an ever closer union among the peoples of Europe, the Treaty itself constituted the charter for a common market. That fact is worth emphasizing, because, in order to understand clearly the difficulties in developing, and the scope of, the various Community policies which are analyzed in this book, it must be borne in mind that the EEC Treaty was conceived so as to govern only relations between Member States up to the common market stage. However, through its Article 235, it gave Member States the possibility to act in the fields not provided by it by taking unanimously the appropriate measures to attain one of its objectives. This has allowed the Member States to implement a large number of Community policies without amending the Treaty.

The Treaties of Paris and Rome each set up different executive organs. The latter were merged by the Treaty of 8 April 1965 establishing a single Council and a single Commission of the European Communities. Since 1 July 1967 there has therefore been only a single Council of Ministers and a single Commission, with the latter inheriting the powers of the ECSC High Authority, of the EEC Commission and of the Euratom Commission. At the time, the merger of the institutions was regarded as the first stage in the merger of the three European Communities into a single **"European Community"**. This has not been done, but the Treaty on European Union gave this name to the revised European Economic Community (Art. G.).

The Treaties establishing the Communities were amended to some extent, notably as regards their provisions relating to the functioning of the institutions, by the Treaty concerning the Accession to the European Economic Community of Denmark, Ireland, the United Kingdom and Norway. That Treaty was signed in Brussels on 22 January 1972 and brought into force on 1 January 1973, but only for three countries, as a referendum in Norway had ruled out that country's accession.

In parallel with the creation of the Community's own resources by the Decision of 21 April 1970, the Member States agreed to amend the Treaties in order to increase the European Parliament's budgetary powers. In fact, a first Budget Treaty was signed on 22 April 1970 and entered into force on 1 January 1971, but the European Parliament felt that it did not increase its powers sufficiently. The Commission decided that the Parliament was right and put forward proposals for a further extension of the Parliament's budgetary powers. The second **Budget Treaty** was the result. That Treaty, amending Certain Financial Provisions of the Treaties establishing the European Communities and of the Treaty establishing a Single Council and a Single Commission of the European Communities, was signed on 22 July 1975 and entered into force on 1 June 1977. In addition to the creation of a new institution, the Court of Auditors, it conferred on the Parliament the exclusive right to give a discharge to the Commission in respect of the implementation of the budget and, "if there are important reasons", to reject the budget as a whole.

The Treaties establishing the Communities were once again amended as to their institutional clauses, by the Treaty concerning the Accession of the Hellenic Republic to the

---

1   See the chapter on customs union.
2   See the chapter on the common market.

European Economic Community and to the European Atomic Energy Community, signed in Athens on 28 May 1979. By that Treaty the "Nine" became "Ten" from 1 January 1981. They became "Twelve" as from 1 January 1986 by virtue of the Acts of Accession of Spain and Portugal, signed in Madrid and Lisbon respectively on 12 June 1985.

An important amendment of the Treaties establishing the European Communities took place on 1 July 1987 with the entry into force of **the Single European Act**[1]. Supplementing in particular the EEC Treaty, the Single Act committed the Community to adopt measures with the aim of progressively establishing the internal market over a period expiring on 31 December 1992. At the same time it consecrated the European Council, European cooperation on foreign policy and social and economic cohesion between Member States. Lastly, it confirmed the Community's competence in numerous fields: social, environmental, research and technology.

But it is the **Treaty on European Union**, signed in Maastricht on 7 February 1992, that marks a new stage in the process of creating an ever closer union among the peoples of Europe. The Union is founded on the European Communities and supplemented by new policies and forms of cooperation. The essentially economic character of the Communities is surpassed, in order to allow the establishment of an entity with global character. According to Article B of the Treaty, the Union sets itself the following objectives:

— to promote economic and social progress which is balanced and sustainable, in particular through the creation of an area without internal frontiers, through the strengthening of economic and social cohesion and through the establishment of economic and monetary union, including ultimately a single currency;
— to assert its identity on the international scene, in particular through the implementation of a common foreign and security policy including the eventual framing of a common defence policy, which might in time lead to a common defence;
— to strengthen the protection of the rights and interests of the nationals of its Member States through the introduction of a citizenship of the Union;
— to develop close cooperation on justice and home affairs;
— to maintain in full the "acquis communautaire" and build on it with the aim of ensuring the effectiveness of the mechanisms and the institutions of the Community.

The Maastricht Treaty covers, encompasses and modifies the previous Treaties. The Clauses modifying the Treaty on the European Economic Community (now called the European Community) are gathered under article G, those concerning the Treaty on the European Coal and Steel Community make up article H and those relating the European Atomic Energy Community form article I. In fact, the new Treaty separates the European construction into three pillars or edifices, distinguished mainly on the basis of the decision-making process: the main pillar or edifice, which is the European Community; the pillar or edifice of justice and home affairs; and the pillar or edifice of the common foreign and security policy

---

1   OJ L169, 29.06.1987.

(CFSP)[1]. Even within the main edifice - the European Community - the TEU has brought about profound changes, since it has renovated certain Community policies and has instituted several others. The renovated policies concern professional training, economic and social cohesion, research and technological development and environment protection. The new fields of Community action cover education and youth, culture, public health, consumer protection, transeuropean networks, industry and development cooperation.

The European Union was enlarged to fifteen Member States, on 1st January 1995, by way of the Treaties of Accession of Austria, Sweden and Finland, signed on 24 June 1994 at the European Council meeting in Corfu[2]. The Accession Treaty of Norway had also been signed at that occasion, but, again, the Norwegian people voted against membership of the Union by a majority of 52.8%.

One characteristic common to the Treaties establishing the European Communities is that they are not conventional international treaties which create rights and obligations for the States alone. These Treaties and the **legislation derived from them** engender rights and obligations not only for the Member States but also for their nationals. This "**direct effect**" of Community law means notably that any person may ask his judge to apply the Community law which contradicts the national law[3]. Citizens may thus invoke Community law before national courts and, if necessary, before the Court of Justice of the European Communities.

Since the citizens have rights and obligations deriving from the European Treaties, they can rightly claim the transparency of these texts. However, one of the most frequent criticisms regarding the text of the Treaty on European Union is its apparent lack of clarity and the technocratic obscurity which engulfs it. It is true that Maastricht did not have the courage to return the texts of the Treaties of Paris and Rome back on the drawing boards, probably through fear of getting totally bogged down. On the other hand, considerable changes have been made to the Treaties, although the old article numbering has been retained and ambiguities remain on some provisions. As a consequence, the Union's basic Treaties are very difficult to read and understand, which is hardly likely to mobilize public opinion in their favour. The Intergovernmental Conference of 1996, requested by the TEU itself, must try to redress this situation.

European Community and European Union

One often hears nowadays about the three "pillars" of the European Union, the first being the European Community (EU), the second the common foreign and security policy (CFSP) and the third justice and home affairs (JHA). We should say, however, that the image of the EU as three pillars minimizes the place of the Community, which is preponderant, since it contains all common and Community policies instituted in the framework of the three original Treaties and all the legislation adopted on their bases since 1952.

The European Union is better visualized **as an on-going construction.** In this image, the European Community constitutes the main edifice, solid and functional, which, nevertheless, is still in a state of horizontal and vertical construction. Next to it, the CFSP and the JHA are still plans drafted under the Treaty on the European Union. Their edifices need to be patiently built with political and legal measures.

---

1   While the Community policies and procedures constitute the bulk of this book, the new policies and procedures are examined in its final two chapters.

2   OJ L1, 01.01.1995.

3   Judgment of 5 February 1962, case 26/62, Van Gend & Loos, ECR 1963, p.1.

A closer look at the metaphorical image of the European construction shows that the main edifice, that of the Community, is divided horizontally by floors. The floor of the common market is built on the foundations of the customs union. This contains, apart from the four fundamental freedoms (free movement of goods, persons, services and capital), numerous horizontal and vertical compartments, which contain the accompanying policies that constitute the bulk of this book. The compartments of coal, steel and nuclear energy, covered by the ECSC and Euratom Treaties, are also found on these first floors of the Community edifice.

The floor of economic and monetary union is now being built on the floor of the common market and, therefore, on the Community edifice. Certain tools and materials were already there, thanks to the European Monetary System and to the free movement of capital, but the Treaty on European Union has drawn the architectural plans and the "memorandum of understanding" that the builders (European institutions and Member States) need to respect in order to succeed in the construction. If certain builders (Member States) advance faster than the others, they might find themselves alone on the "penthouse" of the Community edifice, which will shelter the single currency. The others will continue to work inside the lower floors, until the time that they are ready to join the leaders in the penthouse of the communal edifice.

Apart from the main edifice, which is itself, as we see, under construction, building also started, as of November 1, 1993, on the edifices of the CFSP and the JHA. The architects are the same - the heads of States or Governments meeting within the European Council. The principal craftsmen are also the same - the Council, the Commission and the European Parliament. But the working methods for building these new edifices differ from those used to build the main edifice: notably the Commission is not alone at the origin of every new action or decision, the European Parliament is consulted but is not really engaged in the decision-making process, and the decisions taken are not submitted to the control of the Court of Justice. The method of building these new edifices depends, thus, much more on intergovernmental cooperation rather than on the interaction of the institutions. This does not prevent these new edifices under construction, like the main edifice of the Community, from being **under the roof of the European Union**.

The "European Community" exists thus and grows under the roof of the "European Union". This is also true for the other two Communities, that of coal and steel and that of atomic energy, which are often confounded in "the Community". It is correct to speak about the "Community" in respect of everything that happened and that was built up until the 1st November 1993. It is even correct to speak about the "Community" for measures taken after that date by following the Community procedure on the basis of the EC Treaty (but also the ECSC and EAEC Treaties). It must be noted, in this context, that the European Community has an international legal personality, which includes the capacity to conclude agreements, whereas the Union does not have such a personality. The term "European Union" should, however, be used for all measures that concern the new edifices of the construction and, in general, for designating the organization of European countries, which have decided to create an ever closer union among their peoples, covering relations much broader than the economic relations governed by the original Community.

The principles of subsidiarity and proportionality

According to the Treaty on European Union, the Community shall act within the limits of the powers conferred upon it by the Treaty on European Union and of the objectives assigned to it therein. In areas which do not fall within its exclusive competence, the Community shall take action, in accordance with the **principle of subsidiarity**, only if and in so far as the objectives of the proposed action cannot be sufficiently achieved by the Member States and can therefore, by reason of the scale or effects of the proposed action, be better achieved by the Community. Any action by the Community shall not go beyond what is necessary to achieve the objectives of the Treaty (Art. 3b EC). This principle means that the Community must not undertake or regulate what can be managed or regulated more efficiently at national or regional levels. This is a principle inherent in any construction of a federal type and must be exercised in a spirit of cooperation between the various levels of power.

On the basis of a Commission Communication of 27 October 1992, the Edinburgh European Council in December 1992 clarified the three legal concepts contained in Article 3b EC, stipulating that:

— the Community shall only act when the **competence** to do so has been conferred upon it by the Treaties. The rule is therefore national competence and the exception Community competence. However, there are no clearly established boundaries between the exclusive competence of the Community (smooth operation of the internal market and of common policies, certain social and environmental measures...) and the competence shared with the Member States (economic and social cohesion, industrial, research and consumer policy...), thus giving rise to a second postulate, namely that:

— the Community shall only act when an objective can be better attained at Community than at national level. In fields not falling into its exclusive competence scope, the Community must, therefore, carry out in each individual case a "comparative efficiency test" to determine whether the Member States have the means to attain the common objectives in a satisfactory manner. Should a proposal pass this test, the nature and intensity of Community action still has to be determined; this is the aim of the third postulate, which states that:

— the means employed by the Community must be in proportion to the pursued objective. The **principle of proportionality** applies both in the field of exclusive competence and in that of shared competence. This principle implies that, if a Community action proves to be necessary to attain the objectives of the Treaty, the Community institutions should further examine two points: firstly, they must determine whether legislative action is required or whether other sufficiently effective means can be used (financial support, encouragement of cooperation between Member States by a Recommendation, incentive to take action by a Resolution...); secondly, if it appears necessary to take legislative action, they must seek the legal instrument leaving the greatest freedom to the States, regions, individuals and companies (mutual recognition rather than the harmonization of legislation, framework directive rather than detailed regulations...).

The Court of Justice has consistently held that the choice of the legal basis must be based on objective factors, which are amenable to judicial review. Among those factors are included in particular the purpose and content of the measure[1]. Difficulties arise if the measure in question pursues several aims for which different legal bases can be selected. According to

---

1   See Case C-295/90, Parliament v Council, ECR 1992, I-4193.

the Court, in that case, the principal aim of the measure should determine the choice of the legal basis[1].

In order **to implement the principle of subsidiarity** contained in Article 3b EC, the following procedures and practices are applied in light of the conclusions of the Edinburgh European Council (December 11 and 12, 1992): the Commission shall conduct wide-ranging consultations and present whenever necessary reference documents (Green Papers) prior to proposing legislative texts; in the explanatory memorandum accompanying its proposals, the Commission shall include a "subsidiarity recital" summarizing the objectives of the proposed measure, its effectiveness and why it is necessary; the Council shall verify that the Commission's proposal is in accordance with the provisions of Article 3b, on the basis of the preamble and the explanatory memorandum of the proposal; the Council's decision on the aspects relating to subsidiarity shall be taken at the same time as that on the substance of the proposal and in accordance with the rules laid down in the Treaty.

The European Commission applies already the principles of subsidiarity and proportionality both to direct its initiatives and to evaluate the need for Community legislation, both future and existing. This is reflected in the appreciable drop in the number of new proposals and in the withdrawal or amendment of existing instruments. In its November 1995 report entitled "Better law-making", the Commission places the accent on "doing less but doing it better", by being more selective in making proposals and by establishing ongoing and open dialogue with the citizens, the Member States and all relevant circles, through communications such as Green and White Papers and policy statements[2].

The Community's decision-making process

We have seen that the Treaties establishing the Communities defined the objectives to be attained, laid down the rules to be implemented, set out timetables to be met and established an institutional framework which provides the Communities with an original decision-making and legislative system. That system, which we shall now examine, is based on cooperation and dialogue between three institutions, namely the Commission, the European Parliament and the Council, and in which two other institutions participate, viz. the Economic and Social Committee usually and the Committee of the Regions in a large number of instances. Complex and balanced relations have developed over the years between the first three institutions, with the situation evolving in particular towards the affirmation of the Parliament's powers.

The initiative for the Community's decision-making procedure lies with the Commission. It prepares all proposals for Council Regulations, Directives and Decisions. The Commission's role is not only technical but also political, as it chooses and prepares the ground on which the construc-

---

1   See Case C-155/91, Commission v Council, ECR 1993, I-963.
2   COM (95) 580, 22 November 1995.

tion of the Community is undertaken. Moreover, under Article 149 EC, unanimity is required of the Council for an act constituting an amendment to the Commission proposal, thus consecrating the role entrusted to the Commission of guardian of the common interest. Even a qualified majority within the Council cannot alter what the Commission considers to be in the common interest in its proposal. Unanimity is required within the Council for giving an interpretation of the common interest which differs from that of the Commission, and that occurs rather rarely. Most often it is the Commission which, when preparing its proposal, takes into consideration the often divergent interests of the Member States and endeavours to isolate the Community interest.

It goes without saying that the Community interest may not harm an **"essential interest"** of a Community State, but the definition of an "essential interest" is inevitably subjective. Each Member State has a natural tendency to exaggerate its own problems and minimize those of the others. In other words the Community decision-making process is frequently bound to come to a deadlock, and it has to be emphasized that it is through the joint mediation efforts of the Commission and the Council Presidency that the deadlock can on most occasions be broken. On the one hand the majority has to be persuaded to make the necessary concessions to accommodate the minority and on the other hand the Member State which is upholding an extreme or isolated position has to be persuaded that the general advantages of an agreement are more important than its individual interests. Even although they first and foremost assert the interests of their respective governments, the members of the Council are nevertheless obliged to respect the objectives and needs of the EU as a whole. This is what distinguishes the Council from an intergovernmental conference.

It is worth identifying the major stages of a Council meeting. Each Minister arrives in Brussels with a highly technical dossier prepared by his department, which has followed the proceedings in Coreper[1]. Each Minister sets out his position, which is normally a starting point for negotiation, in other words extreme. The others try to distinguish what is essential to him from what he will be prepared to relinquish. After this round of comments the Presidency summarizes the various positions, tries to piece together the points of convergence and asks all parties to re-examine the points where opinions differ. During the second round of comments one or more delegations announce concessions, coupled with conditions. The meeting is then adjourned to give the Commission and the Presidency the opportunity to draft a compromise. The Commission may amend its proposal to take the compromise into account, and the round of comments resumes. If it is not yet total agreement, at least the positions have moved closer and the solution is becoming easier. The drafting of compromises and rounds of comments have to be continued until all details are settled. So as not to part empty-handed, Ministers are thus obliged to sit until very late at night or to extend the meeting for several days, at which point it becomes a **"marathon session"**.

---

1   See the section on the Council under the next title.

Save where otherwise provided in the Treaties, the Council's decisions are taken either by unanimity or by a **qualified majority**. The latter is calculated on the basis of votes allocated to each Member State under Article 148 EC, as modified by the Decisions adjusting the instruments concerning the accession of new Member States to the European Union[1]. The total number of votes in the Council is increased to 87. For a qualified majority, 62 votes in favour are required where the acts are adopted on a proposal from the Commission; in other cases the 62 votes in favour must be cast by at least 10 Member States. Germany, France, Italy and the United Kingdom each have ten votes, Spain eight, Belgium, the Netherlands, Greece and Portugal five, Sweden and Austria four, Denmark, Finland and Ireland three and Luxembourg two.

In the Community of Twelve the qualified majority was attained when 54 votes were counted, constituting 71% of the 76 votes. Two big countries could, thus, ally with a "small" one and block a decision. But with the envisaged accession of four States (Austria, Sweden, Finland and Norway), with whom negotiations had been successfully concluded in March 1994, 27 out of 90 votes would be needed to block a decision and the "big countries" would have to ally with one or two more "small" countries. The United Kingdom and, to a certain extent, Spain, refused to accept this solution obliging their partners (old and new), to conclude the "Ioannina compromise", which may thwart the Community decision-making process as much as the infamous "Luxembourg compromise". It is interesting to examine the one and the other.

During the first two stages of the transitional period to customs union, the Treaty of Rome required unanimity for most Council decisions. Although transition to the third stage, on 1 January 1966, was to permit a considerable extension of the possibility of majority decisions, application of the majority rule became the central issue in a dispute between France, led by General de Gaulle, and the Commission, led by Walter Hallstein. Following the 1965 end to the crisis, known as the "empty chair" crisis because of the policy pursued by France during it, the Council, meeting in Luxembourg, issued the following text, known as the **"Luxembourg compromise"**, concerning the mechanism for taking decisions within the Council: "Where, in the case of decisions which may be taken by majority vote on a proposal of the Commission, very important interests of one or more partners are at stake, the Members of the Council will endeavour, within a reasonable time, to reach solutions which can be adopted by all the Members of the Council while respecting their mutual interests and those of the Community, in accordance with Article 2 of the Treaty. With regard to the preceding paragraph, the French delegation considers that where very important interests are at stake the discussion must be continued until unanimous agreement is reached. The six delegations note that there is a divergence of views on what should be done in the event of a failure to reach complete agreement. The six delegations nevertheless consider that this divergence does not prevent the Community's work being resumed in accordance with the normal procedure".

Subsequently it was not France alone which invoked the Luxembourg declaration, i.e. essential national interests, to block Community decisions. With the entry of the United Kingdom into the Community France even lost its status of going it alone. This often led to decisions being taken on the basis of the "lowest common denominator", with unanimity being achieved only by removing certain parts of the proposed legislation, which one or other country opposed, or by reducing the scope of the proposal as a whole, with unwelcome consequences on the conduct of Community affairs.

In order to solve the problem of the new blocking minority, the Ministers of Foreign Affairs, at their informal meeting of 26 and 27 March 1994, came to the so-called **"Ioannina compromise"**, which, as amended after the decision of the Norwegian people not to accept the accession of their country to the EU, stipulates that, "if members of the Council representing a total of 23 to 25 votes indicate their intention to oppose the adoption by the Council of a decision by qualified majority, the Council will do all within its power to reach, within a reasonable time and without prejudicing the obligatory time-limits laid down by the

---

1   OJ L1, 01.01.1995.

Treaties and by secondary legislation, such as those in Articles 189b and 189c of the Treaty establishing the European Community, a satisfactory solution that can be adopted by at least 65 votes[1]. Put more simply, this means that two "big" countries and a "small" country may still block a Council decision despite the increase in the number of small countries in the enlarged Union. The decision-making process of the Union may, thus, be hindered again.

And yet, the Community decision-making process has undergone some changes over the last few years that have sought to achieve greater suppleness and democratization. These changes were enacted firstly by the 1987 Single Act, which extended the range of qualified majority voting within the Council subject to the procedure of cooperation with the European Parliament, particularly in fields touching upon the completion of the internal market and economic and social cohesion, and secondly by the Maastricht Treaty, which further broadened the scope of qualified majority voting and introduced the co-decision making procedure.

Article 189b, inserted at Maastricht, defines the **co-decision procedure** with the European Parliament, procedure which applies mainly in the fields of internal market, including the harmonization of standards and technical regulations, free movement of workers, right of establishment, services, actions for the encouragement of education, culture and health, consumer protection, guidelines for trans-European networks, the research framework programme and general action programmes for the environment. Regulations, Directives and Decisions adopted under the Article 189b procedure are signed by the President of the European Parliament and the President of the Council.

The stages of the co-decision procedure are as follows:
— the Commission submits a proposal to the European Parliament and the Council;
— the Council, acting by a qualified majority after obtaining the Opinion of the European Parliament, adopts a common position. The common position is communicated to the European Parliament;
— if, within three months of such communication, the European Parliament:
  a) approves the common position, the Council definitively adopts the act in question in accordance with that common position;
  b) has not taken a decision, the Council adopts the act in question in accordance with its common position;
  c) confirms, by an absolute majority of its component members, its rejection of the common position, the proposed act is deemed not to have been adopted;
  d) proposes amendments to the common position by an absolute majority of its component members, the amended text is forwarded to the Council and to the Commission, which delivers an opinion on those amendments. The last is the most frequent possibility.

Matters obviously become more complicated if the Parliament proposes major amendments to the Council's common position. The latter can naturally, acting by a qualified majority, approve all the amendments if the Commission agrees with them, or act by unanimity if the Commission has delivered a negative opinion. In this case, it amends its common position in consequence and adopts the act in question. If, however, the Council does not accept all of the amendments tabled by the Parliament, the President of the Council, in agreement with the President of the European Parliament, convenes forthwith a meeting of the **Conciliation Committee**, composed of the members of the Council or their representatives and an equal number of representatives of the European Parliament. The Committee then has the task of reaching agreement on a joint text, by a qualified majority of the members of the Council or their representatives and by a majority of the representatives of the European Parliament.

---

1   OJ C1, 01.01.1995.

If, within six weeks of its being convened, the **Conciliation Committee** approves a joint text, the European Parliament, acting by an absolute majority of the votes cast, and the Council, acting by a qualified majority, have a period of six weeks from that approval in which to adopt the act in question in accordance with the joint text. If one of the two institutions fails to approve the proposed act, it is deemed not to have been adopted. This is also the case if the Conciliation Committee does not approve a joint text, unless the Council, acting by a qualified majority within six weeks of expiry of the period granted to the Conciliation Committee, confirms the common position to which it agreed before the conciliation procedure was initiated, possibly with amendments proposed by the European Parliament. In this case, the act in question is finally adopted unless the European Parliament, within six weeks of the date of confirmation by the Council, rejects the text by an absolute majority of its component members, in which case the proposed act is deemed not to have been adopted. The Parliament, thus, has the last word in the co-decision procedure.

It can be seen that the co-decision procedure can become very complicated indeed; but, it has worked well so far. Indeed decisions have been taken fairly quickly as a result of a good working relationship between the institutions, based on the interinstitutional agreement on the Rules of Procedure of the Conciliation Committee, concluded on 21 October 1993. It must be said, however, that the European Parliament, in order not to assume the responsibility of blocking a decision, may be led to accept a common position of the Council that it does not approve entirely.

Article 189c, inserted at Maastricht, defines the **cooperation procedure,** where the Council has the final say, but Parliament is involved in the legislative process by means of its two readings and the proposal of amendments to the Council's common position. It is used mainly in the areas of transport, Social Fund, vocational training, trans-European networks (except guidelines), implementing decisions on economic and social cohesion, implementation of research and environment programmes, development cooperation, certain measures concerning economic and monetary union and the Agreement on social policy adopted by 14 Member States, excluding the United Kingdom.

The main stages in the cooperation procedure are as follows:
a) the Council, acting by a qualified majority on a proposal from the Commission and after obtaining the Opinion of the European Parliament, adopts a common position;
b) the Council's common position is communicated to the European Parliament. If, within three months of such communication, the European Parliament approves this common position or has not taken a decision within that period, the Council definitively adopts the act in question in accordance with the common position;
c) the European Parliament may, within the period of three months, by an absolute majority of its component members, propose amendments to the Council's common position. If the European Parliament has rejected the Council's common position, unanimity is required for the Council to act on a second reading;
d) the Commission, within a period of one month, re-examines the proposal on the basis of which the Council adopted its common position, by taking into account the amendments proposed by the European Parliament. The Commission forwards to the Council, at the same time as its re-examined proposal, the amendments of the European Parliament which it has not accepted, and expresses its opinion on them. The Council may adopt these amendments unanimously;
e) the Council, acting by a qualified majority, adopts the proposal as re-examined by the Commission. Unanimity is required for the Council to amend the proposal as re-examined by the Commission. By picking out the Parliament's amendments, the Commission plays an arbitration role, but the last word in this procedure belongs to the Council.

It should be noted that the **budgetary procedure**, based in particular on the Treaty of 22 July 1975, gives wider powers to the European Parliament. The European Commission prepares a preliminary draft Community budget which it submits to the Council. The Council then adopts a draft budget based on the Commission's draft and forwards it to the Parliament for a first reading. The Parliament, by means of amendments, can propose modifications and increases, up to a maximum level, for the "non-compulsory" category of expenditure[1]. The Council acts on these amendments and proposed modifications and returns the draft budget to the Parliament for a second reading. At the end of the second reading the Parliament can either adopt the budget or reject it en bloc, as it did in 1980. Such a decision makes it necessary to begin the procedure afresh through the submission of new proposals by the Commission. Indeed, according to the Court of Justice, if there is a disagreement between the two arms of the budgetary authority, the budgetary procedure cannot be completed[2].

All these complicated procedures certainly do not contribute to the transparency and speed of the Community's decision-making process. Indeed, there is no apparent logic in the correlation between the various procedures and different fields of activity. Three different procedures apply in the three equally important sectors of agriculture, transport and the internal market (the consultation, cooperation and co-decision procedures respectively). Fields which are closely linked, such as transport and trans-European networks, are subject to different procedures (cooperation and co-decision respectively). Several different procedures may apply within a single policy area, such as the environment or research. In addition, the unanimity rule has been maintained under the TUE in many cases, without any consistent underlying principle. It is clear that the legislative processes need to be radically simplified, with regard to the concept of a hierarchy of acts, a matter which the Treaty has placed on the agenda of the 1996 Intergovernmental Conference.

The Community legal system

Whereas the Treaties serve as plans for the construction of Europe and the cement for it is the economic and social cohesion between Member States which unites them in the will to live and work together, the bricks for the construction are constituted by an increasing number of Community legal acts adopted by the Council and the Commission. Article 189 of the EC Treaty provides for five forms of legal act, each with a different effect on the Member States' legal systems: some are directly applicable in place of national legislation, while others permit the progressive adjustment of that legislation to Community provisions.

The **Regulation** has a general scope, is binding in all its elements and is directly applicable in each Member State. Just like a national law, it gives rise to rights and obligations directly applicable to the citizens of the European Union[3]. Regulations enter into force on a date which they lay down or, where they do not set a date, on the twentieth day following their publication in the Official Journal of the European Communities. The regulation substitutes European law for national law and is therefore the most effective legal instrument provided for by the Treaty.

The **Directive** binds any Member State to which it is addressed with regard to the result to be achieved, while leaving the national authorities jurisdiction as to the form and methods used. It is a sort of Community framework law and lends itself particularly well to the harmonization of

---

1   See the headline on Parliament in the next part of this chapter.
2   Judgment of 7 December 1995, case C-41/95, Council v Parliament).
3   See on this subject, notably, the judgments of the Court of Justice of 14.12.1971, case 43/71, Politi, ECR 1971, p. 1049 and of 7.2.1973, case 39/72, Commission v Italy, ECR 1973, pp. 114-115.

laws. It defines the objective or objectives to be attained and leaves it to the Member States to choose the forms and instruments necessary for complying with it. Although they are generally published in the Official Journal, Directives take effect by virtue of being notified to the Member States to which they are addressed. The latter are obliged to adopt the national measures necessary for implementation of the Directive within time-limits set by it, failing which they are committing an offence.

According to the constant jurisdiction of the Court of Justice, in the absence of measures transposing a directive within the prescribed period, the directive cannot on its own impose duties on an individual and cannot therefore be relied on in proceedings against him (absence of "horizontal" direct effect)[1]. However, by virtue of the "Francovich" jurisdiction of the Court, in certain circumstances Community law requires the Member States to compensate for damage sustained by individuals by reason of their failure to transpose a directive where its purpose is to confer rights on them[2].

The **decision** is binding on the addressees it indicates, who may be one, several, or even all the Member States or one or more natural or legal persons. This variety of potential addressees is coupled with a variety in the scope of its contents, which may extend from a quasi regulation or a quasi directive to a specific administrative decision. Its taking effect for its addressees results from its communication rather than publication in the Official Journal. In any case, according to the Court of Justice, a decision can produce direct effects creating for the individuals rights that national jurisdictions must safeguard[3].

In addition to these legal acts, the effects of which are binding on the Member States, the Community institutions and, in many cases, the citizens of the Member States, the Council and the Commission can adopt **Recommendations** suggesting a certain line of conduct and **opinions** assessing a current situation or certain facts in the Community or the Member States. These instruments enable the Community institutions to adopt positions in a non-binding manner, i.e. without any legal obligations for the addressees - Member States and/or citizens. Furthermore, the Council and the European Parliament adopt **Resolutions**, which are also not binding, suggesting a political desire to act in a given area.

While Resolutions and opinions are published in the "C" series (communications) of the Official Journal of the European Communities (OJ), binding acts and recommendations - as well as **common positions** and **common actions** of the common foreign and security policy and of justice and home affairs (Art. J.2, J.3 and K.3 of TEU) - are published in the "L" series (legislation) of the OJ. It is the binding instruments that constitute Community law, that is, the law adopted by the institutions in order to pursue the objectives of the European Treaties, giving certain rights and obligations to the citizens and obliging the Member States to adapt their legislation and/or the administrative practices.

---

1   Judgment, 26 February 1986, Case 152/84 Marshall and Judgment, 14 July 1994, Case C-914/92, Faccini Dori v Recreb.

2   Judgment, 19 November 1991, joined Cases C-6/90 and C-9/90, Francovich and Bonifaci, ECR 1991, p. I-5357.

3   Judgment of 6 October 1970, case 9/70, Grad, ECR 1970, p. 838 and judgment of 12 December 1990, joined cases 100/89 and 101/89, ECR 1990, p. I-4647.

Community law is uniformly and entirely valid throughout the Community and cannot be invalidated by the individual law of one Member State. It ensues from the Treaties and the constant decisions of the Court of Justice that this law has **precedence over national law**, even the constitutional law, of the Member States, whether it predates or postdates Community legislation. In fact, the Member States have definitively transferred sovereign rights to the Community they created, and they cannot subsequently go back on that transfer through unilateral measures which are incompatible with the concept of the Community[1].

The situation in the Union is a unique one, in that the application of Community law depends, by and large, on the separate jurisdictions of the Member States. It is not for the Community to seek a harmonization which would eliminate the distinctive features of national jurisdictions. However, both the European institutions and the Member States have a duty to ensure that Community law is respected and to take the necessary steps when it is violated: this is a fundamental requirement of any legal system. The European Court of Justice has observed that domestic laws must be reconcilable with the need to apply Community law uniformly so as to avoid unequal treatment of economic operators[2]. In case of conflict of laws, the national judge must, according to the Court, not apply any contrary clauses of the national law, whether these are prior or subsequent to Community law[3].

Community law evolves extremely rapidly. Several hundreds of Community acts are adopted and amended each year. The scope of those acts obviously varies from case to case. Some have a very specific scope or a scope limited in time. Very many regulations, notably in the area of the common agricultural policy, merely implement basic Regulations. It is obviously these last regulations, the directives and decisions that form the Community policies, which we shall examine in this book. As these acts have been amended several times since first adopted, we shall often refer in the footnotes, in addition to the Official Journal containing the basic instrument, to the OJ containing the most important or most recent amendment thereto.

In a Declaration attached to the Treaty on European Union, it is agreed that the Intergovernmental Conference convened in 1996 will examine to what extent it might be possible to review the classification of Community acts with a view to establishing an appropriate hierarchy between the different categories.

The Community finances

The conventional international organizations such as the UN or the OECD are financed by contributions from their member countries. In most instances their financial requirements amount to staff and operational expenditure: if they are entrusted with operational tasks, their financing is generally provided on an "à la carte" basis by those member countries which decided on those tasks. It is virtually never a question, in such organizations, of financial transfers or even of financial compensation. The European Community, on the other hand, although far from being a

---

1   Judgment of 15 July 1964, case 6/64, Costa/ENEL, ECR 1964, p. 1160.
2   Judgment given on 21 September 1983 on Joined Cases 205/82 and 215/83, Deutsche Milchkantor, ECR 1983, p. 2633.
3   Judgment of 9 March 1978, case 92/78, Simmenthal v Commission.

federal type of organization, pursues certain federal objectives, and its expenditure in the main corresponds to a transfer of resources from the national to the supranational level. Indeed, since 1970, the Community controls its own ressources.

The first genuine European tax was introduced with the creation of the ECSC. Article 49 of the Treaty of Paris stipulates that the High Authority (now the Commission) is "empowered to procure the funds it requires to carry out its tasks by imposing **levies on the production of coal and steel**". It may itself determine the mode of assessment and the amount of that tax. The levies are "assessed annually on the various ECSC products according to their average value; the rate thereof shall not, however, exceed 1 per cent". The system applied in this connection by the Commission is similar to the VAT system. The levy is applied to undertakings in the steel and coal sector. Since 1994, the Commission has gradually reduced the levy, thus leading to its total elimination when the ECSC Treaty expires (23 July 2002)[1].

Provision had been made in the EEC Treaty (Article 201) for replacing the Member States' initial contributions (determined on a scale according to GNP shares or other criteria) by own resources after establishment of the Common Customs Tariff (CCT). The transfer of **customs revenue** to the Community budget by Decision of 21 April 1970 was the logical outcome of the attainment, provided for in the Treaty, of a genuine customs union[2]. In such a union the country of import of goods from a third country is not always the country of destination of those goods. The revenue from customs duties are therefore often collected in a country other than the country of destination or of consumption. Only the payment of that revenue to the customs union, in this instance to the Community, makes it possible to neutralize that effect.

However, the importance of customs duties is diminishing inasmuch as they are being progressively abolished or reduced under the General Agreement on Tariffs and Trade (GATT) and the various tariff concessions granted to the least developed countries[3]. For that reason it was decided, in 1970, to use a proportion of the **value added tax (VAT)** as an additional source of Community financing. That tax, which has a uniform basis of assessment, affects all citizens of the European Union and takes fairly accurate account of the economic capacity of the Member States, as it is levied at the consumption level. The "**uniform base**", which was adopted for calculating the proportions of the VAT yield which countries must pay to the EU, is made up of all taxable supplies of goods and provisions of services at the ultimate stage in the Union. It therefore does not depend on the amount of the VAT itself, the rates of which vary from Member State to Member State[4].

The Fontainebleau European Council in June 1984 set the amount of VAT which the Member States were to pay to the Community at 1.4% maximum. But it quickly became clear that the own resources fixed in 1984 were not sufficient to cover Community expenditure. Learning from that situation, the Brussels European Council from 11 to 13 February 1988 reached agreement on the Commission proposals (Delors package), which took tangible form in the Council Decision of 24 June 1988 on the system of own resources[5]. Customs duties on products within the province of the ECSC Treaty now constitute Community own resources. A new own resource was added to the others, grounded on an additional base representing the sum of the Member States' GNPs at market prices. Each Member State contributes to this fourth resource (21.4% of total revenue) in accordance with its wealth.

In order to give tangible form to the Maastricht commitments, particularly as regards economic and social cohesion, the creation of an environment stimulating Europe's competitiveness and development of Community action on the external front, the Commission proposed the doubling of the financial allocation in 1997 compared to its 1992 level (**Delors package II**). The European Council, meeting in Edinburgh on 11

---

1   OJ L315, 08.12.1994.
2   OJ L94, 28.04.1970.
3   See the chapters on customs union and on the European Union in the world.
4   See the chapter on taxation.
5   OJ L185, 15.07.1988.

and 12 December 1992, agreed to raise the ceiling on own resources from 1.20% of the Community's GNP in 1993 to 1.27% in 1999. A Council Decision of 31 October 1994 fixed the level of own (Community) resources available for the period 1995-99 and the structure of the Community financing system[1].

As far as Community expenditures are concerned, we should note that they have increased between the early eighties and the early nineties from 1.7 to 2.4% of all public expenditure in the Member States. They still represent, however, little more than one percent of the cumulative Gross Internal Product of the Member States. More than 90% of the receipts of the European Union are redistributed to the Member States and serve to finance the objectives of the various common and Community policies. Thus, out of a total of ECU 86.5 billion for commitments of the 1996 budget, 40.8 billion (47%) were allocated to the common agricultural policy, 29.1 billion (33.6%) to the Structural Funds, 5.3 billion (6%) to other internal policies and somewhat less than 5.3 billion (6%) to external action of the Union[2]. It is interesting to note that the general budget of the Community covers as guarantee lenders when the Community floats an issue under one of its financial instruments, such as the balance of payments facility or the financial assistance for Central and Eastern European countries. A Guarantee Fund for external actions is designated to reimburse the Community's creditors in the event of default by the recipient of a loan given or guaranteed by the Community in a non-member country[3].

The **management of the Community budget** is entrusted to the Commission and is exercised according to a Financial Regulation[4]. Like other public funds the European Union budget runs the risk of having fraudsters enrich themselves at its expense or embezzle the levies which normally should be transferred to the Union. However, the fight against fraud cannot be led from Brussels alone. Indeed, roughly 80% of expenditure is handled by tens of thousands of national, regional or local officials. Responsibility for ensuring that the funds are properly used rests, therefore, with the national authorities in the first place and it is essential that complementary action be developed at Union level through close cooperation between the Member States and the Commission. This partnership is based on the provisions of Article 209a of the EC Treaty, which specifies the obligations of the Member States in matters of fraud prevention and institutionalizes cooperation between the competent national bodies, with the help of the Commission, and of Title VI of the EU Treaty, which provides for various forms of cooperation in the fields of justice and home affairs.

In this context, the Commission has developed an effective information system based on the IRENE database, which stores the cases of fraud and irregularities reported by national authorities in any budgetary area. It has established an anti-fraud strategy and an annual work programme in this field[5]. The Commission has also set up an Advisory

---

1   OJ L293, 12.11.1994.
2   OJ L22, 29.01.1996.
3   OJ L293, 12.11.1994.
4   OJ L356, 31.12.1977 and OJ L240, 07.10.1995.
5   COM (94) 92 and COM (95) 23.

Committee for the coordination of fraud prevention, which provides a forum in which the most important cases of fraud can be tracked and horizontal matters relating to prevention and prosecution can be discussed[1]. Finally, the Commission adopted a Regulation concerning irregularities and the recovery of sums wrongly paid in connection with the financing of the structural policies[2] and a Regulation concerning similar arrangements for the Cohesion Fund[3].

However, the anti-fraud strategy necessitates an active cooperation between national and Community administrations. Indeed, as national customs officers are in reality Community customs officers, so national anti-fraud officers should also be agents of the management of the Community budget. On the basis of this assumption, the Regulation on the protection of the Communities' financial interests seeks to protect taxpayers' money more effectively by introducing a common legal framework to combat the waste and misuse of Community resources[4]. It applies to irregularities involving budget expenditure or revenue in all areas covered by Community policies. It is based on a common definition of irregularity encompassing the various types of fraud affecting the Community budget and establishes appropriate administrative penalties to be applied uniformly in all Member States in accordance with the same principles and methods. To amplify the Regulation, a Convention on the protection of the Community's financial interests drawn up on the basis of Title VI of the TEU requires Member States to establish a specific criminal offence of "fraud against the Community's financial interests" and provides for convergence in respect of penalties[5]. A Protocol to this Convention deals specifically with fraud against the Community budget involving corruption of European or national civil servants or Members of the European institutions.

The Actors

The protagonists of European construction are the main organs of the Community, called in the Treaties "institutions", and the consultative organs, that we examine below in the order that they intervene in the decision-making process of the Union: the European Council, which gives the impulses to European affairs; the European Commission, which makes the proposals for the actions to be undertaken; the Economic and Social Committee and the Committee of the Regions, which give their opinion on these decisions; the European Parliament and the Council of Ministers, which take the decisions; and the Court of Justice and the Court of Auditors, which control the legality of these decisions.

Behind the main actors, however, stand the crowd artists, who are indispensable for legitimizing the actions undertaken by democratic institutions in a democratic context. These crowd artists are the citizens of the Union, whose role in the European construction should not be minimized.

The citizens

All Europeans take part in the construction of Europe: the housewife filling her basket with products from the four corners of the European

---

1   OJ L61, 04.03.1994.
2   OJ L178, 12.07.1994.
3   OJ L191, 27.02.1994.
4   OJ L312, 23.12.1995.
5   OJ C316, 27.11.1995.

Union; the motorist choosing the car which suits him without regard to its provenance; the worker employed by a Community firm in his country or the firm's country; the businessman rushing across borders to conclude deals with foreign partners; the student spending his holidays in a neighbouring country to learn its language and thus perfect his education; the pensioner from a northern country who spends the whole year dreaming of his holidays in a country of Southern Europe; the citizen of one of those countries who aspires to study at close quarters the lifestyle and culture of his neighbours, etc. They all construct the large house that is Europe without giving it much thought.

The use of goods, services and the opportunities offered by our European partners alone makes the construction of Europe progress. Each time we choose this or that product or service, we unknowingly contribute our grain of sand to the mortar necessary to cement our common construction. We are not aware of the importance of these acts because we find them as natural as the air we breathe. In fact, they have become as vital to our lives as that air.

Imagine for a moment, though, our indignation, our anger, if we were to lose the possibility of freely choosing our consumer goods and those who supply the various services. Can you imagine a government which would dare to deprive us of those goods and those freedoms which have become so indispensable to us, a government which would dare to reconstruct the protectionist barriers of yesteryear? If you cannot imagine it, you believe, quite rightly, that the tide of history is irreversible and that the construction of Europe is here to stay. More than an interested spectator, more even than a crowd artist aware or unaware of his acts, you are certainly a supporter prepared, if necessary, to defend to the utmost the construction of Europe.

That construction has placed Europe yet again in the forefront of the world theatre. We are experiencing a great moment in human history. We are present at, and are taking part wittingly or unwittingly in, an experience that will leave its mark on the history of the planet for a long time, the gradual and free unification of nations, which were hostile to each other until very recently. The **key word of this experience is freedom**: freedom of movement of persons, of goods, of services and of capital, freedom of States and their people to belong or not to the Union. Economic and political freedom is the water for the mortar of the construction of Europe which will sooner or later accommodate all the peoples of Europe, heirs to a common civilization the very cultural diversity of which is its strength and wealth. The citizens who love these freedoms are conscious or unconscious supporters of European construction.

It is clear from the foregoing that the citizens are silent, but vital, actors in the construction of Europe. Nothing lasting could have been built, in fact, without Europeans wanting to live together in peace. The opinion polls known as "Eurobarometers", which are carried out regularly under the auspices of the Commission, show that, in early 1994, the EU citizens were convinced by four-to-one (54% against 13%) that EU membership was a "good thing" rather than a "bad thing", (but, in early 1991, the "supporters" represented over 70% and the "opponents" less than 8%). For problems as serious as unemployment or the fight against terrorism and crime, two citizens out of three are disposed to entrust their fate to the Union rather than to their national government. The European public is even largely in favour of projects which give rise to thorny problems for the EU machinery, such as the creation of a single currency, the common defence or the foreign policy.

Nevertheless, in spite of the 650 or so journalists accredited to the Commission, the European public is still ignorant and ill-informed about the construction of Europe. In the "Eurobarometer" surveys, three fourths of the public say that they are not well informed about the institutions and policies of the European Union. Few and far between are the EU topics which make the headlines in the printed press and even more rarely radio and television headlines. Worse still, it is the crises, the temporary set-backs, which make the headlines, because they are more sensational than the very many successes secured after patient negotiations which nevertheless affect the day-to-day lives of citizens, on occasion much more than the laws adopted by the national parliaments.

It has to be acknowledged, however, that these subjects are difficult for the general public to understand and to that end further efforts will have to be undertaken both by the Union and Governments to educate citizens about Community affairs. The debates set in motion in the Member States during the ratification procedures for the Maastricht Treaty demonstrated the wish of European citizens for greater democratization and transparency of Community activities. The Birmingham European Council of 16 October 1992 declared that the Community can only forge forward with the support of its citizens and undertook to make the work of the Community institutions transparent and the decisions as close as possible to the citizen.

The stakes are high, because once the citizen understands better the importance of European construction for his well-being and his liberties, he will become more than a spectator or passive actor in that construction; he will become a militant for the unification of Europe. He will, for example, lodge more complaints with the Commission when he regards a measure taken by a national, regional or local authority as contravening Community law. He will thus make them comply more fully with that law and more prepared to provide their bricks for the construction of Europe.

The European Council

Everyone has seen the "family photo" taken at the periodic meetings of the Heads of State and of Government of the Community Member States. These meetings are amongst the rare occasions when the Community remains in the spotlight for two days. Quite rightly so, as the European Council is the architect of European construction. It draws up the political plans for further discussions and resolves the most important problems of construction. Begun on an informal basis, it is now explicitly provided for in Article D of the Treaty on European Union.

As early as 1957 a meeting of the Heads of Government of the "Six" was held in Paris in order to accelerate the conclusion of the Treaties of Rome. Subsequently, meetings of Heads of State (e.g. the President of the French Republic) or of Government, styled "Summit Conferences", were held at irregular intervals, usually on France's initiative. These intervals grew shorter and shorter in line with the attainment of customs union, the concretization of enlargement of the Community and progress towards economic integration in areas not covered by the Treaties, necessitating personal intervention by the Heads of Government to enable major political decisions to be taken.

It was at the Paris "Summit" in 1974 that the Heads of Government decided to meet three times a year and, whenever necessary, "in the Council of the Communities and in the context of political cooperation". The "European Council", as it quickly became known, has since then periodically brought together the Heads of Government, the Ministers for Foreign Affairs, the President and one Vice-President of the European Commission - and only them - to discuss subjects of common interest not yet covered by any legal obligation, to lay down guidelines and provide impetus for major political and institutional developments: direct elections of the European Parliament, completion of the internal market, treaty on European Union.

Being a venue where package deals can be struck, and thus being free from the unwieldiness that sometimes paralyses the proceedings of the Council of Ministers, the European Council often acts as an appeal body for politically and economically important business which is deadlocked by the subordinate bodies: achievement of the major prototype for nuclear fusion, known as "JET", European Monetary System, United Kingdom contribution to the Community budget.

It had been feared at the outset that the dealings in the European Council might distort the Community's decision-making process and sterilize the work of the traditional institutions. Those fears proved groundless. First and foremost, the institutions prepare and follow the work of the European Council through the Ministers for Foreign Affairs and the President of the Commission. The Commission is in a position to play the initiative role conferred upon it by the Treaties in preparations for meetings of the European Council. Secondly, the Heads of State and of Government do not adopt legal acts formally binding the Member States. Their deliberations result in the publication of joint declarations containing either guidelines and general directives for future EU action or decisions on political cooperation. These declarations have undeniable political validity, but no legal validity. As we shall see in this book, they give the political impetus necessary for several Community policies, but the latter are constructed with Community provisions adopted subsequently in accordance with the procedure laid down in the Treaties.

The European Council is above all a forum for free and informal exchanges of views between the leaders of the Member States both on political cooperation (coordination of foreign policies) and on Community issues. Its strength is its spontaneity and its informality, which bring about a sort of esprit de corps on the part of Europe's political leaders. Although there have been European Council meetings which have not yielded spectacular results, or indeed any results, the European Council's balance sheet is generally positive. It has resolved several issues which threatened the Community's solidarity and progress, it has provided the impetus for new Community policies and it has established the collective responsibility of the leaders of European diplomacy vis-à-vis the major European and world problems.

The European Commission

The Commission of the European Communities, now referred to as the European Commission or simply the Commission, is the issue, as we have seen, of the merger in July 1967 of the bodies of the three European Communities. The number of its Members has grown with the successive enlargements of the Community, but as a general rule the Commission is made up of two Commissioners for each large Member State and one for each of the smallest Member States. Articles 156 to 163 of the EC Treaty, as amended after the accession of three new Member States, stipulate that the Commission shall consist of 20 members appointed, for a period of five years, by common accord of the governments of the Member States after approval by the European Parliament and shall perform its duties completely independently, in the general interest of the Community.

Approximately 18000 permanent officials, independent of the governments of their respective countries, work under their responsibility. They are divided into more than twenty-four Directorates-General, each of which is responsible for a Community policy, corresponding to the ministries of a national government. And yet the Commission's staff is smaller than that of a good number of national ministries, and furthermore, twenty per cent of the staff is involved in the linguistic work which is absolutely essential to ensure equality of treatment of the nine official languages of the Community.

The Commission is the driving force for the construction of Europe. This **initiative role** falls to it from the fact that, under the Treaties, it alone can **make proposals** with a view to the taking of Community decisions. No other body and no individual State can replace the Commission in this task. It alone can amend its proposal, with the sole exception of there being unanimity in the Council to do so. Even in the course of deliberations and negotiations within the Council, it is the Commission which can revise its proposal in order to encourage concessions here and there and to reach agreement. The Commission can therefore paralyze the Community's decision-making process, just as it can expedite it, which it has always done. Year in, year out, it submits some 700 proposals to the Council.

The power of initiative, which is held by the Commission, is particularly important for the development of the Community policies which constitute the European construction. For policies which were not required and therefore not covered by the Treaties - industrial, regional, monetary, energy and environmental policies - everything had to be done. On the basis of the political impetus granted by the Heads of Government at their Summit Conferences and subsequently at European Council meetings, it was for the Commission to make proposals to the Council for implementing them. If the Commission had not exercised its power of initiative wisely, nothing would have been done and progress towards the construction of Europe would have been blocked.

The Commission plays a **normative role** as guardian of the Treaties and the "acquis communautaire" (i.e., all the Community's legislation). One of its main tasks is to ensure proper application by the Member States of the provisions of the Treaties and of secondary legislation. For that purpose it has investigative power which it exercises on its own initiative or in response to a request from a government or to a complaint from an individual. If, following its investigation, the Commission considers that Community provisions are being infringed, it invites the State charged to submit its comments within a given period. If the State in question does not comply with the provisions or if the explanations that it provides do not convince the Commission, the latter issues a reasoned opinion to which the Member State is obliged to conform within the prescribed time-limit, failing which the Commission refers the matter to the Court of Justice, which arbitrates the dispute and, more often than not, sanctions the irregularity as noted by the Commission and then requires that the recalcitrant Member state conforms to the provisions. There are often differences of opinion between the Member States and the Commission, but the Commission's impartiality has never been called into question.

Furthermore, the Commission plays a **normative role** in the administration of the **safeguard clauses** provided for in the Treaties or in the provisions relating to Community policies. Here also an independent, objective arbiter is necessary in order to assess whether particular difficulties or special circumstances may authorize a Member State to derogate from the rules of the Treaty or from acts relating to Community policies. This task is entrusted to the Commission both by the Treaties and by the provisions of secondary legislation. In performing that task the Commission obviously takes into consideration the vital interests of the Member State which feels that it is suffering damage in a particular situation, but it surrounds itself with precautions and conditions so that prejudice to the functioning of the common market or to a Community policy - and therefore to the common interest - is limited in scope and time.

The Commission is also the **executive body** of the Community and plays, therefore, an **administrative role**. The Treaties confer upon the Commission extensive powers of execution to ensure the attainment of the objectives set out in them: achievement of the common market, control of the rules of competition, supply of fissile materials, etc. But the Commission's powers are constantly increased by the exercise of powers conferred to it, in the name of the Member States, by the Council for the implementation of Community policies. It is the Commission, either alone or assisted by a committee made up of representatives of the governments, in accordance, as appropriate, with the procedures of the Advisory Committee, the Management Committee (which can annul the decision of the Commission, at the qualified majority of its members) or the Regulatory Committee (which must approve the decision of the Commission, at the qualified majority of its members)[1], which implements Council Decisions and manages the Community budget and in particular the various Community Funds: ECSC loans, European Agricultural Guidance and Guarantee Fund (EAGGF), European Regional Development Fund (ERDF), European Social Fund (ESF), European Development Fund (EDF) and the research and technological development programmes.

Finally, the Commission plays a **representative role** by ensuring the representation of the European Union in third countries and in many international organizations. Acting on behalf of the EU on instructions from the Council, the Commission negotiates tariff agreements, for example under the General Agreement on Tariffs and Trade (GATT), trade agreements, association agreements and even, in practice, the agreements on the accession of new Member States to the European Union.

As the Commission's powers increase, so criticism of it also increases: not so much on account of any inefficiency, which would be very difficult to prove, given the very numerous initiatives it takes each year, nor on the grounds of its partiality vis-à-vis one or other State,

---

1   See the Council Decision called "comitology" Decision, OJ L197, 18.07.1987.

but rather because of its **independence**, which some see as a lack of control over its acts and proposals. Such criticism is totally unfair. The Commission is probably the best monitored executive body in the world.

First, there is the self-monitoring exercised both at political level by the presence amongst the Commissioners of dignitaries from all Member States and at administrative level through the composition of the Commission departments. The official of nationality A who is preparing a Community legal instrument is supervised by his superior, of nationality B, the latter in turn by his Director, of nationality C, and all of them by the Director-General, of nationality D. Once the Commission departments have prepared a draft, they unofficially consult the experts from the Member States and the representatives of any occupations which might be concerned by its implementation. The draft thus examined and re-examined is submitted by the competent Commissioner to his fellow Commissioners, who decide by a simple majority, often after arduous discussions and usually after amendments to the draft to take into account its implications for other Community policies.

The proposal adopted by the Commission is then submitted, depending on the procedure, either to the European Parliament and to the Council for decision or to the first for opinion and to the second for decision and, very often, to the Economic and Social Committee and to the Committee of the Regions for an opinion. Detailed discussions begin within the working party of competent national experts, who prepare the Council's decision, the relevant Parliament Committee and the groups of experts of the Economic and Social Committee and of the Committe of the Regions. The interest groups, alerted in good time of this preparatory work, lobby these various technical and political experts and, if the issue is important, public opinion. The text ultimately adopted by the Council alone or by the Council and the Parliament takes into account all these different points of view. In any case, it is false to refer to "decisions taken by the technocrats of Brussels". It is true that the technocrats propose the Community measures; but it is the political institutions representing the democratically elected governments (the Council of Ministers) and the citizens of the Member States (the European Parliament) that take the decisions.

After all these successive controls of the Commission proposal, one could perhaps talk of the slowness of the decision-making process, but certainly not of working in an ivory tower or of lack of monitoring of the Commission. In more general terms, the Commission is officially controlled by the European Parliament, which can pronounce a vote of censure against it and force it to resign, and unofficially by the European Council which, if it disapproves its initiatives, could also press for its resignation. That has never happened. On the contrary, both the control body democratically elected by the peoples of Europe and the Community's supreme political body have on several occasions expressed their satisfaction at the work carried out by the Commission. The latter is, moreover, the natural ally of both in any initiative they wish to take to press ahead with the construction of Europe. The Member States themselves, particularly when they have differences of opinion, ask for the moderating intervention of the Commission.

The Economic and Social Committee

Article 18 of the **ECSC Treaty** set up a Consultative Committee attached to the High Authority (Commission) which the latter was obliged to consult under various Articles of the Treaty and in all cases in which it considered that appropriate. Composed of equal numbers of producers, workers and consumers and dealers in coal and steel products, that Committee, which still operates under the ECSC Treaty, was the precursor to the Economic and Social Committee (ESC) set up under Article 193 of the EEC Treaty and Article 165 of the Euratom Treaty.

The Committee is the official body which enables the Community institutions to evaluate and take into account, when preparing Community decisions, the **interests of the various sectors of industry**. Its members, who are nominated by the Member States and appointed by the Council after consulting the Commission, have to provide a wide representation of the various categories of economic and social life. The 222 members of the ESC voluntarily divide into three groups: the Employers' Group (known as "Group I"), which is made up of representatives of industry, banking or financial institutions, transport operators' federations, etc.; the Workers' Group (known as "Group II"), mainly composed of representatives of trades union organizations, and the Various Interests Group (known as "Group III"), which comprises representatives of agriculture, skilled trades, small and medium-sized undertakings, the professions, consumers' associations and organizations representing various interests, such as the families or ecological movements.

The Committee must be consulted by the Council or by the Commission in certain areas provided for by the Treaty on European Union. The Committee may be consulted by these institutions in all cases where they consider it appropriate. Furthermore, the ESC may issue an opinion on its own initiative when it considers such action appropriate (Art. 198 EC). Whether they are requested by the Commission or the Council or issued on its own initiative, the Committee's **Opinions** are not binding on the institutions. However, the Committee plays the part of a forum in which the points of view of the various socio-professional categories, rather than national arguments, are expressed officially and come face to face. Those Opinions reflect the concerns of public opinion and provide valuable indications of the opposing arguments, of the divergences of interests and of the possibilities of reaching agreement at Community level. For that reason the Commission often adjusts its proposals to take into account the positions of the "grassroots" of the Community. In this way the Committee influences decisions and makes its contribution to the construction of the Community. Furthermore, it associates the economic operators who are ultimately the most directly concerned by the practical effects of Community measures with the European reality.

The Committee of the Regions

The Treaty on European Union officially acknowledges the role played by regions in the Community through the creation of an advisory committee made up of representatives of regional and local bodies (Art. 198a EC). The 222 members of the Committee and an equal number of alternate members (Germany, France, Italy, the United Kingdom each 24; Spain 21; Belgium, Greece, Netherlands, Portugal, Austria and Sweden 12; Denmark, Ireland and Finland 9; Luxembourg 6) are appointed for four years by the Council, acting unanimously.

The Committee of the Regions must be consulted by the Council or the Commission on matters relating to education, culture, public health, European networks and the Structural Funds. It can be consulted in all other cases considered appropriate by one of the two institutions. It can also issue an own-initiative opinion when it considers that specific regional interests are at stake (Art. 198c). The Committee of the Regions thus involves regions and local authorities in the decision-making process and speaks on their behalf on all policies concerning them, and not just on those where consultation is compulsory.

When the Economic and Social Committee is consulted pursuant to Article 198, the Committee of the Regions is informed by the Council or the Commission of the request for an opinion. A protocol on the Economic and Social Committee and on the Committee of the Regions moreover stipulates that the two have a common organizational structure.

The European Parliament

The Treaty establishing the **European Coal and Steel Community** stipulated that the extensive powers it was conferring on the High Authority would be subject to public control by a **"Common Assembly"** representing "the peoples of the States brought together in the Community". Composed of 78 Members, that Assembly held its first meeting on 10 September 1952. With the creation, in 1957, of the European Economic Community and the European Atomic Energy Community, the Common Assembly constituted, at its request, an enlarged Assembly, composed of 142 Members, for the three Communities. Holding its inaugural part-session in Strasbourg on 19 March 1958, the Assembly two days later gave itself the name of "European Parliamentary Assembly". Four years later, on 30 March 1962, it decided to take the name **"European Parliament"**.

During the early years of European construction, the Members of the European Parliament were appointed by the national parliaments and had to be members of them. Although it was provided for by the Treaties of Paris and Rome, election of the European Parliament by **direct universal suffrage** only became a reality twenty-five and twenty years respectively after their signing. The green light for direct elections was given by the Conference at the Paris Summit on 9 and 10 December 1974. On 25 July 1978 the Council adopted a Decision setting the period from 7 to 10 June 1979 for the first direct election. The Treaty on European Union stipulates that the European Parliament should draw up proposals for elections by direct universal suffrage in accordance with a uniform procedure in all Member States.

The number of Members of the European Parliament has increased with the successive enlargements of the Community and, now, of the European Union. After the last enlargement, the number of seats was increased to 626. Germany has 99 seats, France, the United Kingdom and Italy each have 81 seats, Spain 60, the Netherlands 25, Belgium, Greece and Portugal 24, Sweden 22, Austria 21, Denmark and Finland 16 each, Ireland 15 and Luxembourg 6.

The direct election made the European Parliament the first real multinational legislative assembly in the world and consolidated its role in the construction of Europe. In fact, although under the original Treaties the Parliament's role was purely advisory, it has not ceased growing, by virtue of the increasing political influence it has gradually managed to secure. At present it exercises four functions: legislative, budgetary, political and supervisory.

The European Parliament's first task under the Treaties establishing the Communities, that of **consultation**, whereby Parliament gives its opinion on Commission proposals, was strengthened by the Single Act of 1987 which introduced a cooperation procedure and by the Treaty on European Union, which added a co-decision procedure[1]. Article 138b provides, in fact, for the participation of the European Parliament in the process leading up to the adoption of Community acts through exercise of its powers under the procedures laid down in Article 189b and 189c (co-decision and cooperation) and through giving its assent in certain areas of legislation or issuing advisory opinions. Furthermore, the Parliament has the right to give or withhold its **assent** as regards the conclusion of international agreements, the accession of new Member States and the association of third countries. Although they do not yet match the powers of a national parliament, the European Parliament's legislative powers nevertheless resemble those of the Senates which exist in some Member States. It has to be said, moreover, that the national parliaments rarely exercise their powers to the full, subject as they are to the will of the parties which support the governments, which submit legislative drafts to them.

As regards **budgetary functions**, the Parliament, in accordance with the basis of the second budget Treaty of 22 July 1975, has to give its agreement to any major decision involving expenditure to be borne by the Community budget. It is effectively the Parliament which, at the end of a conciliation procedure with the Council, adopts or rejects the budget proposed by the Commission. Thus, it exercises a democratic control on the own resources of the Community. The increased importance of the Parliament in the budgetary process, reflected in the Treaty on European Union (Art. 201 and 209 EC), particularly as regards the power to give a discharge to the Commission, makes the European Parliament's budgetary role comparable to that of the national parliaments which, although they have more rights than it in constitutional terms, often exercise them less vigorously than it does.

However, the Parliament's budgetary powers differ according to the type of expenditure. For "**compulsory expenditure**" (CE), i.e. expenditure resulting from the Treaties and the decisions adopted pursuant thereto (roughly 50% of appropriations, made up chiefly of those relating to the common agricultural policy), the Parliament may propose modifications provided that they do not increase the total volume of the budget. They are then deemed to be accepted if the Council does not reject them by a qualified majority. For "**non-compulsory expenditure**" (NCE), i.e. expenditure which is not the automatic consequence of the various Community provisions (in particular, appropriations allocated to the European Social Fund, research, energy, etc.), the Parliament may not only modify its apportionment but also increase its volume, up to a given limit which depends on the Community's economic situation. That limit may be amended by the Parliament by mutual agreement with the Council.

That budgetary procedure has often been attended by conflicts between the two institutions, as the Parliament wants to use its budgetary powers to influence Community policies and considers as an unjustified restriction of its powers the, somewhat arbitrary, separation of expenditure into compulsory and non-compulsory. Still, the Court of Justice did not justify the President of the European Parliament in his revolt against the Council, manifested in his final adoption of the 1995 budget, although the two institutions had not reached prior agreement as required by Article 203(9) of the EC Treaty[2]. However, the Interinstitutional Agreement of 29 October 1993 on budgetary discipline, which lays down the financial perspective until 1999[3], and the Interinstitutional Declaration of 6 March 1995

1   See the title above on the Community's decision-making process.
2   Judgment of 7 December 1995, case C-41/95, Council v Parliament.
3   OJ C331, 07.12.1993.

on the inclusion of financial provisions in legislative instruments, created the conditions for an era of budgetary peace, at least until the revision of the Treaty, which could comprise Article 203.

The **political function** of the Parliament is also essential. As it represents 370 million citizens and is the European forum par excellence, the Parliament is quite naturally the major contractor for the construction of Europe. It calls upon the other protagonists, the Commission and the Council, to develop or alter existing policies or to initiate new ones: transports, environment, workers' rights, human rights in the world... This function of the European Parliament was consecrated by the Treaty on European Union which gives it the right to request that the Commission submit any appropriate proposals on matters on which it considers a Community act is required (Art. 138b). In addition to the many reports of the Commission, the European Council, itself, reports to the European Parliament on each of its meetings and annually on the progress achieved by the Union.

The activity of the European Parliament Committees, which monitor Community affairs in detail on a continuous basis, has contributed a great deal to developing the European Parliament's influence. These Committees produce reports on any subject which they feel warrant the attention of the Community institutions and invite the relevant Members of the European Commission to go and state their views or give explanations before them and/or before the European Parliament at the time of the vote. The Opinions, Reports and Resolutions of the Parliament, prepared by the specialist Committees, are very often followed by the European Commission, and if appropriate by the Council, as they show not only a political desire to make the construction of Europe progress, but also thorough knowledge of the complicated issues involved in that construction.

The **monitoring function** of the Parliament is exercised in particular vis-à-vis the Commission. Under the Treaties the Commission is answerable to the Parliament alone, so as to obviate its bowing before the will of the governments or of some of their number. Every Member of the Parliament may raise any point relating to the activity of the Commission and call it to account by means of Written or Oral Questions. Each year the Parliament puts some 3,000 questions, nine-tenths to the Commission and the others to the Council. These questions enable the Parliament not only to keep closely abreast of any new development in Community policy, but also in many instances to initiate such developments.

The Commission has to account to the European Parliament, defend its position before parliamentary commissions and in plenary sessions and submit to the Parliament each year a "General Report on the Activities of the European Union". The European Parliament may, moreover, pass a motion of censure against the Commission by a two-thirds majority and thus compel it to resign. The President and the other members of the Commission are subject as a body to a vote of approval by the European Parliament. The term of office of the Commission has been increased to five years, to run concurrently with the Parliament's term.

The European Parliament appoints an **Ombudsman** empowered to receive complaints from any citizen of the Union or any natural or legal person residing or having its registered office in a Member State and concerning instances of maladministration in the activities of the Community institutions or bodies, with the exception of the Court of Justice and the Court of First Instance acting in their judicial role[1]. In cases where the Ombudsman establishes that maladministration has occurred, he refers the matter to the institution concerned, which has three months in which to inform him of its views (Art. 138e EC). The European Parliament may,

---

1   OJ L54, 25.02.1994 and OJ L113, 04.05.1994.

moreover, set up a temporary Committee of Inquiry to investigate alleged contraventions of or maladministration in the implementation of Community law (Art. G. 138c). These procedures may help bring the European construction closer to the citizen.

The Council

The Council of the European Union, composed of Ministers of Members States and usually called Council of Ministers or simply Council, is the Union's **main decision-making body**. It alone, in some cases, or with the European Parliament, in many areas[1], adopts the instruments of secondary legislation on proposals from the Commission. In practice, important decisions are taken either **unanimously**, in which case the vote of the smallest country is as powerful as that of the largest and any country can block the Community process, or by a **qualified majority**, under the conditions explained in the heading on the Community's decision-making process.

Although "the Council" is referred to in the abstract, there are in reality several distinct **specialized Councils**: Council of Ministers for Agriculture, for Finance, for Transport, for Industry, etc. Each Council is composed of the Ministers with responsibility in the matter. On occasion two or three Councils meet on the same day, for three months of the year in Luxembourg and the rest of the time in Brussels, where the Council Secretariat has its headquarters. Although issues are discussed by the Ministers responsible, decisions can be taken by any Council whatsoever, and this is often the "General Affairs" Council, which brings together the Ministers for Foreign Affairs. The latter are to some extent considered the "main" representatives of the Member States on the Council.

The **Council Presidency** changes every six months to another country in alphabetical order, and it is therefore the Minister of the country holding the Presidency who chairs each Council meeting[2]. The rotation of the Presidency has the disadvantage of frequently coinciding with a period of (pre-electoral or electoral) political instability in the country exercising it, but has the advantages of stimulating an emulation among the Member States and giving each country a chance to prove its efficiency in promoting European affairs. The frequency of Council meetings varies according to the sector. Some Councils meet every month, viz. the "General Affairs", Foreign Affairs and "Agriculture" Councils. Others meet three or four times a year, in particular the Economic and Financial Affairs, Social Affairs, Transport and Budget Councils. Yet others meet in the light of working requirements. This applies to the Industry, Energy, Regional Development and Fisheries Councils.

At Council meetings the Commission is represented by the relevant Commissioner and often by its President. During the, on occasion heated, discussions in the Council, the Commission's role is to try to find the common denominator of the general interest of the Union and to submit

---

1   See the title above on the Community's decision-making process.
2   Concerning the order of the exercise of the Presidency see OJ L1, 01.01.1995.

proposals during the meeting which take account of that general interest. The role of the Council Presidency, assisted by its General Secretariat, is to reconcile all the national interests with the Community interest. The roles of the two institutions are therefore complementary and equally difficult. Is it surprising that for a decision to be taken that is regarded as fair by all Member States the meeting may become animated, extend late into the night and even into the subsequent days, on occasion becoming a "marathon session"? Anyone who is surprised is forgetting the difficulties which the national governments very often have in having important laws passed by their national parliaments. After all, the heated discussions concern the transfer of bricks of sovereignty from each member's house to the construction of the communal house.

What is more a cause for surprise is the fact that the Council, despite its composition of national governments which are naturally inclined to defend the national interest, manages to keep its role as a Community institution seeking and ultimately finding the **common denominator** of problems. Every Council decision is tangible evidence of the Member States' will to live and build together. That will is not the fruit of chance, but of a thorough knowledge of each other's problems and interests. That knowledge is gained especially in the Council. At their numerous formal meetings, held usually in Brussels and three months a year in Luxembourg, and during their informal meetings, held at the invitation and in the territory of the Council Presidency, Ministers form friendships and make alliances for the defence of common causes.

Those friendships and alliances also play a very important part in the very numerous specialist **working parties** on the various subjects, composed of members of the national civil services, which discuss the Commission's proposals and prepare Council decisions. The numerous meetings each year of senior officials responsible for agriculture, industry, transport, economic affairs, etc., of the Member States help to align points of view and facilitate the Community progress. However, the national civil services remain the most ardent defenders of national causes and measures, as each brick added to the communal house removes a little of their jurisdiction and authority. That is why on many occasions problems which have remained unresolved at national experts level find a solution in political compromises secured in the Council of Ministers.

An important part in preparing those compromises is played by the Permanent Representatives Committee **(COREPER)**. Not provided for in the Treaties establishing the Communities, but charged with certain work by the Ministers as early as January 1958, Coreper gradually developed without a clearly defined status. It was the "Merger" Treaty of 8 April 1965 and latterly the Treaty on European Union which consecrated Coreper's role in these terms: "A committee consisting of the Permanent Representatives of the Member States shall be responsible for preparing the work of the Council and for carrying out the tasks assigned to it by the Council" (Art. 151 EC).

Coreper's tasks are, however, much more complex than is revealed by that text. When a Commission proposal or memorandum is submitted to it, the Council entrusts its examination either to the Permanent Representatives Committee or, if an agricultural problem is involved, to the Special Committee on Agriculture (SCA). As the pivot between the technical and political levels, Coreper is assisted by the many working parties referred to above, which examine each issue and report to it. Coreper itself sits in two parts: Coreper Part 1, which is composed of the Deputy Permanent Representatives and examines technical questions on the whole, and Coreper Part 2, which is composed of the Ambassadors themselves and deals with political questions on the whole. The Council General Secretariat assists Coreper and the working parties in carrying out their tasks, and the European Commission participates in all the meetings to explain its positions.

After examining an issue Coreper either submits a report to the Council, preparing the ground for its discussions by drawing attention to the political aspects which warrant particular attention, or, if unanimous agreement has been reached between the Permanent Representatives and the Commission representative, recommends that the Council adopt the prepared text "as an 'A' item", i.e. without discussion. In both cases the Council's work is much lighter owing to Coreper's intervention.

The Court of Justice

The general task assigned to the Court of Justice of the European Communities by the Treaties of Paris and Rome is to **ensure that the law is observed** in a uniform manner in the interpretation and application of the Treaties, of the legal acts and of the decisions adopted by the Council and the Parliament or by the Commission. In a community of States the common rules might, if they were controlled only by national courts, be interpreted and applied differently from country to country. Community law might therefore no longer be applied uniformly. That was the reasoning behind the establishment of a Court of Justice of the Community as from the creation of the ECSC.

With its seat in Luxembourg, the Court is composed of as many Judges as there are Member states, plus one to make the number odd - currently fifteen Judges - and nine Advocates-General. The task of the latter is to study the issues and present to the Court publicly and impartially the conclusions they have reached. They are all appointed for six years by mutual agreement of the Member States.

Being the supreme court of the Communities, it gives a coherent and uniform interpretation of Community law and ensures that it is complied with by all the Member States and their citizens. Apart from the tendency of States to interpret that law in their interest, it is new law and not always well known. The national judges, who are the judges of first instance of the rules and behaviour relative to Community law, may, in cases where Community law is also involved, turn to the Court of Justice by means of a **referral for a preliminary ruling** to ask it to adopt a position on the interpretation or evaluation of the validity of Community provisions. Although they are normally optional, referrals for a preliminary ruling are obligatory where judicial remedy under national law is no longer possible, i.e. when the court which has to apply the Community law is taking its decisions in the final instance. Through its preliminary rulings, the Court plays the role of a legal council whose opinions are binding on the parties concerned. The referral for a preliminary ruling is appreciated by the national courts and stimulates the cooperation between them and the ECJ.

In the legal field itself the Court reviews the legality of Community acts. **Proceedings for annulment** may be brought against the decision-making institutions (Council or Council/Parliament and Commission) either by a Member State or, in certain instances, by an individual, or even by another institution. The aim of these proceedings is to annul those acts of the institutions which are at variance with the provisions of the Treaties or their spirit, which exceed their rights or which do not comply with the procedure laid down. If the action is well founded, the Court declares the act in question to be void. Proceedings for annulment are therefore the means to monitor both the conformity of the acts of the Community legislator with the Treaties and the legality of individual Commission decisions and regulations, as well as to resolve interinstitutional disputes affecting the very exercise of the powers devolving upon each of the institutions from the Treaties. The control of the legality of the acts of the institutions likens the Court to a constitutional jurisdiction.

Proceedings for failure to act, on the other hand, are aimed at securing a ruling where the Council or the Commission has failed to meet its obligation to act, thus infringing the provisions of the Treaties. Such proceedings may also be initiated by a Member State, and possibly by individuals, or another Community institution. These proceedings are admissible only if the institution in question has first been called upon to act. Thus, for example, in September 1982 the European Parliament brought an action for failure to act against the Council for failing to establish the framework for the common transport policy[1]. In November 1993, the Parliament, on the basis of Article 175 of the EC Treaty, brought an action against the Commission for failure to present the proposals necessary for the establishment of the free movement of persons within the internal market[2].

The Court also has jurisdiction to rule on proceedings brought against Member States which do not meet the obligations imposed on them by the Treaties or secondary legislation. **Proceedings for infringement** may be brought by Community institutions (in practice, the Commission), a Member State or an individual. Referral to the Court by the Commission is the final stage in an **action for infringement**, taking place following an unsuccessful formal notice to the Member State from the Commission. If a State does not comply with an initial judgment, new proceedings may be brought, at the end of which the Court will rule that there has been a violation of the obligations deriving from its initial judgment. The new Article 171 of the EC Treaty allows the Commission to bring the case of a Member State which has failed to comply with a ruling of the Court of Justice before the Court and to specify the amount of the lump sum to be paid by the Member State concerned. If the Court finds that the Member State has indeed failed to comply with its judgment, it may impose a lump sum of penalty payment. The efficiency of Community law can nevertheless be guaranteed concurrently by the national courts and through referrals for preliminary rulings if a citizen feels that he has been injured by the incriminated act.

Disputes falling within the unlimited jurisdiction of the Court are made up in particular of cases relating to non-compliance or to the interpretation of the Community's rules of competition. Hearing an appeal by undertakings penalized by the Commission, the Court gives a ruling on the merits of the Commission's decision and on the appropriateness of the penalty imposed on the undertaking. The Court also judges disputes which call into question the Community's civil liability as a result of damage caused by one of its institutions or staff in the exercise of their duties.

The judgments of the Court of Justice reflect the vitality of Community law. They reinforce the strength of the law and provide it with the necessary authority vis-à-vis governments, national judiciaries, parliaments and citizens. Through its judgments and interpretations, the Court of Justice promotes the emergence of a genuine European law to which all are subject: European institutions, Member States, national courts and each individual. It therefore has to be regarded as a leading actor in the construction of Europe.

Pursuant to the Single Act, on 24 October 1988 the Council adopted, at the request of the Court, a Decision establishing a **Court of First Instance (CFI)** of the European Communities[3]. The CFI was then consecrated by the Treaty on European Union (Art. 168a EC). The CFI is intended to improve the legal protection of the man in the street and to enable the Court - by relieving it of the examination of the facts in complex areas - to devote itself

---

1   OJ C267, 11.10.1982, see the Chapter on transport.
2   OJ C1, 04.01.1994, see the title on citizens' rights in the chapter on the EU and the citizen.
3   OJ L319, 25.11.1988.

to its task, which is to ensure uniformity of interpretation of Community law. The CFI has jurisdiction in all actions brought by natural or legal persons and cases relating notably to agriculture, fisheries, the European Funds (regional, social), transport and State aids[1]. The judgments of the CFI, made up of fifteen members and normally sitting in chambers, can form the subject of appeals, confined to points of law, to the Court of Justice.

The European Court of Auditors

The Treaty amending Certain Financial Provisions of the Treaties establishing the European Communities and of the Treaty establishing a Single Council and a Single Commission of the European Communities (second Budget Treaty), which was signed on 22 July 1975 and entered into force on 1 June 1977, stipulated, **inter alia**, that a Court of Auditors should be established. That Court took the place, as from 25 October 1977, of the Audit Board of the EEC and Euratom and of the auditors of the ECSC as the body responsible for the external supervision of the general budget of the Community and of the ECSC's operating budget. The Treaty on European Union transferred the provisions relating to the Court of Auditors from the Title on financial provisions to that on institutional provisions (Art. 188 a,b,c).

The number of members of the Court of Auditors is the same as the number of Community Member States. They are appointed by the Council, acting unanimously after consultation of the European Parliament. A declaration annexed to the Treaty on European Union calls on the other Community institutions to consider, together with the Court of Auditors, all appropriate ways of enhancing the effectiveness of its work.

The Court **examines the accounts** of all administrative expenditure and revenue of the Community and of all bodies set up by the Community, such as the European Centre for Vocational Training and the European Foundation for the Improvement of Living and Working Conditions. The Court of Auditors verifies that **revenue has been received and expenditure incurred in a lawful and regular manner** and makes observations on the financial management of the Community budget, especially on the part of the Commission.

The Court of Auditors may also submit observations on specific questions and deliver an opinion at the request of a European institution. Lastly, it may carry out investigations in the Member States in respect of operations which the latter carry out on behalf of the Union, such as the collection of customs duties and the management of the appropriations of the European Agricultural Guidance and Guarantee Fund. The special reports of the Court of Auditors are acknowledged to be a valuable input for Parliament's debates on the discharge to be given to the Commission for its execution of the budget.

The bolstering of the Court of Auditors' role testifies to the will of the European Institutions, in particular the European Parliament, and of the Governments of the Member States to extend and improve financial control owing to the increasing size of the Community budget, which is a direct consequence of the development of the various common and Community policies which we are examining in this book.

---

1   OJ L144, 16.06.1993.

General bibliography on the EU

□ CARTOU Louis, *L'Union européenne; traités de Paris, Rome, Maastricht*, Dalloz, Paris, 1994.

□ COMMISSION EUROPÉENNE, *La Commission européenne 1995-2000*, OPOCE, Luxembourg, 1995.

   –   *Les finances publiques de l'Union européenne: Les caractéristiques, les règles et le fonctionnement du système financier européen*, OPOCE, Luxembourg, 1995.

□ CONSTANTINESCO Vlad, KOVAR Robert, SIMON Denys (sous la dir. de): *Traité sur l'Union européenne. Commentaire article par article*, Economica, Paris, 1995.

□ CORBETT Richard, *The Treaty of Maastricht. From Conception to Ratification. A Comprehensive Reference Guide*, Longman Group, Harlow, Essex, 1994.

□ CORBETT Richard, JACOBS Francis, SHACKLETON Michael, *The European Parliament*, Cartermill Publishing, London, 1995.

□ CURTIN Deirdre, Van EMPEL Martijn, VOLKER Edmond, WINTER Jan, *Leading Cases on the Law of the European Communities*, Kluwer Law and Taxation Publ., The Hague, 1994.

□ DEGRYSE Christophe, *Dictionnaire de l'Union européenne. Politiques, Institutions, Programmes*, De Boeck/Université, Bruxelles, 1995.

□ DEHOUSSE Renaud, *La Cour de justice des Communautés européennes*, Montchrestien, Paris, 1994.

□ DRUESNE Gerard, *Droit et politiques de la Communauté et de l'Union européenne*, Presses Universitaires de France, Paris, 1995.

□ DUTHEUIL DE LA ROCHERE Jacqueline, *Introduction au droit de l'Union européenne*, Hachette, Paris, 1995.

□ DUBOUIS Louis, GUEYDAN Claude, *Grands textes de droit communautaire et de l'Union européenne*, Éditions Dalloz, Paris, 1996.

□ EDWARD David, LANE R. C., *European Community Law. An Introduction*, Butterworth/Law Society of Scotland, Edinburgh, 1995.

□ EDWARDS Geoffrey, SPENCE David (edit.): *The European Commission*, Longman Group Limited, Harlow, Essex, 1994.

□ FONTAINE Pascal, *L'Union européenne*, Éditions du Seuil, Paris, 1994.

□ GAUTRON Jean-Claude, *Droit européen*, Dalloz, 1994.

□ HARTLEY Trevor C., *The Foundations of European Community Law*, Clarendon Press, Oxford, 1994.

□ LASOK Dominik, *Law and Institutions of the European Union*, Butterworths, London, 1994.

□ LAURSEN Finn (ed.), *The Political Economy of European Integration*, European Institute of Public Administration, Maastricht, 1995.

□ MAJONE Giandomenico, *La Communauté européenne: un État régulateur*, LGDJ Montchrestien, Paris, 1996.

- MATHIEU Jean-Luc, *L'Union européenne*, Presses universitaires de France, Paris, 1994.

- O'KEEFFE David, TWOMEY Patrick M. (ed.), *Legal Issues of the Maastricht Treaty*, Wiley Chancery Law Publ., Chichester, West Sussex, 1994.

- O'NEILL Aidan, *Decisions of the European Court of Justice and their Constitutional Implications*, Butterworths Law Publ., Sevenoaks, Kent, 1994.

- POLLARD David, Ross Malcolm, *European Community Law. Text and Materials*, Butterworths, Sevenoaks, Kent, 1994.

- QUERMONNE Jean-Louis, *Le système politique de l'Union européenne*, Éditions Montchrestien, Paris, 1994.

- SCOTTO Marcel, *Les institutions européennes*, Le Monde Éditions, Paris, 1994.

- TOULEMON Robert, *La construction européenne: histoire, acquis, perspectives*, Éditions de Fallois, Paris, 1994.

- WEATHERILL Stephen, BEAUMONT Paul, *EC Law. The Essential Guide to the Legal Workings of the European Community*, Penguin Books, London, etc., 1994.

- WEATHERILL Stephen, *Law and Integration in the European Union*, Clarendon Law Series, Oxford University Press, Oxford, 1995.

- WESTLAKE Martin, *The Commission and the Parliament. Partners and Rivals in the European Policy-making System*, Butterworths Co, London, 1994.

    - *A Modern Guide to the European Parliament*, Pinter Publishers, London, 1994.

1. CUSTOMS UNION

A customs union is an economic area whose members agree, by treaty, to refrain from imposing any customs duties, charges having equivalent effect or quantitative restrictions on each other and to adopt an external common customs tariff in their relations with third countries. The customs union introduced by the EEC countries in July 1968 is thus fundamentally different from a free-trade area such as the European Free Trade Association (EFTA). Although a free-trade area also involves the reduction, between member countries, of customs duties and charges having equivalent effect on the area's originating products, each State maintains its own external tariff and customs policy with regards to third countries. Thus, only those goods made in the territory of the free trade area can move freely, i.e. duty free, whereas freedom of movement is applicable in a customs union regardless of the origin of goods.

The founders of the Community had, from the start, far more ambitious goals than the EFTA countries. They wanted to create a politico-economic framework in which goods, services and capital could be traded freely. In economic integration, they foresaw not only a formula offering economic advantages, but also the means to set up the conditions for political union in Europe. In order to achieve this, a sound foundation was required. Customs union was, accurately enough, such a foundation; although it was not completed in 1968, it allowed for unprecedented trade growth in Europe and the superposition of the entire European construction. In fact, all the Community policies examined herein would be unthinkable were they not based on customs union.

Internal frontiers, which should have disappeared within the Community many years ago, bore witness to the uncompleted state of customs union. The completion of the internal market, examined in the next chapter, finally put the finishing touches to customs union, an essential element of the internal market.

Economic and legal framework

Before the Community treaties came into force, every country pro-tected its national production with customs tariffs, preventing the import of goods at prices lower than those of the national production, and quan-titative restrictions, preventing the import of certain products in quantities exceeding those which were necessary to satisfy local demand not covered by national production. Thus, a country would import the quantities and qualities not normally supplied by its internal production. As industry was well protected, it saw no need to make large scale efforts to modernize or reduce production costs. The European consumer, faced with a limited choice and high prices for low quality goods, was the main victim of this situation. Customs union, aimed at correcting such a situation, is the foundation of the ECSC, EAEC, and the EEC.

The Tariff Union of the ECSC and EAEC

In his historic declaration of 9 May 1950, Robert Schuman said: "the circulation of coal and steel within acceding countries will immediately be freed of all customs duties...". In fact, article 4a of the **ECSC Treaty** prohibited import or export duties, charges having equivalent effect and quantitative restrictions. Entering into force the moment the common market was established, this prohibition was enforced on 10 February 1953 for coal, iron ore and scrap iron, and on 1 may 1953 for steel. The elimination of customs duties and charges having equivalent effect was problem-free and, by 1954, had yielded good results in terms of trade intensification. As seen in the chapters on industry and energy, the steel, iron and coal markets have certainly faced serious problems, first in the 60s and then in the 80s. These were, however, structural problems faced by all Community industries at the same time and not economic or administrative problems caused by customs union. On the contrary, the latter enabled the industries of Member States to face together the coal crisis of the sixties and the steel crisis of the eighties and to allow for survival of the fittest regardless of national interests[1].

As requested by article 93 of the **EAEC Treaty** (Euratom), the Member States abolished between themselves, on 1 January 1959 (one year after the entry into force of the Treaty) all customs duties on imports and exports or charges having equivalent effect, and all quanti-tative restrictions on the import and export of goods and products which come under the provisions of the chapter on the nuclear common market. These products were to circulate freely on the markets of new Member States a year after their accession. As seen in the chapter on energy, the common market in nuclear products works well as a whole.

The customs union of the EC

According to article 9 of the EEC Treaty, the Community is based upon a customs union which covers all trade in goods and which involves the prohibition between Member States of customs duties on imports and exports and of all charges having equivalent effect, and the adoption of a common customs tariff in their relations with third countries. In a free-trade area (EFTA), only those goods produced (or having undergone substantial processing) in the territory of the Member States can move freely, whereas the customs union created by the EEC covers "all trade in

---

1   See the chapters on industry and on energy.

goods". This means that products coming from a third country can move freely within the Community if the import formalities have been complied with and any customs duties or charges having equivalent effect which are payable have been levied in the importing Member State (article 10).

Articles 13 and 14 of the treaty provided that **customs duties and charges having equivalent effect** to customs duties on imports were to be progressively abolished during the twelve-year transitional period from 1 January 1958 to 31 December 1969. Although article 4, paragraph 3 does give the Member States the option of varying the rate of reduction of customs duties according to product (should a sector have difficulties), the reduction was constant and problem-free. The rate of tariff dismantling was even accelerated by two Council decisions, and completed 1 July 1968; 18 months ahead of schedule. This demonstrates that there were no major problems, as any country's objection would have prevented the change of schedule provided by the Treaty. The new member States of the Community had a five-year transitional period to eliminate customs duties in intra-Community trade. This was also problem-free.

The accelerated accomplishment of the tariff union was a success for the Community; it meant that, as of 1 July 1968, free movement of goods had been achieved, although only partially. By this date, intra-Community trade had been freed of customs duties and quantitative restrictions on imports and exports. However, **other trade obstacles,** such as charges having equivalent effect to customs duties and measures having equivalent effect to quantitative restrictions, were far from gone.

The proper functioning of the tariff union required the elimination of such obstacles by the end of the transitional period. In fact, the push for their elimination had not really started yet. The removal of the classical instruments of economic protectionism revealed the extent of the arsenal of sophisticated measures hidden in the most diverse rules still wielded by national administrative departments. Because a great number of such trade barriers were hidden and varied from one State to another, and, because their removal required the laborious harmonization of the Member States' legislation, it was to be a very difficult but necessary task in order to complete the Common Market; their restrictive effects were often more damaging than customs duties and quantitative restrictions. In fact, while customs barriers raised the price of imports or quantitatively limited them, charges having equivalent effect could completely block the import of a product. Fortunately, such extreme cases were rather limited. However, as seen in the chapter on the common market, the elimination of non-customs barriers to trade took three times as long and as much energy as did the elimination of customs barriers.

The economic results of the free circulation of goods were indisputable despite the incompleteness of such free circulation; from 1958 to 1972, while trade between the six founding member-States and the rest of the world had tripled, intra-Community trade had increased ninefold. Such exceptional trade growth was a key factor to economic development and the raising of the standard of living in all member countries. Thanks to the fact that enterprises faced increased competition in their principal markets, the stimulative effect of a wider market created a feeling of confidence which resulted in investment growth. Consumers emerged the overall winners; supply was more diverse and products cheaper than before tariff dismantling.

Sceptics, saying that it was smooth sailing for the EEC as long as the sea of international economy was calm, waited for the results of the first storm. It came in 1973; the energy crisis and the hard years that followed shook customs union considerably but it emerged intact. Admittedly, because of the depression's tenacity and structural nature, the difficulties faced by several of the Community's industrial sectors heightened **protectionist tendencies**, resulting in an increase in the number of grievances for trade restrictions (art. 30 to 34) filed to the Commission by various interested parties. But even in the worst moments of the economic crisis, no Member State ever questioned the existence of the Community.

In the eventuality of a **grievance for trade restrictions**, the Commission examines its validity and, pursuant to article 169 of the treaty, calls upon the concerned State to amend or suppress a rule or practice contrary to Community law. If the country concerned does not comply with this request, the Commission brings the matter before the Court of Justice, whose opinion is binding as much for the Member State as it is for Community Institutions. It must be said that the majority of these cases are settled after notice is given by the Commission to the Member State in question.

In 1973, the Commission created an Advisory Committee on Customs Matters to advise and assist it in the management of customs union. Due to the importance which indirect taxation has now acquired in the smooth operation of the Single Market, the Commission has replaced it with an Advisory Committee on Customs Matters and Indirect Taxation[1]. This Committee strengthens the dialogue between the various parties to customs union and is made up of representatives of professional organizations or of consumers concerned by customs and fiscal problems and established at a Community or international level.

Intra-Community trade

Theoretically, the Community having laid down the foundations of customs union and the CCT having replaced national tariffs, a large part of border formalities should have been eliminated since 1968. In reality, customs union and the common transit procedure have only had a limited effect thanks to the imagination and inventiveness of national administrative departments which replaced them with a plethora of documents to be completed at borders. Every form, every stamp, has had a reason: tax collection, statistics, customs checks aimed at preventing the import of banned products, etc. But each stamp meant time and money to the Community's carriers and exporters. The Single Act of 1987 was needed to eliminate checks at internal frontiers and thus to complete customs union.

Elimination of internal frontiers

The Treaty of Rome provided for the suppression of internal customs duties and quantitative restrictions to trade as well as the elimination of all measures likely to affect freedom of trade. It expressly noted the necessity of "reducing formalities imposed on trade as much as possible" (art 10). In reality, as soon as tariff dismantlement was accomplished, the

---

1   OJ L241, 30.08.1991.

"document war" stepped up between Member State administrations anxious to protect national production and at the same time justify their existence as much as possible. The Commission, primarily, and the Council waged a "war of attrition" on this "build-up of paperwork" which reached a successful conclusion on January 1, 1993.

Since January 1, 1993, no customs formalities are required for trade within the Community[1]. The Community henceforth only forms one single frontier-free area for the purposes of the movement of goods under cover of the TIR and ATA carnets[2]. This saves a great deal of time for economic operators and thus helps cut the cost of transporting goods within the Community. However, in order to have free circulation of persons and goods exactly as in an internal market, Community law must be enforced in a comparable way in all Member States and this is not the case yet.

In order to guarantee the free movement of persons provided for by Article 8A of the Treaty, a Council Regulation of December 19, 1991 abolished with effect from January 1, 1993 controls and formalities appertaining to cabin and hold baggage of persons taking an intra-Community flight and the baggage of persons making an intra-Community sea crossing[3]. Although customs checks of persons have disappeared since the 1st January 1993, the non-suppression of identity checks has provoked much criticism on the part of citizens and the European Parliament and has led the latter to introduce against the Commission the procedure provided for in Article 175 of the EC Treaty[4].

The abandonment of customs formalities, as of 1st January 1993, has necessitated the establishment of a system for collecting statistical information on exchanges of goods between Member States directly from undertakings (**INTRASTAT**). The amendments to customs legislation following the completion of the internal market have necessitated the updating of the regulations on the completion of statistics on the trading of goods with non-member countries[5].

The removal of internal borders has affected the profession of **customs and forwarding agent** and several jobs have simply disappeared. The Member States and the Community have taken measures to facilitate the adaptation of this profession to the internal market. These measures include assistance in the places the most affected by the abolition of customs formalities, thanks notably to the INTERREG initiative, and aid for the reconversion and restructuring of the companies concerned with the aim of preserving the maximum number of jobs[6].

Veterinary and plant health legislation

This legislation is important not only for the internal market, but also for the environment and human health. It is in the interest of all Member States to strengthen their common legislation in these fields and, at the same time, not to upset intra-Community trade of foodstuffs. To this end, the Commission created an Internal Veterinary and Plant Health Inspec-

---

1   OJ L78, 26.03.1991 and OJ L249, 28.08.1992.
2   OJ L78, 26.03.1991 and OJ L216, 03.08.1991.
3   OJ L374, 31.12.1991 and OJ L185, 04.07.1992.
4   See the title on citizens rights in the chapter on the European Union and the citizen.
5   OJ L118, 25.05.1995.
6   OJ L394, 31.12.1992.

tion Office. This Office has been entrusted with the internal and external organization and implementation of inspection measures, checks and monitoring in the veterinary (including fishery products) and plant health fields in accordance with Community regulations, thus ensuring the uniform application of these.

The **plant health arrangements** which came into force on 1 June 1993 have made it possible to remove all physical obstacles to trade of plants and plant products[1]. These arrangements include the rules applicable to the intra-Community trade of plants and plant products imported from third countries, the standards for the protection of the environment and human health against harmful or undesirable organisms, the reduction in number of plant health checks by setting up a Community inspectorate, and by initially moving the checks from the border to the place of destination. The Community Plant Variety Office supervises the protection of plant varieties in the Community[2].

By setting the permitted levels for certain harmful organisms, a 1977 Directive better protects European forests from disease; amended in 1990, it also removes the need for plant health checks in intra-Community trade[3]. By prohibiting the marketing and use of certain substances, this Directive protects human health and, in certain cases, the environment[4]. The placing of plant protection products (pesticides) on the market is regulated by an EC Directive[5]. The Community rules on the marketing and use of **pesticides** containing dangerous substances is becoming more and more strict[6], to the point of banning the use of DDT in the Community. Maximum levels for pesticide residues in and on certain products of plant origin and foodstuffs are fixed at Community level[7]. The marketing of feeding stuffs[8] and of agricultural and vegetable seeds and propagating material are also regulated[9].

Since January 1, 1992, veterinary checks at intra-Community frontiers have been abolished and are instead carried out at the point of departure[10]. At the same time, the Community has switched from a system characterized by a policy of systematic preventive vaccination against foot and mouth disease, which could act as an obstacle to the free movement of animals and products, to a policy of non-vaccination and slaughter in the event of an infection source appearing. A Directive aims at the protection of animals during transport[11]. It lays down journey-time limits, rest times, and watering and feeding intervals. Another Directive lays down conditions for the production and marketing of fresh meat[12]. The Veterinary and Phytosanitary Inspections Office is responsible for the monitoring of all slaughterhouses approved in the Member States for intra-Community trade, as well as of all establishments manufacturing meat products.

1   OJ L376, 31.12.1991 and OJ L96, 22.04.1993.
2   OJ L227, 01.09.1994 and OJ L258, 25.10.1995.
3   OJ L26, 31.01.1977 and OJ L92, 09.04.1994.
4   OJ L33, 08.02.1979.
5   OJ L230, 19.08.1991 and OJ L227, 01.09.1994.
6   OJ L221, 07.08.1986 and OJ L211, 23.08.1993.
7   OJ L221, 07.08. 1986, OJ L350, 14.12.1990 and OJ L197, 22.08.1995.
8   OJ L86, 06.04.1979.
9   OJ 125, 11.07.1966 and OJ L187, 16.07.1988.
10   OJ L395, 30.12.1989 and OJ L268, 14.09.1992.
11   OJ L340, 11.12.1991 and OJ L148, 30.06.1995.
12   OJ L121, 29.07.1964 and OJ L243, 11.10.1995.

Veterinary checks on animals from third countries is organized at Community level[1]. Veterinary import procedures for animals and animal products from third countries have been computerized (Shift System), thus ensuring smooth operation of the internal market[2]. Numerous problems have appeared, however, after the elimination of controls at internal frontiers. In order to establish mutual trust, it is necessary to have a system of identification of animals traded in the internal market.

In the **veterinary field**, the efforts of the Community are mainly geared towards protecting the health of animals and consequently human health. But the eradication of the principle animal diseases prevalent in the Community also contributes to the smooth operation of the internal market. There are Community measures on the struggle against classical swine fever[3], African swine fever[4] and foot-and-mouth disease[5]. Given the importance of animal health, the Community contributes financially to the eradication of such diseases as brucellosis, tuberculosis, bovine leucosis[6] and classical swine fever[7]. The Community also covers various veterinary activities with a view to ensuring the rational development of the livestock production sector and the raising of productivity[8]. Thus, Community Directives deal with additives for feedingstuffs[9], undesirable substances and products in animal nutrition[10], arrangements for approving and registering certain establishments in the animal feed sector[11] and the organization of official inspections, both at external frontiers and inside the Community, in the field of animal nutrition[12]. Community rules prohibit the use in stockfarming of certain substances having a hormonal, thyrostatic and beta-agonists having an anabolic effect[13]. They also prevent meat imports from third countries, which do not prohibit the fattening of livestock with hormones, causing loud complaints of these countries, notably the United States.

The epidemic of bovine spongiform encephalopathy (BSE - "**mad cow disease**") in the United Kingdom is characteristic of the problems that an animal disease can present to a customs union. After having denied for several years that this disease was transmissible to man, the British Government acknowledged, in March 1996, that there was a possible link between the disease of bovine animals fed on meal made from contaminated meat or slaughter by-products and the Creutzfeldt-Jakob disease of human beings. Having taken the opinion of the Standing Veterinary Committee of the Union, on 27 March 1996, the Commission, in the consumers' interest, took a safeguard decision temporarily banning export of bovine animals, meat and meat products from the United Kingdom to other Member States and third countries[14]. On 3 April 1996, the Council agreed on a set of measures involving additional health measures, as well as market support measures examined in the chapter on Agriculture. In the

1   OJ L373, 31.12.1990 and OJ L265, 08.11.1995.
2   OJ L243, 25.08.1992.
3   OJ L47, 21.02.1980 and OJ L166, 08.07.1993.
4   OJ L168, 28.06.1985.
5   OJ L315, 26.11.1985.
6   OJ L24, 27.01.1987.
7   OJ L34, 05.02.1987.
8   OJ L224, 18.08.1990.
9   OJ L270, 14.12.1970 and OJ L350, 31.12.1994.
10   OJ L38, 11.02.1974 and OJ L104, 23.04.1994.
11   OJ C348, 28.12.1993.
12   OJ L265, 08.11.1995.
13   OJ L125, 23.05.1996.
14   OJ L78, 28.03.1996.

field of the customs union, the Council also adapted to the new situation preexisting Directives concerning the movement of feed materials and the marketing of compound feedingstuffs[1]. Despite the prohibition of exports of bovine animals over the age of 6 months, of meat and specified meat products from the United Kingdom as well as the prohibition of feeding ruminants with animal waste of mammalian origin in the Community, the beef market collapsed in the whole Community. This demonstrates the fact that in a customs union the market problems of a Member State are in reality problems of the single market.

Administrative cooperation

Since they collect customs duties, which must be paid in the Community budget, and guard the external frontiers against illicit trading, the customs officers of the Member States act, in fact, in the name of the Community and must apply the Community law. The efficiency of customs union depends as much on homogeneous rules as on the quality of its operational structures. As essential elements of these structures, the customs authorities of the Member States must be open to cooperation both among themselves and with the Commission in the spirit of Article 5 of the EC Treaty. This is the objective of the Council Regulation on the **mutual assistance** between the Member States' administrations and on their collaboration with the Commission to ensure the proper application of customs and agricultural regulations[2].

Modern administrative management increasingly uses computerized methods. With rationalization in mind, the Council decided the coordination of computerized administrative procedures (CD project)[3]. In this context, several computerized links have been developed. Updatings of the Community's integrated tariff (Taric), which is managed centrally by the Commission, are made available to the Member States by electronic data transfer **(TARIC interface)**. A centralized system for automatic tariff quota management communicates electronically with national administrative departments **(Quotas)**. The electronic mail system known as **Scent** (system for a customs enforcement network) is designed to pass urgent messages concerning cases of fraud. A computerized customs information system (CIS) purports to step up the fight against fraud at the Community's external frontiers. CIS is founded on a convention established on the basis of Article K.3 of the TEU (justice and home affairs cooperation)[4]. It is set up and maintained by the Member States' customs administrations to help prevent, detect and prosecute serious offences against national and Community laws.

The abolition of administrative procedures on crossing the internal frontiers of the Community heightens the risk of fraud if equivalent control measures are not applied by all the Member States. Administrative cooperation must encourage a comparative level of checks, thus guaranteeing mutual trust and competition. To this effect, the Commission conducts in partnership with the Member States, an action programme entitled "Customs 2000"[5]. The actions of the programme are focused on the following areas: ensuring the openness in the implementation of Community law by the customs administrations of the Member States; strengthening the common training policy put in place by the MATTHAEUS

---

1   OJ L125, 23.05.1996.
2   OJ L144, 02.06.1981.
3   OJ L33, 08.02.1986.
4   OJ C316, 27.11.1995.
5   COM (95) 119, 04.04.1995.

Programme[1]; developing and spreading use of the best new working methods, based in particular on information technology; ensuring dialogue between customs authorities and customs users, notably small and medium enterprises.

Trade with non-member countries

Apart from removing obstacles to intra-Community trade, customs union includes the harmonization of customs regulations on trade with non-member countries. The efforts aimed at implementing such regulations in the European Union are taking shape in two directions. On the one hand, the Community has established, and manages, a Common Customs Tariff (CCT); on the other hand, Community rules fit into an international context, whose evolution they must follow, and to which they must progressively adapt. Thus, arrangements agreed in the context of GATT and, henceforth, of the World Trade Organization must be transposed into Community law. A true internal market, free of frontiers, presupposes that the external relations of the Member States be regulated in the same way.

For this purpose, the **Community Customs Code** groups together and presents all of the provisions of customs legislation governing the Community's trade with third countries [2]. By regrouping some 75 Regulations adopted between 1968 and 1992, it aims to improve the clarity of Community customs regulations and remove the risk of divergent interpretations or legal vagueness. The Code is divided into three parts:
— the basic rules of customs legislation: customs territory of the European Union, customs tariff, customs value, goods origin;
— rules relative to customs destinations with economic impact: customs systems with economic impact (free zones, temporary admission, processing under customs control), instances of goods redirection or destruction; and
— rules relating to customs debt and appeals against decisions taken in customs matters.

Common Customs Tariff

The difference between a Customs Union and a tariff union, such as the EFTA, is the existence of a single external tariff applied by all Member States to imports coming from third countries. Such imports only have to clear customs once and can then move freely within the common customs area. Reaching an agreement on a single external tariff, however, required a complex striking of balances and compromises, given the different national interests, that is, the different products that each country wished to protect. The common customs tariff is therefore a major achievement by the Community.

---

1   OJ L187, 13.07.1991.
2   OJ L302, 19.10.1992, OJ L253, 11.10.1993 and OJ L162, 30.06.1994.

For the member countries, the CCT meant the loss of both customs revenue which, since 1975, has been a resource of the Community budget, and the option of carrying out an independent customs policy. No member country can unilaterally decide on or negotiate tariff matters; all changes to the CCT are decided by the Council following negotiation (if necessary) and proposal by the Commission. All bilateral (between the EU and non-member countries) and multilateral (GATT) negotiations are carried out by the Commission.

Because CCT is closely linked to the concept of the ECU, **new rates** are used to convert it into national currencies in order to determine the tariff classification of goods and CCT duties whenever there are bilateral central rate adjustments within the European Monetary System[1]. These new rates, along with all tariff changes in the course of the preceding year, including those resulting from regulations on agricultural matters and international negotiations, are incorporated in the annual edition of the Common Customs Tariff, published by the Office for Publications of the Communities and applicable as of 1 January every year[2].

Since 1995, the customs tariff of the European Union takes account of the outcome of the GATT Uruguay Round. In principle, for each item and sub-item of the tariff nomenclature, both the autonomous rates and the conventional rates resulting from the GATT negotiations are indicated. The difference between the two categories of rates is becoming increasingly noticeable, as the outcome of the Uruguay Round means further reductions in the conventional rates, reductions that will, moreover, continue in the years to come. Several technical annexes to the CCT set out the specific import regimes, such as the import regime for certain agricultural products or the regime for pharmaceutical substances which may benefit from an exoneration on duties.

The Commission and the Member States cooperate to ensure the proper and uniform application of the **CCT's nomenclature**. This customs instrument is very important, not only for the collection of customs duties, but also for a number of Community spheres of activity, such as the preparation of foreign trade statistics and the proper application of various measures regarding commercial, agricultural, fiscal or monetary policy. This activity takes the form of the adoption of Commission regulations, the finalization of explanatory notes or classification slips in the customs nomenclature[3]. The Community uses the same nomenclature as its main trading partners, thus facilitating trade negotiations. It is called the **Combined Nomenclature (CN)** because it meets the Community's tariff and statistical requirements simultaneously[4].

In parallel with the introduction of the CN, the **Integrated Community Tariff (Taric)** database was established, in order to indicate, in relation to each CN code, the Community clauses applicable to the goods of this code. It incorporates import provisions not included by the CN, such as tariff quotas and preferences, the temporary suspension of autonomous CCT duties, anti-dumping duties and countervailing duties[5]. Thus, Taric spans all the Community measures applicable to trade and provides national administrations with information on all Community measures relating to internal and external trade. It is published annually, but any modification is immediately transmitted by electronic way to competent administrations[6].

Before effecting any customs operation, it is first necessary to proceed to the "customs classification" of the goods concerned. Classification, has a determining effect on the proper functioning of agreements between the Community and certain exporting countries on the

---

1   See the chapter on Economic and Monetary Union.
2   OJ L319, 30.12.1995, see also the title on GATT in the chapter on the EU in the world.
3   OJ L256, 07.09.1987 and OJ L103, 22.04.1994.
4   OJ L160, 26.06.1990 and OJ L241, 22.09.1993.
5   OJ L256, 07.09.1987 and OJ L347, 28.11.1989.
6   OJ C141, 24.05.1994.

trade of textile products. The level of detail of the combined nomenclature has resulted, principally for those SMEs without computer systems, in a complexity and multiplication of the lines to be declared. Operators can request binding tariff information from the authorities in the Member States with responsibility for the classification of goods under the customs nomenclature [1]. This information indicates the tariff heading to be used for specific goods in all of the Member States. It therefore makes a vital contribution to the legal security of economic operators and greatly facilitates imports and exports.

Economic tariff matters

As of 1968, the Member States are not entitled to unilaterally carry out customs policy, i.e. : suspend customs duties or change CCT. Only the Council can waive the normal application of CCT by means of regulations adopting various tariff measures. Such measures, whether required under agreements or introduced unilaterally, involve reductions in customs duties or zero-rating in respect of some or all imports of a given product. They take the form of Community tariff quotas, tariff ceilings or total or partial suspension of duties.

The most important tariff concessions are granted by the Community in the context of the **General Agreement on Tariffs and Trade (GATT)**. In the course of several international negotiations, namely: the "Dillon Round" (1960-62), the "Kennedy Round" (1964-67) and the "Tokyo Round" (1973-79), substantial reductions of customs duties were made on most industrial products. The "Uruguay Round", which was launched on 20 September 1986 and was concluded on 15 December 1993, has achieved major tariff reductions on the part of the 117 participating countries in the sectors of industry, agriculture and services. It has also imposed new rules and disciplines to international trade.

The European Union can raise customs duties on products whose protection has been bound ("consolidated") under GATT only if it offers its trading partners equivalent compensation. However, the Council may adopt unilateral protective measures on imports when these present a serious risk to European production. Such measures may not be directed at a single country or be limited to one or more Member States. However, according to the rules of GATT, quantitative restrictions are applied "erga omnes", i.e. to all producing countries without distinction. The EU can also protect itself against unfair trading practices by applying the anti-dumping procedures included in GATT provisions. Pursuant to these provisions, the EU can fix countervailing duties if goods are offered in the European market at a substantially lower price than in the producing country[2].

As part of its development aid policy, the European Union applies **generalized tariff preferences** on imports from developing countries (LDCs). To the African, Caribbean and Pacific States (ACP), signatories of the Lomé Convention, the EU grants free access to the near-totality of their imports, with the exception of textile products and of the agricultural products, that are subject to common market organizations[3].

Following the accession to the EEC of the UK and Denmark, both former **European Free Trade Association (EFTA)** members, free trade agreements were concluded between the Community and the EFTA countries in order to avoid the erection of new obstacles to trade. As a result of these agreements, trade between the two groups of countries tripled from 1974 to 1984. These bilateral agreements have been replaced, since 1st January 1994, by the Treaty on the European Economic Area (EEA), which, after the accession of Austria, Sweden and Finland to the EU, brings together the Fifteen with Norway, Iceland and the

---

1   OJ L160, 26.06.1990.
2   See the section on Commercial Policy in the Chapter on the European Union in the World.
3   See the section on development aid in the chapter on the EU in the world.

Liechtenstein in a vast economic zone guaranteeing the four fundamental freedoms of a common market. The free trade arrangements are gradually being extended to the countries of Central and Eastern Europe in the framework of European agreements.

Several **tariff quotas and ceilings** are opened every year, under bilateral agreements with non-member countries or on a unilateral basis in order to secure the Community supply situation for certain products. For the same reason, and also in many cases with the aim of encouraging Community industry to use or introduce new technology, the Council **temporarily suspends**, every year, duties on about 1800 products or groups of products, mainly chemicals and products of the electronics or aircraft industries. Tariffs are also suspended on a number of agricultural and fishery products, to improve the supply of certain types of food and honour preferential commitments entered into with certain non-member countries.

The legislation on preferential tariff measures resulting from agreements concluded between the EU and States or groups of States with which contractual relations are maintained has been consolidated to a few main multiannual Regulations[1]. The full application of CCT is thus limited to trade with North America, Australia and South Africa. Although CCT has become less important, customs union, supported by the instruments of trade policy which accompany it, ensures sufficient protection from the import of cheap industrial goods. In the **textile** sector, customs duties are generally supplemented by agreements on voluntary restraint of exports negotiated as part of the Multifibre Arrangement (MFA). In the **steel** sector, agreements on voluntary restraint have also been concluded with the principal producing countries. As seen in the chapter on **agriculture**, the agricultural market is protected by a special system, now based more and more on customs duties in application of the GATT agreements.

General customs legislation

Customs union requires more than just having a common customs tariff; it must be applied according to identical rules throughout all Member States. Failure to do this could result in different values for customs purposes or different rules on the release of goods for circulation according to the importing Member State. The Customs Code of the European Union, which groups together all the provisions of the Community's customs legislation, aims precisely at removing the risk of different interpretations of EU rules in trade between the Member States and third countries.

The **customs territory** of the Community is defined by a Council Regulation[2]. It states inter alia that the coastal Member States' territorial sea is part of the Community's customs territory. This is of particular importance to the fishing and off-shore activities of Member States. Another Regulation lays down provisions relating to the place of introduction to be taken into consideration for the determination of value for customs purposes[3]. **Value for customs purposes** can sometimes have a greater impact on trade than customs duties. A Council Regulation specifies the method by which such value is determined, the customs clearance criteria

---

1   OJ L189, 23.07.1994 and OJ L199, 02.08.1994.
2   OJ L197, 27.07.1984.
3   OJ L335, 12.12.1980 and OJ L267, 29.09.1990.

for goods finished or processed out of their country of origin, and the conditions under which goods are temporarily exempt of import duties[1].

A Regulation on **checks for conformity** of products imported from third countries with the rules of the Community Directive on product safety, aims to ensure an efficient and coherent management of the common external frontier and to equalize the conditions of competition between Community products and imports[2]. It enables the customs authorities of the Member States to temporarily suspend the customs clearance procedure in cases where imported products present characteristics which may constitute a direct health or safety hazard.

The Community law has harmonized the legislative, regulatory and administrative provisions on: the **customs treatment** of goods entering the Community's customs territory and on the **temporary storage** of these goods[3]; **goods brought into** the customs territory of the Community until such goods have received a destination for customs purposes[4]; **returned goods** in the customs territory of the Community[5]; admission to **free circulation** of goods[6]; and **relief from customs duties**[7].

As regards exports, various Community Regulations govern the **export procedures** of Community goods[8]; the **deferred payment of customs duties** on imports or exports[9] the **refund or remittance** of these duties[10]; and the **post-clearance collection** of export duties not imposed on goods entered for a customs procedure[11]. Furthermore, a Decision adopted on the basis of Article J.3 of the Treaty (common foreign and security policy) and a Regulation (EC) set up a Community regime for the control of **exports of dual-use goods**, i.e. goods used for both civil and military purposes[12].

Of capital importance to the administration of customs union and to the legal security of individuals are the common rules concerning the origin, liability and settlement of **customs debt**[13], those providing the definition of **persons liable for payment** of a customs debt[14] and those defining the conditions under which a person may submit a **customs entry**[15].

As mentioned in the previous part of this chapter, close cooperation between national administrations, organized by the Commission, is needed to prevent infringements of customs rules and other conditions for access to the Union market. Priority areas include fraud prevention, protection of intellectual property rights - particularly trade marks, designs and copyright - and measures to combat counterfeiting.

The **action to combat fraud** in trade with non-member countries is organized by a Council Regulation on the mutual assistance of the administrative authorities of the Member States and on their collaboration with

---

1   OJ L134, 31.05.1980 and OJ L112, 25.04.1985.
2   OJ L40, 10.02.1993.
3   OJ L194, 06.08.1968.
4   OJ L367, 31.12.1988.
5   OJ L89, 02.04.1976 and OJ L105, 22.04.1986.
6   OJ L205, 13.08.1979 and OJ L281, 12.10.1990.
7   OJ L105, 23.04.1983 and OJ L46, 18.02.1994.
8   OJ L83, 30.03.1981.
9   OJ L146, 02.06.1978.
10 OJ L175, 12.07.1979 and OJ L352, 13.12.1988.
11 OJ L197, 03.08.1979.
12 OJ L367, 31.12.1994 and OJ L90, 21.04.1995.
13 OJ L201, 22.07.1987.
14 OJ L102, 21.04.1988.
15 OJ L350, 27.12.1985.

the Commission to ensure the proper application of customs or agricultural rules[1]. Common protection against the unfair trading practices of non-member countries is covered by a Council Regulation of 1 December 1986 which lays down measures preventing imports and prohibiting the release for free circulation of **counterfeit and pirated goods**[2]. The Community, however, lacks uniform penal provisions to prevent the infraction of customs legislation.

Origin of goods

The rules of origin determine to what extent products coming from third countries may be exempt of duty by determining the degree of processing or transformation they have undergone. These rules, which are now contained in the Community Customs Code, are important for the proper application of preference systems and several provisions of the commercial policy of the European Union. In order to prevent fraud arising from irregularities of origin, it is necessary to determine uniformly the origin of goods obtained entirely in a certain country, as well as the origin of goods obtained in a country after substantial transformation of raw materials and semi-products originating in other countries. Thus, goods admitted under preference agreements must come entirely from the exporting country or, if imported from a third country, have undergone substantial processing or finishing. A Council Regulation defines for purposes of non-preference traffic, the concept of the origin of goods[3].

The origin of several categories of products has also been determined autonomously by Council regulations. Such definitions are used for non preferential traffic. Other provisions determine the rules of origin on a conventional basis within the framework of preference agreements between the Community and certain countries, namely the ACP[4]. The action to combat fraud in the field of rules of origin is mainly concerned with **textile products imported** from developing countries[5]. For Community exports, the Commission adapted the model certificate of origin to the overall frame recommended by the UN[6].

Customs procedures with economic impact

Common customs regulations, uniformly applicable in the Community's trade relations with other countries, involve setting up various customs procedures with economic impact. Using Directives, the Council harmonized the legislative, regulatory and administrative provisions relative to **customs warehouses** procedures, **free zones** procedures[7], and usual forms of handling, which can be undertaken in customs warehouses

---

1   OJ L144, 02.06.1981 and OJ L90, 02.04.1987.
2   OJ L341, 30.12.1994. See also the title on Community finances in the Introduction.
3   OJ L148, 28.06.1968 and OJ L54, 28.02.1991.
4   OJ L290, 23.10.1990.
5   OJ L84, 31.03.1978 and OJ L360, 23.12.1983.
6   OJ L59, 05.03.1981.
7   OJ L58, 08.03.1969 and OJ L225, 15.08.1988.

and free zones[1]. In 1983, the Council adopted a Procedure allowing the **processing of goods under customs control** before their release for free circulation in order to avoid, by use of tariff measures, the processing operations of certain imports, such as certain petroleum products, taking place in third countries rather than in the Community[2]. To facilitate the use of containers in, for example, combined road/rail carriage, the Council defined on 13 July 1987 a regulatory system for the **temporary admission of containers**[3]. Bearing the mark of their member State, the containers are deemed to meet the conditions of free circulation provided by articles 9 and 10 of the EEC Treaty.

Of particular interest are **inward processing arrangements** allowing for the temporary release for free circulation of products coming from third countries processed in a member State and re-exported to a third country. The Member States must properly apply these procedures especially when the inward processing deals with agricultural products and when compensating products are released for free circulation in a Member State other than where the processing took place[4]. In an attempt to lighten the formalities for those involved, a Commission Regulation sets specific provisions applicable to certain inward processing arrangements or processing under customs control carried out in a customs warehouse, free warehouse or free zone[5].

The reverse mechanism, **outward processing arrangements**, is of interest to many European enterprises which, in the context of the international division of labour, export goods with a view to re-importing them following processing, working or repairs. This alleviates the enterprise's production costs and thus favours production in the EU. Established in 1982 as part of the multifibre arrangement for textile and clothing products[6], outward processing relief arrangements were expanded, in 1986, to **standard exchange arrangements**[7] and, in 1988, to **triangular traffic** covering two Member States[8]. The Member States can check the relevant documents in order to ensure that the compensating products have been manufactured using goods temporarily exported[9]. The outward processing arrangements have been adapted to the internal market and cover tariff concessions for the Central and Eastern European countries[10].

Appraisal and outlook

The first ten years of the European Economic Community were the years of glory for customs union. The removal of customs duties and quantitative restrictions on imports and exports and the introduction of a common customs tariff are some of the Community's main accomplishments. They ruled out any "national preference" and gave rise to the "Community preference". They provided formidable stimulus to intra-

---

1 OJ L143, 29.06.1971 and OJ L225, 15.08.1988.
2 OJ L272, 05.10.1983 and OJ L78, 26.03.1991.
3 OJ L196, 17.07.1987.
4 OJ L188, 20.07.1985 and OJ L210, 31.07.1991.
5 OJ L151, 15.06.1991
6 OJ L76, 20.03.1982. See "Sectoral Commercial Policy Measures" in the chapter on the EU in the world.
7 OJ L212, 02.08.1986.
8 OJ L174, 06.07.1988.
9 OJ L304, 01.11.1990.
10 OJ L322, 15.12.1994.

Community trade and, as provided by the EEC Treaty, were the foundation for the common market and all Community policies examined herein.

What the Treaty had not foreseen was the tenacity of the national administrative authorities who quickly found obstacles other than those of customs to hinder trade between Member States, protect national production and, leaving, justify their existence. The protection of national production by means of barriers to intra-Community trade was unhealthy because it raised the price of goods by 5 to 10%. The existence of customs at the Community's internal frontiers proved to generally ill-informed citizens that customs union, in the making since 1958, and the Community as a whole did not exist.

And yet customs union, although incomplete, was well and truly in place and through the abolition of customs duties and quantitative restrictions, had contributed to the material well-being of the Member States' citizens. But the latter had already forgotten the situation existing prior to customs union and were ignorant of its benefits. Human nature often takes progress for granted and forgets both what went before and the efforts for change. Barely a third of a century ago, no-one would have imagined that products from all over the continent would be available at an affordable price in a local store, or that millions of tourists would cross borders every year without any formality.

The customs union has now been completed and is seen most strikingly in the disappearance of customs checks at the frontiers between Member States. The abolition of customs checks at internal frontiers was achieved thanks to the abolition of the Single Administrative Document, a far-ranging reform of indirect taxation, examined in the Chapter on Taxation and the entry into force of a series of provisions reorganizing fiscal, veterinary, phytosanitary, sanitary and safety checks and the collection of statistical data. The most meaningful aspect of this process is the lightening of the administrative burden of companies carrying out intra-Community sales and purchases, with the abolition of some 60 million customs administrative documents.

It goes without saying that the abolition of customs formalities at internal frontiers must be counterbalanced by the reinforcement of measures at external frontiers: administrative cooperation must ensure that differences in regulations do not give rise to fraud or problems for consumers; customs checks at the Community's external frontiers will have to be strengthened for imports from third countries; national security problems (crime, drugs, terrorism, firearms traffic) will have to be settled jointly and by a detailed exchange of information between the police and security forces of the Member States and, to a certain extent, with other neighbouring countries; and common policies will be necessary regarding citizens of non-member countries circulating within the Member States.

The priority here is to coordinate the rules governing the latter's entry, residence and eligibility for employment as well as the arrangements on refugees, extradition, visas and the right to asylum. It can be seen that these are subjects relating both to the third pillar of the Union, as judicial and home affairs, and to the first pillar, as important elements of the free circulation of persons in the internal market. It is important that they be considered under this second aspect, so as that the measures concerning them be taken by the Community procedure, which avoids the problems connected with the intergovernmental process.

In addition to the internal environment of the Union, the international environment of customs and commerce has been profoundly modified in the nineties. The opening up of free international trade to the Central and East European countries as well as those of the former Soviet Union and the entry into force of the new GATT agreements have been powerful catalysts in the globalization of trade. At the same time, however, there has been a growing globalization of illicit traffic in all areas, such as drugs, arms, nuclear material and protected animal species. From a customs viewpoint, this requires strengthened cooperation and mutual assistance between the customs administrations of Community countries and those of third countries, notably those of other European countries.

The big challenge of the Member States customs officers, who are in fact customs officers of the Union, is to ensure a high quality of control at the external frontier, which facilitates the free flow of traffic while being applied in an effective, efficient and homogeneous manner. A delicate balance needs to be struck by the customs officers between ensuring minimum disruption to legitimate trade and free circulation of persons on the one hand, and the need to detect and deter fraud on the other. In order to maintain their confidence in the functioning of the customs union and the internal market, citizens must feel that the administration of Community law is as reliable and effective as that of their own national Regulations. Therefore, customs officers at the external frontiers of the European Union must obtain equivalent results, both in terms of control and trade facilitation. This will avoid trade deflection and distortion of commercial flows with the rest of the world. In this way, customs union will mature into what the founding fathers of the Community wished it to be: a firm foundation stone for the common market.

Bibliography on Custom Union

◻ BHAGWATI Jagdish, "Regionalism versus Multilateralism", in *World Economy*, Oxford, Vol. 15, N 5, September 1992, pp. 535-555.

◻ BIZAGUET Armand, *Le grand marché européen de 1993*, PUF "Que sais-je?", 4ème édition réfondue, Paris, 1993.

◻ COMMISSION EUROPÉENNE, *L'union douanière dans le cadre du grand marché*, COM (1990) 572.

- *Nomenclature combinée des Communautés européennes: notes explicatives*, OPOCE, Luxembourg, 1991.

- *Les contrôles vétérinaires et phytosanitaires*, OPOCE, Luxembourg, 1993.

- *Suppression des contrôles aux frontières - Situation au 1er janvier 1993*, Série "Marché intérieur", Vol. 2, 1993.

- *TARIC: tarif intégré des Communautés européennes*, OPOCE, Luxembourg, 1994.

□ DENOEL Xavier, "Les accords de réadmission du Benelux à Schengen et au-delà", in *Revue trimestrielle de droit européen*, N° 4, 1993, pp. 635-653.

□ DEVUYST Youri, "GATT Customs Union Provisions and the Urugay Round: "The European Community Experience", in *Journal of World Trade*, Geneva, Vol. 26, N 1, February 1992, pp. 15-34.

□ *Douane. Réglementation communautaire et nationale*, Ed. F. Lefèbvre, Levallois, 1993.

□ GIFFONI Massimo, *Droit douanier de la l'Union européenne et aspects économiques*, deuxième édition, Commission européenne, OPOCE, Luxembourg, 1995.

□ GOYBET Catherine, "Les zones de libre-échange: nouveau sujet de tension entre les Quinze", in *Revue du Marché commun et de l'Union européenne*, Paris, N° 395, février 1996, pp. 77-80.

□ KOWALCZIK Carsten, *Welfare and Customs Unions*, National Bureau of Economic Research, Cambridge, MA, 1990.

□ "L'intégration économique comparative", in *Revue internationale des sciences administratives*, numéro spécial, 57/04, 1991, pp. 589-752.

□ PLUMMER Michael, "Efficiency Effects of the Accession of Spain and Portugal to the EC", in *Journal of Common Market Studies*, Oxford, Vol. 29, No 3, March 1991, pp. 317-325.

□ PRAHL H., *Douanes et accises*, Presses universitaires de Bruxelles, Bruxelles, 1993.

□ RAVILLARD Patrick, *La répression des infractions douanières dans le cadre du grand marché intérieur*, GNL Joly éditions, Paris, 1992.

□ VAULONT Nikolaus, "La suppression des frontières intérieures et la réglementation douanière communautaire", *Revue du marché unique européen*, N° 1, 1994, pp. 51-70.

□ WILLIAMS David, "A Wider European Customs Union", in *Intertax*, Deventer, N 3, March 1993, pp. 123-127.

2. COMMON MARKET

The creation of a single European economic area based on a common market was, from the very beginning, a fundamental objective of the European Community. Article 2 of the Treaty of Rome, establishing the European Economic Community, set out that objective as follows: "The Community shall have as its task, by establishing a common market and progressively approximating the economic policies of Member States, to promote throughout the Community a harmonious development of economic activities, a continuous and balanced expansion, an increase in stability, an accelerated raising of the standard of living and closer relations between the States belonging to it".

Establishment of the common market first required the elimination of all import and export duties in force between Member States before the foundation of the Community. We saw in the previous chapter how the Member States effectively removed the customs barriers even before expiry of the period laid down by the Treaty and how, immediately after tariff dismantling, they began erecting other barriers between them, in particular technical barriers which were even more difficult to cross than customs ones. In the first section of this chapter we shall look at how the Member States decided to complete the common market and what measures they decided to take to eliminate technical obstacles to trade and to open up their public contracts. In this chapter we shall also examine the measures aimed at the free movement of persons, services and capital, which, together with the free movement of goods, constitute the basic elements of the common market.

The common market which was completed in 1992 is a very important stage in European integration. Underlying it there is a range of basic freedoms: the free movement of goods, persons, services and capital. Their implementation first and foremost makes it possible to allow the production factors of work and capital to operate without hindrance. Undertakings can manufacture and sell their production in accordance with a system of free competition in the Member State in which conditions are most advantageous for them. They can set themselves up wherever they wish in the common market and can call on a multitude of sources of capital which exist in every Member State. Consumers have a free choice of better quality and/or lower price products, manufactured in the Member States. Workers have free access to jobs wherever demand is strongest and thus benefit from better working conditions and remuneration. They can establish themselves with their families in any of the member countries and take up employment there. The key word for the common market is, as we can see, freedom.

Completion of the internal market

After the completion of customs dismantling in July 1968[1], the European Commission recorded, in a 1970 memorandum on industrial policy[2], that, in spite of the undeniable liberalization of trade between the Member States, their six markets taken together were far from resembling a single market. The proof lay in the differences in the level of prices between member countries for similar products. The Commission attributed the inflexibility of prices in part to differences in mentalities and traditions, inadequate knowledge of partners' products, routine loyalty to habitual products, the lack of adaptation of a country's products to the tastes and habits of consumers in the others and the various strategies adopted by producers and distributors from the member countries. To a large extent, however, the inflexibility of prices stemmed from the compartmentalization of markets owing to the old and new barriers which the national authorities had erected to replace the customs barriers and against which the Commission was even then beginning to wage war.

Fifteen years later, in its 1985 "white paper" on completing the internal market[3], the Commission again recorded that the "common" market was far from resembling a single market for a number of reasons, the main ones being:
— customs delays and the administrative charges weighing on intra-Community trade;
— the differences between plant-health and veterinary standards, necessitating checks at borders;
— the formalities carried out at borders for statistical purposes;
— national differences in technical rules and standards for industrial products;
— the lack of openness of public contracts to foreign suppliers;
— restrictions on the freedom to provide certain services, in particular financial services, and on freedom of establishment with regard to certain activities;
— differences between the rates of VAT and excise duties, governed by the "rule of destination" and which have to be adjusted at the border of the Member State of destination;
— the application of monetary compensatory amounts to intra-Community trade in certain agricultural products in accordance with the rules of the common agricultural policy, and
— road transport licences and the checks on the conformity of vehicles with the various national regulations.

We examined the first three causes of the non-completion of the internal market in the chapter on customs union. We shall now expand on the next three, relating to technical barriers to trade, the opening-up of public procurement, freedom to provide services, in this chapter. The last three relate, in order, to taxation policy, agricultural policy and transport policy and they will be examined in the corresponding chapters. Only by tackling all these barriers is it possible to have a market which is genuinely single in all respects, a real "Europe without frontiers".

It is useful to define here the concepts of "common market", "single market" and "internal market" which are used almost synonymously but which have significant nuances of meaning. The **common market** is a stage

---

1   See the chapter on customs union.
2   See the chapter on industry.
3   COM(85)310 final.

in economic integration which, in the words of a Court of Justice ruling, aims to remove all the barriers to intra-Community trade with a view to the merger of national markets into a **single market** giving rise to conditions as close as possible to a genuine **internal market**[1]. The single market is consequently the continuation of the common market and the end point of the process is the internal market. In other words, the common market is a stage on the way to an internal market which, according to Article 7a of the EC Treaty, comprises "an area without internal frontiers in which the free movement of goods, persons, services and capital is ensured in accordance with the provisions of this Treaty". The following pages give an illustration of the obstacles which the Community had to clear during the common market stage in order to reach the goal of a single market, which is similar but not identical to a genuine internal market.

During the first decade of its existence the Community negotiated two very important hurdles towards its economic integration: the achievement of customs union, involving the abolition of customs duties and quantitative restrictions between Member States and the establishment of a common customs tariff, as well as the definition of a common agricultural policy necessary for the free movement of agricultural goods between Member States. These vital achievements were decided upon by the six original Member States in a favourable economic climate and a stable monetary environment guaranteed by the Bretton Woods system.

In August 1971, however, the United States had decided to dismantle the international monetary system, based on the Bretton Woods agreements, which had ensured, until then, the monetary stability indispensable to the functioning of the European common market. Unharnessed, the international speculation had, then, thwarted the first attempt to create an economic and monetary union in Europe. Moreover, the oil crises of 1973 and 1979 had shaken the European economies[2]. Thus the Europe of the early '80s had sunk into "**Euro-slump**" and "**Euro-pessimism**".

It was in this atmosphere that Europe's politicians understood that the only salvation for the European economies would be a forward leap by economic integration. At the instigation of H.D. Genscher, German Minister of Foreign Affairs, and his Italian colleague, E. Colombo, the European Council in Stuttgart on June 19, 1983 adopted a **Solemn Declaration on European Union**. One of the important points of this Declaration was the "completion of the internal market in accordance with the Treaties, in particular the removal of the remaining obstacles to the free movement of goods, capital and services, as well as the further development of a common transport policy."

A few months after that Solemn Declaration, on 14 February 1984 the **European Parliament**, on the basis of an initiative by Altiero Spinelli, adopted by a large majority a draft Treaty on European Union which had been submitted to the Parliaments and Governments of the Member States. This draft both sought to complete the common market and sketched out the later stages, culminating in political union.

However, in January 1985, a new Commission had taken up its duties, and its President, **Jacques Delors**, had presented to the European Parliament the main guidelines for its action over the following four years. President Delors refused to succumb to "Euro-pessimism". The Community needed to re-discover firmness of speech and action, speak with one voice and return to the path of imagination and assume the offensive. Internally, it was more than time to put an end to the image of a feudal Europe which offered only barriers, customs,

---

1   Judgment of May 5, 1982, case 15/81
2   See the chapters on EMU and on energy.

formalities and red tape. All internal European borders should be eliminated by the end of 1992.

The magic date of 1992 was thus pronounced. From the texts of the Treaties to the successive declarations of European Council meetings since 1982, the need to complete the internal market had been asserted at the highest level. To attain that objective a deadline and a detailed programme had been lacking. The Commission had taken up that challenge and provided the missing part. It had started, in that connection, from the broadest possible interpretation of the challenge: to create a genuine common market without internal borders by the end of 1992.

To the above end, on 14 June 1985 the Commission forwarded to the European Council a **"white paper" on completing the internal market**[1]. That programme for the elimination within seven years of all physical, technical and fiscal obstacles was characterized in particular by: a more flexible approach to harmonization methods; the deliberate rejection of all easy ways out, which would in practice result in maintaining controls on trade at the internal borders; the adoption of a precise and binding timetable, which was indispensable to the success of the programme, the importance of which lay in its overall approach and in the balance of interests involved. The white paper therefore listed a battery of some 300 legislative texts aimed at removing barriers to trade.

The Milan European Council (28 and 29 June 1985) welcomed the programme established in the white paper and decided, by a majority of its members, to call an inter-governmental conference with the brief of drawing up a draft Treaty covering, on the one hand, political cooperation and, on the other, the amendments to the EEC Treaty required for the completion of the internal market. The Commission's proposals for a "single framework" for the amendment of the EEC Treaty and for political cooperation were central to the proceedings of the Conference. The "single framework" advocated by it met with the approval of the European Council at its meeting in Luxembourg on 2 and 3 December 1985 and was finalized in the form of a **"Single Act"** by the Ministers for Foreign Affairs meeting in Intergovernmental Conference on 27 January 1986.

The Single European Act, which entered into force on July 1, 1987, made significant changes to the Community's institutional system. By re-establishing majority voting by the Council, it put the Community in a position to take decisions more efficiently and to act more rapidly and more democratically. In addition it provided for the European Parliament to play a fuller part in the decision-making process through the cooperation procedure. Let us now look at how the Single Act succeeded in creating the Single Market.

Removal of technical barriers to trade

What is meant by technical obstacles to trade? In all Community countries industrial products and foodstuffs are subject to legislation which obliges them to satisfy certain criteria or to meet certain standards and technical specifications. This legislation is necessary for various reasons: the rationalization of industrial production, safeguarding the safety of workers, protection of the health of consumers and the reduction of

---

1   COM(85)310 final.

environmental pollution. The problem for the common market was not the existence of **national regulations**, but the differences between them and also the fact that those measures could be used to protect the national market from products from other Member States which were subject to different standards.

The disparity that existed between countries in terms of technical requirements stemmed from historical and economic considerations. A country in which a product was imported rather than manufactured tended to impose stringent requirements on it and checks prior to its being placed on the market, without concerning itself greatly about the economic cost which that represented. On the other hand a producer country of an industrial product tended to take into consideration the economic implications of requirements and controls, an excessive stringency of which would penalize its industry. In any case, the various technical regulations could hinder trade even more than customs duties. Indeed, even a high customs tariff could be paid and a product originating in one country could enter the market of another, whereas if a product did not comply with the technical rules its entry to that country's market was completely blocked.

The result was that the industrialist who wished to export to the other EEC member countries was obliged to bear additional research, development and production costs in order **to comply with all the national standards** which his products had to satisfy. Thus the disparity of the legislation within the Community compelled producers to manufacture different components, increase their production lines, diversify their stocks according to country of destination and to have specialized distribution and after-sales services for each country.

All the above made production on the Community scale more costly than it should have been and promoted large undertakings rather than small and medium-sized undertakings. Large undertakings, in particular multinationals, had the structure, experience and personnel required to meet the specific requirements of the markets in several countries and could spread the additional costs over long runs in such a way that they represented a negligible fraction of the unit cost of the product. For SMEs, however, the additional costs represented a substantial fraction of the production unit cost and could be prohibitive for any exports.

However, under a judgment of the Court of Justice of 17 December 1981 the authorities of the importing State are not entitled unnecessarily to require technical or chemical analyses or laboratory tests when the same analyses or tests have already been carried out in another Member State and their results are available to those authorities or may at their request be placed at their disposal[1]. If they do require such analyses or tests to be carried out unnecessarily, they are infringing Articles 30 to 36 of the EEC Treaty (quantitative restrictions and measures having equivalent effect) and are liable to be called to order by the Commission[2]. Article 36 allows some restrictions on imports on grounds of public morality, public policy or public security, but specifies that they must not constitute disguised restrictions on trade between Member States[3]. According to the Court of Justice, willing to ensure the survival of

---

1   Judgment of 17 December 1981, Case 272/80.
2   See, for example, ruling Commission/Germany, Case C-62/90.
3   See in this context the Judgment of the Court on German beer, case 178/84, ECR 1987, p. 1227.

a company cannot be a justification founded on this Article[1].

The free movement of goods within the Community established by Articles 30 to 36 is in actual fact safeguarded by the **infringement procedures** introduced by Article 169 of the Treaty. The Commission invokes those procedures whenever it records an infringement of Community provisions attributable to any authority whatsoever of a Member State. It may consider a case as a matter of routine in the light of information provided by Members of the uropean Parliament or published in the press or in the official journal of a Member State. Usually, however, a **complaint** is brought before it by an economic operator, an association or even another Member State in respect of draft standards or technical rules of a Member State. In 1995, the Commission still found itself confronted with more than 1000 cases of barriers to trade, a figure illustrative of the persistence of protectionist tendencies among national authorities. A supplementary problem was the not complete or correct transposal of the directives relating to the realization of the single market[2]. At the request of the Commission, the Council, in June 1995, agreed on the principle that penalties be applicable for breaches of Community law in the internal market[3].

Harmonization of legislation

The removal of technical obstacles to trade in **industrial products** is traditionally based on Article 100 of the Treaty, which provides for the **approximation of** such **provisions** laid down by law, regulation or administrative action as they directly affect the functioning of the common market. In this way the Commission has for many years been trying to align national regulations on Community standards agreed upon by the Council. Such alignment is not, however, as easy as it seems at first sight. As technical regulations relate to production systems and consequently investments already made, and as their harmonization sometimes entails the need for industrialists in some Member States to change their production systems by means of new investment expenditure, it can be understood why the removal of technical obstacles to trade forms the subject of interminable discussions. Each member country tries to persuade its partners that its own technical regulations are the best and should be adopted by the Community.

The laborious procedures involved in the approximation of laws lead to results which are unspectacular, but very useful for economic integration. Once the standards are the same in all member countries, type approval of a product granted in any member country is recognized by all the others. The industrialist need only guarantee that all examples of a product will conform to the prototype which has been approved. Exam-

---

1   Judgment of 28 March 1995, case C-324/93.
2   COM (95) 500, 07.06.1995.
3   OJ C188, 22.07.1995.

ples which do not conform may not be sold anywhere in the common market, nor on the producer's home market. Conversely, no Member State may apply more stringent national rules to oppose the importation or use of products which meet Community requirements.

Until now some 250 **directives on the harmonization of laws** have thus been adopted by the Council, a large number of which have on several occasions been adapted to technical progress. They harmonize the national laws in fields as diverse as motor vehicle equipment, foodstuffs and proprietary medicinal products. Thus, considerable progress has been made in the motor vehicle sector, in particular as a result of the entry into force of the EC type-approval for passenger cars[1]. In the foodstuffs sector a body of Community inspectors is responsible for evaluating and checking the control systems in the Member States[2]. Directives have been adopted in the particularly sensitive areas of colourings and sweeteners[3]. The harmonization work relating to pharmaceutical products has culminated in the creation of the single market in medicinal products and in the establishment of a European Agency for the Evaluation of Medicinal Products[4].

However, whilst some problems were being resolved through such harmonizations, the Member States, tempted by protectionism, in particular in the gloomy economic climate of the '70s, were adopting new legislation and creating further technical obstacles to trade. The Community Institutions' laborious work to remove those obstacles therefore resembled the endless tasks of the Danaides. For that reason, the Commission considered a fresh approach to the problem. For that it relied upon the case-law of the Court of Justice. In its judgment of 20 February 1979 in the "**Cassis de Dijon**" case (concerning the sale in Germany of blackcurrant liqueur produced in France), the Court of Justice gave a very broad definition of the obstacles to free trade which were prohibited under **Article 30 et seq.** of the Treaty[5]. It stated that any product lawfully manufactured and marketed in a Member State should in principle be admitted to the market of any other Member State.

According to another Court judgment, to escape the reach of Article 30, national provisions must not discriminate against the traders to whom they apply or have the effect of discriminating between the marketing of national products and that of products from other Member States[6]. Even if they are applicable without distinction to domestic and imported products, national regulations may not create obstacles unless they are necessary to satisfy mandatory requirements and are directed towards an objective of general interest which is such as to take precedence over the requirements of the free movement of goods, which is one of the basic rules of the Community. In plain language, a country must not bar the way to

---

1   OJ L225, 10.08.1992.
2   OJ L290, 24.11.1993.
3   OJ L237, 10.09.1994.
4   OJ L214, 24.08.1993.
5   Judgment of 20 February 1979, Case 120/78, ECR 1979, p. 649.
6   Judgment given on 24 November 1993, Joined Cases C-267/91 and C-268/91, Keck and Mithouard, ECR 1993, p. I-6097.

competing products from another Member State solely because they are slightly different from domestic products. If it does so, the Commission will take proceedings against it as far as the Court of Justice, where it stands every chance of being condemned on the basis of existing case law.

Prevention of new technical obstacles

In parallel with application of the "Cassis de Dijon" principle, and in accordance with the old adage that prevention is better than cure, the Commission secured the adoption by the Council of a procedure for the prevention of new technical obstacles to trade. A Council Directive of 28 March 1983 laying down a **procedure for** the provision of **information** in the field of technical standards and regulations is a vital instrument for preventing the appearance of new obstacles to trade. The Commission must be notified of these and can thus notify the other Member States and request amendments before their entry into force[1]. In 1994, the Council extended the concept of "technical rule" so as to include, in particular, technical specifications linked to tax measures and voluntary agreements[2]. A similar information procedure exists in the framework of the EEA agreement. Transparency is thus ensured throughout the European Economic Area.

Between the entry into force of the information procedure and the end of 1994 the Commission received more than 2900 notifications, approximately 25% of which gave rise to the issuing of reasoned opinions calling upon national authorities to amend certain proposed rules owing to the obstacles they were likely to create. The information procedure is therefore a vital instrument for preventing the emergence of new obstacles to trade which can result from technical standards or rules. Furthermore, it is a priority instrument for the establishment of a technical environment common to all undertakings and capable of initiating, maintaining or strengthening their competitiveness on the internal market or on external markets.

New harmonization method

As regards the existing rules and standards, in a communication to the Council in January 1985 the Commission stated that the technical harmonization work undertaken in the Community, in spite of the very positive and significant results achieved, needed to be updated as regards methods and procedures. It accordingly submitted a proposal to the Council, which on 7 May 1985 adopted a **new approach** to technical harmonization and standards[3].

This method does not rule out the harmonization of laws, which, by virtue of Article 100a of the Treaty, can henceforth be achieved by a qualified majority, but it simplifies and facilitates it. In cases where mutual recognition cannot be applied, because divergences are too great between the essential aims of different national laws, legislative harmonization is

---

1   OJ L109, 26.04.1983 and OJ L81, 26.03.1988.
2   OJ L100, 19.04.1994.
3   OJ C136, 04.06.1985.

confined to the adoption of the **essential safety requirements** (or other requirements in the general interest) with which products put on the market must conform, and which should therefore enjoy free movement throughout the EU. The European standardization establishments then prepare technical specifications, which the manufacturers need in order to produce and put on the market products which comply with the essential requirements laid down by the directives. No mandatory nature is attributed to these technical specifications, which retain their status as voluntary standards. This means that the producer has the right not to manufacture in accordance with the standards, but that he is responsible for proving that his products comply with the "essential requirements" of the Community Directive. On the other hand the national authorities are obliged to recognize that products manufactured in conformity with harmonized standards are **presumed to conform** to the essential requirements laid down in the Directive.

According to the Court of Justice, it is acceptable for only a minimum degree of harmonization to be brought about by a Directive based on Article 100a[1]. In other words, the use of Article 100a as a legal basis does not necessarily entail full harmonization of the conditions of competition. The Court, thus, acknowledges that the degree of harmonization sought at Community level may give rise to less favourable treatment of domestic products which meet only the minimum requirements laid down by a Directive.

The new approach to technical harmonization has given rise to fresh dynamism in the removal of technical barriers to intra-Community trade. Many directives are adopted under it, relating, for example, to the safety of machines[2], appliances burning gaseous fuels[3] and footwear[4]. The **marking provisions** of all "new approach" Directives were consolidated by a Directive of 22 July 1993[5].

Standardization and certification

The key to implementation of the new approach to technical harmonization is standardization, i.e. the establishment of standards which determine the specifications for industrial production. The standards are adopted by bodies recognized by the official authorities, with the task of ensuring that those standards are the result of agreement of all parties concerned: producers, users, consumers, administrations, etc. It was the above mentioned Council Directive of 28 March 1983 laying down a procedure for the provision of information in the field of technical standards and regulations which defined a genuine **Community standardization policy** providing industry with a common technical environment[6]. Subsequent to that Directive the Commission signed contracts with the European Committee for Standardization (CEN), the European Committee for Electrotechnical Standardization (CENELEC) and the European Telecommunications Standards Institute (ETSI) relating to the administration of that procedure in the field of standards. Thereafter

---

1   Judgment given on 22 June 1993, Case C-11/92, The Queen v Secretary of State, ex parte Gallagher.
2   OJ L183, 29.06.1989 and OJ L175, 19.07.1993.
3   OJ L196, 26.07.1990.
4   OJ L100, 19.04.1994.
5   OJ L220, 30.08.1993.
6   OJ L109, 26.04.1983.

the new harmonization method, based on the Council Resolution of 7 May 1985, entrusted those European bodies with the task of elaborating technical specifications which met the essential requirements laid down by the technical harmonization Directives.

In order to be able to exercise their positive effects, European standards must, however, be certified. In other words, it is not enough for a product to comply with a European standard for all public and private contracts to be open to it; that conformity must also be certified and recognized by the relevant bodies. Reciprocal recognition of certificates of conformity with rules and standards is therefore essential to the free movement of goods. Hence, on 21 December 1989, the Council adopted a Resolution on a global approach, laying down the guiding principles for the European policy on the **mutual recognition** of tests and certificates[1].

This Resolution has made it possible to set up the European Organization for Testing and Certification (EOTC), whose memorandum of understanding was signed on April 25, 1990 by the Commission, EFTA, the CEN and CENELEC. The Council has also adopted conformity assessment procedures, intended for use in the technical harmonization Directives for the marketing of industrial products[2]. The principle of mutual recognition enables, especially in sectors which have not been harmonized at Community level, the competent authorities of importing Member States to recognize technical specifications, standards and rules applicable in other Member States and the validity of tests carried out by approved laboratories in other Member States offering adequate guarantees of reliability and efficiency.

In general, the Community, in application of the proportionality principle, chooses the mutual recognition approach in order to solve a problem of diversity of technical rules, because this method of intervention is the least burdensome for the market. Mutual recognition is intended to ensure the free movement of goods and products of all kinds, thereby avoiding unnecessary recourse to harmonization by specific legislative measures. It guarantees the preservation of national diversity and of the various traditions and customs, and contributes towards increasing the range of products available to European consumers. On the external level, this mutual recognition of the methods and structures of conformity within the Community facilitates access to the European market for products from third countries. In return, the Community negotiates similar recognition with the latter. It should be noted, however, that economic operators often prefer to mutual recognition a formal and complete harmonization at Community level, because it offers increased legal security.

In any case, there are still many different national technical standards which, despite the principle of mutual recognition, continue to be an obstacle to trade. So that the Community can administer in a transparent and practical way the mutual recognition of national legislation derogating from the principle of the free movement of goods, Member States must, according to a procedure for the exchange of information, notify the Commission of any measure obstructing the free movement of a model or type of product that is lawfully manufactured or marketed in another Member State[3].

Community-wide protection of **intellectual and industrial property** has a role to play in breaking down barriers to the free movement of goods and services[4]. The Court of Justice has established the principle that copyright, like other industrial and commercial property rights, falls within the scope of the Treaty and that, consequently, any discrimination on grounds of nationality in the national laws governing the extent or exercise of such rights is prohibited[5]. However, standardization and the protection of intellectual property rights, which pursue different objectives (dissemination of technology in the public interest in the

---

1   OJ C10, 16.01.1990.

2   OJ L380, 31.12.1990.

3   OJ C200, 22.07.1994.

4   See the chapters on competition and on the EU and its citizens.

5   Judgment given on 20 October 1993, Joined Cases C-92/92 and C-326/92, Phil Collins v Imtrat and Patricia v EMI Electrola.

first instance and protection of private property in the second) must be able to co-exist in the Community's industrial environment. It is particularly essential that European standards, which are derived from Community Directives, be placed at the disposal of those wishing to use them on equal, reasonable and non-discriminatory terms[1].

In a July 1995 Green Paper, the Commission invites a discussion on the necessity and the content of a Community initiative on "utility models", which offer legal protection for industrial property at a lower level than that afforded by patents and are often used to protect technical inventions which are not particularly innovative, such as mechanisms or tools[2]. In another Green Paper, of 6 March 1996, the Commission calls for consultations with interested parties on legal protection in the internal market of encrypted services which use coding as a means of ensuring payment of a fee: traditional encrypted broadcasts (pay TV, digital TV, etc.) and certain information society services (video on demand, interactive teleshopping, etc.).

The affixing and use of the **Community trade mark** attests to the conformity of industrial goods with Community standards and Member States are thus obliged to accept on their territory any product complying with the CE marking[3]. A Community trade mark may consist of any signs capable of being represented graphically, particularly words, including personal names, designs, letters, numerals, the shape of goods or of their packaging, provided that such signs are capable of distinguishing the goods of one undertaking from those of other undertakings. Registered in accordance with the conditions contained in the Regulation of 20 December 1993, the Community trade mark provides uniform protection throughout the Community, which can be obtained by means of a single procedure[4]. This protection enables the proprietor to prevent any other person from using the mark for the same products or services or for similar products if there is a danger of confusion. The Community trade mark is granted (registered) for a period of 10 years , which is renewable, by the Office for Harmonization in the Internal Market (OHIM). Its protection on all the territory of the Union is reinforced by the existence of quasi-judicial bodies - the Boards of Appeal of the Office for Harmonization in the Internal Market - whose decisions may be challenged before the Court of Justice.

With the completion of the Community policies on standardization and certification all the elements are now in place to ensure smooth operation of the internal market in the field of industrial products. However, the elements of standardization (certification of manufacturing processes, product certification, tests, metrological checks, accrediting of certification and testing bodies...) must also be **elements of the quality**, of the characteristics and performance of a product or service. Standardization and quality improvement are, in fact, inseparable and both contribute to the correct operation of the internal market and the fostering of industrial competitiveness. In a Resolution of June 18, 1992, the Council confirmed that a need existed for high-quality European standards, for the reinforcement of the actual availability of these standards at national level by their systematic transposition and for encouragement of the use of

1   COM (92) 445.
2   COM (95) 370, 19 July 1995.
3   OJ L220, 30.08.1993.
4   OJ L11, 14.01.1994 and OJ L131, 15.06.1995.

standards as an instrument of economic and industrial integration[1]. In addition, European standardization and conformity instruments are invaluable tools in the implementation of other Community policies (e.g. environment, energy, foodstuffs quality, safety at workplace).

Public procurement

Covering the requirements of the official authorities - works and supplies of all sorts for the services of the central civil service, regional and local authorities and for official undertakings and bodies - accounts for 15% of the economic activity of the Member States. If, therefore, a genuine Single Market is to exist, the public sector will have to be opened to intra-Community trade and competition. At the end of the '80s only 2% of the needs of the official authorities were covered by undertakings from a Member State other than that of the official authorities concerned, in spite of the price, quality and service advantages that they could offer. This was paradise for inefficient suppliers of goods and services who had connections with the civil administration, but public administrations were jeopardizing their own efficiency.

Thus the advanced technology industries, of particular interest to the public sector, were suffering from discrimination in favour of traditional industries, as the latter had benefited from the liberalization of trade. In some sectors, such as the aeronautical sector, the transport equipment sector and the sector of certain capital goods, procurement by public bodies constituted the largest, if not the sole, part of the market, made a monopsony of that market and virtually excluded it from the common market. However, State support could not offset the walling-off effects of the markets of high technology industries, as those industries were the very ones most in need of a large market and the economies of scale that it could offer.

If this situation had not been put right, the Community would have ended up specializing in the traditional production of consumer goods and would have left the production of high technology goods to American and Japanese undertakings. In that way the chances of Europe's genuine technological, and even political, independence would have been reduced. What had to be done in that situation? In the '70s a start was made to harmonization, by means of Council directives, of national legislation on public works contracts and supply contracts.

Public works contracts

The first of those directives, adopted on 26 July 1971, is a Directive concerning the abolition of restrictions on **freedom to provide services** in respect of public works contracts and the award of public works contracts to contractors acting through agencies or branches[2]. Another Directive of

---

1   OJ C173, 09.07.1992.
2   OJ L185, 16.08.1971 and OJ L1, 03.01.1994.

the same date concerns the coordination of procedures for the **award of public works contracts** in the Member States. That coordination consists of the publication of notices of public works contracts in the Official Journal of the Communities so that all those interested in the Member States are informed at the same time. It also comprises common rules on the selection of candidates and on the award of contracts. An Advisory Committee for Public Works Contracts was then instructed to examine application of the Directive by the Member States[1].

Through successive modifications the scope of the Directive concerning the coordination of procedures for the award of public works contracts was extended to cover private undertakings engaging in civil engineering works and certain building works which are directly subsidized to more than 50% and to concessions for the performance of public works. The threshold as from which public contracts are subject to the arrangements of the Directive is set at ECU 5 000 000. The procedures for the award of public works contracts are transparent, as the Directive provides, **inter alia**, for advance information in the Official Journal on the main features of future contracts, in order to enable undertakings to prepare their tenders properly, and the publication of the results of contracts awarded. The Directive also stipulates that official authorities must refer to European standards and technical specifications agreed upon at European level which must be met by the undertakings performing contracts. Public works contracts were thus half-opened in 1971 and completely opened in 1993 by a Directive which coordinates and codifies the procedures for the award of public works contracts[2].

Public supply contracts

The liberalization of public supply contracts began with a Directive of December 21, 1976 and was completed in 1993 by the codification of this Directive and of its successive amendments[3]. In accordance with that Directive, States, public bodies, etc., which propose to award a supply contract in excess of 200,000 ECU have to publish a notice in the Official Journal of the European Communities in accordance with a uniform model annexed to the Directives. That model is designed to provide undertakings concerned with all the information they need to be able to propose their candidacy, where restricted procedures are involved, or their tender, where an open procedure is involved. The contracting authorities are obliged to treat all undertakings on an equal footing and, for selecting a tender, to apply identical criteria, published in advance, to all. The products covered by the Directive include everyday supplies necessary for the functioning of services, such as hospital equipment, scientific research equipment and goods necessary for army maintenance which are not specifically military.

---

1   OJ L185, 16.08.1971 and OJ L13, 15.01.1977.
2   OJ L199, 09.08.1993.
3   OJ L13, 15.01.1977 and OJ L199, 09.08.1993.

In December 1976 the Council also decided to give the Advisory Committee for Public Works Contracts responsibility for dealing in addition with the problems of applying the "supply" Directive. Its name was changed to the **Advisory Committee for Public Contracts**. Since then it has monitored the functioning of the Community Directives, ensured that they are applied uniformly in the Member States and examined complaints from undertakings claiming injury at the hands of an irregular procedure for awarding a contract[1].

Public utility and service sectors

To complete the opening up of public contracts, the Directive of 21 December 1976 had to be supplemented in order to put up for Community tender the supply and works contracts in the **water, energy, transport and telecommunications sectors**, which were initially excluded from Community legislation on public procurement. This was achieved by a Council Directive of September 17, 1990 on procedures for the award of contracts in the four sectors[2]. It applies to the contracting entities in these sectors which, by virtue of the existence of exclusive government-regulated networks or concession rights, cannot normally resist political pressure to "buy national".

The bodies in question and the activities concerned include the railway companies, port and airport authorities, gas and electricity distributors, undertakings which extract oil and gas, and suppliers of telecommunications, water and urban transport services. Supply contracts of over ECU 400 000 (600 000 for telecommunications) and works contracts exceeding ECU 5 million awarded by those bodies are subject to the Directive. All entities operating in objectively similar situations in different Member States are treated equally. Contracts must be awarded under proper commercial conditions and in accordance with the principle of non-discrimination by virtue of a flexible system introducing Community publication of invitations to tender, specification of the supplies and works adapted to encouraging tenders, and common rules applicable to all potential participants in the EU.

The transparency of and non-discrimination in public service contracts are guaranteed by a Council Directive of June 18, 1992 on the coordination of procedures for the conclusion of these contracts at national, regional and local levels[3]. Specific arrangements, introduced by this Directive, seek to ensure maximum transparency in the sectors best suited to cross-border transactions and consequently considered priorities: maintenance and repair, computer technology, advertising, architecture, engineering and some financial services. The "non-priority" services - the hotel business, education and training, social services and legal services - on the other hand, are subject to minimum transparency requirements.

The Directive of 17 September 1990 on the procurement procedures of entities operating in the water, energy, transport and telecommunications

---

1   OJ L152, 12.06.1987 and OJ L338, 28.11.1987.
2   OJ L297, 29.10.1990 and OJ L164, 30.06.1994.
3   OJ L209, 24.07.1992.

sectors was amended in 1993, in order to extend its scope to cover purchases of services supplied in those same sectors[1]. As Community service contracts in the above-mentioned sectors are opened up to third-country suppliers of services and tenders, the amended Directive provides the possibility of safeguard measures being taken in relation to third countries which fail to grant reciprocal access to Community firms.

Compliance with the Community law on public procurement

In order to monitor compliance with Community legislation, the Commission instituted a system for checking that the execution of projects or programmes financed from the Structural Funds and the other Community financial instruments is carried out in compliance with the Community rules on public procurement[2]. It also strengthened its measures against infringements of the rules governing public procurement on the basis of the proceedings for failure to act, as provided for in Article 169 EEC.

For its part, the Council adopted a Directive relating to the application of review procedures to the award of public supply and public works contracts[3]. The Directive provides that contractors and suppliers shall have effective remedies whereby alleged infringements by a contracting authority of Community law in the field of public procurement can be sanctioned at any stage whatsoever in the procedure for the award of a contract.

Legal recourse in the public utility sectors is provided by a Directive coordinating the various legislative, regulatory and administrative provisions relating to the application of Community rules on procedures for the award of contracts in the sectors of water, energy, transport and telecommunications[4]. It seeks to ensure that effective and rapid means of recourse exist both at national and Community level as regards procedures for the award of contracts in these sectors. It defines a conciliation procedure to which parties can have recourse to find an amicable settlement to any disputes regarding the application of rules governing public contracts and introduces a mechanism for the rapid correction of clear and evident offences.

The European Union opens up its public contracts to third States which take similar action. Thus the Community and the USA reached, an Agreement, in 1995, on government procurement. This Agreement gives effect in the area of government procurement to the commitments made in the Uruguay Round of multilateral negotiations and to the results of the bilateral negotiations conducted in this area between the Community and the United States[5]. Nevertheless, there exist some restrictions of access to certain public contracts from tenderers from the US[6].

A **public procurement observatory** is responsible for monitoring the liberalization of this sector within the Community and the effects of the process on third countries. The fact should not be hidden, however, that it is difficult to remove totally the tendency towards favouritism for public undertakings. The removal of the last vestiges of the past will require an "effort to educate" the public contracting authorities on the part of the Governments of the Member States under the auspices of the Community Institutions. With this aim in mind, the Commission runs training measures and information campaigns for the parties involved in this field and monitors the implementation in the Member States of the recommendation on the standardization of contract notices[7].

In the long term, if one excludes the current expenses of the public authorities (rental, heating, insurance, etc.), which correspond to local procurement and may be estimated at approximately 20% of total public procurement, 80% of the goods and services procured by

1   OJ L199, 09.08.1993.
2   OJ C22, 28.01.1989.
3   OJ L395, 30.12.1989 and OJ L1, 03.01.1994.
4   OJ L76, 23.03.1992.
5   OJ L134, 20.06.1995, see also the heading on the General Agreement on Tariffs and Trade in the chapter on the European Union in the World.
6   OJ L183, 02.08.1995.
7   OJ L305, 06.11.1991.

the authorities should be accessible to suppliers in every Member State; that means virtually ECU 500 billion, or 12% of the European Union's GDP.

Free movement of workers

One of the great successes of European integration has been to transmute economic migratory movements of the postwar period into free movement of persons. The freedom of movement of workers allows EU citizens to seek, within the Union, better living and working conditions than are available to them in their region of origin. It therefore boosts greatly the chances of improving the standards of living of the individual. At the same time, freedom of movement reduces social pressure in the poorest regions of the European Union and allows the living conditions of those remaining to improve. In the richest regions and countries, migration provides the labour vital to their further economic development. In the EU in general it facilitates the adjustment of the labour supply to the variations in the demand from undertakings and opens the way for more coherent and more effective economic policies on European scale.

However, although the free movement of workers has advantages, it also has disadvantages. In a number of instances it entails a painful uprooting, at least initially, a more than cold welcome from the indigenous population, the impoverishment of regions of emigration in terms of their most dynamic human capital and an overloading of the social services in the areas of immigration. The free movement of labour within the European Union is therefore no panacea. It has to be channelled and supported by social measures in favour of migrant workers and their families. It has above all to be coupled with an efficient regional policy capable of creating jobs in the less favoured regions of the Union to provide employment for the labour available **in situ**. Under these conditions, freedom of movement is an acquired right of EU workers.

Article 8a of the Treaty gives every citizen of the Union the right to move and reside freely within the territory of the Member States. This right contributes to a concrete and practical expression of European citizenship. The challenge to the Union now is, however, to create a real European mobility area, in which freedom of movement becomes not only a legal entitlement but also a daily reality for people across Europe. This calls for a complex interaction of policies, some of which are explained below and some in the chapter on social progress.

The common labour market

Article 69 of the **ECSC Treaty** commits the Member States to removing any restriction based on nationality upon the employment in the coal and steel industries of workers who are nationals of Member States and have "recognized qualifications in a coalmining or steelmaking occupation", subject to the limitations imposed by the basic requirements of health and public policy. That provision was repeated in virtually the same terms in Articles 96 of the **EAEC Treaty** (Euratom), although the latter also called upon the Council to adopt a directive on free access to skilled employment in the field of nuclear energy, which it duly did in July 1962[1]. Limiting free movement to skilled labour was logical for the sectoral Treaties, which could only deal with economic activities which they governed.

The **EEC Treaty** had the objective, as regards workers, of creating a common labour market, which meant the free movement of labour within the Community and the abolition of any discrimination based on nationality between workers of the Member States as regards employment, remuneration and other conditions of work and employment. Under Article 48 freedom of movement of workers entails the right, subject to limitations justified on grounds of public policy, public security or public health to accept offers of employment actually made, **to move freely** within the territory of Member States for this purpose, **to stay** in a Member State for the purpose of employment and **to remain** in the territory of that Member State after having been employed in it. The Council, acting in accordance with the procedure referred to in Article 189b (co-decision with the Parliament) and after consultation of the Economic and Social Committee, shall adopt, in the shape of Directives or Regulations, the measures necessary to gradually achieve the free movement of workers.

As early as 1961 the Council adopted a Regulation relating to preliminary measures for the achievement of freedom of movement of workers within the Community and a Directive on the procedures and administrative practices relating to the introduction, employment and residence of workers from one Member State and their families in the other Member States. Those measures were supplemented in March 1964 and completed on 15 October 1968[2]. Thus freedom of movement of workers was achieved, from the legal point of view, at the same time as customs union, and therefore in advance of the timetable laid down in the Treaty.

Shortly after, in June 1970, the Commission adopted a Regulation, based on Article 48 of the EEC Treaty, on the right of workers to remain in the territory of a Member State after having been employed in that State[3]. That Regulation guarantees that the worker can continue to reside, in the country in which he has settled, on the occasion of his termination of work. That takes specific form in the automatic renewal of the residence permit held by the person concerned as an employed person. The members of his family resident with him enjoy that right even after his death.

The Court of Justice has consistently held that the rules on equal treatment prohibit not only overt discrimination but also **any form of concealed discrimination** which is based on various distinction criteria but has the same effect[4]. However, discrimination exists only where different rules are applied to comparable situations or the same rule is applied to different situations. For instance, where direct taxes are concerned, the Court has ruled that the provisions of the free movement of workers do not in principle preclude the application of national rules under which a non-resident working as an employed person in a Member State is taxed more heavily on his income than a resident in the same employment[5].

The principle of the free movement of workers applies equally to **nationals of third countries**, who stay lawfully in a Member State. Indeed, according to a Judgment of the Court

1   OJ L57, 09.07.1962.
2   OJ L257, 19.10.1968 and OJ L1, 03.01.1994, pp. 325, 572.
3   OJ L142, 30.06.1970.
4   See, e.g., case 65/81, ECR 1982, p. 33 and case 137/84, ECR 1985, p. 2681.
5   Judgment of 14 February 1995, case C-279/93, Finanzamt Köln-Altstadt v R. Schumacker.

of Justice, a firm established in a Member country, which employs lawfully and habitually non-member country nationals, may detach them in another Member State in order to provide services[1]. The principle of free movement applies also to all cases of posting of workers taking place in the framework of a transnational provision of services[2].

Article 48(4) of the Treaty excludes employment in the **national public service** from the principle of the free movement of workers. However, with a view to achieving a single market, the Commission decided in March 1988 to promote the free access of citizens of the Member States to posts in the public sector of other Member States through systematic action directed first towards areas which were sufficiently remote from the specific activities of the public service that they would only in very rare cases be covered by Article 48(4), e.g. bodies responsible for administering commercial services, public health care services, teaching in State educational establishments and research for non-military purposes in public establishments[3]. Moreover, according to the Court of Justice, given the fundamental character of the principles of free movement and of equal treatment, the derogations based on Article 48(4) should not exceed the aims of this exception to the rule[4].

The principle of free movement of workers cannot be hindered by the **rules of sports associations**. In the Bosman judgment, which revolutionized European sport customs, the Court of Justice held, indeed, that Article 48 EC applied to the collective rules adopted by private sports associations since the exercise of sport as an economic activity was covered by Community law[5]. In particular, the Court held that by preventing or deterring nationals of a Member State from leaving their country of origin the transfer rules constituted an obstacle to the free movement of workers. According to the Court, the rules in question are not likely to provide encouragement and financing for small clubs training young players, since there was no guarantee that they would collect such fees and since the amount of the fees bore no relation to the costs actually incurred for the training. The Court also held that under Article 48 no rules could require clubs to field, for a given match, only a limited number of professional players who were nationals of other Member States, but it admitted that the nationality requirement was justified in the case of matches between the national teams of different countries.

Social security for migrant workers

Adequate protection by European provisions in the field of social security is a pre-condition to the effective use of the right to move and to stay within the Union. Without such protection, persons moving across frontiers to work or to look for a job, would risk losing all or part of their rights acquired or in the process of being acquired under national legislation (for example to pensions, health insurance, unemployment benefits or family benefits). Thus, Article 51 of the EEC Treaty provided for the adoption of the measures necessary for that purpose through arrangements to secure for migrant workers and their dependents: (a) aggregation, for the purpose of acquiring and retaining the right to benefit, of all periods taken into account under the laws of several countries, and (b) payment of benefits to persons resident in the territories of Member States. Thanks to the system established since 1958, migrant workers have had the same social security rights as nationals of the host country, the children of migrant workers are entitled to the benefits granted in the country in which they are resident and retired workers are entitled to pensions calculated on the basis of all their years of work in Community countries.

---

1   Judgment given on 9 August 1994 in Case C-43/93, Vander Elst v OMI.
2   OJ C187, 09.07.1993.
3   OJ C72, 18.03.1988.
4   Judgment of 12 February 1974, case 152/73, Sotgiu, ECR 1974, p. 153.
5   Judgment of 15 December 1995, case C-415/93, Jean-Marc Bosman.

The detailed rules for applying social security schemes to employed persons and their families moving within the Community were elaborated in Regulation N° 1408/71[1] and its implementing Regulation, N° 574/72[2], which replaced the 1958 Regulations. On the basis of those Regulations, repayments in respect of health care provided for members of the family resident in a Member State other than that in which the worker is employed and insured are made entirely to the institutions of the country of residence. Pensions of similar nature acquired in the various Member States may be aggregated, but the person concerned may not obtain total benefits in excess of the highest pension he would have obtained if he had spent his whole insurance career under the legislation of any one of the States in which he had been employed. The unemployed person who leaves for another Member State to seek employment receives, for a maximum period of three months from the date of departure, the benefits of the country in which he was last employed, to be paid for by that country. Family allowances are granted under the legislation of, and at the rate laid down in, the country of employment. According to the Court of Justice, such allowances are not subject to requirements as to minimum period of residence[3].

In 1981 the arrangements laid down in Regulation N° 1408/71 were extended to cover **self-employed persons** and their families[4]. In 1986 the situation of persons pursuing activities as employed persons or as self-employed persons in the territories of two or more Member States was regulated[5]. Insured persons staying temporarily in a Member State other than the one in which they are insured, for tourist or employment purposes, may be admitted to hospital or receive refunds in respect of urgent medical care in the host State on presentation of a special form (E 111), to be replaced by a **European card for provision of immediate care**[6].

In some forty years of European action in the field of the free movement of persons, many obstacles have been removed to this fundamental freedom of the EC Treaty. However, there still remain some obstacles which discourage people from moving within the Union. As will be seen under the heading of social protection in the chapter on social progress, the overall approach in this field is not aimed at harmonizing the Member States' systems of social protection, but at achieving effective coordination of these systems throughout the Union, so as not to discourage the free movement of workers.

Other measures in favour of migrant workers

To facilitate the mobility of workers within the Community it was also necessary to ensure and encourage the **education of the children** of migrant workers. That was achieved

---

1   OJ L149, 05.07.1971 and OJ C242, 19.09.1995.
2   OJ L74, 27.03.1972 and OJ C260, 05.10.1995.
3   Judgment given on 10 March 1993, Case C-111/91, Commission v Luxembourg, ECR 1993, I-840.
4   OJ L143, 29.05.1981.
5   OJ L355, 16.12.1986.
6   OJ 75, 16.08.1962.

in a Council Directive of 25 July 1977[1], which obliges the Member States to treat the children of migrant workers in the same way as the children of national workers, including as regards the aid granted by the public authorities to school pupils and to students. Two Resolutions of 22 May 1989, on school provision for gypsy and traveller children and on school provision for children of occupational travellers respectively, provide for measures to be taken by the Community and the Member States to resolve the specific problems of those poorly educated peoples[2].

For the creation of a common labour market, it was also necessary that potential migrant workers have at their disposal information which is as comprehensive as possible regarding the number and nature of jobs available in the Community and the qualifications required. Article 49 of the Treaty itself called upon the Council to set up appropriate machinery to **bring offers of employment into touch with applications for employment**. A large part of the Council Regulation of 15 October 1968 on freedom of movement for workers within the Community was in fact given over to bringing vacancies and applications for employment into touch and clearing them through a European system for the International Clearing of Vacancies and Applications for Employment (SEDOC). In 1993, SEDOC has been replaced by a new system for matching job applications and job vacancies, **EURES** (European Employment Service)[3]. It has the task of exchanging the kind of information covered by the 1968 Regulation in order to make such information available to potential users[4].

EURES is a network of some 400 advisers, coming from the national employment services, employer organizations, trade unions, regional administrations and universities, specially trained to deal with the needs of transnational job-seekers and job-providers. The core of the network is a computerized databank providing information on transnational job and recruitment opportunities, as well as information on living and working conditions in the countries of the Union, from accommodation to contract law and taxation. The European Commission ensures the coordination of the network. EURES serves both as an employment service at the scale of Europe, having as task to inform, counsel and place job seekers on the territory of the European Economic Space, and as a forum for the examination, at operational level, of all questions relating to employment in Europe. By encouraging transfrontier recruitment and acquisition of qualifications, this network makes a real contribution to the creation of a European labour market.

Freedom of establishment and recognition of diplomas

The free movement of persons pursuing activities as self-employed persons is treated in the EU in accordance with the same principles as the free movement of employed persons. In both cases the basic principle is equality of treatment with nationals. **Freedom of establishment** includes the right to take up and pursue activities as self-employed persons and to set up and manage undertakings, in particular companies or firms within

---

1   OJ L199, 06.08.1977.
2   OJ C153, 21.06.1989.
3   OJ L257, 19.10.1968 and OJ L245, 26.08.1992.
4   OJ L274, 06.11.1993.

the meaning of the second paragraph of Article 58 EC, i.e., companies established under the conditions laid down for its own nationals by the law of the country where such establishment is effected, subject to the provisions of the Chapter of the Treaty relating to capital. It also extends to what is known as freedom of secondary establishment, i.e. the setting up of agencies, branches or subsidiaries (first paragraph of Article 52).

Under Article 56, the principle of freedom of establishment does not concern national provisions providing for special treatment for foreign nationals on grounds of public policy, public security or public health. A Council Directive of 25 February 1964 contains an enumeration of the circumstances which cannot be invoked as grounds for refusal of entry or deportation and a series of rules concerning the procedure which must be followed where nationals of Member States may be refused entry or deported[1].

Right of establishment

Right of establishment entails permanent establishment in a Member State in order to pursue an economic activity in that State. However, **freedom to provide services** chiefly concerns the pursuit of an economic activity by a person in another Member State without having the principal or secondary place of business in that State. Giving a clear definition of what should be understood by establishment and by provision of services within the meaning of the EC Treaty is not so easy. In fact, the situation of the person who establishes himself is characterized by the fact that he creates a permanent link with the country of establishment, unlike the provider of services who, conversely, retains his link with another country.

The right for nationals of EU Member States to work or pursue activities as self-employed persons in the Member States means the **right to enter and to reside** in the member country in which they wish to work or pursue those activities. Under the Council Directive of 21 May 1973 on the abolition of restrictions on movement and residence within the Community for nationals of Member States with regard to establishment and the provisions of services, the following are entitled to enter and to reside: Community nationals wishing to enter a country to work as employed persons, to establish themselves there in order to provide services or receive such services in that country, and their spouses, children and other **members of their families**[2]. Nationals of one Member State have the right to remain in the territory of a Member State after having pursued activities as self-employed persons in that State[3]. The right of residence is certified, for those concerned, by a residence permit for a national of a Member State of the European Economic Community which is issued by the authorities of the country of residence on presentation, by the interested party, of an identity card or passport[4].

1   OJ 56, 04.04.1964 and OJ L14, 20.01.1975.
2   OJ L172, 28.06.1973.
3   OJ L14, 20.01.1975.
4   OJ L180, 13.07.1990.

In Articles 54 and 63, the Treaty stipulated that the Council would, acting on proposals from the Commission, draw up programmes for the **abolition of restrictions** on freedom of establishment and freedom to provide services. Indeed, on 18 December 1961 the Council adopted two general programmes for the abolition of restrictions on freedom of establishment and freedom to provide services respectively. However, through its judgment of 21 June 1974 in the **Reyners case** (Dutch legal practitioner wishing to pursue his profession in Belgium), the Court established the direct effect of Article 52. It held that any individual may, on the basis of Article 52 of the Treaty, demand directly the same treatment as is applied to nationals[1]. After that judgment, the abolition of discriminatory practices is effected directly on the basis of the provisions of the Treaty, and it is pointless adopting directives, such as those mentioned below, to liberalize the various occupations.

After removing obvious discriminatory practices, there does, however, remain one other **possibility of obstacles**. The numerous requirements of States with regard to the training of employed and self-employed persons, and the detailed arrangements for pursuing industrial and commercial activities, even although they are not in themselves discriminatory, can impede the free movement of persons, if only because they differ from country to country and oblige the individual to take a new examination which may constitute a serious obstacle to freedom of establishment. That is why Article 57 of the Treaty, as amended at Maastricht, empowers the Council, acting in accordance with the procedure referred to in Article 189b (co-decision) to issue directives for the mutual recognition of diplomas, certificates and other evidence of formal qualifications and for the coordination of national provisions concerning the taking up and pursuit of activities as self-employed persons. However, the Council, acting unanimously on a proposal from the Commission and after consulting the European Parliament, decides on directives the implementation of which involves in at least one Member State amendment of the existing principles laid down by law governing the professions with respect to training and conditions of access for natural persons. In the case of the medical, the allied and pharmaceutical professions, the progressive abolition of restrictions shall be dependent upon coordination of the conditions for their exercise in the various Member States (Article 57, paragraphe 3).

Recognition of diplomas

The mutual recognition of diplomas, certificates and other evidence of formal qualifications is linked on the one hand to freedom of establishment and on the other to vocational training, which is examined in the chapter on social progress. In spite of this dual interest, very little progress had been made until recently in the field of the mutual recognition of diplomas. In fact in the mid-'70s the Community embarked on a long journey into the related fields of comparability and the **mutual recognition of diplomas**. A series of Council Decisions set up advisory committees on training, and a series of Directives was aimed at the mutual recognition of diplomas, certificates and other evidence of formal qualifications, comprising measures to facilitate the effective exercise of freedom of establishment and freedom to provide services in respect of: doctors[2], nurses[3], dental practitioners[4], veterina-

---

1   Judgment of 21 June 1974, Case 2/74, ECR 1974, p. 631.
2   OJ L167, 30.06.1975 and OJ L165, 07.07.1993.
3   OJ L176, 15.07.1977.
4   OJ L233, 24.08.1978.

rians[1], midwives[2], architects[3] and dispensing chemists[4]. In parallel the Council decided, on 16 July 1985, to lay down provisions relating to the comparability of vocational training qualifications in the hotel-restaurant, motor vehicle repair and construction sectors[5].

Finally, with a view to completion of the internal market, the Community came upon the inspiration which made that laborious work obsolete, namely a **general system for the recognition of higher-education diplomas** awarded on completion of professional education and training of at least three years' duration[6]. The salient features of the Directive, adopted by the Council on 21 December 1988, are the following: the principle of mutual trust amongst the Member States; the principle of the comparability of university studies between Member States; the mutual recognition of diplomas without prior harmonization of the conditions for taking up and pursuing occupations, and lastly the principle that any divergence between Member States, in particular as regards training, will be offset by vocational experience. This system means, provided that the persons pursuing a profession fulfil certain minimum conditions as to qualifications, experience and professional education, that their qualifications will be recognized in all Member States and they will be authorized to pursue their activities without restriction.

A similar system relates to diplomas and certificates awarded on completion of **professional education and training of fewer than three years** of higher education or not covered by higher education. It covers two training levels: higher education or post-secondary diplomas where course duration is less than three years and secondary education diplomas. It also applies to certain non-graduates who have acquired professional experience[7]. There is provision for link-up between the two systems in order to cover professions which fall under the first system in one Member State and under the second in another.

With these two general systems for the recognition of diplomas, any EU national has the right to have vocational qualifications obtained in another Member State recognized in respect of any host Member State which regulates any activity whatsoever in its territory. In instances where significant differences in the duration of the training and education exist, or substantial differences in the content of the training and education acquired, the host Member State may require proof of vocational experience or adaptation training or a competence test.

1   OJ L362, 23.12.1978.
2   OJ L33, 11.02.1980.
3   OJ L223, 21.08.1985.
4   OJ L253, 24.09.1985.
5   OJ L199, 31.07.1985.
6   OJ L19, 24.01.1989.
7   OJ L209, 24.07.1992 and OJ L184, 03.08.1995.

Freedom to provide services

Article 59 and the third paragraph of Article 60 provide that restrictions on "freedom to provide services" within the Community which are not applicable to nationals shall be "abolished in respect of nationals of Member States who are established in a State of the Community other than that of the person for whom the services are intended". Under Article 60 of the EEC Treaty, **services** shall be considered to be "services" where they are normally provided for remuneration, in so far as they are not governed by the provisions relating to freedom of movement for goods, capital and persons. A definition which is formulated in a negative form, viz. to the effect that provisions of services are the forms of self-employed activities not governed by other provisions of the Treaty, lacks clarity. Article 60 specifies, however, that the provisions on the free movement of persons covered all activities of an industrial or commercial character or of craftsmen and the activities of the professions.

The activity must be limited in time, must normally be pursued against payment and must involve some form of foreign aspect, unless the border is physically crossed. The person providing a service may, in order to do so, temporarily pursue his activity in the State where the service is provided, under the same conditions as are imposed by that State on its own nationals (third paragraph of Article 60). Services provided under a contract outside the country of establishment may be of a long duration. There is nothing, moreover, to preclude an activity for the provision of services from being of a magnitude such as to necessitate the acquisition of goods in the country of provision of services. However, to constitute a provision of services, the person providing the service must remain established in his own country and his services must cross borders. The rules of the Treaty nevertheless cover situations where it is the person receiving the services who crosses the border, such as a tourist, and situations where both the person receiving and the person providing the service remain in their respective countries, such as consultation by correspondence.

It can be seen that the distinction between freedom of establishment and freedom to provide services is not obvious. However, that no longer has any practical relevance since a judgment of the Court of Justice of 3 December 1974 in the **Van Binsbergen** case established the direct applicability of the prohibition on discrimination in respect of the provision of services[1], just as the Reyners case had done for freedom of establishment. No individual liberalization Directives are therefore necessary. Indeed, according to recent Court case-law, Article 59 in itself grants operators properly established in their country of origin the right to supply services in another Member State without the latter being able to prevent the exercise of that right on the grounds that the conditions of supply are different there[2]. Only overriding reasons relating to the public interest may justify an exception to that principle, provided that it is proportionate to the aim in view. Thus, the Court has acknowledged that safeguarding the financial sector's reputation may constitute an imperative reason for action in the public interest and may justify restrictions on the freedom to provide financial services[3]. However, as confirmed by the Court in a recent case, a Member State cannot be denied the right to take measures to prevent the exercise by a person providing services whose activity is entirely or principally directed towards its territory of the freedoms guaranteed by the Treaty for the purpose of avoiding rules which would be applicable to him if he were established within that Member State[4]. In this context, the Commission

1   Judgment of 3 December 1974, Case 33/74, ECR 1974, 1299.
2   Judgments of 25 July 1991, cases C-288/89 and C-353/89.
3   Judgment of 10 May 1995, case C-384/93, Alpine Investments BV v Minister van Financiën.
4   Judgment of 5 October 1994, Case C-43/93, TV 10.

adopted on 6 December 1993 an interpretative communication concerning the free movement of services across frontiers[1].

Services represent almost 60% of the value added of the Community economy and cover a vast spread of economic activities, from banks and insurance to transport and tourism, not to mention data-processing and management consultancy. They therefore play an increasingly large part in the economy and employment and are a linchpin for smooth operation of the EU's internal market.

Financial services - banks, insurance companies and stock exchanges - which are closely monitored by the official authorities, are particularly important, as they constitute a vast potential market and are indispensable activities for the proper functioning of the other economic sectors. The European Union has to reconcile two contradictory requirements in these cases, viz. the need to maintain very stringent criteria for control and financial security and the need to leave the branch concerned enough flexibility for it to be able to meet the new and ever-more complex requirements of its customers throughout the European market. The approach pursued therefore involves confining harmonization to the basic aspects of financial security and solvency and, for the rest, applying the rule of mutual recognition as far as possible on the same basis as for trade in goods.

In accordance with the principle of **mutual recognition**, if a financial service is lawfully authorized in one Member State it must be open to users in the other Member States without having to comply with every detail of the legislation of the host country, except those concerning consumer protection. Control has to be exercised by the Government in the territory of which the company providing the services is established, with the authorities of the country in which the service is performed merely ensuring that certain basic rules relating to commercial conduct are observed. This system applies both to the traditional fields of transport, insurance and banking and to the new fields of services, such as information technology, marketing and audiovisual services. Harmonization of legislation is henceforth necessary only in very specific instances, to facilitate the exchange of services. Nevertheless, a Green Paper of the Commission seeks to identify consumers' requirements and concerns in the field of financial services, particularly when these services are sold at a distance[2].

Banking

As regards banks, the Council, after abolishing restrictions on freedom of establishment and freedom to provide services in respect of self-employed activities of **banks and other financial institutions**[3], adopted, in 1977, a first Directive on the coordination of the laws, regulations and administrative provisions relating to the taking up and pursuit of the

---

1   OJ C334, 09.12.1993.
2   COM (96) 209, 22 May 1996.
3   OJ L194, 16.07.1973.

business of credit institutions[1]. A second Directive in this field, adopted by the Council in 1989, permits the mutual recognition of supervision systems, i.e. application of the principle of supervision of a credit institution by the Member State in which it has its head office, and the issue of a **"single bank licence"** which is valid throughout the Community[2]. The single licence authorizes a bank established in a Member State to open branches without any other formalities or to propose its services in the partner countries. It also contains provisions relating to the reciprocity governing the opening in the Community of subsidiaries of banks from non-member countries. So as to dispel uncertainties on the interpretation of the Second Banking Directive, the Commission has mapped out the legal framework in which a Member State may invoke the concept of the general good in order to prevent a credit institution lawfully established and authorized in another Member State from providing services[3].

A 1992 Directive permits the **supervision** of credit institutions on a consolidated basis[4]. It defines the object of supervision, consolidation methods and the sharing of responsibilities between Member States for the monitoring of multinational groups, particularly financial companies whose main activity is the holding of interests in credit establishments or other financial establishments. The object of supervision is solvency, the match between own funds and risks and non-financial interests.

On the other hand, a Directive on the monitoring and controlling of **large exposures of credit institutions** seeks to ensure that the Member States control excessive concentrations of exposures to a single client, thus avoiding losses that might threaten the solvency of a credit institution and have repercussions on the entire financial system[5]. In particular it stipulates that the large exposures of credit institutions should not exceed 40% of equity capital during a transitional phase, subsequently reduced to 25%, that credit institutions must notify the authorities when they fall to 10% of equity capital and that their aggregate total should not exceed 800% of equity capital.

A Directive on **deposit-guarantee schemes** is designed to protect depositors in the event of an authorized credit institution failing[6]. It stipulates that there must be a guarantee scheme in all Member States, financed by the banking sector and covering all deposits up to ECU 20 000 per depositor (ECU 15 000 in Spain, Portugal, Greece and Luxembourg). The scheme is expected to cover depositors not only in institutions in the Member State which authorize them but also those in branches of such institutions set up in other Member States. A similar scheme will soon be set up providing for minimum **compensation for investors** in the event of the failure of an investment firm, authorized to provide services throughout the Union, to honour its debts[7].

Other vital factors for the European banking system are: the Directive on **annual accounts** and consolidated accounts of banks and other credit institutions[8]; the Directive on the obligations of branches established in a Member State of credit institutions and financial institutions having their head offices outside that Member State regarding the publication of **annual accounting documents**[9]; the Directive on the own funds of credit institutions, the Community definition of which is vital to the harmonization necessary for mutual recognition[10]; and the Directive on the **solvency ratio** for credit institutions, establishing a minimum level for that ratio and the method of calculating the ratio to be observed between own funds

1   OJ L322, 17.12.1977 and OJ L168, 18.07.1995.
2   OJ L386, 30.12.1989 and OJ L110, 28.04.1992.
3   OJ C291, 04.11.1995.
4   OJ L110, 28.04.1992.
5   OJ L29, 05.02.1993.
6   OJ L135, 31.05.1994.
7   OJ C320, 30.11.1995.
8   OJ L372, 31.12.1986 and OJ L1, 03.01.1994.
9   OJ L44, 16.02.1989 and OJ L1, 03.01.1994.
10   OJ L124, 05.05.1989 and OJ L110, 28.04.1992.

and risk assets and off-balance-sheet items[1]. These various Directives complete the arrangements introduced, in particular through the second banking Directive which introduced freedom of establishment and freedom to provide services on the basis of recognition of the authorization granted by the country of origin.

In the European internal market, the transparency, performance and stability of cross-border payment systems should match the properties of the best domestic payment systems. To this effect, a draft Directive requires banks to execute transfers within reasonable time-limits (five banking business days for the originator's institution and one banking business day for the beneficiary's institution), makes double-charging illegal, requires the reimbursement of the full amount (up to a limit of ECU 10 000) in the event of non-execution of transfers and enhances transparency concerning the conditions applying to transfers[2]. A Commission notice supplementing the proposal of this Directive provides a framework allowing banks to set in place cooperation arrangements aimed at making cross-border credit transfers more efficient without unduly restricting competition, particularly concerning market access and price competition[3].

A related area, of great interest to travellers in particular, is that of the use throughout the Community of magnetic-stripe and microcircuit **payment cards**. These cards are increasingly used in the Member States for obtaining cash from automatic cash dispensers or for paying for products or services directly and electronically at sales-point terminals or even at home. Achievement of the internal market requires Community action to ensure the interconnection of networks and the mutual opening-up of magnetic card systems, the liberalization of electronic payments from all administrative constraints and an appropriate balance between the interests of the various parties (industries, companies providing services, financial institutions, consumers and traders). So as to encourage the interconnection of the networks, the Commission issued Recommendations: on a European Code of Conduct concerning in particular relations between financial institutions, traders and service establishments, and consumers[4], on consumer protection in the field of the new payment systems, and in particular the relationship between cardholder and card issuer[5]; and on the transparency of bank charges relating to cross-border transactions[6].

Insurance

In the field of insurance too, the Council, after adopting, in 1973, a first Directive on the coordination of laws, regulations and administrative provisions relating to the taking-up and pursuit of the business of **direct insurance other than life insurance**[7], adopted, in 1988, a second Directive amending the first to facilitate the effective exercise of freedom to provide insurance services[8]. It provides in particular for very liberal arrangements for covering major industrial and commercial risks, together with adequate protection for minor consumers. The Council already, in 1987, adopted two Directives supplementing and clarifying the provisions of the first coordinating Directive as regards **credit insurance** and **suretyship insurance** on the one hand[9] and **legal expenses insurance** on the other[10].

A third coordination Directive in the area of direct insurance other than life insurance provides for a single authorization system enabling a

1   OJ L386, 30.12.1989 and OJ L85, 03.04.1996.
2   OJ C353, 30.12.1995.
3   OJ C251, 27.09.1995.
4   OJ L365, 24.12.1987.
5   OJ L317, 24.11.1988.
6   OJ L67, 15.03.1990.
7   OJ L228, 16.08.1973 and OJ L168, 18.07.1995.
8   OJ L172, 04.07.1988.
9   OJ L185, 04.07.1987.
10 Ibid.

company with its registered office in a Community Member State to open branches and operate services in all the Member States without the need for authorization procedures in each country[1]. It is designed to ensure the free movement of insurance products within the Community and give those taking out insurance the opportunity to do this with any Community insurer, thus finding the cover best suited to needs, while enjoying an adequate level of protection. An Insurance Committee set up by a Council Directive of December 19, 1991 has been given the brief of helping the Commission exercise the implementation powers conferred on it by the Council in the field of direct insurance[2].

With particular reference to insurance against **civil liability in respect of the use of motor vehicles**, the Council adopted, in 1972, a Directive on the approximation of the laws of the Member States relating to insurance against civil liability in respect of the use of motor vehicles, and to the enforcement of the obligation to insure against such liability. That Directive in particular abolished "green card" checks at borders between Member States. That first Directive was supplemented in 1984 in order to afford adequate protection for the victims of road accidents, irrespective of the Member State in which the accident occurred[3]. The third Directive in the field of insurance against civil liability in respect of the use of motor vehicles, adopted by the Council on May 14, 1990, seeks to provide better protection for accident victims and insured persons. It imposes compulsory cover for all passengers of the vehicle, covering the entire territory of the Community, including cases where the passenger is the owner, the holder of the vehicle or the insured person himself[4]. A Commission Decision, annexed to the Multilateral Guarantee Agreement between national insurers' bureaux signed in Madrid on March 1991, requires Member States to refrain from making any checks on insurance against civil liability in respect of vehicles which are normally based in a Member State or in certain third countries[5].

As regards the business of **life insurance** and the pursuit thereof, a first Council Directive coordinated the provisions of the Member States relating to it[6]. The second directive in this field, adopted in 1990, seeks to ensure the effective freedom to provide services in the field of life insurance, offering policy-holders the choice between all the different types of contract available in the Community[7]. It provides for the system of free provision of services through brokers, in light of the extension of its application scope to group insurances and the need to guarantee the independence of brokers in all the Member States. In order to avoid sources of distortion of competition, the taxation arrangements are those of the Member State of the commitment, i.e. of the policy-holder. The third coordination Directive for provisions relating to direct life insurance supplements the first two, coordinating the basic rules of prudential and financial supervision and providing for single authorization valid throughout the Community, along with the checking of all of a broker's activities by the Member State of origin[8].

For **insurance companies themselves**, a Council Directive of December 19, 1991 lays down harmonized rules and establishes greater transparency and easier comparability of annual and consolidated accounts of these companies[9]. With a view to encouraging cooperation between undertakings in the insurance sector, a Council Regulation stipulates that the Commission can grant derogations, under certain conditions, to certain types of agreements, decisions and concerted practices in the insurance field, under application of Article 85, paragraph 1 of the Treaty[10]. This Regulation is intended to cover cooperation on the drafting

1   OJ L228, 11.08.1992.
2   OJ L374, 31.12.1991.
3   OJ L103, 02.05.1972 and OJ L8, 11.01.1984.
4   OJ L129, 19.05.1990.
5   OJ L177, 05.07.1991.
6   OJ L63, 13.03.1979 and OJ L168, 18.07.1995.
7   OJ L330, 29.11.1990.
8   OJ L360, 09.12.1992.
9   OJ L374, 31.12.1991.
10   OJ L143, 07.06.1991.

of standard insurance terms, the joint cover of certain types of risks, the settlement of claims, the checking and acceptance of safety equipment and registers of heightened risks and the information systems which relate to them. The Commission determines the conditions which must be fulfilled for the exemption to apply automatically to these agreements[1].

Stock exchanges and financial services

Community law on stock exchanges and other securities markets is directed towards widening the range of investments at Community level while protecting investors. A 1979 Directive coordinated the conditions for the admission of securities to **official stock exchange listing**[2]. Two Council Directives, adopted in 1993, established the **single market in securities**. By virtue of the first of these Directives, investment services in the area of securities can be freely conducted, although monitored, throughout the EU financial area[3]. An investment firm in any Member State can carry out its activities anywhere in the European Union on the basis of a single authorization (called a "European passport) issued by the Member State of origin. The conditions governing authorization and business activity have been harmonized for this purpose. Prudential supervision, based on uniform rules, is carried out by the authorities of the home Member State, but in cooperation with the authorities of the host Member State. Investment firms have right of access to all the regulated markets in the EU. Minimum transparency rules designed to guarantee investors a sufficient level of protection must be respected on regulated markets.

The equity capital of investment firms and credit establishments must be adequate to guarantee market stability, guarantee an identical level of protection against bankruptcy to investors throughout the European Union and to ensure fair competition between banks, subject to specific prudential provisions, and investment societies on the securities market. In order to fulfil these objectives, the second 1993 Directive lays down minimum initial capital requirements and sets the equity capital which must permanently be held in order to cover position, settlement, exchange and interest rate risks[4].

The investors are protected by means of adequate and comprehensive information on transferable securities such as to enable them to evaluate the risks involved, and thus encourage them to invest. A 1982 Directive specified the information to be published on a regular basis by companies the shares of which have been admitted to official stock-exchange listing[5], and a 1988 Directive specified the information to be published when a major holding in a listed company is acquired or disposed of[6]. Another Directive coordinates the requirements for the drawing-up, scrutiny and distribution of the **listing particulars** to be published for the admission of securities to official stock exchange listing[7]. It provides for the mutual recognition of listing particulars where application for the admission of securities is applied for simultaneously or within a short interval in at least two Member States and for the official listing in a Member State, without publication of new listing particulars, of companies

---

1   OJ L398, 31.12.1992.
2   OJ L66, 16.03.1979 and OJ L62, 05.03.1982.
3   OJ L141, 11.06.1993.
4   Ibid.
5   OJ L48, 20.02.1982 and OJ L1, 03.01.1994.
6   OJ L348, 17.12.1988 and OJ L1, 03.01.1994.
7   OJ L100, 17.04.1980 and OJ L135, 31.05.1994.

already listed, either in another Member State or on a junior market in the same Member State. The time of publication of prospectuses must be the time when transferable securities are offered to the public for the first time[1]. Concessions are provided for small and medium-sized undertakings and exclusions exist for certain types of offer or certain types of security.

A central factor for the proper functioning of the internal market in transferable securities is the Directive relating to **undertakings for collective investment in transferable securities (UCITS)**[2]. It co-ordinates the rules governing such undertakings in the Member States with a view, on the one hand, to approximating the investment policies and the conditions of competition between these UCITS at Community level and, on the other hand, to achieving effective and more uniform protection of shareholders in such undertakings. To ensure that this coordination was totally efficient, restrictions on the free movement of shares in UCITS were abolished.

In order to combat fraudulent use of privileged stock exchange information which certain individuals can obtain, ensuring them of substantial profits to the detriment of other investors, the Council adopted, in November 1989, a Directive coordinating the regulations on **insider dealing**[3]. By combating such dealings, the Directive is aimed at promoting the proper functioning of transferable securities markets in the Community. The adoption of a Protocol to the Convention of the Council of Europe on Insider Trading in order to ensure the precedence of the Community arrangements within the Community made it possible for the Member States to sign that Convention.

Free movement of capital

Freedom of capital movement is another essential component for the edifice of the large European internal market. The liberalization of payment transactions is a vital complement to the free movement of goods, persons and services. Borrowers - notably SMEs - must be able to obtain capital where it is cheapest and best tailored to their needs, while investors and suppliers of capital must be able to offer their resources on the market where there is the greatest interest. That is why it is important that the Member States free capital movements and allow payments to be made in the currency of the Member State in which the creditor or beneficiary is established.

The rules relating **to transfers of "capital" and of "payments"** formed the subject of very detailed provisions in Articles 67 and 73 and 106 and 221 respectively of the EEC Treaty as well as in Annex III to that Treaty. The principle of the free movement of capital was set out in the Treaty(Article 67), but in a more limited way than for goods and workers, "to the extent necessary to ensure the proper functioning of the common market." Those rules were laid down in detail in three Council Directives[4]. The rules guaranteed Community citizens the right to effect all payments of capital movements relating to the provision of services and to the free movement of workers. The same was true to a large extent of transfers of capital linked to establishment (direct investment, capital movements of a personal nature and movements linked to trade in goods). On the other hand, capital movements concerning long-term credit relating to commercial transactions or the purchase of unlisted securities were liberalized only in 1987[5].

---

1   OJ L124, 05.05.1989.
2   OJ L375, 31.12.1985 and OJ L168, 18.07.1995.
3   OJ L334, 18.11.1989 and OJ L1, 03.01.1994.
4   OJ 43, 12.07.1960, p.919, OJ 9, 22.01.1963, p. 62, and OJ 125, 17.08.1963, p.2240.
5   OJ L332, 26.11.1982.

All previous directives were repealed by the Directive of 24 June 1988, which ensures the **full liberalization of capital movements**[1]. Under this Directive, all restrictions on capital movements between persons (natural or legal) resident in Member States were removed in the beginning of the nineties. Monetary and quasi-monetary operations (financial loans and credits, operations in current and deposit accounts and operations in securities and other instruments normally dealt in on the money market) in particular are liberalized. A specific safeguard clause allows Member States to restore restrictions on short-term capital movements if their monetary or exchange-rate policies are disturbed. Such measures must, in all circumstances, be authorized by the Commission, but the Member State may, on the grounds of urgency, adopt such measures itself as interim protective measures.

The possibility of concerted Community action to deal with external monetary or financial disturbances is also provided for. Consultation takes place within the Monetary Committee and the Committee of Governors of the Central Banks on the initiative of the Commission or of any Member State. It relates to any measure to be taken to counteract any difficulties encountered. The possible measures here are mainly coordinated provisions of monetary and exchange-rate policy. However, if such measures prove to be inadequate, the possibility is not ruled out of the concerted regulation of short-term capital movements from or to third countries.

The Directive contains some provisions on **relations with third countries** with regard to capital movements. The principle of "erga omnes" liberalization is incorporated in the Directive. The Member States must endeavour to attain the same degree of liberalization, with regard to third countries, as that which applies within the Community. However, that provision does not prejudice the other provisions which exist or may be adopted in related areas (right of establishment, provision of financial services and admission of foreign securities to national capital markets) and which bring into play in particular a **requirement of reciprocity**. In this connection, a Commission report of 15 July 1992 pointed to a wide variety of arrangements applied by third countries to Community financial institutions and stressed the need to improve the situation through negotiations rather than through measures designed to limit or suspend access to the Community market.

However, **Articles 73a to 73h of the EC Treaty**, which have replaced Articles 67 to 73 of the EEC Treaty, go even further than the 1988 Directive in the liberalization of capital movements. The principle of the free movement of capital and payments is now expressly laid down in the Treaty. Article 73b declares, in fact, that all restrictions on the movement of capital between Member States and between Member States and third countries are prohibited. The main change as compared to the previous situation is the extension in all but a few cases of the obligation to liberalize capital movements to and from third countries. Nevertheless, Article 73f authorizes temporary safeguard measures to be taken where they are justified on serious political grounds or where capital movements to and from third countries cause serious difficulties for the functioning of economic and monetary union. In addition, Article 73d authorizes Member States to take all requisite measures to prevent infringements of national law and regulations, in particular in the field of taxation and the prudential supervision of financial institutions. According to the Court of Justice, the export of important amounts of money may be subjected to a prior declaration, so

---

[1]   OJ L178, 08.07.1988 and OJ L1, 03.01.1994.

that the national authorities may exercise effective supervision in order to prevent infringements of their laws and regulations[1].

On the basis of these provisions and of those liberalizing banking, stock-exchange and insurance services, the Community financial market has been completely liberalized since January 1, 1993. European undertakings and individuals have access to the full range of options available in the Member States as regards banking services, mortgage loans, securities and insurance. They are able to choose what is best suited to their specific needs or requirements for their daily lives and for their occupational activities in the large market. The Court has held that the free movement of capital and loans should not be restrained by national provisions which are likely to deter the parties concerned from approaching banks established in another Member State[2].

The European financial area must not, however, be exploited for the purposes of **laundering money** generated by criminal activities. With a view to nipping such practices in the bud, the Council adopted a Directive on June 10, 1991, applicable to credit establishments and financial institutions, including life insurances[3]. Under the terms of this Directive, the Member States must make provision for measures such as identification of customers and economic beneficiaries, the conservation of supporting documents and registrations of the transactions, the informing of the relevant authorities of suspected laundering operations and the obligation for the institutions covered to set up training programmes for their employees and apply internal checking procedures. The Member States must, furthermore, apply the appropriate measures to ensure that these provisions are fully applied, thanks notably to the determination of applicable sanctions. A contact committee will have the task of contributing to the harmonized implementation of national measures through regular consultations between representatives of the Member States and of the Commission.

Trans-European Networks

The integration of national markets through the completion of the internal market can only have full economic and social impact if operators enjoy trans-European transport, telecommunications and energy networks which optimise use of the various legal instruments governing the operation of this market. With a view to enabling citizens, economic operators and regional and local authorities to derive full benefit from the setting up of an area without internal frontiers, the Community strives to promote the interconnection and inter-operability of national networks and access to these networks. It takes account in particular of the need to link island, landlocked and peripheral regions with the central regions of

---

1   Judgment of 23 February 1995, joined cases C-358/93 and C-416/93, Bordessa and Others.
2   Judgment of 14 November 1995, case C-484/93, Peter Svenson.
3   OJ L166, 28.06.1991 and OJ L1, 03.01.1994.

the Community (Art. 129b of the EC Treaty). Infrastructure construction must comply with complicated sets of rules and regulations, which usually differ from one Member State to the next. To speed up the implementation of networks, and to encourage public-private partnerships, these complex rules and procedures should be streamlined, by having one approval procedure instead of requiring a series of different approvals for each element of the project, for example.

In order to achieve these objectives, the Community:
— establishes a series of guidelines identifying projects of common interest and providing the objectives, the priorities, the general lines of Community action and coordination with national decisions. These guidelines are adopted in accordance with the procedure contained in Article 189b (co-decision Council-Parliament) and require the approval of the Member State in question:
— adopts measures designed to harmonize technical standards;
— supports the financial efforts made by the Member States for projects of common interest, by carrying out feasibility studies and granting loan guarantees or interest rate subsidies. These decisions are taken by the Council in cooperation with the Parliament pursuant to the procedure of Article 189c;
— contributes to the financing of specific projects in the area of transport infrastructure through the Cohesion Fund (Art. 129c).

For **transport**, the emphasis is placed on creating high-level service or utility networks alleviating congestion, namely motorways, high speed trains, the organization of air space and combined forms of transport. New or better designed infrastructures should permit: better, safer travel at lower cost in order to improve competitiveness; effective regional planning in order to avoid a concentration of wealth and population; and bridge-building towards Eastern Europe.

As regards **telecommunications**, the priority objectives are the development of Community wideband networks - called "information highways" - and the creation of telematic networks between government departments - vital for the advancement of information society and for the running of the internal market - particularly in the fields of customs, indirect taxation, statistics and border checks.

In the **energy** sector, the chief aim is the gradual integration of natural gas and electricity networks, heightening energy supply security of all regions of the Union and ensuring international competitiveness of European firms, which are big consumers of energy.

Joint **environmental projects** consist of joint action by Member States to devise projects of common interest for protecting or improving the environment, including waste management and water policy.

A **declaration of European interest** should help mobilize private funding of projects falling into the Community programme of trans-European networks[1]. The most obvious expression of common interest is the identification of investment projects for the creation of trans-European networks. This identification could in spite of the risks inherent to big transnational projects, mobilize companies in the sector, network operators and suppliers of equipment in all the Member States. This is why the Commission's White Paper on growth, competitiveness and employment, submitted to the European Council in December 1993, points at the trans-European networks as important means of attaining these objectives[2].

The financial instruments which can facilitate the realization of these networks are notably the Cohesion Fund, certain actions provided for

1   OJ C124, 06.05.1993.
2   COM (93) 700, 5 December 1993 and COM (93) 632, 22 December 1993.

under the Structural Funds Regulations for the period 1994-99, the loans of the European Investment Bank and the loan guarantees of the European Investment Fund. A Council Regulation lays down the legal rules for the granting of Community financial assistance in the field of trans-European networks[1]. It defines the types of aid, the project selection criteria and the procedures for examining, assessing and monitoring applications for funding. The Community support can take the form of contributions to feasibility studies, interest-rate subsidies, loan guarantees and, in duly justified cases, direct grants to investments.

The Essen European Council, of December 1994, adopted operational conclusions, concerning particularly the management vehicles for individual projects and the examination of a "network approach" for environmental projects. It confirmed a revised list of fourteen priority transport projects and ten priority energy projects. It has also stressed the importance of traffic management systems, particularly in the case of air traffic. With regard to funding, the European Investment Bank is to create a special window for financing the networks, and the European Council called on the Council to adopt the necessary decisions to top up the funds currently available for the trans-European networks.

Appraisal and outlook

It took nearly a quarter of a century after the removal of customs duties and quantitative restrictions between Member States to complete the tandem of customs union and common market. And yet "Target 1992" which appeared so monumental, important and difficult to attain when set by Commission President Delors at the beginning of 1985 seemed to shrink to minute proportions when actually attained. 1992, which should have been the year of the completed internal market, became the year of Maastricht and its consequences. At the beginning of 1992, the press switched the spotlight to the major objectives of the Maastricht Treaty, which had just been signed. In the middle of the year, attention of public opinion was focused on the Danish "no" vote in the referendum on the Maastricht Treaty. The end of the year was dominated by the ratification score table of the Maastricht Treaty. Against this backdrop, Target 1992 passed almost imperceptibly and now all attention is focused on the problems of the passage to the single currency, thus confirming what is said in the introduction of this work, namely that the press and public opinion are much more interested in the Community's problems than in its achievements.

And yet the achievement of an internal market is a substantial one. On January 1, 1993, eighteen States - the Community Twelve having drawn along with them the six EFTA countries - swept aside the frontiers which had separated them for centuries. They abolished border-crossing formalities and substituted a single goods certification system for the 18 compul-

---

1　OJ L228, 23.09.1995. See also the chapters on industry (telecommunications), transport and energy.

sory ones previously existing. They thus created an economic area of 375.000.000 inhabitants in which goods move freely without checks at internal frontiers. This reduces the manufacturing and transport costs of goods. The abolition of customs documents and of controls at frontiers allows time reductions of deliveries to other Member States of up to 48 hours. This, together with the abolition of technical barriers to trade, facilitates exports and the realization of important economies. The reduction of administrative and financial costs of intra-Community trade and the realization of economies of scale tend to liberate the dynamism and the creativity of European economic operators and to give them a solid base from which to tackle international competitiveness.

In banking and insurance sectors, where obstacles to cross-border trade were particularly pronounced, the increase in cross-border competition is reflected in a growing number of branches and outlets in other Member States of the Union. The liberalization of capital movements contributes to an improvement of the allocation of resources within the Union. Public procurement in all Member States is open to tenders from all Community undertakings. European consumers now enjoy a huge choice of high quality goods and services at the best possible prices. The free movement of workers, freedom to provide services and freedom of establishment for self-employed persons constitute basic rights, guaranteeing the citizens of the Community the right to pursue an occupation and protecting them against any interference with those freedoms by a national public service. The citizen of a Member State, be he worker, businessman or tourist, can no longer be regarded as an alien in another Member State, but as a Community citizen, and no discrimination against him is permitted. The one outstanding failure to date is the maintenance of physical controls on the free movement of people at the internal frontiers of non-Schengen countries. Although the psychological impact of this gap on the citizens is quite important, its economic impact is limited as the most economically significant parts of Community legislation in this area, i.e.; recognition of the rights of movement and of establishment, are already in place.

The completion of the internal market has furthermore brought about substantial progress for the majority of the Community's policies examined in this book. It has prompted a high degree of fiscal harmonization, thereby removing fiscal frontiers. It has created a need for strengthened economic and social cohesion and therefore prompted a major step forward for the Community's regional and social policies. It has reinforced the legal foundations of consumer and environmental protection policies and those of research and development policies. In the space of just three years, it has led to more progress in transport policy than in the previous thirty. Lastly and perhaps most importantly, it sped up decisions on the march forward of the Community. Consolidation of the Single Market was the driving force behind the Maastricht agreements, designed to build economic and monetary union and political union on its foundations. Even although these new objectives are contested by some, all agree on the need for consolidation of the single market, which thus becomes an unquestionable "acquis communautaire".

However, the task to integrate the internal market is not yet complete. The priority is now to make it work efficiently. This implies, in particular, adequate implementation of the measures to complete the internal market in every Member State, effective opening-up of public contracts, further mutual recognition of standards, more transparent rules for the internal market and simplification of the taxation system. New procedures and work methods must be introduced, the transparency of the Community legislation be increased and wide-ranging cooperation established, in the form of a partnership between national and Community authorities on the management of Community provisions and programmes and on the checks and inspections indispensable if the internal market is to operate smoothly. The transparency and effectiveness of penalties for failure to comply with the obligations arising out of the Community law in the internal market field must also be improved. Last but not least, the single market must be supplemented by the single currency and continually adapted to technological change and to the information society. The stakes are high. They involve new employment opportunities, access to an enormous range of products from all Member States, travel with no borders, more and better audiovisual programmes, freedom for all, be they students, travellers, self-employed or retired, to settle in the place of their choice in the Community.

With particular reference to businessmen, they must achieve business-Europe, that is to say regard Europe as their internal market and organize their administration, production, commercial strategies and cooperation across borders. For them, too, the stakes are vital. They involve the modernization, profitability and expansion of their undertakings. There is no doubt that in the vast arena of the single market, in which all protectionist measures will have disappeared, efficient and dynamic undertakings will have everything to win. As will be seen in the chapter on industry, the Community helps businesses and particularly SMEs striving to adapt to the conditions of the Single Market.

The completion of the internal market will also step up the competition pressure on the Community's weakest regions and countries. They must gradually move away from activities procuring short-term advantages such as wage costs but which, due to their low technological content, do not enjoy a bright future. Economic restructuring, however, is all the more difficult for countries with retarded development, which no longer grasp the traditional instruments of manipulation of their economies: customs policy, commercial policy and competition policy. The following chapter will reveal the risk that these difficulties will increase with the adoption of the single currency, given that the weakest States will no longer be able to manipulate currency exchange rates and budgetary deficits to support their industries, albeit on a temporary basis. As will be seen in the chapter on regional development, greater effort will thus have to be invested in economic and social cohesion, in step with the effort for monetary integration, so as to allow the most feable to participate in the next phase.

In the hurdle-race of European integration, six have left first and have arrived alone at the term of the customs union. Their success has convinced the hesitating ones, who have joined them and, thus, fifteen have arrived at the term of the single market. Now, some are already preparing for the run to the next term, that of the single currency, while others shout to them not to harry, to wait for the new partners coming from the East who have not yet arrived at the term of the single market. Who is right? What are the hurdles and what are the prizes of the next stage of European integration? What will happen if they do not come all together at the term of the next stage? These are some of the questions, which the next chapter endeavours to answer.

Bibliography on the Common Market

□ BELLANDO Jean-Louis, BOUCHAERT Hervé, SCHOR Arman-Denis, *L'assurance dans le marché unique*, Collection "Les Études de la Documentation Française", Paris, 1994.

□ BENETT Roger, *Selling to Europe. A Practical Guide to Doing Business in the Single Market*, 2nd edition, London, 1993.

□ BRUNELLI Pierre, *Marchés publics et Union européenne. Nouvelles règles communautaires*, Éditions Continent Europe, Paris 1995.

□ CARSWELL Lucie A., de SARREAU Xavier, *Law & Business in the European Single Market*, Law Journal Seminars Press, New York, 1993.

□ CEN, *Standards for Access to the European Market. The Technical Programme*, Comité Européen de Normalisation, Brussels, 1993.

□ COCKFIELD Lord, *The European Union. Creating the Single Market*, Wiley Chancery Law, Chichester, 1994.

□ COMMISSION EUROPÉENNE, *Une nouvelle politique communautaire de normalisation*, OPOCE, Luxembourg, 1993.

  – *Un marché commun des services - Situation au 1er janvier 1993*, Série "Marché intérieur", Vol. 1, 1993.

  – *Tirer le meilleur parti du marché intérieur: Programme stratégique*, COM(93)632, Bruxelles, le 22 décembre 1993.

  – *Le marché intérieur de la Communauté: rapport 1993*, COM (94) 55 du 14.03.1994.

  – *Les marchés publics en Europe: Les directives*, OPOCE, Luxembourg, 1994.

□ COX Andrew, *The Single Market Rules and the Enforcement Regime after 1992*, Earlsgate Press, Winteringham, S. Humberside, 1993.

□ CRANSTON Ross (ed.), *European Banking Law. The Banker-Customer Relationship*, The Lloyd's Press Ltd, London, 1993.

□ EUROPEAN COMMISSION, *The Opening up of Public Procurement*, OOPEC, Luxembourg, 1993.

□   EGAN Manus, RUSHBROOKE Justin, LOCKETT Nicholas, *EC Financial Services Regulation*, Chancery Law Publ., Chichester, 1994.

□   GOLDMAN B., LYON-CAEN A., VOGEL L., *Droit commercial européen*, Dalloz, Paris, 1994.

□   JORGE Henrique Machado, *Assured Performance. The Role of Conformity Assessment in Supporting the Internal Market*, Édité par le CEPS, Bruxelles, 1995.

□   MATTERA Alfonso, *Le marché unique européen; ses règles, son fonctionnement*, Jupiter, Paris, 1990.

□   MOLINIER Joël (sous la dir. de), *La dimension externe du marché unique européen*, Presses de l'Université des sciences sociales de Toulouse, Toulouse, 1994.

   –   *Droit du marché intérieur européen*, LDG, Paris, 1995.

□   NICOLAS Florence, REPUSSARD Jacques, *Des normes communes pour les entreprises*, Commission européenne, OPOCE, Luxembourg, 1995.

□   O'CONNOR R. M., *Standards, Technical Regulations and Quality Assurance*, Commission EC, Luxembourg, 1993.

□   PELKMANS Jacques, EGAN Michelle, *Fixing European Standards: Moving beyond the Green Paper*, Centre for European Policy Studies, Brussels, 1993.

□   PERTEK Jacques, *L'Europe des diplômes et des professions*, Éditions Bruylant, Bruxelles, 1994.

□   SERVAIS Dominique, *Un espace financier européen*, quatrième édition, Office de publications officielles des Communautés européennes, Luxembourg, 1995.

□   SOUSI-ROUBI Blanche, *Droit bancaire européen*, Dalloz, Paris, 1995.

□   TREPTE Peter-Armin, *Public Procurement in the EC*, CCH Editions Ltd, Bicester, 1993.

□   VINOIS Jean-Arnold, "Les réseaux transeuropéens: une nouvelle dimension donnée au Marché unique", in *Revue du Marché unique européen*, Paris, N 1, 1993, pp. 93-125.

3. ECONOMIC

AND MONETARY UNION

Economic and monetary union (EMU) is an advanced stage of economic integration involving a common monetary policy and closely coordinated economic policies of the Member States. EMU has to be based on a common market in goods and services, but is itself necessary for the proper functioning of the common market, as exchange-rate variations between Member States' currencies hinder the interpenetration of capital markets, disturb the common agricultural market and prevent the common industrial market from wholly resembling an internal market.

The Treaty of Rome did not provide for the monetary organization of the Community, first because that Treaty was establishing a common market rather than an economic and monetary union and, secondly, because at the time of drafting of the Treaty an international monetary organization existed, namely the Bretton Woods system, which ensured the convertibility of all the currencies of the West at fixed parities.

It was just at the time when the Bretton Woods system collapsed, in early 1971, that the Member States of the Community began their effort to organize their monetary affairs in an economic and monetary union. With hindsight, that initial effort looks like a headlong rush without sound foundations, as it was not based on a common market. However, that initial effort enabled the Members States to acquire precious experience and devise instruments and mechanisms which were, in 1979, transposed to the European Monetary System, have been improved over time and will thus be used for the second effort at establishing an economic and monetary union in the '90s.

That second effort has more chances of succeeding than the first. The internal market has now been completed, the Member States have close links in all the fields which we are examining in this work and they have engaged themselves by Treaty to strive for the convergence of their economies. The economic and monetary union introduced by the Treaty on European Union represents a new and very important stage in the process of European construction. It constitutes a progressive, disciplined and irreversible commitment to adopt a single currency administered by a single central bank. The Maastricht Treaty which, through the single currency, will end currency fluctuation margins - still possible within the EMS - will eliminate monetary insecurity from the internal market.

Economic and legal framework

The customs union removed the risk of seeing barriers erected between the countries of the Community which would deprive their industries or their markets of supplies, but it cannot prevent monetary variations, which can create obstacles which are just as insurmountable as customs barriers, if not more so. In fact, **the devaluation** of the currency of a country which is a member of a customs union has an equivalent effect to imposing customs tariffs on all imported products and subsidizing that country's exports. Conversely, **the revaluation** of a member country's currency means restricting its exports and encouraging its imports, and these are factors which unfairly impede the economic operators of countries with strong currencies.

During the stage of the customs union, exchange rate variations are still possible and, to a certain extent, desirable, because the Member States conserve the autonomy of their economic policies and can, by means of those variations, adjust their economies to the new conditions of competition prevailing between themselves and with the rest of the world. During the stage of the common market, however, the exchange rate variations become more and more inconvenient for the partners. Indeed, in order to create the conditions of a single market, the partners adopt a great number of common or Community policies and, thus, lose a good deal of the possibility of autonomous management of their economies. This would not be particularly inconvenient if the single market resembled in all to an internal market, according to the definitions given in the previous chapter, since then the loss of national autonomy would be compensated by an increment of collective disciplines in the economic and monetary fields. But exactly, in order for the single market to become a real internal market, it must be completed by a single currency. This is the reason why, in view of the completion of the single market, the Member States of the Community decided in Maastricht to engage themselves in the track of economic and monetary union.

Grounds for EMU

A non-completed single market is exposed to monetary and economic problems. On the **monetary level**, the devaluation of the currency of a Member State can provide a competitive advantage to its industries, whereas the revaluation of the currency of another Member State may handicap its exports. In both instances, moreover - whether upward or downward change in the value of certain Community currencies - there is an exchange risk in the event of credit sales to a Community partner, and this greatly restricts the use of that system in intra-Community trade. In fact, an exchange-rate adjustment, even a moderate one, may substantially alter the contractual obligations of European firms and at the same time affect the relative wealth of citizens and the purchasing power of consumers.

Currency fluctuations can also penalize both investors who have financed their **foreign investments** by exporting capital from their countries and those who have had recourse to the resources of the host country. In the first case, devaluation of the currency of the country in which the investment took place or revaluation of the currency of the investor's country erodes the repatriated capital and profits. In the second case, devaluation in the investor's country or revaluation in the host country means higher amortization and therefore a greater investment cost than expected. For all those reasons, European undertakings would have continued, without monetary union, to seek their external financing on their domestic markets only.

Exchange risks, thus, limit **interpenetration of financial markets** and therefore economic growth in the European Union. Diversification of investment possibilities, coupled with the absence of exchange risks in an EMU, would tend to increase capital supply. An increase in their external sources of financing would help undertakings reach the dimensions required by the common market. By virtue of greater competition, the financial institutions would be induced to grant more favourable financing terms, thus facilitating their expansion, especially into other Member States.

From the **economic point of view**, if the internal market is divided into autonomous markets as a result of divergent economic policies followed by the Member States, the advantages expected of it, in particular economic growth and economic stability, are greatly reduced. In fact, the interdependence of the economies of members of a common market accelerates the **transmission of cyclical fluctuations** and of the effects of measures intended to deal with them. Attainment of the economic objectives of a Member State depends to a large extent on economic conditions in the other Member States. An unfavourable economic situation in one Member State leads to a reduction in its imports from the other members of the common market, which are affected in turn. On the other hand, a favourable economic situation in one member country has positive effects on the economies of the others and feedback effects on the former. Thus, one can see the importance to all Member States of the coordination of their economic policies. If there is no such coordination, the differences in economic development which take the form of high interest rates in some Member States and low rates in others and, conversely, of low exchange rates in the former and high exchange rates in the latter can result in undesirable capital movements, that is to say from the poorest to the richest countries.

Negative effects can also ensue from **divergences in national short-term economic policies**. If, for example, a Member State wishes to pursue a deflationary policy by raising interest rates, whilst another Member State wishes to follow an expansionist policy with low interest rates, capital may emigrate, for short-term investments, from the second country to the first and prevent the attainment of the objectives of both. Even when they pursue the same objectives, but by different means, two Member States of the common market can give rise to undesirable movements of capital. If, for example, a State imposes quantitative restrictions on credit in order to pursue a deflationary policy, whilst another raises interest rates, capital from the first may go to short-term investment in the second, causing balance of payments problems in the first and inflationary pressure in the second.

It can be seen that the increasing interpenetration of the economies leads to a **lessening of the independence of national short-term economic policies.** If this loss of independence were not offset by the introduction of Community policies, control of the economy of the European Union as a whole would become increasingly difficult. In fact, the semi-integration, or imperfect integration, which characterizes a common market generates situations which are unstable, and in the long term intolerable, for Member States' economic policies. Those policies are no longer up to dealing with short-term economic situations because, on the one hand, some of their causes lie abroad and, on the other hand, some economic policy instruments are already out of the reach of the national authorities, including customs duties, import restrictions and export inducements.

If economic conditions in the common market are to resemble those in an internal market, it is first and foremost necessary to eliminate exchange-rate adjustments, which disrupt trade and investment through their unpredictable effect on profitability. To this end, the Member States must impose the full and irreversible conversion of their currencies at fixed parities or, better, adopt a single currency. In either case, they would thus establish a monetary union within which transaction costs (the costs of foreign-exchange transactions or the costs of exchange-rate cover, which are estimated to be 0.3-0.4% of the Union's gross domestic product), would disappear altogether. The second possibility, however, would have some additional advantages. The single currency would permit a genuine comparison of prices of goods and services within the single market, it would become one of the main exchange and reserve currencies in the world and it would allow Europeans to pay for their imports from third countries in their own currency. By greatly facilitating the functioning of the single market, the single currency would provide a stable macroeconomic environment, which would be of considerable benefit to undertakings. This environment would foster trade, improve the allocation of resources, encourage savings, enhance growth and in the end create more employment.

Certainly, all these benefits would be derived from the economic and monetary union under certain **conditions**. This should encompass only countries well managed economically; hence the need for an economic union, within which Member States would have undertaken to scrupulously observe certain criteria ensuring monetary stability, price stability, sound public finances and, thus, sustainable growth. The observance of these criteria would be based on two foundations: a focal point for the coordination of economic policies (the Council of Economics and Finance Ministers), responsible for defining the broad guidelines of economic policy and having the means at its disposal to apply pressure on participating countries to meet their commitments; and an independent monetary institution, which would bring together the central banks of the Member States and the European Central Bank and would determine the Union's monetary policy.

All this would certainly mean the **loss of monetary sovereignty** of the countries participating in the final phase of the EMU and even some loss of their economic sovereignty. In fact, the exchange rate instrument could not be used anymore by one of these countries experiencing particular difficulties; but, this instrument could provide only a temporary relief to this country and would create problems to the other members of the Union, which would certainly prefer to grant their unfortunate partner a financial assistance. Moreover, in a context of globalization of the markets, of interdependent economies, of freedom of goods and capital movements, a totally autonomous economic policy is no longer possible. There is a need for convergence of economic policies of the Member States in view of their alignment with the best track record. The Member States of the EMU would, thus, lose prerogatives, which in practice they could not use. On the other hand, they would have a **collective responsibility** with regard to economic and monetary policies of the Union and would, therefore, exercise an enlarged joint economic and monetary sovereignty.

The march towards EMU

The EEC Treaty obviously did not aspire to creating an economic and monetary union. It merely set forth a number of general principles relating to the **coordination of economic and monetary policies** required for the proper functioning of the common market. To be fair to the authors of the Treaty, it was difficult for them to lay down specific monetary policy measures when their avowed objective was to establish a common market rather than an economic and monetary union. To start down that path required a major political decision.

Instead of taking such a decision, the Member States of the Community reaffirmed, in a non-binding Community act of **22 March 1971, their resolve** to go beyond the EEC framework and to attain by stages economic and monetary union through the close coordination of their economic and monetary policies. When their venture foundered in the international monetary chaos prevailing at the time, they quietly put it on the back burner for several years and decided, on 18 December 1978, to strengthen their monetary links within a **European Monetary System** (EMS).

These ventures were, of course, very useful, as they made it possible to draw up certain economic and monetary integration mechanisms, but they lacked solid foundations, as they were embarked upon before the common market had been completed and were not enshrined in a basic Community law, that is to say a new Treaty. That is why the Committee for the Study of Economic and Monetary Union, set up by the Hanover Council of 27 and 28 June 1988 and chaired by Jacques Delors, placed emphasis, in its report of 12 April 1989, on the necessity to open negotiations on a new Treaty which would ensure continuity in the process of the establishment of economic and monetary union. The European Council was persuaded, and decided, in Madrid on 26 and 27 June 1989, that the first stage of EMU would begin on 1 July 1990, calling upon the relevant bodies to convene an intergovernmental conference to determine the subsequent stages within the framework of a treaty on economic and monetary union. This conference, along with the parallel one on political union, got down to work in December 1990 and succeeded in drawing up a draft Treaty on European Union which was adopted by **the European Council meeting at Maastricht** on 9 and 10 December 1991 and which aims among other things, at the creation of an economic and monetary union. In what follows the evolution of the Community towards monetary union will be examined.

Monetary policy

In the beginning of the Community there was the **Bretton Woods system**! That small town in the north-east of the United States owes its fame to the signing, on 22 July 1944, of agreements which were to govern the international monetary system for a quarter of a century. The agreements set out three main principles: the convertibility of currencies between one another, the equilibrium of balances of payments and the maintenance of fixed parities, which meant that it was for each country to defend the parity of its currency, as defined by a certain weight in gold.

The Bretton Woods System

The official authority of the system, the **International Monetary Fund** (IMF), confirmed the amendments of parities communicated to it, usually after the fact, and acted as a foreign exchange office for the central banks. Member countries could, against payment of a quota (a quarter of which was theoretically payable in gold) open in the IMF "ordinary credits" in foreign currencies which they needed. But the IMF was really under American control, by virtue of the 31% of the votes held by the United States in its Governing Board and of the dollar's role in the system.

The **special role of the dollar** in the international monetary system was not featured in the Bretton Woods Agreements. It had started with an improved Gold Standard. Practice established a Gold Exchange Standard whereby the central banks could keep as reserves either gold or certain currencies which could in principle be converted into gold. In fact it was especially the dollar, and secondly the pound sterling, which were universally accepted, after the war, as international means of payment by the same token as gold. Since the price of gold was unreasonably low, international transactions were settled in dollars rather than in gold and one had thus **de facto** entered a "dollar system".

Under that system one country, **the United States,** was in practice exempt from maintaining the equilibrium of its balance of payments and could therefore conduct its monetary policy in the light of its national political objectives. In effect, the role of the dollar gave the United States an exceptional advantage in terms of trade, as it could purchase other countries' products by issuing excessive quantities of paper money, and it enabled American multinationals to purchase numerous European undertakings cheaply. The exodus of dollars, through the balance of payments deficit, also allowed the Americans to maintain, at low cost, military personnel and governments which were well disposed towards them in a number of countries in the world.

In any event, a huge mass of dollars accumulated from year to year outside the United States and especially in Europe. Exporters who had sold their businesses to American multinationals, the Arab emirs, who sold oil, and other individuals or companies held dollars which they deposited in banks as short-term investments. Those dollars in circulation outside the United States gradually established a market independent of any monetary authority, the "**Euro-dollar market**". It should also be noted that the foreign exchange markets of the EEC countries operated on the basis of the dollar, as European currencies were quoted on those markets in dollars, and offsetting of purchases and sales of European currencies was settled in dollars.

The 1971 Resolution

The Community countries therefore had every reason to put up a common front against the dollar and try to tighten the monetary links between them. To that end the "Barre Plan" of 4 March 1970 and the "**Werner Report**" of 8 October 1970 proposed the attainment by stages of economic and monetary union within the Community. Acting on a proposal from the Commission based on the "Werner Report", the Council and the Representatives of the Governments of the Member States expressed their political will to establish economic and monetary union in accordance with a **plan by stages** beginning retroactively on 1 January 1971[1] At the conclusion of that process the Community should have constituted an area within which persons, goods, services and capital could move freely, forming a single currency area within the international system and possessing such powers and responsibilities in economic and monetary matters as would enable its institutions to administer the union.

But Europe had not foreseen the reaction of the rest of the world to its intentions. In the two weeks following the Resolution of the EEC countries to put their monetary affairs in order, those countries were faced with such an influx of short-term capital that some of them were obliged to take emergency measures that were at variance with the intentions expressed in their Resolution, especially as regards the narrowing of the margins of exchange rate fluctuations between the currencies of the Community.

The most serious blow to the monetary union of the EEC was to come five months after the March 1971 Resolution. On 15 August 1971 - an historic date for the international monetary system - the United States Administration announced its decision completely to suspend the convertibility of the dollar into gold, to allow its exchange rate to fluctuate and to protect the US market against imports from the rest of the developed world. The United States thus delivered the coup de grace to the Bretton Woods system. Simultaneously they were delivering such a severe blow to the economic and monetary union of the EEC that union had to be buried for ten years, even though the Member States were loath to admit it.

In accordance with the invitation from the Council of 21 March 1971, the Governors of the Central Banks of the Member States decided, in fact, to reduce, as from 24 April 1972, the margins of fluctuation between the Community currencies to 2.25%. This was how the Community's **monetary snake** was born. The snake was to operate in a tunnel represented by the fluctuation margins of 4.5% between Community currencies and the dollar. But the snake did not stay in the tunnel for long. On 12 March 1973 the Council, noting the difficulties in complying with the fluctuation margins of Community currencies against the dollar, decided to leave the central banks free not to intervene when the exchange rates for their currencies reached the margins of fluctuation against the dollar. One could then speak of "**snake without a tunnel**".

The international monetary crisis accentuated by the 1973 oil crisis, which had itself been prolonged by the 1975 economic recession, both increased the structural differences

---

1   OJ C28, 27.03.1971.

and imbalances within the newly enlarged Community. Differences in competitiveness and variations in the ability to meet increased demand and to withstand inflation exacerbated the divergences between the Member States' economies. Although it was pursuing monetary union, the Community in fact divided into two monetary areas: that of the snake and that of floating exchange rates. The snake itself, although more binding than the floating exchange rates, had become extremely unstable since coming out of the tunnel. Nothing now limited its contortions.

Speculators were the masters of the game. It only needed a large number of them to be sellers, at a given moment, of a currency deemed to be the weakest in the snake for that currency to reach its floor. It was for the monetary authorities of the country under fire from speculation to stop the fall in their currency by buying it in against their cash holdings in foreign currency. The fate of the currency under attack then depended on the volume of the foreign exchange reserves which its central bank had at its disposal and could sacrifice. Thus most European currencies joined the floating exchange rate system one after the other. Initially that arrangement brought a degree of relief by alleviating the central banks of the impossible task of supporting their weak currencies. In due course, however, there being no mechanism obliging States to pursue stringent, convergent monetary and economic policies, those States sooner or later resorted to the currency creation anticipated by the speculators and became more and more engulfed in inflation, social pressure, economic stagnation and unemployment.

Thus the objectives which had been set for the first stage of economic and monetary union could not be attained, and the transition to a genuine second stage, envisaged for early 1974, never took place. Although the first attempt to create an economic and monetary union failed, the experience acquired in that attempt was valuable to the Community. The instruments introduced in 1972, viz. the monetary snake, that is to say the band for Community fluctuation with its intervention and short-term support mechanisms, the European Monetary Cooperation Fund (EMCF) and the European unit of account were tried out successfully, improved and passed on to the European Monetary System (EMS).

European Monetary System

From July 1978 the European Council, at the instigation of Valéry Giscard d'Estaing, then President of the French Republic, and of Helmut Schmidt, then Chancellor of the Federal Republic of Germany, laid the groundwork for the introduction of an improved monetary system. Thus, on 18 December 1978 the Council adopted a Regulation relating to the European monetary system and another changing the value of the unit of account used by the EMCF[1]. Whereas at world level, since 1971, a country's monetary authorities have no longer been obliged to intervene to influence the exchange rate of their currency, the EMS exchange rate mechanism introduced, for member currencies, an obligation to limit fluctuations between the latter to certain fluctuation margins.

In its initial stage the EMS was in reality an improved, more flexible and more sound "snake". The maximum margin tolerated between two currencies in the system remained 2.25%, just as in the snake (6% for the weaker currencies), but a currency's exchange rate fluctuations were no longer calculated, as in the snake, in relation to each of the other currencies in the system, but in relation to the European monetary unit. The latter was thus used as a unit of account to establish exchange rate margins and to trigger compulsory intervention similar to that under the snake.

---

1   OJ L379, 30.12.1978.

But the EMS disposes normally of much more refined mechanisms than those of the snake. **Central rates** are used to determine the grids of bilateral parities, viz. between each of the currencies in the system. Margins of fluctuation of normally 2.25% (6% for some feeble currencies) are fixed around these bilateral rates. The central rates are adjusted in accordance with a joint procedure involving all countries participating in the exchange mechanism as well as the European Commission. A "divergence indicator" based on the ecu is used to detect divergences between Community currencies and to prevent the appearance of the spot margin which triggers compulsory intervention. The "divergence threshold" is set at 75% of the limit of the maximum margin of fluctuation of each currency against the ecu.

Where a currency crosses its **divergence threshold**, the "alarm bell" sounds and the authorities which issue the currency in question are supposed to act to eliminate, through appropriate measures, the tension on the foreign exchange markets. Moreover, where a currency crosses its divergence threshold, "voluntary" interventions are in principle made in the currencies of the other countries participating in the system. On a second level, where a currency threatens to burst through its "floor" or "ceiling" because its exchange rate is more than 2.25% (or 6% for the weaker currencies) from the central rate set in relation to the other currencies, compulsory interventions are also in principle made in the currencies of participating countries.

The unit of account used in the European Monetary System has developed a great deal. Yet the ecu (English initials of the **European Currency Unit**, calling to mind, in French, the old gold coin used for centuries) was initially identical to the European unit of account (EUA) used in the snake system, apart from the fact that it involved a review clause whereby changes could be made to its composition. In common with the EUA, the ecu is based on an assortment, or "basket", of different national currencies, the initial composition of which was determined on the basis of objective criteria relating to the economic importance of each Member State, in particular its gross national product, its intra-Community trade and its contribution to the short-term financial assistance mechanism. Thus, the basket is composed of some 32% DM, 20% FF, 11% UKL, 10% HFL, 8% BF, etc.

The value of the ecu varies according to the weighted trend of the exchange rates of the currencies in the **basket** and it is therefore more stable than the value of each of the currencies taken separately, because upward or downward trends of various currencies in the basket offset one another. The exchange value of the ecu in a national currency is equal to the sum of the exchange values of the amounts which compose the ecu. Those exchange values are calculated daily by the Commission and published in the Official Journal of the European Communities ("C" series).

In addition to its general functions as a unit of account, in particular for expressing the amounts in the general budget of the Communities and the common prices for agricultural products, the ecu is the central element of the European Monetary System. Thus, the ecu is used as the common denominator in the exchange rate grid for Community currencies, as the basis for establishing the indicator of divergence between Community currencies, as the denominator for intervention operations and as a means of settling credit or debit balances between the central banks. In 1994, the existing rules on the definition of the ecu were consolidated, in order to replace them by a single definition compatible with Article 109g of the EC Treaty and to clarify and simplify Community legislation[1].

In 1985 a **mobilization mechanism** was introduced, permitting any central bank faced with a need for intervention currency temporarily to mobilize ecu in exchange for dollars or Community currencies, and the official ecu circuit was opened to central banks from third countries and international monetary establishments[2]. On 12 September 1987 the "Basle/Nyborg" Agreement strengthened the cooperation links within the EMS. The **multilateral supervision** procedure was reinforced, the scope of any realignments was limited and differences in interest rates became the main instruments to combat tension within the parity grid.

In general the EMS has shown the importance of the **collective discipline** framework which it helped to establish. In an international monetary environment disturbed by the second oil crisis, the sustained rise in the dollar in the early '80s, its spectacular fall after February 1985 and the stock exchange crisis of October 1987, the EMS satisfactorily fulfilled its main objective of establishing close cooperation leading to an area of monetary stability in Europe. By obliging the countries which are party to it to comply with an explicit exchange rate discipline, it made a decisive contribution in the fight against inflation.

Over the years, however, the EMS became a genuine mark zone, in which discipline was notably guaranteed by the German Central Bank, the famous Bundesbank, familiarly called "Buba". This discipline gave good results until the end of the '80s, but, since 1990, two important phenomena have started eroding this discipline within the EMS: the complete liberalization of capital movements within the Community, which reinforced the speculative capacity of financial intermediaries; and the cost of reunification, which has resulted in an increasing budgetary deficit in Germany. No system of monetary cooperation can function, however, when the State which issues the reference currency can not guarantee its stability. Just as the inflation drift in the United States put an end to the Bretton Woods system, so the German interest rate drift has caused the rupture of the EMS.

Thus, during the second half of 1992, uncertainties surrounding the process of ratification of the Maastricht Treaty, currency turmoil and doubts surrounding the outcome of the Uruguay Round placed the EMS exchange rate mechanisms under severe strain. In July 1993, more severe pressures developed within the exchange-rate mechanism with massive speculative attacks against the weaker currencies. Under these circumstances, the Ministers and central bank governors of the Member States decided, on 2 August 1993, to widen temporarily the fluctuation margins within the exchange-rate mechanism to 15% either side of the bilateral central rates.

The officially expressed will of the Finance Ministers is to maintain the EMS, even if they need to give it more flexibility for a certain time. However, the governments of the Member States seem to be in no hurry to return to the narrow bands of 2.25%. If, as is likely, the two main causes

---

1   OJ L350, 31.12.1994.
2   OJ L290, 01.11.1985.

of the monetary tension were the divergent course of recession in the different Member States and the conflict between German monetary policy and the Bundesbank's intervention obligation within the EMS, then returning to the old system without first tackling its inherent problems will leave currencies open to attacks in the future. The exchange-rate fluctuations which are now allowed have, however, negative effects on economic growth and the internal market. While the terms of exchange are improved in those countries whose currencies are depreciated, they encounter inflationary and budgetary pressures. On the contrary, the countries whose currencies are appreciated experience a serious handicap of their exports. The inability of the EMS to circumscribe monetary disturbances in the single market proves that the single currency is an essential complement of this market.

The monetary system under European Union

The Treaty on European Union provides for the eventual introduction of a single monetary policy based upon a single currency managed by a single and independent central bank. The primary objective of the single monetary policy and exchange rate policy shall be to maintain price stability and, without prejudice to this objective, to support the general economic policies in the Community, in accordance with the principle of an open market economy with free competition. These activities of the Member States and the Community shall entail compliance with the following guiding principles: stable prices, sound public finances and monetary conditions and a sustainable balance of payments (Art. 3a EC).

Although economic and monetary union has to be envisaged as a single process, there are, in fact, three phases involved. The first phase, marking the beginning of the whole process, came with the entry into force of the Directive on the complete liberalization of capital movements in July 1990. The central objectives of this phase are greater convergence of economic policies and closer cooperation between central banks, incorporating greater consistency between monetary practices in the framework of the EMS[1].

During this phase, Member States must adopt multiannual programmes intended to ensure convergence, in particular with regard to price stability and sound public finances. The Council is responsible for assessing the progress made with regard to economic and monetary convergence and the progress made with the implementation of Community law concerning the internal market (Art. 109e EC). In order to promote coordination of the policies of Member States to the extent needed for the functioning of the internal market, provision is made for a **Monetary Committee** with advisory status. The Member States and the Commission each appoint two members of the Monetary Committee (Art. 109c EC).

As provided for in Article 109g of the Treaty, the **composition of the basket of the ecu** was "frozen" on 1 November 1993, the date of the entry into force of the Maastricht Treaty, on the basis of the composition of the

---

1   OJ L78, 24.03.1990.

basket (in amounts of each national currency) defined on 21st September 1989 at the occasion of the entry into the basket of the peseta and the escudo. No other change in the composition of the basket of the ecu is allowed until the ecu gives way to the single currency, the Euro. On the other hand, the percentage weight of the currencies composing the basket may change in line with their fluctuations in the exchange-rate market. Consequently, the possible devaluation of a weak currency will not entail a corresponding devaluation of the ecu, because the amount of the deval-ued currency in the basket will remain the same, but its percentage share in the basket will diminish. This will automatically increase the weight of stronger currencies and will mean a "harder" ecu, more resistant to devalu-ation.

The **second stage** of economic and monetary union began on 1st January 1994. During this stage, the Treaty on European Union compels each Member State to endeavour to avoid excessive public deficits and initiate steps leading to independence of its central bank, so that the future monetary union encompasses only countries which are well managed economically. A Council Regulation lays down detailed rules and defini-tions for the application of the excessive deficit procedure, including the definition of public debt, as well as rules for the reporting of data by the Member States to the Commission[1].

In the process leading to the independence of central banks, the Treaty prohibits them from granting governments overdraft facilities or any other type of credit facility and from purchasing public sector debt instruments directly from them (Article 104). A Council Regulation clarifies certain implications of this prohibition, making it clear that the holding until maturity of public-sector debt instruments purchased prior to 1st January 1994 is not prohibited and that the central banks may therefore keep them in their portfolio until maturity[2].

Together with the prohibition on the direct monetary financing of public deficits and in order to submit public borrowings to market disci-pline, the Treaty provides that public authorities may not have privileged access to financial institutions, unless this is based on prudential consid-erations (Article 104a). The Treaty seeks, thus, to institutionalize a sort of market-induced budgetary control. To this effect, a Council Regulation defines the terms "privileged access", "financial institutions", "prudential considerations" and "public undertakings"[3].

Following the provisions of Article 109f (EC), the Committee of Gov-ernors of central banks and the European Fund of Monetary Cooperation were dissolved in January 1994. They were replaced by a **European Mone-tary Institute** (EMI), with its seat in Frankfurt. The EMI has its own resources consisting of contributions from the central banks based on a key identical to that for the future European Central Bank (50% population - 50% GDP)[4]. It is directed and managed by a Council, consisting of a President and the Governors of the national central banks, one of whom

---

1   OJ L332, 31.12.1993.
2   Ibid.
3   Ibid.
4   Ibid.

shall be Vice-President. It shall monitor the functioning of the European Monetary System and facilitate the use of the ecu. It shall strengthen cooperation between the central banks as well as coordinating the monetary policies of the Member States. It must, in particular, be consulted by the authorities of the Member States on any draft legislative provision within its field of competence[1]. The EMI will thus help to achieve the necessary conditions for moving to the third stage of the EMU, in particular by strengthening the coordination of monetary policies with the aim of ensuring price stability and by making the necessary preparations for introducing the European System of Central Banks, carrying out a single monetary policy and creating a single currency. In fact, the EMI monitors the economic and monetary policies of the Member States "ex ante" (autumn) and "ex post" (spring). It has prepared a payment-system arrangement for a single monetary policy and large-value transactions (Target). It is studying the institutional and logistical aspects of the issuing, sorting and handling of European banknotes.

In **preparation for the move to the third stage**, the Commission and the European Monetary Institute shall report to the Council on national legislation linked to the achievement of economic and monetary union and progress towards a high degree of convergence assessed by reference to **four specific criteria**: a rate of inflation which is close to that of the three best performing Member States in terms of price stability; a government budgetary position without a deficit that is excessive, meaning a government deficit not exceeding 3% of GNP and total government debt not greater than 60% of GNP (subject to an appraisement by the Council deciding by qualified majority); the durability of convergence achieved by the Member State being reflected in the long-term interest rate levels; and the observance of the normal fluctuation margins provided for by the Exchange Rate Mechanism of the European Monetary System, for at least two years (Art. 109j and Protocol on the excessive deficit procedure). This last condition has lost its importance since the normal fluctuations margins have been enlarged to 15%. Concerning the assessment of the progress made in achieving price stability, a Regulation provides for Member States to draw up their consumer price indices on a comparable basis[2].

It must be noted that the decision for a Member State entering the final stage of the EMU will be based on a political appreciation taking into account at the same time the indicators provided for in the Treaty, the expected trends and the exceptional circumstances that may justify an economic result which does not satisfy a certain criterion. In fact, the question for each Member State will be whether the advantages expected from the diminution of the uncertainty and the cost of transactions outweigh the disadvantages of not being able to follow a common monetary policy. The answer will depend on the will of the country which, at a certain moment, does not still fulfil the required conditions, to make the necessary efforts to reduce its budget deficit and its foreign debt. When that effort has enabled the Member State in question to enter the "virtuous

---

1   Ibid.
2   OJ C84, 06.04.1995.

circle", its situation could evolve rapidly and be submitted to the Community for examination. However, the convergence criteria must be scrupulously observed not only for entering the third stage but also for participating on a lasting basis in monetary union.

Member States not able to adopt the single currency from the start will be given a derogation which implies that the provisions on monetary policy and on sanctions with respect to excessive deficits do not apply to them (Art. 109k). Ratification of the Treaty implies an irrevocable commitment by the Member States to move to the third stage if they satisfy the necessary conditions. This applies also to new members of the Union, such as Austria, Sweden and Finland. However, two protocols attached to the Treaty allow the United Kingdom to reserve its decision concerning its participation to the third stage and Denmark a similar exception if, after a referendum, it decides not to move to that stage. Countries benefiting from an "opt-out" and those which do not meet the criteria from the outset will nevertheless participate in all the procedures (multilateral surveillance, excessive deficit...) designed to facilitate their future participation. The Governors of their central banks will be members of the ECB General Council.

From the start of **the final stage** of EMU, the Community will have a single monetary policy and a single currency - the Euro. This implies a new institution, the **European Central Bank (ECB)**, which will replace the EMI and will form, together with the central banks of the Member States, the **European System of Central Banks (ESCB)**. Neither the ECB nor national central banks shall seek or take instructions from governments or Community institutions (Art. 107). The total independence of the European Central Bank is the touchstone of the Community's new monetary policy. According to the German concept, which has shown its worth through the independence of the Bundesbank, currency is something much too serious to leave in the hands of politicians who, legitimately worried about unemployment, are tempted to manipulate the currency to kick-start the economy without drawing on the lessons of the past. Democratic control can and must be exercised a posteriori by the dismissal of the governors of national central banks, members of the ECB board, who are judged by their governments to have failed in their task.

All central banks, including those not participating in the single monetary policy, will be members of the **ESCB** from the start of the third stage. The primary objective of the ESCB shall be to maintain price stability. Without prejudice to this objective, the ESCB shall support the general economic policies in the Community with a view to contributing to the achievement of the objectives of the Community as laid down in Article 2. The basic tasks to be carried out through the ESCB shall be: to define and implement the monetary policy of the Community; to conduct foreign exchange operations consistent with the provisions of Article 109; to hold and manage the official foreign reserves of the Member States; and to promote the smooth operation of payment systems (Art. 105). However, exchange policy with regard to the currencies of third countries (US dollar, Japanese yen...) is determined by the Council after consultation of the ECB (Article 109).

The **ECB** will make regulations and take decisions necessary for carrying out the tasks entrusted to the ESCB (Art. 108a). The ECB will have the exclusive right to authorize the issue of bank notes within the Community. The ECB and the national central banks may issue such notes. Member States may issue coins subject to approval by the ECB of the volume of the issue (Art. 105a). The ECB will be consulted on any proposed Community act and may submit opinions to Community institutions or to national authorities on matters within its field of competence (Art. 105).

The capital of the ECB will be held by the national central banks in proportion to the individual countries' demographic and economic weight. The external foreign reserves of the **national** central banks will be pooled at the ECB within certain limits. The decision-making bodies of the ECB will be the Governing Council and the Executive Board. The policy of the ECB aiming at ensuring price stability will be formulated by the Governing Council, which will be composed of the fifteen Governors of the central banks of the Member States and of the members of the executive Board. The executive Board, consisting of the President of the ECB, the Vice-President and four other members, will implement the ECB monetary policy and will give the necessary instructions to the national central banks.

At the start of the third stage the Monetary Committee will be replaced by an **Economic and Financial Committee**. The Member States, the Commission and the ECB will each appoint no more than two members of the Committee. This will have the following tasks: to deliver opinions at the request of the Council or of the Commission, or on its own initiative for submission to those institutions; to keep under review the economic and financial situation of the Member States and of the Community and to report regularly thereon to the Council and to the Commission, in particular on financial relations with third countries and international institutions; to contribute to the preparation of the work of the Council on EMU; to examine, at least once a year, the situation regarding the movement of capital and the freedom of payments and to report to the Commission and to the Council on the outcome of this examination (Art. 109c).

At the starting date of the third stage, the Council shall, acting with the unanimity of the Member States without a derogation, on a proposal from the Commission and after consulting the ECB, adopt the conversion rates at which their currencies shall be irrevocably fixed and at which irrevocably fixed rate the single currency, renamed **Euro**, shall be substituted for these currencies (Art. 109l). The actual currency composition of the basket shall not be changed (Art. 109g) and its external value shall not be modified, but the ecu shall then be replaced by the Euro and this shall become a currency in its own right (Art. 109l). The Euro will, in fact be the currency of those Member States which participate fully in the single monetary policy. The SME will continue to exist in order to limit the fluctuations between the single currency of these Member States and the currencies of the Member States with a derogation. The right of vote of the latter will be suspended for all questions relating to the single currency.

The introduction of the single currency of the EU or of certain Member States will inevitably involve, however, a number of practical questions, such as the design, the production and distribution of means of payment (bank-notes and coins), use of the currency, price adjustments and practical consequences for enterprises. These questions are examined in a communication of the Commission[1]. Taking account of these difficulties, the Commission, after receiving the report of the "Maas" expert group, ap-

---

1   OJ C153, 04.06.1994.

pointed specifically to examine practical issues of the EMU, suggested a reference scenario in three phases for the **introduction of the single currency**[1]. The scenario of the Commission was closely followed by the technical report on the same subject, presented on 14 November 1995, by the European Monetary Institute and by the scenario that the Council, on its turn, presented to the European Council.

On this basis, the European Council, meeting in Madrid on 15 and 16 December 1995, confirmed that **1 January 1999 will be the starting date for stage three** of EMU, in accordance with the convergence criteria, timetable, protocols and procedures laid down in the Treaty. It also decided that, as of the start of stage three, the name given to the European currency shall be the Euro, a name that symbolizes Europe and must be the same in all the official languages of the European Union, taking into account the existence of different languages. The Council, in the composition of Heads of State or Government, will confirm as early as possible in 1998 which Member States fulfil the necessary conditions for the adoption of the single currency (Phase A).

Stage three will thus begin on 1 January 1999 with the irrevocable fixing of conversion rates among the currencies of participating countries and against the Euro (Phase B). From that date, monetary policy and the foreign exchange rate policy will be conducted in Euros, the use of the Euro will be encouraged in foreign exchange markets and new tradeable public debt will be issued in Euros by the participating Member States. A Council Regulation will provide the legal framework for the use of the Euro, which, from this date, will become a currency in its own right, and the official ecu basket will cease to exist. The European Central Bank will have to be created early enough so as to allow preparations to be completed and full operation to start on 1 January 1999.

By **1 January 2002** at the latest, Euro banknotes and coins will start to circulate alongside national notes and coins, which will start to be withdrawn (Phase C). At most six months later, the national currencies will have been completely replaced by the Euro in all participating Member States and the changeover will be complete. Thereafter, national banknotes and coins may still be exchanged at the national central banks. The European institutions are aware of the practical and psychological problems of an upheaval of this magnitude and without precedent. Although surveys show that the majority of European citizens are in favour of the single currency, they also show some fears, particularly as to the risk of conversion errors, transition costs, effects on employment and understanding of new prices. This is why, the Commission prepares a communications strategy in order to win public support and stimulate technical preparations for the passage to the Euro.

In moving to the third phase of EMU, the Member States will undoubtedly lose the autonomy of their monetary policy, since they will no longer be at liberty to use the two main levers of this policy, the exchange rate and the interest rate (a freedom which they had already lost to a large extent, due to the interdependence of the European economies). At the

---

1   COM (95) 333 final, 31.05.1995.

same time, however, they lose responsibility for the parity of their currency and the equilibrium of their balance of payments, while henceforth enjoying shared responsibility for the parity of the Euro against the currencies of third countries and the equilibrium of the collective balance of payments of the countries entering the third phase of EMU. The countries moving on to this phase have in fact already got their economies under control as regards inflation, external debt and public sector deficit and thus collectively share the advantages of belonging to a strong currency zone, the Euro zone.

Economic policy

The Member States signatory to the EEC Treaty were not prepared to abandon their sovereign powers in economic or monetary matters in favour of the Community. Accordingly, the Treaty was confined to defining the objectives to be pursued in national economic policies, including full employment, a stable level of prices and currency and equilibrium of the balance of payments. Elaboration and implementation of economic policy as such, however, remained exclusively within the jurisdiction of the Member States.

However, the **Treaty of Rome** had considered it desirable that the Member States regard their conjunctural policies as a matter of common concern. Article 103 stipulated that they should consult each other and the Commission on the measures to be taken in the light of the prevailing circumstances. Pursuant to that provision of the Treaty, the Commission endeavoured, even from the period of transition towards customs union, to ensure the coordination of economic policies by annually adopting appropriate Recommendations to the Member States. At that time the Council met twice a year to examine the economic situation in the Community and to invite the Member States to implement the conjunctural policies set out in particular in the Commission's guidelines. But it very quickly became clear that the progress made in the field of the coordination of economic policies fell far short of expectations.

In 1974, the Council set up an **Economic Policy Committee** for Short-term Economic and Financial Policies[1]. That Committee, which consists of one representative for each Member State and a Commission representative, has the task of preparing the meetings of the **ECOFIN Council** (Economic and Financial Affairs). It is also responsible for the exchange, on a reciprocal and continuing basis, of information on decisions or measures envisaged by the Member States which could have a considerable effect on the economies of the other Member States or on the internal or external equilibrium of the Member State concerned or which could give rise to a considerable gap between the development of the economy of a country and the jointly defined medium-term objectives.

The Community's economic policy did not really get off the ground until the Member States decided to undertake the attainment of economic and monetary union. More than other Community policies, the economic policy is indispensable to attainment of such union, as it constitutes one of its two aspects. The task assigned to it by the Resolution of the Council and of the Representatives of the Governments of the Member States of 22 March 1971 on the attainment by stages of economic and monetary union was the **convergence of the economies** of the Member States, which is an extremely difficult task considering the structural disparities between the economies which were to participate in that major undertaking. However, the experience acquired during the first attempt of the Community at

---

1   OJ L63, 05.03.1974.

economic and monetary union, should be precious for the second attempt based on the Treaty on European Union.

This fresh endeavour, like the first, twenty years before, has started in an environment of economic and monetary crisis. The persistence of the crisis between 1991 and 1993 exacerbated an already difficult labour-market situation. The need to face up to the crisis and to the deterioration in employment and working conditions led the Commission to draw up a White Paper on the medium-term strategy for promotion of growth, competitiveness and employment , which contains a clear presentation of the structural problems facing the Community and proposes concrete solutions for addressing the issues raised[1]. According to the Commission, the sustainable development of the European economies and the increase of labour intensity require a strategy based on three inseparable elements: (a) the creation and the maintenance of a macroeconomic framework which, instead of constraining market forces, as has often happened in the past, supports them; (b) determined actions in the structural area aimed at increasing the competitiveness of European industry, at removing the rigidities which are curbing its dynamism and preventing it from reaping the full benefits of the internal market; (c) active policies and structural changes in the labour market and in the regulations limiting the expansion of certain sectors (notably the service sector) making it easier to employ people and increasing the employment component of growth.

Largely following the ideas of the Commission, the European Council, in December 1993, decided to implement an action plan directed, in the short term, at reversing the unemployment trend and, by the end of the century, at significantly reducing the number of unemployed. The plan disposes of around ECU 20 billion per year and must, in particular, stimulate the setting up of big equipment and communication networks, in order to improve the competitiveness of the economy and the functioning of the internal market. Both, the White Paper and the action plan of the European Council are vital elements in the EU's strategy for steering the economies of the Member States back onto a path of growth and employment creation, as well as for allowing them to attain the objectives of economic and monetary union.

Economic convergence in the European Union

In contrast to monetary policy, Member States will retain ultimate responsibility for economic policy within the economic and monetary union provided for by the **Treaty on European Union**. They will, however, be required to act in such a way as to respect the principle of an open market economy where competition reigns, to regard their economic policies as a matter of common concern and to conduct them with a view to contributing to the achievement of the objectives of the Community (Art. 102a and 103). Herein lies the originality of the model for European Economic and Monetary Union; a union of independent States with sig-

---

1   COM (93) 700, 5.12.1993.

nificantly different development levels but which want to be partners in the pursuit of common goals.

Budget policy is perhaps the area in which differences of opinion between Member States are still at their strongest. This stems from the fact that the budget is the most characteristic manifestation of national sovereignty in economic terms. The budget is in fact the main instrument of orientation of the economy in general and of individual government policies, such as regional social and industrial policies, etc. Through its expenditure side the budget has a direct influence on public investment and an indirect influence, through aids of all sorts, on private investment. Through its revenue side the budget acts on savings and on the circulation of currency. A State's budget policy may pursue short-term economic objectives (avoidance of a recession or stemming of inflation) or structural improvement objectives pertaining to the national economy and implemented through productive investments. Clearly, although it is difficult, coordination of budget policies is most important for the economic convergence sought by the Maastricht Treaty.

In the second phase of EMU, i.e. since the 1st January 1994, economic policies of the Member States shall be coordinated at Community level. A Council Decision of 1990 is directed towards the attainment of progressive convergence of economic performance of the Member States[1]. To this effect the Council (ECOFIN), acting by a qualified majority on a recommendation from the Commission, formulates, each year in the spring, a draft for the **broad guidelines of the economic policies** of the Member States and of the Community, and reports its findings to the European Council. This discusses a conclusion on the broad guidelines of the economic policies of the Member States and of the Community. On this basis, the Council, acting on a qualified majority endorses the broad guidelines of economic policy, which lay down the common objectives in terms of inflation, public finance, exchange rate stability and employment (Art. 103,2).

The Council, on the basis of reports submitted by the Commission, monitors economic developments in each of the Member States and in the Community as well as the consistency of economic policies with the broad guidelines **(multilateral monitoring).** It is based on convergence programmes presented by each Member State which specifically aim at addressing the main sources of difficulty in terms on convergence (Art. 103,3). It also involves a review of budgetary policies, with particular reference to the size and financing of deficits, if possible prior to the drafting of national budgets. The regular monitoring of economic and monetary policies of the Member States by the European Monetary Institute, mentioned in the previous part of this chapter, is an integral part of the general monitoring procedures.

Where it is established that the economic policies of a Member State are not consistent with these guidelines, the Council may, acting by a qualified majority, make the necessary recommendations to the Member State concerned. It may decide to make its recommendations public (Art. 103, 4). The Council may, acting unanimously on a proposal from the

---

1   OJ L78, 24.03.1990.

Commission, decide upon the measures appropriate to the economic situation, in particular if severe difficulties arise in the supply of certain products. Where a Member State is in difficulties or is seriously threatened with severe difficulties caused by exceptional occurrences beyond its control, the Council may, acting unanimously on a proposal from the Commission, grant, under certain conditions, Community financial assistance to the Member State concerned (Art. 103a).

As the secondary legislation necessary for implementing the second stage of EMU was adopted in full in 1993, certain restrictions on financing public deficits came into force on 1 January 1994, including the bans on direct financing of deficits by central banks (Art. 104 EC) and on any form of privileged access by the public to financial institutions (Art. 104a)[1]. The Council recommendations designed to bring to an end the excessive deficits are adopted by qualified majority in accordance with Article 104c(6) of the EC Treaty.

The broad guidelines of the economic policies for 1996, adopted by the Council on 10 July 1995, consider it essential for the recovery to be turned into strong, sustainable, non-inflationary medium-term growth which respects the environment[2]. The Council demands sustained efforts to consolidate public finances in most Member States, as well as nominal wage trends consistent with the price-stability objective and real wage terms below the increase in productivity in order to strengthen the profitability of employment-creating investment. According to the Council, this strategy may reduce unemployment and allow the high degree of convergence necessary to facilitate the move to the third stage of EMU. The Commission recommendation for the broad guidelines of the economic policies for 1997 confirms in essence the guidelines adopted by the Council in 1995[3].

From the third phase of EMU, budgetary policies of the Member States will be constrained by three rules: overdraft facilities or any other type of credit facility from the ECB or national central banks to public authorities (Community, national or regional) will be prohibited (Art. 104); any privileged access of public authorities to the financial institutions will be banned (Art. 104a); neither the Community nor any Member State will be liable for the commitments of public authorities, bodies or undertakings of a Member State (Art. 104b).

The Commission monitors the development of the budgetary situation and the level of government debt in the Member States with a view to identifying gross errors. In particular it examines compliance with **budgetary discipline** on the basis of the following two criteria: a) whether the ratio of the planned or actual government deficit to Gross Domestic Product exceeds a reference value (3% of GDP), unless either the ratio has declined substantially and continuously and reached a level that comes close to the reference value or, alternatively, the excess over the reference value is exceptional and temporary and the ratio remains close to the reference value; b) whether the ratio of government debt to gross domestic product exceeds a reference value (60% of GDP), unless the ratio is sufficiently diminishing and approaching the reference value at a satisfactory pace (Art. 104c and Protocol on the excessive deficit procedure).

If a Member State does not fulfil the requirements under one or both of these criteria, the Commission shall prepare a report. The report of the Commission shall also examine whether the government deficit exceeds

---

1　OJ L332, 31.12.1993.
2　OJ L191, 12.08.1995.
3　COM (96) 211, 15 May 1996.

investment expenditure and take into account all other relevant factors, including the medium term economic and budgetary position of the Member State. The Council shall, acting by a qualified majority on a recommendation from the Commission, and having considered any observations which the Member State concerned may wish to make, decide after an overall assessment whether an excessive deficit exists. Where the existence of an excessive deficit is decided, the Council shall make recommendations to the Member State concerned with a view to bringing that situation to an end within a given period. If there is no effective action in response to its recommendations within the period laid down, the Council may make its recommendations public.

If a Member State persists in failing to put into practice the recommendations of the Council, the Council may decide to give it notice to take, within a specified time limit, measures for the deficit reduction which is judged necessary in order to remedy the situation. If the Member State fails to comply with the decision of the Council, the latter may decide to apply or intensify one or more of the following measures: to require that the Member State concerned publish additional information, to be specified by the Council, before issuing bonds and securities; to invite the European Investment Bank to reconsider its lending policy towards the Member State concerned; to require that the Member State concerned make a non-interest-bearing deposit of an appropriate size with the Community until the excessive deficit has, in the view of the Council, been corrected; to impose fines of an appropriate size (Art. 104c).

Balance of payments problems

A member country of the Community may, like any country, find itself faced with serious **short-term economic problems**. Such problems, which can have consequences for the balance of payments of a member country, are particularly significant for the Community, as they may force that Member State to take protectionist measures, which are at variance with the freedom of trade provided for in the Treaty of Rome. That is why Community legislation lays down measures which must be taken by the country in question and by the Community Institutions to help it cope with its problems without jeopardizing the proper functioning of the common market.

Article 109h of the Treaty stipulates that "where a Member State is in difficulties or is seriously threatened with difficulties as regards its balance of payments... and where such difficulties are liable in particular to jeopardize the functioning of the common market... the Commission shall immediately investigate the position of the State in question and the action which... that State has taken or may take" and "shall state what measures it recommends the State concerned to take". If the action taken by the Member State and the measures suggested by the Commission do not prove sufficient to overcome the difficulties which have arisen or which threaten the Member State, the Commission recommends to the Council the granting of **mutual assistance.** This may take the form of the granting of limited credits by other Member States and/or recourse to other international organizations, as well as measures needed to avoid deflection of trade where the State which is in difficulties maintains or reintroduces quantitative restrictions against third countries. If the mutual assistance recommended by the Commission is not granted by the Council or if the mutual assistance granted and the measures taken are insufficient, the Commission authorizes the State which is in difficulties to take **protective measures**, the conditions and details of which the Commission determines. Such authorization may be revoked and details may be changed by the Council acting by a qualified majority.

Article 109i of the Treaty stipulates that where a sudden crisis in its balance of payments occurs and a decision within the meaning of Article 109h is not immediately taken, the Member State concerned may, as a precaution, take the necessary protective measures, while ensuring that such measures cause the least possible disturbance in the functioning of the common market and are not wider in scope than is strictly necessary to remedy the immediate difficulties. The Commission and the other Member States must be informed of such protective measures not later than when they enter into force. The Commission may recommend to the Council the granting of mutual assistance under Article 108 or the amendment, suspension or abolition of the measures taken by the State in difficulties. In the third stage of EMU, these provisions will no longer be relevant for the Member States participating fully in the single monetary policy. They may, however, be granted the financial assistance provided for in Article 103a.

Financial solidarity

Although the Treaty of Rome made vague provision for short-term financial assistance in the event of difficulties for a Member State, it made no provision whatsoever for medium-term financial assistance. In the context of the plan to attain economic and monetary union by stages, the Council decided, in 1971, to set up machinery for **medium-term financial assistance**[1]. In 1988, it decided to introduce a single mechanism for medium-term balance of payments financial support in the Member States[2]. That Decision provides that where a Member State is in difficulties or is seriously threatened with difficulties as regards its balance of payments, it may have recourse to the Community machinery for mutual assistance, i.e. ask its partners for medium-term credit. The granting of such credit is decided upon by the Council acting by a qualified majority. The decision on the granting of financial support fixes the amount and the terms of the credit and determines what undertakings in respect of economic policy the recipient Member State must enter into.

Credits under the medium-term mutual assistance system may be granted for two to five years. They are granted in installments, and the Council decides on the release of each installment after verification has shown that the debtor country has fulfilled its economic commitments during the previous period. No single country may obtain more than 50% of the total amount of medium-term financial support available, so that the machinery may be used by several States simultaneously. Before Community assistance is granted to a Member State which is experiencing balance of payments difficulties, the possibilities offered by other assistance systems, such as those of the International Monetary Fund, have to be examined. Following the satisfaction of these conditions Greece was granted a loan of 2.2 billion ECU

---

1 OJ L73, 27.03.1971.
2 OJ L178, 08.07.1988.

in February 1991[1] and Italy received, in January 1993, a loan of 8 billion ECU[2].

The main Community instrument of financial solidarity is however the **European Investment Bank** (EIB). The Treaty on European Union reaffirms the EIB's task, as a Community financial institution, of contributing to the balanced development of the Community and the implementation of its policies. Thanks to its high credit rating, the Bank borrows on the best terms on the capital markets worldwide and on-lends to the Member States and their financial institutions - which distribute these global loans to SMEs. The EIB is a major source of finance for new industrial activities and advanced technology in sectors such as the motor vehicle industry, chemicals, pharmaceuticals, aeronautical engineering and information technologies. It also contributes to the establishment of trans-European telecommunications and energy networks, reinforcement of industrial competitiveness, environmental protection and cooperation in the development of third countries. However, the priority task of the EIB is to contribute to the development of the least favoured regions of the European Union. These contributions account for around 70% of its financings in the Community.

In December 1992, the Edinburgh European Council assigned the EIB the management of a new **temporary lending facility** of 5 billion ECU (increased to 8 billion by the Copenhagen European Council in June 1993). The purpose of this new mechanism, called "Edinburgh facility" is to finance up to 75% of the cost of infrastructure projects, particularly those relating to trans-European networks. Furthermore, a decision in principle was taken by the same European Council to set up a **European Investment Fund** (EIF) with a capital of 2 billion ECU contributed by the EIB (40%), the Commission (30%) and public and private financial institutions (30%). The EIF can offer guarantees of some 10 billion ECU and thus provide support to projects worth up to 20 billion ECU. The EIF is intended to facilitate the financing of major infrastructure projects in trans-European networks and improve access to financial markets for SMEs, particularly those in areas eligible for regional aid[3]. However, the Fund operates on a commercial basis and therefore seeks to obtain an appropriate return on its operations. The agreement on the European Economic Area includes a financial mechanism, management of which is also entrusted to the EIB. This mechanism boosts support for the development of the Community's least favoured regions.

---

1   OJ L66, 13.03.1991.
2   OJ L22, 30.01.1993.
3   OJ L173, 07.07.1994, see also the heading on enterprise funding in the chapter on industry.

Appraisal and outlook

The effort of establishing an economic and monetary union began on 1 January 1971, which saw the start of the first Community effort to establish an EMU as a follow-up to the Werner Plan and to the Resolution of the Council and of the Representatives of the Governments of the Member States of 22 March 1971. That first attempt did, of course, fail, because it was premature in view of the international monetary situation, which was perturbed by the convulsions of the dollar, and of the state of economic integration in the Community, which had newly completed its customs union. There was a desire to leave the common market stage standing and go straight to the EMU stage. Those illusions were quickly lost, and the race was abandoned at the end of the first lap. But the effort was not in vain. It was during that first stage of the first effort at establishing an EMU that the instruments and mechanisms were implemented, in particular the monetary snake, the European unit of account and the European Monetary Cooperation Fund, which developed, in 1979, into the European Monetary System, which have shown their advantages and their disadvantages and which thus serve the second effort at establishing an EMU, in the '90s.

The EMS made it possible to attenuate the variations in the nominal and actual exchange rates of currencies participating in the exchange rate mechanism, to lower inflation levels and to approximate interest rate levels. We must not, however, delude ourselves. The EMS does not irrevocably fix the exchange rates of participating currencies; it merely limits the variations in those rates. The ecu which is the principal instrument of the system, is not a real currency; it is a basket made up of currencies of the Member States, the weight of which can change as a result of the different performances of the national economies. This is what happened in the second half of 1992 and the first half of 1993 and shook the system. As long as the possibility exists of separate changes in the parity of a national currency or of a divergence of the exchange rates between Community currencies, the person wishing to invest or sell on credit in a partner country is not as at ease as when investing or selling in his own country. This unease makes the freedom of movement of goods, services and capital imperfect. For the conditions obtaining in the European Union to be comparable to those obtaining in the single market of a State, the single market of the Union must be supplemented by a single currency. This is sought by the Maastricht Treaty.

There are those who believe that the various national currencies are necessary for as long as differences in economic development between the Community Member States continue. They thus defer until far in the future the attainment of monetary union, once those differences have been ruled out. They forget that differences in economic development exist even between regions in a single State. Why does a poor region not have balance of payments problems vis-à-vis the country of which it is part? Because when its imports from the rest of the country exceed its exports, the difference is paid for in the national currency by regional savings, capital transfers for investments from other regions or, lastly, national aid. As balance of payments problems do not exist between the regions of a State, they should not exist between the States of a genuine economic and monetary union, that is to say a union in which economic and monetary conditions are identical to those that exist in a national State. In such a union it should be as easy for an Englishman to pay a Dutchman as for a northern Italian to pay a southern Italian. Investment by a German in France should be made under conditions of simplicity and security similar to those for investment by a Walloon in Flanders.

At the beginning of the 19th century, in an era not so distant from our own, the German States - and they numbered more than 300 - each had its own currency and therefore its own monetary policy. To guarantee the revenue of its sovereign, each of those States had its own central bank, its own tax system and, of course, its own customs protection against the rest of the world, including the Teutonic world. The economic and monetary chaos prevailing as regards France's German-speaking neighbours was such that Voltaire had stated that the German nation was condemned to eternal poverty. What would Voltaire have said if he could have seen, a century-and-a-half later, the strength of the German economy and especially of the German mark? Would he not have made the connection between the blossoming of Germany and the economic and monetary integration established by Bismarck and completed towards the end of the 19th century? Will it not seem equally absurd, a hundred years from now, that each European State at the end of the 20th century had its own currency and its own monetary policy?

That is all very well, but it is no easy operation in the present state of economic integration in Europe to abolish all the national currencies in favour of a European currency. That would entail abolishing national monetary policies and even the Member States' balances of payments, which would cease to have any meaning. It can be done, but on two conditions: the Member States' budget policies have to be closely coordinated and resources have to be transferred from the richest to the poorest regions of the Community. Otherwise the current structural imbalance between the Member States would be liable to worsen within the union. In fact resources will be transferred within EMU by means of the Community budget and within the framework of the regional and structural policies which we are examining in this work.

Those policies and the corresponding Funds become increasingly important as European integration progresses. The doubling of the Structural Funds between 1988 and 1993, decided upon in December 1988, enabled the poor regions of the Community to participate smoothly in the completion of the internal market. The fresh doubling of the Structural Funds between 1994 and 1999, decided upon in July 1993, should help these regions to take part in Economic and Monetary Union too. However, the doubling of the Community effort must, at least, be equalled by a national effort which would guarantee a sufficient economic growth in the poorest regions. In fact, endogenous forces of growth must be strengthened by improving the competitiveness and enhancing the dynamism of the national economies, which will in turn require fiscal consolidation.

Provided that these conditions are satisfied, the advantages of economic and monetary union could considerably outweigh the costs. The main cost of EMU will be the loss of the nominal exchange rate as an instrument for fine-tuning the economy. But already little use is made of this instrument by the Member States and the European Union will always be able to adjust its exchange rate vis-à-vis the rest of the world. At the same time, the bind of the balance of payments on current account will be lifted for each Member State individually. This will be a great advantage, notably for Member States currently experiencing difficulties in this area. However, balance of current payments will continue to have a constraining effect on the Union as a whole. Therein lies the importance of close coordination of economic and monetary policies.

Price stability is a vital prerequisite for EMU, but will also bring benefits for the economy, enabling, for example, efficient use of the pricing mechanism for the allocation of resources. National budgetary policies and consequently government finances will be subject to certain constraints, since the convergence criteria must be strictly and fully respected, both before and after the changeover to the single currency. But thanks to the disappearance, on the other side of the equation, of exchange rate risks and inflation, interest rates will fall appreciably, generating a considerable bonus for the national budgets of many countries, bonus which will outweigh the loss of income generated by the issue of currency. The most direct "static gain" consists of the ending, within a unified market, of all transaction costs inherent in the use of several currencies, costs representing between 0.3 and 0.4% of the GDP of the Union. These gains would be particularly welcomed by travellers, who lose important amounts in the exchange of their currency for those of the countries they visit. "Dynamic gains" could take two forms: those resulting from heightened productivity and those generated by the attenuation of the uncertainties concerning the long-term evolution of exchange rates.

In addition, the Euro will allow a better balance of the international monetary system, dominated since half a century by the dollar, which serves as a reference currency for almost 60% of world trade, whereas American exports represent around 12% of world exports. Thanks to the single currency, the European Union may play a role in the international monetary system commensurate with its economic and commercial weight (18% of world exports). The single currency will also protect the single market against the fluctuations of the other monetary zones.

Contrary to popular opinion, for countries to make the transition to the final phase of EMU, it will be less a case of entering a Mark zone than of leaving one to join the Euro zone. As demonstrated by the monetary events of 1992 and 1993, the European countries are, whether they like it or not, currently in a Mark zone and must follow or suffer the consequences of the interest rate policy unilaterally decided by the Bundesbank. In contrast, in the European Central Bank, the governor of the "Buba", even if he still has the weight of the German economy behind him, could easily find himself in the minority up against his colleagues from the other central banks taking part, on the same footing as him, in the Board of Governors of the ECB. Copying this same German model, the ECB will be just as independent from the German government as from the governments of the other Member States. There is therefore every reason to hope that the monetary policy of European Union will be much more inspired by the common interest than monetary policy within the European Monetary System where each central bank and each government can, in the final analysis, follow the monetary policy best suited to the interests of its own country.

There must, however, exist a framework for the exchange-rate relations between participants and non-participants in the third stage of EMU. This framework should, on the one hand, promote the convergence process in non-participating Member States, particularly with a view to enabling them to join the single currency as soon as possible and, on the other hand, allow the efficient and orderly functioning of the single market through exchange rate stability and thus guarantee against competitive devaluations of the currencies not participating in the third stage.

Bibliography on the EMU

◻ BROWER Frank, LINTNER Valerio, NEWMAN Michael (ed.), *Economic Policy Making and the European Union*, Federal Trust, London, 1994.

◻ BUITER Willem, CORSETI Giancarlo, ROUBINI Nouriel, "Excessive Deficits: Sense and Nonsense in the Treaty of Maastricht", in *Economic Policy*, N° 16, April 1993, pp. 58-100.

◻ BUSCH Andreas, "The Crisis in the EMS", in *Government and Opposition*, Vol. 29, N 1, 1994, pp. 80-96.

◻ CARAVELIS Georges, *European Monetary Union*, Avebury, Aldershot, Hants, 1994.

◻ COMMISSION EUROPÉENNE, *Croissance, Compétitivité, Emploi: les défis et les pistes pour entrer dans le XXIe siècle* (Livre blanc), OPOCE, Luxembourg, 1994.

    – *Livre vert sur les modalités de passage à la monnaie unique*, COM (95) 333 final du 31.05.1995.

◻ COWIE Harry, PINDER John (ed.), *A Recovery Strategy for Europe*, Federal Trust for Education and Research, London, 1993.

◻ FEDERAL TRUST, *Towards the Single Currency*, Federal Trust Papers 2, London, 1995.

◻ FLOC'HLAY Jean-Michel, *L'Union économique et monétaire*, Comunica, Fontenay-sous-Boix Cedex, 1994.

    – *La monnaie unique. Pourquoi? Comment?*, Eudyssée Éditions, Lagny-sur-Marne, 1996.

◻ GIAO Dao Dang, *Le système monétaire international et l'Europe; du Sterling Standard à l'Union économique et monétaire*, STH, Paris, 1994.

□   GRETSCHMANN Klaus (ed.), *Economic and Monetary Union: Implications for National Policy-Makers*, Martinus Nijhoff Publ., Dordrecht, 1993.

□   GROS Daniel, *Towards Economic and Monetary Union: Problems and Prospects*, *CEPS, Brussels, 1996.*

□   HEALEY Nigel (ed.), *The Economics of the New Europe*, Routledge, London, 1995.

□   JACQUET Pierre, "La désunion monétaire européenne", in *Politique étrangère*, 58e année, N° 1, Printemps 1993, pp. 43-53.

□   LAMBRECHTS Marc, LOVENS Pierre François, *Monnaies en crise: le SME, le dollar, les spéculateurs*, Publication de l'Echo, Bruxelles, 1993.

□   LASTRA Rosa Maria, "The Independence of the European System of Central Banks", in *Harvard International Law Journal*, Vol. 33, Nr 2, Spring 1992, pp. 475-519.

□   LELART Michel, *La construction monétaire européenne*, Bordas/Dunod, Bruxelles, 1994.

□   LIGOT Maurice, *Les problèmes monétaires de l'Union européenne: dévaluations compétitives et monnaie unique*, Délégation pour l'Union européenne de l'Assemblée Nationale, Paris, 1995.

□   PERRUT Dominique, *L'Europe financière et monétaire: Règles, opportunités, stratégies*, Nathan, Paris, 1993.

□   RAYMOND Robert, *L'unification monétaire en Europe*, Presses Universitaires de France, Paris, 1993.

□   ROSE A. K., SVENSSON L.E.O., "European Exchange Rate Credibility before the Fall", in *European Economic Review, Vol. 38, N° 6, June 1994, pp. 1185-1216.*

□   SANDHOLTZ Wayne, "Choosing Union: Monetary Politics and Maastricht", in *International Organization*, Vol. 47, Nr. 1, Winter 1993, pp. 1-39.

□   SCHOR Armand-Denis, *La monnaie unique*, PUF, "Que sais-je?", Paris, 1995.

□   STUYCK Jules (ed.), *Financial and Monetary Integration in the European Economic Community*, Kluwer Law and Taxation Publ., Deventer, ND., 1993.

□   TSOUKALIS Loukas, *The New European Economy; the Politics and Economics of Integration*, 2nd edition, Oxford, Oxford University Press, Oxford, 1993.

□   USHER John, *The Law of Money and Financial Services in the European Community*, Oxford University Press, Oxford, 1994.

□   WILDAVSKY Aaron, ZAPICO-GOÑI Eduardo (ed.), *National Budgeting for Economic and Monetary Union*, Martinus Nijhoff, Dordrecht, 1993.

4. REGIONAL DEVELOPMENT

The notion of regional development, aiming at the creation, maintenance and management of localization conditions for economic activities, is a postwar concept. It stems from the observation that, contrary to given natural factors such as climate, geography and mineral resources, economic conditions for localization can be influenced by a deliberate policy undertaken by official authorities. Every Member State, along with the European Union itself, presently has a regional policy aimed at enhancing the development of less-favoured regions by means of transferring resources from prosperous regions.

The regional policy of the EU does not seek to supersede national regional policies; the Member States, through their own regional policies, are the first ones who must solve the problems in their regions by promoting infrastructures and financially supporting job-creation investments. However, Community regional policy must coordinate national regional policies by formulating guidelines and establishing certain principles in order to avoid competition for assistance between Member States. It must also coordinate the various policies and financial instruments of the EU to give them a "regional dimension" and thus more impact on regions most in need of care.

The main objective of European regional policy is the reduction of existing regional disparities and the prevention of further regional imbalances by transferring Community resources to problem regions using financial instruments such as the European Regional Development Fund. European regional policy has grown in importance since the Treaty made it an essential instrument of economic and social cohesion, itself necessary for the progress of economic and monetary union, implying the convergence of the Member States' economies. Indeed, the regional policy of the Union must promote the concept of European solidarity by completing and guiding the action of the Member States in view of a balanced European integration, profitable not only to the poor regions, but also to the rest of the Union.

Economic and legal framework

Throughout history, the economic map of Europe was shaped by localization factors such as the nature and topography of land, climate, waterways and natural protection from invaders. Having remained basically unchanged for centuries, these factors attracted people living primarily off the land to certain regions rather than others. The industrial revolution profoundly changed the economic geography of Europe; industry was attracted to certain regions by the existence of energy sources (coal), raw materials (metals), waterways, harbour sites and cities. The other factors still played a role of course, but it was progressively reduced.

People followed businessmen; so too did the State. It brought with it the infrastructure, public utilities and administrative fabric absolutely necessary for industrial growth. **Infrastructure**, in the broad sense of the word, includes means of transport, communication and telecommunication, housing, and any facilities allowing for the creation or extension of towns. Public utilities which are related to them range from such classical services as the distribution of water and electricity, to universities, research and training centres, as well as various elements related to the quality of life such as park maintenance, cultural and leisure facilities, etc.

Each of these economic, administrative, cultural and social factors create "external economies", i.e. advantages resulting from a combination of factors without imposing specific costs on undertakings. Other conditions being equal, it is not surprising to see businessmen going wherever they can find external economies and large markets, made up of large population concentrations. In fact, modern firms tend to seek a combination of favourable features, including infrastructure and human resource endowments, when taking their decisions about where to locate. The problem is that uneven patterns of development, historically, have resulted in widely different endowments in infrastructures (transport, energy, telecommunications) and in human capital (the knowledge and skills accumulated in the workforce).

Moreover, since innovation has evolved into a continuous process requiring the rapid introduction of each new advance, the economic success of a region depends to a large extent on the possibilities available for securing access to innovation and technological developments on an ongoing basis. The problem for weaker regions is that the productive base consists largely of small and medium-sized firms, usually working in traditional sectors and lacking an outward-looking perspective. In many regions, highly qualified people are in short supply and ancillary services, such as banking, are inadequate, thus inhibiting innovation. In fact, most factors which favour RTD and innovation (organization, management, commercial, financial and technical skills required to introduce a new or improved product or process onto the market) are almost always found in developed regions.

These factors and trends of the **concentration of economic activities** are so compelling that opposing them would be in vain were it not for the fact that they have certain limits and lead to adverse trends which could eventually be used. At a certain point, external economies can thus become diseconomies when pollution and communications congestion lead to costs and discomfort for undertakings and people employed by them. Above all, factors of localization of economic activities are not immutable; the localization factors of today replace the waning ones of yesterday. The structural changes upsetting European industry will certainly affect the localization of economic activities. The localization demands of the post-industrial society will certainly not be those of the industrial society.

The phenomenon of globalization of economies and markets, which involves the intensification of international competition through the emergence of a potentially unique worldwide market for an expanding range of goods and services, brings out the importance of regional policy. In this context, international competitiveness is based much less on static comparative advantages of the regions, such as territorial concentration and endowment in natural resources, and increasingly more in qualitative dynamic parameters, such as factor mobility, social consensus, pertinent information and the capacity to combine factors effectively, which offer the possibility of decentralized economic growth, if canalized by an adequate policy.

The Member States and the European Union can profit from these trends and changes to balance their regions better. This time, they must precede businessmen and people in order to defeat their inertia and to make sure that necessary movements are not carried out in a disorderly fashion as were the preceding ones. By taking care of their problem regions, the States and the EU can help them to both develop their markets for the benefit of all and better balance their economies in the light of future changes. The **Committee of Regions** set up by the Treaty on European Union and consecrating the role of regional authorities in the institutional system of the Union, should play an important role in the forecasting of regional tendencies and in the management of structural interventions of the EU[1].

Problem regions

All the Member States of the European Union are experiencing variations in the levels of development and living standards from one region to another and the gaps are wider still when measured across the Union as a whole. At the beginning of the nineties, some 52% of the total population of the Union lived in problem regions. The per capita gross domestic product (GDP) in the ten poorest regions of the Union, was only about one quarter of that in the ten richest regions. Unemployment in the ten regions worst hit was up to seven times greater than in the ten most fortunate regions. From one country to another the ratio of young people receiving vocational training was about 1 to 2, the ratio for basic infrastructure about 1 to 3 and the ratio for grants for research and technology about 1 to 7.

The reform of the Community's structural funds, dealt with in the third part of this chapter, defined three types of "problem" regions: regions

---

1   See the sub-title on the Committee of Regions in the introduction.

whose development is lagging behind, areas where declining industrial activities are dominant and those where agriculture dominates. The feature which these three types of regions have in common is their excessive dependence on a limited range of traditional economic activities which can no longer provide sufficient productivity, employment and income. The consequence is phenomena common to all these regions, namely per capita GDP below the Community average, high and prolonged unemployment and a continuous outward population flow.

Regions whose development is lagging behind, termed "Objective 1 regions" under the reform of the structural funds, were generally defined as those where per capita GDP is at least 25% less than the Community average. Their geographical scope spans all of Greece, Portugal and Ireland and large chunks of Spain and Italy, Corsica, the French Overseas Departments, Northern Ireland, the Highlands and Islands, the new German Länder, the Belgian Hainaut, the Austrian Burgenland and the regions of very low population density of the Scandinavian countries. These regions are faced with a combination of handicaps: insufficient or run-down infrastructure - transport, energy or telecommunications; weak or outdated industrial structures whose production methods often fall short of the mark and whose products are ill-adapted to the marketplace; agriculture where archaic structures prevail; population exodus combined with urban decay; and high rates of unemployment particularly among young people and unqualified or poorly qualified workers. All of the regions whose development is lagging behind are situated at the periphery of the country to which they belong and/or of the European Union. A quarter of the population of these regions live on islands, some of which are very small (Greek islands) or very far from the heart of the Union (Canaries, Azores, Madeira, Overseas Departments). This is an additional development handicap, for remoteness from the main centres of economic activity and the main centres of consumption renders their products less competitive and makes them less attractive to private investment.

Declining industrial areas, eligible under Objective 2 of Community regional policy, are regions where a large segment of the working population is employed in declining industrial sectors: steel-making, coal-mining, iron mines, shipbuilding, textiles. In most cases, the decline of these areas is due simply to exhaustion of the natural resources, to competition from substitutes or from third countries where raw materials and labour are cheap and to production capacity which outstrips both internal and external demand. In general, these regions have an average population density which is very high (occasionally more than 1,000 inhabitants per km^2). This is often the cause of major planning problems, due notably to difficulties which arise from over-population, abandoned industrial sites and pollution. However, the labour market situation remains the most preoccupying problem in these regions, thus making the reduction of unemployment the principal aim of Community policy.

The rural areas eligible under Objective 5b of the Community's regional policy are situated in twelve Member States outside the regions whose development is lagging behind. Poor diversification of industry and services and an absence of new employment creation have led to the depopulation of these areas over the last thirty years. They currently cover more than 20% of the Union's territory, but account for only 9% of its population. The handicap of low population density - occasionally dropping to less than 20 inhabitants per km^2 - is aggravated by insularity, remoteness from economic centres, a mountainous situation and other obstacles in the path of access to the EU's internal market. However, the relatively untouched ecological resources of rural areas represent an asset both for local people and for the city dwellers who come to spend time in the country. They are consequently a resource for the development in these regions of tourism, craft industries and high technology SMEs with non polluting workshops.

Regions with very low population density (less than 8 inhabitants per km^2) which are situated in the north and east of Finland and the northern half of Sweden, are eligible under Objective 6 of the regional policy. As well as suffering from depopulation problems, these regions are also disadvantaged by their peripheral location and by the harsh arctic or subarctic climate.

It should be noted in this connection that an increasingly acute problem for the European Union is the excessive concentration of populations and economic activities in areas where tertiary activities are predominant; very often coinciding with **large urban and industrial centres**. Although large urban concentrations also exist in the poorest regions of the Union (Athens in Greece and Naples in southern Italy), the problem is especially found in the central and richest regions. The common characteristics of these large centres are: depopulation of the core and overpopulation of the outlying districts, increasing difficulties in executing infrastructure works and maintenance of the territory, air pollution and a general depreciation of the environment. These problems, being a consequence of the rift in the EU between rich and poor regions, the solutions are to be sought along three main lines: Community economic policy measures favouring the poorest Member States, regional policy measures favouring problem regions, and environmental policy discouraging the setting up of industry in over populated regions.

Reasons for European action

Although regional development actions have always existed, the concept per se of a regional policy is quite recent and was not widespread before the creation of the EEC. In one way or another, however, since the sixties, each Member State carries out its own regional policy. Each of these policies generally aims at favouring the development of the national territory's less prosperous regions by means of **transferring resources** from regions which are well off. The means normally used by Member States to remedy regional problems are of two types: firstly, improving the infrastructure and the social and cultural development of backward regions, and secondly, various premiums, subsidies and tax incentives for the siting of undertakings in these regions. The general objective of these measures is to create or reestablish a better distribution of economic activities and population over the national territory. To do this, certain governments also try to discourage investments in highly developed regions. The advantages of such measures are twofold: favouring the transfer of resources towards poor regions while halting the disproportionate expansion of congested regions.

Clearly, it is primarily up to the national administrative authorities to solve the problems of their regions, namely by promoting infrastructures. The scale of the effort required to stimulate economic activity in the least advanced regions means that public funds must be used in conjunction with private investment. Even **regional aid**, when judiciously applied, is a vital instrument to regional development and to continued and balanced expansion within the European Union. But given the possibility of competition, by virtue of economic integration itself, between the various regions in order to attract Community and foreign investments, the advantages granted can go beyond compensation for material difficulties faced by investors in the areas to be promoted. Thus, part of the aid granted would merely become a reciprocal neutralization. Member States would start to outbid each other with no change made to the overall importance of investment flows which, on a European scale, could be mobilized to favour regional development. The national regional actions would simply be more expensive and grant unwarranted profits to benefitting undertakings. The prime objective of EU regional policy is to confront and coordinate national regional policies by formulating guidelines and setting priorities at European level which effectively help close the gap between regions.

But the EU also has its own responsibility in matters of regional development. The very essence of economic integration is the optimization of **market mechanism** effects on a European scale. But a market policy based on some sort of spontaneous balance between the various economic parameters essentially benefits rich regions. Indeed, prior to the creation of the common market, economic activities had developed in a national context; certain activities usually grouped in certain regions were protected from international competition by customs barriers. With the opening of frontiers, European and foreign (American, Japanese...) undertakings are normally set up in European regions where infrastructure is most developed, where labour is most qualified, and where the economic environment is most adapted to their activities. Concentration invites concentration.

Indeed, the wider European market reinforces the polarization of preexisting economic activities and thus accelerates the agglomeration and **concentration process**. If measures were not taken at national and European level, the completion of the internal market would tend further to widen existing inequalities in the distribution of economic activities throughout the Community territory. That is why, the objective of economic and social cohesion, implying the desire to reduce disparities between the various regions of the Community, was introduced by the Single Act. But, since Maastricht, the stakes have been raised. Now, the foundations must be laid for an economic and monetary union in accordance with very strict criteria of "economic convergence".

Of course, the achievement of economic and monetary union promises enhanced prospects for the developed and the less favoured regions alike. The reduction of trans-frontier transaction costs and the elimination of exchange rate risk may promote regional specialization and intra-Community trade in goods and services. The weaker regions can benefit from this specialization by exploiting more fully their comparative advantages. Furthermore, a general expansion of trade is likely to be beneficial for economic growth which provides in turn favourable conditions for lagging regions to catch up. Finally, increased capital mobility encouraged by fixed exchange rates and the tendency towards quasi-uniform inflation rates may equalize interest rates for any given level of risk, which should favour the less developed regions where capital is often relatively scarce and capital costs, therefore, relatively high.

At the same time, however, Member States will lose certain fiscal and monetary policy options as well as the ability to adjust the exchange rate. Exchange rate flexibility is important in that, in principle, it enables a country, through devaluation, to offset a loss in international competitiveness in a relatively painless manner. As such, it facilitates short-term adjustment to general, or country-specific economic shocks. The removal of the possibility of exchange rate adjustment, therefore, represents a more important loss to the least developed countries of the Union, which must carry out the most important structural changes. Those countries must invest most, while spending least so as to conform with the Maastricht criteria.

In addition, those countries could **lose the advantage of lower labour costs.** As long as markets were protected, salaries in certain countries were much lower than in others, compensating for the lower productivity of a labour force that was not very qualified. But in a common market, and even more in an economic and monetary union, freedom of movement for workers, better information on respective situations, and common union demands tend to align revenues towards the levels already attained in the more prosperous regions; a positive result from a social point of view but one which engenders inflationist tendencies and creates difficulties for undertakings in areas where productivity is too low. If these undertakings have to shut down, the workers lose their jobs and their revenue increase is merely an illusion.

From both an economic and social point of view, neither the weakest member countries nor the European Union can tolerate for long that a substantial part of their patrimony be vowed to underdevelopment. The prosperity of certain areas of the union cannot be paid for by the decline or stagnation of other areas. Furthermore, because the most fruitful trade is always carried out between developed partners, the asymmetrical evolution of areas is contrary to general interest. In so far as progression towards economic and monetary union is sought, the harmonious development of all areas is thus necessary, requiring substantial European effort. Recognizing this necessity, the Maastricht Treaty created a specific instrument, the Cohesion Fund, and the Edinburgh European Council, at the end of 1992, agreed to increase Community resources in favour of economic and social cohesion in the perspective of EMU.

First steps of a policy

The treaties establishing the ECSC and EEC recognized the existence of regional disparities and aimed for harmonious economic development in the Community. Article 54 of the ECSC Treaty enabled the Commission to facilitate the financing of programmes creating new activities which are economically healthy and likely to ensure the productive re-hiring of labour made available by the introduction of new processes, techniques or equipment in the coal and steel industry.

The EEC Treaty stated in its preamble that its signatories were anxious to strengthen the unity of their economies and to ensure their harmonious development "by reducing the differences existing between the various regions and the backwardness of the less favoured regions". It also stated in article 2 that the Community should have as its task, among others, to promote throughout its territory a harmonious development of economic activities. But the Treaty's enthusiasm in favour of regional development essentially stopped right there. In its body, it limited itself to authorizing both the European Investment Bank to finance projects for developing less developed regions (article 130) and the other Community institutions to provide for certain derogations to Community regulations in order to protect these regions (articles 39, 75 and 80). The most important of these derogations is the one provided in article 92, according to which national aids to promote the economic develop-ment of areas where the standard of living is abnormally low or where there is serious underemployment may be considered to be compatible with the common market.

These sparse provisions implied, but could not constitute, a Community regional policy. Therefore, as of the moment it was set up, following the merger of the three Community executives in July 1967, the European Commission dedicated itself to demon-strating the necessity of a regional policy and to defining what it would consist of. This policy neither could nor should substitute national regional policies, but should have the legal means to coordinate them efficiently and the financial instruments to complete them. These aspirations of the Commission were echoed by the **Resolution of 22 March 1971** taken by the Council and the Representatives of the Governments of the Member States on the step by step achievement of economic and monetary union. It provided for necessary structural and regional actions within the framework of a Community policy having the appropriate means, so that they can also contribute to the balanced development of the Community in order to solve the most important problems[1].

During the Paris summit conference of October 1972, the Heads of State and Govern-ment recognized that Community regional policy was a necessary element to reinforce the Community and defined the steps to be taken: the coordination of the regional policies of the Member States and the setting up of a Regional Development Fund. Thus, the Council adopted on 18 March 1975 a Regulation creating a **European Regional Development Fund (ERDF)**[2], its related financial provisions and a decision creating a **Regional Policy Commit-tee**[3].

It was these provisions that really permitted Community regional policy to take off. Unfortunately, this coincided with the beginning of the economic recession, which especially worsened regional problems in areas of old industrialization. Therefore, regional policy instruments and means devised well before 1975 did not satisfy the Commission for very long. On its request, the Council adopted in 1979 a Resolution on the new guidelines of Community regional policy[4] and modified twice, at the beginning of the 1990s, the ERDF Regulation. These changes brought definite improvements in both budget allotment and the Commission's initiative and responsibility in fixing Community regional priorities. At the same time, the Community by the Integrated Mediterranean Programmes (IMP) granted a particular effort for Mediterranean areas in view of its expansion to include Spain and Portugal[5].

Economic and social cohesion

By the mid-1980s however, the Community's effort to reduce the disparities in its areas appeared inadequate in the light of its goal of completing the internal market. The **Single European Act**, setting this goal, introduced regional policy in the Community's basic texts

1   OJ C28, 27.03.1971. See the previous chapter.
2   See the title on ERDF at the end of this chapter.
3   OJ L320, 11.12.1975 and OJ C195, 24.07.1984.
4   OJ C36, 09.02.1979.
5   OJ L197, 27.07.1985.

and recognized its role in reinforcing its economic and social cohesion[1]. It also requested that the Commission submit to the Council a comprehensive proposal aimed at implementing, in the structure and rules for the operation of existing structural Funds, the necessary changes to define, rationalize and coordinate their operations. But, the Commission was not satisfied with a simple rationalization and coordination of structural Fund operations. In its February 1987 communication "Succeeding the Single Act - a new frontier for Europe", it requested the doubling of the financial allotment of these Funds until 1993 in order to ensure the problem-free completion of the internal market.

The European Council of Brussels, from 11 to 13 February 1988, agreed with the Commission by accepting the **"Delors I Package"** on the reform of Common Agricultural Policy, Community financing and the reform of structural funds. The Council then adopted on 24 June 1988 a framework regulation on the new tasks of structural funds[2] and, on 19 December 1988, four regulations implementing provisions of the framework regulation concerning each of these Funds and the coordination of their operations[3]. The new Community regional policy thus took off on 1 January 1989 with an endowment of some ECU 64 billion for the 1989-1993 programming period; but its limits could already be seen in 1992. Created to enable backward areas to partake in the completion of the internal market of the Community without damage, it was no longer sufficient to enable them to participate in the effort for the creation of the European economic union in the 90s.

Taking into consideration this requirement, the Treaty of Maastricht states in its Article B that strengthening of economic and social cohesion is a fundamental objective of the Union. Article G. 130a specifies that in order to promote its overall harmonious development, the Community shall develop and pursue its actions leading to the strengthening of its economic and social cohesion, aiming, in particular, at reducing disparities between the levels of development of the various regions and the backwardness of the least-favoured regions, including rural areas. Although all Community policies can contribute to reinforcing economic and social cohesion, as is stated in Article G. 130b, a major role is, certainly, played by the **Structural Funds** (European Agricultural Guidance and Guarantee Fund, Guidance Section; European Social Fund; European Regional Development Fund), which may be grouped together (Art. G. 130d).

Closely following the Commission Communication "From the Single Act to Maastricht and beyond: the means to match our ambitions " (**Delors II Package**), the Edinburgh European Council on 11 and 12 December 1992 agreed to devote a cumulative amount of 141.471 billion ECU (1992 prices) to structural actions in the period 1994-1999. This represents an average of around 25 billion ECU a year from 1993 to 1999, compared to 13 billion ECU from 1988 to 1992. In 1993, the last year of the old programming period, expenditure in structural measures accounted for 31% of the total as against 51% for agriculture. By 1999, the figure will have risen to 36%, while the share of spending on agriculture will have declined to 46%. This financial effort should make a major contribution to economic and social

---

1   OJ L169, 29.06.1987.
2   OJ L185, 15.07.1988.
3   OJ L374, 31.12.1988.

cohesion in the Community. To that end, the Council adopted a series of Regulations amending and improving the rules and operating provisions to govern the Structural Funds from 1994 to 1999[1].

The situation in which certain Member States find themselves necessitates special efforts to promote economic and social cohesion and thus enable them to comply with the convergence criteria required for passage to the third stage of Economic and Monetary Union. Indeed, among these criteria is, in particular, the one on curbing public deficits. In order to satisfy this condition, the less wealthy countries must apply very strict budgetary disciplines, whereas they need, at the same time, to pursue and even increase public investments in order to close the prosperity gap with the other Member States.

To elude this contradiction, Article G. 130d and a Protocol annexed to the Treaty of Maastricht have provided for the creation of the **Cohesion Fund**. This must contribute financially to projects in the fields of the environment and transport infrastructure for trans-European networks in Member States whose per capita GNP is less than 90% of the Community average (Greece, Spain, Portugal and Ireland) and which are implementing a programme aiming to fulfil the conditions of economic convergence announced in Article 104c of the EC Treaty. Taking into consideration the specific needs of less wealthy countries, the Member States have, moreover, declared their intention to allow a greater margin of flexibility in allocating financing from the Structural Funds, to adjust levels of Community participation in the context of programmes and projects of these Funds and to study all the measures necessary for economic and social cohesion. In particular, the Community co-financing rate for the Cohesion Fund should be between 80 and 85%. The resources available from the Cohesion Fund for the period 1993-1999 should rise to ECU 15 billion (1992 prices)[2].

All the projects financed by the Cohesion Fund in the fields of environment and transport must contribute to the overall economic development of the Member State concerned, thereby strengthening the economic and social cohesion of the Union. It is therefore laid down that projects must be of a sufficient scale (at least ECU 10 million) to have a significant impact in the field of environmental protection or in the improvement of trans-European transport infrastructure networks. The granting of assistance from the Fund is also conditional on the beneficiary Member State making a real effort not to run up an excessive public deficit. If a country refuses to bring its public finances under control, assistance from the Fund may be suspended.

For the four least wealthy countries in the Community, the cumulative financing from the Cohesion Fund and the Structural Funds will result in the near doubling of commitments under the new programming period. Furthermore, these four countries have access to a financial mechanism set up by the EFTA countries participating in the European Economic Area (ECU 900 million in grants and interest subsidies equal to 2 points over 10 years on EIB loans totalling ECU 1500 million). Lastly, these countries, as

---

1   OJ L193, 31.07.1993 and OJ L337, 24.12.1994.
2   OJ L130, 25.05.1994.

the problem regions of other countries, will benefit from the stimulation provided by pooling the experiences, know-how and innovative capacity available in the Union, through the coordination of national and Community policies.

The evolution of the Community's regional policy, from the viewpoint of its two main aspects built up over the years and confirmed in Maastricht, namely the coordination of national and Community policies and the coordination of the Community's financial instruments, is analyzed below.

Coordination of national and Community policies

Today's economic challenges are numerous: rapid technological developments, changes in systems of production and organization, competition and competitiveness, globalization of economies, displacement of production and so on. In this context, the objective of economic and social cohesion means a great deal more than the mere redistribution of funds to the poorest Member States and regions. It requires coherent action through a coordination of national and Community economic policies. The Community's regional policy complements that of the Member States and places them in a European context. It also has clear links with other Community policies, such as agriculture, fisheries, environment, trans-European networks, which also make their contribution to economic and social cohesion.

The first part of Community regional policy is also the oldest, as the Treaty of Rome gave the Commission the right to monitor the **regional policies of the Member States**. Article 92 states that any aid which distorts or threatens to distort competition by favouring certain undertakings or the production of certain goods shall, in so far as it affects trade between Member States, be incompatible with the common market. But in the very same article (92), paragraphs 3(a) and (c) specify that the following may be considered to be compatible with the common market: "aid to promote the economic development of areas where the standard of living is abnormally low or where there is serious underemployment" and, more generally, "aid to facilitate the development of certain economic activities or of certain economic areas, where such aid does not adversely affect trading conditions to an extent contrary to the common interest".

Transparency of regional aid

It is first for the European Commission to state its position on the compatibility or incompatibility of a given regional aid with the common market. Article 93 states that the Commission shall, in cooperation with the Member States, keep **under constant review all systems of aid** existing in those States. It must be informed, in sufficient time to enable it to submit its comments, of any plans to grant or alter aid. The Member States notify the Commission of proposed levels of regional aid and the latter either approves or amends them, often to lower levels, in the Decisions taken under Articles 92 and 93. The Member

State concerned shall not put its proposed measures into effect until the procedure initiated by the Commission has resulted in a final decision. If the State concerned does not comply with this decision within the prescribed time, the Commission or any other interested State may refer the matter to the Court of Justice directly, which happens quite often.

The Commission's task was not at all simple from the outset. It had to assess and attempt to coordinate aid which was often rather "murky", and of which it was difficult to get a clear picture. Its services began by trying to establish maximum levels of subsidy equivalent which should not be exceeded in the various regions, but it proved to be impossible to put an exact figure to the aggregate impact of the various regional measures. Furthermore, it would have been politically sensitive to try to divide up regions into those which could receive high levels of aid and those which could receive little or no aid, particularly since there was no method for assessing the handicaps of a given region for which the aid was supposed to compensate. Any attempt to impose a uniform model for regional development measures would have been unacceptable to national and regional authorities, whose responsibility it was first and foremost to solve regional problems, and would also have been an impossible task, for the variety of problems encountered made it very difficult to suggest a single solution.

It was against this backdrop that the Commission tried to assume the role assigned to it by the Treaty of Rome. In June 1971, it consequently informed the Council that from January 1, 1972 it would apply, in order to implement the tasks assigned to it by the provisions of the Treaty, **certain principles** to general regional aid systems either in force or introduced at a later stage in the central regions of the Community and that it would be desirable for the Member States to undertake to respect these principles. On October 20, 1971, government representatives of the Member States, meeting within the Council, adopted a First Resolution on general regional aid systems. Under this Resolution, the Member States undertook to make general regional aid systems more transparent, more specific from the territorial and sectoral viewpoint and to stop trying to outbid one another by setting a ceiling for the density of aid at least in the most heavily industrialized regions of the Community, termed **"central regions"** due to the fact that they are geographically close one to the other and to the industrial heartland of Europe, the Ruhr[1].

This was the first and last such Council Resolution, which has remained in force and has been supplemented by various Commission Communications clarifying the way in which Article 92, paragraph 3 of the Treaty should be applied. Thus, in 1978, the Commission redefined the existing **coordination principles** and added to their implementation methods, notably the common method of assessing aid intensity[2]. The ceilings set in this Communication which were revised on 21 December 1993 in parallel with the adoption of new rules for the Structural Funds for the 1994-1999 planning period, act as maximum limits reflecting the nature and seriousness of regional problems throughout the Community.

The successive enlargements of the Community have boosted its regional diversity and accentuated the need for new instruments to control regional aid. At the same time, Article 130A, introduced into the Treaty by the Single European Act, gave fresh impetus to the aim of stronger economic and social cohesiveness and stipulated that the Community should attempt to close the gap between its regions and help the less-favoured regions to catch up. In response to these requirements, the Commission adopted new methods of application of Article 92, paragraph 3 sub (a) and (c)[3]. Using these methods, it can **examine the socio-economic situation** of a particular region in its national and Community context. As a conse-

---

1   OJ C111, 04.11.1971.
2   OJ C31, 03.02.1979 and OJ C212, 12.08.1988.
3   OJ C163, 04.07.1990.

quence, it can check, in the interests of the Community, that considerable regional disparity exists and, if this is the case, authorize the Member State in question to pursue a national regional policy regardless of its level of economic development; but, even in that case, the Community context is taken into consideration.

The Commission insists that a differential of regional subsidization is created in favour of the least developed regions of the Union in order to strengthen its regional cohesion. Commission guidelines therefore specify in detail the regions of the Union which may be eligible for regional aid. The respective ceilings for national State aids are set country by country on an individual basis. Under Article 92,3 (a), aid for investments in the least developed regions of the Union may be up to 75% of the cost and, under certain conditions, temporary operating aids may also be granted. In practice, however, the 75% ceiling is rarely reached as the countries concerned lack the necessary financial resources.

Coordination instruments for national policies

The **Community Support Frameworks** (CSF) and the **Single Programming Documents** (SPD), which are a reference framework for structural fund aid[1], also act as a coordination instrument for regional policy. On the basis of the CSFs and the SPDs, the Commission determines priority operation areas for the Fund and possible resource levels which will be allocated to regional development under regional aid systems or public infrastructure work. Indeed, the Commission's role during negotiations for the adoption of CSFs and SPDs is not simply to distribute funds, but also to bring the European "value added" by proposing adjustments in the measures being implemented by the Member States on the basis of the precise criteria for assistance from the Structural Funds and the priorities of Community policies. As a general rule, the **Regional Policy Committee**, set up by a Council Decision of March 18, 1975[2], gives its Opinion on the CSFs and SPDs. The Member States are thus kept informed of one another's development programmes[3]. Coordination of regional policies is also one of the tasks of the **Committee of Regions**, set up by the Treaty on European Union[4]. This Committee expresses the viewpoint of the local authorities, notably on five Community policies: education, culture, public health, the trans-European networks, economic and social cohesion.

The Commission uses a **data bank** to assess regional development programmes and regional aid systems. This data bank contains regional economic indicators such as productivity, employment and migration, produced by the EEC's Statistical Office with the help of national research institutes. On the basis of the data thus collected, the Commission, after consulting the Regional Policy Committee, draws up every three years a **progress report** on the situation and socio-economic evolution of the Community's regions. This report, the production of which is stipulated in the new ERDF Regulation[5], acts as groundwork for EU regional policy guidelines and for ERDF operations.

A report on the economic situation of the regions is also given in the **regional development studies**. The Commission, on the basis of Article 10 of the ERDF Regulation, finances

---

1   See section on the method for structural operations.
2   OJ L73, 21.03.1975.
3   OJ C96, 17.04.1989.
4   See the introduction to this book.
5   OJ L374, 31.12.1988 and OJ L193, 31.07.1993.

two types of regional policy studies. The first is closely connected to Regional Fund operations and seeks to boost the efficiency with which its resources are used. The second is designed to help the Commission and the Member States draw up new strategies and define regional development activities. These consist of **innovative measures** (pilot projects, networks for cooperation and the exchange of experience, feasibility studies) intended to generate new policies through a Community-wide experimental approach. For instance, interregional cooperation innovative schemes and urban development pilot projects have paved the way to the Community initiatives INTERREG and URBAN. Four priorities have been laid down for innovative measures between 1994 and 1999: interregional cooperation inside and outside the Community, planning of the Community territory, innovation in regional economic development and development of urban policies.

In the framework of the innovative measures the Commission devised a programme of studies called "**Europe 2000+**", designed as a town and country planning at European level. It offers local, regional and national authorities a means of giving greater weight to land use considerations in their policies within a Community context and developing exchanges of experience in this field. The first report "Europe 2000+" was presented in October 1991 and the second in October 1994. The latter highlights the disparity between the low rate of interregional mobility of the population and the high rate of job mobility resulting from the free movement of capital and technological developments. It also points to the need to take account of the impact of the large trans-European networks, which will have significant structural effects and should be completed by measures allowing the regions traversed to take advantage of their impact. Finally, it urges the Member States to cooperate on transnational spatial planning areas in order to deal with wider problems such as the protection and development of the Alps and of the Baltic, Atlantic and Mediterranean coasts.

Coordination of Community policies

The studies and innovative actions mentioned above help coordinate the regional policies of the Member States and also the regional impact of the various Community policies. Since any economic activity is of necessity localized in one area, the majority of the Community's measures, be it in agriculture, industry, transport or research, have an impact at regional level. The Community's regional policy consequently, following the guidelines defined in the Council Resolution of February 6, 1979[1], attempts to ensure consistency between regional objectives and those of other Community policies through the method of **regional impact assessment** (AIR). The purpose of assessing Community measures from a regional viewpoint is to correct any negative regional effects which they may have or to enhance any positive ones.

In the operations of the Structural Funds, particular attention is devoted to compliance with rules governing the protection of the environment, competition (Articles 92 and 93 EC) and public procurement. The new programming documents for the period 1994-1999 contain precise stipulations on these three areas. The Commission, in partnership with

---

1   OJ C36, 09.02.1979.

national and regional authorities as well as parties most closely involved in a project, including non-governmental environmental organizations, appraises the environmental aspects of the programmes and monitors those measures which could have indirect effects on the environment[1].

The possibilities for coordinating the objectives and means of **enterprise policy** with those of regional policy have been given careful consideration by the Commission[2]. In 1984 it began the process of creating **Business and Innovation Centres (BICs)** in towns and cities of the Community. The BICs are professional structures which offer a multiservice assistance to innovative SMEs. Their integrated range of business services includes: basic assistance with management, technical approval, innovation, marketing strategy, raising of capital, development of business skills; SME access to venture capital; and provision of premises for SMEs. The 110 BICs on the territory of the Union and in several Central European countries are linked in a European Business and Innovation Centre Network (EBN) which helps them with their management and promotes cooperation. Around two thirds of the Centres are cofinanced by the ERDF.

Finally and most importantly, Community policies are coordinated through "**Community initiatives**", dealt with in the following part of this chapter. According to Article 11 of the Regulation implementing the coordination of the structural funds[3], Community initiatives seek to: contribute to resolving serious problems directly related to the implementation of other Community policies; promote the application of Community policies at the level of the regions; or favour the solving of problems common to certain categories of regions. For example, the initiatives LEADER, in the agricultural sector and PESCA, in the fisheries sector, stimulate ideas and promote innovative methods of dealing with the key problems of European cohesion.

Coordination of financial instruments

In addition to the Cohesion Fund, which is outlined above in the title on economic and social cohesion, and the European Regional Development Fund (ERDF) which as seen below is the central instrument of Community regional policy, the Community has a range of financial instruments which can support operations in regional economies: the EAGGF Guidance Section, the Social Fund, ECSC and Euratom loans and the **European Investment Bank**.

The latter is the longest standing regional development instrument, for in Article 130 of the Treaty of Rome it was called upon to ensure balanced and smooth development of the common market in the interests of the Community. As a consequence, prior to the creation of the Regional Fund, the Bank was responsible for the bulk of Community regional infrastructure action - roads, motorways, telecommunications, electricity stations and so on. Even after the creation of the ERDF, almost 75% of EIB financing in the Community contributes to regional development, although they pursue other objectives such as those of promoting SMEs and trans-European networks. The EIB notably supplies long-term capital for the financing of infrastructure projects in the fields of transport, energy and telecommunications.

---

1   COM (95) 509, 22 November 1995.
2   See the chapter on industry.
3   OJ L374, 31.12.1988.

EIB operations always take the form of loans at rates close to those practised on the financial markets where it raises its funds. Since the EIB is a bank, it does not grant interest-rate reductions, but the financial institutions in the Member States and notably those whose vocation is regional development can borrow from the Bank and on-lend at more favourable terms. Some of the loans do have interest-rate subsidies attached, funded by the Community budget[1].

The new Article 198e of the Treaty, inserted at Maastricht, confirms that the loans and guarantees of the EIB will facilitate projects for developing less-developed regions, for modernizing or converting undertakings or for developing fresh activities as well as for projects of common interest to several Member States. This Article makes specific reference to the desired interaction between EIB operations and Structural Funds measures, stating that "in carrying out its task, the Bank shall facilitate the financing of investment programmes in conjunction with assistance from the Structural Funds and other Community financial instruments", which concern regions whose development is lagging behind and declining industrial areas. The Bank also plays an active role in the financing of trans-European networks and thus in the implementation of the support instruments financed by the Community budget: interest rate subsidies on its own loans, co-financing of feasibility studies and co-financing of guarantee funds.

The measures implemented under Articles 54 and 56 of the ECSC Treaty are particularly well adapted to the problems of predominantly industrial regions, for the coal and steel industries are very often situated in regions which face specific difficulties due to their dependence on these declining industries. **ECSC operations**, which take the form of non-repayable aid, guarantees, normal or "soft" loans, therefore have a regional role to play. The most vital ones, from a regional viewpoint, are the reconversion loans granted by the Commission to help fund programmes to create, either in the coal and steel industries or in any other industrial sector, new economically viable activities or to transform companies which could provide productive jobs for the workforce released by the profound upheaval in the coal or steel industries[2]. However, the Commission decided to suspend, as of 1 January 1995, application of Article 56 of the ECSC Treaty on the financing of vocational training aid, since the Member States can apply to the European Social Fund to finance such measures.

Reform of the Structural Funds

Since the creation of the Regional Fund in March 1975 and more especially since the adoption by the Council in February 1979 of the "guidelines for Community regional policy"[3], the Commission has attempted to coordinate the different Community mechanisms, at least for projects receiving its support. But this task was complicated by the fact that the financial instruments then existing each operated on the basis of their own Regulation, following separate objectives. There was no binding Community provision stipulating that they should be coordinated. The Commission proposed that this shortcoming be corrected when the struc-

---

1   See the chapter on Economic and Monetary Union.
2   OJ C188, 28.07.1990 and OJ C59, 06.03.1992.
3   OJ C36, 09.02.1979.

tural funds were reformed as part of the process of completing the internal market, placing the emphasis on the need to coordinate their operations. The Brussels European Council of February 11-13, 1988 upheld this view and the Council consequently adopted on June 24, 1988 Regulation 2052/88 on the tasks of the structural funds and their effectiveness and on coordination of their activities between themselves and with the operations of the European Investment Bank and the other existing financial instruments[1].

In December 1992, the Edinburgh European Council set the Community's financing arrangements for the period up to the end of the century. For all of the Structural Funds, the planned commitments for 1994 and 1999 are ECU 141,471 million, or one-third of the Community's expenditure over this period (Delors II package). In order to make allowance for the new priorities of the Community on economic and social cohesion defined in a Protocol of the TEU, heighten the efficiency of the Structural Funds on the basis of the experience acquired since their reform and coordinate them with the newly created Cohesion Fund and the Financial Instrument for Fisheries' Guidance (FIFG), the Structural Fund regulations were amended. The amendments consolidate and improve the fundamental principles laid down in 1988, that is, concentration on the least-favoured regions, partnership, programming and additionality[2].

The new regulations thus define the **priority objectives** for the Structural Funds, for the 1994-1999 financial period:

— **Objective 1**: promote development and structural adjustment of regions whose development is lagging behind (ERDF, ESF and EAGGF-Guidance). A budget of 96.346 billion ECU, i.e. 70% of the total, is reserved for these regions;
— **Objective 2**: conversion of regions, frontier-zone regions or parts of regions (including employment centres and urban communities) seriously affected by industrial decline (ERDF and ESF);
— **Objective 3**: combat long-term unemployment, facilitate the occupational integration of young people and the integration into the employment market of the socially excluded (ESF);
— **Objective 4**: facilitate the adaptation of workers to industrial change and the evolution of production systems;
— **Objective 5a**: speeding up adaptation of agricultural structures (EAGGF-Guidance) and fishery structures (EAGGF-Guidance and FIFG);
— **Objective 5b**: facilitate the structural adjustment of rural areas (EAGGF-Guidance, ESF, ERDF and FIFG);
— **Objective 6**: promote the development of regions with extremely low population density and harsh climate of the Nordic countries.

Objectives 1, 2, 5b and 6 are of a specifically regional nature. They only apply to certain eligible regions or parts of regions. On the other hand, Objectives 3, 4 and 5a cover all of the Community. For Objectives 1 and 5b, eligibility of regions is determined for a period of six years and the CSFs

---

1   OJ L185, 15.07.1988 and OJ L1, 01.01.1995.
2   OJ L193, 31.07.1993.

cover the same period. For Objectives 2 and 4, however, programming is in two three-year phases.

Method of structural operations

In order to attain the objectives stated above, the work of the Structural Funds is based on four principles: the **concentration** of measures on the above-mentioned objectives; **programming**, which results in multiannual development programmes; additionality; and partnership. **Additionality** means that Community action is viewed as a complement to the corresponding national action or a contribution to it; it must bring added value to national initiatives. It is based upon partnership between the Commission, the Member State in question and the authorities and competent bodies, including the economic and social partners, appointed by the latter at national, regional, local or other level. The **partnership** focuses upon preparation, including the financing of preparatory research, financing of action, follow-up, including the financing of in-the-field technical assistance, and assessment of its impact. Technical assistance of various forms can be given at any stage of a programme and include any measure allowing the Member States to use the Structural Funds in an optimal way.

With the aim of simplifying and accelerating the programming procedure, the Member States submit to the Commission their draft operational programmes along with their **regional development plans**. The latter incorporate a description of the main thrusts of regional development, the activities falling under these and use to be made of Community financial assistance. Plans submitted under Objectives 1, 2, 5b and 6 must also incorporate an assessment of the environmental situation and of the environmental impact of the planned actions, along with the provisions taken to involve environmental authorities in the preparation and implementation of these plans. The Commission evaluates the proposed plans and action and draws up, with the agreement of the Member State in question, the **Community Support Framework (CSF)** for Community structural operations. This Framework includes: (a) ex-ante evaluation of the planned objectives, quantifying, insofar as their nature permits, the progress to be made in relation to the existing situation in the period in question, and the priorities for Community operations; (b) forms of operations; (c) the indicative financing plan in which the amount of operations and sources are specified; (d) the duration of these operations. Instead of a CSF, the Commission may, at the request of the State concerned, adopt a **Single Programming Document (SPD)**, which is produced by a simplified procedure whereby the strategic priorities, programming procedures and aid granted are all included in a single document. A CSF or an SPD can, if necessary, be revised and adapted on the initiative of a Member State or the Commission with the agreement of the former in light of new pertinent information and results observed in the course of implementing the relevant actions.

Community financial instruments can either co-finance the operational programmes of appropriate aid systems or projects or can grant a global subsidy managed by an intermediary appointed by the Member State with the approval of the Commission. An **operational programme** is a collection of multi-annual measures which can be implemented through use of one or several Community financial instruments. It allows the financing of actions and projects selected by national or regional authorities. **The global subsidy**, for its part, is granted to an intermediary organization and can help the introduction of various services for businesses operating in the industrial, craft, agricultural or tourism sectors and can smooth SME access to the capital market. It can cover all financial engineering operations which are of particular interest to SMEs.

Commitment appropriations for the structural funds were doubled in real terms between 1987 and 1992 and will again be doubled between 1993 and 1999 to reach 30 billion ECU in 1999. Levels of Community support are adjusted to suit the seriousness of the problem, the specific nature of the action, the financial capacity of the Member State in question and the specific interest of the activities from a Community and regional viewpoint. However, there are certain ceilings: 75% of the real cost and, as a general rule, at least 50% of the public expenditure for the measures applied in the regions covered by Objective 1; and 50% at the most of the total cost and, as a general rule, at least 25% of public expenditure for measures applied in regions covered by the other objectives. In exceptional, duly justified cases, the Structural Fund contribution can rise to 85% of total cost for actions in the Objective 1 regions of the four Member States which are beneficiaries of the Cohesion Fund (Spain, Portugal, Greece and Ireland). In accordance with the commitment made by the Edinburgh European Council, the Commission shall ensure that the resources committed in these countries under Objective 1 and from the Cohesion Fund are doubled in real terms between 1992 and 1999.

The **regions covered by Objective 1** are regions with a level II area under the Nomenclature of Territorial Units for Statistical Purposes, the per capita GDP of which is less than 75% of the Community average. They are listed in the Annexe to Regulation 2052/88, amended in 1993. The Italian Abruzzi, which have attained the 25% threshold, have been admitted to the list for a transitory period of three years. Eligible regions on the list now include the new German Länder and East Berlin, Flevoland in the Netherlands, the Hainaut in Belgium and the adjacent French districts of Valenciennes, Douai and Avesne, along with Merseyside and the Highlands and Islands in the UK. In 1995, the Austrian region, Burgenland, was also declared eligible under Objective 1. In these regions the emphasis is on catching up: direct investment in production to create lasting jobs; the infrastructure required for economic development, including that under the trans-European networks; various services to SMEs to make the most of local and regional potential; investment in infrastructure for education and health; vocational training and employment aids; various rural development measures.

Declining industrial areas and frontier-zone areas covered by Objective 2 must belong to a territorial unit of level III under the Nomenclature and must meet each of the following criteria: a percentage of industrial employment and an average rate of unemployment higher than the Community average and a decline in industrial employment compared with 1975. In these regions measures are centred on employment and the establishment of firms under favourable conditions: investment in new productive activities; infrastructure, particularly for the restoration of industrial sites and the protection of the environment; various services for SMEs; research and development; vocational training; employment aids.

The **rural areas** which are eligible under Objective 5 must be situated outside the Objective 1981 regions and must be characterized by a low level of socio-economic development, assessed on the basis of per capita Gross Domestic Product. They must also meet at least two of the three following criteria: a) high level of agricultural employment in total employment; b) low level of farm income; c) low population density and/or a trend towards major population outflow. In such zones measures are primarily intended to promote alternative activities in rural environment: investment, particularly in infrastructure, to create jobs outside agriculture and protect the environment; various services for SMEs; research and development; training; various rural development measures.

The **regions with very low population density** eligible for Community assistance under Objective 6 are situated in the north and east of Finland and the northern half of Sweden, except for certain coastal strips. They have a population of eight or less per km^2 and are also disadvantaged by their peripheral location and by the harsh arctic or subarctic climate.

In order to monitor and evaluate the efficient implementation of Structural Fund aid, the 1988 regulations led to the creation, for each CSF and each operational programme, of a **monitoring committee**, made up of those responsible at regional and national level, along with representatives of the Commission. The amendments to these regulations adopted in 1993 further strengthen the role of the monitoring committees. They notably enable them to adapt the financial plans of the CSFs and SPDs while respecting the financial allocation granted by the Commission. Information and publicity measures carried out by the Member States are integrated into the operational activities of the Structural Funds[1]. Evaluation activities are reinforced in the new programming and, in line with the logic of the subsidiarity principle, the Member States assume main responsibility for them. In contrast, a new provision enables the Commission to take fraud prevention measures and notably requires down the systematic transmission of information (reports of irregularities, administrative and legal monitoring).

Community Initiatives

Outside the CSFs, the three structural funds operate individually or collectively to support programmes of Community interest (Community initiatives). The Commission is empowered by the Council to launch "Community initiatives" with a view to easing the application of Community policies at regional level and to ensuring that the undertakings in regions whose development is lagging behind and in declining industrial areas can take advantage of the opportunities generated by the completion of the internal market. Whereas Community Support Frameworks are underpinned by national development plans, Community initiatives are transnational programmes whose objectives are the same for all of the eligible regions as they aim at resolving problems which have a particular relevance for the Community. However, by way of application of the principles of partnership and subsidiarity, national, regional or local authorities are deeply involved in drawing up and implementing Community initiatives, in particular through the operational programmes which they submit to the Commission.

Adopted by the Commission in June 1994 after consultation with other Community institutions and the Member States, the Community initiatives for the 1994-99 programming period, pursue to a large extent the objectives of the initiatives developed successfully during the previous programming period[2]. Their objectives are summarized below.

INTERREG II has three distinct strands as it combines the functions of Interreg I and Regen. One aim is to develop cross-border cooperation and help areas on the Union's internal

---

1   OJ L152, 18.06.1994.
2   OJ C180, 01.07.1994.

and external frontiers to overcome the specific problems arising from their comparatively isolated position vis-à-vis other national economies and the Union as a whole. ECU 2.4 billion are allocated to this strand out of which 1.8 billion have to go to Objective 1 regions. The second aim, with an allocation of ECU 500 million, is to fill gaps in energy networks and provide interconnections with wider European networks. The third strand, with an allocation of ECU 415 million aims at improving international cooperation on water management (controlling floods and droughts) and at achieving a better balance in spatial development.

LEADER II continues the efforts of Leader I for rural development by financing skill acquisition by local actors and the realization of certain investment programmes and joint projects involving parties in two or more Member States. The emphasis is put on the innovative nature of projects. Rural areas in regions eligible under Objectives 1 and 5(b), and exceptionally, some adjoining rural areas, are eligible for Leader II. This initiative disposes of ECU 1.4 billion, of which ECU 900 million is to go to Objective 1 regions. An additional ECU 230 million is used to support local integrated development initiatives.

REGIS II groups together the specific measures of Regis I and action eligible for assistance under Poseidom, Poseima and Poseican in order to foster closer integration into the EU of the most remote regions, i.e. the French overseas departments, Madeira, the Azores and the Canary Islands (Poseidom, Poseima and Poseican programmes). The planned allocation for Regis II is ECU 600 million.

The **employment and development of human resources** initiative supports a revival of employment, greater social solidarity throughout the Union and equal opportunities for women on the labour market. It integrates action to help three categories of persons facing particular difficulties on the labour market. In particular, it aims at promoting equal opportunities for women with regard to employment (NOW), access to the employment market for handicapped and disadvantaged persons (HORIZON) and integration into the labour market of young people without qualifications (YOUTHSTART) and people in danger of social exclusion (INCLUSION). The planned allocation of this Initiative is ECU 1.4 billion, out of which ECU 800 million should go to Objective 1 regions.

ADAPT is an initiative financed by the European Social Fund and covering all the Community territory in order to further the new Structural Fund Objective 4 (adaptation to industrial change)[1]. With an allocation of ECU 1.4 billion, Adapt aims at: adapting workers to change; improving the competitiveness of firms through training; preventing unemployment by improving qualifications; and creating new jobs and fresh activity. An additional strand, Adapt-Bis, allocated ECU 170 million, supports job-creation related to the information society.

The **SME** initiative is intended to boost the dynamism of small and medium-sized enterprises, particularly in regions where development is lagging behind, and so facilitate their adjustment to the requirements of the single market and international competition[2]. Furthermore, the SME initiative covers the objectives of three former Community Initiatives contributing to the modernization of businesses; STRIDE on strengthening technology in less-favoured regions; PRISMA on improving business services; and TELEMATIQUE on promoting the use of advanced telecommunications services. Only SMEs situated in areas eligible under Objectives 1, 2 or 5(b) can qualify for financial assistance from the Structural Funds under the SME initiative, which disposes of ECU 1 billion, of which ECU 800 million must go to Objective 1 regions.

URBAN, having an allocation of ECU 740 million, including ECU 400 million for Objective 1 regions, steps up pilot and innovative actions led by the Commission in neighbourhoods in crisis in big and medium cities characterized by social exclusion. It supports schemes for economic and social revitalization, the renovation of infrastructures and facilities and environmental improvement.

PESCA, with an allocation of ECU 280 million, half of which is to go to Objective 1 regions, seeks to strengthen and diversify the economies of areas heavily dependent on the fisheries sector by accompanying change in this sector by local development initiatives[3]. It contributes to diversify areas dependent on fisheries in regions eligible for Objectives 1, 2 or 5(b) through the development of job-creating activities.

An **Initiative in Northern Ireland**, disposing of ECU 300 million, aims at consolidating the reconciliation process and supporting the economic rehabilitation of this region. The

---

1   See the chapter on social progress.
2   See the heading "Business financing" in the chapter on industry.
3   See the title on structural policy in the chapter on fisheries.

Initiative finances actions for the development of employment, urban and rural regeneration, development of cross-border relations, social inclusion and industrial development, notably through the promotion of SMEs.

Four specific initiatives will be pursued until the end of 1999 in the following sectors: coal (RECHAR), steel (RESIDER), shipbuilding (RENAVAL), textiles (RETEX) and conversion of military industries (KONVER). In addition, during the GATT negotiations, the Council of Ministers agreed to assist the necessary adjustments of the Portuguese textile industry by a specific initiative to that end.

ERDF

The reform of the structural funds as embodied in Regulation 2052/88 clearly brought a need for revision of each of the individual funds, including the **European Regional Development Fund (ERDF)**. This was done by a Regulation of December 19, 1988[1]. This was the third major overhaul of the ERDF since its creation in 1975, demonstrating both the Community's growing commitment to regional development and its increased experience on this matter.

The beginnings of the Regional Fund were relatively modest. Quite apart from its insufficient budget during its first years of operation, the ERDF had a handicap which was unique among the Community's financial instruments: the allocation to the Member States of **quotas**, which had to be respected in the sharing out of the Fund's aid and which turned it into a financial instrument at the service of the regional policies of the Member States rather than the Community's regional policy. The Commission had no qualms about putting its finger on this weakness of the Regional Fund and fighting to adapt its means to its targets. The first unambitious reform of the ERDF in February 1979 gave the Commission a "non quota" section for the financing of specifically Community measures, designed to supplement or reinforce the application of other Community policies. When the ERDF was reformed for a second time, in June 1984, the system of national quotas was replaced by a **system of brackets** which defined, for each Member State and for a period of three years, upper and lower limits of aid which could be granted. This led to greater flexibility in the management of the Fund and therefore to higher concentration of its operations in the less prosperous countries.

The third reform of the ERDF, in December 1988, an offshoot of the structural fund reform, abolished the compulsory breakdown of ERDF resources, replacing it with an **indicative allocation** decided upon by the Commission[2]. The new ERDF Regulation is characterized by considerable flexibility at operational level. The Fund can make use of all forms of financial operation, such as co-financing of regional operational programmes, regional aid systems and major projects for infrastructures and productive investments, the granting of global subsidies and support for technical assistance and for preparation and assessment measures.

The Regulation of the ERDF was again amended in July 1993, as part of the revision of the Structural Funds[3]. It extends the scope for assistance to take better account of the specific needs of the regions, particularly those eligible under objective 1, by including investment in education and health and stressing the importance of certain priority areas such as technological research and development and the extension of trans-European networks. New forms of assistance are also provided for, such as global grants for Community initiatives.

Within the framework of the task entrusted to it by Article 130c of the Treaty, the ERDF participates in the financing of: (a) productive investment to permit the creation or maintenance of permanent jobs; (b) invest-

1   OJ L374, 31.12.1988.
2   OJ L374, 31.12.1988.
3   OJ L193, 31.07.1993.

ment in infrastructure relating to the particular needs of Objective 1, Objective 2 and Objective 5(b) regions; (c) the development of indigenous potential in the regions by means of measures which encourage and support local development initiatives and the activities of SMEs, involving in particular, assistance towards services for enterprises, financing the transfer of technology, improvement of access for enterprises to the capital market and direct aid to investment; (d) in the regions designated under Objective 1, investment in the field of education and health; (e) measures in the field of research and technological development; (f) productive investment and investment in infrastructure aimed at environmental protection; (g) regional development operations at Community level, in particular in frontier regions; and (h) preparatory, appraisal, monitoring and evaluation measures.

Appraisal and outlook

One of the basic aims of the Treaty of Rome was to reduce the gap between the different regions of the Community and close the development lag of the least favoured. However, the Community has only had a regional policy worthy of the name since the middle of the seventies. Up until 1974, the Community used financial instruments not specifically intended for regional development to support national regional policies. The Commission, under the powers which it held by virtue of Articles 92 et seq. of the EEC Treaty, tried through assessment of regional aid granted by the Member States to coordinate regional aid systems, with the aim notably of preventing the States outbidding one another in an attempt to attract foreign investment.

It was the prospect of a Single Market by 1992 that cracked the whip in the area of Community regional policy. The Single European Act acknowledged the major contribution which such a policy could make to improving the economic and social cohesion of the Community and provided for reform of the structural funds with a view to rationalizing and coordinating their operations. The Brussels European Council of February 11-13, 1988 went one step further, backing the Commission in its request for the doubling of the structural fund resources between then and 1993. This was the starting point for the Community's new regional policy based notably on the coordination of its financial instruments and the coordination of national and Community policies to help regions which need an extra push towards economic prosperity.

The reform of the Structural Funds has led to better integration of the various actions conducted under the banner of structural policies and contributed to the concept of an all-round, consistent strategy for economic and social cohesion in the Community. The basic principles of the reform, such as concentration of efforts, programming and additionality have on the whole given satisfactory results, particularly in areas facing industrial decline (Objective 2). Following the revision of the Structural Funds in July 1993, the efficiency of structural policies was boosted through the simplification of programming and decision-making procedures, the complementarity of Community and national activities and more partnership, including better involvement of social partners in the drafting and management of operational programmes.

Since 1 November 1993, the Treaty on European Union has provided both a frame of reference and support for the Community regional policy, notably by establishing economic and social cohesion as a fundamental objective of the Union, creating the Cohesion Fund, setting up the Committee of the Regions and promoting trans-European infrastructure networks. At the same time, the objective of economic and social cohesion has become even more imperative. As seen in the Chapter on economic and monetary union, such union, implying abandon of the use of exchange rate adjustment as a means of rebalancing the national economy, would not be feasible without an efficient regional policy revolving around sufficient capital transfers from the richer to the poorer regions of the EU. The problem for the least-favoured regions is, in particular, to ensure that striving to stabilize the budget does not choke off the investment in basic infrastructure, education and training which those regions require and that the search for monetary equilibrium does not raise the cost of credit to firms.

Far from being a distant objective, then, the reduction of regional imbalances is a prerequisite for any economic and political progress in the European Union. No community is sustainable or justifiable if there are major disparities between the standards of living of the people belonging to it and if certain of its members have the impression that the pooling of resources is only in the interests of the others. Furthermore, the capital transfers carried out in the framework of an efficient regional policy should not simply be seen by the well off as an offering to the less fortunate in the Union. They are also in the economic interests of the more prosperous States, since they develop markets for their products, and in their ecological interest, for in generating a better economic balance of the EU they will tend to relieve its ecological problems. In general, structural action contributes to stimulate growth in the whole Union.

Taking into consideration such arguments, the Edinburgh European Council agreed to the near doubling of the allocation to the Structural Funds and the Cohesion Fund for the four Member States eligible for funding from the latter during the period 1993-1999 in relation to the previous programming period. By the end of the decade, the Union's regional policies are likely to finance around 5% of investment in Objective 1 regions which could rise to between 7 and 13% in the four poorest Member States, beneficiaries of the Cohesion Fund. The additional resources are accompanied by a strengthening of procedures designed to improve the efficiency of regional development programmes. Used to finance new infrastructures, such as the trans-European networks, and additional productive investment, these resources can be expected to accelerate the process of transformation and modernization of the Union's weakest regions.

It should be noted that, in the wake of the globalization of economies and markets, it is no longer possible to divide industry and geographical areas into clearly identified and relatively independent segments. European firms are engaged in production both within the Union and in third countries. Their competitiveness depends more and more on their capacity to combine relevant information and factors. This could create potential for decentralized industrial growth provided appropriate support is given, particularly at regional level. Indeed, the four weakest Member States - with the support of the Structural Funds - are investing more heavily than the other countries of the Union, notably in transport and telecommunications infrastructure. Since the latter investments embody the latest technology, the weaker regions achieve relatively high rates of access to the digital services which are essential for the information highways of the 21st century.

However, structural change is a slow process, especially with regard to the Union's most backward regions. The performance of Ireland, Spain and Portugal has been most encouraging, since the annual growth of their economies has averaged 0.75% to 1.75% points above the rate for the Community between 1986 and 1992. The situation in Greece, in Southern Italy and Northern Ireland, on the other hand, is considerably less encouraging and the economic performance of these regions seems to be deteriorating in comparison to the rest of the Union. For such regions the Community policies may not be sufficient. Other conditions need to be satisfied before some of these regions are able to reduce the gap with the rest. Certainly, Member States' own policies to promote development in their regions have an important role to play; constraints of a social, political or institutional nature holding back the growth of their prosperity must be tackled. The challenges faced by these regions in the framework of EMU fully justify the Community effort to assist them. This effort cannot, however, replace the national effort and the necessary behavioural changes and government policies, concerning, in particular, proactive employment policies.

The enlargement of the EU to three new Member States enhances the continental nature of its regional policy and gives a new dimension to its problems of regional development. The particular difficulties in the sparsely populated, climatically extreme regions of Northern Scandinavia have to be accommodated. In general, however, the accession of Austria, Sweden and Finland will not contribute to a widening of regional disparities, since their average level of GDP per head is almost the same as that of the Union. Quite different will be the situation with the accession to the EU of the countries of Central and Eastern Europe, envisaged for the end of the century. Then, the disadvantaged regions would become far more numerous. Although the general application of the cohesion policy throughout the Union should be maintained, a concentration on the least wealthy regions would probably be necessary.

Bibliography on regional policy

□ AMIN Ash, TOMANEY John (ed.), *Behind the Myth of European Union. Prospects for Cohesion*, Routledge, 1995.

□ BUZELAY Alain, HANNEQUART Achille, *Problématique régionale et cohésion dans la Communauté européenne*, Economica, 1994.

□ CHARPENTIER Jean, ENGEL Christian (sous la dir. de), *Les régions de l'espace communautaire*, Presses Universitaires de Nancy, Nancy, 1992.

□ COMMISSION EUROPÉENNE, *Révision de la réglementation applicable aux Fonds structurels*, COM (93) 67.

- *Le fonctionnement des Fonds structurels communautaires 1994-1999*, COM (93) 124.

- *Programmes de développement régional*, OPOCE, Luxembourg, 1994.

- *Europe 2000+. Coopération pour l'aménagement du territoire européen*, OPOCE, Luxembourg, 1994.

- *L'Europe au service du développement régional*, OPOCE, Luxembourg, 1994.

- *Guide des initiatives communautaires 1994-1999: Fonds structurels communautaires*, OPOCE, Luxembourg, 1994.

□ EUROPEAN COMMISSION, *New Location Factors for Mobile Investment in Europe*, OOPEC, Luxembourg, 1993.

- *Guide to Financial Engineering Techniques Used by the European Commission in the Context of Regional Policy*, OOPEC, Luxembourg, 1994.

- *Trade and Foreign Investment in the Community's Regions: The Impact of Economic Reform in Central and Eastern Europe*, OOPEC, Luxembourg, 1993.

- *The Structural Funds in 1994*, OOPEC, Luxembourg, 1996.

□ DREVET Jean-François, *Aménagement du territoire. Union européenne et développement régional*, Éditions Continent Europe, Paris, 1995.

□ GRANRUT Claude du, *Europe, le temps des régions*, Librairie Générale du droit et de la Jurisprudence, Paris, 1994.

□ HANNEQUART Achille (ed.), *Economic and Social Cohesion in Europe; A New Objective for Integration*, Routledge, London, 1992.

□ HEBRARD Joël, "Aménager l'Europe de demain. Une vision différenciée et intégrée de l'espace européen", in EUREG: *Europäische Zeitschrift für Regionalentwicklung*, Stuttgart, N° 1, 1994, pp. 9-14.

□ HOLLAND Stuart, *The European Imperative. Economic and Social Cohesion in the 1990s*, Ed. Spokesman, Nottingham, 1993.

□ LEONARDI Robert, NANETTI Raffaella (ed.), *Regional Development in a Modern European Economy. The Case of Tuscany*, Pinter Publishers, London, 1994.

□ MORTENSEN Jorgen (ed.), *Improving Economic and Social Cohesion in the European Community*, MacMillan Press, London, New York, 1994.

□ PRESTON Jill, *Regional Policy*, Longman Group, Harlow, Essex, 1994.

◻ ROBINS Nick, "The EU Structural Funds and Environmental Policy", in *European Trends. The Economist Intelligence Unit*, London, N° 1, 1994, pp. 95-104.

◻ RYLAND Diane, "The Cohesion Fund: A Question of Balance", in *European Environmental Law Review*, London, Vol. 3, N° 9, October 1994, pp. 263-266.

◻ SAINT-OUEN F., "De l'Europe des États à l'Europe des Régions?", in *Relations internationales*, N° 73, printemps 1993, pp. 81-94.

5. SOCIAL PROGRESS

Given the varied economic structures of the Community Member States, their social problems were from the outset - and still are to some extent - quite different. It would not have been possible at the start - and that still holds true - to entrust the European Institutions with the task of solving all the Member States' social problems. Such a solution depends to a great extent upon economic policy, which is still to a large degree in the hands of the individual governments. But as European integration advances and the Member States delegate significant economic and monetary policy instruments to the European Union, the latter commits itself increasingly to the advancement of social progress for all the peoples who make it up. Thus, whilst the Treaty of Rome relied above all on the functioning of the common market to improve living and working conditions in all Member States, the Treaty of Maastricht assigns to the Community the task of actively promoting economic and social cohesion within the Community.

Considerable progress was, it is true, made within the framework of the EEC Treaty as regards the four facets of Community social policy, viz.: the free movement of workers (discussed in the chapter on the common market), employment policy, vocational training and the improvement of living and working conditions. But the differences in social progress between Member States widened in line with the enlargement of the Community. In the promised economic and monetary union those differences will not be able to continue without giving rise to tension within the Union.

The Community Charter on the fundamental rights of workers adopted by the European Council in December 1989 is therefore the bedrock for the construction of a social area, which is vital to the progress of the EU. It clearly states that workers' aspirations, interests and rights will be guaranteed in the Single Market. The Social Charter of the Community fixes the main principles on which the European model of labour law is founded. Although it also concerns freedom of movement, employment matters and vocational training, the Charter insists mainly on the improvement of living and working conditions and it is therefore examined in more detail under that title. All the Member States except the United Kingdom have agreed to implement the 1989 Social Charter.

Economic and legal framework

The objectives of the social policy are very close to those of the regional policy. The latter is directed towards improving the lot of the least-favoured regions of the European Union, the social policy that of its poorest citizens. Both seek to resolve the economic and social imbalances in the Union and to ensure that the advantages ensuing from the functioning of the common market are shared amongst all the countries and all the citizens. Several of their measures are complementary, and their financial instruments must be closely coordinated in order to put them into effect.

Reasons for a European social policy

A Community social policy, which was necessary for the social cohesion of the Community as early as the stage of the progressive implementation of the common market, is provided for in vague terms in the EEC Treaty. Although its signatories stated that they were resolved to ensure social progress by common action and affirmed as the essential objective the improvement of the living and working conditions of their peoples, they remained entirely independent in the field of social policies. They placed their faith above all in the automatic improvement of social conditions, relying on the **knock-on effect that economic integration would produce**. They were not wrong in that, but they were not completely right either.

It is certain that the progressive integration of the economies in itself promotes the approximation of several aspects of the social systems of the States of the Community. The closer the economies become, the more the social problems are similar and the more similar, not to say common, solutions become necessary. The most characteristic social features of the Community during the first thirty years of its existence have been the moderate growth of the population, increased life expectancy and shorter working life, the widespread extension of compulsory education and the mass entry of women into economic activities. In addition to those general phenomena there have been structural changes within sectors and sectoral movements from agriculture to industry and from the latter to the service industries. It is therefore not by chance that the problems of employment, social security and the vocational training of certain categories of workers (the young, the old and women) are priorities in every Member State. Economic integration does not mean that national social systems will be wiped out automatically. These systems, which are the result of national traditions and an important factor in competitiveness, are highly resistant to change. Any alignment of Member States' social systems must take account of specific national features and preserve a delicate and complex balance between them.

The free movement of workers and transnational trades union contacts have promoted a degree of **upward levelling** of wages, social benefits and social protection. Increased prosperity did not, however, resolve all the Community's social problems; it even made some of them more acute or gave rise to new ones, viz. problems of the regions and categories of persons who did not participate fully in the general progress; problems of structural unemployment; problems relating to the distribution of income and wealth; conflicts between economic and social values and, on occasion, dramatic changes in lifestyle with negative consequences for the behaviour of young people.

To attain social cohesion in the Union minimum social standards are needed, having regard to differing national systems and needs, and to the relative economic strengths of the Member States. The establishment of a framework of basic minimum standards provides a bulwark against using low social standards as an instrument of unfair economic competition and protection against reducing social standards to increase the competitiveness of the businesses of one Member State. These basic standards should not over-stretch the economically weaker Member States, but they should not prevent the more developed Member States from implementing higher standards.

A dynamic social policy is inseparable from an efficient industrial policy. Adequate vocational training for workers and the improvement of the occupational and geographical mobility of labour are prerequisites for the efficiency of European industry. Likewise, Community aid granted to workers who have to leave certain activities - for example textiles, clothing or agriculture - make it possible to absorb economic changes without any social unrest. Conversely, aid to industries in crisis situations - for example the steel industry or shipbuilding - have a direct social impact, as they make it possible to protect jobs.

Technological progress and improved training lead to the strengthening of the requirements as regards social justice, to worker participation and to the improvement of the quality of life and of work. At the same time, however, technological progress gives rise to numerous structural changes accompanied by tension on the labour market. It is therefore essential that social progress keeps in step with technological progress. Furthermore, a common approach must be taken to these phenomena so as not to give rise to distortions of competition within the common market. In fact, given the increasing economic interdependence of the member countries, any one of their number which decided to carry out a social reform on its own might handicap some of its industrial sectors or even its economy in general.

At the dawn of the 21st century, the European societies are faced with new challenges. The globalization of trade and production, the impact of new technologies on work, society and individuals, the persistent high level of unemployment and the ageing of the population are all combining to put unprecedented strains on the economic and social fabric of all the Member States. While the basic responsibility in these areas lies with the

Member States, full cooperation between them, within the Union, plays an important role in ensuring that the national systems of social protection do not develop in ways which conflict with overall Union employment objectives or standards, distort conditions of competition, or inhibit the free movement of people within the Union. This is why, Article 2 of the Agreement on Social Policy gives the Union a role in supporting and complementing the activities of the Member States.

A hesitant start

The Treaty of Rome had two series of social provisions spread over two groups of articles: one relating to the free movement of workers (Articles 48 to 51) and the other concerning what it called "social policy" (Articles 117 to 128). The latter group was virtually confined to the retraining and resettlement of workers with the help of a European Social Fund in order in particular to facilitate the free movement of those workers. There was a basic difference between the provisions of the two groups of articles. Those relating to the free movement of workers were subject to the normal institutional mechanism for Community decisions, involving a Commission proposal, consultation of the European Parliament and the Economic and Social Committee and, lastly, a decision by the Council in the form of a regulation or a directive. The institutional procedure governing the European Social Fund was the same, but the social provisions, concerning inter alia employment, labour law and working conditions, vocational training and social security, only provided for close cooperation between Member States, which the Commission was given the task of promoting by making studies, delivering opinions and arranging consultations (Article 118).

The Commission did not take long to voice its opposition to those contradictions in the social provisions of the Treaty of Rome. Its grievances were echoed at the Conference of Heads of State or of Government in the Hague in December 1969, which recognized the need to reform the Social Fund, and at the Paris Conference in October 1972, which designated full and better employment as basic objectives of the Community's social policy. The Heads of State or of Government then stressed that vigorous action in the social field was, in their view, as important as the achievement of economic and monetary union, and called upon the Community Institutions to adopt, after consultations with both sides of industry, an action programme laying down concrete measures in the social field and corresponding resources, in particular within the framework of the Social Fund.

This programme, which was adopted by the Council on 21 January 1974, was a turning point in the Community's social policy from two points of view: first, it meant that the Community's States recognized that a purely national social policy could no longer be conducted in a Europe progressing towards integration; secondly, the 1974 programme made the social policy into a complex policy integrated in the Community's general policy. Of course it still, in line with the Treaty, aimed at protecting migrant workers and improving training and occupational mobility within the Community, but it was extended to cover new areas such as employment and the improvement of living and working conditions.

That policy needed a new or adapted financial instrument. Practice had shown, according to the Commission, that assistance from the European Social Fund, granted on the basis of excessively stringent criteria, was inflexible, belated and burdensome. Thus the Fund could not cope with unemployment stemming from the fact that manpower was not adapted to the rapid development of technology. It was inefficient because the automatic nature and thin spread of the assistance granted did not make more effective targeted measures possible. Lastly, and above all, the task of the Fund was denatured by the **practice of the fair return**, i.e. the States' requirement that they recover, through Social Fund aid, the total amount of their contributions to its functioning. These various shortcomings were recognized by the Heads of State or of Government of the Community who, at the Summit Conference held in the Hague in December 1969, stated that they were aware of the need to transform the ESF within the framework of a closely harmonized social policy of the Member States. The **reform of the Social Fund**, which involved a mini-revision of the EEC Treaty, formed the subject of a Council Decision of 1 February 1971 which replaced the assistance granted on the basis of Article 125 of the Treaty by a new system of aids. That reform was not, moreover, the last, because, yet again at the instigation of the Commission, the operating rules of the Social Fund were simplified in 1977 and its tasks were revised in 1983[1].

Social cohesion in the European Union

The effort to complete the internal market at the end of the 1980s was to mean a fresh start for the Community's social policy and its financial instrument, the ESF. The **Single European Act** and, later on, the Treaty on European Union stated that "in order to promote its overall harmonious development, the Community shall develop and pursue its actions leading to the strengthening of its economic and social cohesion" (Article 130a), and "Member States shall pay particular attention to encouraging improvements, especially in the working environment, as regards the health and safety of workers, and shall set as their objective the harmonization of conditions in this area, while maintaining the improvements made" (Article 118a). For that purpose the Council, acting by a qualified majority in cooperation with the Parliament adopts by means of directives, minimum requirements, having regard to the conditions and technical rules obtaining in each of the Member States.

The **Structural Funds**, and especially the European Social Fund, represent the main instruments for promoting cohesion within the Union. With a view to strengthening the Community's economic and social cohesion, the European Council on 11 and 12 February 1988 had agreed to double the commitment appropriations for the Structural Funds in 1993 as against 1987, which meant a considerable increase in the European Social Fund's appropriations. As we saw under the heading of coordination of financial instruments in the chapter on regional development, the ESF henceforth has had to contribute to the attainment of the Objectives set out in Regulation 2052/88 on the tasks of the Structural Funds[2].

In keeping with the reform of the Structural Funds, which constituted the financial side of economic and social cohesion, the European Council, despite the opposition of Mrs. Thatcher, who was then Prime Minister of the United Kingdom, agreed in December 1989 on the **Community Charter of the fundamental rights of workers**, which represented the legal side of social cohesion and stressed particularly the improvement of living and working conditions: social protection; freedom of association and of collective bargaining; equal treatment for men and women; information, consultation and participation of workers; the protection of health and safety at the workplace; and the protection of children and adolescents, the elderly and the disabled. The Commission, which had proposed the Charter, proposed immediately after its adoption by the majority of heads of State of Government, a series of Community laws in order to bring it into force. But due to the unanimity rule required and the negative position of the United Kingdom, very few social measures were adopted before the completion of the internal market which they should in principle follow in step. In order to get out of the impasse, the Eleven on the one hand and

---

1   OJ L289, 22.10.1983 and OJ L370, 31.12.1985.
2   OJ L185, 15.07.1988.

the United Kingdom on the other signed at Maastricht a Social Protocol allowing the former to adopt alone the social measures that they deemed useful.

The **Agreement on social policy** concluded by eleven Member States -which were joined after their accession by Austria, Sweden and Finland - is attached to the Treaty of Maastricht and is the sole example of a Community regime where one Member State does not share the others' objectives. According to this Agreement, the Community and the Member States have as their objectives the promotion of employment, improved living and working conditions, proper social protection, dialogue between management and labour, the development of human resources with a view to lasting high employment and the combating of exclusion.

With a view to achieving these objectives, the Council, taking account of national conditions, particularly as regards contractual relations, the interests of SMEs and the need to ensure the competitiveness of the Community's economy, adopts by means of directives minimum require- ments for gradual implementation. The Council, composed of fourteen Ministers, acts in accordance with the procedure referred to in Article 189c (cooperation with the European Parliament) requiring a qualified majority of the Fourteen in the following fields: improvement of the working environment to protect workers' health and safety; working conditions; the information and consultation of workers; equality between men and women with regard to labour market opportunities and treatment at work; the integration of persons excluded from the labour market.

However, unanimity of the Fourteen is required in the following fields: social security and social protection of workers; protection of work- ers where their employment contract is terminated; representation and collective defence of the interests of workers and employers, including co-determination but excluding salaries, right of association and the right to strike; conditions of employment for third-country nationals legally residing in Community territory; financial contributions for promotion of employment and job-creation.

In a communication of 14 December 1993 on the application of the Agreement on social policy, the Commission points out that legislative proposals in the social policy field will be governed either by the provi- sions of the EC Treaty, where such proposals address all the Member States, or by the Protocol on social policy from which the United Kingdom is excluded[1]. In deciding which procedure to adopt, the Commission takes into consideration certain elements: the nature of the proposal, the attitude of the social partners to it, the need to ensure that the social dimension progresses at the same pace as other Community policies, and hence the possibility for the Council to reach decisions by qualified majority, the desire to ensure that all workers throughout the Community benefit from the proposed measures, and the possibility for all the Member States to move forward together. The Commission tries to promote those legal instruments which allow a unanimous adoption and as a last resort pro- ceeds to a change of the legal base of its proposal in order to reach an

---

1   COM (93) 600.

agreement by the eleven (now the fourteen). In any case, the measures taken under the Agreement on social policy are actually Community measures and the Court of Justice is therefore competent to interpret them and rule on their validity.

It goes without saying that the path towards the harmonization of social conditions in the European Union will be long and difficult; the British Government even qualified it at Maastricht as "suicidal", because, in its opinion, it would increase the cost of labour in Europe. However, as we will immediately see, the Community of Twelve has already accomplished some progress in many of the areas in question. The Commission's White Paper on European Social Policy sets out its approach to the next phase of social policy development (1995-99) and seeks to trace a way forward for the Union[1]. A resolution adopted in Council by eleven members, within the framework of the Protocol on Social policy, stresses that the Commission's White Paper represents an important contribution to the development of social policy in the Union[2]. The Council lists some central objectives towards which such a policy could be directed: improving the competitiveness of the Union and increasing the opportunities for job-creating growth; protecting the rights of employees by means of minimum social standards; respecting the principles of subsidiarity and proportionality; promoting convergence rather than unification of national systems; strengthening the social dialogue; and meshing of economic and social measures. Taking account of these guidelines, the Commission set out a detailed work programme in the social field for the period from 1995 to 1997, which shall be subject to an annual adaptation[3]. This programme focuses on a number of major issues: employment, education and training, consolidation and development of social legislation, equal opportunities for women and men and an active society for all.

Employment policy

At the same time as it was integrating its labour market, as we saw in the chapter on the common market, the Community was struggling against the problem of unemployment. This problem became a matter of serious concern for all the countries of the Community around the mid-'70s. Until then employment problems in the Community merely consisted of structural and regional imbalances in a general context of full employment. A series of very variable economic factors led to the **rapid deterioration of the employment situation** in the Community, viz.: the October 1973 oil crisis and the fivefold increase in energy prices in the space of few months, the inflation and economic recession of the late '70s and early '80s, lively competition from recently industrialized countries with cheap labour, a degree of saturation of demand in Europe for industrial goods and

---

1   COM (94) 333, 27 July 1994.
2   OJ C368, 23.12.1994.
3   COM (95) 134, 12 April 1995.

the evolution of the economy and of European companies towards a post-industrial stage. Many jobs thus became superfluous and disappeared. Others were created, but required new qualifications which most of the unemployed did not possess. At the same time, women, most of whom had previously stayed at home, joined the labour market in force.

Having averaged close to 10% for a decade, unemployment in the Union now stands at around 11% and is seen as its gravest social problem. The economic and social costs of this unemployment are enormous. They include not only the direct expenditure on providing social security support for the unemployed, but also: the loss of tax revenue which the unemployed would pay out of their income if they were working; the increased burden on social services; rising poverty, crime and ill-health. Special concern focuses on the lack of prospects for new entrants to the labour market, especially young people and women and for people excluded from regular work.

Overall EU employment performance is markedly worse than in the United States and Japan. Thus, in 1994, the unemployment rate rose to just over 11% in the Union, compared with less than 6.5% in the United States and under 3% in Japan. Levels of social solidarity are certainly higher in Europe as compared with the United States and Japan; but such solidarity has been mainly passive. It is devoted to maintaining the incomes of large groups in society, but little efforts are made to adapt the broader employment environment and the legal and fiscal systems to the new economic and social realities.

Now it is clear that reducing unemployment necessarily requires **pro-active labour market policies**. A radical new look is needed at the whole range of available instruments which can influence the employment environment, whether these be regulatory, fiscal or social security incentives. The educational system, labour laws, work contracts, contractual negotiation systems, the social security system and business management form the pillars of the "employment environment" in each Member State and combine to give each of them a distinctive appearance. According to the subsidiarity principle, the vast bulk of these measures will be for individual Member States to decide upon in responding to their diverse national situations. However, the Union can and must play an important role by: firstly, providing a forum where a common broad framework strategy can be agreed; and secondly, by underpinning national measures with complementary financial support through the European Social Fund (which represents 13% of all Member States' expenditure on active labour market policies).

In July 1994, the Commission presented this new approach in a White Paper on European Social Policy[1], which is closely allied to the White Paper on growth, competitiveness and employment[2]. In both Papers, the Commission underlines the need, within the framework of vigorous action to tackle unemployment, for more active labour-market policies, for priority to be given to training geared to the kind of jobs available, for an early

---

1   COM (94) 333, 27 July 1994.
2   COM (93) 700, 5.12.1993. See the chapter on EMU.

response to technological change, and for improvements to employment services or agencies.

In Essen in December 1994, the European Council adopted, as proposed by the Commission, recommendations for national employment measures in five key areas: improving employment opportunities for the labour force through initial and further training; increasing the employment intensiveness of growth through more flexible organization of work, wage restraint to encourage job-creating investment and the promotion of local employment initiatives; reducing non-wage labour costs sufficiently to ensure a real impact on recruitment decisions; improving the effectiveness of labour-market policies by making them less dependent on passive support and by facilitating and encouraging access to employment; and multiplying measures to help groups hard hit by unemployment, such as young people, women or the long-term unemployed.

The Essen European Council had asked the Member States to integrate the recommended action points into their policies by means of multiannual programmes for employment and had also called on the Council and the Commission to report on their implementation. Reporting in this context on employment in Europe in 1995, the Commission noted the momentum which had built up under the strategy mapped out in Essen, taking the form more especially of Member States' multiannual employment programmes[1]. Noting the cooperation of all parties involved in the creation of new jobs, the Madrid European Council, in December 1995, pointed out the priority spheres of action in Member States' multiannual employment programmes: stepping up training programmes; rendering more flexible the organization of work; continuing the wage restraint; promoting local employment initiatives; and converting passive policies to protect the unemployed into active job-creation measures.

Institutional machinery

Thanks to a **levy system** on the production of the industries concerned, the ECSC was better placed than the EEC to cope with the employment problems. Article 56 of the ECSC Treaty contained provisions on employment in the coal and steel industries. Originally that Article provided for measures only in the event of the introduction of new processes or equipment, within the framework of the common market, resulting in a significant reduction in the labour requirements of those industries and regional difficulties in re-employing redundant workers. But in 1960 the provisions of Article 56 were extended to cover instances where fundamental changes, not directly connected with the establishment of the common market, in market conditions for the coal or the steel industry should compel some undertakings permanently to discontinue, curtail or change their activities[2].

The common intervention system applicable to **ECSC redeployment aid** makes provision, for the five standard situations in which workers obliged to leave their jobs early may find themselves (early retirement, unemployment, resettlement, conversion and training), for aids linked with uniform duration limits and standard limits on the maximum amounts granted. These "traditional" aid programmes are supplemented by aid under the steel industry social measures[3] and under the coal industry social measures[4].

1   COM (95) 396, 26 July 1995.

2   OJ C276, 24.10.1980 and OJ C340, 31.12.1980.

3   OJ L335, 23.12.1994.

4   OJ C108, 16.04.1994.

The Commission is now examining the best means of transferring ECSC social aid into the European Social Fund under the EC regime, in anticipation of the expiry of the ECSC Treaty in 2002. It has already decided to suspend application of Article 56 of the ECSC Treaty as regards joint financing of vocational training and employment aid programmes, which will henceforth be funded by the ESF[1]. Useful lessons can probably be learned from experience gained with the ECSC which has operated in exceptionally close association with the social partners and with co-financing from the industries concerned. This system has cushioned the social impact of tremendous job losses over the past thirty years in these industries.

Unlike the ECSC Treaty, the EEC Treaty did not prepare the Community Institutions sufficiently to cope with the employment problems which had been plaguing the Community since the mid-'70s. Of course Article 118 gave the Commission the task of promoting close cooperation between States in the social field with regard to employment inter alia. To do so, however, it could act, in accordance with that Article, only by making studies, delivering opinions and arranging consultations. The Commission has not only exhausted all those possibilities, but it has also gone beyond what the Treaty asked of it.

In view of mutual information and concertation, the Commission set up a programme of employment statistics, and publishes reports on employment forecasts for each sector, based on national work and containing homogeneous quantitative data[2]. It keeps a continuous inventory of the measures taken in the countries of the Community to tackle the employment crisis and manages a Mutual Information System on Employment Policies (**MISEP**) to collect, exploit and disseminate the information through a network of national correspondents. The **Observatory and documentation system on employment** links the MISEP system with two networks which furnish the information available within the Member States: the network of employment coordinators (NEC), made up of national civil servants; and the European system of documentation on employment (SYSDEM), made up of correspondents belonging to universities and research centres.

The Commission examines the information thus obtained, studies the trends which affect employment in the Member States and publishes reports and bulletins assessing the rapid changes currently taking place in the Union's labour market[3]. It proposes to establish a specific legal basis for the activities of analysis, research and cooperation in the field of employment, in order to foster a more effective partnership of all those involved in employment policy[4]. Already, the Commission organizes two or three meetings a year of Heads of Employment Departments (**Standing Committee on Employment**) to provide them with an opportunity of discussing the employment situation, the measures taken in each country and the objectives and priorities for Community measures in the field[5]. This Committee is concerned essentially with the preparation and follow-

---

1   OJ C178, 30.06.1994.
2   OJ L351, 20.12.1991.
3   See, e.g., COM (95) 465, 11 October 1995.
4   COM (95) 250, 13 June 1995.
5   OJ L273, 17.12.1970 and OJ L21, 28.01.1975.

up of European Councils, which, as mentioned above are increasingly interested in employment problems.

Community initiatives on employment

On the basis of Article 118 EEC, which enjoined it to promote a close cooperation among the Member States in the field of employment without having recourse to formal legislation, it had the Council adopt guidelines for a Community labour market policy[1] and a series of Community Resolutions and programmes in the field of employment. These Council Resolutions aimed at: Community action to combat unemployment[2], the promotion of **employment for young people**[3], combating unemployment amongst women[4], the contribution of local job-creation schemes to efforts to combat unemployment[5], tackling long-term unemployment[6], promoting the integration or reintegration of women in active life[7] and assisting the long-term unemployed[8]. Despite their non-compulsory character, these Resolutions have had some practical effects. Thus, the Resolution on the promotion of employment for young people gave rise to many initiatives of the European Social Fund, whether measures in favour of young people establishing undertakings, innovative practices on the part of undertakings or aid for the integration of disadvantaged young people. The Resolution on long-term unemployment led to a job creation programme being adopted for specific groups of long-term unemployed (**ERGO**).

Likewise, local job-creation schemes formed the subject of an important action programme for the local development of employment (**LEDA**) aimed at pinpointing and removing the obstacles to those schemes. The Commission also set up a system for exchanges of information for local employment initiatives (**ELISE**) and a support programme for innovative local or regional job creation schemes (**SPEC**). On the basis of these last experiences, the Commission presented in a communication the elements of a European strategy for encouraging **local development and employment initiatives**[9]. These are viewed in terms of local projects calling for a legal and financial partnership between the public and private sectors and geared to meeting new needs such as, home-help services, child care, assistance for young people facing difficulties, cultural heritage, crafts and tourism, waste management, protection and conservation of natural areas. The European Council of Cannes, in June 1995, stressed the importance of local employment initiatives.

---

1   OJ C168, 08.07.1980.
2   OJ C186, 21.07.1982.
3   OJ C29, 04.02.1984.
4   OJ C161, 21.06.1984.
5   Ibid.
6   OJ C2, 01.01.1985.
7   OJ C333, 28.12.1988.
8   OJ C157, 27.06.1990.
9   COM (95) 273, 13 June 1995.

Two important Community initiatives on employment were launched in 1994 in the context of economic and social cohesion[1]. The initiative on **Employment and Development of Human Resources** aims to improve access to employment for certain disadvantaged groups: the women (Employment-NOW); the disabled, the long-term unemployed, the socially excluded (Employment-HORIZON); and the young unemployed (Employment-YOUTHSTART). The **ADAPT** initiative aims to assist workers at risk of unemployment through industrial change to adapt to new working practices and methods. Both initiatives place emphasis on developing a strong transnational and innovative dimension and are designed to have an important catalytic effect on national, regional and local efforts to promote employment and to improve the quality and standards of training provision.

The actions of the European Social Fund

Due to the reservations of the United Kingdom, the only important modifications made in Maastricht to the social provisions of the Treaty concern the European Social Fund. Implementing decisions concerning the ESF are henceforth adopted by the Council acting in accordance with the procedure referred to in Article 189c (cooperation). The tasks of the Funds now cover not only the promotion of easier employment of workers and their geographical and occupational mobility within the Community, but also workforce adaptation to industrial changes and to changes in production systems, in particular through vocational training and retraining (Article 123 EC).

However, the social problems which Member States face and for which the Social Fund is designed show little sign of improvement. Unemployment in the EC is on the increase. The labour market is not functioning as it should to reap the potential benefits of the Single Market. The European Commission therefore proposed and the Council adopted, on July 20, 1993, more sweeping changes to the Social Fund's regulations than those concerning the other two structural Funds[2].

Assistance to the unemployed naturally is the EC's and therefore the Social Fund's top priority. The **new Objective 3** of the Structural Funds covers measures to combat long-term unemployment and to promote the vocational integration of young persons on the labour market (i.e. the former Objectives 3 and 4). The Objective's main innovation is that it explicitly provides for initiatives designed to promote the integration on the labour market of persons who run the risk of being excluded from any social protection. The increase in long term unemployment and the great difficulty that young people fresh on the job market have in finding employment have aggravated the problem of social exclusion. The latter is therefore mentioned explicitly in the new Objective.

---

1   OJ C180, 01.07.1994, see the heading on Community Initiatives in the chapter on Regional Development.
2   OJ L193, 31.07.1993. See the chapter on Regional Development.

Employment in the EC is affected from a qualitative angle by changes in demand, technological progress, external competition, and new and revised EC policies. Industrial changes and new production systems affect, to varying degrees, all economic activities, large as well as small enterprises and the different local labour markets in Europe. A qualified work force is an essential component in the competitiveness, productivity and quality of companies. Effective access to continuing training and re-training is needed to increase the ability of workers, especially those whose skills are inappropriate or those employed in undertakings experiencing particularly difficult adaptation problems.

The Structural Funds' **new Objective 4** seeks to prevent exclusion from the labour market, by making it easier for workers to adapt to changes in industry and production systems in the EC, whenever fresh skills are required. The new Objective's priorities are as follows: training in relation to the introduction, use and development of new or sophisticated production methods; training to enable SMEs to adapt to new forms of cooperation with large groups, particularly in the field of sub-contracting.

In addition to assistance under Objectives 3 and 4, which concern the Community as a whole, the Fund must also give its support to operations which are of particular importance to the regions of Objectives 1, 2, 5b and 6. The prime aims of Social Fund assistance in these regions are to stabilize and promote employment, by means of continuing training initiatives for persons who are in employment or who have recently lost their job, and to facilitate industrial and urban restructuring or rural adjustment and diversification. Social Fund assistance will also have to be available, within this context, to develop human potential in the fields of research, science and technology.

Education, vocational training and youth

The problems of employment and vocational training are related, as very often the jobs offered require qualifications which those seeking employment lack. That is why employment and vocational training policies are also linked. In fact, training is an instrument of active labour market policy. Measures which promote training or vocational retraining at the same time promote the employment or re-employment of workers in sectors where qualified labour is needed. Many workers cannot secure employment without acquiring a specialization, but they cannot acquire specialization through experience until they have found a job. Education or vocational retraining is in practice the only way out of this vicious circle. Breaking this vicious circle is vital as workers should be able to change more frequently jobs throughout their working lives in the future.

Vocational training is not only a basic human right, enabling workers to realize their full potential, but also a prerequisite for technological progress and regional development. Indeed, a skilled, adaptable and mobile workforce is the base of a competitive economy. It allows industries and regions to adapt rapidly to the requirements of technology and market trends and thus to become or remain competitive. Unemployment is in fact rife especially in the traditional industries in decline (steel, shipbuilding, textiles), whilst the new industries (information technology, aerospace) are badly in need of qualified labour. Tomorrow's trades will require the autonomy, the independence of spirit, the analytical ability and the capacity to make diagnoses, qualities which depend on knowledge. The new qualifications can help the European economy to effect the necessary structural changes in the post-industrial era and enable it better to face competition from the newly industrialized countries. The EU's objective should therefore be to develop human resources throughout people's working lives, starting with basic education and working through initial training to continuing training.

According to the Social Charter of 1989, every worker must have the right to vocational training throughout his working life. There can be no discrimination as regards this entitlement on the grounds of nationality. Public authorities, companies or social partners must make facilities for continuing training readily available, so that everyone can retrain, do further training or acquire new knowledge to keep up with technological progress.

The foundations of training and education policies

In 1975, the Council set up an organ of Community policy on professional training, namely the European Centre for the Development of Vocational Training (**CEDEFOP**). Since 1994, it is located in Thessaloniki[1]. Cedefop's programme of work focuses on two priority areas, namely qualifications and vocational training systems. The former is essentially concerned with the transparency of qualifications and new occupations at European level and the impact of new forms of work organization and qualifications on training systems. The latter is concerned with strategies for the optimum combination of types and phases of training with a view to achieving a lifelong learning process and with improved teacher training. Under the EEA Agreement, its member countries are entitled to participate in Cedefop projects.

Underlying cooperation in the field of education is the collection and dissemination of information on the programmes and projects of the various higher education establishments in the Member States. An Education Information Network in the European Community, set up by the Commission in 1981 under the name of EURYDICE, is available to users with responsibilities in the field of education, such as the Community Institutions, national authorities and officials responsible for higher education in the Member States[2].

Amongst European actions in the university field one must include the Convention setting up the **European University Institute in Florence**[3]. The Institute specializes in research in four areas, viz.: history and civilization, economics, law and political and social science. The task of the Institute is to contribute to the development of the cultural and scientific heritage of Europe, as a whole and in its constituent parts. The Institute runs interdisciplinary research programmes on the main issues European society has to address, especially those involving European integration. Its research work has to cover the great movements and institutions which characterize the history and development of Europe. The Commission contributes financially towards the Institute's scientific and research activities, namely the research library and European library (Eurolib programme). In addition, the Commission covers the cost concerning the historical archives of the European Communities, which are managed by the Institute.

---

1   OJ L39, 13.02.1975 and OJ L30, 09.02.1995.
2   OJ C336, 19.12.1992.
3   OJ C29, 09.02.1976.

The Treaty on European Union has consecrated Community action in the fields of education, vocational training and youth. This action must, however, fully respect the responsibility of the Member States for the content of teaching, the organization of education systems and vocational training and their cultural and linguistic diversity. The new Article 126 specifies that the Community contributes to the development of **quality education** by encouraging cooperation between Member States and, if necessary, by supporting and supplementing their action in the fields of: teaching and dissemination of languages; mobility of students and teachers; cooperation between educational establishments; exchanges of information and experience; and the development of distance education. Incentive measures shall be adopted by the Council acting in accordance with the procedure referred to in Article 189b (co-decision with the European Parliament).

According to Article 127 of the Maastricht Treaty, the Community implements a **vocational training policy**, which supports and supplements the action of the Member States and which aims to: facilitate adaptation to industrial changes, in particular through vocational training and retraining; improve initial and continuing vocational training in order to facilitate vocational integration and reintegration into the labour market; facilitate access to vocational training and encourage mobility of instructors and trainees; stimulate cooperation between educational or training establishments and firms; and develop exchanges of information and experience on issues common to the training systems of the Member States. The Council adopts measures necessary to the achievement of these objectives acting in accordance with the procedure referred to in Article 189c (cooperation).

In several resolutions and conclusions the Council called on the Commission, the Member States and interested organizations to work towards greater coherence at Community level between vocational training programmes, and to promote the development of European cooperation in this field, the transfer of innovation and the development of applied research with a view to supporting modernization, adaptability and quality in vocational education and training[1]. The Council also recommended that Member States gear their vocational training policies to ensure that every worker has access to **continuing vocational training** throughout his or her working life, in accordance with the principle set out in the Community Charter of the Fundamental Social Rights of Workers[2]. Some innovative projects in this field were carried out in 1996, the European Year of Lifelong Learning[3]. Responding to the concerns voiced on several occasions by the Council of Ministers and the European Council, the Commission presented, in November 1995, a White Paper on the need to strengthen training and education policies in the face of the challenges posed by the advent of the information society or the "learning society"[4].

Education and training programmes

To attain the new objectives of the Treaty on European Union, while ensuring the continuation of the Community programmes on education

---

1   OJ C186, 08.07.1993, OJ C374, 30.12.1994 and OJ C207, 12.08.1995.
2   OJ L181, 23.07.1993.
3   OJ L256, 26.10.1995.
4   COM (95) 590, 29 November 1995.

and training, the European Parliament and the Council adopted, on a Commission proposal, a new five-year programme (1995-1999) in the field of education, entitled "Socrates", which forms an integral part of a package including the "Leonardo da Vinci" programme concerning vocational training and "Youth for Europe III". In fact, Socrates and Leonardo take up and innovate the preceding Erasmus, Lingua, Comett, Petra, Force and Eurotecnet programmes. The Union's new generation of education and training programmes is designed to develop a European dimension of education from the primary school to the university and to establish a genuine European market in skills and training.

The **SOCRATES** programme, endowed with ECU 850 million, comprises measures and projects intended to promote transnational cooperation **in the field of education**, centred around three themes: cooperation in higher education through the promotion of student and teaching staff mobility, the establishment of university networks and the incorporation of the European dimension into all levels of study (previous Erasmus and Lingua programmes); cooperation in secondary school education through the promotion of partnerships between schools in different Member States and networks of schools for the joint pursuit of educational projects, with special reference to languages, the new information technologies, cultural heritage and environmental protection (Comenius programme); and measures applicable to all levels of education, concerning the promotion of language skills, open and distance education, and exchange of information and experience[1].

The **LEONARDO** programme (1995-1999), which is endowed with ECU 620 million, is developed in synergy with the Structural Funds of the Union and especially, as far as the ESF is concerned, with the objectives 3 and 4, and is designed to promote and support quality and capacity of innovation **in the field of training**[2]. It emphasizes the need for a balance between initial training, continuing training and lifelong learning and provides support for the development of language skills and the dissemination of innovation. Leonardo's measures are fourfold: support for the improvement of Member States' vocational training systems and arrangements; support for the improvement of vocational training actions, including university/industry cooperation for the benefit of companies and employees; support for the development of language skills, knowledge and the dissemination of innovatory measures; accompanying measures (cooperation network, information, monitoring, assessment).

Since 1964, a major action programme entitled "**Youth for Europe**" has supported the promotion of youth exchanges in the Community outside the context of education. This programme provides, on the one hand, for direct support for project-centred youth exchanges and mobility or projects enabling young people to participate in voluntary service activities in the educational, cultural, social and environmental protection fields and, on the other hand, for Community aid to promote short study visits, further training and pilot projects for youth workers. Youth for Europe III

---

1   OJ L87, 20.04.1995.
2   OJ L340, 29.12.1994.

embraces all the Community's activities so far for young people, more particularly the action programme for the vocational training of young people and their preparation for adult and working life (PETRA)[1]. It extends the scope of the earlier measures, while providing positive action for disadvantaged young people. In addition to exchange schemes for young people and the training of youth leaders, the programme provides for initiatives which require creativity and solidarity with a view to promoting a sense of European citizenship among young people and making more information available to them. On the basis of the experience of the "Youth for Europe" programme, the Commission considers the prospects for the development of European voluntary service for young people between the ages of 18 and 25 enabling them to participate, for a period of six months to one year, in a social or humanitarian project in a Member State other than the one where they reside[2].

One specific programme, adapted to the particular needs and situation of the countries in Central and East Europe is the **Trans-European Mobility programme for University Studies (TEMPUS)**. The second phase of the programme (1994-1998), TEMPUS II, concerns the countries of Central and Eastern Europe eligible for financial aid under the PHARE programme as well as some independent States of the former Soviet Union eligible for the TACIS programme[3]. It aims at promoting the development of higher education systems in the eligible countries by means of partnership projects between institutions of these countries and similar institutions in the countries of the European Union. These projects can be part of the networks formed as part of the ERASMUS, COMETT and LINGUA programmes. The following people are entitled to receive assistance towards mobility: students in higher education and teachers in the eligible countries who want to complete a period of study in a university in a Member State, and students and teachers in the Community who want to study or teach in an eligible country; students, teachers or training officers who want to complete practical training courses in the Member States, or, conversely, in one of the eligible countries; young people and youth organizers who want to take part in the activities of university associations and in studies on higher education and training systems. The **European Training Foundation**, established in Turin, endeavours to play a part in developing vocational training systems in the countries of Central and Eastern Europe and in the Independent States of the former Soviet Union[4].

The Community has commenced negotiations with Cyprus and Malta for a cooperation in the fields of education, training and youth in the framework of Community programmes. It has already concluded agreements for cooperation in the fields of higher education and vocational training with the United States[5] and Canada[6]. These cooperation programmes seek to encourage, on the one hand, exchanges of knowledge,

---

1   OJ L87, 20.04.1995.
2   COM (95) 727, 24 January 1996.
3   OJ L122, 07.05.1992 and L112, 06.05.1993.
4   OJ L131, 23.05.1990 and OJ L216, 20.08.1994.
5   OJ L279, 22.11.1995.
6   OJ L300, 13.12.1995.

students and staff and, on the other, interaction between higher education establishments, training providers and undertakings in the EU, the USA and Canada.

Living and working conditions

In article 117 of the EEC Treaty the States of the Community agreed on "the need to promote improved working conditions and an improved standard of living for workers, so as to make possible their harmonization while the improvement is being maintained". They believed, at the time when the Treaty was drafted, that such a development would ensue not only from the functioning of the common market, which would favour the harmonization of social systems, but also from the procedures provided for in the Treaty and from the approximation of provisions laid down by law, regulation or administrative action. Under Article 118a of the EC Treaty, "Member States shall pay particular attention to encouraging improvements, especially in the working environment, as regards the health and safety of workers, and shall set as their objective the harmonization of conditions in this area, while maintaining the improvements made". In order to achieve this objective, the Council adopts by means of Directives minimum requirements for gradual implementation, acting in accordance with the procedure referred to in Article 189c (cooperation).

As can be seen, therefore, the concern of the European Union for the living and working conditions of its citizens is not new and its commitment in this respect has grown apace with economic integration. Thus, in the **Community Charter of fundamental social rights**, adopted by the Strasbourg European Council on 8 and 9 December 1989, the Member States agreed that the development of a large European labour market should bring about an improvement in the living and working conditions of workers in the Community. These fundamental rights are: freedom of movement, employment and fair pay, the improvement of living and working conditions, social protection, freedom of association and of collective bargaining, vocational training, equal treatment for men and women, information, consultation and participation of workers, the protection of health and safety at the workplace, and the protection of children and adolescents, the elderly and the disabled.

But the Social Charter only laid down the principles. In order to implement it, Directives had to be unanimously adopted by the Council. However, the United Kingdom, which had opposed the adoption of the Charter, also contested the justification and the usefulness of binding Community rules. This deadlock had to be broken. As was seen under the heading of social cohesion in the European Union, the solution found in Maastricht was for the Twelve, in a Protocol, to authorize eleven Member States (fourteen after the accession of three new Member States) to have recourse to the institutions, procedures and mechanisms of the Community for the purposes of taking among themselves and applying as far as they are concerned the acts and decisions required for giving effect to the 1989 Social Charter.

The instruments of the policy

By a Council Regulation of 26 May 1975 the Community created a **European Foundation for the Improvement of Living and Working Conditions**, with a three-party structure, which is located in Dublin (Ireland)[1]. Its tasks are to develop and to pursue ideas on the medium and long-term improvement of living and working conditions in the light of practical experience and to identify factors leading to change. It has to advise the Community institutions on foreseeable objectives and guidelines by forwarding in particular scientific information and technical data. The Foundation's four-year programme for 1993-1996 covers six main subject areas: social cohesion; access to employment; innovation and organization of work; human relations in businesses, social dialogue and industrial relations; health and safety; socio-economic aspects of the environment; equal opportunities for women and men.

The European Foundation for the Improvement of Living and Working Conditions is not the Community Institutions' only adviser on the matter. The oldest and most institutional, being provided for in the Treaty of Rome, is the **Economic and Social Committee**. The ESC is composed of employers' representatives, workers' representatives and other interest groups and it delivers Opinions on Commission proposals and may also issue Opinions on its own initiative.

Even before it prepares a proposal, the Commission often consults the numerous **advisory committees**, composed of both sides of industry, set up over the years (on vocational training, freedom of movement, problems of safety and health at the workplace, steel, fisheries, etc.). The Commission has also set up Joint Committees on Social Problems of Agricultural Workers[2], on Social Questions arising in Inland Water Transport[3], on Railways[4] and on Social Questions in Road Transport[5].

Social dialogue

The legal process has difficulty in keeping pace with events in European integration, technological change and organization of work. These changes require new mechanisms of social progress parallel to legislation and State regulation. The social and cultural traditions of the Member States make it possible to build a European model of consensus, reconciling economic effectiveness and social solidarity. The **social partners** can play a crucial role in this process, both through cooperation between the State, employers and the trade unions on economic and social policies, and through the establishment of relations based on agreement between employers and the trade unions.

The social dialogue which was under way from the beginning of the Community, particularly in the coal and steel sectors, was consecrated first by the Single Act and then by the Treaty on European Union, which commits the Commission to develop the dialogue between management and labour at European level which could, if the two sides consider it desirable, lead to relations based on agreement (Article 118b). At European level the social partners are represented by the European Trade Union

1   OJ L139, 30.05.1975 and OJ L41, 23.02.1995.
2   OJ L243, 05.09.1975.
3   OJ L297, 06.11.1980.
4   OJ L8, 10.01.1985.
5   OJ L317, 28.11.1985.

Confederation (ETUC), the Union of Industries of the European Community (UNICE) and the European Centre of Public Enterprises (CEEP).

The social dialogue entered a new stage on October 31, 1991 with the conclusion of an agreement making explicit provision for contractual relations at Community level. This agreement was a major source of inspiration for the social agreement adopted in Maastricht by eleven Member States. The latter stipulates that the Commission consults management and labour on the possible direction of Community action in the field of social policy and on the content of any planned proposals. Dialogue between management and labour at Community level can lead to the conclusion of agreements either in accordance with the procedures and practices specific to management and labour and to the Member States, or by a Council decision in accordance with the clauses of Article 4, paragraphe 2, of the agreement on social policy.

The Commission used the procedure provided by the social protocol in order to achieve Community action on the issue of reconciling work and family life, particularly concerning parental leave, action opposed by the United Kingdom since 1984. In fact, the social partners negotiated and signed, on 14 December 1995, a collective agreement, that entitles both male and female workers to unpaid **parental leave** of at least three months' duration and to time off work in the event of an unforeseen family emergency. The social partners asked the Commission to submit their agreement to the Council, in the form of a proposal for a Decision, so as to make it legally binding on all the Member States except the United Kingdom. The Commission proposed to that effect a Directive having as a legal basis Article 2(4) of the Agreement on social policy[1].

The social partners helped draw up the White Paper of the Commission on growth, competitiveness and employment. They now contribute to the implementation of the employment strategy as defined by the Essen European Council by submitting reports to the European Council. On 20 October 1995, the Commission and the social partners inaugurated, in Florence, the European Centre for Industrial Relations (ECIR)[2].

Worker participation

Worker participation can be understood in two ways: (a) information, consultation and participation in the business's decision-making process; and (b) the employees' financial participation in the business's capital and/or profits. Either way, worker participation is a very controversial subject and varies significantly from Member State to Member State. The European Union therefore is proceeding very slowly in this area.

The 1989 Social Charter stipulates that information, consultation and participation for workers must be developed along appropriate lines, taking account of the practices in the various Member States. Such information, consultation and participation must be implemented in due time, particularly in the following cases:
— when technological changes which, from the point of view of working conditions and work organization, have major implications for the work-force, are introduced into undertakings;
— in connection with restructuring operations in undertakings or in cases of mergers having an impact on the employment of workers;

1   COM (96) 26, 31 January 1996.
2   COM (95) 445, 25 December 1995.

— in cases of collective redundancy procedures; and
— when workers, especially transboundary ones, are affected by the employment policies of the company where they are employed.

The Directives discussed under the following heading concerning large scale redundancies and the maintenance of workers' rights in the event of company takeovers stipulate that the workers must be informed and consulted in good time, so that they can make constructive proposals. By the same token, the 1989 Directive on the improvement of the health and safety of workers at work, also makes worker participation compulsory.

However, these Directives do not cover the vast majority of cases of restructuring, mergers, corporate reorganization or the introduction of new work or manufacturing methods. The information and consultation of workers in these cases is pursued by the first Directive adopted by the Council under Article 2 of the Agreement on social policy annexed to the EC Treaty, which excludes the United Kingdom. This Directive provides for the establishment of a **European Works Council** or a procedure for the purposes of informing and consulting employees in European-scale undertakings[1]. The companies or groups of companies concerned are those with more than 1000 employees in total in the Community and with at least two establishments in different Member States, each employing at least 150 people. The Directive also covers undertakings or groups of undertakings with headquarters outside the territory of the Member States (in this case the United Kingdom counts as a non-member country), in so far as they meet the above criteria. The Directive provides for the establishment, at the initiative of the company or group management or at the written request of at least 100 employees or their representatives in at least two Member States, of a "special negotiating body" with the task of concluding an agreement between the management and the employees' representatives, on the scope, composition, powers and term of office of the European committee to be set up in the undertaking or group, or the practical arrangements for an alternative procedure for the information and consultation of employees.

The Council's draft Regulation on the statute of a **European limited liability company** also provides for worker participation[2]. This does not concern the day-to-day running of the company for which the management is responsible, but the monitoring and development of corporate strategies. Several forms of participation are possible: including the workers in the supervisory or administrative body; having a separate body to represent the work force of the European company; other forms of participation as agreed between the managerial or administrative bodies of the founding companies and the company's work force, as long as there is the same amount of information and consultation as for the separate body. But in spite of this flexibility, worker participation is the most controversial subject in the draft Regulation on the European company.

The Commission tries to break the deadlock in the Council as regards a series of proposals, including the one on the European limited liability company, containing specific provisions on the question of employee participation. Given that a legal framework already exists at transnational level thanks to the European Works Council, the Commission initiated consultations with the social partners on the advisability and possible direction of Commu-

---

1   OJ L254, 30.09.1994.
2   OJ C138, 29.05.1991 and OJ C176, 08.07.1991.

nity action in the field of employee information and consultation in national undertakings[1]. In the event of adoption of a global approach on employee participation, the specific provisions linked to the proposals could be withdrawn and steps could be taken to unblock these proposals.

Worker participation in the company's capital and profits is an even more controversial issue. Some see this as relinquishing management control, diminishing the shareholders' authority and "forfeiting dividend income". Others believe that allowing employees to share in the profits makes for greater flexibility in their earned income, has a stabilizing effect in macro economic terms and is a motivating force resulting in greater productivity and consequently in an improved financial performance. The Commission agrees with the latter point of view and has put forward to the Council a recommendation which it has adopted, concerning the promotion of employee participation in a company's capital and profits[2]. The recommendation asks the Member States to: ensure that they have the appropriate legal structures for implementing various forms of financial participation effectively; consider the possibility of offering tax or other incentives for doing this; encourage the distribution of information about participation and about the experiences of other countries in the Community; and make sure that the social partners have a wide enough range of formulae to choose from based on consultations between employers and employees or their representatives. In any event, companies and employees alike must be able to decide freely whether or not to take part in this.

Social protection

Social security costs (medical care, unemployment benefits, family allowances, pensions, etc.) are an important aspect of the cost of production. That is why, during the negotiations preceding the drafting of the EEC Treaty, some governments had argued that, in a common market, conditions of competition would be more favourable for countries whose social security costs were lower. The "Spaak Report", which was the basis for the negotiations, dealt with this issue, affirming that the differences in social security costs were offset by the general conditions of trade, in particular the exchange rate, and that it was neither possible nor necessary to eliminate them by means of a specific overall action. Thus, the Treaty did not call for harmonization, but for **close cooperation in the social field** (Article 118). Thus the Community confined itself, in the field of social protection, to problems peculiar to certain categories of workers, e.g. migrants, as we saw under the heading of free movement of workers in the chapter on the common market, and women, as will be seen under the heading of equal treatment of men and women.

However, ever since 1992 when the effects of the economic crisis started to really make themselves felt in Europe, social protection has been a controversial issue. Some people claim that the onerous burden of social protection in Europe has resulted in a loss of international market share, as the "labour" element in costs is very high compared with that in the newly industrialized countries. Others claim that the countries in the South of the Community benefit from **"social dumping"** in that they derive competitive advantage from their social charges being on average lower than in the countries in the North. Although there is an element of truth in these claims, their fears are exaggerated. The social protection and the social rights of workers in Europe are the envy of workers in the rest of the world. As soon as their economic and social development permits, these workers will certainly demand similar social cover. What is more, when the level of social protection is low, so too are the qualifications and motivation of the work force. The competitive advantage arising from

---

1   COM (95) 547, 14 November 1995.
2   OJ L245, 26.08.1992.

lower labour costs is to a large extent wiped out by lower productivity. Indeed, productivity is the key to competitiveness and high labour standards are an integral part of the competitive formula.

The fact is, however, that labour markets do not work efficiently in Europe, with a lack of flexibility - more particularly in terms of the organization of working time, pay and mobility - and an inadequate match of labour supply to the needs of the market, especially as regards workforce skills and qualifications. This rigidity is the root cause of what are relatively high labour costs, which have risen at a much greater rate in the EU than among its trading partners. These high labour costs incite firms to substitute labour by more capital-intensive factors. In SMEs, in particular, controls, forms and checks related with social protection are viewed as an additional labour cost and trigger a psychological reaction against the idea of recruiting labour.

Some countries have tried to solve these problems by reducing social protection, but without much success. The increase in poverty and in income disparities that result tend to nourish social tensions and reduce the quality of life in urban centres. There are no miracle remedies, but a need to reform in depth the systems of social security by the introduction of a greater flexibility in the organisation of work and in the distribution of work time, by a reduction of the cost of work and by the promotion of better qualifications and of active employment policies.

As is said in the Commission's White Paper of December 1993 on Growth, Competitiveness and Employment, the new model of European solidarity calls for less passive and more active solidarity. Solidarity, first of all, between those who have jobs and those who do not, expressed in a sort of European social pact adapted to the specific circumstances of each country and each business, thanks to which the new gains in productivity would essentially be applied to forward-looking investments and to the creation of new jobs. Solidarity between men and women making it easier to reconcile family life and working life. Solidarity also between generations, with an eye to the repercussions of a demographic trend and of unemployment, which jeopardize the social security systems. Solidarity, once again, between the more prosperous regions and the poor or struggling regions. Solidarity, lastly and most importantly, in the fight against social exclusion, which splits society in two and imposes renovation of stricken urban areas, construction of subsidized housing and adaptation of education and training systems.

In fact, the avowed aim of the countries in the European Union is to promote improved living and working conditions for workers (art. 117 EC). This means that social protection must be harmonized upwards so that any temporary advantage arising from relatively low social contributions is reduced. This objective is contained in the 1989 Social Charter, where it is stated that "in accordance with the rules pertaining in each country... every worker in the European Community has the right to adequate social protection and, regardless of his status or the size of the company in which he works, must be entitled to adequate social security benefits; those persons not in the labour market, because they have not been able to find work, who have no means of support must be entitled to sufficient benefits and resources, as appropriate to their personal situation".

Thus the Social Charter requires the Member States to provide adequate social protection for their workers but does not ask for the existing systems to be harmonized. As these systems reflect the traditions and existing social benefits of each individual State, it is not easy to change them. However, in an internal market and even more in an economic and monetary union, differences between the various social security systems can constitute distortions of competition, hinder the free movement of labour and exacerbate regional imbalances. Therefore, without changing the actual social security systems, there needs to be a strategy whereby their objectives are brought into alignment. In 1990, the Commission set up a system for mutual information on social protection (the MISSOC programme), which is run by a network of national correspondents and coordinated by the European Social Security Institute.

As part of the implementation of the Charter of workers' fundamental social rights, in 1992 the Council adopted two important recommendations[1]. The first is aimed at helping the most disadvantaged by inviting the Member States to recognize a general right to guaranteed resources and benefits for anyone living in a Member State who has insufficient means. The second is aimed at promoting a harmonization of social protection objectives and policies, so that the free movement of people is not impeded by the different levels of social protection in the Member States and social protection is not adversely affected by competition between the various national systems. This last Recommendation is particularly important because the Member States acknowledge in it that comparable trends lead to common problems and challenges (unemployment, ageing, changing family structures) and that a single market can be created while maintaining the diversity of social protection systems in the Member States, mainly as regards the arrangements for financing and organizing them. This means that diversity may exist in the short-run, but that the long-term objective of the Union is the convergence of social protection systems. In view of this objective and the changes made necessary by the deteriorating relationship between the size of the labour force and the number of pensioners, the Commission launched a debate on the future of social protection, particularly concerning its financing and the way to make it more employment-friendly[2].

The Community has already made headway when the term "social protection" is taken in its broadest sense to cover social security and the right to work. An important Community measure for the social protection of employees is the Directive on the approximation of the laws of the Member States relating to **collective redundancies**[3]. Employers who envisage such redundancies have to hold consultations with workers' representatives on the possibilities of avoiding or reducing such redundancies. Moreover, the employer has to notify any proposed collective redundancy to the competent official authority and may not implement it before the expiry of a period of 30 days which the authority uses to try to find solutions to the problems that have arisen and/or to lessen the impact of the redundancies. This Directive is particularly important for workers employed by multinational companies which operate in one or more EU countries, as, by laying down provisions common to all Member States it prevents multinationals from taking advantage of differences between national laws.

In the same vein, on 14 February 1977 the Council adopted a Directive on the approximation of the laws of the Member States relating to the safeguarding of employees' rights in the event of **transfers of undertak-**

---

1   OJ L245, 26.08.1992.
2   COM (95) 466, 31 October 1995.
3   OJ L148, 22.02.1975 and OJ L245, 26.08.1992.

ings, businesses or parts of businesses[1]. Before any such amalgamation, the workers' representatives have to be informed of the reasons for it and of its consequences for the employees and of the measures envisaged in their favour. In principle, the workers' rights and obligations are transferred to the new employer for at least a year and agreement on the conditions of the takeover has to be reached in consultation with the work force. Failing agreement between the employer or employers and the workers, an arbitration body gives a final ruling on the steps to be taken in favour of the workers.

In the United Kingdom, worker representation traditionally depends on the employer's recognition of unions, so that an employer who does not recognize a union can escape the information and consultation duties provided by the two Directives above. The Court of Justice upheld the Commission's view, asserting that a representation scheme not dependent on the employer's will is necessary for compliance with the Directives; otherwise, the Directives would have no practical effects[2].

But the workers' interests also need to be protected **in the event of the insolvency** of their employer, especially where the employer's discontinuation of payment does not lead to the opening of insolvency proceedings owing to a lack of assets which can be distributed or where assets are not sufficient to cover outstanding claims resulting from contracts of employment or employment relationships, even where the latter are privileged. For that reason, a Council Directive of 20 October 1980 obliges Member States to set up guarantee institutions independent of the employers' operating capital so that their assets are inaccessible to proceedings for insolvency[3]. In such an eventuality, those institutions must, within certain limits, settle the claims of employees arising prior to the insolvency of the employer, including contributions under social security schemes.

A Directive on the **protection of young people at work** prohibits work by children (less than 15 years of age or still subject to compulsory full-time schooling), with the exception of certain cultural, artistic or sporting activities and, for children of at least 14 years of age, combined work/training schemes, in-plant work-experience schemes and certain light work[4]. The Directive asks Member States to strictly regulate work done by adolescents of more than 18 years of age, by imposing specific rules in respect of working time, daily rest periods, weekly rest periods and night work, and laying down technical health and safety standards.

In the single market, social protection must also cover **atypical work**, i.e. other forms of work than that for an indefinite period, such as work for a specific duration, interim work, temporary work and seasonal work. These different forms of work enable companies to organize their work and their production in such a way as to improve productivity and thus become more competitive. Similarly, they enable workers to adapt the hours they work to suit their personal and family circumstances. But in a single market, certain essential conditions must be determined both to

1   OJ L61, 05.03.1977.
2   Judgments given on 8 June 1994, Cases C-382/92 and C-383/92, Commission v United Kingdom.
3   OJ L283, 20.10.1980.
4   OJ L216, 20.08.1994.

avoid distortions of competition and to protect the workers who opt for or accept (for want of something better) these new forms of work. These two objectives are contained in the draft Directives on atypical work[1]. They are aimed at guaranteeing the same conditions of social protection, in particular social security, vocational training, health and safety, for interim and specific duration workers and those on fixed term contracts as for workers employed full-time for an indefinite period. The Council has adopted a Directive on the health and safety of workers with a fixed-duration employment relationship or a temporary employment relationship[2]. Concerning the other draft Directives, which are blocked in the Council, the Commission has initiated the procedures provided by the Agreement on social policy.

Contract duration is but one of the areas where there have been changes in the organization of work in Europe. Alongside traditional work practices, recent years have seen the growth of **new forms of work**: homeworking (out-workers), part-time work, job sharing, job splitting, being "on call", distance working... These new work forms have arisen as a result of new technologies, to accommodate companies' needs for flexibility and to meet the personal and family demands of many workers. However, they can obscure the situation of these workers if there is no written proof of the essential points of the employment relationship. Therefore, on 14 October 1991, the Council adopted a Directive relating to the drawing up of a written declaration regarding an employment relationship[3]. It stipulates that an employer shall notify an employee of the essential aspects of the contract or employment relationship by written declaration not later than two months after the commencement of employment. More specifically, they cover the place of work, the nature of the work and the category of employment, the duration of the employment relationship, the number of hours worked and paid holidays, pay and social rights.

A Directive concerning certain aspects of the **organization of working time** lays down a basic set of minimum provisions covering more particularly: the maximum weekly working time (48 hours), the minimum daily rest period (11 uninterrupted hours), the minimum period of paid leave (4 weeks), conditions relating to night work and the maximum period of such work (8 hours), and breaks in the event of prolonged periods of work[4]. Although, in theory, most workers in the European Union enjoy better social protection than is embodied in the European Directive, in practice no Member State implements all its provisions. The Directive will thus exercise a pressure on the Governments of the Member States to better guarantee the rights of workers.

With the progressive ageing of Europe's population, the **problems of retirement and post-retirement** become increasingly acute and require cooperation between Member States. In response to this, the Council adopted on November 26, 1990 a Decision on measures in

---

1   OJ C224, 08.09.1990.
2   OJ L206, 29.07.1991.
3   OJ L288, 18.10.1991.
4   OJ L307, 13.12.1993.

favour of the elderly, covering a range of initiatives to be implemented at Community level in the period from January 1, 1991 to December 31, 1993[1]. In a Resolution on **flexible retirement arrangements** the Council wants older people to continue to play an active part in society and maintain a link with the labour market[2]. It emphasizes that a flexible retirement policy could constitute a rational response to changing demographic patterns and to labour-market changes, but that flexible retirement arrangements are a matter for each Member State, bearing in mind the principle of subsidiarity. However, it calls on the Commission to promote exchanges of information and to examine whether measures taken by the Member States need to be completed.

The determination of wages is the sole responsibility of the Member Stages. Wages are, in fact, usually determined within the framework of collective bargaining or by reference to such bargaining by various practices in the Member States. The notion of a **guaranteed minimum wage** depends on different criteria in the Member States of the EU and its definition is left to them. However, the Commission and the Member States are expected to implement the engagement taken in the Community Charter of the Fundamental Social Rights that workers are assured of an **equitable remuneration** (which is a different notion from the minimum wage), meaning a reward for work done which is fair and sufficient to enable them to have a decent standard of living[3]. This would tend not only to guarantee a fundamental human right but also to avoid distortions of competition and to promote transparency in the European work market.

Equal treatment for men and women

Article 119 of the EEC Treaty, with which feminist movements in Europe are very familiar, stipulates that "each Member State shall during the first stage" of customs union "ensure and subsequently maintain the application of the principle that men and women should receive **equal pay for equal work**", which means "(a) that pay for the same work at piece rates shall be calculated on the basis of the same unit of measurement"; and "(b) that pay for work at time rates shall be the same for the same job". Article 119 defines pay as "the ordinary basic or minimum wage or salary and any other consideration, whether in cash or in kind, which the worker receives, directly or indirectly, in respect of his employment from his employer". The Treaty's concern for equality stems from the fact that competition between Community countries could be distorted by the employment in some of them of women who were paid less than men for the same job. Moreover, unequal conditions of employment and remuneration between the sexes could be eliminated only through Community action, as no country could go it alone with a reform which would be likely to alter conditions of competition to its detriment, in particular in industries employing large numbers of women.

In 1960 the Commission of the EEC addressed a Recommendation to the Member States for the implementation of Article 119, stating that, unlike Article 117 and 118, Article 119 did not merely set out objectives for the harmonization of other social policies, but laid down the obligation for them to act so that the principle of equal pay was applied. On the basis of that Recommendation, the Council adopted in 1961 a Resolution calling upon the Member States to take the measures necessary for the application of Article 119, with the deadline being deferred until 31 December 1964. Despite this Council Resolution, the original Member States did not hasten to take the legislative and administrative measures necessary in order to implement the principle of non-discrimination based on the sex. However, the Court of

---

1   OJ L28, 02.02.1991.
2   OJ C188, 10.07.1993.
3   OJ C248, 11.09.1993.

Justice in three famous judgments bearing the name of Gabrielle Defrenne, air hostess of Sabena, established that Article 119 had a horizontal direct effect and could be evoked in national courts, but that it needed interpretation by the Community legislative authority, particularly concerning indirect or disguised discriminations and equal working conditions other than payment[1].

The opinion of the Court was listened to by the Commission and finally by the Council in the social action programme of 1974[2]. Thus, on 10 February 1975 the Council adopted a Directive on the approximation of the laws of the Member States relating to the application of the **principle of equal pay** for men and women[3]. The purpose of that Directive was to eliminate any discrimination on grounds of sex as regards all aspects and conditions of pay. It called on the Member States to "cleanse" their legal provisions of all discriminatory aspects and to repeal all collective or contractual provisions that were at variance with the principle of equal pay. The social agreement concluded by eleven Member States in Maastricht stipulates that equal pay means that pay for the same work at piece rates shall be calculated on the basis of the same unit of measurement and that pay for work at time rates shall be the same for the same job. The Court of Justice, on its part, established that the employers' contributions in favour of a pension scheme should be considered as part of gross payment and that, in this context, the burden of proof of non-discrimination based on sex should be borne by the employer[4].

Equal pay was only one battle won in the war against discrimination against women which, according to a 1975 memorandum from the European Commission, was based on historical and cultural causes and was reinforced in practice by the education system, inadequate vocational guidance and the restrictive role imposed on women as wives and mothers. Thus, in 1976 the Council adopted a Directive on the implementation of the principle of equal treatment for men and women as regards **access to employment, vocational training and promotion**, and working conditions[5]. That Directive prohibits any indirect discrimination, i.e. the ways in which women are disadvantaged in relation to men in spite of apparently equal treatment, viz.: individual or collective contracts concerning employment and working conditions. For example, according to the ECJ, a discriminatory recruitment system is contrary to the 1976 Directive[6]. However, in the "Kalanke" case the Court held that national rules giving absolute and unconditional priority to women holding the same qualifications as their male counterparts would also entail sex-based discrimination[7]. Given that the Kalanke judgment created a great uncertainty as regards the legitimacy of quotas and other forms of positive action in favour of women, the Commission in a communication of March 1996 on

1   Judgments : of 25 May 1971, ECR 1971, p. 445; of 8 April 1976, ECR 1976, p. 455; and of 15 June 1978, ECR 1978, p. 1365.
2   OJ C13, 12.02.1974.
3   OJ L45, 19.02.1975 and OJ L1, 03.01.1994.
4   Judgment of 11 March 1981, Worringham, ECR 1981, p. 767 and judgment of 17 October 1989, ECR, p. 3199.
5   OJ L39, 14.02.1976.
6   Judgment of 30 June 1988, ECR 1988, p. 3559.
7   Judgment of 17 October 1995, case C-450/93, Kalanke, OJ C315, 25.11.1995.

the interpretation of the judgment considers that the Court has not condemned the implementation of positive action measures in general, but
only a rigid quota system under which there is no possibility of taking
particular individual circumstances into account. It, therefore, proposed
an amendment of the 1976 Directive in this sense[1]. A specific Directive
provides for the implementation of equal opportunity and also the protection of pregnant women working in the agricultural sector[2].

Two Council Directives concern the progressive implementations of
the principle of equal treatment for men and women: one in matters of
social security[3], the other in occupational social security schemes[4]. The
principle of equal opportunity means that there is no discrimination based
on sex especially as regards the scope and the conditions governing the
right to any work regime; the calculation of contributions; the calculation
of benefits and the conditions governing the duration and preservation of
pension rights. According to the ECJ, the provisions concerning social
security do not apply to women who have never been employed, those
who do not look for a job and those who have voluntarily stopped working[5]. On the contrary, again according to the Court, the principle of
non-discrimination applies indifferently to both men and women. Indeed,
in its "Barber" judgment the Court of Justice held that any sex discrimination in the granting or calculation of an occupational pension, notably the
differentiation of the age of pension according to the sex, is prohibited by
Article 119[6]. As the Barber judgment has important financial implications
for the professional schemes of social security, the Commission proposes,
for this reason as well, the amendment of the 1976 Directive, in order to
adapt it to the new interpretation of Article 119[7].

Following on from the action programme implementing the Charter
of the Fundamental Social Rights of Workers, the Council adopted a
Directive on the measures to be taken to improve the health and safety
protection of women workers who are pregnant, have just given birth or
are breast-feeding[8]. These measures on the one hand prohibit the dismiss-
ing of the women workers in question and their exposure to specific agents
or working conditions which could endanger their health and safety, and
on the other ensure the preservation of the rights derived from the employment contract and of maternity leave of at least fourteen consecutive
weeks. In addition, according to the ECJ, the non-recruitment of pregnant
women or the laying off of women who have a bad health condition after
having given birth are discriminatory and cannot be tolerated[9]. In another
connection the Council recommended to the Member States to take or to
encourage initiatives allowing parents to educate well their children[10].

---

1   COM (96) 88 and 93, 27 March 1996.
2   OJ L359, 19.12.1986.
3   OJ L6, 10.01.1979.
4   OJ L225, 12.08.1986.
5   Judgment of 27 June 1989, ECR 1989, p. 1963.
6   Judgment given on 17 May 1990, Case C-262/89, Barber v Guardian Royal Exchange, ECR 1990, 1889.
7   OJ C218, 23.08.1995.
8   OJ L348, 28.11.1992, see also the section on safety at work.
9   Judgments of 8 November 1990, ECR 1990, I-3941 and I-3979.
10   OJ L136, 08.05.1992.

Under these provisions any woman who feels that she is the subject of discrimination on grounds of sex or her matrimonial or family situation may bring proceedings before the national courts and enjoy, in so doing, legal protection against any attempt at reprisals on the part of her employer. She can directly, or through the Commission, bring the matter before the Court of Justice of the European Communities. According to the case-law of the Court of Justice, national courts must be consistent in ensuring the full effect of Community rules, where necessary disregarding any national provisions to the contrary[1]. Following the "Bilka" judgment, the national court must determine if a discriminatory practice is objectively justifiable on reasons other than the sex and if it is proportionate[2].

But equal treatment for men and women would lead to a high level of female unemployment as long as the occupational qualifications of the sexes were not the same, especially in an employment crisis situation. For that reason, the Commission adopted a Recommendation on vocational training for women[3] and the Council adopted Resolutions on action to combat unemployment amongst women[4] and on the reintegration and late integration of women into working life[5]. In that context, the Commission developed an initiative, known as **IRIS**, aimed at managing a network of demonstration projects concerning the vocational training of women[6]. An action programme has also existed since 1985 on equal opportunities for girls and boys in education[7]. As was mentioned above under the heading of employment, the Community initiative Employment-NOW is particularly aimed at the professional training of women. The great strides that have been made towards equal opportunities for girls and women in education have laid the foundation for a major step forward in the next decade.

On the basis of a Council Recommendation concerning the encouragement of positive actions in favour of women[8], the Community has implemented since 1982 four action programmes designed to promote equality of opportunity between men and women. The fourth action programme (1996-2000), adopted by the Council in December 1995, sets out to ensure that equal opportunities are taken more into consideration in defining and implementing the relevant policies at all levels - Community, national and regional[9]. The programme focuses on six objectives: mobilization of all the actors in economic and social life for the promotion of equal opportunities; promotion of equal opportunities in a changing economy; reconciliation of family life and work; promotion of a gender-balance in decision-making; rendering conditions more conducive to exercising equality rights; implementing, monitoring and assessing equal opportunities measures.

The gender balance of sexes in economic activities is likely to be deeply affected by structural economic change, in particular the growing role of services, the new technologies and the new flexibilities of work contracts that public and private enterprises are seeking. This is especially relevant to homeworking and teleworking, which offer significant opportunities for women, but under certain conditions. As is said in the Commission's White Paper of July 1994 on European Social Policy, positive and sustained action is needed to maximize the opportunities and reduce the dangers. A Resolution of the Council and of the representatives of the Member States on equal participation by women in an employment-intensive economic growth strategy aims at improving the flexibility of working hours, promoting a high level of skills among women and encouraging self-employment and the creation of businesses by women[10].

Responding to a Council Resolution, the Commission adopted, on November 27, 1991, a Recommendation combined with a Code of Good Practice on the protection of the dignity of women and men at work in which it invites the Member States to take steps with a view to improving the prevention of and fight against all forms of **sexual harassment**[11] . Another

1   Judgment given on 25 July 1991, Case C-345/89, Stoeckel, ECR 1991, I-4047.
2   Judgment of 13 May 1986, Bilka-Kaufhaus, ECR 1986, p. 1607.
3   OJ L342, 04.12.1987.
4   OJ C161, 21.06.1984.
5   OJ C333, 28.12.1988.
6   OJ C184, 14.07.1988.
7   OJ C166, 05.07.1985.
8   OJ L331, 19.12.1984.
9   OJ C306, 17.11.1995.
10   OJ C368, 23.12.1994.
11   OJ C157, 27.06.1990 and OJ L49, 24.02.1992.

Council Resolution aims at a balanced participation of women and men in decision-making in the political, economic, social and cultural fields[1]. A Resolution of the Council and the representatives of the governments of the Member States calls on the latter to take action aimed at promoting and disseminating a diversified and realistic image of men and women in advertising and the media[2]. More generally, the Commission proposes incorporating equal opportunities for women and men into all Community policies and activities[3].

Measures in favour of the disabled

The disabled are another category of persons to which the European Union pays particular attention. The Community is home to some 30 million people who have a physical or mental handicap making their socio-economic integration problematic. The first action programme, adopted by the Council in 1981, was directed towards the economic and social integration of disabled people. In that connection, on 24 July 1986 the Council adopted a Recommendation on the employment of disabled people[4], and the Commission established a databank concerning the problems of and technical aids for the disabled in the Community (**HANDYNET**).

In 1987, the Council adopted an action programme to promote the integration of handicapped children into ordinary schools[5]. In 1993, it launched the second Community action programme for disabled people (**HELIOS**), the main objective of which is the establishment of a coherent overall policy based on the innovative experiences of the Member States as regards training, occupational rehabilitation, economic and social integration and the autonomy of handicapped people[6]. HELIOS has set up a Community network of training and occupational rehabilitation centres and experiences. The aim of this programme is to give handicapped people maximum autonomy in such areas as mobility, transport, access to buildings and public services and accommodation. The HANDYNET system, which has been developed as part of the HELIOS programme gives priority to providing information on technical aids for the handicapped ("Handyaids")[7].

A Resolution adopted by the Council and by the Education Ministers meeting within the Council seeks to step up the promotion of full integration of handicapped children and young people into the ordinary education system, through developing cooperation between all relevant bodies and tapping the potential offered by new technologies in the educational field[8]. The Community initiative Employment-HORIZON, in accordance with the objectives of the Structural Funds, strives to ease the integration of handicapped people and certain disadvantaged groups through the provision of correctly adapted training[9].

In the framework of the research programme on applied technology, the Council launched, in September 1993, a Community technology initiative for disabled and elderly

1   OJ C168, 04.07.1995.
2   OJ C296, 10.11.1995.
3   COM (96) 67, 21 February 1996.
4   OJ L225, 12.08.1986.
5   OJ C211, 08.08.1987.
6   OJ L56, 09.03.1993 and OJ L316, 09.12.1994.
7   OJ L393, 30.12.1989.
8   OJ C162, 03.07.1990.
9   See the heading above on Community intiatives on employment.

people (TIDE)[1]. It seeks to promote the development and supply of technical aids, the pooling of information and experience in this area, and the application of new technology to facilitate communication, mobility and employment for the disabled.

Action to combat poverty

Another category of people which attracts the EU's attention is that of the economically and socially disadvantaged. The standard of living has certainly improved in every Community State since its inception. Economic expansion and social progress have made it possible to attain a major part of the objective of the Treaty of Rome of promoting improved living conditions in the States of the Community so as to make possible the harmonization of those conditions while the improvement is being maintained. But each Member State still has pockets of poverty characterized by very low income owing to lack of education, inadequate professional qualifications, poor living conditions, ill health and a socio-cultural environment lacking in economic motivation. It is estimated that the income of about 15% of the European Union's population is less than half the average income of the country in which they live.

Article 2, point 2 of the **Agreement on Social Policy** gives the Union a specific role in supporting and complementing the activities of the Member States as regards the integration of persons excluded from the labour market. In compliance with the principle of subsidiarity however, initiatives to combat poverty and social exclusion are primarily the preserve of the Member States' local, regional and national authorities. The European Union can only complete and stimulate the work of the Member States in these fields by promoting the exchange of information, the comparison of experiences, the transfer of know-how and the demonstration of the validity of the projects based on partnerships. To this end, the Commission put forward a proposal for a medium-term action programme[2].

The most specific Community action to improve living conditions is in the sectors covered by the ECSC Treaty. The Commission funds, with the assistance of intermediary banks, the construction, modernization and, exceptionally, purchase of subsidized housing for employees in the coal and steel industries[3]. That activity is based both on the social concern to improve workers' accommodation and the desire to increase productivity by accommodating workers near the workplace and, moreover, in regions in economic decline.

In the framework of the EC Treaty the Community has launched numerous initiatives to help combat poverty and social exclusion. Since 1987, it has distributed food surpluses within the framework of winter aid campaigns for the most needy organized by non-governmental organizations (NGOs). It has supported the work of the European Anti-Poverty Network and has established a permanent dialogue with this group. It has channelled the resources of the Structural Funds towards the development of the less favoured regions and towards the vocational integration of the most vulnerable groups of society. As of 1994, the Fund's Objective 4 specifically covers the vocational integration of socially excluded persons. The Community initiative on "employment and human resources" can also make a major contribution to combating exclusion. The URBAN initiative, on its part, can help in a number of inner-city neighbourhoods where an accumulation of exclusion factors exists.

1   OJ L240, 25.09.1993.
2   OJ C34, 02.02.1994.
3   OJ C34, 04.02.1993.

Safety and health at work

The Community has for a long time been involved in the area of worker safety. The ECSC and Euratom Treaties assigned tasks to the Community institutions in this field. Article 46 of the **ECSC Treaty** called upon the High Authority (Commission) to "obtain the information it requires to assess the possibilities for improving working conditions and living standards for workers in the industries within its province, and the threats to those standards". Article 55 called upon it to "promote technical and economic research relating" inter alia "to occupational safety" in those industries. ECSC "social research" has developed from multiannual programmes decided upon by the Commission in the fields of hygiene and safety in mines, the effort to combat pollution at the workplace and ergonomics[1]. A safety and Health Commission for the Mining and Other Extractive Industries prepares opinions and makes proposals to the Governments in those fields[2].

By virtue of the powers conferred on it by the **Euratom Treaty** (Articles 2 and 30 to 39), the Community has been able to implement an efficient policy for the protection of workers and the general public against the risks linked with radioactivity. The Council Directive of 1 June 1976 laying down the revised basic standards for the health protection of the general public and workers against the dangers of ionizing radiation strengthened and improved the practical organization of radiation protection in the Community[3]. That was highly appropriate at a time when public opinion was beginning to worry about the consequences of radioactivity for the environment and human health. In the health field, a Council Directive (Euratom) of 3 September 1984 lays down basic measures for the radiation protection of persons undergoing medical examination or treatment[4].

For the remainder of the economy covered by the EEC Treaty, it is the field of road transport, characterized by very special working conditions, which has served as a bridgehead for measures to humanize work[5]. In other fields the social action programme of January 1974 had to be awaited for Member States to begin targeting a general improvement in working conditions. That was when they decided to set up an Advisory Committee on Safety, Hygiene and Health Protection at Work[6]. In June 1978 the Community adopted a first programme of action on safety and health at work, and on 27 February 1984 it adopted a second programme[7]. On the basis of those programmes, Directives were adopted concerning the protection of workers from various risks, viz.: exposure to chemical, physical and biological agents at work[8], the major accident hazards of certain industrial activities[9], exposure to metallic lead and its ionic compounds at work[10], exposure to asbestos at work[11] and, finally, exposure to noise at work[12].

After Article 118A of the Treaty, which was added by the Single Act, had increased the Community's authority as regards the health and safety of the work force, in 1987 the Commission adopted a new programme, which was ratified by a Council Resolution on 21 December 1987, on the safety, hygiene and health at the place of work[13]. At the same time the Commission set up a mutual information system for legislative and ad-

---

1   OJ C257, 14.10.1986.
2   OJ 28, 31.08.1957.
3   OJ L187, 12.07.1976 and OJ L246, 17.09.1980.
4   OJ L265, 05.10.1984. See also the chapter on energy.
5   See the chapter on transport.
6   OJ L185, 09.07.1974.
7   OJ C67, 08.03.1984.
8   OJ L327, 03.12.1980 and OJ L356, 24.12.1988.
9   OJ L230, 05.08.1982.
10 OJ L247, 23.08.1982.
11 OJ L263, 24.09.1983 and OJ L206, 29.07.1991.
12 OJ L137, 24.05.1986.
13 OJ C28, 03.02.1988.

ministrative acts of the Member States concerning health and security of workers at the place of work[1].

As part of this new programme, on 12 June 1989 the Council adopted a **Framework Directive** on the introduction of measures to encourage improvements in the safety and health of workers at the workplace[2]. This Directive lays down three main principles: the employer's general obligation to guarantee the workers' health and safety in all work-related aspects, in particular by preventing professional risks, by keeping the work force informed and by training; the obligation of every worker to contribute to the health and safety of himself and others by using the work facilities correctly and respecting the safety instructions; the absence or limited liability for employers for things caused by abnormal unforeseen circumstances or exceptional events. By laying down the main principles concerning health and safety at work in the Community, the 1989 Directive is the foundation on which all other directives on the matter are superimposed.

This is particularly the case as regards the individual Directives laying down minimum requirements on: workplaces[3]; work equipment and machinery and personal protective equipment[4]; the manual handling of loads involving some kind of risk - notably of dorsal/lumbar damage - for workers and work using display screens[5]; exposure during work to carcinogenic agents and biological agents[6]; minimum health and safety requirements on temporary and mobile sites[7]; safety and/or health signs in the workplace[8]; the protection of workers in the mineral-extracting industries by forging[9]; and the protection of workers in surface and underground mineral-extracting industries[10]. Workers having an interim or specific duration work relation must enjoy the same health and safety conditions as the other workers of an undertaking[11]. One Directive which is as much part of the 1989 general Directive on the improvement of workers' health and safety as of the action programme on equal opportunity for men and women is the one aimed at improving the health and safety of pregnant workers and workers who have recently given birth or are breastfeeding[12]. These Directives represent major steps forward, even in the Member States with the highest standards.

In 1994, the Council approved a Regulation establishing a European Agency for Health and Safety at Work, based in Bilbao[13]. Its main tasks are the collection and dissemination of technical, scientific and economic information on health and safety at work, the promotion of and support for exchanges of information and experience between Member States, the provision of information necessary for the Commission in the preparation and evaluation of legislation and the establishment of a network linking Member States' national networks.

The **fourth Community programme** concerning safety, hygiene and health at work (1996-2000) aims to consolidate and implement existing legislation, to evaluate the impact on safety and health of other Community policies, and to develop awareness-raising activities and other non-legislative measures, including: preparation of guidance notes and core information material; enhancement of information, education and training; investigation of

---

1   OJ L183, 14.07.1988.
2   OJ L183, 29.06.1989.
3   OJ L393, 30.12.1989.
4   OJ L393, 30.12.1989 and OJ C246, 22.09.1995.
5   OJ L156, 21.06.1990.
6   OJ L196, 26.07.1990, OJ L374, 31.12.1990 and OJ L155, 06.07.1995.
7   OJ L245, 26.08.1992.
8   Ibid.
9   OJ L348, 28.11.1992.
10 OJ L404, 31.12.1992.
11 OJ L206, 29.07.1991.
12 OJ L348, 28.11.1992. See the heading above on the equal treatment of men and women.
13 OJ L216, 20.08.1994 and OJ L156, 07.07.1995.

key problem areas such as violence at the workplace, stress and specific measures in favour of women; a new SAFE (Safety action for Europe) programme aimed at providing support for projects designed to improve working conditions, disseminate information and improve knowledge of European legislation, with particular reference to SMEs[1].

Public health protection

Significant links exist between public health and social and environmental policies. These include the adverse effects of poverty, unemployment and social exclusion on health; the increasing pressures on health and social protection systems caused by demographic changes, notably the ageing of the population; the role of preventive and rehabilitative health programmes in fostering social integration; the impact of environmental conditions on public health; and the specific health problems and needs arising from increased mobility within the Union and migration into it.

Public health was brought fully into the action scope of the European Union by Article 129 EC, added in Maastricht, which states that health protection requirements must form a constituent part of the Community's other policies. This Article invites the Community to contribute towards ensuring a high level of human health protection by encouraging cooperation between the Member States and by fostering cooperation with third countries and the competent international organizations. Community action is directed towards the prevention of diseases, in particular the major health scourges, including drug dependence, by promoting research into their causes and their transmission, as well as health information and education. Incentive measures are adopted by the Council acting in accordance with the procedure referred to in Article 189b (co-decision with the European Parliament).

To accompany the entry into force of the Treaty on European Union, the Commission, at the request of the Council, laid down the **framework for action in the field of public health**[2]. Referring to the communication of the Commission, the Council identified priority areas for action such as: cancer; drug dependence; AIDS and other transmissible diseases; health promotion; education and training; disease surveillance; and the collection of reliable health data[3]. Other Council Resolutions aim at the integration of health protection requirements in Community policies and at the impact on human health of the free movement of medicinal products[4]. In the framework for action in the field of public health, the Parliament and the Council have adopted a programme of action on health promotion, information, education and training (1996-2000)[5]. Its aim is to promote the "health promotion" approach in national health and to encourage the adoption of healthy lifestyles and behaviour.

---

1   COM (95) 282, 12 July 1995.
2   COM (93) 559, 24.11.1993.
3   OJ C165, 17.06.1994.
4   OJ C350, 30.12.1995.
5   OJ L95, 16.04.1996.

On the basis of Article 118a of the Treaty, which was added by the Single Act, the Community had already taken certain initiatives in the field of public health protection. As regards acquired immune deficiency syndrome (**AIDS**), the Member States decided, first, to introduce a procedure for the periodical and rapid exchange of epidemiological data at Community level and machinery for the exchange of information on national measures taken[1]. Then, in the framework of programme against AIDS they decided on the establishment of an epidimiology network in the Community[2]. The programme of Community action on the prevention of AIDS and certain other communicable diseases (1996-2000) focuses on information, training, education, surveillance and monitoring of communicable diseases, support for persons with HIV/AIDS and combating discrimination[3].

The third action plan to **combat cancer** ensures, until 2000, the continuity of the programme launched in 1987 and is intended to reduce mortality and morbidity due to cancer[4]. In the framework of that programme the Council adopted a Resolution on banning smoking in places open to the public[5], a Directive concerning the labelling of tobacco products[6] and a Directive concerning the maximum tar content of cigarettes was adopted by the Council on May 17, 1990[7]. A Directive is being prepared laying down restrictions on the advertising of tobacco products in the press and by means of bills and posters, as well as another completely prohibiting television advertising of tobacco. The attack on smoking of the Community, following that of the United States, is sending shivers down the spine of the international tobacco industry.

For the **prevention of drug dependance,** the Member States agreed, in 1987, to set up a customs cooperation. The European Monitoring Centre for Drugs and Drug Addiction was established in Lisbon in 1994[8]. The Community action programme on the prevention of drug dependence (1996-2000) aims to help in combating drugs by encouraging cooperation between Member States, supporting their action and promoting coordination of their policies and programs with a view to preventing dependence linked to the use of narcotics and psychotropic substances and associated use of other products for similar purposes[9].

Appraisal and outlook

Considering that it started off virtually without resources, the Community's social policy has covered a lot of ground. Its greatest success is undoubtedly the achievement of a common labour market, which we examined in the chapter on the common market. By virtue of the Community regulations adopted in their favour, migrant workers originating in the poorest regions of the Community enjoy fair conditions compared with nationals of the host country with regard to access to employment, social security, the education and vocational training of their children, living and working conditions and the right to exercise union rights.

Although the employment policy which the Community implemented as from the mid-1970s did not succeed in eliminating the scourge of unemployment, it nevertheless provided a framework for the Member States' policies on the matter in such a way as to obviate disastrous

1   OJ C197, 27.07.1988 and OJ C329, 31.12.1990.
2   OJ C15, 18.01.1994.
3   OJ L95, 16.04.1996.
4   Ibid.
5   OJ C189, 26.07.1989.
6   OJ L359, 08.12.1989.
7   OJ L137, 30.05.1990.
8   OJ L36, 12.02.1993 and OJ L341, 30.12.1994.
9   OJ C34, 07.02.1996.

antagonism, especially for the poorest. It also managed to improve the conditions of the unemployed, in particular the most vulnerable, young people and women, by contributing to the financing of vocational training programmes targeted on them. As a result of the numerous reforms of the European Social Fund, in particular that of 1988 which doubled its resources, the education and vocational training policy now has an efficient instrument which can come to the assistance of the neediest layers of the population, in particular those in the regions whose development is lagging behind.

The **social bedrock** which is thus being built is indispensable for the construction of the single market and even more so for the construction of economic and monetary union. No progress can be made towards the latter if there is not at the same time progress towards social union, which will level out the differences in the social achievements and rates of social progress of the Member States. Otherwise the fears of some of "social dumping" and the fears of others of "permanent handicap" will become increasingly strong. In order to calm these fears, the European Union must strengthen its **economic and social cohesion**, conceived as the fruit of an increase in the capacity for endogenous development rather than a mere redistribution of income. Thus on the one hand the Structural Funds can contribute to approximating the development opportunities of the EU's Member States and regions, notably as regards infrastructure and access to vocational training. On the other hand, the working conditions and representation of workers must be examined, using consultation and legislation. Making optimum use of the gains through an active employment policy and adequate vocational training, the concrete achievement of the free movement of persons, improved protection of the health and safety of workers at the workplace, solidarity and the social dialogue are the objectives of the social bedrock of the internal market, the essential elements of which feature in the Community Charter of fundamental social rights.

It must be said, however, that in the single market context, the Community is making slower progress in the social field than in the economic one. This is due in part to the fact that although the Single European Act introduced the rule of majority voting for most of the harmonization Directives required for the completion of the internal market, it upheld the rule of unanimity in the field of social legislation. As a consequence, a Member State opposed to interventionism in the social field can block a great many of the Commission's proposals in this area. The Maastricht agreement opened the way to a reinforcement of the Community's social dimension and an increase in measures in such important areas as social exclusion, the disabled, poverty, and integration of migrants from non-member countries.

The United Kingdom will have to assess if it wants and if it can stay isolated on this matter which is of primary importance to its workers and Trade Unions. However, the rift should not be exaggerated. Measures have already been taken within the Community context - and therefore with the participation of the United Kingdom - concerning the improvement of the living and working conditions of workers. Such solidarity can be reproduced in the future.

After all, the United Kingdom, like all the other countries in the Community, will have to follow the German model if they wish to address the challenge of industrial change. Unless they want to specialize in sectors of activity with low added value, the public and private managers in the countries of the Community will have to ensure that their employees receive continuing training and are part of every stage of technological change. In the final analysis, the high productivity of European workers - a product of motivation and education - is the Community's only weapon when confronted with the ever more cutthroat competition from the newly industrialized countries with low labour costs.

Indeed, the Community has to address major industrial change both of a quantitative and qualitative nature: the globalization of production and markets, the acceleration of technological change and changes of production systems. These factors as a whole are having a profound effect on the Community's industrial scene, and a significant impact on employment and the dynamic of human resources in the Community. The Community's social policy must anticipate the changes in employment and in future requirements for qualifications, it must adapt workers' qualifications to future changes and minimize the economic and social cost of changes already occurring. In the final analysis, if the Community's international competitivity is to be safeguarded in order to reduce and prevent unemployment, the Member States and the Community must increase their work forces' competitivity by adopting effective social policies based on motivation and qualifications.

While wealth creation is essential for social progress, this progress cannot be founded simply on the basis of the competitiveness of economies, but also on the efficiency of European society as a whole. This efficiency, on its part, can only be based on a well-educated and highly motivated and adaptable working population. Economic and social progress must, therefore, go hand in hand to preserve the shared values which form the basis of the European social model. These include democracy and pluralism, respect of individual rights, free collective bargaining, the market economy, equality of opportunity for all, social welfare and solidarity.

Bibliography on social policy

□ ARCHER W. H., RABAN A. J., *Working in the European Union. A Guide for Graduate Recruiters and Job-Seekers*, EURES, European Commission, OOPEC, Luxembourg 1995.

□ CARRAUD Michel, *Droit social européen*, Publisud, Paris, 1994.

□ CEDEFOP, *Training and the Labour Market*, OOPEC, Luxembourg, 1995.

□ COMMISSION EUROPÉENNE, *Livre vert sur la politique sociale européenne; options pour l'Union*, OPOCE, Luxembourg, 1993.

  − *Politique sociale européenne; une voie à suivre pour l'Union (Livre Blanc)*, OPOCE, Luxembourg, 1994.

  − *L'éducation et la formation face aux défis technologiques, industriels et sociaux: premières réflexions*, COM (94) 528 du 23 novembre 1994.

  − *Intégration européenne et marché de l'emploi*, OPOCE, Luxembourg, 1994.

  − *L'emploi en Europe*, OPOCE, Luxembourg, 1995.

  − *La protection sociale en Europe*, OPOCE, Luxembourg, 1996.

□ DREZE Jacques, *Pour l'emploi, la croissance et l'Europe*, De Boeck-Wesmael, Louvain-la-Neuve, 1995.

□ EUROPEAN COMMISSION, *Your Social Security Rights when Moving within the European Union*, OOPEC, Luxembourg, 1995.

□ EUROPEAN SOCIAL OBSERVATORY, *Economic and Monetary Union and Social Protection*, European Social Observatory, Brussels, 1995.

□ FRAZIER Carole, *L'éducation et la Communauté européenne*, CNRS Éditions, Paris, 1995.

□ GOLD Michael (ed.), *The Social Dimension. Employment Policy in the European Community*, Macmillan Press Ltd., London, 1993.

□ GUERY Gabriel, *Vivre l'Europe sociale*, Bordas/Dunod, Paris, 1994.

□ JACOBS Antoine, ZEIGEN Hans, *European Labour Law and Social Policy*, Tilburg University Press, Tilburg, 1993.

□ MOUSSIS Nicholas, *Access to Social Europe: Guide to Community Legislation and Programmes*, European Study Service, Rixensart, 1994.

□ SEUL Otmar (sous la dir. de), *Participation par délégation et participation directe des salariés dans l'entreprise*, Chlorofeuilles, Nanterre, 1994.

□ STRAUSS Sabine, "Enseignement et construction européenne", *L'Europe en Formation*, N° 299, Hiver 1995-1996, pp. 25-34.

□ TELO Mario (sous la dir. de), *Quelle Union sociale européenne? Acquis institutionnel, acteurs et défis*, Éditions de l'Université de Bruxelles, Bruxelles, 1994.

□ TEYSSIE Bernard, *Code de droit social européen*, 2e édition, Éditions Litec, Paris, 1994.

6. TAXATION

The EEC Treaty was very cautious as regards tax harmonization. What it wanted above all was the introduction and observance of the rule of fiscal neutrality in Community trade, i.e. equal tax treatment for domestic production and imports from member countries. Beyond that, the Treaty merely invited the Commission to examine how turnover taxes could be harmonized. The Treaty did not call for any harmonization or other Community action with regard to direct taxes.

The fiscal objectives of the Treaty were attained rapidly. Cumulative multi-stage taxes, which did not guarantee fiscal neutrality, were replaced by a new turnover tax, value added tax, and the structures of that tax were harmonized in all Community Member States, old and new. The principle of fiscal neutrality was thus guaranteed, but at the price of maintaining tax barriers, which were necessary for the collection of VAT and excise duties in the country of destination of goods.

In the single market goods must be able to move completely freely, and to achieve this, tax has to be imposed on them in the country of origin or in that of destination. This led, at the end of the 1980s, to the alignment of VAT and excise duties. At the same time the harmonization of direct taxes has begun, especially those on companies and savings, in order to make the growth of companies and capital movement independent of tax considerations. Tax harmonization should henceforth be regarded as a coherent entity and should progress at the same tempo as economic integration. Basically the approximation of the Member States' tax systems can be completed only through the approximation of their economies.

Economic and legal framework

Having economic and social structures which differed in many ways, the States which were to form the Community also had rather dissimilar tax systems, both as regards financial policy, that is to say in particular the composition of the tax burden as between direct and indirect taxes, and the technical organization of taxation. In the short term there was no question of tackling those disparities themselves. It was a matter of little by little trying to level out the underlying economic and social differences before aiming at the final objective of Community fiscal policy, viz. : making a single fiscal territory of the European Community.

But pending such unification, if the Member States of a common market had absolute freedom in the fiscal field, they could very quickly replace the customs barriers to trade by tax barriers; they could in fact, while lowering their customs duties in accordance with the Community timetable, raise their domestic fiscal duties in such a way that the total burden on imports remained unchanged. It was therefore necessary that indirect taxes, in particular turnover tax, have no influence on intra-Community trade flows. In other words, **fiscal neutrality** between domestic production and imports from the partner countries was needed. To secure fiscal neutrality in a common market the turnover tax of the country of origin or of the country of destination would have to be imposed on all goods.

If the rule of **the tax of the country of origin** were adopted, there would be a danger of creating trade flows based artificially on the difference in the taxes rather than on the difference in comparative costs, but there would be pressure on the Member States to approximate the rates of their taxes, and fiscal frontiers could be removed, as imported goods would already have paid taxes at the rate of the country of origin. If, on the other hand, the system of the **tax of the country of destination** were applied, production could be concentrated where the comparative economic advantages were greatest rather than where taxation would be lower, as all products in competition on a market, whether of domestic origin or imported, would be uniformly subject to the tax on consumption in force on that market. However, under that system the tax barriers would have to be maintained in order to levy the taxes of the country of destination on imported goods and the Member States would not be encouraged to approximate the rates of their taxes. This was the price which the founder Member States, in light of the low level of integration of their economies, paid in opting for the system of taxation in the country of destination.

Even if the system of the tax of the country of destination were imposed uniformly, fiscal neutrality could still not be ensured if some countries in the common market applied a system of **cumulative multi-stage turnover tax**, which was the case in five of the original six Community countries. Under that system tax was levied on the product for each transaction and therefore its total size was not only a function of its rate but also of the number of transactions which had been carried out up to the stage of final distribution. A product was therefore taxed less heavily if it was manufactured by a vertically integrated undertaking than where it was manufactured and distributed by various small undertakings. It is immediately evident that such a system would distort competition in the common market by favouring integrated large undertakings originating in certain member countries or third countries. In addition, such a system would not make possible genuine fiscal neutrality in international trade, as it is very difficult to monitor each product at every stage of manufacture and distribution in order to ascertain the exact amount of the tax it has borne.

Fiscal neutrality

Recognizing this difficulty, Article 97 of the EEC Treaty allowed Member States which levied a turnover tax calculated on a cumulative multi-stage tax system to establish average rates for products or groups of products in the case of internal taxation imposed by them on imported products or of repayments allowed by them on exported products. But the Treaty did not provide any rule for establishing average rates. It merely prohibited the application of such average rates from resulting in products imported from the other Member States being liable to taxation in excess of that imposed on similar domestic products (Article 95) and from resulting in the repayment of taxation on products exported to Member States at a rate that exceeds the taxation actually imposed (Article 96). Those were at liberty to establish the average rates of their multi-stage taxes.

It quickly became clear that on the entry into force of the Treaty the States which applied the cumulative multi-stage tax system were below the ceilings, as they did not, on average, repay as much turnover tax as that actually levied on exported products and did not, on average, apply as high a tax on imported products as that applied to similar domestic products. They therefore had room to manoeuvre to improve the competitive position of their undertakings in line with progress on customs dismantling. Furthermore, they could easily exceed the ceilings laid down by the Treaty as it was virtually impossible to establish accurately what tax had been imposed directly or indirectly on similar domestic products.

Having been invited, in Article 99 of the Treaty, to consider how the laws of the Member States concerning turnover taxes could be harmonized, soon as the EEC Treaty entered into force, the Commission submitted to the Council, in June 1964, a proposal for a first Directive on the harmonization of legislation of Member States concerning turnover taxes. It was in reality a matter of the general use in all Member States of a common system of **tax on value added**. It was adopted by the Council on 11 April 1967, together with a Directive on the structure and detailed rules for applying the common VAT system[1].

A major step was thus made towards **fiscal neutrality** in the common market, which however could not be fully attained unless all indirect taxes were harmonized. In fact, there were still very important specific taxes on consumption, known as **excise duties**, whose structures and levels varied greatly in the countries of the Community. Those differences stemmed not only from historic reasons, but also from economic and social ones. Given that the main raison d'être of excise duties was their yield, States had a tendency to impose higher levels on certain products of major consumption, and those products were not necessarily the same in every State. Some goods were regarded as luxury products in some States but not in others. Lastly, if a Member State of the Single Market taxed heavily certain products which are dangerous to health, such as alcoholic drinks, in order to restrain their consumption, whereas another country preferred to attack other products, such as tobacco products, illegal traffics might develop between the two countries frustrating the objectives of both.

Be that as it may, the differences between Member States in excise duty structures could give rise to significant disturbances in conditions to competition, especially where products heavily taxed in one State mainly came from the others. In such instance consumption naturally moved towards alternative products, as is the case with wine and beer. In the interest of the proper functioning of the common market and the attainment of the Community agricultural, energy and transport objectives, the structures of those taxes needed to be harmonized. That was the second priority task which the Commission tackled during the '70s, but with much less success than it had in the field of turnover taxes, harmonization of the structures of which continued during the '70s and '80s with the adoption of several directives establishing the uniform basis of assessment of VAT.

Taxation and conditions of competition

Just behind the harmonization of the structures of all indirect taxes came, of course, the harmonization of their rates. It is obvious that in order to create completely impartial conditions of competition in the common market a common system of taxes on consumption is needed, comprising

---

1   OJ 71, 14.04.1967.

not only the same structures, but also very approximate levels, indeed standard wherever possible. In effect, the different rates of taxes could have a different influence on the consumption of various products in the common market and could distort the conditions of competition between the undertakings of the Member States. Where the tax burden on a product is lower in one country than in another, if the other **conditions of competition** are identical in both countries, the undertakings which manufacture the product in the first country are in a much more favourable competitive position than their counterparts in the second country, as they can have increased demand and high profits in their principal market.

Moreover, there are grounds for questioning whether, in spite of the harmonization of tax structures and the alignment of indirect taxation, fiscal neutrality exists, when some States have much more recourse than others to direct taxes not eligible for equalization at frontiers. It is true that such States tax the products of their partners less than do those which have more recourse to indirect taxes, but the terms of trade and productivity offset to a large extent the fiscal disparities of Member States' companies. Moreover, States clearly apply certain categories of tax on the basis of historic habit, sociological structure and economic conditions. Some mainly apply indirect taxes, which are easily collected, whilst others have greater recourse to direct taxation, which is fairer from the social viewpoint. The European Union States will for a long time to come have to have **sufficient autonomy in the tax field** so that they have enough room for manoeuvre to act in the light of their economic situations. Harmonization of direct taxes can therefore only be a long-term objective of European tax policy.

However, **some harmonization of direct taxation** is necessary for several reasons. First, so that conditions of competition are not distorted in the European Union, production costs and the profitability of invested capital must not be influenced too differently from country to country by taxation. Thus, lower company taxation in one State than in the others is tantamount to a subsidy which is incompatible with the common market. Capital movements and the siting of undertakings can also be influenced by the disparate levels of direct taxation in the countries of the EU and by the more or less strict application of the rule of deduction at source. Countries which have high taxes on company revenue or which do not give favourable treatment to reinvested profits may, if there is no monetary equalization, lose capital to countries in which company taxation is more favourable. Such capital movements are undesirable, as they do not lead to optimum use of financial resources and production factors in the EU.

Tax barriers, such as the taxation of an appreciation of assets in the event of a merger or double taxation in the event of deduction at source, impede **concentrations**, which are necessary to enable Community small and medium-sized undertakings to adapt to the dimensions of the common market and to make them competitive on the world market. Disparities in direct taxes work to the advantage of **multinational undertakings**, as they are better able to concentrate their profits in the State which taxes them least. For that purpose they use holding companies, transfer prices within the group and international debenture loans. The holding companies are established in countries with low taxation, known as tax havens. They group, by various means, a large proportion of the profits of their subsidiaries established in countries with normal taxation and reinvest them in the same or other companies. One means of concentrating profits in low-taxation countries is the practice of transfer prices between units within the same group, which can vary greatly from market prices.

It can be seen from the foregoing that the requirements for tax harmonization increase together with progress towards economic integration. Whilst fiscal neutrality in a customs union is ensured by the harmonization of the structures of turnover tax and excise duty, in a common market and even more so in an economic and monetary union gradual harmonization of the levels of those taxes and even of direct taxation are necessary in addition.

Indirect taxation

Indirect taxes are those on turnover, production or consumption of goods and services - regarded as components of cost prices and selling prices - which are collected without regard to the achievement of profits, or indeed income, but which are deductible when determining profits. Customs duties are a form of indirect taxation. That is why, as a result of their removal in a common market, Member States are more tempted to replace customs barriers to trade by fiscal barriers, i.e. by internal duties. That danger was foreseen in the EEC Treaty, Articles 95 to 98 of which contained provisions to obviate it, together with Article 99, which called upon the Commission to consider how the legislation of the various Member States concerning turnover taxes, excise duties and other forms of indirect taxation, including countervailing measures applicable to trade between Member States, could be harmonized in the interest of the common market.

Indeed, the Commission assisted by two committees of experts, examined the harmonization of indirect taxation and, particularly, of **cumulative multi-stage taxes**. That system, which was practised by five of the six countries of the Community as originally constituted, had the specific characteristic of levying turnover tax on raw materials, semi-processed products, component parts and finished products each time they were sold by one firm to another. The consequence was that the taxes on the various stages of production of a product burdened its consumer price all the more inasmuch as it had taken numerous transactions to manufacture and distribute it. That is why, in the countries which applied that system of indirect taxation, there was a tendency to integrate vertically every stage from the production of the raw material up to and including the retail trade in a product. That was an incitement to an artificial concentration of undertakings, as such a concentration was often sought not for its genuine economic merits, but for its tax advantages. It goes without saying that the integrated undertaking, which enjoyed advantages under the tax system, could oust its small competitors from the market.

Moreover, given the inherent complexity of cumulative taxes, the fixing of average levels for compensation measures at frontiers in respect of such taxes did not rule out the unfavourable treatment of imports and the favourable treatment of exports. As a result, the Commission was already convinced, at the beginning of the 60s, that the only radical solution to the problems arising from cumulative multi-stage taxes was the adoption by all Member States of a system of turnover taxes which did not distort conditions of competition either within a country or between Member States. Such a system was the tax on value added.

Value added tax

When it was adopted for the first time, in France in 1954, value added tax (VAT) was regarded as merely another tax on turnover or on consumption and did not attract the attention of other countries. It was only from 1962, with the publication of two reports ordered by the Commission recommending its adoption by all Member States, that its interest for the Community was understood. Acting on the basis of Commission proposals, the Council adopted on 11 April 1967 two Directives on the harmonization of legislation of Member States concerning turnover taxes[1]. Those two Directives laid the groundwork for the common value added tax system and a third one, adopted in 1969, introduced it in the tax systems of the Member States[2].

According to Article 2 of the first Directive of 1967, VAT is a **general tax on consumption**, i.e. a tax on all expenditure on goods and services. The tax is levied at every stage of an economic activity on the value added at each stage. It is paid by all those involved in the production and distribution of a product or service, but it is not an element in the costs of those intermediaries and does not appear as an item of expenditure in their returns, as it is not they who bear the tax, but the end consumer.

The tax is **proportional to the price** of the products and services irrespective of the number of transactions which have taken place at the stages preceding that to which it is applied. At the time of each transaction, the sum of VAT, calculated on the price of the good or service, is reduced by the sum of the taxes previously paid on the cost of the various components of the cost price. The total sum which changes hands at each stage in the production or distribution includes the VAT paid up to that point, but the amount of the tax is recovered at each sale, except for the final sale to the **final consumer**, who purchases the product or service for his private use. The tax is paid to the State by the vendor in each transaction. However, the latter does not bear the burden of the VAT, as his purchaser has advanced the full amount of the VAT to him. Tax paid at previous stages, on deliveries made or services rendered to the taxable person, and the tax paid on imports, is deductible from the turnover tax of that taxable person.

Given this **deductibility of taxes already paid**, VAT is neutral from the point of view of domestic competition, i.e. it does not favour vertically integrated undertakings, as did the cumulative multi-stage taxes. But VAT is also neutral from the point of view of international competition, since it cannot favour domestic products. In fact, even before the 1992 harmonization, which, as will be seen below, removed all discrimination, imports were taxed in the country of consumption to the same extent as similar domestic products, and exports were excluded from taxation by means of

1   OJ 71, 14.04.1967 and OJ L145, 13.06.1977.
2   OJ L320, 20.12.1969.

tax credits or refunds to exporters of tax paid on all elements of the cost of the exported product. Calculation of the tax paid was easy, as it appeared on all invoices and documents accompanying the product. The exporter was credited with the tax he had paid for the purchase of products for exportation against the VAT he had to pay on his domestic transactions. If the amount credited for exportation was higher than the amount of the VAT on his domestic transactions, the difference had to be refunded to the exporter. Thus, as will be seen in the next section, these procedures were simplified from January 1993, enabling the abolition of border controls.

The replacement of cumulative multi-stage taxes by value added tax eliminated the main resource of discrimination within the meaning of Articles 95 and 96 of the EEC Treaty. But, as the two Directives of 11 April 1967 did not resolve all the structural problems of value added tax, they left in existence the possibility of many significant differences of opinion as to the **scope of the tax**, particularly as regards taxable persons, taxable or exempt transactions, the methods of calculating basic taxable amounts and the special schemes. Article 19 of the second Directive of 1967 merely stated that those differences should be progressively restricted or abolished.

It took some ten years plus a new Directive, the sixth on the harmonization of turnover taxes, to achieve that goal. This Directive established a package of common rules making it possible to define the scope of the tax and the method of determining tax liability, i.e. the territorial application of the tax, the taxable persons, the taxable transactions, the place of applicability of such transactions, the chargeable event, the taxable amount, the detailed procedures for applying rates of taxation, the exemptions and the special schemes. In Community jargon all these rules are known as "**the uniform basis of assessment of VAT**", and that basis is particularly important in that VAT is a basic source of revenue of the Community. The sixth Directive on the harmonization of the laws of the Member States relating to turnover taxes, which was adopted on 17 May 1977, repealed the second Directive of 1967 and filled the gaps it had left, notably in the fields of the **provision of services**, agricultural production, small undertakings and exempt activities and operations. The 1977 Directive was amended in 1995 in order to simplify the tax treatment of a number of transactions and thus improve the functioning of the internal market in the benefit of the economic operators and the administrations of the Member States[1].

The sixth Directive firms up the definition of the provision of services and establishes the place in which they are to be taxed: as a general rule this is the place where the person supplying the services has his principal place of business or the permanent establishment from which the services are provided. As regards **farmers**, it confers on the Member States the right to apply to them, in accordance with a common method of calculation, a flat-rate scheme to offset the deductible tax on their purchases and the services supplied to them by third parties. With regard to **small undertakings**, it lays down that the Member States may apply simplified schemes

---

[1]   OJ L145, 13.06.1977 and OJ L102, 05.05.1995.

for charging and collecting tax. In addition, the sixth Directive provides for a complete system of **exemptions** both for activities within the country and for transactions linked with importation, exportation and international trade in goods.

However, with the implementation of the sixth Directive, the work on harmonizing the Member States' laws on turnover tax structures was not at an end. A number of the provisions of the Directive still needed to be thrashed out. Thus, the sixth Directive had laid down the principle that any taxpayer was entitled to the deduction or refund of VAT in whichever country he incurred expenditure subject to tax. An eighth Directive on the matter, adopted by the Council in 1979, lays down the common arrangements for the refund to **taxable persons not established in the territory of the country** of VAT borne by them on imports or purchases of goods or services in a Member State[1]. The thirteenth Directive, adopted in 1986, does likewise for refunds to **taxable persons not established in Community territory**[2]. The tenth Directive applies VAT to the **hiring out of moveable tangible property**[3].

Removal of fiscal frontiers

One of the main challenges of 1992 was in the tax field. Prior to 1992, goods and services moving within a Member State were taxed differently from those which were exported. On exportation the product benefited from full tax remission and was in return subject to the VAT of the country of import at the frontier crossing. The tax was paid to the country in which the goods arrive at the final consumption stage.

The protection which that system afforded against tax evasion and avoidance depended on the **frontier controls**. Without a check at the border to ensure that the goods which were the subject of an application for the reimbursement of tax had actually been exported, it would be all too easy for dishonest operators to invoice goods at the zero rate for exportation and subsequently resell them on the internal market, either free of tax, which would place their competitors in a disadvantageous position with regard to price, or by including the tax component in the price, but keeping its amount for themselves. That would not only have constituted a loss of tax revenue for the exporting State, but also a source of serious distortion of trade. For the authorities of the importing State, on the other hand, frontier controls were used to tax imported goods at the rates prevalent in the country in question, so as to collect the revenue due to them and, at the same time, make sure that these products did not unduly compete with national products.

However, the export refunds and import taxes which accompanied intra-Community trade, and the resultant controls, constituted what came to be known as "**fiscal frontiers**". To remove those frontiers, it was vital that cross-border trade be treated in the same way as purchases and sales within a State.

---

1   OJ L331, 27.09.1979.
2   OJ L326, 21.11.1986.
3   OJ L208, 03.08.1984.

In its "White Paper" of June 1985[1] the Commission actually proposed that cross-border sales and purchases be treated exactly the same as sales and purchases within a Member State. As far as the Commission was concerned that meant that as from 1 January 1993 all sales of goods and services should be taxed at the rate of the country of origin[2]. But the Council did not follow the Commission's lead. In conclusions of 9 October 1989 adopted unanimously (necessary condition in order to counter the proposal of the Commission), it emphasized that the introduction of a system of taxation in the country of origin, proposed by the Commission, presupposed that conditions would be fulfilled which could be satisfied by 1 January 1993. In order to achieve by that date the effective removal of the frontiers for undertakings and participants, while observing the economic neutrality of the common VAT system, the Council therefore considered it necessary to continue, for a limited period, to levy VAT and excise duty in the State of consumption.

In June 1991, the Council reached an overall political agreement on the detailed content of the temporary system. These arrangements were then embodied in Council Directives. A Directive on the **approximation of VAT rates** completes the common VAT system, amending the Directive of 17 May 1977[3]. It stipulates that, during the operational period of the transitional VAT arrangements (from 1 January 1993 to 31 December 1996), the Member States shall apply a standard VAT rate of at least 15%. In fact, the standard VAT rate varies between 15 and 25% in the Member States. Thus, in 1994, it was 25% in Denmark, 21% in Ireland, 19.5% in Italy, 18.6% in France, 18% in Greece, 17.5% in the United Kingdom and the Netherlands, 16% in Portugal and 15% in Germany, Spain and Luxembourg. All the higher VAT rates existing in several Member States have been abolished, leading to a significant fall in consumer prices in some sectors, such as automobiles.

The Member States however enjoy the option of applying, alongside the normal rate, one (or two) **reduced rates**, equal to or higher than 5%, applicable only to certain goods and services of a social or cultural nature. Examples include foodstuffs, pharmaceuticals, passenger transport services, books, newspapers and periodicals, entrance to shows, museums and the like, publications and copyright, subsidized housing, hotel accommodation, social activities and medical care in hospitals. The preservation of the zero and extra-low rates (below 5%) is authorized on a transitional basis, along with reduced rates on housing other than subsidized housing, catering and children's clothes and shoes.

The sixth Directive on VAT was amended in 1991 to supplement **the common system of VAT**[4]. The amendment establishes the basic rules for the transitional VAT system which will apply in principle until December 31, 1996. The new scheme dispenses with customs procedures. Intra-Community trade in goods between taxable bodies is subject to taxation of the goods acquisition in the country of destination. In the case of sales between companies subject to VAT, i.e. the vast majority, the vendor exempts the deliveries made to clients in other Member States. In his VAT return, he indicates, in a separate box, the total of his exempted intra-Community sales. In another return (usually quarterly), he lists the VAT number of his

---

1   See the chapter on the common market.
2   OJ C250, 19.09.1987.
3   OJ L316, 31.10.1992 and OJ L390, 31.12.1992.
4   OJ L376, 31.12.1991 and OJ L384, 30.12.1992.

customers in the other Member States and the total amount of his sales to each of them during the period in question. The purchaser applies VAT to his purchase in another Member State, termed an "acquisition". He must declare the total amount of these acquisitions in a separate box in his normal VAT return and can request the deductibility of this VAT in the same return.

Individuals travelling from one Member State to another pay VAT there where they purchase the goods and are no longer subject to any VAT-related taxation or any border formality when they cross from one Member State to another. The system of travellers allowances is thus abolished as far as intra-Community travelling is concerned. Under certain conditions, the Member States will be able to authorize duty-free sales until July 1, 1999. However, tax free purchases in intra-Community travel are limited to ECU 90, whereas allowances for travellers arriving at the Community from third countries can be as high as ECU 175[1].

In the framework of the transitional system, the seventh VAT Directive has introduced certain special systems. For **remote sales** (mail order) of an undertaking to individuals and other non-taxable bodies, VAT is counted at the rate in force in its Member State, except when its sales in the Member State of destination are above a certain limit (generally, ECU 100,000 per year) or if it prefers taxation in that State. **New vehicles** (cars, boats, aircraft) which form part of the operating stock of the vendor and which do not have a mileage of more than 3,000 kilometres are taxed in the country of registration, i.e. in the purchaser's country of origin, whereas second-hand vehicles are subject to the VAT rates practised in the country of the vendor. **Institutional non-taxable bodies** (government authorities) and **exempted taxable bodies** (banks, insurance companies...) are able to purchase goods in other countries, paying the VAT applicable in the country of origin, provided that their purchases do not overstep a certain threshold to be set by each Member State. For **second-hand goods, works of art, collectors' items and antiques**, sales between individuals are free of VAT and those realized by second-hand dealers and tradesmen are taxed in the Member State of destination on the dealer's profit margin and not on the total value of the goods[2].

On 1 January 1993, the new arrangements provided for in the transitional VAT regime came into force and, as a result, the charging of VAT on imports within the Community and the associated customs-based formalities ceased to exist. The transitional VAT arrangements are functioning satisfactorily overall. However, some mechanisms of the transitional VAT arrangements have proved to be complicated, particularly for small and medium enterprises, and the deterrent effect of some of the rules remains an obstacle to the development of trade between Member States. Likewise, the justification of the intra-Community nature of operations and the burden of identification and declaration are real difficulties encountered by traders, demonstrating that enterprises and consumers still do not enjoy all the expected advantages of the single market. This is why, the Commission recommended to the Member States a simplification of the taxation on small and medium enterprises[3].

The abolition of frontier controls and the resultant fraud risk require cooperation between government authorities in the area of indirect taxation. Such cooperation got off the

---

1   OJ L60, 03.03.1994 and OJ L365, 31.12.1994.
2   Ibid.
3   OJ L177, 09.07.1994.

ground in 1992. It revolves primarily around regular exchanges of data between the relevant authorities of the Member States on intra-Community trade[1]. The backbone of the system is an on-line network linking the relevant administrations of the Member States("Scent-taxation"), enabling rapid and efficient information exchange designed to combat fraud in the VAT and excise-duties fields. In order to offer certain national civil servants in charge of indirect taxation additional training so as to prepare them for the work arising from the internal market, the Matthaeus-Tax programme finances exchange schemes and vocational training programmes of the Member States[2].

Excise duties

In a fiscally integrated Community a number of major special taxes on consumption (excise duties), i.e. taxes on the consumption of certain products, yielding substantial revenue to the States, must be maintained alongside VAT. Excise duties make it possible to impose a much larger tax burden on a small number of products than that borne by the vast majority of goods which are only subject to VAT, which has very few, and fairly low, rates. If the various excise duties in the Community States were abolished, the resultant losses of revenue would have to be offset by increasing VAT rates, which would be certain to have an inflationary effect on their economies. Thus, for example, manufactured tobacco products and mineral oils bear, without major drawbacks, very high taxes which on average yield more than 10% of the tax revenue of the EU States. To replace that revenue by other revenue would entail not only fiscal, but also economic and social disruption.

Moreover, within the overall context of a tax scheme, excise duties constitute **flexible components** which can easily be manoeuvred if further tax revenue is needed. As they are separate taxes, excise duties can easily be adapted to the various economic, social and structural requirements. Lastly, they can be levied specifically in order to reduce consumption of certain products, such as tobacco products and alcoholic drinks, for public health reasons, and petroleum products for reasons of energy savings and to reduce energy dependence.

But if some excise duties had to be maintained in the Community, **their structures had to be harmonized** first so as to remove taxation indirectly protecting national production or in excess of that imposed directly or indirectly on similar domestic products (Article 95 EEC), and then, **their rates had to be harmonized** so as to eliminate, in trade between Member States, taxation and tax refunds as well as frontier controls which disturbed the free movement of goods within the common market.

Article 99 of the EEC Treaty gave the Commission a brief to consider how the legislation of the Member States concerning excise duties could be harmonized in the interest of the common market. Furthermore, the Resolution of the Council and of the Representatives of the Governments of the Member States of 22 March 1971 on the attainment by stages of economic and monetary union provided that, during a first stage of three years, beginning on 1 January 1971, the Council, on a proposal from the Commission, would act on measures relating to the harmonization of the scope, basis of assessment and mode of levying excise duties, in particular those which have an appreciable influence on trade. In order to meet the

---

1   OJ L24, 01.02.1992.
2   OJ L280, 13.11.1993.

commitments entered into under that Resolution, the Commission forwarded to the Council on 7 March 1972 five proposals for Directives on the harmonization of excise duties. Examination by the Council of the Commission proposals revealed that the Member States were much less willing to harmonize their specific taxes on consumption than they had been as regards their turnover taxes. Faced with that situation, the Commission utilized the **judicial process**. In 1978 it brought five cases against various States under Article 169 of the EEC Treaty for failure to fulfil their obligations under Article 95 in the field of alcoholic drinks. In fact, alcoholic drinks belong to a single family, whether distilled like spirits or fermented like wine and beer. Was it pure chance that excise duty in the United Kingdom was five times higher on wine than on beer or that brandy in France enjoyed rates which were at least 30% lower than those applied to whisky? On 27 February 1980, the Court of Justice sided with the Commission to condemn such practices.

Despite the Commission's efforts and several fresh rulings against various Member States by the Court of Justice, a political compromise only emerged ten years later as part of **the removal of fiscal frontiers** necessary for the achievement of the Single Market. The 92/12 Directive defines the **general arrangements** for the holding and movement of products subject to excise duty from 1 January 1993[1]. In contrast to the harmonized VAT system, the general arrangements for excise are definitive. The taxable event takes place at the stage of manufacture in the Community or of import into the Community from a third country. The tax is payable when the product is put up for consumption and must be acquitted in the country of actual consumption. The Member States have the option of introducing or maintaining taxation on other products and services, provided however that this taxation does not give rise to border crossing formalities in trade between the Member States.

Excise duties are paid by the consignee in the country of destination and the appropriate provisions are taken to this effect. For commercial operations, the Community system is similar to that applied within a State; the movement of products subject to suspended excise duty is through interconnected bonded warehouses and is covered by an accompanying document which has been harmonized at Community level. The payment of the excise due in the State of destination can be assumed by a fiscal representative established in this State and designated by the consignor. The appropriate provisions are taken to enable the exchange of information between all the Member States concerned by the movement of goods subject to excise with a view to ensuring effective fraud control. Individuals can purchase the products of their choice in other Member States, inclusive of tax, for their personal use[2].

Directive 92/78 harmonizes the excise-duty structures on **manufactured tobaccos** in the Member States, with the retail sales price taken as the calculation basis. Directive 92/79, on the approximation of excise-duty rates on cigarettes, stipulates that total excise duty (specific duty plus proportional duty calculated on the basis of the maximum retail sales price, before VAT) must constitute at least 57% of the sales price. Directive 92/80, on the approximation of taxes on manufactured tobaccos other than cigarettes (cigars, cigarillos, tobacco for rolling cigarettes and other tobaccos for smoking), sets minimum total excise duties for these products, but grants the Member States the option of applying them either as specific excise duty per unit, or proportional excise duty calculated on the basis of the

---

1   OJ L76, 23.03.1992 and OJ L365, 31.12.1994.
2   OJ L76, 23.03.1992 and OJ L390, 31.12.1992.

maximum retail sales price, or a combination of the two. The Directive on taxes which affect the consumption of manufactured tobacco was consolidated in 1995[1].

Directive 92/81, on the harmonization of excise-duty structures on **mineral oils**, generally makes them subject to specific excise duty calculated per 1000 litres of the product (or, for heavy fuels, liquefied petroleum gas and methane, per 1000 kilograms). Directive 92/82 stipulates minimum excise duties for mineral oils at the following levels: 337 ECU per 1000 litres for leaded petrol; 287 ECU per 1000 litres for unleaded petrol; 245 ECU per 1000 litres for diesel and paraffin used as fuel; 18 ECU per 1000 litres for domestic oil, diesel and paraffin used for fixed engines; 13 ECU per 1000 kilograms for heavy fuel; 100 ECU per 1000 kilograms for liquefied petroleum gas and methane used as fuel; 36 ECU per 1000 kilograms for liquefied petroleum gas and methane used for fixed engines; and 0 ECU for liquefied petroleum gas, methane and paraffin used for heating. A 1994 Directive clarifies the special arrangements applicable to mineral oils and simplifies the administrative procedures connected with their implementation[2]. A 1995 Directive establishes common rules for the tax marking of gas oil and kerosene which have not borne duty at the full rate applicable to such oils when used as propellants[3].

Directive 92/83 covers the harmonization of excise-duty structures on **spirits and alcoholic beverages**. Directive 92/84 sets minimum excise duties on spirits and alcoholic beverages at the following levels: 550 ECU per hectolitre of pure alcohol; 45 ECU per hectolitre for intermediary products; 0 ECU for wine; 1.87 ECU per hectolitre per degree of alcohol in the finished product for beer[4].

The objective of the Lisbon Conference is to assess the performance of the Community's current excise system and to assist the Commission in its task in formulating an excise policy for the future. This policy should, on the one hand, secure tax revenues and guarantee sound economic conditions at national level, and, on the other, remain consistent with the wider policies of the European Union, particularly health, energy, environment and the common agricultural policy[5].

Other indirect taxation

Various indirect taxes whose harmonization is important for European construction also exist in addition to value added tax and special taxes on consumption. Examples of these are taxes on insurance policies and taxes on motor vehicles intended for the carriage of passengers, which vary greatly between Member States. The most significant from the point of view of competition, however, are capital duty and stamp duty levied on shares in registered capital (shares and securities), as their diversity can give rise to double taxation and distortions of competition and constitute obstacles to the free movement of capital.

In order to prevent such problems, a 1969 Directive concerning indirect taxes on the **raising of capital** provided for the harmonization of capital duties and the abolition of stamp duties, which were deemed to be undesirable from the economic point of view[6]. However, when that Directive was applied it became clear that capital duties could be set at too high a level, especially in certain company-restructuring operations. For that reason it was supplemented in 1973 concerning the field of application of the **reduced rate of capital duty**[7]. In 1985 it was amended to facilitate the contribution of risk capital to undertakings by reducing their fiscal burden[8].

1   OJ L291, 06.12.1995.
2   OJ L316, 31.10.1992 and OJ L365, 31.12.1994.
3   OJ L291, 06.12.1995.
4   OJ L316, 31.12.1992.
5   COM (95) 285, 13 September 1995.
6   OJ L249, 03.10.1969.
7   OJ L103, 18.04.1973.
8   OJ L156, 15.06.1985.

Direct taxation

Taxes on the revenue of undertakings and private individuals, which are not incorporated in cost prices or selling prices and the rate of which is often progressive, may be regarded as direct taxes. The two important categories of direct taxes are **income tax and capital gains tax**. Article 98 of the Treaty prohibits, as regards such taxes, countervailing charges at frontiers, i.e. the application of remissions and repayments in respect of exports to other Member States. Derogations may not be granted unless the measures contemplated have been previously approved for a limited period by the Council. Apart from that provision the Treaty of Rome did not deal with direct taxes and did not call for them to be harmonized.

Whilst the harmonization of indirect taxes was necessary from the outset to avoid obstacles to trade and to free competition and later to make the removal of fiscal frontiers possible, the harmonization of direct taxes did not appear indispensable in the common market. It gradually became clear that the free movement of capital and the rational distribution of production factors in the Community required a **minimum degree of harmonization of direct taxes**. If one wishes to approximate Member State's economic policies, one must start by coordinating the fiscal instruments used by them. Also if the wish is to facilitate the creation of internationally competitive industrial undertakings, the taxation of companies operating in several Member States must not place them at a disadvantage in relation to those restricting their activities to the purely national level. The Commission tabled proposals in this connection as long ago as 1969. The Council needed 21 years (!) of debate before it could approve these proposals, vital for transnational cooperation and company merger.

The first Directive adopted by the Council on July 23, 1990 relates to the taxation system applicable to the **capital gains generated upon the merger**, hiving off, transfer of assets, contribution of assets or exchange of shares between two companies operating in different Member States[1]. National regulations consider this type of operation as a total or partial liquidation of the company making the contribution and subject it to capital gains tax, set in an artificial manner, since it compares the market value of the good in question (the company itself, or a building, land, a share package) to the value entered in the balance sheet, traditionally underestimated. Such a calculation is unjust insofar as no liquidation is taking place in effect; rather two companies from different Member States are forming closer links. The Community solution consists of no longer taxing the capital gain at the time when the merger or contribution of assets takes place but rather when it is collected. This solution would be of major interest for the formation of "European companies", insofar as such companies usually result from the merger of companies originally established in different Member States.

---

1   OJ L225, 20.08.1990.

The second Council Directive of July 23, 1990 relates to the common fiscal system applicable to **parent companies and subsidiaries** situated in different Member States[1]. There can be little doubt that the decision by an undertaking to set up a subsidiary in another Member State of the Community is adversely affected by the fact that the dividends of the latter would be subject to tax in the country where it has its domicile for tax purposes, to corporation tax and, in the Member State where the subsidiary is domiciled, to a non-recoverable withholding tax. The Directive abolishes withholding taxes on dividends distributed by a subsidiary to its parent company established in another Member State.

On July 23, 1990, representatives of the Member States also signed an agreement providing for the introduction of an **arbitration procedure** in the event of disagreement between the tax authorities of the Member States relating to a cross-border operation[2]. This will ensure the avoidance of double taxation arising when an adjustment to the profits of a company carried out by the tax authority of one Member State is not matched by a similar adjustment in the Member State of the partner company. Such double taxation would penalize European transnational cooperation. A time limit has been placed on the procedure, so that lengthy delays lasting for several years and generating additional costs cannot develop. The company concerned by the measures in question becomes rapidly a party to the procedure and consequently has an opportunity to put its viewpoint forward.

The guiding principle of Community policy in the field of direct taxation is to eliminate the double taxation of cross-border activities whilst ensuring taxation at least once. Concrete measures, such as the proposed Directives for interest and royalties, the offsetting of losses and the extension of the parent-subsidiary and merger Directives have been tabled by the Commission. These measures enjoy the support of economic operators since they would make a significant contribution to improving the tax environment in which cross-border activities are planned and executed. However, adoption of these measures would only go part of the way towards resolving the problem of double taxation. The guidelines laid down in the Commission communication to the Council and Parliament in response to the Ruding report provide a detailed blueprint for further Community action in this field[3]. This action would take the form of either a general obligation to abolish all cross-border double taxation or a phased approach the priorities for which would have been set by mutual agreement with the Member States.

In the "Schumacker" case, the Court of Justice found that, although direct taxation does not as such fall within the competence of the Community, the powers retained by the Member States must nevertheless be exercised consistently with Community law, and in particular with the rules governing the free movement of workers, which require the abolition of any discrimination based on nationality[4]. Thus, tax benefits granted only to residents of a Member State can constitute indirect taxation by reason of nationality, but only where different rules were applied to comparable situations or the same rule was applied to different situations. Where direct taxes are concerned, however, the Court found that the situations of residents and non-residents are not, as a rule comparable and, therefore, a resident can be taxed by a Member State more heavily on his income than a resident in the same employment.

Effort to combat tax avoidance

The most important and urgent problems for the Community in the area of direct taxation were posed by international tax avoidance. In addition to the substantial budgetary losses for States and the fiscal injus-

---

1 OJ L225, 20.08.1990.

2 Ibid.

3 SEC (92) 1118, 26 June 1992.

4 Judgment of 14 February 1995, case C-279/93, Finanzamt Köln-Altstadt/R. Schumacker.

tice, international tax avoidance generates abnormal capital movement and distortions of conditions of competition. The particularly important aspects from the international point of view are : the concealment by some taxpayers of their taxable activities beyond the borders of their States in countries in which the level of taxation is low or the risk of discovery small; the possibilities of avoidance open to multinational companies, especially through the manipulation of transfer prices between undertakings in the same group; and the tax arrangements for holding companies, which is a problem outside the European Union's remit, as a large number of those companies are established in tax havens outside the Union.

Bilateral agreements did, of course, exist in this field, but as a result of the increasingly complex nature of the modern company, the prevention of international tax evasion and avoidance necessitated, to be effective, organization on an international, and above all on a Community scale. Thus, the Council had adopted the principle of a first common action in a Resolution of 1975 with a twofold aim: regarding the basis of assessment, to make correct assessments for taxes on income or profits, and regarding recovery, to support prosecutions of persons guilty of tax avoidance[1].

With a view to the legal implementation of the 1975 Resolution, in 1977 the Council adopted a Directive concerning mutual assistance by the competent authorities of the Member States in the field of direct taxation[2]. That Directive introduced a procedure for the systematic exchange of information directed towards enabling them to effect a correct assessment of direct taxes in the Community. The exchange of information may take place at the request of the Member State concerned, but it is also provided for where that State has no grounds on which to base its request. Thus, the exchange of information without request may be automatic, in certain cases decided upon by mutual agreement between the authorities concerned, or spontaneous, where one competent authority feels that it has certain information likely to interest another Community tax authority, for example where there are grounds for supposing that there are artificial transfers of profits within groups of enterprises. For that purpose the Directive established a procedure for cooperation between the Member States and the Commission which enables them to inform each other of their information and experiences notably in the field of transfer prices. In a 1984 Resolution the Council expressed the desire that the administrative procedures in intra-Community trade be computerized[3]; this is now taking place.

However, the liberalization of capital movements as from 1 July 1990, in accordance with the Directive of 24 June 1988[4], has **increased the risk of tax evasion**. In fact, Community residents can henceforth freely transfer their savings to bank accounts in any Member State without the corresponding income necessarily being declared to the tax authorities of the State of residence. Since, in several Member States, there is no "withholding tax" on bank interest paid to non-residents, investment would tend towards those States, thus avoiding any taxation. Such capital movements, motivated purely by tax considerations, would be at variance with the optimum allocation of resources, which is the objective of establishing a Community financial area. Moreover, as in the global economy capital has become very mobile, the States have a tendency to displace the tax burden towards less mobile bases, such as work. Thus, between 1980 and 1993, the implicit tax burden on capital in the EU has decreased by more than one tenth while the implicit tax burden on work has increased by one fifth[5]. Any new increase on the tax burden on work could drive economic activity towards the black market and/or aggravate the effects on the costs of labour and employment.

---

1   OJ C35, 14.02.1975.
2   OJ L336, 27.12.1977 and OJ L76, 23.03.1992.
3   OJ C137, 24.05.1984.
4   See the chapter on the common market.
5   SEC (96) 487, 20 March 1996.

It would therefore be necessary, to lessen the risk of tax distortion, evasion and avoidance, to intensify the exchange of information between tax authorities on the basis of the Directive of 19 December 1977 and to remove the encouragement to invest in a Member State which applies a more favourable tax scheme than the Member State of the investor by introducing in all the Member States a relatively low withholding tax. That twin objective is aimed at by the Council in its conclusions of 13 December 1993 on the **taxation of savings**. Interest received by Community residents is to be subject either to withholding tax at a minimum rate of 15% or to notification of the tax authorities of the country of residence. In addition, Member States should act in concert to prevent tax evasion towards third countries, which erodes their tax revenues and even their fiscal sovereignty.

The question of greater harmonization of direct taxes will doubtless be placed on the EU's agenda at an advanced stage towards economic and monetary union. In the meanwhile, the regular meetings between the Directors General of direct taxation represent a cooperation instrument which could be used for the gradual coordination of national fiscal policies.

Appraisal and outlook

The aim of creating a unified fiscal area in the European Union is ambitious, even if unification means the harmonization of national tax laws rather the creation of a federal tax system. Fiscal unification can only be achieved progressively, in line with the approximation of the national economies. Naturally, for as long as the tax schemes are not closely harmonized, they will have different influences on conditions of competition between identical economic activities in the Member States, which activities will have to bear different tax burdens. But distortions of competition caused by heavier taxation in some States than in others, are usually offset by superior public services and or favourable exchange rates. If there were no such counterbalances in a common market in which there is freedom of establishment, undertakings would of preference go and establish themselves in the member country which offered the best tax conditions for them or for their products. No such phenomenon occurred in the Community. Although corporation tax rate and value added tax rates are very different in the various Member States, there has not been a consequent migratory tendency from some States towards others on the part of undertakings.

It was, however, a matter of urgency for the common market to harmonize turnover tax structures and consequently to achieve fiscal neutrality, i.e. equal tax treatment of domestic products and products imported from the Member States. That was to a large extent achieved with the adoption of the VAT system by all the original Member States at the beginning of the '70s and by the new Member States after their accession. Such a close harmonization of turnover taxes as that resulting from the adoption by all Member States of the value added tax with a uniform basis of assessment was not called for by the Treaty. The Community therefore went beyond what was required of it.

Nevertheless, not all the Community's tax problems were resolved. Firstly, the structures of all taxes on consumption needed to be harmonized. Although the harmonization of the structure of turnover tax made good progress, in particular after the adoption of the sixth VAT Directive, harmonization of excise duty was confined to a few measures concerning specific taxes on manufactured tobacco. The Commission proposals on the matter, dating from March 1972, were shelved in the Council, allowing the Member States to engage in conduct which did not comply with Article 95 of the Treaty, i.e. to levy higher internal taxes on products from other Member States than those levied on similar domestic products. Faced with a political stalemate, the Commission was constrained to pursue the judicial process to win respect of the Community provisions by the recalcitrant Member States.

Twenty years later (!), under pressure from the completion of the internal market which required the abolition of fiscal frontiers, the Member States have finally agreed to harmonize their excise duties, thus proving that when the political will exists, the technical problems of European integration can always be overcome. The harmonization of VAT rates and of excise-duty structures and rates, achieved in 1992, meant a great deal of upheaval in the tax revenue of the Member States, heavily drawn from indirect taxation. However, despite the reservations and the predictions of doom among some fiscal experts, they have been able to carry out this harmonization without major upset, and this in a dreary economic climate.

The harmonization of indirect taxation is very important, not just for the smooth operation of the internal market but also for the alignment of economic conditions in the Member States. The new VAT and excise arrangements will enable companies to sell, purchase and invest in all the Member States without being subject to controls or formalities arising from the crossing of borders. Individuals can purchase goods in all the Community countries and, without restriction, bring them back for their personal consumption without any checks or taxation on border crossing.

The definitive VAT system, which should enter into force on 1 January 1997 and include the payment of VAT in the country of origin, should satisfy certain essential criteria. First of all, it should be as simple as possible for enterprises, particularly SMEs, in order to make Community firms more competitive both within the internal market and in other markets by cutting costs of transactions. Moreover, the definitive system should preserve the neutral effect of VAT on competition as regards the origin of goods and services. It should also satisfy Member States' justified budgetary interests by avoiding falls in tax revenue throughout the Community and shifts in tax revenue between Member States. Last but not least, the definitive system should be simple and transparent, thus promoting voluntary compliance with the law and allowing a concentration of resources on the detection and combating of fraud.

As regards **direct taxation**, the harmonization process will of necessity take even longer. It has to be said that such harmonization is not as vital to economic integration as is the harmonization of indirect taxation. Differences between the Member States' direct taxes do not disturb intra-Community trade to the extent that differences in indirect taxation do. Only the harmonization of corporation tax and tax on savings is really indispensable for enabling companies in the various Member States to enjoy fair conditions of competition and for capital movement to be free from distortions resulting from taxation. Fiscal differences between the Member States can influence investment location and lead to distortions of competition. The abolition of dual taxation on cross-border operations begun in 1990 must therefore be continued so that companies view their investments in the different Member States as investments in a domestic market.

Some very important areas of direct taxation, such as personal income tax, are not directly targeted by the harmonization process, and the inclination to align the rates and the progressivity effect is markedly less. So long as the economic and monetary union is not completed, Member States, in application of the principle of subsidiarity, must keep enough room for manoeuvre to be able to conduct their budgetary and economic policies. During those first stages, however, a procedure for the coordination of national fiscal policies would have to be introduced to enable those policies to converge progressively in parallel with the convergence of economic policies. Indeed, all Member States have common problems, notably that of capital evasion to fiscal paradises and even that of competition among themselves in order to attract capital while penalizing their work-forces. If they put together part of their sovereignty so as to take collective measures, Member States could better face international competition and avoid seeing the money market forces do away with that sovereignty. At the end of the day, the tax harmonization process must progress at the same tempo as the economic integration process, so as to concur within the economic and monetary union.

Bibliography on fiscal policy

□   BROOD Edgar (et al.), "Capital Contribution Tax in the EC", in *EC Tax Review*, 1993/2, pp. 96-106.

□   CALLEJA D., VIGNES D., WÄGENBAUR R., *Dispositions fiscales, rapprochement des législations*, Vol. 5 du "Commentaire Megret" sur le droit de la CEE, Université Libre de Bruxelles, Bruxelles, 1993.

□   COMMISSION EUROPÉENNE, *Conclusions et recommandations du comité de réflexion des experts indépendants sur la fiscalité des entreprises*, OPOCE, Luxembourg, 1992.

   -   *Suppression des contrôles aux frontières: contrôle des marchandises, contrôle des personnes, taxe sur la valeur ajoutée, droits d'accises*, OPOCE, Luxembourg, 1993.

-    *La fiscalité dans l'Union européenne*, SEC (96) 487 final, 20 mars 1996.

□   COOPERS & LYBRAND, *EC Initiatives in Direct Taxation and the National Responses*, Kluwer Law and Taxation Publishers, Deventer, ND., 1992.

□   DEVEREUX Michael, "Does a Monetary Union Require International Fiscal Policy Co-ordination", in *Economic and Social Review*, 23/01, 1991, pp. 35-54.

□   EUROPEAN COMMISSION, *Options for a Definitive VAT System*, OOPEC, Luxembourg, 1995.

-    *Towards Greater Fiscal Discipline*, OOPEC, Luxembourg, 1995.

□   GIOVANNINI Alberto, SPAVENTA Luigi, *Fiscal Rules in the European Monetary Union: A No-entry Clause*, Centre for Economic Policy Research, London, 1991.

□   GUIEU Pierre, "L'élimination des barrières fiscales et l'harmonisation de la TVA", in *Revue du marché unique européen*, Paris, 1-1991, pp. 11-63.

□   MARCHAIS Isabelle, *La fiscalité et le Grand Marché de 1993*, 2 volumes, Impact Europe, Bruxelles, 1992.

□   MAUBLANC Jean-Pierre, "1992 ou la mise en place du nouveau régime de la TVA sans frontières", in *Revue du Marché commun et de L'Union européenne*, Paris, N 367, avril 1993, pp. 335-342.

□   TERRA Ben, KAJUS, Julie, *Introduction to Value Added Tax in the EC after 1992*, Kluwer Law and Taxation Publishers, Deventer, ND.,1992.

□   *TVA 1993; conséquences pratiques de l'adaptation au marché unique*, Éditions Francis Lefèbvre, Paris, 1992.

□   VALENDUC Christian, "L'harmonisation fiscale et la construction européenne", *Courrier Hebdomadaire du CRISP* (Centre de recherches et d'informations socio-politiques), N° 1441/42, 1994.

□   VAN DEN BEMPT, "National Fiscal Policies in an Economic and Monetary Union", in *European Business Journal*, London, Vol. 3, Nr. 1, 1991, pp. 10-18.

□   VAN DER PLOEG Frederick, "Fiscal, Stabilisation and Monetary Integration in Europe: A Short-Run Analysis", in *Economist*, Leiden, Jaarg. 140, Nr. 1, 1992, pp. 16-44.

□   VANDERSTICHELEN Benoit, *Nouveau régime TVA*, Éditions Delta, Bruxelles, 1993.

□   VILLEMOT Dominique, *La TVA européenne. Les régimes de TVA applicables aux échanges avec les autres États membres de la CEE*, Presses Universitaires de France, Paris, 1994.

7. COMPETITION

Competition policy is essential to the achievement and maintenance of the single market. It ensures the competitive conduct of undertakings and protects the interests of consumers by enabling them to procure goods and services on the best terms. It promotes economic efficiency by creating a climate favourable to innovation and technical progress. It prevents anti-competitive practices on the part of companies or national authorities which might choke off the competitive dynamics generated by the completion of the single market. In fact the driving force for the economic benefits which are expected to derive from the completion of the single market is the possibility of undertakings to compete on equal terms on the markets of all the Member States.

While preventing market compartmentalization from being restored by means of international agreements and while preventing market enlargement from securing windfall profits for dominant undertakings, the competition policy of the EU has to establish for European industry the legal framework and economic conditions which enable it to develop and modernize to cope with international competition. That is why, whilst action is taken without respite against improper agreements or conduct on the part of (in many instances large) undertakings which try to corner a share of the common market and the corresponding profits, agreements and practices which enable SMEs to cooperate with one another and to form concentrations without damaging the interests of consumers or trade between Member States are concurrently permitted, even without prior notification to the Commission.

Just as important to the proper functioning of the internal market are the Community rules governing State aid, public undertakings and national monopolies. Those rules seek to prevent Member States from using such means to promote their national industries to the detriment of their competitors and, ultimately, of the single market. All the same, those rules have to be complied with, which accounts for the need for a neutral and respected referee placed above the scrum of national interests. The EEC Treaty allocated that role to the European Commission. This is indeed one of the few areas in which the Commission has autonomous, supranational power and may transcend its initiative role to take on that of direct

decision. Under the control of the Court of Justice, it establishes Community law on competition which provides a framework for and orientates
national laws.

Economic and legal framework

Before the opening up of frontiers to intra-Community trade and
competition, prices in some countries and in some sectors were maintained
artificially at a level which allowed marginal undertakings to survive. The
consumer bore the burden of protecting them. In other sectors, unprofitable undertakings were supported by aids of all kinds, and it was therefore
the taxpayer who kept them alive. Hence, both consumers and taxpayers
had a great interest to see the non profitable undertakings disappear from
the market thanks to the fair play of competition. However, national rules
alone cannot ensure competition in a common market. They must be
completed by Community rules to cover cases where trade between the
Member States is affected and, therefore, there is Community competence.

The European competition policy must ensure the unity of the common market by preventing undertakings from dividing it up amongst
themselves by means of precautionary agreements. It must obviate the
monopolization of certain markets by preventing major undertakings
from abusing their dominant position to impose their conditions or to
acquire their competitors. Lastly, it must prevent governments from distorting the rules of the game by means of aids to private sector undertakings or discrimination in favour of public undertakings.

Buoyancy of competition in the large market

The very essence of the large market of the European Union is the
liveliness of competition. The large market actually enables undertakings
to produce on a large scale, to put in hand modern methods of production
and to reduce their costs, to the benefit of consumers. Thanks to the
common market, consumers have a choice between domestic products and
products from partner countries, imported free of quantitative restrictions
and customs duties. Their choice naturally turns towards better-quality
products, taking into account their price, irrespective of their provenance.
Consumers are therefore the judges of the performance of undertakings in
the large market. The least viable undertakings are obliged to modernize
or close their doors.

It has to be stressed that, in spite of the disappearance of unviable
firms in the common market, the number of undertakings actually in
competition with one another in a specific market increases and the possibilities for market domination decrease, as partners' products compete
with domestic products on equal terms. National monopolies become
oligopolies and the number of firms in oligopoly-type markets increases.

This results in a tendency towards a drop in the economic clout of national monopolies and oligopolies.

The increase of competition as a result of the creation of the common market involves the upheaval of supply conditions, the renunciation of traditional habits and behaviour and, in some instances, the loss of monopoly profits. Such developments cannot leave businessmen indifferent. Their attitude may be positive or negative. In most cases they will endeavour to preserve or even increase their share of the market by reducing their cost prices by restructuring, investment outlay and rationalizing production and distribution methods. Such an approach is in the interest both of consumers, who benefit from plentiful supply on the best possible conditions, and of businessmen themselves, as they learn to live with the common market and to cope better with international competition. Some businessmen, however, might react negatively to the changed behaviour imposed by the common market. To counter intensified competition, they might try to strengthen existing national agreements or to establish new agreements at European level. Other producers, having a dominant position on a specific market, might attempt to monopolize it by acquiring their competitors.

Restrictive practices

Monopolization of a market can be achieved in two ways: by agreement or by concentration. **An agreement** is defined as an understanding between undertakings which remain autonomous, for the purpose of specific behaviour on the market, in particular the restriction of competitive practices. **Concentrations** eliminate the autonomy of participating undertakings by grouping them under a single economic administration, notably by integrating capital and management. It can be seen that agreements have the effect of imposing a specific behaviour, whilst concentrations entail changing the structure of undertakings.

Agreements are conservative in nature, as they are generally intended to protect what already exists, even less viable undertakings. By artificially limiting competition between participating companies, agreements isolate them from the pressures, which would normally push them to conceive new products or more efficient production methods. On the other hand, concentrations mostly contribute to eliminating (through mergers) the least viable and least efficient undertakings. Agreements are only exceptionally in the interest of the consumer and may be permitted if they are directed towards research, specialization and cooperation to improve production and distribution methods. Concentrations, on the other hand, are in principle acceptable, as the market, extended by economic integration, calls for larger undertakings and because, through the improvement of structures, rationalization of production and the securing of internal economies, they reduce production costs to the advantage of the consumer. However, where concentrations exceed certain limits, they begin to present dangers, as the very large undertaking can exploit its dominant market position to remove all competition. For that reason, European institutions must monitor not only agreements, but also concentrations.

In order to ensure that undertakings operating in the internal market enjoy the same conditions of competition everywhere, efforts have to be made to combat not only unfair practices on the part of undertakings, but also discriminatory measures on the part of States. Economic integration and the increasing liberalization of international trade have greatly weakened the classical methods of commercial protection, viz. high customs duties and quantitative restrictions on imports as well as technical barriers to trade. For that reason, States have more frequent recourse to **aids** as an instrument of economic policy, especially given that increased competition and more rapid technological change reveal structural weaknesses in several sectors and regions of the EU. Some aids are doubtless justified on the grounds of social policy or regional policy, while others are necessary to direct undertakings towards the requisite adjustments at an acceptable social cost. But the Member States' aid policies are often aimed at artificially ensuring the survival of sectors undergoing structural difficulties. Such aid measures run counter to the changes to the production structures inherent in technological progress and their social cost is often greater than the sums allocated to them, as they block production factors which could be better employed elsewhere. In addition, such uncoordinated measures at European level lead to spiralling aid, as each country finds itself obliged to follow in its neighbour's footsteps whenever the latter supports an economic activity. All these reasons necessitate European control of national aids.

One of the most intricate problems in the field of competition is posed by **public and parapublic** undertakings. Member States use them as instruments for attaining various economic, political and social objectives such as directing investment towards certain sectors or regions, administering certain unprofitable public services, handling certain economic activities regarded as strategic, acting as the nation's standard bearer in the arena of international competition and employ persons who do not find jobs in the private sector. In return for the manifold services they render to governments, the latter tend to discriminate in favour of public undertakings. The various privileges which are granted to them can distort conditions of competition vis-à-vis undertakings in the private sector of their own nationality and those of their partners in the common market. This latter aspect of relations between Member States and their public undertakings is of particular interest to the European institutions.

Foundations of the European policy

Agreements (in principle), concentrations (in some instances), protectionist national aids and discrimination in favour of public undertakings are incompatible with the common market. They must be controlled by the European institutions on the basis of European criteria, because the Member States' competition policies, even when they are stringent, are not efficacious at European level.

Article 3 of the EEC Treaty, given over to the principles of the Community, provides for the institution "of a system ensuring that competition in the internal market is not distorted", and the whole chapter on competition allocates to the Community the task of organizing intra-Community trade, free from tariff barriers, on the basis of the law of supply and demand. Article 85, relating to agreements, Article 86, concerning dominant positions, and Article 92, dealing with aids granted by States, are probably the best known articles in the Treaty of Rome. We shall examine them in the next three sections of this chapter.

The competition rules of the Treaty have been interpreted and applied through Council regulations and Commission regulations as well as through general communications and individual decisions of the Commission. Thus, Regulation N° 17 of 1972, first Regulation implementing Articles 85 and 86 of the Treaty, sets out the Commission's supranational powers, which are essential for the existence of Community competition policy[1]. These powers, which affect the Member States and their nationals, are examined below. In a Communication dated July 26, 1991 containing guidelines on the application of the Community competition rules in the telecommunication sector, the Commission specifies the legal and economic principles of its action in this field[2].

Competition policy affects virtually all the **other Community policies**, which must comply with its rules. This is true in particular of industrial policy, as regards structural and sectoral measures, regional policy, as regards development aid for the poor regions, energy and transport policies, as regards the major public and multinational undertakings in those sectors, and agricultural and fisheries policies, as regards common market organizations.

Since 1 January 1994, the competition rules of the European Union have been extended to the whole European Economic Area (EEA). Articles 85 and 86 of the EC Treaty, which ban agreements and abuse of dominant position respectively, are therefore now applicable in Norway, Iceland and Liechtenstein in accordance with Articles 53 and 54 of the EEA Agreement. The Europe Agreements concluded with the countries of Central and Eastern Europe include rules of competition, which are essentially the same with those of the EC Treaty. Less strict rules of competition are contained in the association and cooperation agreements concluded with the independent States of the former Soviet Union. An Agreement between the European Communities and the Government of the United States of America is intended to promote cooperation and coordination between the competition authorities of the two parties[3].

Powers of the Commission

In carrying out the tasks assigned to it under Article 89 and by the provisions adopted pursuant to Article 87 of the Treaty, the Commission may **gather all necessary information** from the governments and competent authorities of the Member States and from undertakings or associations of undertakings. If, in any economic sector, the trend of trade between

---

1   OJ 13, 21.02.1962 and OJ L377, 31.12.1994.

2   OJ C233, 06.09.1991.

3   OJ L95, 27.04.1995.

Member States, price movements, inflexibility of prices or other circumstances suggest that competition is being restricted or distorted, the Commission may conduct a general inquiry and in the course thereof may request undertakings in the sector concerned to supply the information necessary for the application of Articles 85 and 86, in particular on all agreements, decisions and concerted practices normally exempt from notification. It may also request undertakings or groups of undertakings whose size suggests that they occupy a dominant position within the common market or a substantial part thereof to supply such particulars of the structure of the undertakings and of their behaviour as are requisite to an appraisal of their situation in the light of Article 86 of the Treaty.

The national competition authorities, national and Community courts and the Commission each assume their own tasks and responsibilities, in line with the principles developed by the case-law of the Court of Justice of the European Communities. A Commission Communication of February 1993 aims at reinforcing the cooperation between itself and the national courts[1]. The Commission underlines that it is the administrative authority responsible for the implementation and for the thrust of competition policy in the Community and for this purpose has to act in the public interest. National courts, on the other hand, have the task of safeguarding the subjective rights of private individuals in their relations with each other. In this way, national courts are able to ensure that the Community competition rules are respected for the benefit of private individuals. Where the application of Articles 85 and 86 causes them particular difficulties, national courts may consult the Commission on its customary practice in relation to the Community law at issue. In a communication adopted on 31 October 1995, the Commission explains how it intends to assist national courts in the State aid field (Article 93(3) of the EC Treaty).

In accordance with Articles 53 and 54 of the Agreement on the European Economic Area, the European Commission must verify whether the cases referred to it come under these articles. It must act in cases likely to affect inter-State trade within the EEA, and also when the practices in question threaten to upset trade between one of the EU States and one or several of the EFTA States, on condition that the companies in question achieve over 67% of their combined turnover for the EEA on the territory of the EU. On the other hand, the EFTA Surveillance Authority decides in cases involving firms whose turnover on EFTA territory is equal or above 33% of turnover on EEA territory, except when trade within the EU is affected. Responsibility is shared out in the same way for negative clearance applications concerning a dominant position. Community-scale concentrations naturally remain under the responsibility of the Commission. The latter has laid out in a Regulation the details of the implementation of the competition rules established in the EEA Agreement[2].

The Commission may be **apprised of restrictive behaviour** in various ways: through articles in the press, questions put by Members of the European Parliament or contacts with interest groups, in particular those involved in consumer protection. Very often, moreover,

---

1   OJ C39, 13.02.1993.
2   OJ L336, 31.12.1993.

the Commission receives formal complaints concerning restrictive behaviour from a party with a legitimate interest in the matter, e.g. the government of a Member State, a professional organization, an undertaking or an injured private individual.

In order to combat cartels more effectively, the Commission intends no longer to fine firms party to an illegal cartel which furnish it with detailed information about the cartel provided certain conditions are met, notably that the firm is the first one to cooperate. The Commission also intends to grant substantial reductions in fines in the case of firms which, once the investigation is completed, are the first to come forward, provide confirmation that the infringement took place or accept the facts as alleged[1].

If it feels that the commercial practices of which it has learned in whatever manner pose problems with regard to the rules of competition, the Commission normally wishes to gather further information on the matter. The Commission may send written **requests for information** not only to the undertakings being investigated, but also to third parties which may be able to clarify certain points in the matter, e.g. competing undertakings, trading partners or associations of undertakings. When the Commission sends a request for information to an undertaking or association of undertakings and when a request for the establishment of infringement or of a negative clearance or a notification is submitted to the Commission, a copy must be forwarded to the competent authorities of the Member States, which are kept regularly informed of the procedures. But the Commission may establish direct links with the nationals of those States. It may in particular oblige the undertakings of a Member State to supply all information and documents which it considers necessary, subject to daily penalty payments. It may also impose fines where the information supplied is incorrect, misleading or incomplete.

The Commission has the power to send officials empowered by it to the headquarters of undertakings to gather the information it needs in situ. If there is a risk that, having been forewarned, the undertaking may destroy the proof of the infringement, the Commission carries out a **surprise inspection**. The undertaking visited is not obliged to admit the officials who go on an inspection visit, but the Commission may, in such case, take a formal decision ordering it to submit to inspection, if necessary using the threat of penalty payments[2]. Officials carrying out an inspection visit are authorized to examine the books and other business records of the company, to take copies of or extracts from them, to ask for explanations and to enter any premises, land or means of transport belonging to the undertaking. In such cases, as in that of written requests for information, undertakings which, although submitting to inspection, provide the documents requested in incomplete form are liable to be fined[3].

After examining the information collected, the Commission may reach the conclusion that the rules of competition of the Treaty have indeed been infringed. In that case it must inform the parties concerned of the grounds for complaint that it feels it has to uphold with regard to their behaviour or send them a written statement known as a **"statement of objections"**. It attaches thereto a list of documents which constitute its file on the matter concerned. A specific time-limit - one or two months, depending on the complexity of the matter - is granted to the parties concerned to reply in writing to the Commission's allegations. In order to prepare their reply, the parties concerned may examine the files in the Commission's premises, except for certain confidential documents concerning, for example, the professional secrets of third undertakings or the Commission's internal notes.

Depending on the complex nature of the matter, one, two or even more years may be required for the Commission to reach a final decision. During that time the behaviour in question may cause serious and irreparable damage, for instance to a complainant, whose livelihood may even be threatened, or be completely at variance with the general public interest. In urgent cases of this kind the Commission has the power to act immediately and adopt **protective measures** to put a stop to the restrictive behaviour. Such measures, also called "interim", do not prejudge the final outcome of the matter.

Where, in its final decision, it establishes that there is infringement, the Commission orders the undertaking or the parties concerned to put an end to it without delay. If the parties have of their own volition already put an end to the infringement in the course of the appraisal proceedings, the decision may merely record that the behaviour in question constituted an infringement. If appropriate, the Commission also has the power to order a

---

1   OJ C341, 19.12.1995.
2   See, for example, OJ L121, 06.05.1992.
3   See, for example, OJ L305, 21.10.1992 and OJ L294, 15.11.1994.

positive action on the part of the undertakings involved, such as providing a customer with supplies.

The Commission has the power to **impose fines** of up to ECU 1 million or up to 10% of the total turnover achieved by each of the undertakings concerned during the preceding business year (with the amount imposed being the higher of those two figures) where those undertakings intentionally or negligently infringed the provisions of Articles 85 (1) or 86. The imposition or non-imposition of a fine, and the amount thereof, depend in particular on the gravity of the infringement, its duration and the size of the undertakings involved. An intentional infringement usually leads to a heavier fine than when undertakings are simply guilty of negligence. Practices which have already in the past been frequently punished by the Commission also carry heavier fines, as the earlier decisions of the Commission and of the Court of Justice should have alerted undertakings to the unlawful nature of such behaviour. But instances of recalcitrant undertakings are relatively rare. As a general rule the undertakings in question voluntarily eliminate restrictive practices, resulting in the unofficial shelving of the matter by the Commission.

Commission action in the area of competition is controlled, from the legal standpoint, by the **Court of Justice**, which can rescind or amend any formal Commission decision, i.e. negative clearances, decisions granting or refusing an exemption, orders to put an end to infringements, etc. The Court may also confirm, reduce, repeal or increase the fines and penalty payments imposed by the Commission. Any natural or legal person in respect of whom a decision has been taken may institute proceedings before the Court, as may any other person directly and individually concerned by a decision of which he is not the addressee.

The Commission's competition policy is controlled, from the political standpoint, by the **European Parliament**, which adopts positions on its guidelines. In 1971 the Parliament called upon the Commission to submit an annual report to it on its activities in the sphere of competition. Since then the Commission has submitted to it annually a voluminous report, which accompanies its General Report on the Activities of the Communities and is valuable for any student of EEC competition policy as well as for any undertaking which wishes to enjoy the possibilities afforded by the large market, especially from the point of view of cooperation with its counterparts in other countries, without infringing the rules of European law.

European law and national law

In the field of competition, national competence and Community competence are autonomous and parallel, the latter being defined by the criterion of the effect of trade among Member States. In a concrete case there may be juxtaposition of the validity of European law and national law. In such a case, **European law takes precedence** over national law. In its judgment in the Bayer AG case the Court found that application of the Community rules of competition does not in principle rule out application of the law of the Member States, but that in the event of conflict, Community law takes precedence.

National authorities may take action against an agreement, pursuant to national law, even where the position of that agreement with regard to Community rules is pending before the Commission. However, the decision resulting from a national procedure may not run counter to the Commission's decision. Where the latter precedes the national decision, the competent authorities of the Member State are obliged to observe its effects. Where, on the other hand, the Commission's decision postdates the national decision and is at variance with its effects, it is for the national authorities to take appropriate measures.

The Court of Justice has consistently held that government measures could be regarded as contrary to the competition rules laid down in the EC Treaty, if they were to impose or encourage the conclusion of agreements contrary to Article 85, to heighten the effects of an agreement (e.g. by guaranteeing provisions of an existing agreement in a given market) or to delegate to private operators the power to take concerned decisions on economic action. On the other hand, national legislation could not be regarded as contrary to the Community rules merely because it had restrictive effects on competition similar to those resulting from measures prohibited by Article 85[1].

The Member States cannot do anything against Commission decisions, whereas the Commission can request the competent authorities of the States concerned to proceed with any verification it deems necessary or to collect fines or penalty payments it has imposed. National courts have the right to refer matters of Community law to the Court of Justice of the European Communities for a preliminary ruling. Appeal courts are obliged to request a preliminary ruling where a decision on the point at issue is necessary to enable them to deliver their judgment. In the Communication on **cooperation with domestic courts**, mentioned above, the Commission encourages courts in the Member States to make greater use of their jurisdiction to apply Articles 85 and 86 of the EEC Treaty[2].

As regards **national aids** and discrimination in favour of **public undertakings**, on which the Member States are responsible for infringements of the free-competition arrangements, the precedence of Community law on competition is even more clear-cut. Likewise, it is quite evident that law must be applied by supranational bodies with the power to compel national authorities to comply with their decisions.

Prohibited agreements and permissible cooperations

Article 65 of the **ECSC Treaty** prohibits all agreements between undertakings, decisions by associations of undertakings and concerted practices tending directly or indirectly to prevent, restrict or distort normal competition (price-fixing; restriction or control of production; technical development or investment, and the sharing of markets, products, customers and sources of supply). However, the Commission may authorize specialization agreements, joint-buying or joint-selling agreements in respect of particular products, and agreements strictly analogous to them if it finds that such agreements will make for a substantial improvement in the production or distribution of the products in question and that they are not liable to give the undertakings concerned the power to determine the prices, or to control or restrict the production or marketing, of a substantial part of the products in question or to shield them against effective competition.

The Commission may impose fines not exceeding twice the turnover on the products which were the subject of an agreement on any undertaking which has entered into an agreement which is automatically void, or has enforced or attempted to enforce, by arbitration, boycott or any other means, such an agreement or an agreement for which it has refused or revoked authorization. If the purpose of the agreement or practice is to restrict production, technical development or investment, the fines may be raised to 10% of the turnover of the undertakings in question and the periodic penalty payments to 20% of the daily turnover.

---

1   Judgments of 17 November 1993, cases C-2/91, C-185/91 and C-245/91.
2   OJ C39, 13.02.1993.

The EEC Treaty is just as stringent with regard to agreements as the ECSC Treaty. Its famous **Article 85** declares that all agreements between undertakings, decisions by associations of undertakings and concerted practices which may affect trade between Member States and which have as their object or effect the prevention, restriction or distortion of competition within the common market shall be prohibited as incompatible with the common market and automatically void, and in particular those which: (a) directly or indirectly fix purchase or selling prices or any other trading conditions; (b) limit or control production, markets, technical development, or investment; (c) share markets or sources of supply; (d) apply dissimilar conditions to equivalent transactions with other trading parties, thereby placing them at a competitive disadvantage; (e) make the conclusion of contracts subject to acceptance by the other parties of supplementary obligations which, by their nature or according to commercial usage, have no connection with the subject of such contracts.

However, under **paragraph 3 of Article 85**, the Commission may declare the provisions of paragraph 1 of that Article inapplicable in the case of any agreement or category of agreements between undertakings, any decisions by associations of undertakings and any concerted practice or category of concerted practices, on the following conditions: that they contribute to improving the production or distribution of goods or to promoting technical or economic progress, while allowing consumers a fair share of the resulting benefit, and that they do not afford such undertakings the possibility of eliminating competition in respect of a substantial part of the products in question. Where these requirements are met, the Commission can issue a **negative clearance**, either on an individual basis or by way of a group exemption.

Not all agreements between Community undertakings are prohibited - far from it. Most are even desirable with a view to improving the structures of European industry, as we see in the relevant chapter. In parallel with the elimination of situations incompatible with the system of competition and market unity, the Commission has in fact always pursued a policy of encouraging cooperation between undertakings where, in its opinion, such cooperation is compatible with the common market and can produce favourable economic effects.

Notification and negative clearance

To be able to judge on the compatibility or non-compatibility of agreements with the common market, the Commission has to distinguish them. It was for that purpose that it required, under Regulation N° 17 of 1962[1], the notification of agreements (apart from some which were exempt), in particular: international agreements for the purpose of establishing restrictions on competition (price-fixing, sharing of markets, discounts and selling conditions, rationalization, standardization, etc.): agreements involving only undertakings from one Member State, but with implications for intra-Community trade, and agreements in which third-

---

1   OJ 13, 21.02.1962.

country undertakings participate, insofar as they may affect intra-Community trade.

If they do not fall into one of many category exemptions which we shall see below, agreements between undertakings and decisions by associations of undertakings (e.g. professional associations) must be submitted to the Commission for a decision stating that they do not in any way infringe Article 85 paragraph 1 (**negative clearance**) or that, while they come under Article 85 paragraph 1, they fulfil the requisite conditions for exemption under Article 85 paragraph 3. Notification has to be given in writing on an official form drawn up by the Commission, known as **"Form A/B"**[1]. This form, which is adapted to the requirements of undertakings, enables the Commission to have available to it immediately all information essential for the appraisal of notified agreements. Notification need not be given by all participants in an agreement, but the notifier must be party to the agreement for it to be able to benefit from immunity with regard to fines. The Form A/B may also be used for applications and notifications relating to Article 86 of the EC Treaty, as well as for those relating to Articles 53 and 54 of the Agreement on the European Economic Area (EEA).

The complement to compulsory notification, which is also provided for in Regulation N° 17/62, is the negative clearance by which the Commission states formally that the agreement does not contravene the rules of competition. The Commission must first give interested third parties the opportunity to submit their observations. To that end, it publishes in the Official Journal of the European Communities ("C" series) the main details of the matter. Interested third parties are allowed a period to react to that publication. A second formality to be completed before a negative clearance is issued is the consultation of the authorities of the Member States meeting, for that purpose, in the Advisory Committee on Restrictive Practices and Dominant Positions. At the end of those formalities three scenarios are possible, viz. (a) the Commission finds that the agreement, decision or practice does not infringe Article 85 paragraph 1, in which case it issues a **negative clearance;** (b) the Commission considers that the agreement in question infringes Article 85 paragraph 1 but that the conditions are satisfied for granting an exemption under Article 85 paragraph 3, in which case it adopts a formal decision for an **individual exemption,** or (c) it considers that those conditions have not been met, in which case it addresses to the undertakings concerned a **statement of objections.**

Throughout the years, the Commission has endeavoured to specify, in a double series of measures, some of which were individual and some general, those agreements not covered by the prohibition in Article 85 paragraph 1 and those which, although covered by the prohibition, were likely to be removed from it. Individual exemption decisions do not lend themselves to ill-considered generalization, as the conditions for exemption can only be specific on a case-by-case basis. However, some types of clearly defined agreements were approved as time went on for exemptions in categories.

The "de minimis" rule

In May 1970 the Commission published a communication concerning **agreements of minor importance** which do not fall under Article 85 paragraph 1 of the Treaty, as they do not appreciably affect competition within the common market or trade between Member States. This "de minimis" rule applies to agreements between undertakings which satisfy

---

1   OJ L377, 31.12.1994.

certain market-share and turnover criteria. Those criteria were revised upwards in 1977 and yet again in 1986[1]. In the latter Notice the Commission takes the view that an agreement is not likely, as a general rule, to affect market conditions appreciably where the market share held by the undertakings concerned does not exceed 5% of the total market for the goods or services subject to the agreement in the common market and their aggregate annual turnover does not exceed ECU 200 million. Whatever the nature of the agreement in question, if the two criteria are met the undertakings need not, as a general rule, concern themselves about any applications of Article 85 paragraph 1 and can therefore refrain from notifying the agreement to the Commission.

The derogation from notification of agreements of minor importance is chiefly of interest to SMEs, as it enables them to avoid the laborious procedure of notification-negative clearance and to cooperate without fear of infringing the rules of the common market. Furthermore, several regulations, referred to below, concerning exemptions by category, are first and foremost of interest to SMEs, either because of the activity considered or owing to the implementing conditions (market share and turnover).

Permitted contractual relations

Agreements between undertakings are not regarded as restricting competition and, therefore, do not need to be notified to the Commission where their purpose is a **form of authorized cooperation,** such as: the joint carrying out of comparative studies on undertakings and economic sectors, the joint preparation of statistics and models, the joint study of markets, cooperation on accounting, joint financial guarantees, the joint execution of research and development contracts, projects or commissions, the joint use of means of production, storage and transport and, under certain conditions, the joint performance of orders, joint selling, joint after-sales and repair service and joint advertising[2]. In order to lift any doubts the Commission specified in two communications the characteristics of very common contractual relations concerning exclusive representation and subcontracting, which do not fall under the prohibition of Article 85, paragraph 1.

In the communication relating to **exclusive representation** contracts concluded with sales agents which was published in 1962[3], the Commission stipulated that a contract concluded with a commercial agent who negotiates business on behalf of a principal is not covered by Article 85 paragraph 1. A trader is regarded as a "commercial agent" only if he does not accept any liability for the financial risks involved in the transactions and if he in fact acts only as a simple middleman for the principal. Obviously, one has to ascertain whether or not there is economic integration between the agent and the principal, and to judge that the Commission attaches greater importance to economic reality than to the legal form of

---

1   OJ C231, 12.09.1986.
2   OJ C75, 29.07.1968.
3   OJ 139, 24.12.1962.

relations between undertakings. Thus, the distributor who holds, as owner, a considerable stock of the product covered by the contract or who, at his own expense, provides a significant service to his clientele free of payment or who himself determines the selling prices or the other conditions of the transaction, is regarded as a self-employed trader, in which case Article 85 paragraph 1 applies. However, Article 85 paragraph 1 does not apply in relations between a parent company and its subsidiary, where the latter is not free to determine its action on the market.

In December 1978 the Commission published a communication on the appraisal of **subcontracts** with regard to the provisions of Article 85 of the Treaty[1]. Through that communication the Commission wanted to encourage the development of an industrial practice which is of importance in intra-Community relations and corresponds to abilities peculiar to small and medium-sized undertakings. Subcontracting usually involves, for a small undertaking, known as the "subcontractor", performance of an order for a large undertaking, known as the "principal", in accordance with the directives of the latter. The Commission establishes the principle that the making available to the subcontractor of know-how (whether patented or not) or equipment of the principal may constitute a valid basis for the obligation to supply to the latter only manufactured objects or work executed and does not restrict competition within the meaning of Article 85.

Exemption of categories of agreements

Whereas the contractual relations mentioned above are not prohibited by Article 85, paragraph 1, the contractual relations mentioned under this heading are in principle prohibited but can be exempted from the prohibition. As we saw above, Article 85 paragraph 3 lists four conditions which have to be met for an exemption to be granted by the Commission to an agreement or concerted practice which would restrict competition within the meaning of Article 85 paragraph 1. We also saw that the Commission, after notification of the agreement, may grant an exemption on an individual basis. As a general rule, however, the requirements for exemption are laid down in the regulations exempting certain categories of agreements. A 1965 Council Regulation lays down the conditions under which the Commission may declare by way of regulation that the provisions of Article 85(1) do not apply to certain categories of agreements and concerted practices[2].

These Commission Regulations identify clearly-defined categories of agreements which automatically benefit from the exemption provision of Article 85 (3). Where the requirements set out in a Regulation are met, an agreement does not need to be notified to the Commission and may be implemented without further ado. These block exemption Regulations are particularly useful for SMEs and were in many respects specifically designed for their benefit. In many Regulations, maximum thresholds for

1   OJ C1, 03.01.1979.
2   OJ 36, 06.03.1965.

turnover and/or market share have been set at levels at which SMEs are likely to be the principal beneficiaries.

A first group of block exemption regulations concerns the **cooperation agreements**. A Commission Regulation of 19 December 1984 thus exempts from application of Article 85 paragraph 1 **specialization agreements,** i.e. agreements under which the parties mutually undertake not to manufacture certain products themselves in order to specialize in the manufacture of other products[1]. Although competition is restricted, as the parties refrain from the independent manufacture of certain articles, exemption by category was introduced to allow SMEs to improve their production process and to strengthen their competitive position vis-à-vis larger undertakings. That is why, if the agreement is to enjoy category exemption, it is necessary, inter alia, for the market in the products forming the subject of specialization not to represent more than 20% of the total market in such products and for the aggregate turnover of the participating undertakings not to exceed ECU 500 million.

Another Commission Regulation of 19 December 1984 gives exemption, under certain conditions, to categories of **agreements on research and development** of products or processes as part of a specific programme[2]. Joint exploitation of the results of such agreements is authorized only where the know-how resulting from the R & D carried out jointly makes a significant contribution to technical or economic progress and is a determining factor in the manufacture of new or improved products. The Regulation contains a detailed list of authorized restrictions and obligations, such as those directed towards strengthening cooperation between the parties in the field of R & D, and provisions concerning the scope of the new technology or granting limited territorial protection to the parties. Details are also listed of the provisions which must on no account appear in agreements if the parties are to benefit from exemption by category (blacklist).

A Commission Regulation of 1992 seeks to encourage cooperation between joint ventures of a **cooperative character**. Such enterprises now enjoy a block exemption which, as will be seen below, applies to specialization agreements, research and development agreements, patent licensing agreements and know-how licensing agreements. In a Communication on the same day, the Commission informs interested industrial and commercial circles of the criteria upon which the assessment of joint ventures of a cooperative character will be assessed[3].

The first case concerning cooperative joint ventures is particularly significant as an indicator of the Commission's attitude on their behalf. The companies Philips, Thompson and Sagem decided to set up a cooperative joint venture for the development, manufacture and sale of active matrix liquid crystal displays for screens, and the Commission approved the operation. Its decision indicated clearly that, although the parent companies were competitors as regards screens in general, the joint venture was a means of introducing more quickly into Europe a new technology, the development costs of which were very high, and this in an area in which there was considerable technical and industrial uncertainty and in

1   OJ L53, 22.02.1985.
2   OJ L53, 22.02.1985 and OJ C83, 11.04.1986.
3   OJ L21 of 29.01.1993 and OJ C43, 16.02.1993.

which competition was increasingly worldwide. The Commission's positive attitude to strategic alliances and, in particular, to cooperative joint ventures was also demonstrated in the adoption of a number of formal exemption decisions, including the one concerning the strategic alliance between the United Kingdom telecommunications operator British Telecom and the United States long-distance telecommunications company MCI[1], and the one authorizing the setting-up by Exxon and Shell of a joint venture in the petrochemicals industry[2].

A second group of Commission regulations and communications concerns **distribution agreements**. Under a Regulation of 22 June 1983 the Commission applied Article 85 paragraph 3 of the Treaty to categories of **exclusive distribution agreements** concluded between a supplier and one or more distributors[3]. Some manufacturers, in particular of high-technology products, want their products to be sold by "approved" qualified resellers. Although they restrict competition, such agreements have beneficial effects on distribution within the common market, because the (exclusive) distributor in principle knows the market much better than the supplier, who may be established in another country. Several conditions are laid down for category exemption, the main one being that, in addition to the "official" network through which the exclusive distributor imports goods into a given territory, there is a "parallel" network through which another trader established in that territory imports goods that he has acquired from a third party established outside that territory. Any clause aimed at preventing parallel imports renders exemption by category inapplicable.

Thus, the new Regulation on the exemption of certain categories of **motor vehicle** distribution and servicing agreements sets out to boost competition in motor vehicle distribution by changing the balance between the various interests involved[4]. It is designed in particular to: give dealers, most of whom are SMEs, greater commercial independence from manufacturers, notably by granting them, under certain conditions, the right to sell other manufacturers' cars and by drawing up a black list of anticompetitive clauses which are prohibited; provide better protection for the right of independent suppliers of spare parts to supply resellers of their choice and to place their trade mark; and increase consumer choice by prohibiting certain practices designed to prevent parallel imports and by requiring dealers to honour guarantees and to perform free servicing regardless of where in the common market the vehicle was purchased.

Another Commission Regulation exempts from application of Article 85 categories of **exclusive purchasing agreements**, under which a reseller is obliged to purchase supplies exclusively from a manufacturer or a specific other supplier (a wholesale supplier, for example), without, however, being allocated an exclusive sales territory[5]. If that manufacturer or supplier has managed to corner the maximum sales points or the most important sales points in a given territory, his competitors may have great difficulties in selling their products in that territory. The longer the exclusive purchasing obligation and the wider the range of products involved,

1   OJ L223, 27.08.1994.
2   OJ L144, 09.06.1994.
3   OJ L173, 30.06.1983 and OJ C101, 13.04.1984.
4   OJ L145, 29.06.1995.
5   OJ L173, 30.06.1983 and OJ L1, 03.01.1994.

the more serious the barrier to the entry of competitors to the market. For that reason, in addition to various other conditions for applying that category exemption, the maximum length of the exclusive purchasing obligation has to be limited to five years (renewable) and the range of products covered by the obligation has to be confined to products which are linked by virtue of their nature or of commercial practice.

As exclusive purchasing agreements concerning **beer** sold for consumption on the premises (in particular in cafés) and **fuels** sold in service stations entail substantial financial commitments on the part of suppliers, special obligations apply to such agreements, especially as regards the maximum duration of the exclusive place, which may be ten years. In order to be exempt from the ban, exclusive supply agreements for beer concluded by breweries must meet certain criteria defined by the Commission[1].

A third group of exemption regulations concerns **industrial property rights**, which take on increasing importance in the single market. They include patents, copyright, trade marks, rights of representation, filed designs and, by analogy, technical know-how. The detailed procedures for acquiring and using those rights are determined by the law of each Member State, which is perfectly legitimate but can pose problems if the holder of an industrial property right uses it abusively to compartmentalize the common market or to restrict competition on it. The exemptions granted by the Commission to agreements in the industrial property field therefore try to reconcile the requirements of competition in the common market with conditions on the world market in the high-technology sectors.

Thus **patent licensing agreements,** which grant exclusive rights to licensees for the manufacture and/or sale of patented products and which can cause problems for the common market owing to the territorial protection which they impose, can also have beneficial effects, in particular for SMEs, which cannot otherwise have access to new technology or do not have the financial resources to exploit their inventions. For that reason, in 1984 the Commission adopted a Regulation exempting certain categories of patent licensing agreements, subject to certain conditions[2]. As regards territorial protection, that Regulation allows each party to be protected against active or passive competition from the other party throughout the duration of the agreement. The licensee must also be protected against active competition from other licensees throughout the duration of the agreement, but after five years from the date on which the product was placed on the market, all licensees must have the right to supply the product on the territory of other licensees in response to unsolicited demand from customers established in those territories ("passive sales").

Franchise agreements for distribution and services, which mainly involve the exploitation of industrial or **intellectual property right licenses** (trade marks, distinguishing signs or know-how) for the sale of goods or the provision of services to end users, generally have a positive effect on competition. They improve distribution in that they give the franchiser the possibility of creating a uniform distribution network with limited outlay, which can promote access to the market for new competitors, in particular small and medium-sized enterprises, which can team up with large undertakings while keeping their independence and specializing. The Commission accordingly adopted, in 1988, a Regulation exempting categories of franchise agreements for distribution and services[3]. Exemption is applicable only when certain conditions are satisfied, for example the possibility for the franchisee to sell to other franchisees and the obligation on the franchisee to provide a guarantee throughout the Community[4]. Exclusive purchasing is authorized only for products in respect of

1   OJ C121, 13.05.1992.
2   OJ L219, 16.08.1984 and OJ L214, 08.09.1995.
3   OJ L359, 28.12.1988.
4   See, for example, OJ L20, 25.01.1994.

which it is not possible to formulate objective quality specifications. An obligation of non-competition is, however, regarded as non-restrictive, even during a period of up to one year after expiry of the contract.

Unpatented technical know-how, contained in specifications of manufacturing processes, recipes, formulae and designs, is increasing rapidly in the Community, as are agreements for its exploitation. Know-how is defined as a grouping of technical information which is substantial, secret and identified in an appropriate manner. Although they may impede competition by imposing territorial limits, **know-how licensing agreements,** like patent licensing agreements, have beneficial effects on the economy, as they facilitate the transfer of technology and promote innovation, particularly as regards SMEs. Accordingly, on 30 November 1988 the Commission adopted a Regulation exempting certain categories of these agreements[1]. Such agreements may include territorial protection of the licensor and of the licensee (the one vis-à-vis the other as regards any exploitation of the invention) for a period of ten years from the first licensing agreement concluded for each protected territory within the Community. Between licensees, the authorized duration of protection is ten years for exploitation or active sales and five years for passive competition, in both cases as from the date of the first licensing agreement concluded for the same technology with regard to a given territory within the Community.

A new Commission Regulation provides automatic exemption from the prohibition on restrictive practices to **technology transfer** agreements, whether these are "pure" or "mixed" patent licensing and know-how licensing agreements[2]. It thus helps to promote the spread of new technologies within the European Union and benefits the vast majority of economic operators. It provides for a threshold, however, namely a 40% market share, beyond which companies do not benefit from the Regulation if they have obtained exclusive licences and thereby cornered the relevant market and prevented access by third parties to the new technologies.

The regulations cited above, and regulations on exemption by category dealt with in the sections on insurance (in the chapter on the common market) and air transport (in the chapter on transport), authorize, under certain conditions, the forms of cooperation between undertakings which are the most commonplace and which do not restrict competition in a manner which is incompatible with the rules of competition of the Treaty. They thus govern the vast majority of cases of agreements existing in the Community. The Commission can therefore give its undivided attention to the prohibited agreements examined below, which are usually secret and which really impede free competition and trade in the common market.

Prohibited agreements

We shall not attempt, here, to describe all the forms of horizontal agreements which are prohibited by the rules of competition of the Treaties. Specialist works have to be consulted on the subject. Moreover, each case differs depending on the product concerned, the market involved and the imagination of the executives of the participant undertakings. We shall confine ourselves to a few characteristic cases of agreements incompatible with the common market, as emerging from Commission decisions. The Commission judges the advantages and disadvantages of an agreement or category of agreements not on the basis of purely legal criteria, but also using the criterion of the general interest of the producers and consumers

---

1   OJ L61, 04.03.1989 and OJ L21, 29.01.1993.
2   OJ L31, 09.02.1996.

in a sector. Also, it applies the "de minimis" rule, discussed above, to agreements which infringe the rules of competition but the economic impact of which is insignificant.

The Commission acts cautiously with regard to agreements which it considers incompatible with the Treaty. It tries to gather indisputable evidence of the infringement of Article 85 paragraph 1, which can, on occasion, take several years, as nowadays restrictions of competition rarely take the form of written agreements obliging contractors to carry out unlawful acts on pain of penalty. They usually take the form of concerted practices based on "gentlemen's agreements", material evidence of which is difficult to find. The Commission's cautious approach on the matter - outlined under the heading of the powers of the Commission - has the disadvantage of being slow, but it adds weight to its decisions which are usually upheld by the Court of Justice in the event of the undertakings charged bringing proceedings before it. Those decisions therefore make clear the Community's policy on major types of prohibited agreements.

The sharing of markets is particularly restrictive of competition and at variance with the objectives of the common market, as agreements based on the principle of reciprocal respect of national markets for the benefit of the participants established there have the effect of obstructing intra-Community trade in the products concerned. Through the system of fixing supply quotas on the basis of the total sales of members of the agreement, those members waive the freedom to apply an independent sales policy, but have, on the other hand, the possibility of applying a prices policy shielded from the competition of their partners. The following are celebrated cases of penalized market-sharing agreements: the case of the Community quinine producers, who had decided amongst themselves, by gentleman's agreements, on price regulation and quotas covering all their sales on the internal markets and abroad[1]; and the case of the major sugar undertakings, which controlled intra-Community trade in sugar for human consumption[2]. More recently, in November 1994, the Commission decided to impose the highest fines ever (ECU 248 million) on 9 associations of undertakings and 33 European cement producers, parties to a general market-sharing agreement aimed at protecting national or domestic markets and concluded under the aegis of Cembureau, the European Cement Federation[3].

Agreements on the fixing of prices or of other conditions of transactions seriously limit competition, as they prevent purchasers from benefiting from the competitive behaviour that producers would have shown had the agreement not existed. As they are coupled with reciprocal respect for national markets, they are also likely to have an adverse effect on intra-Community trade. The Commission has therefore prohibited: concerted practices for the purpose of the application by the participating undertakings, on the same dates and in respect of the same categories of product (colorants), identical rates of price increases[4]; horizontal price fixing agree-

1   OJ L192, 05.08.1969.
2   OJ L140, 26.05.1973.
3   OJ L343, 30.12.1994.
4   OJ L195, 07.08.1969.

ments and horizontal exclusive dealing agreements in the crane-hire sector in the Netherlands (Van Marwijk/FNK-SCK)[1] and the market-sharing and price-fixing cartel of 14 PVC producers. The re-adoption by the Commission of its 1988 decision in this case, after its annulment by the Court of Justice on procedural grounds, demonstrates its determination to take action against such restrictive agreements, which infringe the basic rules of competition, by imposing substantial fines on those involved[2].

Restrictions on access to the market by new entrants are also prohibited. Access to the market can be impeded where a large number of retailers on this market are tied by an obligation to sell only the products of the manufacturer with which they have a contract or vertical arrangements having a similar exclusionary effect on third parties. This is why, the Commission prohibited the agreement between Langnese (Unilever) and Schöller, which occupy a duopolistic position on the German impulse ice cream market, and the Court of First Instance confirmed the prohibition[3]. In other cases, new competitors can be prevented from entering the market through a horizontal agreement or concerted practice, as in the aforementioned case of the Dutch crane-hire market[4].

Isolation of a market within the Community can also occur, without exclusive business relations being agreed upon as in the previous case, through agreements concluded between producers from a Member State in order to grant habitual customers **rebates whose levels are fixed collectively** on the basis of total purchases from those producers during the reference period. This was the case of the agreement of German manufacturers of ceramic tiles[5]. The aggregation of the discount bases induced customers not to consider offers, even if more favourable, from producers in the other Member States, so as to group their purchases with producers participating in the agreement and thus secure the highest possible levels of rebate.

Joint selling is, as a general rule, permitted by the Commission in the context of association agreements, as referred to above. The same is not true, however, of **joint sales agreements** through which the participating undertakings share amongst themselves, in accordance with a specific scale, the total quantity of products on offer through a sales point at uniform prices and on uniform sales terms. The three factors together - the action of the joint body, the apportionment of supply quotas and price-fixing - prevent any competition between the participants on the markets concerned and deprive purchasers of any choice between different offers. For that reason, the Commission penalized the three main French fertilizer producers, the purpose of whose cooperation was to ensure the distribution of their complex fertilizers in Germany solely through the intermediary of a joint commercial company called "Floral"[6].

Joint purchasing agreements may also result in a restriction of competition where the large purchasing capacity of the participating undertakings enables them to abuse their strength vis-à-vis the suppliers. That was the case with the wholesalers participating in the Dutch cooperative VBA, the world's largest flower auction, who had undertaken not to market any products other than those supplied through the VBA[7]. On the other hand, the Commission authorized the Eurovision system of joint purchasing of broadcasting rights for international sporting events. Although the system restricts competition, because of the combined purchasing power enjoyed by the European Broadcasting Union, the Commission accepted it, because it contributes to the development of a genuine European broadcasting

---

1   OJ L312, 23.12.1995.
2   Judgment of 15 June 1994, Case C-137/92P and OJ L239, 14.09.1994.
3   Judgments of 8 June 1995, cases T-7/93, Langnese-Iglo and T-9/93, Schöller, ECR 1995.
4   OJ L312, 23.12.1995.
5   OJ L10, 13.01.1971.
6   OJ L39, 15.02.1980.
7   OJ L262 of 22.09.1988.

market and facilitates cross-border broadcasting, particularly important for the members of the EBU from smaller countries[1].

The most complicated cases are those of **exclusive distribution agreements,** which are covered by a category exemption, but not where they provide for absolute territorial protection **which prevents parallel imports.** This is the case of agreements which stand in the way of the distributor re-exporting the products in question to other Member States or of such products being imported from other Member States in the concessionaire's area and being distributed there by persons other than the concessionaire. Commission policy on the matter was clearly set out in its decision of 23 September 1964 in the "Grundig-Consten" case[2], essentially upheld by the Court of Justice in its judgment of 13 July 1966. The Commission continues to fight against distribution systems which impede parallel trade, such as that of the German company Tipp-ex, which prevented its distributors from reselling products in other Community Member States[3], or that of BASF, which prevented its exclusive distributor in Belgium and Luxembourg of Glasurit car refinishing paints to export those products to the United Kingdom[4].

There are, of course, several other types of unauthorized horizontal agreements, such as those which fix discriminatory conditions in transactions with third parties competing with each party, or those aimed at ousting a current competitor from the market or closing it to a potential competitor. Other types of agreements which are normally exempt are liable to come within the scope of Article 85 paragraph 1 if they restrict competition and are not covered by the "de minimis" rule, e.g. joint advertising agreements, if they prevent the participants from also promoting their products independently; agreements for the use of a common quality label, if that label may not be used by all manufacturers whose products meet the quality standards in question, and even agreements on the exchange strategy of the participants. In the event of doubt as to the legitimacy of an agreement, undertakings concerned that wish to avoid fines would be well advised to notify the agreement to the Commission.

Market domination

We shall see in the relevant chapter that, from the point of view of the Community's industrial and enterprise policies, concentrations of small and medium-sized undertakings into larger units are in principle desirable and should be encouraged, as they lead to economies of scale, rationalization of the production and distribution of products in the common market and promote technical progress. But if the concentration exceeds certain limits, which vary from sector to sector, it may result in the formation of

---

1   OJ L272, 04.11.1993.
2   OJ L161, 20.10.1964.
3   OJ L222, 10.08.1987.
4   OJ L272, 15.11.1995.

monopolies or, more often, oligopolies and the consequent restrictions of competition and intra-Community trade. That occurs in particular where an undertaking which dominates a sector by virtue of its size and economic strength acquires the smaller undertakings in competition with it one by one. The ECSC and EEC Treaties provided for this instance, the former in a much clearer manner than the latter.

Under Article 66, which is one of the most important of the ECSC Treaty, any transaction which brings about a concentration between undertakings at least one of which is engaged in production in the coal or the steel industry, whether it is effected by merger, acquisition of shares or parts of the undertaking or assets, loan, contract or any other means of control, shall require the prior authorization of the High Authority (Commission). The severity of the ECSC Treaty with regard to concentrations stems from the historic circumstances under which it was framed. Article 66 had the objective of satisfying not only German and French public opinion, but also the occupying forces in Germany, which were dominated by the United States. A significant aspect of the Allies' policy towards the occupied Germany had been to dismantle the major "Konzerne" of its heavy steel industry ("trust-busting"), in particular in the coal and steel sector. But little by little the High Authority and the Commission, which succeeded it after 1967, influenced by the development of the coal and steel market, departed from a strict interpretation of the Treaty. As a general rule the Commission tends to align the policy with regard to concentrations which is pursued in the coal and steel sectors on the policy pursued in the sectors covered by the EEC Treaty, i.e. it tries to strike a balance between the severity of the ECSC Treaty and the tolerance of the EEC Treaty with regard to concentrations.

Exploitation of a dominant position

Article 86 of the EEC Treaty stipulates that "any abuse by one or more undertakings of a dominant position within the common market or in a substantial part of it shall be prohibited as incompatible with the common market in so far as it may affect trade between Member States". Apart from the fact that Article does not prohibit the obtaining of a dominant position, but only abuse thereof, it leaves several issues obscure, although they are now clarified by various standard Commission decisions and judgments of the Court of Justice.

First, **domination of a given market** cannot be defined solely on the basis of the market share held by an undertaking or of other quantitative elements, but also in the light of its ability to exercise an appreciable influence on the functioning of the market and on the behaviour of other undertakings. In its judgment of 14 February 1978 in the case of "United Brands Company v. Commission" the Court upheld and enlarged the definition of the dominant position adopted by the Commission as early as its decision of 9 December 1971 in the "Continental Can Company" case[1]. It thus stated that the dominant position referred to in Article 86 "relates to a position of economic strength enjoyed by an undertaking which enables it to prevent effective competition being maintained on the relevant market by giving it the power to behave to an appreciable extent independently of its competitors, customers and ultimately of its consumers".

---

1   OJ L7, 08.01.1972.

The definition of **the relevant market** or of the market in question is also of great importance, as the more strictly that market is defined in time and space, the greater the likelihood that a dominant position can be identified in the common market. In its judgment of 13 February 1979 in the "Hoffman-La Roche v. Commission" case, the Court of Justice felt, in common with the Commission[1], that each group of vitamins constitutes a separate market and that one product can belong to two separate markets if it can be used for several purposes[2]. The Court held that actual competition must be able to exist between products which belong to the relevant market, which presupposes an adequate degree of interchangeability between such products.

As regards the concept of the **apportionment of trade between Member States,** which is the same for Articles 85 and 86, the Commission and the Court of Justice are in agreement that a concentration in which an undertaking which occupies a dominant position in the common market or in a substantial part of it will always be of importance for trade between Member States. In its judgment of 13 July 1966 in the "Grundig-Consten" case the Court opined that the concept of damage to trade between Member States should be seen as a question of "whether the agreement is capable of constituting a threat... to freedom of trade between Member States in a manner which might harm the attainment of the objectives of a single market between States"[3]. It goes without saying that abuse of a dominant position is judged all the more harshly because it tends to compartmentalize the relevant market and make economic interpenetration more difficult. That was the case with British Leyland, which refused to issue type-approval certificates for left-hand-drive "Metro" vehicles in order to prevent the re-importation of such vehicles from other Member States[4].

Lastly, as regards the concept of **abuse of a dominant position,** Article 86 is more explicit, as it stipulates that "abuse may in particular, consist in: (a) ... imposing unfair purchase or selling prices or other unfair trading conditions; (b) limiting production, markets or technical development ...; (c) applying dissimilar conditions to equivalent transactions with other trading parties ..." and "(d) making the conclusion of contracts subject to acceptance by the other parties of supplementary obligations" which have no connection with such contracts.

In its aforementioned judgment in the "Hoffmann-La Roche" case the Court of Justice for the first time gave a general definition of abuse by stating that it is an "objective concept relating to the behaviour of an undertaking in a dominant position which is such as to influence the structure of a market where, as a result of the very presence of the undertaking in question, the degree of competition is weakened and which, through recourse to methods different from those which condition normal competition in products or services on the basis of the transactions of commercial operators, has the effect of hindering the maintenance of the degree of competition still existing in the market or the growth of that competition". In the British Midland/Aer Lingus case, the Commission showed its determination to proceed

1   OJ L223, 16.08.1976.
2   Judgment of 13 February 1979, case 85/76, ECR 1979, p. 461.
3   Cases 56, 58/64, Consten-Grundig v Commission, ECR 1966, p. 299.
4   OJ L207, 02.08.1984 and case 226/84, British Leyland PLC v Commission, ECR 1986, p. 3263.

against any airline or any other holder of a dominant position which tries to stand in the way of the development or maintenance of competition[1].

The "United Brands Company" judgment defines the scope of the concept of abuse by confirming the obligation for an undertaking in a dominant position to respect the principle of proportionality when it imposes restrictions on its resellers, even if in so doing it is pursuing legitimate objectives such as maintaining the quality of its products or protecting its commercial interests[2]. Such objectives cannot, a fortiori, be invoked when in reality their purpose is to eliminate competitors. Hence Tetra Pak, the largest Community producer in the milk carton industry, was censured for having obtained an exclusive licence concerning technology for a method of sterilizing cartons for long shelf-life milk[3]. Technological prominence may even entail certain obligations for undertakings in a dominant position vis-à-vis their competitors. In 1984 the Commission obliged IBM to communicate systematically in good time to its competitors in the Community appropriate information on its interfaces in order to enable them to connect their products to its large medium-sized data-processing systems and to its network or systems interconnection system. In July 1994, the Commission in cooperation with the American Department of Justice obtained an important undertaking from Microsoft, the world's leading software producer, concerning the granting of software licences to microcomputer manufacturers in proper terms.

Generally speaking, an undertaking in a dominant position may abuse its power on the market in one of the following ways: by setting the prices on the dominated market or by "tying" the products or services of this market to other products or services (for example, the railway traction services in Germany offered by the Deutsche Bahn to specialized operators in the combined transport of goods operating in the port of Rotterdam[4]); by imposing on its customers exclusive purchasing agreements for a category of products (such as the vitamins in the Hoffmann-La Roche case); or by attempting to eliminate competition by "predatory pricing", i.e. by selling below cost for a short period of time until the competitors are driven out of the market.

It is certain that the Commission and the Court regard it as an abuse where an undertaking in a dominant position strengthens that position by means of a concentration or of the elimination of competitors, with the result that competition, which continued in spite of the existence of the dominant position, is virtually eliminated as regards the products concerned in a substantial part of the common market. The Commission accordingly imposed heavy fines on: AKZO Chemie, which is the chemical division of the Dutch multinational group AKZO, for having abused its dominant position on the organic peroxides market by trying to eliminate a small competitor from the market by applying prolonged, selective price-cuts designed to damage its business[5], and British Sugar plc for implementing a series of abuses designed to eliminate a smaller competitor from the retail sugar market[6]. On July 24, 1991, the Commission imposed a record fine on Tetra Pak for having deliberately attempted to eliminate its actual or potential competitors, in breach of Article 86 of the EEC Treaty and this after its first condemnation seen above.

1   OJ L96, 10.04.1992.
2   Judgment of 14 February 1978, case 27/76, ECR 1978, p. 207.
3   OJ L272, 04.10.1988 and case T-51/89, ECR 1990, II-309.
4   OJ L104, 23.04.1994.
5   OJ L374, 31.12.1985 and judgment of 3 July 1991, case C-62/86, Akzo Chemie v Commission, ECR 1991.
6   OJ L284, 19.10.1988.

In the aforementioned judgment in the Hoffmann-La Roche case , the Court of Justice felt that the prohibitions listed in Article 86, in spite of that Article's necessarily vague wording, did not show the indeterminate and unforeseeable nature alleged by Roche. According to the Court an undertaking which dominates a market must take that fact into account and itself seek legal security by requesting a **negative clearance** of the Commission, as provided for in Article 2 of Regulation N° 17/62. As the Court stressed in its judgment of 19 June 1978 in the BP v. ABG case, such a clearance would not, however, free the Commission from its obligations peculiar to the market, where the competitive position of operators is particularly threatened, to comply scrupulously with Article 86 of the Treaty. The Court thus confirmed that the purpose of Article 86 is to preserve an effective competition structure in the common market, especially where it is jeopardized by the elimination of independent economic operators by an undertaking in a dominant position.

Concentrations in the Single Market

Concentrations are arrangements whereby one or more persons or undertakings acquire control of a company and thus change the structure of undertakings and of the market they operate in. The most important forms of concentrations of undertakings are the holding of a company in the authorized capital of another company or of other companies, the total or partial acquisitions by a company of the assets of other companies and, lastly, the merger of two or more companies which are legally independent into a new company. Concentrations allow economies of scale to be obtained, production and distribution costs to be reduced, profitability to be improved and technical progress to be speeded up. All of that facilitates the international competitiveness of Community undertakings and may provide consumers with part of the benefits of economic integration. It is, however, obvious that where concentrations exceed certain limits they can lead to monopoly or oligopoly structures which restrict competition and jeopardize consumers' interests.

As mentioned above, Article 86 of the Treaty prohibits abuse of a dominant position, but not its existence or creation. As quite distinct from the ECSC Treaty on this point, the EC Treaty does not require the authorization of the Commission for a concentration transaction which may lead to the creation of a dominant position. That special characteristic of the EC Treaty could lead to the following paradox: if two or more undertakings wanted to initiate simple horizontal cooperation between themselves, they would be subject to the prior authorization procedure for agreements based on Article 85 and laid down in Regulation N° 17/62. If, on the other hand, one of them wanted to acquire the other or others, they would not be subject to any control, as Article 86 does not require any.

However, the Commission undertook to fill the legislative vacuum in the EEC Treaty on the basis of Article 3 (f) thereof. In the Commission's view, since the EEC Treaty has the objective of ensuring the functioning of an undistorted system of competition, the exploitation of a dominant position should be regarded as abusive if it in practice prevented that undistorted competition from functioning. A concentration of undertakings that results in the **monopolization of a market** should therefore be dealt with as abuse of a dominant position within the meaning of Article 86.

For the first time in 1971 the Commission translated that interpretation into fact by adopting a Decision applying Article 86 in the case of the concentration of an undertaking occupying a dominant position, namely Continental Can Cy, with a competing undertaking[1]. Domination of the market was not defined by the Commission solely on the basis of the market share held by the grouped undertakings, but also on the basis of the advantages held by the group over most of its competitors by virtue of its size and economic, financial and technological strength. The Commission concluded that Continental Can Cy had abused its dominant position by taking control of one of its potential main competitors, thus strengthening the said dominant position in such a way that competition in a substantial part of the common market was virtually eliminated with regard to the products concerned. The judgment delivered by the Court of Justice on 21 February 1973 declared the Commission's decision void on the grounds that the market in question had not been sufficiently demarcated, but confirmed the correctness of the Commission's approach to the application of Article 86 to abuse of the dominant position by the concentration. The Court in fact stated that "abuse may therefore occur if an undertaking in a dominant position strengthens such a position in such a way that the degree of dominance reached substantially fetters competition, i.e. that only undertakings remain in the market whose behaviour depends on the dominant one"[2].

With the support of the Court of Justice, the Commission could henceforth exercise an **a posteriori control of concentrations** of undertakings, one of which had already achieved a dominant position. However, knowing that "prevention is better than cure", the Commission wanted a preventive policy in the field of concentrations. After securing the support of the Heads of State and Government at their Paris meeting in December 1972, it prepared a proposal for a **Regulation on the control of concentrations** of undertakings, which it submitted to the Council in July 1973. It took sixteen years of discussion in the Council and several amendments to the Commission proposal for it finally to be adopted on 21 December 1989[3].

Compulsory notification covers mergers involving undertakings whose aggregate worldwide turnover exceeds ECU 5 thousand million (general threshold), where the turnover in the EEC countries of at least two of those undertakings exceeds ECU 250 million, and this involves some 50 to 60 cases of mergers a year. The national authorities keep their power of investigation and authorization if two-thirds of the activities of each of the companies concerned take place in a Member State. The regulation on mergers is fully in tune with the principle of subsidiarity. The Commission only takes action on mergers if they have a Community dimension and on restrictive practices only if they affect trade between Member States; in these cases its position, its experience and its powers of inquiry place it at the best level to assess the factors involved. Moreover, the Commission can authorize a national anti-cartel office to investigate a concentration

---

1   OJ L7, 08.01.1972.
2   Case 6/72, Europemballage Corporation v Commission, ECR 1973, p. 215.
3   OJ L395, 30.12.1989 and OJ L257, 21.09.1990.

which may have significant effects on a local market. In the cases notified to it the Commission has three weeks to announce to the undertakings and Member States concerned that it will be carrying out an inquiry. Thereafter, it has three months to rule in favour of or against the proposed merger. The Commission has to base its decision principally on criteria of competition, but may also take into consideration other factors, such as economic and technical progress.

To ensure the effective application of the principle of compulsory notification, the Commission adopted in July 1990 a Regulation covering, among other points, time limits and hearings, the form, content and other **provisions relating to notifications**[1]. This Regulation was supplemented by two Communications of the Commission relating respectively to secondary restrictions on merger operations and the definition of merger and cooperation situations falling under the scope of the basic regulation[2]. Notifications relating to the 1989 Regulation on the control of concentrations between undertakings and to Article 57 of the EEA Agreement must be submitted in the manner prescribed by Form CO, drawn up by the Commission[3].

The procedures established for dealing with notifications enable the Commission to make effective use of its new powers in this area. The Commission grants authorization, within the space of a month, to the vast majority of operations which do not create or reinforce a dominant position in the common market or a substantial part of it[4]. Only when serious doubts exist as to the operations' compatibility with the common market does it decide to open a detailed investigation as provided for in the second part of the procedure.

Until the end of 1995, the Commission had prohibited only three concentration operations: the take-over of de Havilland by Aérospatiale and Alenia, justified by very high market shares in a global market, high barriers to entry and the maturity of the market; the joint venture, Holland Media Groep (HMG), because it would be uniquely able to offer advertisers coordinated scheduling on the Dutch television market; and the creation of the joint venture Nordic Satellite Distribution (NSD), because it would reinforce the anti-competitive effects foreclosing the Nordic satellite television market. Still, in those cases, the Commission invited the parties concerned to propose appropriate amendments to their projects rendering them compatible with the common market. Thus, the Regulation on mergers does not prevent undertakings from entering into strategic alliances; it allows them to seek complementarities, acquire an international dimension, penetrate new markets and take advantage of the single market, without jeopardizing competition within it. However, with a Green Paper of 31 January 1996, the Commission launched a wide-ranging debate on the review of the Merger Regulation, centred mainly on the thresholds above which the Commission has exclusive competence, i.e. a worldwide turnover of ECU 2 billion (instead of ECU 5 billion) and an individual turnover of ECU 100 million (instead of ECU 250 million) in two EU countries.

---

1   OJ L219, 14.08.1990 and OJ L336, 31.12.1993.
2   OJ C203, 14.08.1990.
3   OJ L377, 31.12.1994.
4   See, for example, OJ L239, 07.10.1995, (Swissair-Sabena).

State intervention

Competition in the common market can be distorted not only by the machinations of undertakings, but also by State intervention. The arguments adduced by governments for intervening in economic activities are numerous, but they all have a politico-social ring: to prevent the closure of undertakings which might give rise to collective redundancies, which are unacceptable in social and regional terms. At national level, undertakings experiencing difficulties make public opinion and the official authorities aware of their predicament, especially where traditional activities are involved, or big business, when they are regarded as "flagship undertakings".

The social and regional consequences of structural changes should indeed be attenuated, but the changes themselves should not be opposed by artificially ensuring the survival of sectors in decline. The question should be asked, on a case-by-case basis, whether aid is really essential, rather than a radical change in production methods, and whether aid for an industry in difficulty in one common market Member State might not harm the interests of the same industries established in the other Member States. It is, indeed, obvious that State intervention may involve a conflict of interests between the economic operators benefiting from such intervention and their competitors in the other Member States, which will be placed in a less favourable position and will press their governments to redress the situation. Unilaterally conceived State initiatives cannot, therefore, but trigger retaliation from partner countries and lead to costly operations for everyone. In order to avoid squandered resources, therefore, a "code of good conduct" is needed for the Member States in this area.

To that end, Article 92 of the EC Treaty stipulates that "any aid granted... which distorts or threatens to distort competition by favouring certain undertakings or the production of certain goods shall, in so far as it affects trade between Member States, **be incompatible with the common market**". Given the high degree of integration of the Community's economy, most national subsidies are likely to be considered trade-distorting, even for products which are not exported to other Member States, if they compete on their home market with imports from other Member States. The form of the aid is irrelevant: for example outright grants, soft loans, tax concessions, guarantees, the supply of goods or services at less than cost are all subject to Community State aid control. However, an important innovation was introduced in 1992 with the adoption of the **"de minimis" rule** under which aid of less than ECU 50 000 over three years is judged not to affect trade between Member States and thus need no longer be notified to the Commission.

Paragraph 2 of Article 92 considers that the following shall be **compatible with the common market**, provided that it is granted without discrimination related to the origin of the products concerned: **aid having a social character** granted to individual consumers, aid to make good the damage caused by natural disasters or exceptional occurrences and aid granted to certain areas of Germany affected by the division of that country (before 1991). Article 92 paragraph 3, for its part, stipulates that the following may be considered to be compatible with the common market: aid to **promote the economic development of areas** with economic or social problems; aid to promote the execution of an important project of common European interest or to remedy a serious disturbance in the economy of a Member State; aid to facilitate the development of certain economic activities or of certain economic areas, where such aid does not adversely affect trading conditions; aid to promote culture and heritage conservation[1]; and such other categories of aid as may be specified by decision of the Council acting by a qualified majority on a proposal from the Commission.

So that the Commission may adopt a position on the possible application of one of the above derogations from the incompatibility of aid, the Member States are obliged, under Article 93 paragraph 3 of the EEC Treaty to **inform it in sufficient time**, through a detailed questionnaire, of any plans to grant new aid or alter existing aid. Such aid may not be granted by Member States until the Commission has taken a final decision on it. In case the Member States fail to fulfil their obligation to notify proposals to grant aid, the Commission reserves the right to take a provisional decision requiring them to recover, with interest, any aid paid illegally pending a final decision by it on the compatibility of the aid with the common market[2]. The Commission has a period of two months to adopt a position on any proposed system of aid notified to it. Before the end of that period, it either informs the Member State concerned of its decision not to oppose implementation of the aid project or it initiates the procedure laid down in Article 93 paragraph 2 of the EEC Treaty with regard to it.

Under the procedure, the Member State concerned is given notice to submit its comments within a given time-limit, normally set at one month. The other Member States are also invited to submit their comments on the proposed aid in question, as are other interested parties, which are apprised through **publication in the Official Journal of the European Communities.** In the light of those comments, the Commission may decide either not to object to the proposed aid or to require that it be abolished or to call for certain alterations to be made to it. In the event of aid having been granted illegally to the beneficiary, the Commission is entitled to **require that the Member State which granted it unduly recover it** . Aid is granted illegally if it is awarded without prior notification to the Commission or before the Commission has taken a final decision or, again, if it is granted in contempt of the decision taken by the Commission regarding it. If the Member State concerned is not in agreement with the Commission's decision it may, within two months, refer the matter to the Court of Justice.

A Court of Justice ruling of February 14, 1990 provided some highly useful clarifications to the State aids vetting system and more specifically: to the procedural rules of Article 93, paragraph 3, which oblige the Member States to inform the Commission of planned State aids so that it can take a decision on their compatibility prior to implementation; and to the obligation for the Member States to demand repayment of aid not eligible for one of the dispensations provided for under Article 92 and which is consequently incompatible with the common market[3]. In another judgment the Court specified that only benefits granted directly or indirectly out of State resources are to be regarded as aid within the meaning of Article 92(1)[4]. According to the Court, if a firm in receipt of State aid has not brought direct

---

1   Point inserted at Maastricht.
2   OJ C156, 27.06.1995.
3   Case C-301/87, France v Commission, OJ C61, 10.03.1990.
4   Case 88/77, Van Tiggele, ECR 1978, p. 25.

annulment proceedings under the second paragraph of Article 173 of the EC Treaty against a Commission decision declaring the aid to be unlawful (even though it was fully informed of the decision) within the periods prescribed, that firm cannot plead that the Commission decision is unlawful[1].

The Commission processes one thousand aid applications every year. Half of these are made up of aid for the manufacturing industry and services. The other half consists of aid in the sectors of agriculture, fisheries, transport and coal-mining. The annual total amount of aid in the Community stands at around ECU 90 billion, around 40% of which goes to manufacturing. All the Member States grant aid to their companies, but the percentage of GNP absorbed by this aid varies from 2% to 4%, with the highest percentage granted by the most wealthy countries. Major differences also exist in the form taken by subsidies. Whereas in Spain, for example, assistance consists almost exclusively of financial aid, in Germany, tax incentives are most used. All these types of aid, useful or otherwise, have one thing in common: they distort competition between undertakings, some of which enjoy subsidies or tax reductions while others do not. It is this harmful impact on competition which prompts the Commission to take action on behalf of the Community, particularly when the aid granted runs counter to the cohesion objective because it is at the detriment of the poorer regions of the Community.

Aid of a regional character was examined in the chapter on regional development, under the heading "coordination of policies". The following paragraphs look at other State operations: general aid, sectoral aid, national monopolies and public undertakings.

General aids

Aid from which any undertaking whatsoever can benefit, without regard to its geographical location or to the sector to which it belongs, is regarded as general aid. Owing to this lack of a specific character, such aid cannot lay claim to an exemption provision provided for in the Treaty. The Commission has to be able to verify, prior to their being granted, that general aids are in response to genuine economic or social needs, that they lead to an improvement in the structures of beneficiary undertakings and that they do not give rise to problems at Community level.

The completion of the internal market fuels competition and thus pushes for an increase in State aids. The Commission is trying to put a brake on this trend. It discourages so-called "general" aid, making it clearly understood to the Member States that this category of aid, which does not pursue clearly defined objectives, is not compatible with the internal market. For that reason, it requires Member States, when applying general aid arrangements, either to notify it in advance of the relevant regional or sectoral programmes or, if there are no such programmes, to inform it of significant individual cases. It also tries to obviate an excessively high

---

1   Judgment given on 9 March 1994, Case C-188/92, ECR 1994, I-833.

intensity of aid (aggregation) for a single undertaking under various aid schemes.

The Commission systematically prohibits **State export aid** within the Community and normally prohibits aid which does not have a **counterpart in the Community interest**. Aid on which no time limit is placed and which is required to support current activities ("**operating aid**") is just as unacceptable as aid for intra-Community exports. As to the problem of State **participation in the capital of undertakings**, the Court of Justice confirmed, in a series of judgments delivered in 1985 and 1986, that such contributions were indeed likely to be State aids coming within the scope of Article 92 et seq. of the EEC Treaty.

However, certain general aids are granted to achieve **legitimate objectives** and may be approved by the Commission under certain conditions. In addition to regional development aids, this is generally the case for research and development aids, aids in favour of small and medium-sized enterprises, environmental protection aids, vocational training aids and aids for job creation programmes for the unemployed.

Thus, the Commission established since 1986 a Community framework for State **aids for research and development**. Under the new framework for this type of aids, preference is given to projects in favour of SMEs, to undertakings investing in the less developed regions of the Union or which fit into the 1994-98 framework programme for research and technological development with its specific priorities[1]. In order to reduce red tape, prior notification is required only for individual research projects costing more than ECU 25 million and benefiting of more than ECU 5 million in aid.

The framework for aid to **small and medium-sized enterprises,** drawn up by the Commission on May 20, 1992, includes in this category independent companies with fewer than 250 employees and/or turnover of less than 20 million ECU or a balance sheet result of less than 10 million ECU[2]. Consistency between policy in favour of SMEs and the principle of economic and social cohesion is provided by variations in the proportion of aid permitted. Thus, in regions not eligible for regional aid, the permitted aid proportion is restricted to 7.5% (but can rise to 15% for small companies with up to 50 employees). In regions eligible for regional aid, the permissible aid ceiling stands at 10% or 15%, depending on the seriousness of the problems faced by the areas in question. Advice, training and technology transfer aid are accepted in all types of area and can reach proportions of 50%.

The Commission authorizes subsidies helping companies adapt to **environmental protection** standards and notably those encouraging them to make efforts in relation to the requirements of the fifth programme on the environment and environmentally sustainable development[3]. The Community framework is designed to ensure that State aid granted for environmental purposes complies with the "polluter pays" principle and

---

1   OJ C45, 17.02.1996. See the chapter on research.

2   OJ C213, 19.08.1992.

3   OJ C72, 10.03.1994.

is consistent with the internal market and the Community's competition policy.

Aids granted to assist companies facing a particularly difficult market situation, such as structural overcapacity, are accepted only in exceptional circumstances as part of a wider plan to reduce the overcapacity. In July 1994, the Commission adopted guidelines on State aid for **rescuing and restructuring firms** in difficulty, which set out its approach to examining aid of this type, in particular: there must be a restructuring plan capable of ensuring the viability of the firm; aid must be limited to the strict minimum needed for implementing the plan; criteria ensuring that the distortion of competition will be strictly limited must be met[1]. Aid to finance **social measures** exclusively for the benefit of employees who are displaced by restructuring are not taken into consideration in determining the size of any capacity reduction required.

So as to help Member States devise **employment aid** measures in response to the guidelines on employment set out in the White Paper on growth, competitiveness and employment and confirmed at the Essen and Cannes European Councils, the Commission set out, in July 1995, the guidelines by reference to which it assesses the compatibility of such aid with the EC Treaty[2]. It gives sympathetic consideration, on the one hand, to aid which, subject to certain ceilings, aims to create new jobs in SMEs and in regions eligible for regional aid, and on the other, to aid which is intended to encourage the recruitment of certain categories of workers experiencing particular difficulties in entering or re-entering the labour-market.

Sectoral aids

In principle, sectoral aids pose fewer problems than general aids, in that their field of application and scope are more clearly delineated. The Commission's policy on sectoral aids involves recognizing that the problems facing these industries may, depending on the case, justify the granting of State aid while ensuring that such aid does not unduly delay the necessary changes, does not distort competition to an extent counter to the common interest and is in line with the attainment of the Community's objectives, or at least will not hinder that goal.

The Commission takes particular care to ensure that public funds are not used to confer undue advantages on certain undertakings at the expense of competing undertakings. The symbiosis of national economies in the common market is reflected by very similar economic developments in the Member States, even although their economic structures are not homogeneous. The difficulties justifying intervention by a Member State are often to be found in some or all of its partners. A "**Community framework**" encompassing national measures should therefore be elaborated when conditions so permit. Such a framework should include guidelines for the objectives to be attained at Community level and a description

---

1 OJ C368, 23.12.1994.
2 OJ C334, 12.12.1995.

of how to achieve that. The framework for aids to sectors in crisis takes varying legal forms, but is generally based on the criterion of "overcapacity", for which the definition and implementing provisions have gradually been refined to take fuller account of the features of the specific market in question such as progress in production technologies and the degree of globalization.

In the field of **aid to shipbuilding**, seven directives have succeeded one another since the early '70s. The seventh, whose validity was extended from year to year until the of September 1996, was aimed at directing State aid, whose ceiling was set at 9%, towards the building of the types of vessels for which Community yards were relatively more competitive[1]. This Directive was replaced, since the 1 October 1995, by a Council Regulation on aid to shipbuilding, which implements the provisions of the OECD Agreement on respecting normal competitive conditions in the commercial shipbuilding and repair industry[2].

The rules for **aids to the steel industry** introduced in 1981[3] seem to have met those objectives. Although balance has not been restored between supply and demand on the steel market and in spite of the fragile nature of some undertakings, the closures made in return for aid approved under the rules have allowed a restructuring of the industry, enabling it in time to regain its financial autonomy. In 1991, the Commission renewed for five years the rules for aids to the steel industry, with some changes and clarifications relating to research and development aid, regional aid and aid granted to companies in the new German Länder[4]. However, the new steel industry crisis at the beginning of the 90s led a number of Member States to notify to the Commission restructuring and privatization plans comprising aid elements that were incompatible with the aid code. In each case, the essential condition for authorization by the Commission, requiring the unanimous assent of the Council to an exemption from Community policy on aid to the steel industry pursuant to Article 95 of the ECSC Treaty, is that the aid has to be offset sufficiently by capacity reductions in order to further the process of stabilizing the Community steel industry[5].

The textiles-clothing sector, which has also been the subject of considerable restructuring, has to a large extent regained the level of competitiveness required to ensure its economic success and viability on the Community market and can therefore no longer be regarded as a sector in crisis. However, the system for monitoring aids to **synthetic fibres** producers, which was introduced in 1977 and is renewed on a year-to-year basis, favours aid which seeks to re-absorb over-capacity through restructuring or reconversion of the industry[6]. According to the new code on aid to the synthetic fibres industry, adopted by the Commission on 16 January 1996, the intensity of any authorizable aid is geared to company size and depends on the existence of a structural shortage of the product, a significant reduction in production capacity or the lack of any significant increase in capacity.

In 1988, moreover, the Commission decided to introduce a framework for aids to the **motor vehicles** sector in order to monitor the various types of aid granted to producers in that sector, including assistance received through Community funds[7]. In the early 90s , the crisis affecting almost the whole of European industry has resulted in greater overcapacity in the motor vehicle industry, necessitating strict control of aid in this sector and, therefore, an extension of the validity of the aid framework[8]. However, the Court of Justice annulled the indefinite extension of the validity of this framework[9]. Following this judgment, the Commission decided to extend, retroactively from 1 January 1995, the validity of the framework on State aid to the motor vehicle industry and proposed that the framework be reintroduced in a slightly modified form for a further period of two years from 1 January 1996.

---

1   OJ L380, 31.12.1990 and OJ L351, 31.12.1994.
2   OJ L332, 30.12.1995. See the heading on shipbuilding in the chapter on industry.
3   OJ L228, 13.08.1981.
4   OJ L362, 31.12.1991.
5   See, e.g., the exemption in favour of Irish Steel, OJ C13, 18.01.1996.
6   OJ C142, 08.06.1995.
7   OJ C123, 18.05.1989.
8   OJ C81, 26.03.1991 and OJ C36, 10.02.1993.
9   Judgment of 29 June 1995, case C-135/93.

Generally speaking, the Commission is adopting an increasingly re-served attitude to sectoral aid. Fearful that aids to industry may distort competition in the single market, the Commission will continue to try to ensure that aid to undertakings does not constitute the resurgence of protectionist measures in a new form. In fact, an active market penetration strategy, even in a period of economic growth, can seriously damage competitors who do not receive any aid.

Public undertakings

The public sector, made up of public undertakings, joint ventures and undertakings controlled by the public authorities by means of holdings, varies in size from one EU country to another. The larger the public sector, the more difficult it is for the public authorities to resist the temptation to make the undertakings controlled by them the instrument of their eco-nomic policy, giving them, in return, a privileged position in various respects. Although the interpenetration of the Member States' economies reduces the effectiveness of that instrument, and of other instruments of economic policy, an exceptional situation for public undertakings would constitute a serious danger for the free competition in the single market.

Indeed, governments grant certain public enterprises statutory mo-nopoly protection. Such exclusive monopoly rights are awarded for vari-ous public policy reasons, such as ensuring security of supply, providing a basic service to the whole population or avoiding the costs of duplicating an expensive distribution network. Such practices are common, notably for utilities (energy and water), postal services, telecommunications and to some extent in broadcasting, transport (air and maritime), banking and insurance. These exclusive rights could prevent, however, the creation of a real internal market in the sectors in question, if Member States could protect from competition their monopolistic enterprises. Member States must, therefore, not take measures which could lead their public enter-prises enjoying monopoly rights to infringe Community rules on compe-tition, free movement of goods and services.

While remaining neutral with regard to the legal position on owner-ship in the Member States, the EC Treaty stipulates, in **Article 90**, that "in the case of public undertakings and undertakings to which Member States grant special or exclusive rights, Member States shall neither enact nor maintain in force any measures contrary to the rules contained in this Treaty ...". Such undertakings therefore have **the same obligations as private firms,** including those laid down in Article 7 (prohibition of discrimination on grounds of nationality) and 85 to 94 inclusive (rules of competition of the Treaty). Member States may not grant them aids which are incompatible with the common market, disguised, for example, as non-remunerated acquisitions of holdings or as other advantages. Article 90(3) confers on the Commission the task of ensuring the application of these provisions and the power to address directives or decisions to Member States where necessary. The Court of First Instance has held that this power of surveillance enjoyed by the Commission with respect to

Member States entails the application of broad discretion regarding the tasks assigned to the undertakings concerned[1].

However, Article 90 makes a distinction between general public undertakings and **public-utility undertakings**, "entrusted with the operation of services of general economic interest or having the character of a revenue-producing monopoly". Article 90 allows exceptions to the general rule laid down in its paragraph 1, so as not to obstruct "the performance, in law or in fact, of the particular tasks assigned to them". Moreover, the development of Community trade must not be affected to such an extent as would be contrary to the interests of the Community.

In an important judgment, the Court of Justice acknowledged that undertakings of this kind, unlike others, have to subsidize their less viable activities from their more profitable business if they are to provide their services in balanced economic conditions. On the other hand, the exclusion of competition is not justified, according to the Court, in the case of specific services which are dissociable from the service operated in the general interest and meet the special needs of economic operators[2]. In another judgment the Court, after observing that, in the context of competition law, the concept of "undertaking" encompasses any body engaged in an economic activity, regardless of its legal status or the way in which it is financed, held that social security schemes cannot be considered to be undertakings, because they do not exercise an economic activity but fulfil an exclusively social function. They are therefore not subject to the competition rules of the Treaty[3]. The Court recognizes also the public service mission of electricity distribution companies, even if they operate regionally and have no exclusive rights, but holds that account must be taken of the economic conditions in which the undertaking operates[4].

Public undertakings can pose two sorts of problems for the European Union, namely that of the interpenetration of public contracts, which is discussed in the chapter on the common market, and that of the overlapping of nationalization or acquisition of holdings by the State and "disguised" aid to the undertakings concerned. The distinction is in fact difficult to draw between an operation to salvage and replenish capital used up by losses, which is permitted under Article 222, and an aid operation covered by the prohibition in Article 92 paragraph 1. Greater **transparency of the financial relations** between States and their public undertakings is needed, in order to enable the Commission to decide whether transfer of public funds to those undertakings are compatible with the rules laid down in the Treaty.

That is precisely the aim of the Directive of 25 June 1980 which the Commission adopted on the basis of Article 90, paragraph 3, of the Treaty[5]. That Directive obliges Member States to supply the Commission, at the latter's request, with information on public funds made available directly or indirectly to public undertakings, thus covering not only "active transfer" of public funds, such as the provision of capital and the covering of losses, but also "passive transfers", such as the forgoing by the State of income of profits or of a normal return on the funds used. In the initial stages the Commission asked for details of the **financial relations of the public authorities with public undertakings** in sensitive sectors, e.g. motor vehicles, synthetic fibres, textiles machinery, manufactured tobacco and shipbuilding. However, on 24 July 1985 the Commission amended the 1980 Directive to include in its scope

---

1   Judment given on 27 October 1994, Case T-32/93, Ladbroke Racing Ltd v Commission.
2   Judgment given on 19 May 1993, Case C-320/91, ECR 1993 I-2563.
3   Judgment given on 17 February 1993, Joined Cases C-159/91 and C-160/91, ECR 1993, I-664.
4   Judgment given on 27 April 1994, Case C-393/92, ECR 1994, 1477.
5   OJ L195, 29.07.1980.

public undertakings operating in the energy, post and telecommunications, transport and public credit institutions sectors[1].

At the end of the 80s, the Commission had to deal with a number of cases of non-notification of aid to public undertakings, in breach of Community law on State aids. In order to place public and private undertakings on an equal footing, it therefore in a Communication asked the Member States to supply it in a systematic manner, in the framework of an **annual report** information on financial transfers to public undertakings, having an annual turnover of more than ECU 250 million, so as to be able to identify any aid elements which they contain[2]. In a judgment of 16 June 1993 the Court of Justice annulled for procedural reasons the communication on public undertakings. Following this judgment, the Commission amended its Directive of 25 June 1980 on the transparency of financial relations between Member States and public undertakings, incorporating into it the reporting system provided for in the communication of 1991 and designed to identify those cases in which aid is present in financial flows between public authorities and publicly-owned companies. At the same time it amended this communication, which became simply a statement of the Commission's policy on the matter.

The Commission recognizes that the operation of services of general economic interest (in the sense of Article 90(2) EC) must not be prejudiced. However, it is examining on a sector-by-sector basis whether less restrictive practices are possible, how to limit statutory monopoly rights to the essential activities and whether competing services could use existing networks or new technologies would permit the construction of alternative networks. Thus, the Commission Directive of 16 May 1988 on free competition on the Community markets in **telecommunications terminal equipment** (modems, telex and telefax terminals, private satellite stations, etc.) prohibits immediately any exclusive rights to import, market, connect, bring into service and maintain such equipment[3]. Similarly, Commission Directive of 28 June 1990 on competition in the markets of **telecommunications services** provides for the abolition of the exclusive rights for the supply of telecommunications services other than voice telephony[4]. By amending these two Directives, in October 1994, the Commission has paved the way for liberalization in the **satellite telecommunications** sector, thus helping the development of trans-European networks in this sector and preparing the European information society[5]. In any case, the regulatory prerogatives enjoyed by national telecommunications organizations must be dissociated from their commercial activities. Thus, the Court of Justice has held that Article 90(1) could not be relied upon to contest the powers of authorization which a minister exercised in the normal course of his duties and delegated to a national organization[6].

State monopolies of a commercial character

Article 37 of the EEC Treaty added to the general provisions of Article 90 on public undertakings the provision that the Member States would progressively adjust any State monopolies "of a commercial character so as to ensure that when the transitional period has

1   OJ L229, 28.08.1985.
2   OJ C273, 18.10.1991.
3   OJ L131, 27.05.1988.
4   OJ L192, 24.07.1990.
5   OJ L268, 19.10.1994.
6   Judgment given on 27 October 1993, Joined Cases C-46/90 and C-93/91, Lagauche and Others.

ended no discrimination regarding the conditions under which goods are procured and marketed exists between nationals of Member States". That rule allowed of exceptions in order to dispose of agricultural products or obtain for them the best return and in order to enable Member States to comply with their obligations under international agreements.

At the outset virtually all commercial monopolies in the Community presented problems with regard to Article 37. The Commission accordingly, as from 1962, initiated a series of proceedings against Member States which refused or neglected to carry out the progressive adjustment of their monopolies. For a long time those Commission efforts came up against the unwillingness of Member States which administered lucrative monopolies, such as the tobacco and alcohol monopolies, or monopolies regarded as important for national security, like the French oil monopoly. In 1980, some ten years later than the timetable envisaged in Article 37, the final stage of the adjustment of State monopolies of a commercial character was reached, but some Member States are still fighting a rearguard action to protect some of the privileges of their monopolies, such as the exclusive import and export rights for gas and electricity.

Appraisal and outlook

Competition policy has traditionally been seen as a purely national prerogative. The Community is the first group of countries to practice a policy which tries to deal with the impact that distortions of competition have on trade. The basic objective of the Community competition policy is to prevent the unity of the common market from being called into question by measures which have the effect of giving preference to certain economic operators and of restoring the partitioning of domestic markets. In fact, whatever means are used to "organize" a market, i.e. to **correct the rigours of competition**, the undeclared objective most often consists of raising prices and restoring national viability, borne by the consumer or the taxpayer. The methods of weakening competition in a market are agreements between competitors, the elimination of competitors by concentrations or support for national operators by their State.

From the beginnings of the Community an administrative practice developed gradually by the Commission and confirmed by the case-law of the Court of Justice has made it possible to interpret and improve the rules of the Treaty in order to establish a range **of principles of fair behaviour** which, while not hindering the freedom to engage in business, indicates to economic operators the rules to be complied with to ensure that free trade and equal opportunity are guaranteed within the common market. The practices of undertakings directed towards impeding imports or exports, fixing production or sales quotas and generally sharing the market are accordingly actively proceeded against. Agreements which have the effect of concentrating demand on specific producers, and exclusive distribution agreements which prevent traders and consumers from purchasing products in any Member State under the customary conditions there, are also prohibited. Undertakings which practice the prohibited restrictions of competition, thus jeopardizing the unity of the common market, have to expect to have heavy fines imposed on them.

Legal proceedings are also brought against undertakings which abuse a dominant position by refusing to supply a long-standing customer, by applying discriminatory prices, unlawful practices which cause or could cause damage to customers or consumers or, lastly, by concentrations which result in eliminating competition in a market. It would be absurd to take legal action against horizontal agreements between undertakings whilst at the same time permit the monopolization of certain markets through uncontrolled vertical integration of undertakings in a dominant position. However, the risk of monopolization increases as the internal market takes shape. That is why the Regulation adopted in December 1989 introducing the control of major concentration transactions came at just the right time to fill a legal vacuum which had been causing problems for a long time. Application of the Regulation has already demonstrated that it has a crucial role to play in restructuring industry so that it can rise to the challenge of the single market.

The **control of concentrations** does not mean the prohibition of concentrations. Just as concentrations are dangerous when they strengthen the dominant position of major undertakings, so are they desirable when they strengthen the competitive position of small and medium-sized undertakings. Refraining from a strictly legal approach to problems of competition, the Commission conducts in fact two parallel policies: a policy for the elimination of abuse by major undertakings and a policy of encouragement of cooperation and concentration between small and medium-sized undertakings. Thus, through its communications concerning cooperation between undertakings and agreements of minor importance, as well as through its individual decisions, the Commission has made possible very strong cooperation between small and medium-sized undertakings. Its approaches to the problems of specialization, subcontracting and patent licensing are along the same lines. Concerning the behaviour of large enterprises, the Commission follows a double policy. On the one hand, it vigorously pursues all forms of corporate conduct that cause serious restrictions of competition and deprive other firms and consumers of the benefits of an open market economy. On the other, it authorizes certain forms of cooperation (strategic alliances) between firms, taking the view that, provided certain guarantees are given that competition should not be distorted, such cooperation between undertakings can help them adjust to their new economic environment.

As regards State aids, the role of the Community competition policy is not only to prevent national initiatives that are harmful to intra-Community trade or to the economic activity of the other Member States, but also to limit State intervention to aid which fits in with the prospect of adjusting the structures of the Community's production mechanism to changes in demand and to the international division of labour. The Community competition policy is thus not only a necessary instrument of economic and social cohesion, pivotal to the success of the internal market, but also a complement to Community sectoral policies - industrial, energy, agriculture and transport sectors - aimed at improving production structures.

It is no exaggeration to state that the Commission's competition policy has an influence on "industrial morality" in the Community. A very large majority of undertakings - and thousands each year notify their horizontal or vertical cooperation projects - work in close cooperation with the

Commission and, if necessary, rectify their agreements or their competitive practices as soon as the Commission informs them that they are out of order. Others change their agreements themselves as soon as the Commission imposes heavy fines in similar cases. There are just a few undertakings which yield only after lengthy discussions or even following the judgment of the Court of Justice, which always has the last word in problems relating to competition. For its part, the Commission is adopting a pragmatic approach towards increased competition resulting from a number of factors, including rapid technological change, the completion of the single market, the globalization of markets and economic difficulties in several sectors. Indeed, competition policy has a key role to play in promoting sustainable development. It can influence market structure, both by establishing a framework that enables consumers to benefit from the advantages of competition and by screening types of corporate conduct in order to authorize those which are favourable to competition and to prohibit those which do not.

Bibliography on competition policy

□ BOUTERSE Rosita Bianca, *Competition and Integration - What Goals Count?*, Kluwer Law and Taxation Publ., Deventer, 1994.

□ COHEN-TANUGI L., ENCAOUA D., WINCKLER A., SIRAGUSA M., BRUNET F., *La pratique communautaire du contrôle des concentrations. Analyse juridique, économique et comparative Europe, États-Unis, Japon,* De Boeck-Wesmael, Louvain-la-Neuve, 1995.

□ COMMISSION EUROPÉENNE, *Rapport sur la politique de concurrence,* annuel.

  - "Concurrence et intégration; Politique communautaire de contrôle des concentrations", in *Économie européenne,* N° 57, 1994.

  - *Droit du contrôle des concentrations dans l'Union européenne,* OPOCE, Luxembourg, 1995.

  - *La politique européenne de concurrence, 1995,* OPOCE, Luxembourg, 1996.

□ EUROPEAN COMMISSION, *New Industrial Economics and Experiences from European Merger Control. New Lessons about Collective Dominance?,* OOPEC, Luxembourg, 1995.

  - "Competition and Integration - Community Merger Control Policy", *European Economy,* Supplement A, nr. 3/95.

□ GREAVES Rosa, *EC Block Exemption Regulations,* Chancery Law Publ., London etc., 1994.

□ HENRIKSEN U. B., *Anti-competitive State Measures in the European Community - An Analysis of Decisions of the Court of Justice,* Munksgaard, Copenhagen, 1994.

▫ JONES, VANDER WOUDE, LEWIS, *European Community Competition Law Handbook*, Sweet & Maxwell, London, 1994.

▫ KOBIA Roland, *Introduction to the Law, Practice and Policy of State Aids in the European Union*, Institute for European Business Administration, Gand, 1996.

▫ KOCH Roger, *Competition Policy and Law*, Longman Group, Harlow, Essex, 1994.

▫ KORAH, Valentine, *An Introductory Guide to EC Competition Law and Practice*, fifth edition, Sweet & Maxwell, London, 1994.

▫ LEVIE Guy, COUSY Herman (sous la dir. de), *La politique européenne de concurrence en matière d'assurances*, Academia-Erasme, Louvain-la-Neuve, Bruylant, Bruxelles, 1995.

▫ MAITLAND-WALKER Julian, *Competition Laws of Europe*, Butterworths, London, 1995.

▫ PRIESS Hans-Joachim, "Recovery of Illegal State Aid: An Overview of Recent Developments in the Case Law", in *Common Market Law Review*, Vol. 33, N° 1, 1996, pp. 69-91.

▫ ROSE Vivien, *Bellamy & Child Common Market Law of Competition*, 4th ed., Sweet & Maxwell, London, 1993.

▫ THIRY Bernard, VANDAMME Jacques (sous la dir. de), *Les entreprises publiques dans l'Union européenne: entre concurrence et intérêt général*, Éditions A. Pedone, Paris, 1995.

▫ VAN BAEL, Ivo, BELLIS Jean François, *Competition Law of the European Community*, CCH Europe, Bicester, 1994.

▫ ZACHMANN Jacques, *Le contrôle communautaire des concentrations*, Librairie Générale de Droit et de Jurisprudence, Paris, 1994.

8. ENVIRONMENT

U p to the end of the '60s no European country had a clearly defined environment policy. Student unrest in France and Germany in May 1968, the United Nations Conference on the Human Environment, held in Stockholm in June 1972, and the publication in the same period of the report by the Club of Rome on "the limits of growth" alerted European public opinion to the ecological problems of economic development and questioned the hierarchy of the values extolled by the consumer society.

The Governments of the Community States were obliged hastily to design measures against pollution and nuisances so as to open a safety valve to an ecological movement likely to swing the pendulum to the other extreme, to impose "zero growth", to block technological progress and with it, perhaps, economic and social progress. But all the Member States had to act together, as any country which took measures on its own against pollution or nuisances, or measures more stringent than its neighbours, would be likely to penalize its industry, which would have to bear the cost. Having done so, it would be forced to block the placing on its market of more pollutant, noisy or dangerous products from its more lax partners, which would bring the risk of technical barriers to trade.

The Summit Conference of Heads of State and Government held in Paris in 1972 opened the way to the implementation of a common policy on environmental protection. The Commission went to work and prepared wide-ranging action programmes for the reduction of pollution and nuisances and for the management of environmental resources. In record time by Community standards the Community provided itself with many concrete measures, which proves that, when there is pressure from public opinion, political will and the absence of deep-rooted national policies, the European institutions are capable of legislative work comparable to that of an individual State.

The European Union's environment programme now aims at sustainable development, which takes into account the present needs without jeopardizing the development possibilities of future generations. This means that short term economic gains at the expense of the environment should be replaced by a more sustainable model of economic and social development, which may constitute the basis for greater efficiency and competitiveness, both at a Union level and internationally.

Economic and legal framework

European industrial society developed apace for a century (1860-1960) without a second thought for the ecological consequences of its growth. As we saw in the chapter on regional development, economic activities centred on certain places, for geographical and economic reasons, with no regard to the environment. But, virtually every human activity and industrial process affects the natural environment, either through atmospheric or water pollution, noise pollution or even by the destruction of areas and the countryside. Although environmental damage had been going on for a century, it was not until the '60s and '70s that it took on alarming proportions, for three main reasons: increased town-dwelling, very rapid economic expansion and the ill-considered use of new production techniques and of new products, chiefly derived from oil.

After May 1968 in particular people in Europe began giving serious thought to an environment policy, as it could be envisaged that economic growth would run up against two obstacles: upstream, an increasing dearth of non-renewable resources and the gradual destruction of certain areas, and downstream, revolt by ever larger layers of the population, notably amongst young people, against the hierarchy of values imposed by the consumer society. Governments lost no time in adopting an environment policy as a safety valve against a situation likely to become explosive at an early date. The European Commission, although it had no specific brief on the matter under the Treaty, expatiated in loud and clear terms, in July 1971, in a communication to the Council, on the reasons for the Community States all to act together on the environment.

Need for common measures

In fact, in the mosaic of States called Europe the **common market in terms of pollution** was established before the common market in goods. Polluted air and water moved freely across frontiers well before the idea emerged to open them to foreign goods. Each European State was thus immediately concerned by what was happening in its neighbours' countries with regard to the environment. It must not be forgotten that virtually every large lake and large watercourse in Europe is shared by two or more States, that the Mediterranean and the North Sea represent a common heritage for several European States and that those seas, lakes and rivers are used as common dumping grounds for the industrial waste of several countries. In the field of nature conservation and the protection of wildlife, too, a country which protected migratory birds or endangered species would be wasting its time if its neighbours killed them. If the mess was to be stopped, action therefore had to be taken together.

Not only neighbourliness, but the comparable socio-economic development of the European countries, argued in favour of Community action to protect the environment. The **phenomena common** to all European States of the expansion of industrial activities, the increase in the urban population within megalopoles and the drift away from increasingly large tracts of territory originally used and maintained by agriculture required comparable measures and means to be implemented in the Member States to cope with them. Short of seriously affecting the competitive capacity of its economy, no European State could hope to resolve its environmental problems by acting on its own.

The fight against pollution in fact imposes on industrialists certain expenditure to adapt their products or their manufacturing processes. Such expenditure is all the greater, the more stringent the standards laid down by the public authorities. If a State of the Union imposed stringent and **costly anti-pollution measures** on its industry, it might penalize it vis-à-vis its competitors from other States which were less attentive to the damage caused by pollution or which had different ideas as to how to apportion expenditure for the fight against pollution. Competition would therefore be distorted in the common market. It was therefore necessary for the same rules to be imposed on all European producers.

The free **movement of goods** within the common internal market would also be affected if each Member State laid down different standards for products put on sale on its market. The country which laid down more stringent standards than its neighbours, for example on restrictions on the noise of construction plant or on the exhaust emissions of motor vehicles, would impede imports from other countries. Protection against pollution and noise could thus quickly deteriorate into protection against foreign products. In other words, national environment policy could be used to thwart the internal market in a very subtle manner.

One of the most urgent problems calling for a common approach was the elimination of industrial and urban waste. Even if the damaging effect of waste did not go beyond the confines of a region, European action would be necessary if **the elimination or re-use of waste** entailed substantial cost and led to differences between the conditions of production and distribution of certain goods in the common market. The most important waste for the EU is obviously waste whose disposal, owing to its toxicity, non-biodegradability, bulk or whatever reason, requires a solution that goes beyond a region or even a State.

The cost of the overexploitation of natural resources is far greater than the current clean-up activities such as waste and waste-water treatment. Past damage does not only require mounting costs, but the reduced availability and quality of natural and environmental resources represents a handicap for Europe and a reduced capacity for long-term economic prosperity. On the other hand, the new environmental technologies, called "**clean-technologies**", present a dual advantage for European countries. By improving the production process in terms of energy and natural resources efficiency, they can reduce the dependence of the European Union on costly imports. By increasing product lifetime and by facilitating reuse and recycling, clean technologies can make more attractive the labour-intensive activities of control, repair and recycling.

The determination of rules on the environment and the preparation of provisions against pollution necessitate much research. To ensure better use of public resources while avoiding duplication on the part of European laboratories, **very costly environmental research** needs to be coordinated in a Community programme. Likewise, the control of jointly established standards requires the elaboration and implementation of efficient measurement methods recognized by all, the preparation of type-approved apparatus and, on occasion, the setting up of monitoring networks or even joint supervision bodies.

Lastly, it has to be said that the **European institutions are better placed than governments** to have a long-term view of environmental problems and requirements. Even when they are certain of remaining in office for fairly long time, national governments, being preoccupied with short-term problems, are rarely in a position to plan long-term strategies in this non-profit-making sector. Its relative detachment from the day-to-day problems peculiar to the Member States and its right of initiative with regard to the harmonization of legislation make it possible for the European Commission to introduce a long-term programme against pollution before it becomes catastrophic.

Legal context of environmental action

Although the Community had enough economic and political arguments for dealing with environmental problems, it did not initially have a solid legal basis for so doing. In order to set Community objectives for the reduction of pollution and nuisances, reference could only be made to Article 2 of the EEC Treaty, which assigned to the Community the task, inter alia, of promoting "an accelerated raising of the standard of living" of the populations belonging to it. In order to undertake urgent measures to stop the process of deterioration of the environment, the Community provisions had to be based on Article 235, which specifically permits action in areas in which the Treaty has not provided the necessary powers, but which requires unanimity of the Member States, with the slowness that involves.

That general legal framework could be used in the environmental sector, but **political consensus** was still required to be able to act in that new field. Such consensus was achieved at the Paris Summit Conference on 20 October 1972, which urged the Council to adopt at an early date the **programme of action on the environment** submitted by the Commission in 1972. The programme was formally adopted on 22 November 1973. On that occasion the Council declared that the promotion throughout the Community of a harmonious development of economic activities, and a continuous and balanced expansion, which constituted the tasks of the EEC, could from then on not be imagined in the absence of an effective campaign to combat pollution and nuisances or of an improvement in the quality of life and the protection of the environment.

The legal basis of environment policy was considerably enlarged by the Single Act of 1987 and firmly established by the **Treaty on European Union**. The environment is now a Community policy with the following objectives: preserving, protecting and improving the quality of the environment; protecting human health; prudent and rational utilization of natural resources; promoting measures at international level to deal with regional or worldwide environmental problems.

Environment policy is based on the precautionary principle and on the principles that preventive action should be taken, that environmental damage should as a priority be rectified at source and that the polluter should pay (Art. 130r). The Member States finance and implement environment policy. However, without prejudice to the principle that the polluter pays, if a measure involves costs deemed disproportionate for the public authorities of a Member State, the Council, in the act adopting that measure, lays down appropriate provisions in the form of temporary derogations and/or financial support from the Cohesion Fund (Art. 130s).

> Three decision-making procedures are provided for in the field of the environment:
> a) the standard procedure is that set out in Article 189c, namely, the procedure of cooperation with the European Parliament after consultation of the Economic and Social Committee;
> b) the procedure set out in Article 189b (co-decision) is followed for the adoption of general action programmes setting out priority objectives;
> c) the unanimity of the Council acting after consultation of the European Parliament and ESC is needed for: provisions primarily of a fiscal nature; measures concerning town and country planning; and measures significantly affecting a Member State's energy supply (Art. 130s).
>
> The protective measures adopted under Article 130s do not prevent any Member States from maintaining or introducing more stringent protective measures. However, environmental protection can no longer be used as a pretext for technical barriers to trade. Internal market policy and environment policy must therefore march forward side by side. To this end, the Commission adopted on March 26, 1991, the guidelines for a **new legislative model** seeking to reconcile the demands of the environment with those of the market. This model sets two stages for the definition of environmental standards. The first consists of the setting by the Commission of a high-level standard, in accordance with Article 100a, paragraph 3 of the Treaty. This standard will be based on the technology available within a specific time span and which should be applied by all the Member States as rapidly as possible. During the second stage, the Council will set a "target" standard, corresponding to the highest level of protection which can be reasonably envisaged in light of the latest scientific and technological developments. This approach is designed to preserve the unity of the internal market, avoiding a proliferation of national dispensations and, at the same time, to guarantee the EU - which will have the strictest standards - full independence from third countries.

The **fifth Community action programme** on the environment and environmentally sustainable development aims at the objectives fixed by the Treaty on EU[1]. The central theme of the programme is that the objectives set cannot be attained by action at Community level alone but only by a coordinated response in which all levels of society share the responsibility, combined with deeper dialogue with all the parties involved. The programme places strong emphasis on prevention and the integration of environmental concerns into other policy areas, targeting, in particular, industry, energy, transport, agriculture and tourism. It further sets guidelines and objectives, particularly performance targets. Four categories of instruments are proposed for their attainment: legislation; market-based measures (including economic and tax incentives); general supporting measures (improved data, scientific research, technological development, information and training) and financial support mechanisms.

The activities which the Community undertakes or wishes to undertake to protect the environment and conserve nature in Europe and in the

---

1   COM (92) 23 and OJ C138, 17.05.1993.

rest of the world are becoming increasingly costly and must be planned over the long term. Awareness of this provided the impetus for the creation of a financial instrument for the environment, **LIFE**, which seeks to promote the development and implementation of the Community's environment policy and legislation by financing priority projects in the Community and by providing technical assistance to the associated countries of Central and Eastern Europe as well as countries in the Mediterranean region or in Baltic coastal areas[1]. It provides financial assistance for preparatory measures, demonstration schemes, awareness campaigns, incentives, technical assistance and measures necessary for the maintenance or restoration of biotopes, natural habitats and species. In addition to LIFE, Community support through the Structural Funds and the Cohesion Fund facilitates the realization of joint environmental projects (JEPs) in the poorest Member States.

The "polluter pays" and the prevention principles

One of the most important principles, defined as early as the 1973 action programme and clarified in a Council Recommendation of 3 March 1975, was the "polluter pays" principle. This principle, which is mentioned in Article 130r, paragraph 2, of the EC Treaty, means that the cost incurred in combating pollution and nuisances in the first instance fall to the polluter, i.e. the polluting industry. Given, however, that the polluting industry can pass the cost of the prevention or elimination of pollution on to the consumer, the principle amounts to saying that polluting production **should bear: the expenditure** corresponding to the measures necessary to combat pollution (investment in apparatus and equipment for combating pollution, implementation of new processes, operating expenditure for anti-pollution plant, etc.); and **the charges** whose purpose is to encourage the polluter himself to take, as cheaply as possible, the measures necessary to reduce the pollution caused by him (incentive function) or to make him bear his share of the costs of collective purification measures (redistribution function). The Community guidelines on State aid for environmental protection, which we have seen in the chapter on competition, are designed to ensure that aid granted for environmental purposes complies with the "polluter pays" principle.

The Commission should take account, in its proposals, of the micro-economic implications of the various measures envisaged on the environment, by evaluating their cost and, if appropriate, their effect on the prices of the products concerned, giving consideration to the desired objectives on the one hand and to international competitiveness, development and employment on the other. But it is not always possible to **compare the cost of proposed measures with the expected advantages** of a reduction in the social cost of pollution and an improvement in the quality of the environment. Those advantages would have to be interpreted and considered, but their evaluation in monetary terms would pose problems which are particularly difficult to resolve. How can the damage caused by smoke from a factory to the health of neighbourhood residents be measured ? What value do we put on the cleanliness of the sea for a bather ? How do we evaluate the aesthetic damage which an industrial complex causes to a site or landscape ? Clearly, the answers to these questions are

---

1   OJ L206, 22.07.1992 and OJ C184, 18.07.1995.

highly subjective and can be strongly influenced by the interests involved. In order to answer such questions and enable the Union to measure the progress made towards environmentally sustainable development, the Commission establishes green national accounts combined with a series of environmental indicators.

However, the European Union's work on the environment is marked more and more by an integrated, preventive approach taking account of human activities and their consequences for the environment as a whole. The transition towards a more pro-active policy of voluntary prevention is manifested in the Directive on **the assessment of the effects of certain public and private projects** on the environment and on natural resources[1]. According to this Directive, the promoter of the project, whether it be industrial, agricultural or relating to infrastructure, has to supply detailed information on its possible consequences for air, water, soil, noise, wild animals and their habitats, etc. The decision of the public authority as to whether to authorize the project must weigh the economic, social or other advantages of the project against its environmental consequences.

The prevention is also the objective of the Regulation on the "eco-audit" scheme, which allows voluntary participation by companies in the industrial sector in a Community eco-management and audit scheme (EMAS or eco-audit)[2]. This scheme is based on three elements: the establishment and implementation by the companies in question of environmental policies, programmes and management systems for their production sites; systematic, objective and periodical evaluation of the efficiency of these programmes and systems by independent verifiers; and annual information for the general public in the form of "environmental declarations" by companies participating in the system.

Another means for the prevention of pollutions is the "eco-label", which guides the consumers towards "clean" products and thus incites the industrialists to produce them. Indeed, the Regulation relating to the granting of a **Community eco-label** is designed to ensure better consumer information on the environmental impact of products other than foodstuffs, beverages and pharmaceuticals[3]. A competent body appointed by the Member State in which the product is manufactured, placed on the market for the first time or imported is responsible for deciding whether or not to grant the eco-label, after assessment of the ecological performance of the product in accordance with the general principles given in the Regulation and the specific criteria set by the Commission, assisted by a committee of representatives of the Member States. In this way, the Commission established the ecological criteria for several categories of manufactured products, including laundry detergents[4] and indoor paints and varnishes[5].

---

1   OJ L175, 05.07.1985.
2   OJ L168, 10.07.1993.
3   OJ L99, 11.04.1992.
4   OJ L217, 13.09.1995.
5   OJ L4, 06.01.1996.

Notification, information and monitoring

In 1973 the Representatives of the Governments of the Member States meeting in Council adopted an Agreement on information for the Commission and for the Member States with a view to possible harmonization throughout the Community of urgent measures concerning the protection of the environment[1]. That specific instrument of Community policy made it possible for the Commission to receive draft laws, regulations and administrative provisions concerning the environment and intervene if it considered that draft rules did not comply with Community policy.

The number of notifications emanating from the Member States pursuant to the specific Standstill Agreement of 1973 dropped significantly at the end of the '80s, as national drafts were increasingly notified under the Directive of 28 March 1983 laying down a procedure for **the provision of information in the field of technical standards and regulations**[2], discussed under the heading of technical barriers to trade in the chapter on the common market. As the Court of Justice noted in its judgment of 20 September 1988 on the "Danish bottles" cases[3], national environmental measures are likely to affect completion of the internal market and therefore need to be notified under the general notification procedure.

For their own information, the national and Community authorities dispose since 1975 of a common procedure for the setting up and constant updating of an inventory of sources of information on the environment in the Community[4]. A Council Directive of 1991 standardizes and rationalizes the environment reports produced by the Member States[5]. In 1996, a Council decision established a reciprocal exchange of information and data from networks and individual stations measuring ambient air pollution within the Member States[6].

The fifth Community programme of policy and action in relation to the environment and sustainable development is based on a sharing of responsibility between all levels of society and on a closer dialogue between all concerned. This programme established monitoring mechanisms such as the environmental review group, made up of the heads of the departments of the environment in the Member States, which seeks to integrate the environmental objectives of the Union into national policies.

In any event, the Commission receives information on the legislative or administrative intentions of the Member States. It verifies the transposition by the Member States of Community legislation into national law and initiates proceedings against States which either fail to implement Community provisions on the environment in full or correctly or do not give notification of domestic measures on the environment. The Commission has an important ally in the matter, namely the public in the Member States, who are concerned at environmental damage and make a growing number of complaints to it each year. When it receives a complaint from an individual citizen or association, the Commission carries out an inquiry to verify the facts, and if it considers that Community law has been infringed it initiates the procedure provided for in Article 196 of the Treaty.

---

1   OJ C9, 15.03.1973 and OJ C86, 20.07.1974.
2   OJ C109, 26.04.1983.
3   OJ C269, 18.10.1988.
4   OJ L31, 05.02.1976.
5   OJ L377, 31.12.1991.
6   OJ C30, 03.02.1996.

The public was made aware of the importance of environmental protection and of the European dimension of environment policy by the **European year of the environment,** celebrated in 1987[1]. That year saw in particular the operation "Blue flags in Europe", which identifies the cleanest beaches in the Community, and the action "1,000 municipalities for Europe", which awarded prizes for the best cooperation activities between local authorities and environment protection organizations. A 1990 Directive intends to guarantee freedom of access to and dissemination of information on the environment held by public authorities and to set the basic conditions under which information on the environment should be made available to the public[2]. The latter, through pressure that it can exercise on national authorities can contribute a great deal to improving the respect of Community legislation.

In order to reinforce communication with its non-institutional partners (non-governmental organizations, regional and local authorities, industry, etc.) the Commission set up a **General Consultative Forum on the Environment**[3]. Consisting of members from manufacturing industry, the business world, regional and local authorities, professional associations, trade unions and environmental protection and consumer organizations, the purpose of the Forum is to help achieve the objectives of the fifth Community action programme on the environment. In this connection, the Commission has initiated general measures to provide information and raise awareness about the environment[4]. It has also proposed a programme of Community action for the promotion of non governmental organizations which have as primary objective the defense of the environment[5].

The task assigned to the **European Environment Agency,** which is established near Copenhagen, is to provide the Commission and the national authorities with the technical, scientific and economic information necessary for the framing and implementation of measures and legislation relating to the environment[6]. Being a Community body open to third countries because of the multinational character of work on the environment, the Agency is destined to become the hub of a European network for monitoring and obtaining information on the environment.

Environment and Community policies

Article 130r of the EC Treaty, stipulates, inter alia, that environmental protection requirements must be integrated into the definition and implementation of other Community policies. This is meant to ensure environmental protection in all its forms by means of prior analysis of the potential problems in this sector and of the adoption of measures which integrate environmental requirements into the planning and performance of economic and social activities. In fact, many environmental issues such as climate change, acidification and waste management can only be tackled by an interplay between the main economic actors and sectors, not only by legislative means, but also by an extended and integrated mix of other instruments, such as standards, certification systems, voluntary schemes or economic instruments. Therefore, the sustainable protection of the environment depends to a large extent on the policies pursued in the fields

1   OJ C63, 18.03.1986.
2   OJ L158, 23.06.1990.
3   OJ L328, 29.12.1993.
4   OJ C54, 25.02.1993.
5   COM (95) 573.
6   OJ L120, 11.05.1990.

of industry, energy, transport, agriculture and tourism, which are in turn dependent on the capacity of the environment to sustain them.

The **industrial sector** has to take ecological requirements increasingly into account in the choice of products and manufacturing processes. Thus, henceforth the environment is one of the factors making a difference to the competitive position of companies or industries. Below we shall examine the constraints imposed on heavily polluting sectors like the chemicals, steel and detergents sectors. On the other hand, the so-called "Eco-industry" is a rapidly expanding market with increasing importance for Europe. It covers not only the supply of goods and services to firms for pollution control and abatement but also the expenditures made for improving production methods, using energy more efficiently and developing less polluting products. In addition, the harmonization of laws on quality standards for industrial products is in reality targeted on a twofold objective: the uniform protection of man and the Community environment, and the removal of barriers to trade resulting from differences in the standards or technical specifications in Community countries. These two objectives are pursued by environmental control of products and the granting of a Community eco-label[1].

Environment policy has close ties with **energy policy**, as the production and use of energy are amongst the principal sources of air pollution (burning of fossil fuels) and water pollution (through the discharge of cooling-waters and polluting substances by refineries and nuclear power stations). It is obvious that the policy for the rational use of energy and encouragement of soft (non-polluting) energy is first and foremost in the interests of the environment. It should also be noted that, with the exception of the management of radio-active waste, the bulk of Community work on nuclear safety is carried out in the framework of the Euratom Treaty and therefore under energy policy rather than environment policy[2].

The various **means of transport**, particularly in urban areas, are another source of pollution. With the aim of defining a common strategy on transport and environment policies, the Commission adopted a Green Paper in February 1992 on the impact of transport on the environment[3]. After taking stock of the adverse effects of transport on the environment and reviewing trends and forecasts relating to transport demand and traffic volume, the Commission outlines a common strategy for developing transport in an environmentally compatible way.

The Community action programme on the environment is underpinned by a multinational programme of **research in the field of the environment** and the climate covering the study of the natural environment, global change, environmental technologies, space technologies for environmental monitoring and the human dimension of environmental change[4]. The development of clean products and processes in the European Union does not only prevent rapidly increasing clean-up costs but also stimulates the diffusion of Community research to the rest of the world who needs it badly.

The **common agricultural policy** developed during the '70s without any consideration whatsoever for the environment. Thus, it not only resulted in the famous wine lakes and butter mountains, but also in the ill-considered use of pesticides and fertilizers, which are very harmful to the environment. Fortunately, such excesses seem to have been curbed since the mid-'80s, and agricultural and environmental policies now have a common goal, which is to improve the Union's rural area. In this framework, the Council adopted: a Regulation on organic production of agricultural products and its presentation on agricultural products and foodstuffs[5]; a Directive on the marketing of plant pharmaceuticals[6]; and a Directive on the protection of waters against pollution caused by nitrates from agriculture[7].

The sustainable development of resources is fully integrated into the **common fisheries policy** by means of measures taken to conserve resources, preserve marine biodiversity and rationalize fishing. The environmental impact of fisheries is taken into account, in particular,

---

1   OJ L99, 11.04.1992.
2   See the title on the nuclear market in the chapter on energy.
3   COM (92) 46.
4   OJ L361, 31.12.1994. See the chapter on research.
5   OJ L198, 22.07.1991.
6   OJ L230, 19.08.1991.
7   OJ L375, 30.12.1991.

by the systematic consultation of scientific experts when legislative measures on the exploitation of resources are drafted.

Community **regional policy** and environment policy are complementary, as regional aid can help to reverse inordinate urbanization, which gives rise to ecological problems, whilst measures to combat pollution can have a dissuasive effect on the siting of industries in congested regions of the European Union. This is why, as we saw in the chapter on competition, the Community framework of State aids for environmental protection takes account of the fifth environmental programme and encourages the application of the "polluter pays" principle. The Cohesion Fund, the Structural Funds and the Community initiatives, referred to in the chapter on regional development, not only take the environment into account in their economic activities but also attach greater importance to construction of the environmental infrastructure needed to implement the main Directives on sewage and waste management[1].

International cooperation

Some forms of pollution are threatening not only the European ecological systems but also the natural balance of the entire planet, e.g. climate change, ozone layer, bio-diversity). These problems have to be tackled on an international basis. Participation by the Community as such in the work of specialist international bodies geared to preserving the world's natural wealth and preventing barriers to international trade forestalls differences of opinion amongst the Member States and highlights their common interests. Furthermore, active participation by the Community in the work on the environment of other international organizations, such as the OECD, the Council of Europe and the United Nations, enables Community law to follow international thinking in that area. As we shall see in the following sections, the Community as such has signed several international conventions for the protection of the environment.

The agreement on the **European Economic Area** (EEA) between the EU and the EFTA countries institutes, among other things, a close environmental cooperation. Relations between the countries of Western Europe and the countries of **Central and Eastern Europe** have an environmental component, which will be necessary to redress the ecological situation at the same time as the economic situation of those countries. One of the aims pursued by projects supported in the framework of the PHARE programme is directly to improve the environmental situation in the countries aided and even to lay the foundations of a coherent policy in this area. As from 1974 the Community initiated consultations with the **United States** on the environment, and this facilitates cooperation on subjects like the greenhouse effect[2], marine pollution and biotechnology.

The Community as a body participated in the United Nations Conference on the environment and development (UNCED), the so-called "Earth Summit", held in Rio de Janeiro from June 3 to 14, 1992. This conference culminated in the adoption of the Rio Declaration and the "Agenda 21", which is the international community's action programme for the environment and development in the XXIst century and contains a number of innovative features, namely acknowledgment of the need for sustainable development; shared but differentiated responsibility of States; and world partnership. The environmentally sustainable development strategy greatly influenced the Community's fifth programme on the environment. The European Union is actively involved in the international work to follow up the UNCED, particularly in the meetings of the Commission on Sustainable Development which concern forest conservation, the protection of biodiversity, urban and

---

1   See the Commission's communication on cohesion and the environment, COM (95) 509, 22 November 1995.

2   OJ C183, 20.07.1989.

rural environment, land management and coastal resource management of developing countries.

Reduction of pollution and nuisances

The initiatives grouped under this title are directed towards: the fixing of quality objectives for European waters, the control of discharges into the aquatic environment of the European Union, efforts to combat sea and air pollution, the prevention of industrial accidents and efforts to combat noise pollution. These various groups of activity are examined in succession below.

Quality objectives for European waters

Water is an element indispensable not only to human life, but also to many of man's activities, from fishing to industry, by way of agriculture. Water plays an essential role in the natural ecological balance by procuring a substantial proportion of the oxygen necessary for life. Lastly, seas, lakes and rivers are of great value for recreational activities and leisure, which are indispensable for town-dwellers.

The physical interdependence of the various surroundings that make up the aquatic ecosystem, such as surface fresh water, groundwater and sea water, necessitates the coherent management of these resources. The fact that watercourses often cross several countries and that the catchment areas also extend across the territories of several countries dictates the common management of these resources. Comparable, and sometimes common, management of water is indispensable, inter alia, to prevent distortions of competition between major water-using undertakings.

The EU States lay down quality objectives or quality standards so as to manage water rationally and limit water pollution. These objectives, which vary according to the intended use of the water (drinking water, bathing water or water suitable for fish-breeding), lay down the pollution or nuisance levels not to be exceeded in a given surrounding or part thereof. European directives fix certain mandatory values, which must not be exceeded, and some guide values, which Member States endeavour to comply with.

Thus, a Council Directive of 1975 lays down quality standards for **surface water intended for the abstraction of drinking water** in the Member States[1]. It obliges the Member States to take all the measures necessary to ensure that both national surface waters and surface waters that cross frontiers comply with the values laid down. A Directive of October 1979, complementary to the aforementioned one, lays down the methods of measurement and frequencies of sampling and analysis of the quality values required of surface waters intended for the abstraction of drinking water in the Member States[2]. It defines in particular the physical, chemical and microbiological properties required of such water and the

---

1   OJ L194, 25.07.1975 and OJ L377, 31.12.1991.
2   OJ L271, 29.10.1979 and OJ L377, 31.12.1991.

frequency of sampling and analysis of those values. A common procedure exists for the exchange of information on the quality of surface fresh water in the Community[1].

A Directive relating to the quality of **water intended for human consumption** concerns all water supplied directly for human consumption and water used in the food-manufacturing industries[2]. It laid down "mandatory" values and "guide" values i.e. maximum admissible concentrations of numerous undesirable elements for all water supplied for human consumption or used in the food industries, with the exception of natural mineral waters, which are governed by another Council Directive.

As regards **bathing water**, a Directive lays down quality standards for running or still fresh water and sea water in regions in which bathing is authorized or tolerated[3]. The Directive lays down a sampling procedure and fixes the frequency of the checks to be carried out and the methods of analysis to be applied to areas where the number of bathers is highest, and in particular at peak bathing times. The Member States have to forward to the Commission each year a summary report concerning the most significant properties of their bathing waters. The Commission may publish the information obtained, but only with the prior agreement of the States concerned. By retaining such a discretion, the Member States are thereby able to undermine the objectives of the Directive. Nevertheless, this Directive represents an impressive undertaking for cleaning up Europe's coastlines, requiring substantial investment in waste water purifiers and diffusers. However, the Commission reports that while the overall situation of almost 90% of the coastal areas is satisfactory, the quality of only 65% of inland areas is good.

In a Council Directive of 1978 on the **quality of fresh waters capable of supporting fish-life**, the Community States undertook to establish programmes for the protection and improvement of water designated as salmonoid waters and cyprinid waters[4]. A Directive of 1979, on the quality required of shellfish waters, is directed towards protecting and improving such waters in order to permit the development of molluscs in favourable conditions and to contribute to the good quality of edible shellfish[5].

Control of discharges into the aquatic environment

To attain and maintain the water-quality objectives described above, a detailed examination needed to be carried out of the methods that could be used to reduce pollution caused by certain dangerous substances discharged into the European aquatic environment, i.e. inland surface water, groundwater, internal coastal waters and territorial sea waters. Some toxic substances discharged into the water are, of course, chemically or biologically diluted and decomposed until their toxicity disappears, but others are persistent, i.e. they retain their chemical composition, and therefore their danger to the environment and to man, for a lengthy period, which can, in some cases, be several years.

For the above reason, a Council Directive of 1976 on pollution caused by certain dangerous substances discharged into the aquatic environment of the Community is directed towards curbing the process of the deterioration of that environment by **prohibiting or restricting the discharge of toxic substances**[6]. The latter were divided into two lists: a "black list" grouping particularly toxic, persistent and bioaccumulable substances, and a "grey list" which mainly concerned substances whose harmful effects are limited to one locality and depend on the properties of the receiving

1   OJ L334, 24.12.1977 and OJ L355, 28.11.1986.
2   OJ L229, 30.08.1980 and OJ L377, 31.12.1991.
3   OJ L31, 05.02.1976 and OJ L377, 31.12.1991.
4   OJ L222, 14.08.1978 and OJ L377, 31.12.1991.
5   OJ L281, 10.11.1979 and OJ L377, 31.12.1991.
6   OJ L129, 18.05.1976 and OJ L377, 31.12.1991.

waters. The "black list" was, moreover, amended and supplemented several times in the light of the development of scientific and technical knowledge of the toxicity of the various substances[1]. Whether substances from the first list or the second list were involved, the Directive of 1976 provided for authorizations granted for all discharges into Community waters, issued by the competent authority of the Member State concerned for a limited period.

The elaboration of Community standards is a lengthy and complicated process. The Commission has to propose, for each substance from the two lists, the maximum values not to be exceeded in a surrounding, taking into account both the toxicity of the substance, its persistence and its bioaccumulation properties, as well as the best technical means available for disposing of them. Accordingly, in the context of implementing the 1976 Directive, the Council adopted Directives on: **mercury**[2], **cadmium**[3], **hexachlorocyclohexane**[4] and **other dangerous substances** on the "black list" in the 1976 Directive, such as carbon tetrachloride, DDT and pentachlorophenol[5]. All these lists of dangerous substances and the measures necessary for controlling their discharge into the aquatic environment appear fastidious at first sight, but they are costly for polluting undertakings and very useful for consumers, who would otherwise be deprived of water in Europe if they did not exist.

A 1979 Directive on the **protection of groundwater** against pollution, prohibits the direct or indirect discharge (percolation through the soil) of certain particularly dangerous substances into such water and regulating in detail the discharge of certain other less harmful substances[6].

The growing use of chemical compounds in industry, agriculture and in products of household use poses ever-more serious dangers to the environment and human health. Hence, **detergents** are a significant cause of pollution of the Community's aquatic ecosystem. The formation of foam in waters into which detergents are discharged in large quantities limits the contact between water and air, makes oxygenation difficult, jeopardizes the photosynthesis necessary for the life of aquatic flora, has an adverse effect on waste water purifying processes and constitutes a risk of the transmission of bacteria and viruses. For those reasons and in order to prevent technical barriers to trade, as early as November 1973 the Council adopted a Directive on the approximation of the laws of the Member States relating to the placing on the market and the use of detergents[7].

One very dangerous industrial sector for the aquatic environment is that of the manufacture of **titanium dioxide**, which is a pigment used for the manufacture of paints, varnishes, plastics, inks, etc. Untreated waste from factories which produce titanium dioxide is known as "red sludge". The alteration of the colour and transparency of water which it causes leads to the reduction of photosynthesis and phytoplancton and, in the most serious cases, to the disappearance of all life from estuary waters and the waters of the receiving sea. The Council accordingly adopted a Directive, on 20 February 1978, on waste from the titanium dioxide industry, providing for the control by the Member States of the operations for treating such waste[8]. A new Directive sets procedures for harmonizing the programmes for the reduction and eventual elimination of pollution caused by waste from the titanium dioxide industry[9].

More generally, a Council Directive of 1991 contains provisions on the collection, processing and discharge of **urban waste water** and biodegradable water from some industrial sectors, and on the disposal of sludges[10]. In particular, the Directive stipulates that as a general rule, waste water which enters into collection systems must, before disposal, be

1   OJ L181, 04.07.1986 and OJ L377, 31.12.1991.
2   OJ L81 of 27.03.1982 and OJ L377, 31.12.1991.
3   OJ L291, 24.10.1983 and OJ L377, 31.12.1991.
4   OJ L274, 17.10.1984 and OJ L377, 31.12.1991.
5   OJ L181, 04.07.1986 and OJ L377, 31.12.1991.
6   OJ L20, 26.01.1980 and OJ L377, 31.12.1991.
7   OJ L347, 17.12.1973 and OJ L80, 25.03.1986.
8   OJ L54, 25.02.1978 and OJ L32, 03.02.1983.
9   OJ L409, 31.12.1992.
10 OJ L135, 30.05.1991 and OJ L226, 07.09.1993.

subjected to secondary treatment in accordance with a timetable adjusted to the size of the population covered and the type and situation of the collection water. Another Directive concerns the protection of waters against pollution caused by nitrates from agricultural sources[1].

In addition to its own work to combat the pollution of the aquatic environment, the Community participates in the work carried out in the framework of international cooperation, including: the Berne Agreement of 1963 concerning a Commission for the Protection of the Rhine against Pollution[2], the 1976 Bonn Convention on the Protection of the Rhine against Pollution by Chemical Products[3]; the Convention on the International Commission for the Protection of the Elbe[4]; the 1974 Paris Convention for the Prevention of Marine Pollution from Land-based Sources[5]; and the Convention on the protection and use of transboundary watercourses and international lakes[6].

Effort to combat marine pollution

Of all forms of pollution, sea pollution is one of the most dangerous because of its consequences for fundamental biological and ecological balances, the degree of degradation already reached, the diversity of sources of pollution and the difficulty of monitoring compliance with measures adopted. The main sources of sea pollution are land-based ones, i.e. the discharge of effluent from land, which we just examined under the previous title, discharges of waste at sea and the accidental spillage of hydrocarbons.

The danger of serious pollution from **massive discharges of hydrocarbons** for the coasts of the Community States and for the seas surrounding them became a matter of concern to public opinion and the Community Institutions after the shipwreck of the giant oil tanker "Amoco-Cadiz" and the serious pollution of the coasts of Brittany that ensued. In June 1978 the Council set up an action programme of the European Communities on the control and reduction of pollution caused by hydrocarbons discharged at sea[7]. In order to implement this action programme the Commission set up under its aegis an Advisory Committee on the Control and Reduction of Pollution Caused by Hydrocarbons Discharged at Sea[8]. The Council, for its part, established a Community information system (a computerized network of data) for the control and reduction of pollution caused by the spillage of hydrocarbons and other harmful substances at sea[9]. In many instances, the Council reiterated the need for a Community strategy for the integrated management and development of coastal zones based on the principal of sustainability and sound ecological and environmental practice[10].

1   OJ L375, 31.12.1991.
2   OJ L240, 19.09.1977.
3   OJ L210, 19.07.1982 and OJ L183, 14.07.1988.
4   OJ L321, 23.11.1991 and OJ L45, 23.02.1993.
5   OJ L194, 25.07.1975.
6   OJ L186, 05.08.1995.
7   OJ C162, 08.07.1978.
8   OJ L188, 22.07.1980 and OJ L89, 29.03.1985.
9   OJ L77, 22.03.1986 and OJ L158, 25.06.1988.
10   OJ C59, 06.03.1992 and OJ C135, 18.05.1994.

In a Resolution of 8 June 1993, the Council underlines that Community measures on maritime safety and pollution control must apply to all vessels operating in the European Union waters irrespective of their flag. In its view, further EU action in this field should have the following objectives: to tighten up ship inspection and withdraw sub-standard vessels; to improve shipping safety; to identify environmentally sensitive areas, on the basis of current legislation and international guidelines, and to propose specific measures for those areas to the International Maritime Organization (IMO)[1].

In fact, the effort to combat pollution of the seas requires action not only at Community, but at international level too. The Community accordingly participates as such in the international agreements against the pollution of the North Sea and the Mediterranean, including: the Bonn Agreement for cooperation in dealing with pollution of the North Sea by oil and other dangerous substances[2]; the Helsinki Convention on the protection of the Baltic Sea[3]; the Convention for the protection of the marine environment of the North-East Atlantic[4]; the Barcelona Convention on the Protection of the Mediterranean Sea against Pollution[5]; the Protocol concerning cooperation in combating pollution of the Mediterranean Sea by oil and other harmful substances in cases of emergency[6]; and the Protocol for the Protection of the Mediterranean Sea against Pollution from Land-based Sources[7]. The revision of the Barcelona Convention and its Protocols, signed in June 1995, extended its scope to cover coastal zones and introduced sustainable development objectives and principles such as the "polluter pays", prevention, use of the best available technologies and use of impact assessments[8].

Effort to combat air pollution

As will be seen below, the Community has already since the 1980s taken some important measures to combat various air pollutions. It lacked, however, an overall strategy to ensure satisfactory air quality. This strategy was defined in 1995 by a Directive on ambient air quality assessment and management[9]. It provides in particular for: the establishment of objectives for ambient air quality based on the setting of limit values and warning thresholds for the main harmful substances; the assessment of air quality in the Member States on the basis of common criteria; better information for the public; measures to maintain or improve air quality.

Industrial and household activities have recourse to the burning of fossil fuels. Such burning causes the emission into the air of sulphur dioxide ($SO2$), due to the presence of traces of sulphur in the fuel and of very fine particles of partly burned carbon and hydrocarbons which are highly pollutant for the air and highly toxic for human health. Air pollution is obviously much more severe in large urban and industrial conurbations. It is strongly influenced by meteorological and climatic conditions (wind, rainfall, temperature inversions and solar radiation) and can, in turn, influence those conditions. It can have its origins in distant sources of pollution as a result of the long-distant transport of pollutants by the wind.

1   OJ C271, 07.10.1993.
2   OJ L188, 16.07.1984 and OJ L263, 22.10.1993.
3   OJ L73, 16.03.1994.
4   OJ C172, 07.07.1995.
5   OJ L240, 19.09.1977.
6   OJ L162, 19.06.1981.
7   OJ L67, 12.03.1983.
8   COM (95) 202.
9   OJ C216, 06.08.1994.

Now, several of the most industrialized regions of the European Union are situated in frontier areas. **Sulphur dioxide and suspended particulate matter** are carried from one European region to another according to wind direction. The European States therefore had to act in unison to prevent air pollution and at the same time to prevent the effects on the functioning of the common market resulting from barriers to trade in fuels and on the conditions of competition between industries using such fuels. However, prudence was called for so as not to disturb European industry too much.

In 1975 the Council adopted a decision establishing a reciprocal exchange of information and data from networks and individual stations measuring air pollution within the Member States in order to monitor the formation in the air of sulphur dioxide and black smoke and to create a database to make it possible to study the phenomenon of transboundary air pollution. In 1996, the system for the exchange of information was improved, in particular by increasing the number of pollutants covered and the volume of data provided[1].

Thereafter, in 1980 the Council adopted a Directive concerning limit values not to be exceeded and guide values to be used as reference points for air quality with regard to sulphur dioxide and suspended particulates[2]. At the same time the Council adopted a Resolution under which the Member States undertook to restrict, reduce progressively and prevent air pollution by sulphur dioxide and suspended particulates[3].

The 1980 Directive represented a major step forward in Community policy on the protection of the air against pollution, but it was also important in international terms in the context of implementation of the Geneva Convention on long-range transboundary air pollution[4]. A Protocol of this Convention provided for the long-term financing of a cooperative programme for monitoring and evaluation of the long-range transmission of air pollutants in Europe (EMEP)[5]. In the framework of the Geneva Convention the Community undertook a commitment to reduce its total sulphur emissions by the year 2000 to almost 62% below 1980 levels.

In order to attain and maintain air quality standards, a whole gamut of measures to limit the emission of sulphur dioxide and other pollutants is, of course, required. A Council Directive of 24 November 1975 limits the **sulphur content of certain liquid fuels**. The limit values laid down in that Directive became more stringent in 1994[6]. There are also Community Directives limiting emissions of sulphur and other pollutants from industrial plants[7], from large combustion plants[8] and from municipal waste incineration plants[9]. Other Directives relate to air quality standards for nitrogen dioxide[10] the reduction of environmental pollution by asbestos[11] and the control of volatile organic compound (VOC) emissions resulting from the storage of petrol and its distribution to service stations[12].

In 1991, the Council outlined a Community strategy to limit emissions of carbon dioxide and raise energy efficiency. This strategy aims to stabilize **carbon dioxide (CO_2) emissions** in the Community at their 1990 level by the year 2000. It would be based upon regulatory, sectoral and volun-

1   OJ L210, 19.07.1982 and OJ C281, 07.10.1994.
2   OJ L229, 30.08.1980 and OJ L377, 31.12.1991.
3   OJ C222, 30.08.1980.
4   OJ L171, 27.06.1981 and OJ L149, 21.06.1993.
5   OJ L181, 04.07.1986.
6   OJ L307, 27.11.1975 and OJ L74, 27.03.1993.
7   OJ L188, 16.07.1984.
8   OJ L336, 07.12.1988 and OJ L337, 24.12.1994.
9   OJ L163, 14.06.1989, OJ L203, 15.07.1989 and OJ L1, 03.01.1994.
10 OJ L87, 27.03.1985.
11 OJ L85, 28.03.1987 and OJ L377, 31.12.1991.
12 OJ L365, 31.12.1994.

tary measures, such as the Directive to limit carbon dioxide emissions by improving energy efficiency[1] and a mechanism for monitoring CO_2 emissions and other greenhouse gas emissions, which provides for the Member States to compile inventories of CO_2 emissions and national abatement programmes evaluated by the Commission[2]. However, the Commission has proposed a Directive which would introduce a tax on CO_2 emissions and energy designed to encourage consumers to make more rational use of energy and to favour the least polluting energy sources[3]. In conclusions adopted on 15 December 1994, the Council sets out a Community strategy to reduce CO_2 emissions and improve energy efficiency, in particular by fiscal measures.

Another major source of air pollution addressed by the Community is pollution by emissions from motor vehicles. **Carbon monoxide** resulting from the incomplete combustion of organic substances used in fuel was tackled first owing to its adverse consequences for human health and the environment. A Council Directive of 1970 concerning the harmonization of legislation on measures against air pollution by motor vehicle emissions obliged Member States to introduce three types of test to control gas emissions from positive-ignition engines of motor vehicles[4]. The technical controls of vehicles laid down by that Directive led to a significant reduction in emissions of carbon monoxide and unburned hydrocarbons by each vehicle. However, that effect was to a large extent neutralized by the increase in the number of vehicles in circulation in the Community States. For that reason the 1970 Directive was adapted to technical progress on several occasions in order to reduce the permissible levels of carbon monoxide emissions. A Council Directive of 18 July 1989 is directed towards reducing by more than half the air pollution caused by cars below 1.4 litres[5]. Another Directive makes the emission standards applicable to light commercial vehicles as stringent as those in force for private cars[6]. The new limit values, which will be compulsory from 1 January 1996 for new type approvals, will bring about a 50% reduction in pollutant emissions and thus will bring the European standards up to the American federal standards[7].

Another first-category air pollutant is **lead** and its compounds. A large proportion of the total quantity or this element in the air comes from emissions from petrol-engine vehicles. A Council Directive of 1982 lays down a limit value for lead in the air[8]. Compliance with that limit required very costly measures for the Member States motor-vehicle industry. In order to prevent barriers to trade and the upheaval of conditions of competition, it was necessary to proceed in stages with the approximation of the laws of the Member States concerning the lead content of petrol,

1   OJ L237, 22.09.1993, see the programme SAVE in the chapter on energy.
2   OJ L167, 09.07.1993.
3   OJ C196, 03.08.1992 and COM (95) 172.
4   OJ L76, 06.04.1970.
5   OJ L226, 03.08.1989.
6   OJ L186, 28.07.1993.
7   OJ L100, 19.04.1994.
8   OJ L378, 31.12.1982 and OJ L377, 31.12.1991.

allowing the European motor vehicle industry and the petrol production and distribution industry time to adapt to the new conditions. That was done in a 1985 Directive[1] and lead-free petrol won little by little and without problems the markets of the Member States.

As far as **polluting emissions by diesel engines** are concerned, a 1988 Directive provides for a two-step reduction of limit values for emissions by commercial vehicles of three gas pollutants (carbon monoxide, hydro-carbons and nitrogen oxide) and for the introduction of monitoring of particulate emissions by these vehicles[2]. Another Directive monitors the emission of pollutants from diesel engines for use in wheeled agricultural or forestry tractors[3].

Moving above the atmosphere, the stratosphere is also in danger. The **stratospheric ozone layer** is vital to mankind, as it filters a large proportion of the sun's ultraviolet rays. A reduction in that layer could lead to a large increase in the number of skin cancers or considerable damage to agriculture on the planet. Emissions of chemicals such as chlorofluorocarbons (CFCs) and halons already caused, between 1969 and 1986, a 3% reduction of the ozone layer above the northern hemisphere and each spring causes a 50% reduction in that layer above the Antarctic; in addition, they contribute to the "**greenhouse effect**" and hence to global warming. Effective combatting of this phenomenon requires concerted action at international level. The European Union is signatory of the Framework Convention on climate change of the United Nations, the objective of which is to stabilize greenhouse gas concentrations in the air at a level avoiding dangerous climate change[4].

In that connection, particular reference should be made to the Protocol on the control of greenhouse gas emissions, signed at Montreal within the framework of the United Nations Convention on Climate Change. In this framework, a Directive of 1992, on **air pollution by ozone**, established a harmonized procedure monitoring concentrations, exchanging information and informing and warning the population, backed up by mechanisms to coordinate the action taken or planned in the Community against photochemical pollution[5]. In the context of the implementation of the second amendment to the Montreal Protocol, the Community committed itself to stabilize CO_2 emissions at 1990 levels by the year 2000 and to reduce progressively the consumption of chlorofluorocarbons and hydrochlorofluorocarbons leading to a total phase-out by 2015[6].

Chemical substances and industrial hazards

Major pollution of water, air and soil is caused by chemical products discharged in the form of by-products or industrial waste. The Community had first endeavoured to control the pollutant substances enumerated in the lists annexed to the directives concerning water and air quality. But it soon became clear that of the thousands of chemical substances placed on

---

1   OJ L96, 03.04.1985 and OJ L377, 31.12.1991.
2   OJ L36, 09.02.1988 and OJ L40, 17.02.1996.
3   OJ L220, 29.08.1977 and OJ L378, 31.12.1982.
4   OJ L33, 07.02.1994.
5   OJ L297, 13.10.1992.
6   OJ L33, 07.02.1994 and OJ L333, 22.12.1994.

the Community market only a small number had undergone testing which could prove their potential danger to human health and the environment. It became therefore urgent to devise mechanisms for the prevention of possible risks of dangerous substances.

The Council Directive of 1967 on the approximation of the laws relating to the classification, packaging and labelling of **dangerous substances** did not make provision for a procedure for the prevention of hazards before they were placed on the market. This Directive was amended several times to bring it into line with technical progress[1]. The sixth amendment of that Directive, in 1979, provided for a preventive procedure[2]. Each Member State undertook to act as a representative of its European Community partners when authorizing the introduction of a new chemical product into the whole Community market. For that purpose the producer or importer has to provide the State into whose market the product is first introduced with a "**base set**". That dossier is composed of a whole range of information on the physico-chemical properties of the new product concerned, its possible effects on health and the environment, the uses for which it is intended, the quantities produced, the proposed classification and labelling and a general evaluation of the dangers. That information is forwarded to the Commission, which sends it to each Member State and to the Scientific Advisory Committee, which examines the toxicity and ecotoxicity of chemical compounds[3].

A Council Regulation of March 23, 1993 relates to the evaluation and control of the environmental risks inherent in **existing substances**[4]. It seeks to ensure systematic evaluation of the risks arising from substances in the European Inventory of existing commercial substances (**EINECS**) on the basis of information supplied by the manufacturers or importers and covering around 10,000 substances present on the market, with variable degrees of requirements depending on the quantities involved. It provides, notably for systematic data collection, the establishment of lists of substances to be evaluated as a priority and the evaluation of risks, and sets up for this purpose close cooperation between the Member States, the Commission and industry.

The placing on the Community market for use in the Member States of certain dangerous substances and preparations are restricted by a Council Directive of 1976, which has been adapted to technical progress on a number of occasions[5]. Export from and import into the Community of certain dangerous chemicals are governed by a Council Regulation of July 23, 1992 which notably introduces the principle of "prior informed consent", compatible with the procedure established by the United Nations Environment Programme, which consists of granting the authorities of an importing country discretionary power as to whether to accept or refuse import of a substance which is prohibited or strictly regulated by the Community[6].

The classification of a chemical substance as dangerous or harmless obviously necessitates sound laboratory tests. Accordingly, a 1986 Council Directive concerns the harmonization of laws, regulations and administrative provisions of the Member States relating to the application of the principles of **good laboratory practice** and the verification of their

---

1   OJ L196, 16.08.1967 and OJ L381, 31.12.1994.
2   OJ L259, 15.10.1979.
3   OJ L198, 22.07.1978 and OJ L105, 26.04.1988.
4   OJ L84, 05.04.1993.
5   OJ L262, 27.09.1976 and OJ L365, 31.12.1994.
6   OJ L251, 29.08.1992 and OJ L332, 22.12.1994.

applications for tests on chemical substances[1]. The inspection and verification of Good Laboratory Practice are themselves regulated by a Council Directive of 9 June 1988[2].

All these rules cannot in themselves prevent serious industrial accidents which are catastrophic for the environment, like those in Seveso in Italy in 1981 and Bhopal in India in 1984. For that reason, the Council adopted in 1982 a Directive on the **major-accident hazards** of certain industrial activities (Seveso Directive)[3]. With the benefit of the experience gained, a new Directive concerns the control of major accident hazards involving dangerous substances[4]. It aims to improve and reinforce the arrangements for the prevention of such hazards notably through: the submission of safety reports by establishments where dangerous substances are present in large quantities demonstrating that the major-accident hazards have been identified, that the design, construction, operation and maintenance of the installations are sufficiently safe, and that emergency plans have been drawn up; the consideration for major-accident prevention objectives and limitation of the consequences of such accidents in Member States' land-use policies; better public information and consultation.

Another Directive aims at an **integrated pollution prevention and control**[5]. Its across-the-board approach involves the various media (air, water, soil) by applying the principle of the best environmental option, in particular in order to avoid transferring pollution from one medium to another. It provides that the operators of certain polluting plants submit requests for operating permits to the competent authority in the Member States, with the issuing of a permit being conditional on compliance with basic obligations such as not to exceed emission limit values. Provision is also made for informing and consulting the public before issuing the permit.

Effort to combat noise pollution

Noise has intensified considerably with the development of industrialization and urbanization, in particular through the use of increasingly numerous and noisy machines in road transport and air transport. Noise has been the subject of studies which have shown that, depending on its intensity and nature, it gives rise to certain consequences for the person exposed to it, from discomfort to psychological, or even pathological, effects. Action needed to be taken at Community level, as measures taken nationally to reduce noise nuisances could effect the functioning of the common market by creating technical barriers to trade in products subject to anti-noise specifications or distortions of competition between noisy plants, on which different investment or operating costs would be imposed. Although based first and foremost on commercial and economic

---

1   OJ L15, 17.01.1987 and OJ L1, 03.01.1994.
2   OJ L145, 11.06.1988 and OJ L11, 13.01.1990.
3   OJ L230, 05.08.1982 and OJ L336, 07.12.1988.
4   OJ C120, 24.04.1996.
5   OJ C165, 01.07.1995.

considerations, the harmonization of national rules could, and was, to constitute an instrument for combating noise nuisances in the Community.

A 1970 Directive on the approximation of the laws of the Member States relating to the permissible sound level and the **exhaust system of motor vehicles**, which was one of the first Community measures with implications for the environment, laid down the permissible sound levels for the various categories of motor vehicles intended for use on the road and having at least four wheels. It has been adapted to technical progress several times[1]. A 1978 Directive on the permissible sound level and **exhaust system of motorcycles** is aimed at limiting the sound output of these particularly noisy vehicles without disturbing trade between Member States[2].

A significant source of noise is aircraft, the number of which increases each year. Sound pollution in this area needed to be limited, but without giving rise to distortions of competition between aircraft manufacturers and between users (airlines). A 1979 Directive is directed towards limiting **noise emissions from subsonic aircraft** which land in the territory of the Community, and not only those registered in the Member States[3]. A 1989 Directive seeks to limit noise emissions from subsonic **civil jet aircraft**[4] and a 1992 Directive provides for the phasing out of the noisiest of these aeroplanes[5].

Another major source of noise pollution is that of the various **appliances used in the construction sector**. Here, too, the Community needed to be involved in order to avoid technical barriers to trade. Thus through a series of directives, the Council approximated the laws of the Member States relating to the permissible sound power level of: construction plant and equipment[6]; compressors[7]; tower cranes[8]; welding generators[9]; powered hand-held concrete-breakers and picks[10]; hydraulic excavators, rope-operated excavators, bulldozers, loaders and excavator-loaders[11].

Lastly, the Community also aims to reduce noise nuisances outside and inside **dwellings**. One Directive concerns the permissible sound power level of lawnmowers[12] and another the airborne noise emitted by household appliances[13].

Management of environmental resources

The Community environment programme is not confined to the effort to combat pollution and nuisances, but also seeks to make an active contribution to improving the environment and the quality of life through the rational management of space, the environment and natural resources. The measures provided for in that section of the environment programme can be grouped under the headings of the protection of flora and fauna in Europe and the management of waste in the Community. The financial instrument LIFE can finance projects in these areas, such as the conservation of biotopes of particular importance for the Community, projects for

---

1   OJ L42, 23.02.1970 and OJ L371, 19.12.1992.
2   OJ L349, 13.12.1978 and OJ L98, 11.04.1989.
3   OJ L18, 24.01.1980 and OJ L1, 03.01.1994.
4   OJ L363, 13.12.1989 and OJ L1, 03.01.1994.
5   OJ L76, 23.03.1992.
6   OJ L33, 08.02.1970 and OJ L1, 03.01.1994.
7   OJ L300, 19.11.1984 and OJ L1, 03.01.1994.
8   Ibid.
9   Ibid.
10   Ibid.
11   OJ L384, 31.12.1986 and OJ L168, 18.07.1995.
12   OJ L300, 19.11.1984 and OJ L81, 26.03.1988.
13   OJ L344, 06.12.1986 and OJ L1, 03.01.1994.

the conservation of endangered species and the location and restoration of areas contaminated by waste and/or dangerous substances.

Protection of flora and fauna

Species of wild flowers and the animal populations form part of the Community's heritage. Apart from the fact that they represent non-renewable genetic assets, they participate in many natural functions which ensure overall ecological balances, such as the regulation of the development of undesirable organisms, the protection of the soil against erosion and the regulation of aquatic ecosystems. The genetic assets represented by all present-day animal and plant species constitute a resource of ecological, scientific and economic interest of inestimable value for the future of mankind. However, industrialization, urbanization and pollution are threatening a growing number of wild species and undermining the natural balances resulting from several million years of evolution.

For the protection of wildlife, the Community depends on the **work of international bodies**, in particular the Council of Europe, directed towards ensuring the protection of wildlife and the conservation of the characteristic biotopes or ecosystems, in particular in wetlands, which are essential to such life. Most important in that context is the Convention on Wetlands of International Importance Especially as Waterfowl Habitat adopted on 2 February 1971 by the International Conference at Ramsar, in Iran. In 1974 the Commission recommended that the Community States all accede to the Ramsar Convention as a first step towards the protection of European wetlands[1]. In 1982, the Community as such signed the Convention on the Conservation of Migratory Species of Wild Animals, known as the "Bonn Convention"[2], and the Convention on the Conservation of European Wildlife and Natural Habitats, called the "Berne Convention"[3]. Those three Conventions, together with the Conventions for the Conservation of Salmon in the North Atlantic Ocean[4] and for the Conservation of Atlantic Tuna[5], which concern the conservation of fishery resources, were to provide the framework for Community action in the field of the protection of flora and fauna.

In this framework a 1992 Directive aims to protect natural and semi-natural habitats and wild fauna and flora[6]. It provides for the establishment of a European ecological network of special conservation areas, "Natura 2000", made up of sites which are home to types of natural habitats and habitats of species of interest to the Community. The Member States must take appropriate steps to avoid their deterioration or any other disturbances affecting the species.

---

1   OJ L21, 28.01.1975.
2   OJ L210, 19.07.1982.
3   OJ L38, 10.02.1982.
4   OJ L378, 31.12.1982.
5   OJ L162, 18.06.1986.
6   OJ L206, 22.07.1992.

A significant means of protecting wildlife threatened with extinction is to restrict and **control rigorously international trade in plants and animals** belonging to such species and products made therefrom. In 1982, the Council adopted a Regulation on the implementation in the Community of the Convention on International Trade in Endangered Species of Wild Fauna and Flora (CITES). That Convention has the objective of protecting 2.000 species through the stringent control of international trade. Moreover, the Regulation provides for restriction or control measures which go beyond the provisions of the Convention[1].

To implement the international Conventions, the Community has taken specific measures relating to **certain particularly endangered species**. Thus, the Council adopted: in 1979, a Directive on the conservation of wild birds, which establishes the list of species which may be hunted, the list of species which may be marketed and the list of prohibited methods of hunting and trapping[2]; in 1981, a Regulation prohibiting the importation of certain products derived from cetaceans (whales, etc.), in order to contribute to the conservation of such endangered species[3]; in 1983, a Directive prohibiting imports into the Community of skins of harp seal pups and of hooded seal pups, the annual hunt for which had shocked public opinion[4]; and in 1991, a Regulation prohibiting the use of leghold traps in the Community and the introduction into the Community of pelts and manufactured goods of certain wild animal species originating in countries which catch them by means of leghold traps[5]. On the basis of the 1982 Council Regulation on the application of the Washington Convention, the Commission adopted, in 1989, a Regulation prohibiting the issue of import permits for ivory derived from the African elephant, with a view to contributing in that way to putting a stop to the slaughter thereof[6].

The situation of several plant species in Europe and elsewhere in the world is no less worrying, owing to the encroachment on the countryside by towns, soil erosion and soil destruction and the abandonment of rural life by an ever-increasing number of citizens. Thousands of hectares of forests are destroyed in Europe each year by fires and pollution. To put a stop to that catastrophe, the Council adopted two Regulations on the **protection of the Community's forests**: one against atmospheric pollution[7]; and the other against fire[8]. At international level, the Community provides financial and technical support for countries and organizations promoting the conservation and sustainable management of **tropical forests** and their associated biological diversity[9]. The Community has signed together with the Alpine countries the Convention on the protection of the Alps, which aims at safeguarding the Alpine ecosystem and securing environmentally sustainable development for the populations[10].

The Council has also agreed to the European Union's participation in the conclusion of the Convention on the **Conservation of Biological Diversity**, which was drafted under the auspices of the United Nations Environment Programme (UNEP)[11]. The objectives of this Convention are: the conservation of biological diversity; the sustainable use of its components; and the fair and equitable sharing of the benefits arising from

1   OJ L384, 31.12.1982 and OJ L151, 23.06.1993.
2   OJ L103, 25.04.1979 and OJ L164, 30.06.1994.
3   OJ L39, 12.02.1981.
4   OJ L91, 09.04.1983.
5   OJ L308, 09.11.1991 and OJ L184, 20.07.1994.
6   OJ L240, 17.08.1989.
7   OJ L326, 31.11.1986 and OJ L125, 18.05.1994.
8   OJ L217, 31.07.1992 and OJ L93, 12.04.1994.
9   OJ L327, 30.12.1995.
10   OJ L61, 12.03.1996.
11   OJ L309, 13.12.1993.

genetic resources, including, in particular, appropriate access to genetic resources and appropriate transfer of relevant technologies, taking into account all rights over those resources and of adequate funding. The Community supports, in particular, a Protocol to this Convention on the safe transfer, handling and use of modified living organisms resulting from biotechnology.

Management of waste

As the penalty paid for economic development and urbanization, the accumulation of waste destroys the environment and is at the same time proof of regrettable profligacy. Waste of all kinds, i.e. household waste, industrial waste, sewage sludge from waste water, agricultural waste and waste from the extractive industries, accounts for some 2.500 thousand million tons each year. Its treatment provides employment for more than 2 million persons in the European Union and represents an annual turnover of between ECU 100 and 200 thousand million.

Included amongst "waste" are toxic substances and substances which are hazardous for man and the environment, as they can pollute the water table by percolation, contaminate micro-organisms and appear in the food chain through complex and little-known means. But "waste" also includes scrap metal, paper, plastics and waste oils, which can be recycled, which is important in a Europe becoming increasingly poor in raw materials.

In view of the close interdependence of waste management and many industrial and commercial activities, the lack of a Community design for waste management is likely to affect not only environmental protection, but also the completion of the internal market by creating distortions of competition and unjustified movements of investment, or even the partitioning of the market. The objectives of a Community strategy on waste management are therefore: **prevention**, by encouraging the use of products which create less waste ; **increasing its value**, through the optimization of collection and sorting systems; **the laying down of stringent standards** for final disposal, as contained in the Council Directives on new municipal waste-incineration plants[1] and on existing municipal waste-incineration plants[2]; **rules governing the carriage** of dangerous substances, so as to ensure safe and economic carriage and the **restoration of contaminated areas**, taking into account the civil liability of the polluter.

It must be said that the Community has already been pursuing most of those objectives since the mid-'70s, with varying degrees of success. For instance, a Council Directive of 15 July 1975 is aimed at **approximating national laws on waste**, which it defines as "any substance or object which the holder disposes of or is required to dispose of pursuant to the provisions of national law in force"[3]. This Directive is considered as the **"framework Directive" for Community waste policy**. It obliges the Member States to take measures to ensure that waste is eliminated without endan-

---

1   OJ L163, 14.06.1989 and OJ L1, 03.01.1994.
2   OJ L203, 15.07.1989 and OJ L1, 03.01.1994.
3   OJ L194, 25.07.1975 and OJ L377, 31.12.1991.

gering human health and without damaging the environment, and in particular without giving rise to risk to water, air or soil, fauna or flora, without causing discomfort through noise or smell and without affecting areas or landscapes. It also aims to set up an integrated and appropriate network of waste disposal plants, to encourage disposal as close as possible to the waste production site, thus reducing the dangers inherent in waste transport, and to promote clean technologies and products which can be recycled and reused.

A Directive on **toxic and dangerous waste** contains a list of 27 substances the collection, disposal and re-use of which necessitate special precautions[1]. The list includes mercury and cadmium, certain solvents and pharmaceutical preparations, ethers, tar and asbestos. The Directive provides for standard authorization arrangements for plants, establishments or undertakings which store, treat or discharge waste containing such substances. It gives priority to the promotion of clean technologies and of products generating little or less waste and to the establishment of an information system on the Community situation as regards waste management.

In 1990, the Council has better defined the waste management policy[2] and, in 1991, it has adopted a Directive on **hazardous waste**, which has influenced the environment policy in general, because it has necessitated the amendment of many pre-existing Directives[3]. Another Directive provides for measures and methods to prevent or reduce the adverse effects on the environment and human health resulting from such incineration[4]. Concerning the disposal of waste oils, which are very polluting for the water and the soil, a Directive prohibits the discharge into the environment of any semi-liquid or liquid composed wholly or in part of mineral oil or synthetic oil[5]. Another Directive does likewise with regard to polychlorinated biphenyls (PCBs) and polychlorinated terphenyls (PCTs)[6].

Recycling plays an increasingly important role in Community waste management policy. That is especially true of waste paper, which represents between 40 and 50% of the volume and 15 and 20% of the tonnage of urban waste. The recycling of a ton of waste paper, which is less polluting than the manufacturing cycle for pulp, replaces the equivalent of 2 or 3 cubic meters of wood, viz. approximately 15 to 20 small trees. Moreover, it replaces imports in this sector, which is, after the oil sector, the most in deficit in the Community's trade balance. The Council accordingly recommended to the Member States, on 3 December 1981, that every effort be made to re-use waste paper and to use recycled paper[7]. With regard to containers for liquids for human consumption, on 27 June 1985 the Council adopted a Directive directed towards reducing the tonnage and/or volume of such containers in household waste through the implementation of programmes prepared by the Member States[8]. A Directive on packaging and packaging waste aims at preventing the producing of packaging waste, reusing packaging and recycling packaging[9].

In the framework of the internal market and the subsequent removal of border controls, the Council adopted a Regulation on the monitoring and control of **waste transfers** within, on entrance to and exit from the Community[10]. This Regulation seeks to put an end to what has been termed "waste tourism" within the Community and the unrestricted export of waste to the developing countries. In cases of waste transfers between

1   OJ L84, 31.03.1978 and OJ L377, 31.12.1991.
2   OJ L122, 18.05.1990.
3   OJ L377, 31.12.1991 and OJ L168, 02.07.1994.
4   OJ L365, 31.12.1994.
5   OJ L194, 25.07.1975 and OJ L377, 31.12.1991.
6   OJ L108, 26.04.1976 and OJ L377, 31.12.1991.
7   OJ L355, 10.12.1981.
8   OJ L176, 06.07.1985.
9   OJ L356, 31.12.1994.
10   OJ L30, 06.02.1993 and OJ L288, 09.11.1994.

the Member States, a distinction is made between wastes for disposal and those for value addition. For the first category, the principles of proximity, priority to value addition and self-sufficiency apply. For the second, a notification system applies with a follow-up document and the compulsory existence of a contract between the notifying party and the consignee. Although there are exceptions under certain conditions, normally all exports of waste to third countries and imports into the Community of waste from third countries are prohibited. The Community is moreover a party to the Basle Convention on the control of cross-border movements of dangerous wastes and their disposal[1].

Appraisal and outlook

In a European economy which undergoes structural change, the challenge facing those with responsibility for environment policy is to develop instruments which will make it possible painlessly to achieve the objective of growth which is compatible with the essential requirements of the environment. This involves foreseeing the ecological problems of technological development and limiting them from the outset, for example by encouraging the selection of new chemical products before they are launched on the market, the preparation of stringent safety standards applicable to potentially dangerous manufacturing procedures, the disposal of waste without danger to the environment or to human health and the systematic evaluation of the likely impact on the environment of any new economic activity. However, there is no major conflict between economic growth and a healthy and clean environment. The inflationary effect of environment policies is negligible. On the other hand, the "**environment industry**" is probably in a position to help the European economies to restructure themselves on new bases by directing them towards new activities which employ advanced technology and a skilled workforce.

Thanks to the Treaty on European Union, the environment has graduated to the status of full-blooded policy and falls into the priority objectives of the Union. Environmental constraints will have to be integrated into the definition and implementation of other EU policies. Nevertheless, the major concern of environment policy in the European Union is still the **reduction of pollution and nuisances**. The vast majority of the numerous Community provisions on the environment concern the effort to combat the pollution of fresh water and sea water, air pollution, dangerous chemical substances and noise nuisances. The uniform application in all Member States of environmental standards is, in fact, indispensable not only for the preservation of Europe's environment, but also for the good functioning of the internal market and for economic and social cohesion.

It is very difficult to evaluate the specific results of the European measures in this area, first because the quality of the environment is a highly subjective notion and therefore difficult to define, and secondly

---

1   OJ L39, 16.02.1993.

because the policy to combat pollution is a **Sisiphean task**. The quality objectives that it lays down are incessantly thrust aside by economic development and urbanization. It is true that the annual reports of the Commission to the Parliament and the Council on the implementation of the European Community's environment programme show a reduction of ozone-depleting substances and improvements made in water quality and waste management. But progress is made at varying speeds, with the manufacturing sector setting the fastest pace, while progress is slower in transports, agriculture and tourism. In any case, a permanent vigilance is required of citizens, who can lodge complaints with the Commission whenever they observe that European standards are not being complied with by an undertaking or by public or private works in their country or a neighbouring country.

Moreover, the European Union cannot work in isolation in this field. Even if it were to succeed in significantly reducing and preventing pollution in its territory, it would still be open to water and air pollution from the other countries of Europe and the other regions of the world. For that reason the countries of the EU must strive for environmental protection together with other countries in the framework of **international organizations** such as the Council of Europe and the United Nations. Together they can ensure that others comply to a greater extent with the standards obtaining in their countries. Thus, the new economic departure of the **East European countries**, assisted by the countries of the West, must go hand-in-hand with increased consideration of environmental constraints, which have been tragically neglected in the past. The European Environment Agency, which is open to the other countries of Europe, plays an important part in this area.

The environmental interdependence of all the countries in the world is particularly marked with regard to the **greenhouse effect** and its climatic consequences for the globe. It is self-evident that the countries of the European Union cannot take action against that phenomenon other than in the framework of wide-ranging international cooperation. Furthermore, the Union's credibility and efficiency at world level hinges on its ability to adopt progressive internal measures in the field of environmental defence. During the "Earth Summit" in June 1992 in Rio de Janeiro, the Community and the Member States recognized their wider responsibilities to play a leading role in promoting concerted action at global level. The Community's fifth action programme on the environment reflects its commitment to this. The implementation of this programme may translate into practice the theory of sustainable development and constitute the beginning of the solution to the problem of excessive use of natural and environmental resources, which becomes ever more acute at world level.

The need for international cooperation is even more obvious as regards the second aspect of environment policy, namely that of the **management of resources**, in particular fauna and flora. In this area it is the third world which faces some of the most threatening environmental problems and the most serious at world level, viz.: desertification, excessive urbanization, population explosion, extinction of wildlife and destruction of the rainforests. The cooperation and development programmes of the European Union must lend particular attention to these problems, notably that of **rainforests**, which constitute one of the planet's most important natural resources.

However, there is nothing automatic about the move towards sustainable development and, while economic growth and environmental protection are compatible, there is still a need for a Community policy framework in order to improve the quality of the environment. There is need, in particular for market-based instruments such as environmental taxes and charges, e.g. the tax on carbon dioxide emissions and energy. Using instruments of this kind would make it possible to place less reliance on binding administrative and regulatory measures and, as a result of the revenue generated, to reduce certain other statutory contributions and charges, including those that burden labour.

Bibliography on environment policy

▫ ABRAHAM Filip, DEKETELAERE Kurt, STUYCK Jules (ed.), *Recent Economic and Legal Developments in European Environmental Policy*, Leuven University Press, Leuven, 1995.

▫ BRENTON Tony, *The Greening of Machiavelli: the Evolution of International Environmental Politics*, Royal Institute of International Affairs, London, 1994.

▫ BONNEFOI Christine-Marie, *Droit européen de l'environnement*, Delmas, Paris, 1993.

▫ BOY Laurence, "L'éco-label communautaire, un exemple de droit post-moderne", in *Revue Internationale de Droit Économique*, N° 1, 1996, pp. 69-97.

▫ COMMISSION EUROPÉENNE, *La croissance économique et l'environnement: quelques implications pour la politique économique*, COM (94) 465 du 3 novembre 1994.

  – *L'environnement: un enjeu majeur pour la R&D européenne: un aperçu des résultats des programmes de recherche de l'Union européenne dans le domaine de l'environnement*, OPOCE, Luxembourg, 1995.

▫ DEMIRAY David, "The Movement of Goods in a Green Market", in *Legal Issues of European Integration*, Deventer, N° 1, 1994, pp. 73-110.

▫ DE SADELEER Nicolas, *Le droit communautaire et les déchets*, LGDJ Édition, Paris, 1995.

▫ DUERKOP Marco, "Trade and Environment: International Trade Law Aspects of the Proposed EC Directive Introducing a Tax on Carbon Dioxide Emissions and Energy", in *Common Market Law Review*, Dordrecht, Vol. 31, N° 4, August 1994, pp. 807-844.

▫ EUROPEAN COMMISSION, *Waste Management Planning in the European Community*, OOPEC, Luxembourg 1994.

▫ EUROPEAN FOUNDATION FOR THE IMPROVEMENT OF LIVING AND WORKING CONDITIONS, *Industrial Relations and Environmental Protection in Europe*, OOPEC, Luxembourg, 1994.

▫ EUROPEAN ENVIRONMENT AGENCY, *Environment in the European Union, 1995. Report for the Review of the Fifth Environmental Action Programme*, OOPEC, Luxembourg, 1995.

▫ FREESTONE David, "EC Environmental Law after Maastricht" in *Northern Ireland Legal Quarterly*, Belfast, Vol. 45 N° 2, 1994, pp. 152-176.

▫ HANDLER Thomas (ed.), *Regulating the European Environment*, Chancery Law Publishing, Chichester, 1994.

▫ IRWING Alan, GEORG Susse, VERGRAGT Philip, "The Social Management of Environmental Change", in *Futures*, Oxford, Vol. 26, N 3, April 1994, pp. 323-334.

▫ JOHNSON Stanley, CORCELLE Guy, *The Environmental Policy of the European Communities*, Kluwer Law International, The Hague, 1995.

▫ KUNZLIK Peter, *Environmental Policy*, Longman, Harlow, 1994.

▫ *L'actualité du droit de l'environnement. Actes du colloque des 17 et 18 novembre 1994*, Bruylant, Bruxelles, 1995.

▫ LENAERTS Koen "The Principle of Subsidiarity and the Environment in the European Union: Keeping the Balance of Federalism", in *Fordham International Law Journal*, New York, Vol. 17, N° 4, 1994, pp. 846-895.

▫ LONDON Caroline, "Droit communautaire de l'environnement", in *Revue trimestrielle de droit européen*, Paris, année 30, N° 2, avril-juin 1994, pp. 291-325.

▫ MULLARD Sally, "Towards an EU Strategy for Integrated Coastal Zone Management", in *European Environmental Law Review*, London, Vol. 4, N° 1, January 1995, pp. 16-20.

▫ PONS Françoise, *Environment: New Policies of the European Union*, Club de Bruxelles, Bruxelles, 1994.

▫ PORTWOOD Timothy, *Competition Law and the Environment*, Cameron May, London, 1994.

▫ ROGERS Michael, *Business and the Environment*, MacMillan Press Ltd., Basingstone, Hampshire, 1995.

▫ STANNERS David, BOURDEAU Philippe (ed.), *Europe's Environment. The Dobris Assessment*, European Environment Agency, OPOCE, Luxembourg, 1995.

▫ WAELBROECK-ROCHA Elisabeth, VOS Hans, JANTZEN Jochem (et al.), *Potential Benefits of Integration of Environmental and Economic Policies - An Incentive-Based Approach to Policy Integration*, European Communities Environmental Policy Series, OOPEC, Luxembourg, Graham and Trotman, London, 1994.

9. INDUSTRY

The Treaty establishing the European Economic Community regulated the attainment of customs union in great detail with regard to the industrial products of the Member States, but the Community did not, at its inception, have an industrial policy as such. In fact the founding fathers of the EEC had hoped that the liberalization of trade and increased competition could, on their own, bring about the structural changes that Community industry needed. As was explained in the chapter on the common market, this hope was not fully realized because of the persistence of technical obstacles to trade and, therefore, the tardy completion of the single market.

While industrial protectionnism remained, hidden behind technical regulations, the concept of industrial policy had been the subject of repeated controversies in the Community. It took several years' effort, especially by the Commission, for all Member States to agree that a Community industrial policy was necessary, first for the completion of the common market in industrial products and, secondly, to cope with common structural and sectoral problems. The first major aspect of this policy, which is linked with harmonization of legislations and standardization, was dealt with in the chapter on the common market. In this chapter we shall examine structural industrial policy, pertaining notably to small and medium enterprises, and sectoral policy concerning some key sectors of European industry.

A large part of this chapter thus deals with **enterprise policy**, which is connected with industrial policy. In the run-up to the completion of the Single Market, in the early 1990s, the Community has, in fact, paid close attention to small and medium-sized enterprises (SMEs), which account for almost 99% of the industrial fabric of the Community and for 70% of total employment in the private sector of the Member States and which face problems of integration in the Single Market. The enterprise policy, which covers not only industrial firms but also firms in other economic sectors, in particular craft, tourism and distribution businesses, has three main objectives: (a) to provide Community enterprises as a whole with the necessary legal and administrative framework which will enable their activities to develop freely under conditions corresponding to those of an internal market; (b) to create an economic environment which helps firms to develop fully in the single internal market; and (c) to encourage cross-border cooperation between European firms. We examine the Community's enterprise policy in the second part of this chapter.

Economic and legal framework

The European Treaties did not make provision for a Community industrial policy. However, they dealt primarily with the industrial sector of the Member States. Whilst the Treaties establishing the European Coal and Steel Community (ECSC) and the European Atomic Energy Community (EAEC) constituted sectoral policies in the relevant industrial sectors, the Treaty establishing the European Economic Community (EEC) chiefly regulated the common market in industrial products.

Although limited in scope, the ECSC and EAEC (Euratom) Treaties are more precise than the EEC Treaty; they include provisions both on the attainment of the common market and on the structural policy of the sectors to which they relate, and they give powers to the Community Institutions to formulate such policies.

The most comprehensive from the industrial policy standpoint is the **ECSC Treaty**. By endowing the High Authority (Commission) with supranational powers, the Member States made it possible for Community policies to be implemented in the priority areas which coal and steel constituted in the '50s. Owing to this the coal crisis, which came into being in 1958 because of the replacement of coal by oil, was able to be resolved gradually through rationalization and the reduction of production without the serious social problems and intra-European discord to which fierce competition between undertakings and countries could have given rise. The same was true of the steel sector, in which the crisis occurred some ten years after the coal crisis.

Although the European Atomic Energy Community experienced a serious crisis between 1965 and 1977, it was a result less of the failings of the **Euratom Treaty** than of the yearning of some member countries for the supranational powers that they had themselves delegated to the Commission. In fact, as we shall see in the chapter on energy, the Euratom Treaty provides a sufficient framework for a policy in the nuclear industry sector.

For its part, the **EEC Treaty** made no call for an industrial policy. It seemed to trust to the automatic characteristics of freedom of competition and freedom of trade not only for the attainment of the common market in industrial products, but also for the restructuring of sectors and undertakings which was required by the size and dynamic nature of that market. However, although it made no specific reference to an industrial policy, the EEC Treaty contained several important elements of such a policy (rules of competition, tax provisions, approximation of laws). But it wanted it to be very broad-based. It assumed that the abolition of protectionist measures and the opening-up of the markets would provide industrial undertakings with sufficient impetus to overcome their structural problems. That was why the Treaty did not give instructions or powers to the Community Institutions for the planning and execution of industrial structural and sectoral policies.

Since the common market was not fully operational, it could not have as significant an impact on industrial structures as the founding fathers of the EEC had hoped. The industrial sector certainly benefited from customs union, without which the development of the Member States' industries would probably not have been the same. But the impact of the common market varied greatly between sectors. In sectors producing major consumer goods, such as the domestic electrical appliances sector, the common market was attained fairly rapidly and influenced the productivity and structures of these sectors. In other sectors, like the motor vehicle one, customs union led to the interpenetration of markets, further rationalization of production and, ultimately, to the achievement of economies of scale and external economies for the whole sector.

In the absence of a legal basis for a real industrial policy, Community institutions limited themselves to examine industrial developments without being able to influence them. They thus set in place coordinated statistical instruments to measure investment in industry[1], the business cycle in industry and small craft industries[2] and industrial activity[3]. Later on, those industrial statistical surveys were completed with annual surveys of industrial production[4] and of the labour costs in industry and the services sector[5].

A number of measures are necessary to facilitate the process of internationalization by strengthening the ability of European industry to compete both on its own market and globally. As from 1968, with the introduction of the **Common Customs Tariff** and by virtue of its single duties, the Community had available to it a valuable instrument for conducting an effective commercial policy and for pressing on towards the liberalization of international trade. That instrument has been used successfully by the Commission, which has negotiated, on behalf of the Community, the reduction of the customs protection of the major commercial powers within the framework of the General Agreement on Tariffs and Trade (GATT)[6].

However, the easing of the protectionism of others did not suffice to redress the competitive situation of Community industry. To be able to measure up to the American undertakings, - and since the 70s to the Japanese undertakings - European undertakings had to combine the production factors of capital and labour so as to minimize their production unit cost. In other words, they had to find the dimension most appropriate to the new conditions of competition and improve their productivity by seeking new products and new production techniques. But to do so they needed a solid basis for expansion, which only the large European market could offer them.

The challenges of European industry

Completion of the single European market presents businesses with an opportunity to benefit from economies of scale, to cut their administrative and financial costs, to gain easier access to public procurement in other Member States and to cooperate more closely with each other over the frontiers. The advantages from economies of scale for investments on the domestic market are not only relevant for mass production, but also for the development of specialized products. As important as the size of the home market is its quality. The Single Market itself represents an essential step for business to look, think and act strategically beyond national borders. At the same time, greater standardization of products places a premium on product innovation, manufacturing excellence, design and reliability compared with the more traditional factors like proximity to markets, distribution systems and customer loyalty.

Globalization of economies and markets, which involves the intensification of international competition, enables not only greater economies of scale to be reaped but also specialization for more defined market segments. In the context of this globalization, European businesses must be able to face international competition. However, in recent years, Community industry has not only lost market shares as a result of the growing power of the newly industrialized countries, but has also had to give ground to the other members of the Triad: the United States, because of the adverse trend of exchange rate; and Japan, because of a failure to move

1   OJ 131, 13.08.1964 and OJ L1, 03.01.1994.
2   OJ L128, 03.06.1972 and OJ L1, 03.01.1994.
3   OJ L133, 10.06.1972 and OJ L1, 03.01.1994.
4   OJ L374, 31.12.1991.
5   OJ L404, 31.12.1992.
6   See the common commercial policy in the chapter on the European Union in the world.

as quickly into expanding markets. Although it has not deteriorated, apparent labour productivity in Community manufacturing still lags a good way behind that of the US and Japanese industry. Economic operators and public authorities in Europe must therefore pay more attention to the factors influencing productivity: technological development, investment in R&D, the rate of capacity utilization, the cost and skill of the labour force, management skills and the organization of production.

Apart from globalization of markets and competition, European industry must prepare to face the challenge of the **new industrial revolution**, the one resulting from the development of information and communications technologies. These are making the traditional distinctions between electronics, information technology, telecommunications and the audiovisual sectors increasingly obsolete. They are blurring the borderlines between the secondary and tertiary sectors, between industry and services. This will have far-reaching effects on production structures and methods. It will spell changes in the way companies are organized, in managers' responsibilities and in relations with workers, particularly concerning the organization of work. There will therefore be a need for structural adjustment, comprising the steady shifting of resources towards the most productive outlets. Structural adjustment and international competitiveness are closely linked since the ability to produce effectively for markets comes precisely from that speedy adjustment of resources to demand which is the basis of structural adjustment.

An efficient market economy requires that the main initiative and responsibility for **structural adjustment** must lie first with economic operators. The role of public authorities is above all a catalyst and pathbreaker for innovation. Industrial firms should be able to expect from public authorities clear and predictable conditions for their activities. This means that public authorities may take accompanying measures to assist and speed up the process of adjustment, particularly in the area of infrastructural provision (for example, education, energy, telecommunications and research), but can never substitute for the decisions to be made by business. The main question is not whether an industrial policy is opportune, as governments are increasingly having an important influence on industrial development and performance. The real issue is which long-term industrial and technological framework is needed in order to strengthen the optimal allocation of resources by market forces, towards accelerating structural adjustment and towards improving industrial competitiveness.

Industrial competitiveness and Community policy

After the completion of customs union, in July 1968 it became clear that union could not on its own resolve all the problems of the Community's industry. Accordingly, the Commission, in response to the instructions from the October 1972 Paris Summit, forwarded to the Council a communication relating to the Community industrial and technological policy programme[1]. That programme set out the measures required for the elimination of barriers to trade, the progressive and effective opening up of public and semi-public

---

1   Supplement to the Bulletin of the European Communities N° 7, 1973.

contracts, the promotion of competitive undertakings on a European scale and actions to assist sectors experiencing special problems: traditional industries in crisis situations, on the one hand, and high-technology industries whose progress was lagging behind, on the other. It should be noted that the most difficult part of this programme, adopted by the Council in December 1973[1], was the effective attainment of the internal market, as it was, fifteen years later, to form the main subject of a new Commission memorandum, namely the 1985 White Paper, and even of a Community act, viz. the Single Act of 1987, examined in the chapter on the Common Market. In that chapter we saw that most of the objectives of the 1973 industrial programme were attained twenty years later with the completion of the internal market.

Thus, since the beginning of the nineties, **European standardization** has been transformed from a marginal activity to one which is attracting priority attention. Under the new approach to technical harmonization and standardization, legislation is confined to laying down the essential requirements to which products must comply in order to ensure the protection of public health and safety or the protection of the environment and the consumer. European standards provide manufacturers with a set of technical specifications recognized in each Directive as giving a presumption of conformity to the essential requirements. European standards are not only required for the purpose of removing technical barriers to trade; increasingly they are also becoming a key element for the promotion of industrial competitiveness by lowering costs for producers and enabling the emergence of new markets, particularly for developing new technologies.

Very important for European industrial competitiveness is also **public procurement**, which is now opened up thanks to the legislation of the Single Market. Its importance is threefold: firstly, the vast size of public procurement - 16% of GDP - means that market access is very important for all firms; secondly, public procurement may enhance technological capability by increasing the marketable demand of high technology products; thirdly, public procurement being concentrated on relatively small group of sectors, these industries depend on a competitive market for public procurement to develop the necessary products and skills to be successful internationally.

The completion of the internal market has **intensified competition** between European companies. However, it is necessary to ensure that the movements towards concentration which are taking place do not obstruct the free play of market forces. The tendency for certain groups to acquire a dominant position under the guise of achieving a sufficient critical size must be checked. As was seen in the chapter on competition, the Regulation on the control of concentrations put in place the necessary legal instrument for Community treatment of large mergers and acquisitions, allowing however European companies to pursue business strategies, which may safeguard their competitiveness at world level.

In a Communication on "industrial policy in an open and competitive environment"[2], submitted to the Council and approved by it on November 26, 1990, the Commission sets out the approach which it believes the Community should follow as regards industrial strategy in a Single Market. Rejecting the hackneyed debate of "liberalism versus interven-

---

1   OJ C117, 31.12.1973.
2   COM (90) 556.

tionism", the Commission places full responsibility for industrial competitiveness on the shoulders of undertakings, it being understood that government authorities must guarantee them a transparent and predictable environment and outlook for their activities. The strategy is consequently one of permanent adaptation revolving around the principle of free trade and on the competitive operation of undertakings. This strategy is based on three principles: consistent recourse to all policies with a bearing on industrial activity, in particular that of protection of the environment[1]; improved access of Community businesses to non-Community markets and to measures against unfair trading practices and in favour of international industrial cooperation[2]; and the positive adjustment to industrial changes through a consistent approach[3].

With the entry into force, in November 1993, of the **Treaty on European Union**, industrial competitiveness became one of the stated objectives of European integration. Article 3 of the EC Treaty states, in fact, that the action of the Community includes, inter alia, the strengthening of the competitiveness of Community industry. The Title on Industry of the TEU announces that the Community and the Member States must ensure the existence of the conditions necessary for the competitiveness of the Community's industry. For this purpose, in accordance with a system of open and competitive markets, their action aims at: speeding up the adjustment of industry to structural changes; encouraging an environment favourable to initiative and to the development of undertakings throughout the Community, particularly small and medium-sized undertakings; encouraging an environment favourable to cooperation between undertakings; and fostering better exploitation of the industrial potential of innovation and research and technological development policies (Art. 130).

This article forms the legal basis for Community action in the fields of industry and business. It specifies however that it does not provide a basis for the introduction by the Community of any measures which could lead to a distortion of competition. The objectives set out above may be pursued by the following means: the mutual consultation of the Member States and, where necessary, the coordination of their action, in liaison with and upon initiative of the Commission; the coordination with other Community policies and activities; and specific measures in support of action taken in the Member States decided by the Council acting unanimously on a proposal from the Commission after consultation of the European Parliament and the Economic and Social Committee.

By endorsing the Commission's White Paper on growth, competitiveness and employment as the bench-mark for the action taken by the European Union, the European Council, in December 1993, backed an approach to industrial development based on **global competitiveness** as a key factor to value-added and employment. This competitiveness supposes the capacity of the EU, its Member States, its regions, its industries and its businesses, exposed to international competition to secure a relatively high return on the factors of production and relatively high employment levels on a sustainable basis. In order to improve European competitiveness on markets open to international competition, there must

---

1   OJ C331, 16.12.1992.
2   OJ C178, 15.07.1992. See the part on the common commercial policy in the chapter on the EU in the
     world.
3   COM (92) 2000.

be a high level of productivity, allowing better use of the competitive advantages of European regions and industries.

In order to create a favourable environment for targeting industrial policy on such growth areas as the markets in knowledge and culture, health care, biotechnology, environmental protection and top-of-the-range products, the Commission advocated broad action lines: promoting intangible investment, e.g. by exploiting the competitive advantages associated with better protection of the environment; developing industrial cooperation; ensuring fair competition; and modernizing the role of the public authorities, thus relieving businesses of unnecessary bureaucratic burdens[1]. These broad lines of action were endorsed by the Council in a Resolution on the strengthening of the competitiveness of Community industry[2]. The Commission in turn proposed the implementation of a Community action programme to strengthen the competitiveness of European industry[3].

SMEs in the single market

Until recently different definitions of SMEs were used in Community policies (competition, Structural Funds, R&D, tendering for public procurement, etc.). This diversity could give rise to doubts among public authorities and even to confusion among the businessmen concerned. Moreover, the most often, as SMEs were considered the undertakings employing up to 500 people, i.e. 99,9% of undertakings in the EU. Replying to a request by the Council (Ministers of Industry) for clarification of the definitions of SMEs, the Commission adopted a recommendation on the definition of small and medium-sized enterprises[4]. Thereafter, in order to be considered as an SME, an undertaking must have fewer than 250 employees and may not belong to one or more large enterprises. More specifically, an enterprise is considered "medium-sized" if it has more than 50 and fewer than 250 employees, an annual turnover not exceeding ECU 40 million or an annual balance-sheet total not exceeding ECU 27 million. A "small" enterprise must have fewer than 50 employees, an annual turnover not exceeding ECU 7 million or an annual balance-sheet total not exceeding ECU 5 million. Without regard to their turnover, undertakings with fewer than 10 employees are considered to be "micro-enterprises". This definition serves as a reference for Community programmes, policy and legislation concerning SMEs and thus provides an overall framework for all measures aimed at SMEs. It should be noted that with this definition, the Union numbers some 17 million SMEs, providing over 70% of its employment, accounting for 50% of investment and representing 60% of its wealth.

---

1   COM (94) 319, 14 September 1994.
2   OJ C343, 06.12.1994.
3   COM (95) 87, 22 March 1995.
4   OJ L107, 30.04.1996.

In addition to these quantitative and easily verifiable criteria, SMEs are often also identified by qualitative criteria, focusing chiefly on the ownership of their capital, their management and their methods of financing. A SME is often a family business, whose management and ownership are in the hands of the same person(s). Day-to-day running of a SME falls upon the company head, enabling flexibility and rapidity in the decision-making process and a personalized relationship with staff, suppliers and customers. Finally, a SME is heavily dependent on self-financing due to difficult access to the financial markets and it often suffers from limited availability of financial resources. These qualitative identification criteria merge with a small undertaking's main characteristics, characteristics which can occasionally prove a handicap, but which can also be to their advantage.

During the 60s and the 70s economists extolled the advantages of multinational undertakings: scale economies, new production and distribution technologies, modern personnel management, production and distribution planning at European scale... Politicians offered all sorts of advantages to multinational undertakings to incite them to invest in their country or region and thus assist in its development and in the absorption of the redundant manpower of the primary sector. In fact, multinationals -practically all American- mainly exploited the over-valued dollar to buy at a good price European firms and/or eliminate from the markets that interested them the large and medium-sized national companies.

During the 80s the rise of the multinationals had slowed. The European Commission defended more and more vigorously the tendencies of large firms to monopolize certain markets and the tendencies of national and regional authorities to give them large incentives in the form of aids. Trade unions claimed more and more rights and social benefits for European workers. Monetary and monopolistic super-profits started diminishing for the multinationals. Thus, they stopped investing in Europe and started practicing the so-called "social dumping", that is setting up plants in countries with low labour costs.

Now, it is clear that, because of the technological development and the globalization of the markets several traditional industries and "national champions" are in decline, while new industries and operators are emerging, often offering products and services with a higher value-added content. These new operators are quite often small and medium enterprises.

SMEs provide around 70 million jobs, thus representing a growing part (around 72%, of which some 30% is accounted for by firms with fewer than 10 employees) of total employment in the private sector - industry and services - in the European Union. Whether they are themselves producing high technology products and equipment or whether they are using such products and equipment, SMEs have an important growth potential. Between 1988 and 1993, the small and the micro-enterprises created 3 million jobs, one third of which in new undertakings, mainly in distribution and services. On the other hand, under the effects of the recession, the medium-sized and large undertakings lost, during the same period, more jobs than they created.

Although it is clear that economies of scale exist and are very important in certain types of production, such as the production in very large numbers of standard products, it is also clear that the management structures of small undertakings are simpler and more flexible than those of big firms and that this, other things being equal, can be a serious advantage. Social relations are also better in smaller as compared to bigger undertakings. Moreover, small enterprises absorb the most vulnerable categories in the labour market, i.e., women and young persons. Last but not least, SMEs are present in new expanding markets and "market niches", less vulnerable to international competition.

Of course, SMEs also have their weak points, which are notably: (a) the difficulty to face the complicated administrative and legal environment created by the completion of the internal market and the internationalization of production; (b) lack in management training for many businessmen and/or lack of willingness to delegate part of the management to qualified associates; and (c) funding difficulties, despite the increase and the differentiation of sources of financing in the large market. It is clearly more difficult and relatively more costly for SMEs than for large firms to have access to world technological capital, to avail themselves of the most sophisticated management techniques and business services and to find their proper place in the globalized economy and even in the EU's Single Market.

Small and, above all, medium-sized businesses, must, first and foremost, rely on their own efforts to achieve success in the Single Market. In order to succeed they must make the effort to adapt to their new environment by abandoning some of their family-style management habits and/or their production and marketing methods and cooperate with each other in order to overcome some of the handicaps which are attributable to their size, in particular with regard to supply and the distribution of their products over a number of Member States.

In so doing SMEs must, however, be given help by their trade organizations, their governments and the European institutions. In order to fully accomplish their task in the context of the single market, SME trade organizations must collate and distribute to their members all the technical, economic and commercial information which relates to markets in the Member States and which can help to locate fresh business potential. The authorities in the Member States can also provide information and, in some cases, funding for SMEs. Their assistance must be of a limited nature, however, in order not to distort or threaten to distort competition by favouring certain undertakings or the production of certain goods within the meaning of Article 92 of the EEC Treaty. That is why a Community enterprise policy is needed to provide a framework for and coordinate the efforts deployed by the Member States to assist their SMEs.

Enterprise policy

While economic crisis continued and the number of unemployed increased in Europe, in the early 90s, the European Union attached its hopes of recovery more and more on small and medium enterprises (SMEs). Of course, the interest of the Community in SMEs is not new, since it was manifested already in 1986 with the adoption of a first programme in their favour; but, the coming into force of the Treaty on European Union was a turning point for enterprise policy. As was seen above, Article 130 EC states, among other things, that the Community and the Member States shall encourage "an environment favourable to initiative and to the development of undertakings throughout the Community, **particularly small and medium-sized undertakings**".

In October 1992, the Commission set up a **European Observatory for SMEs**. Consisting of a European network of research institutes, this Observatory has the task of helping the Commission devise guidelines for its enterprise policy, notably through an independent annual report on the situation of and prospects for SMEs in the Community. In its third annual report (1995), the Observatory recommends in particular that measures in favour of SMEs be better adapted to the fundamental changes they face, especially the globalization of markets, the development of the information society and the challenges of growth, competitiveness and employment[1].

Since 1990, three multiannual programmes were implemented in favour of SMEs. The **third multiannual programme** (1997-2000) pursues the policy in support of SMEs and introduces a series of new initiatives[2]. Its objectives are: to simplify and improve the administrative and regulatory business environment; to improve the financial environment for enterprises; to help SMEs to Europeanize and internationalize their strategies; to enhance SME competitiveness and improve access to research, innovation and training; to promote entrepreneurship and support special target groups such as craft industries, small firms, women and young entrepreneurs.

The framework of Community enterprise policy was considerably enlarged by a Council Resolution of 22 November 1993 on strengthening the competitiveness of enterprises, in particular SMEs, and developing employment in the Community[3]. Indeed, the Council invites the Commission and the Member States to take a number of administrative and financial measures and actions in the field of research with a view to promoting an environment conducive to the creation and development of SMEs, including the implementation of a Community initiative programme for SMEs and craft enterprises.

Encouraged by the Council, the Commission in a communication of 25 May 1994 therefore proposed the implementation of an **integrated programme in support of SMEs and the craft sector**[4]. The Council agreed to this in October 1994[5]. The integrated programme seeks to bring together, within a coherent global framework, actions taken in a concerted manner by the Member States and the European Union, in order to make it easier for SMEs to take advantage of the opportunities being offered to them and thus make a contribution to solving the unemployment problem. The programme gathers together the various existing initiatives and proposes new ones to be implemented by means of a partnership between all parties concerned with the development of SMEs. The new initiatives are twofold: concerted action and contributions by the European Union.

The aim of concerted action is to encourage mutual consultation between Member States and, where necessary, coordination between them on (a) improving the environment for businesses by simplifying administrative procedures so as to relieve the burden on them and liberate their potential for job creation and (b) stimulating support initiatives for businesses at a national or regional level. The concerted actions began in 1995 with the organization by the Commission of two forums for the exchange of information on best practices, one concerned with simplifying administrative formalities and the other with support measures for setting up companies.

---

1   COM (95) 526, 8 November 1995.
2   OJ C156, 31.05.1996.
3   OJ C326, 03.12.1993.
4   COM (94) 207.
5   OJ C294, 22.10.1994.

The contributions of the European Union to the development of enterprises concern both their legal and fiscal environment and certain more direct support measures. The support measures are intended to meet, in particular, the major objectives set out in the White Paper on growth, competitiveness and employment: improving access to financing and credit, supporting cooperation between firms through initiatives extending further than the first phase of seeking partners, and improving management quality. In a report on the coordination of activities in favour of SMEs and the craft sector, the Commission provided a complete picture of the initiatives in favour of SMEs taken by the European Union under its various policies under the two main headings of the integrated programme: improvements to the legal, administrative, fiscal and financial environment of businesses, and SME support measures[1]

Although for practical reasons we are examining enterprise policy in the chapter for industry, it should be stressed that the policy concerns not just industry but practically every economic sector, in particular craft business and distribution. Indeed, the new policy dovetails with Community policies which predate it, viz. those concerning the operation of the Single Market, economic and social cohesion, research and technological development and environmental protection. Thus, given that it supplements and is itself supplemented by other Community policies, the enterprise policy has three broad objectives, which we shall examine one by one: to create a legal framework which lends itself to the setting up and development of enterprises in the Community; to create an economic environment which will help enterprises reach their full development in the Single Market, and to promote cooperation between enterprises situated in different regions of the Community.

Company law

The objectives pursued by the Community through its efforts at harmonization in the area of company law and accounting are: the mobility of firms in order to allow them to benefit from the advantages of a unified market; the equality of the conditions of competition between firms established in different Member States; the promotion of commercial links between the Member States; the stimulation of cooperation between firms across frontiers and the facilitation of cross-border mergers and acquisitions. Appropriate Community measures are needed to provide for legal structures which facilitate cross-border establishment and investment, and to smooth discrepancies between national systems of company law which discourage or penalize these activities.

European undertakings must have the right to set themselves up easily in the territory of all Member States. To that end, Article 220 of the Treaty of Rome called upon the Member States to enter into negotiations with each other with a view to securing, inter alia, the mutual recognition of companies or firms pursuant to the principle of freedom of establishment within the meaning of Article 48, the retention of legal personality

---

1   COM (95) 362, 8 September 1995.

in the event of transfer of their seat from one country to another and the possibility of mergers between companies or firms governed by the laws of different countries. However, in this case, practice proved to be simpler than what had imagined the authors of the Treaty. In fact, by virtue of the freedom of establishment laid down by the Treaty, undertakings formed in accordance with the law of one Member State do not encounter administrative problems in establishing themselves in the territory of another Member State.

The same cannot be said of the real economic and legal problems of establishment, which cannot disappear by the sole virtue of the provisions of the Treaty. Indeed, as the common market develops, companies see a constant increase in the transnational dimension of their relations with third parties, be they shareholders, employees, creditors or others. That development multiplies the danger of conflict between the various national measures which guarantee the rights of those people, to the very detriment of the people those provisions are meant to protect. It is accordingly understandable that the Community's first effort of structural policy concerned **the coordination of the company law** of the Member States by means of Council Directives, based on Article 54.3.g. of the Treaty, which provides for coordination of the safeguards which are required by Member States of Community companies for the protection of the interests of members and others. It took a panoply of Council Directives, adopted from 1968, to give substance to that Article of the EEC Treaty.

The first Directive lays down a system of disclosure applicable to all companies in order to coordinate safeguards for the protection of the interests of members and others[1]. It obliges Member States to keep a register of companies which anyone may examine and to ensure that certain information is published in a national gazette. Also to protect the interests of members and others, the second Directive provides for the harmonization of the standards and procedures relating to the formation of public limited liability companies and the maintenance and alteration of their capital. An amendment to this Directive, adopted in 1992, aims to ensure that this type of company does not make use of a subsidiary for the acquisition of its own shares[2]. The third Directive introduces into the legal systems of all member countries the procedure for the merger of public limited liability companies, with the transfer of the assets and liabilities of the acquired company to the acquiring company[3]. The sixth Directive regulates the hiving-off process, i.e. the division of an existing company into several entities[4]. The eleventh Directive imposes measures in respect of disclosure in the Member State in which a branch is situated, in order to ensure the protection of persons who through the intermediary of the branch deal with a company who is governed by the law of another Member State[5]. The twelfth Directive deals with single-member private companies and allows, under certain conditions, the limitation of liability of the individual entrepreneur throughout the Community[6].

The fourth, seventh and eighth Directives create a code of European accounting legislation which is harmonized to a great extent, even although it is still far from being complete. The fourth concerns the annual accounts of certain types of companies[7]. It notably authorizes the Member States to simplify accounting requirements for small and medium-sized enterprises, defined according to their balance sheet, their turnover and the number of

---

1   OJ L65, 14.03.1968 and OJ L1, 03.01.1994.
2   OJ L26, 30.01.1977 and OJ L347, 28.11.1992.
3   OJ L295, 20.10.1978 and OJ L1, 03.01.1994.
4   OJ L378, 31.12.1982 and OJ L1, 03.01.1994.
5   OJ L395, 30.12.1989 and OJ L1, 03.01.1994.
6   Ibid.
7   OJ L222, 14.08.1978 and OJ L82, 25.03.1994.

employees (maximum of 50 for small enterprises and 250 for medium-sized). The seventh Directive concerns the consolidated accounts of companies which form part of a "group" of undertakings, i.e. parent companies and their subsidiaries[1]. The consolidated accounts must give a true reflection of a company's assets and liabilities, its financial situation and the results of the various undertakings making up the group. The eighth Directive defines the qualifications of persons responsible for carrying out the statutory audits of accounting documents[2]. These individuals must have received high-level theoretical and practical training, have passed an examination of professional competence and have been approved by the relevant authority in the Member State where they are performing their duties.

It should be noted, however, that accounts prepared in accordance with the accounting Directives and the national laws which implement them do not meet the more demanding standards drawn up by the International Accounting Standards Committee (IASC) in collaboration with the International Organization of Securities Commissions (IOSCO). The European Commission is therefore proposing a strategy for improving the accounting framework for the financial information disclosed by companies in Europe. This strategy, which would be founded on the harmonization of European and international standards, would allow European international companies to prepare a single set of consolidated accounts based only on international accounting standards[3].

Specific Directives, mentioned in the chapter on the common market, deal with the annual accounts and consolidated accounts of banks and insurance undertakings. Other Directives, examined in the chapter on taxation, concern the taxation system applicable to mergers, divisions, transfers of assets and exchanges of shares concerning companies of different Member States and the Community system of taxation applicable in the case of parent companies and subsidiaries of different Member States[4]. These Directives remove the main tax obstacles to cooperation and restructuring of enterprises within the European Union.

The above measures facilitate the interpenetration of markets. But it is also necessary for Community undertakings to be able to cooperate easily amongst themselves, which is by no means straightforward. The various forms provided for by national laws for cooperation between domestic undertakings are not adapted to cooperation at common market level, owing specifically to their attachment to a national legal system, which means that cooperation between undertakings from several countries must be subject only to the national law governing one of the participating undertakings. Economic operators, however, do not readily accept attachment to a foreign legal system, both for psychological reasons and owing to ignorance of foreign laws. Such legal barriers to international cooperation are particularly important where the parties involved are SMEs.

It was therefore necessary to introduce a legal instrument covered by Community law which would make adequate cooperation between undertakings from different Member States possible. This is the purpose of the **"European Economic Interest Grouping" (EEIG)**, an instrument for cooperation on a contractual basis, whose Regulation was adopted by the Council in 1985[5]. The EEIG is not an economic entity separate from and independent of its members, behaving autonomously and trying to make profits for itself. It is a hybrid legal instrument offering the flexibility of a contract and some of the advantages of company status, including notably

1   OJ L193, 18.07.1983 and OJ L1, 03.01.1994.
2   OJ L126, 12.05.1984 and OJ L1, 03.01.1994.
3   COM (95) 508, 14 November 1995.
4   OJ L225, 20.08.1990.
5   OJ L199, 31.07.1985 and OJ L1, 03.01.1994.

legal capacity. It serves as an economic staging post for the economic activity of its members. It enables them, by virtue of pooled functions, to develop their own activity and thus increase their own profits. Each member of the Grouping remains entirely autonomous both in economic and legal terms. That is a pre-condition for the existence of the European Economic Interest Grouping and distinguishes it from any other form or stage of merger. The Grouping ensures the equality of its members. None of them could give the others or the Grouping itself binding directives. Lastly, the Grouping may not seek profit for itself, may provide services only to its members and must invoice them at the cost price. These services can consist of marketing, the grouped purchase of raw materials or the representation of its members' interests.

Natural persons, companies and all other "legal entities" falling under public or private law can form part of an EEIG. Groupings can be created in all sectors of the economy, from agriculture to industry, trade, the craft sector or services. The grouping must incorporate at least two bodies: the board of members and the manager or managers. The board of members is the supreme body. It can take any decision for the purposes of attaining the grouping's objective. The members of the EEIG have considerable liberty to organize its management in line with the needs of the cooperation venture. An EEIG can be constituted without capital; it can even have no assets. Members enjoy a great deal of flexibility regarding how they decide to finance the grouping's activities. An EEIG can, in all the Member States, be a holder of rights and obligations, conclude contracts, be a party to legal proceedings and have its own assets in accordance with the objectives set by its members. Due to its full legal capacity, it is obliged to assume responsibility for its commitments on its own assets. Nevertheless, in the event of default by the grouping, its members are jointly and severally liable with regard to third parties for the debts of the grouping.

The EEIG is the only legal instrument at Community level which offers a framework adapted to cross-border cooperation between companies; but recourse to this instrument is still not massive; 700 EEIGs were created during the first six years of its existence. The Commission therefore decided to create a European network for EEIGs, in order to provide detailed information which can be put to immediate use by firms that wish to expand their activities in cooperation with partners in other countries of the Union. The network, named **REGIE**, aims to help SMEs benefit from practical experience of EEIGs, give them an opportunity to strengthen existing European groupings and help them define their cooperation projects more clearly. A regularly updated database provides a clear picture of the situation as regards EEIGs and is built around the BRE and BC-NET networks, which are the customary channels for promoting cross-border cooperation.

Although transnational cooperation between enterprises now disposes of a legal instrument, a legal framework for the concentration of Community enterprises is still lacking. The body of that framework should, according to the Commission, be the statute of a **European public limited liability company** which it had proposed to the Council as early as 30 June 1970. This was a single statute, directly applicable in all Member States, thus freeing such companies from legal attachment to any one country. European public limited liability companies would be subject to the tax system of the country in which they had the headquarters of their actual administration. Provision was made, for European companies with establishments in several Member States, for the setting up of a European businesses committee with competence for matters concerning several establishments and entrusted with rights of information, consultation and co-decision with regard to such matters.

That proposal gave rise to wide-ranging discussion within the Community on the numerous very important subjects which it covered, such as the conditions for the formation of the European company, its registration, the tax system applicable to it, the protection of the interests of third parties and above all the participation of employees in its management. In order to unfreeze the situation in the framework of the single market, the Commission, twenty years after its initial proposal, forwarded to the Council a new proposal for a Regulation on the Statute for a European company[1]. However, the proposal remains blocked in the Council, despite the fact that the Edinburgh European Council, in December 1992, recognized its importance for the restructuring of European industry and pressed for its quick adoption. In fact, the absence of an instrument for restructuring companies is estimated to cost European business ECU 30 billion a year. In order to break the deadlock in the Council on a series of proposals concerning worker participation, among which the one on the European company statute, the Commission launched the idea in 1995 of adopting a general Directive on information and consultation of workers in national companies - parallel to the European Works Council Directive - and thus dissociate the social issues which are the cause of the blocking of the proposals[2].

The business environment

In the run-up to the completion of the Single Market the Community has endeavoured in particular to remove any obstacles to cross-border business activity, so as to help companies take advantage of new commercial opportunities on partner countries markets and, in general, to improve the environment in which Union business operates. Nevertheless, because of the complex nature of certain European provisions and inadequate knowledge of the European legislation concerned, businessmen often regard that legislation as a brake on or even, in some cases, as a disincentive to the entrepreneurial spirit. The European Union should therefore ensure that the impact of its legislation on enterprises, in particular SMEs, is not in conflict with the objective of seeing enterprises reach their full development in the Single Market.

The European institutions must, first of all, take into account the problems and conditions which are specific to SMEs when drawing up and implementing Community policies (regional, social, research, environment, etc.). This is already being done to a large extent. Since 1986 all proposals presented by the Commission to the Council and to Parliament have been accompanied by an **impact assessment describing its likely effects on businesses**, in particular small and medium-sized enterprises, and on job creation. The "impact form", which must be filled by the services of the Commission that are at the origin of a legislative proposal, allows through a cost/benefit analysis to assess the effects of this proposal on

---

1   OJ C263, 16.10.1989 and OJ C138, 29.05.1991.
2   COM (95) 547, 14 November 1995. See the heading on worker participation in the chapter on social progress.

enterprises, particularly on SMEs. The impact assessment also gives details of the consultations that have taken place with the trade organizations concerned by the proposal. The Community's legislative authorities are thus kept fully informed of all the implications of a proposal as far as enterprises are concerned. Since 1993 the Commission has improved and strengthened the system for assessing the impact of European legislation on businesses, in particular as regards increased openness and the consultation of trade organizations[1]. Thus, the Commission's legislative programme is now published in the Official Journal, indicating all the proposals subject to "preconsultation" and assessing their impact on enterprises[2]. In addition, the Committee for improving and simplifying the environment for enterprises, consisting of representatives of the Member States and representatives of SMEs at European level is charged with carrying out consultations on legislative and administrative provisions which hamper the creation, growth and transfer of enterprises, e.g. in the fields of financial instruments, capital markets, internationalization of activities and statistical reporting obligations[3]. In its report entitled "Better law-making", the Commission places the accent on doing less but doing it better, by being more selective in making proposals and by establishing ongoing and open dialogue with citizens, the Member States and all relevant circles, including obviously businessmen[4].

It is advisable, however, to ensure that Member States do not complicate matters when transposing Community legislation into national law. On 28 May 1990 the Council accordingly issued a recommendation to the Member States to implement programmes of **administrative simplification** covering both new legislative proposals and existing legislation and to examine the impact of all proposed legislation or rules on the administrative burden on enterprises[5]. The Council is asking the Member States to adopt simplification programmes relating both to new legislative proposals and to existing legislation and to assess the impact of any proposed legislation or regulation on the administrative burden of enterprises. In accordance with the principle of subsidiarity, the choice of how such administrative simplification should be achieved is left to the Member States. The Council also invited the Member States to encourage their awarding authorities to facilitate the access of SMEs to public procurement, to reduce the costs incurred by them and to prepare them for effective participation in public procurement procedures.

A Recommendation of the Commission, addressed to the Member States, on the method of taxing SMEs depending on whether they are incorporated or not aims at improving the fiscal environment of SMEs[6]. In order to make it easier for SMEs to finance themselves the Commission recommends to the Member States to set the tax burden on reinvested earnings, in the case of sole proprietorships, at the same level as that applied to non-distributed corporate income. Another Recommendation of the Commission addressed to the Member States, concerning payment deadlines in commercial transactions, aims at reducing the burden on SME liquidity caused by late payments[7]. Lastly, taking account of the fact that 10% of business closures in the European Union have their origin in a badly administered inheritance, the Commission, in a Recommendation on the transfer of enterprises, advocates

---

1   OJ C331, 16.12.1992.
2   OJ C125, 06.05.1993.
3   OJ C294, 22.10.1994.
4   COM (95) 580, 22 November 1995.
5   OJ L141, 02.06.1990 and OJ C331, 16.12.1992.
6   OJ L177, 09.07.1994.
7   OJ L127, 10.06.1995.

changes in the law of succession and easing the taxation burden, in order to facilitate the continuity of enterprises and the jobs which go with them[1].

It is also necessary to improve the **quality and flow of information** on the internal market and other fields of Community policy directed towards enterprises, in particular SMEs. The free movement of persons and goods can be meaningful only if people and firms are kept informed of the possibilities open to them. Similarly, economic operators must be kept informed of the Community structural policies which can provide funding for their projects. Special attention should be paid to the need to inform managers of SMEs in the least-developed regions of the Community, i.e. the least-favoured in terms of access to information on the Community.

Accordingly, in September 1987, the Commission launched the **Euro-Info-Centre** (EIC) network. EICs are designed to respond to SMEs' requests for information covering in particular the internal market (legal, technical and social aspects of Community trade) and the possibility of benefiting from Community funding. Some 230 EICs are disseminated throughout the regions of all the Member States and have centres of correspondence in the EFTA countries, the countries of Central and Eastern Europe and Mediterranean countries. They are integrated in host organizations which have experience in providing information and advice to firms and which are well established in their local environment, e.g. chambers of commerce, local development agencies, trade organizations and business consultants. The EICs have three major objectives: to provide information about all Single Market issues and opportunities of interest to enterprises; to assist and advise businesses on participation in European activities; and to act as a channel of communication between enterprises and the Commission. They constitute a network which can exchange information on Community, national and regional legislation and the procedures which are of direct concern to businesses in their respective regions.

By their nature it is generally more difficult for smaller enterprises to participate in **research and development programmes** (R&TD). Firstly, the administrative costs of applying to participate and organizing the required cooperation are relatively high for SMEs and, secondly, they do not have the same facility of access to long-term finance as larger companies. On the other hand, small businesses often have greater flexibility, creativity and dynamism, characteristics which qualify them well to contribute to the innovative process. The Commission is making considerable efforts to promote SME participation in Community programmes such as BRITE and CRAFT, which are designed to strengthen the scientific and technological basis and, thereby, the competitiveness, of European industry. The **BRITE/Euram** programme (covering advanced materials applications and industrial technologies) provides for feasibility awards for SMEs, to help them find partners for subsequent calls for proposals of applied research. **CRAFT** is designed to enable SMEs which do not have any research and development potential to join together to define a com-

---

1   OJ L385, 31.12.1994.

mon approach and commission a third party (a university, a research centre or a firm) to carry out technological development on their behalf. The EU's fourth R&TD framework programme (1994-98) strengthens and extends to other research themes the CRAFT method and the feasibility premiums granted under the BRITE-Euram programme[1]. In a 1995 Resolution the Council stresses how, with the internationalization and globalization of economic relations, it is necessary to facilitate access to technology for SMEs and invites the Commission to develop measures with the particular aim of increasing participation by SMEs in R&TD programmes[2].

A pilot scheme entitled "**Euromanagement**" purports to assess the impact of European policy in the fields of standardization, certification, quality and safety on SMEs. Under this pilot scheme, 70 information and advice bodies are running activities preparing the heads of SMEs for operation in a large European market through seminars on strategic management or impact, sectoral and regional studies. The results of these actions are disseminated by the Commission as "best-practices" and measures to help SMEs to adapt to changing standardization and conformity assessment requirements. Furthermore, in order to encourage and assist industrial SMEs to participate in measures under the fourth Community research and development programme, a **"Euromanagement R&D"** project enables SMEs wishing to engage in transnational technological cooperation to benefit from the services of specialized consultants. Since 1995 the Euromanagement operation was extended to the field of environmental management and auditing.

In order to grasp the opportunities offered to them by the Single Market and face the problems associated with it, managers of SMEs need suitable training. The level of **vocational training** is often quoted, however, as a weakness of SMEs. The Community has recognized that problem and the importance of preparing the human resources of SMEs to the structural adjustments associated with European integration. The main Community instrument for training is the European Social Fund, within which SMEs gain support for training or retraining to introduce or to improve new management techniques. Objective N° 4 of the Structural Funds as well as Community initiatives SME and ADAPT encourage training, which can help SMEs adapt to single market and global market conditions[3].

Enterprise funding

Many European SMEs experience financing problems, which tend to become more severe. They have less equity capital than their counterparts in the United States or Japan and they are more dependent than large firms on direct institutional finance (bank overdrafts, short and long-term loans), which is more expensive. In a communication of 10 November 1993 on the financial problems experienced by small and medium-sized companies, the Commission notes that the situation could be improved easily by providing them with effective advice regarding both their management methods and their relations with their financial backers[4]. It also stresses the need to extend the range of financial guarantees in line with the availability of loans, examine new possibilities and promote "best practice" through demonstration and pilot projects. Last but not least, the Commission suggests improving coordination and communication between the

1   OJ L222, 26.08.1994 and OJ L306, 30.11.1994.
2   OJ C341, 19.12.1995.
3   See the chapters on regional development and social progress.
4   COM (93) 528.

various European, national, regional and local programmes aimed at strengthening the financial position of SMEs.

SMEs are particularly interested in the possibility of Community funding under the structural policy. The Regulation on the **European Regional Development Fund**[1] provides for a series of measures to support local development initiatives and the activities of SMEs. More particularly, it provides for:

— aid for services for undertakings, notably in the fields of management, market study and research and common services for many undertakings;

— the financing of the transfer of technology, including the dissemination of information and the implementation of innovation in the businesses;

— the improvement of the access of undertakings to capital markets, notably through the provision of guarantees and participations;

— direct aid for investment, in the absence of an aid system; and

— the realization of small dimension infrastructure.

The Business and Innovation Centres (BICs), set up by the Commission and public and private regional partners, are designed to promote business creation and expansion by providing a comprehensive programme of services (training, finance, marketing, technology transfer, etc.) to SMEs which are developing innovatory technology-based projects[2].

Community aid for the setting up of BICs is granted in areas eligible under the ERDF. However, even SMEs situated in fairly prosperous areas have **difficulties with regard to funding**, in particular in terms of start-up capital, and have to pay higher rates of interest than large firms. As stated above, integrating the Community's financial markets in the wake of the completion of the Single Market leads to an improvement in the conditions under which firms have access to capital. However, more specific measures are needed to offset the inadequacies of the financial markets. The Commission is accordingly financing various private projects in this field: a plan to encourage banks, the holders of venture capital, and other intermediaries to establish new start-up capital funds for new and innovative companies (**Seed capital**); a plan which, by the creation of transnational syndicates, seeks to encourage the supply of venture capital for SME innovatory projects involving cross-border cooperation (**Venture Consort**); and a scheme designed to stimulate investment in high technology which meets the financial requirements of the promoters of cross-border technological projects - 14 specialist financial institutions - and of the SMEs taking part in those projects (**Eurotech capital**). The networks created by these three pilot schemes are being extended and consolidated, particularly through the development of expertise and information services. In 1995 the Commission initiated a debate on the creation of new Europe-wide capital markets for smaller entrepreneurially managed growth companies[3].

After the Edinburgh European Council of December 1992 acknowledged the vital role which SMEs can play in economic recovery and job creation, the Copenhagen European Council of June 1993 decided to lighten the burden of interest rates placed on SMEs. The Community budget thus finances 3% interest rate subsidies to loans granted by the European Investment Bank to job-creating SME ventures. Loans totalling

1   OJ L374, 31 December 1988 and OJ L193, 31.07.1993.
2   OJ C13, 17.01.1994. See the title on the coordination of Community policies in the chapter regional development.
3   COM (95) 498, 25 October 1995.

ECU 1 billion, managed by financial intermediaries in the Member States, can thus finance the investment projects of SMEs creating additional jobs. These loans are granted by the EIB for a maximum of five years under the temporary loan mechanism called "**Edinburgh facility**"[1]. The total resources having been used by the end of 1995 and the job-creation objectives having been surpassed, the Commission recommended the extension of the facility[2].

Another one billion ECU, of which 800 million are reserved to regions whose development is lagging behind, is earmarked for the financing of the "**SMEs initiative**" in the framework of the structural policy. This initiative is intended to promote the involvement of SMEs at international level and their capacity to benefit from the dynamics of the internal market[3]. In addition to pursuing some of the aims of the previous Community initiatives STRIDE, PRISMA and TELEMATIQUE, seven priority areas are identified by the new initiative for increasing the competitiveness and the international involvement of SMEs:

— the improvement of the production systems and organization of SMEs (total quality, innovation, advanced telecommunications services);
— consideration of the environment and the rational use of energy;
— strengthening of cooperation between SMEs and research centres;
— facilitating access to new markets, including public contracts and foreign markets;
— developing cooperation between SMEs and with suppliers, subcontractors and customers;
— making available to SMEs appropriate instruments to improve access to finance and credit;
— the improvement of vocational qualifications in these six areas.

In elaborating their operational programmes within the framework of the SMEs initiative, the Member States must select, on the basis of these priority areas, a limited and well balanced list of measures concentrating aids on SME projects. Preference is given to immaterial investments (recourse to external competencies, enterprise strategy plans, systems of total quality) rather than to infrastructures.

Cooperation between businesses

The acceleration of the process of economic integration in the Community is bringing with it faster structural change and greater competitive pressures on businesses. In many situations, cooperation or partnership between businesses in different regions or countries of the Community can help to meet the challenge of the wider market. For one thing, cooperation between smaller enterprises can help them to compete with larger ones, especially of the arrangements concerned are based on complementarity resulting in mutual benefits. Moreover, cooperation can identify and promote potential development opportunities which will enable SMEs to

---

1   OJ L107, 28.04.1994.
2   COM (95) 485, 30 October 1995 and COM (95) 502, 29 November 1995.
3   OJ C180, 01.07.1994, see the title on Community initiatives in the chapter on regional development.

diversify. There are different forms of cooperation, e.g. joint ventures, syndicates, agreements covering non-financial links (the granting/purchasing of licences, the transfer of know-how, marketing, etc.) or the acquisition of holdings. It may be formal, i.e. based on a contract (e.g. via a European economic interest grouping) or informal.

Before taking part in any form of cooperation, firms must of course consider whether that cooperation is legal, since cooperation agreements sometimes give rise to problems in connection with the provisions of the Treaties concerning competition. Such cases are, however, rare. As stated in the chapter on competition, the Commission, in a communication on **agreements of minor importance** which do not fall under Article 85(1) of the Treaty, does not regard an agreement as being likely to affect market conditions appreciably if the market share of the firms concerned does not exceed 5% and if the aggregate annual turnover does not exceed ECU 200 million[1]. By way of further general communications, exempting regulations for specific groups and individual Decisions the Commission has laid down in greater detail the position of the other forms of cooperation in relation to the provisions of the Treaties. Generally speaking, the Commission is in favour of cooperation between Community firms. However, if there is in any individual case any doubt as to whether a cooperation agreement appreciably affects competition and trade between Member States the firms concerned may report the agreement to the Commission and ask for negative clearance.

However, while cooperation between Community firms is regarded as desirable and is generally authorized, it still has to overcome problems of a technical and psychological nature. It is for that reason that the Community should adopt measures to create an environment which lends itself to cooperation between firms. The Community's first expression of interest in cooperation between firms was the **Business Cooperation Centre (BCC)**. It is an exchange network for non-confidential information on cooperation opportunities. Any firm seeking a commercial, technical or financial partner may contact either a network member or the BCC in Brussels, which enters the details of the request and disseminates them via its network of some 250 correspondents in 60 countries.

Whereas the BCC deals with non-confidential request for partnership, there is another Community cooperation instrument to handle confidential information: the **Business Cooperation Network (BC-Net)**, a computerized network of 400 or so business advisers in the public and private sector spread throughout the European Union. Unlike the BCC system, BC-Net cannot be accessed directly by firms; only the advisers can enter confidential offers and requests into the system, using standard cooperation profiles based on a specific nomenclature. The system allows rapid and confidential identification of potential partner firms in other Member States or third countries. BC-Net is expanding rapidly and currently handles some 1 500 cooperation profiles each month.

In the context of economic and social cohesion the Commission has also developed **"Europartenariat"**, which is designed to encourage cooperation between businesses located in regions which are less developed or are undergoing industrial restructuring and others elsewhere in the Community. Europartenariat meetings are held twice a year in various regions of the Community, in the course of which managers of local firms meet potential partners from other Member States. After a preparatory year

---

1   OJ C231, 12.09.1986.

during which enterprises in the chosen region are selected, followed by wide-ranging promotion of their cooperation projects, presented in a multilingual catalogue, Europartenariat culminates with two days of face-to-face contacts between heads of enterprises for the purposes of concluding marketing, financial, technological and other such partnerships.

Another programme seeking to encourage partnership in Europe is **INTERPRISE**. In the framework of this programme, three regions from three Community countries get together for the purposes of organizing a meeting of enterprises with the aim of establishing contact between entrepreneurs who can then forge commercial, technical and financial cooperation. A project between three Community regions can be extended to one or several non-Community regions. Projects supported under INTERPRISE must at the least include the following phases: identification and selection of enterprises in the regions involved which are interested in cooperation with an enterprise in the other participating regions; publication and distribution of a catalogue of interested enterprises and their reasons for seeking cooperation; organization of an event during which face-to-face contact is made between participating enterprises.

In the framework of the PHARE programme, which seeks to encourage economic reform in Central and Eastern Europe, the Commission launched, in 1991, the **JOPP programme** (Joint Venture Phare Programme). It aims to facilitate the creation and development of joint ventures in the countries of Central and Eastern Europe, while encouraging foreign investment and the growth of the competitive sector. Targeted mainly at SMEs, JOPP can intervene at any of the various stages in the creation of a joint venture, from the feasibility study to finding the necessary financial resources for the venture.

The Commission has also drawn up a programme to encourage **transnational subcontracting** and thus create a genuine European market in that field. Effective cooperation between component assemblers and suppliers is one of the essential preconditions for reducing the total time involved in innovation, optimizing R&D expenditure, reducing overheads, ensuring the technical homogeneity of products and improving product quality. The establishment of harmonious and balanced sub-contracting relationships is a prerequisite for heightened competitiveness of Community industry. It falls to the Community institutions to encourage and coordinate the process and provide information in this field, thus creating the conditions for a genuine European sub-contracting market[1]. In a Communication of January 17, 1992, the Commission outlined the initiatives which it intends to conduct in this field. These revolve around the three following thrusts: better market transparency through in-depth analysis of the sub-contracting situation in the Member States and in third countries and through information provision to SMEs, in particular via the Euro Info Centres; the establishment of an appropriate legal framework for sub-contracting; and support for the emergence of partnership between sub-contracting undertakings, especially by interconnecting electronic

---

1   OJ C254, 07.10.1989.

databanks through the SCAN project (Subcontracting Assistance Network).

Sectoral policy

The incentives used by governments to modernize and guide national industries, such as grants to certain research bodies, to documentation centres and centres for the dissemination of knowledge, to productivity centres and to vocational training centres can be counted as sectoral measures. Some such measures are already centralized at European level, as we shall see in the chapter on research policy. The others require Community coordination, inasmuch as they are capable of disturbing conditions of competition on the common market.

But sectoral policy is first and foremost linked with commercial policy. The **commercial policy measures** which have the greatest consequences for industrial sectors are manipulations of the customs tariff, anti-dumping measures, trade agreements and various export incentives. By virtue of customs union, most of those measures are already in the hands of the European institutions. Harmonization or coordination is needed of those which are still in the hands of the individual governments, so that there is no unfair competition between industries in the same sector in the European Union[1].

Also still in the hands of governments are the most direct and best-known sectoral measures, i.e. **aids of every kind**: grants, loans, interest rate subsidies, etc. Aids for the improvement of certain sectors and aids to "infant industries" are characteristic examples of sectoral measures. The main grounds for them are employment, regional development or even national prestige where important undertakings, regarded as "flagship undertakings", are involved. As sectoral aids and the conditions under which they are granted vary greatly from one EU State to another, they may affect trade between Member States and distort or threaten to distort competition.

In fact, as other forms of protectionism recede, the importance of State aids as an anti-competitive mechanism tends to grow. Beyond their negative effect on competition, State aids can also have serious implications for economic convergence within the EU. The four largest Member States account for 88% of all aid granted in the Union. Large and well developed Member States will always be able to outbid less developed Member States on the periphery of the Union. The objective of industrial policy should be to create the conditions which allow better control of such aids. Moreover, the effectiveness of the Community's policies to promote greater cohesion could be improved by a progressive reduction in aid intensities in the central and more prosperous regions.

It is for that reason that Articles 92 and 94 of the EEC Treaty provide for Commission control of the aids which States grant directly or indirectly

---

1   See the section on the common commercial policy in the chapter on the European Union in the world.

to certain undertakings or the production of certain goods. Such aids must be notified to the Commission, which has the power to authorize them or prohibit them in accordance with the criteria laid down in the Treaty or under secondary legislation. Thus, although the most powerful instrument of sectoral industrial policy is still in the hands of the governments, the Commission can invoke the supranational power conferred upon it in this area by the Treaty to prevent such national aids from distorting conditions of competition or running counter to the objectives of the EU's industrial policy[1].

The best way to prevent individual sectoral measures by governments that are harmful to the common interest and at the same time to restructure European industry is the EU's sectoral policy. This has developed in the most vulnerable sectors at international level, either because the markets are saturated (steel, shipbuilding, textiles) or because they are not yet well developed in the European Union (aeronautics, information industries, telecommunications). We shall examine Community policy in those sectors below.

Steel

The steel industry is one of the two strategic sectors governed by the European Coal and Steel Community (ECSC). Those strategic sectors were made subject to common rules and a common authority. Intra-Community trade was liberalized and increased by almost 130% during the first five years of the ECSC's existence. In 1974 Community steel represented approximately 7% of the total industrial production of the Community and employed almost 80,000 workers. The turning point for that industry, as for many others, was the 1973 energy crisis and the 1975 economic recession that ensued. As the crisis developed, the Community assumed ever-increasing responsibilities, enabling it, on the one hand, to stabilize the market in order to remedy the constant deterioration of the financial situation of undertakings and, on the other hand, to encourage the adjustment of industrial structures to the new market conditions. For that reason, in October 1980, with the agreement of the Council of Ministers, the Commission declared a state of "**manifest crisis**" in the steel sector[2]. That situation - which was provided for in the ECSC Treaty - allowed the Commission to lay down compulsory restrictions on steel production and deliveries to the Community. Those restrictions took the form of the quarterly fixing of production quotas, only part of which could be delivered to the Community market.

At the same time (1980) the Commission introduced a Community system for framing national aids to the steel industry. That system was strengthened in 1981 with the entry into force of a stricter "**code of aids**", covering all public financial assistance. Moreover, a precise timetable for the elimination of such assistance was laid down: no further aid could be granted to the steel industry after 31 December 1985[3]. The **restructuring plan** for the Community steel industry thus constituted a coherent package which disciplined steel production and prices as well as the granting of national sectoral and social aids. By allowing the European steel industry to sell its products at more profitable prices, those direct intervention measures facilitated the adjustment of undertakings to the new market conditions. In actual fact, Community discipline made a significant contribution to the recovery of steel prices in the second half of the '80s. Thus, with a view to completion of the internal market, the Commission took the opportunity offered it to abolish as from 1988, following eight years of containment of the steel sector, the quota system and certain accompanying measures[4].

---

1   See the section on State interventions in the chapter on competition.
2   OJ L290 and OJ L291, 31.10.1980.
3   OJ L180, 01.07.1981.
4   OJ C194, 23.07.1988.

However, the steel market is closely monitored, on the one hand, by way of informations that steel companies must communicate to the Commission concerning their investments[1] and, on the other, in the framework of six-monthly **forward programmes** covering market developments and future prospects[2]. These programmes show an improvement of the situation since 1994. That year the steel industry has recorded substantial increases in consumption and prices, caused in particular by the market recovery in various steel-using sectors such as motor vehicles, engineering and electronics. However, since the second half of 1995 a slight slowdown in activity, in particular, in the automobile sector, has led to a more modest increase in steel consumption.

The "social aspect of steel", involving the financing from the ECSC budget of social measures is adapted to the programme on the restructuring of the Community steel industry[3]. It is worth noting that in the mid-nineties the total workforce of the steel industry of the Twelve was just over 300,000 workers. The "external aspect of steel", entails a few tariff quotas and the prior statistical monitoring of imports from Central and Eastern European countries to ensure that they do not harm the Community steel industry[4].

Shipbuilding

The shipbuilding industry - another problem sector - has been losing momentum in Europe since the early '60s. In 1960 the shipyards of the Community countries accounted for half the world production of ships. In 1975 their share of the world market in shipbuilding fell to 22%. As early as that year, half the world production of vessels came from Japanese yards, whilst the shipyards of certain developing countries, such as South Korea, were becoming seriously competitive.

During the same period (1960-1975), the market in shipbuilding underwent a far-reaching structural change owing to the spectacular expansion of oil transport requirements. After the closing of the Suez Canal in 1967, the oil companies ordered increasingly numerous and ever-larger tankers to link the Persian Gulf with Europe and the United States by going round Africa. An excess capacity of means of transport was already becoming apparent as early as 1972, but orders continued for reasons of competition and speculation, leading to a considerable increase in the capacities of European shipyards. The 1973 oil crisis and the ensuing economic recession led fleets which had substantial excess to a massive amount of laying-up and of cancelled orders. Shipyards then found themselves with a large **excess production capacity**, especially with regard to tankers.

In a Resolution adopted on 19 September 1978 the Council laid emphasis on the need to maintain a healthy, competitive shipbuilding industry within the Community whose activity was commensurate with the Community's maritime trade and with its own economic, social and strategic importance[5]. However, in the absence of a legal basis provided by the EEC Treaty, the Council could not or would not take the socio-economic measures necessary for the restructuring of the European shipbuilding industry. Thus, the only means

---

1   OJ L286, 16.10.1991.
2   See for example, OJ C38, 10.02.1996.
3   OJ C146, 26.05.1993. See the chapter on social progress.
4   See the sectoral measures under commercial policy in the chapter on the European Union in the world.
5   OJ C229, 27.09.1978.

available to Community policy in the shipbuilding sector remained the coordination of national aids. Seven successive Directives covered the Community framework for aid to shipbuilding.

By avoiding spiralling aids and by contributing to the restructuring of undertakings, the **Community framework for aid to shipbuilding** made it possible for the European industry to become more competitive. However, owing to the persistence of the economic recession, the situation of shipbuilding both at international and Community level worsened still further during the '80s. The seventh Directive on aid to shipbuilding, whose validity was extended from year to year until the end of 1996, aimed at directing State aid towards the building of types of vessels for which Community yards were more competitive[1]. It was also directed towards increasing efficiency through selectivity, intra-Community competition and the encouragement of continuous restructuring. In addition, the Directive obviously ensured transparency and equal treatment with regard to shipbuilding throughout the Community.

The multilateral negotiations launched in 1989 under the auspices of the OECD between the main producing countries (European Union, Japan, South Korea, Norway, United States), which together account for more than 70% of world shipyard output, led to agreement in July 1994 on the elimination of all obstacles to normal conditions of competition in the sector as from 1 January 1996. Consequently, the seventh Directive was replaced, since the 1 October 1995, by a Council Regulation on aid to shipbuilding, which implements the provisions of the OECD Agreement on respecting normal competitive conditions in the commercial shipbuilding and repair industry[2].

In a communication on Europe's maritime future, the Commission stressed the vital role played by **maritime industries**, which alongside shipbuilding encompass a vast range of products and industries, such as ship fitting, port services and the marine-resource industry, including fisheries and energy[3]. It proposed an industrial policy of the Union for those industries aiming at: the promotion of intangible investment, particularly in the fields of R&D, information and telecommunication technology; the development of industrial cooperation within the Union and with third countries' industries; the implementation of the OECD Agreement respecting normal competitive conditions and the removal of obstacles to the free movement of European products in third countries; and the improvement of port infrastructure in the context of a trans-European network.

Textiles and clothing

The textiles and clothing industries experienced difficulties from as early as the late '60s, as a result in particular of the slow growth of domestic

---

1   OJ L380, 31.12.1990 and OJ L351, 31.12.1994.
2   OJ L332, 30.12.1995. See the heading on sectoral measures of commercial policy in the chapter on the EU in the world.
3   COM (96) 84, 13 March 1996.

demand and the rapid development of exports from the developing countries. In fact those industries, in common with all industries which need neither high technology nor capitalist concentration, lose their competitive advantage in Europe to industries from countries which have a relatively cheap workforce.

The recession of 1974 and 1975 struck the textiles and clothing industries particularly hard, as it coincided with an influx of low-price textile imports. The result was many factory closures and a substantial reduction of the workforce (800,000 jobs lost between 1973 and 1980), creating social problems, especially in some Community regions. The European Social Fund was able to help those who lost their jobs in the textiles and clothing sectors, but such assistance was no more than temporary repair pending a genuine Community textiles policy. Put into effect in the beginning of the eighties this policy had two aspects: an internal aspect and an external aspect.

On the internal level, the Commission established an **inventory of existing national aids** and applied a policy aiming at preventing such aids from giving rise to distortions of competition within the Community or having the effect of transferring labour problems and structural difficulties from one country to another. Several schemes for aid to the textiles and clothing industries were accordingly prohibited or adjusted, and programmes for the orderly reduction of production capacity were able to be agreed on. The system for monitoring aids to **synthetic fibres** producers, which was introduced in 1977 and is renewed on a year-to-year basis, favours aid which seeks to re-absorb over-capacity through restructuring or reconversion of the industry[1]. The Community aid also focused on industrial restructuring and conversion operations in the man-made fibres sector[2]. In the field of technological research, the Community gave its financial support for the implementation, within the framework of the BRITE programme, of several research projects likely to increase the competitiveness of the textiles industry and to encourage the transfer of the results to industry throughout the Member States.

The external aspect of the textiles policy consisted of organizing international trade in textiles in order to provide breathing space for the Community industry without frustrating the industrialization hopes of the developing countries. Such organization was sought within the framework of the General Agreement on Tariffs and Trade (GATT) through the arrangement on international trade in textiles, commonly known as the **"Multifibre Arrangement"** (MFA)[3]. However, the new textiles agreement, concluded within the framework of the Uruguay Round aims at the progressive liberalization of textile and clothing products within the World Trade Organization[4].

The new face of textile and clothing policy was shaped by a Commission Communication of October 1991, confirmed by a Council Resolution of June 1992[5]. On the external front, Community commercial policy focuses on the opening up of non-Community markets and the promotion of Community exports, action to combat dumping and subsidies and fraudulent declarations of origin and the protection of designs and models. On the internal front, the emphasis is placed on the economic diversification of regions which are heavily dependent on the textile and clothing sector.

In pursuit of the latter aim, the Commission launched at the beginning of 1992 the Community initiative **RETEX**[6]. It covers regions falling under

1   OJ C142, 08.06.1995.

2   OJ L326, 22.12.1979.

3   See the title "sectoral measures of commercial policy" in the chapter on the European Union in the world.

4   See the heading on "sectoral commercial policy measures" in the chapter on the European Union in the world.

5   OJ C178, 15.07.1992.

6   OJ C142, 04.06.1992 and OJ C180, 01.07.1994.

Objectives 1, 2 and 5b of the structural policy which are heavily dependent on the textile-clothing sector. It is designed to adapt viable undertakings in all the industrial sectors of these regions, including those in the textile sector. This requires sustained assistance for SMEs in raising their know-how level; the creation of local groups of businesses and cooperation activities in the areas of research and development, new production and marketing methods and so on; the creation of SME outreach and advice teams; temporary contributions to salaries for the purposes of implementing modernization plans; and vocational training of staff threatened by unemployment in the textile sector.

According to the Commission, the European textiles and clothing sector should be integrated in a balanced way into the World Trade Organization system, in order to improve access to third countries' markets[1]. Industrial policy measures relating to exports, industrial cooperation, training and the fight against fraud should be reinforced. European regions most affected by the results of the Uruguay Round and other factors should continue to be supported by accompanying measures. In this context, Community financial assistance is granted to a specific programme for the modernization of the Portuguese textile and clothing industry[2].

Aeronautical sector

With a consolidated turnover of close to ECU 36 billion, at the end of the eighties, the European aeronautical industry is second in the world after that of the United States (ECU 90 billion) and far ahead of that of Japan (ECU 5.5 billion). It employs some 500,000 people in the Community. It is a growth industry whose technology has an impact on a much wider range of industries. In a word, it is the type of industry towards which Europe must turn more and more in order to replace those productions that are transferring to third-world countries in the context of a new international division of labour. However, whilst the European market constitutes 20% of the world market in civil aircraft and aviation, the share of the European industry in the world market is less than 10%. Obviously the American industry is by far the leading world exporter of both civil and military aircraft.

During the '70s the aeronautical industry pushed intra-European collaboration further than any other industrial sector, but on a bilateral rather than Community level (Concorde and Airbus projects). Such bilateral or multilateral projects suffered from contradictions between national policies, the non-existence of a single commercial strategy for the Community and the lack of joint financing. Whilst the Concorde and Airbus programmes were both remarkable technical successes, only the Airbus programme was an immediate commercial success. The arrival on the market of the Airbus A320, a 120-seat short-haul aircraft, deliveries of which began in early 1988, should enable the European civil aircraft industry to increase its share in world deliveries of civil aircraft, with the prospect of increasing it further with deliveries, in the early 1990s, of the large-capacity Airbus (A330) and the long-haul Airbus (A340).

1   COM (95) 447, 11 October 1995.
2   OJ L86, 20.04.1995.

The success of the "**Airbus industries**" consortium troubles the United States, which sees its commercial supremacy threatened in the domain of civil aircraft. In 1987 the United States referred to the GATT Committee on Trade in Civil Aircraft on the matter of inducements which were, in their view, prohibited with regard to the sale or purchase of civil aircraft. The negotiations continued in 1988 bilaterally and multilaterally between the United States and the Community represented by a Member of the Commission and the Ministers for Trade of the four Member States concerned. The negotiations to some extent reduced the differences of opinion between both parties, but the dispute was not settled. It should, however, be noted that although the Community is not directly involved in Airbus or in the alleged inducements, it brings its full weight to bear in the negotiations with the Americans.

The Community policy in the aeronautical industry is based on non-compulsory legislation, on concerted action and consultation between the Member States, particularly concerning external aspects[1]. In addition to genuine liberalization of the aeronautics market, the sector's competitiveness hinges first and foremost on research and development. Since 1989, the Community has been co-financing a **research** programme in the aeronautical sector which is integrated into the BRITE-Euram programme[2]. Such cooperation in the research sphere makes it possible to concentrate efforts in the key sectors of industrial technology which correspond to jointly defined new requirements and to provide for additional financial resources to intensify efforts.

Air traffic is expected to grow by over 5% a year until 2010 and should generate demand for over 17 000 jet aircraft over the next 20 years, a trend which should be paralleled on the engine and component markets. In order to benefit fully from the growth of the demand, European aircraft builders must continue their rationalization and international cooperation activities and improve their research and development efforts. The Commission, in agreement with the Council, pursues a strategy of putting together a package of measures implemented jointly by the industry, the Member States and the Union with a view to boosting the industry's long-term competitiveness[3]. To this end, the Commission set up in 1995 an "Aeronautics task force" to bring together in joint projects of interest to the entire industry the research being undertaken at Community or national level or in the context of specific applications of the information society.

Information industries

Information technologies (IT) now increasingly underpin all production and service industries, and are also the vehicle for a growing number of societal services such as health, education, transport, entertainment and culture. After forty years of quantitative growth, we are at the onset of a qualitative transformation in the impact of information technologies. The **information society** is the dawning of a multimedia world (sound - text - image) representing a radical change comparable with the first industrial revolution. It goes hand in hand with the "non-physical" economy, based on the creation, circulation and exploitation of knowledge, which will be one of the dominant characteristics of the 21st century. The conditions of access to information, to the networks carrying it (broad band networks called "information highways") and to the services facilitating the use of

---

1   OJ C59, 13.03.1975 and OJ C69, 13.03.1977.
2   See the chapter on research policy.
3   COM(92) 164 and OJ C178, 15.07.1992.

the data (including high value-added services, databases, etc.) are vital components of the Union's future competitiveness.

At the instigation of the Commission, the Council had adopted, in 1974, a resolution on a Community policy on data processing[1] and, in 1979, a Community action promoting microelectronic technology[2]. But the first specific measure of the data-processing policy was the Council Decision of 28 February 1984 adopting the first European strategic programme for research and development in information technologies **(ESPRIT)**. Finalized after lengthy consultations with industrialists from the sector, the universities and authorities of the Member States, that first programme, which was funded half by the budget of the Community and half by the industrial sector, was a genuine catch-up strategy in the field of information technologies with a view to curbing the external dependency of European industry.

The overall objective of the multiannual RTD programmes Esprit, which succeed each other since the middle eighties, is to contribute to the healthy growth of the information infrastructure so as to improve the competitiveness of all industry in Europe and to help enhance the quality of life for all citizens by promoting as wide as possible access to the information infrastructure. The networks of excellence launched in the framework of Esprit bring together industry, users, universities and research centres. Supplier enterprises and users form a consortium to pursue demonstrably new RTD, with the users having a particular interest in taking up and exploiting the results of the collaboration.

The new RTD programme in the field of information technologies (1994-1998) fits in fully with the efforts to develop the information society and places emphasis on the information infrastructure, users' and market needs, access to services and technologies, user-friendliness and best practices, with the aim of increasing the competitiveness of industry as a whole[3]. RTD activities are concentrated in particular on: software technologies, fostering European capabilities in emerging software technologies and in distributed information processing; information technology components and subsystems in the key areas of microelectronics, microsystems and peripherals; and long-term research needed to increase the turnover from the laboratory to the market and to build up the scarce expertise underpinning European information technology. Focused clusters aim at achieving a maximum of synergies in this programme. They cover an open microprocessor systems initiative, high-performance computing and networking, technologies for business processes and integration in manufacturing.

Another Community multiannual programme (1996-2000), entitled INFO 2000, intends to stimulate the development of a European multimedia content industry and to encourage the creation, development and distribution of European multimedia products[4]. It aims in particular to encourage the multimedia industry, which consists largely of small and medium-sized businesses, to identify and exploit the new commercial opportunities expected on this market. It focuses on the transition from printed to electronic publishing and the appearance of interactive multimedia information services. The Commission proposes also

---

1   OJ C86, 20.07.1974.
2   OJ C231, 13.09.1979.
3   OJ L334, 22.12.1994.
4   OJ L129, 30.05.1996.

the adoption of a multiannual programme to promote the linguistic diversity of Europe in the information society and to communicate easily with the rest of the world[1].

As part of the moves to set up a European information area where processing of personal data is expected to develop significantly, the Council and the Parliament adopted, in October 1995, a Directive on the protection of individuals with regard to the processing of personal data[2]. While affording individuals in all the Member States an equivalent, high level of protection with regard to the processing of data concerning them, this Directive seeks to ensure the free movement of personal data in the Community and to remove distortions of competition and the resulting risks of relocation.

In its communication of 19 July 1994 entitled "Europe's way to the information society: an action plan", the Commission sets out a detailed work programme based on four complementary approaches: adapting the regulatory framework; information networks, services, applications and content (establishing a European Forum for Basic Services and an Information Society Project Office); social and cultural aspects; and promotion of the information society. This action plan was approved by the Essen European Council in December 1994. Information being linked to telecommunications, many subjects that interest it are touched upon under the following two headings.

Telecommunications

Digital technologies, developped by the information industry, allow the integrated transmission of sound, text and image in one communication system and project Europe into the **information era**, which will radically change the modes of consumption, production and organization of work. On the other hand, advanced communications technologies and services are a vital link between industry, services sector and market as well as between peripheral areas and economic centres. These services are therefore crucial for consolidation of the internal market, for Europe's industrial competitiveness and for economic and social cohesion in Europe. They can also contribute to social progress and to cultural development. Community policy on telecommunications is developing since the '80s around four axes: the creation of a single market of telecommunications equipment, by the way of standardization; the liberalization of telecommunication services; the technological development of the sector with the assistance of Community research; and the balanced development of the regions of the Union by means of trans-European telecommunication networks.

A Council Decision and a Resolution on standardization in the field of information technology and telecommunications pursue the objective of creating a **European market in telecommunications equipment**[3]. Such standardization of information technology and telecommunications prevents distortions of competition and ensures exchanges of information, the convergence of industrial strategies and, ultimately, the creation and exploitation of a vast European IT&T market. The Commission collates requirements with regard to standardization on the part of users and establishes the priorities of a work programme, which is entrusted to the CEN (European Committee for Standardization) and the CENELEC (European Committee for Electrotechnical Standardization), with the participa-

1   COM (95) 486, 8 November 1995.
2   OJ L281, 23.11.1995.
3   OJ L36, 07.02.1987 and OJ C117, 11.05.1989.

tion of the CEPT (European Conference of Postal and Telecommunications Administrations). The establishment in 1988 of the European Telecommunication Standard Institute (ETSI) gave fresh momentum to this work, which is experiencing exponential growth. The emphasis is now placed on the involvement of private organizations representing industry and consumers in the pre-standardization process and in the effective application of harmonized standards in the Member States, including for public contracts.

The regulatory framework for telecommunications terminal equipment follows and affects the new approach to standardization, testing and certification, that we have examined in the chapter on the common market. European institutions and standards bodies endeavour to ensure the coherence with the regulatory framework applicable to information equipment in order to meet the challenge of interoperability. A Directive concerning telecommunications terminal equipment and satellite earth station equipment ensures mutual recognition of their conformity by instituting harmonized certifying, testing, marking, quality assurance and product control procedures[1]. It guarantees the right to connect terminal equipment lawfully placed on the market to the public telecommunications networks without the need for further formalities and establishes the single market for satellite earth station equipment.

The creation of a single market in telecommunications equipment necessitated, however, the progressive **opening of telecommunications markets**, which were traditionally State monopolies. Telecommunications services had to be liberated and conditions of free provision of services by the networks had to be defined. To pursue this objective, which represents the second axis of the Community policy in this sector, the Commission adopted, in June 1990, a Directive based on Article 90 of the EEC Treaty, requiring Member States to introduce arrangements ensuring free competition on the Community market in telecommunications terminal equipment (modems, telex terminals, receive-only satellite stations, etc.)[2]. This Directive gives users the possibility of connecting terminal equipment, which they will henceforth be able to procure freely without being obliged to apply to a single national telecommunications authority. Through its successive amendments, the Directive entitles suppliers of telecommunications services to use capacity on cable television networks for all telecommunications services except voice telephony - primarily data communications, "closed" corporate networks and multimedia services[3]. It also requires Member States to abolish the exclusive and special rights remaining in telecommunications, the restrictions on the installations used for mobile networks and the obstacles to direct interconnection between such networks. Last but not least, the Commission Directive provides for the complete liberalization of voice telephony and telecommunications infrastructures on 1 January 1998.

---

1   OJ L128, 23.05.1991, OJ L290, 24.11.1993 and COM (95) 612, 6 December 1995.
2   OJ L192, 24.07.1990.
3   OJ L256, 26.10.1995 and OJ L74, 22.03.1996.

For its part, the Council adopted in June 1990 the framework Directive on the supply of an **open telecommunications network (ONP)**[1]. Through the use of public telecommunications networks and/or public telecommunications services in the Member States, this Directive seeks to facilitate the provision of services by companies or individuals with their established place of business in a Member State other than that of the company or person for whom the service is destined. The measures developed in that context are aimed at the coordinated introduction into the Community of: a pan-European, land-based public radio paging[2]; a single European emergency call number[3] a common international dialling code (00)[4] and a **European area code** for telephone services with Europe-wide applications[5].

The principles of ONP are already implemented in **packet-switched data services** and **services using the integrated services digital network** (ISDN)[6]; in the services of **leased lines**[7]. in pan-European land-based public mobile communications using cellular, digital telephony or, in other words, **mobile telephone networks**[8]; and in digital European **cordless telecommunications** (DECT)[9].

The same principles will soon be extended to **voice telephony**, which is the major service exploited by telecommunications operators as regards both scale and economic importance[10]. A Council Resolution of 1993 has confirmed the principle of complete liberalization of public voice telephony services, and therefore of the abolition of national monopolies, by 1 January 1998[11]. An additional period of five years, to 2003, may be granted to Member States with less developed networks (Spain, Portugal, Greece and Ireland). In another Resolution, the Council defines the basic principles of a **universal service** for telecommunications in a competitive environment - a minimum service of specified quality to be made available to all users at an affordable price - and gives guidelines on methods of financing the universal service[12]. Indeed, the liberalization of the telecommunications sector means that tariffs will progressively be calculated on the basis of costs and, therefore, that current methods of financing will have to be re-examined.

Having thus paved the way, the European Parliament and the Council adopted, in December 1995, a Directive on the application of **open-network provision (ONP) to voice telephony**[13]. It provides for the harmonization of the conditions of access to and use of public telephone networks

1	OJ L192, 24.07.1990.
2	OJ L310, 09.11.1990.
3	OJ L217, 06.08.1991.
4	OJ L137, 20.05.1992.
5	OJ C318, 04.12.1992.
6	OJ L382, 31.12.1986 and OJ L200, 18.07.1992.
7	OJ L165, 19.06.1992.
8	OJ C329, 31.12.1990 and OJ L8, 12.01.1994.
9	OJ L144, 08.06.1991 and OJ L194, 29.07.1994.
10	OJ C147, 27.05.1993.
11	OJ C213, 06.08.1993.
12	OJ C48, 16.02.1994.
13	OJ L321, 30.12.1995.

and services by other operators. In addition, it pursues three objectives ensuring citizens of the availability of reasonably priced and good quality services at the moment when competition is introduced into the sector: defining the rights of voice telephony users in their dealings with telecommunications bodies; improving access to the public telephone network infrastructure; and providing a harmonized Community-wide voice telephony service.

Reacting to the publication by the Commission of a Green Paper on the liberalization of telecommunications infrastructure and cable television networks[1],the Council noted the consensus in favour of the establishment of an appropriate **regulatory framework** focusing on universal service, licences and interconnection[2]. Key factors in the elaboration of such a framework are notably: the extension of competition to the whole sector; the maintenance and development of a universal service in compliance with the principles of transparency, proportionality and non-discrimination; the establishment of a specific regulation on interconnection; and the guarantee of comparable and effective access to the markets of the Member States and of third countries

The **technological development** in telecommunications - third axis of the Community policy in this sector - is pursued by research in advanced communication technologies and services. The specific R&TD programme (1994-1998) for advanced technologies and communications services (ACTS) aims at consolidating European technological leadership in digital broadband communications and enable effective network management and service deployment in a diverse and competitive communication environment[3]. The main activities of the programme fall in the following six areas which interest directly or indirectly telecommunications: interactive digital multimedia services, including the establishment of European standards for high definition television (HDTV); photonic technologies, including development of the technological basis for deployment of fully optical networks ("Transparent Highways") in Europe by 2000; high-speed networking for broadband services such as videophones, teleworking and multimedia; mobility and personal communication networks; intelligence in networks and service engineering necessary for the equipment and management of communications networks; quality, security and safety of communications services and systems.

The fourth axis of Community telecommunications policy turns round **trans-European telecommunications networks** which are, in reality, national digital networks interconnected, managed in a coherent fashion and using different vectors (cables, terrestrial and satellite radio transmission). With the aid of these networks, it will be possible to transmit a multitude of texts, images and sound transmissions, stored and combined in databases, for use in the most diverse applications (manufacturing activity, education, medical care, leisure, tourism, etc.). These networks will irrigate all economic activities and transform the ways of life and work of European citizens. The guidelines for the development of these networks aim at optimizing the use of Community instruments and financial resources, facilitating the transition to the information society, making European firms more competitive and improving economic and social cohesion[4].

The European Parliament and the Council have already agreed in November 1995 on the guidelines for the development of integrated services digital networks (ISDN) as a

---

1   COM (94) 682.

2   OJ C188, 22.07.1993.

3   OJ L222, 26.08.1994.

4   OJ C134, 06.05.1996.

trans-European network, an important step towards the information society[1]. This first really European network in the field of telecommunications uses digitally the existing infrastructure of the telephone network, thus enabling the transmission of texts, information, sounds and images at a speed of 64,000 bits per second, 12 times the speed of the normal telephone network. Euro-ISDN already offers a wide range of services, designed mainly for enterprises: videosound, videoconference, computerized exchange of data, texts and images, bank transactions at a distance.

Information and telecommunications technologies

The wealth of nations depends, increasingly, on the use of information and knowledge, with the aid of the enormous progress made in information and communications technologies (ICTs). Harnessing the opportunities opened up by the digitalization of information in all its forms (text, image and sound), these technologies are transforming dramatically many aspects of economic and social life, such as working methods and relations, the organization of undertakings, the focus of education and training, and the way people communicate with each other. As an imput to industry as a whole, ICTs are key factors for the competitiveness of European companies. Since they are amongst the highest growth activities, and they are also highly skilled activities, these technologies have a high potential for employment creation.

There is a close correlation between the development prospects of individual technologies and products (telephones, interactive disk readers and combinations thereof), of the programs (computer software, databases, audiovisual programmes, etc.) and of the associated services and networks. The European Union is in a strong competitive position in several of these fields and has every means of retaining or winning a substantial share of the market. It should, however, remove various administrative obstacles to an optimal exploitation of ICTs, create an appropriate regulatory and political environment and encourage the implementation of trans-European telecommunication services.

The work programme (IMPACT II) aims at establishing an internal market in information services[2]. The objectives of the programme are to reduce legal and economic uncertainty in the market, to reinforce the competitive capability of European suppliers of information services, to promote the use of advanced electronic information services in the Community and to strengthen the Community's internal and external cohesion in this area. The measures required to attain those objectives are: the operation of a network of national partners, the European Information Market Observatory; improvement of the synergy between the public and private sectors; specific action for the benefit of libraries; measures to improve users' access to information services, and the promotion of European information services.

The specific research and technological development programme in the field of **telematics applications of common interest** (1994-1998) aims to involve users in all stages of the projects and establish firm partnerships between users and suppliers[3]. It covers four research areas: telematics for services of public interest, such as systems for processing and exchange of information between administrations and telematics in road transport; telematics for knowledge, notably research, education, training and libraries; telematics for improving employment and the quality of life, with particular attention on urban and rural areas, health

1   OJ L282, 24.11.1995.
2   OJ L377, 31.12.1991.
3   OJ L334, 22.12.1994.

care, elderly and disabled people and the environment; and, finally, horizontal RTD activities such as telematics engineering, language engineering and information engineering.

Telematics applications play a central role in the development of trans-European networks. Thus, for the creation of trans-European networks between administrations (TNA)[1], the Council has adopted a multiannual operation supporting the interchange of data between administrations (IDA), particularly those needed for the operation of the internal market and the implementation of common policies[2]. Telematics applications also promote: the interconnection of networks in universities and national research institutes; the interconnection of library services, notably those of national libraries; networks for cooperation between local authorities in tele-working and tele-services; cooperation among staff specializing in public health and tele-medicine; access of handicapped and elderly people to communications and information technologies (TIDE); language-learning and telematics translation services (Euramis); the use of telematics tools in the road transport sector[3]; and the operation of satellite navigation services[4].

A programme for the development of trade electronic data interchange systems (TEDIS) encourages electronic data interchange (EDI) by supporting and coordinating the activities of groups of users in various industrial sectors and also encourages national initiatives to promote such interchanges[5]. Data interchange, particularly important for industrial competitiveness, focuses on telecommunications, legal aspects, security, provision of information for the public, as well as existing or new multisectoral projects. In October 1994, the Commission adopted a communication on the legal aspects of EDI, together with a recommendation for a standard European agreement[6]. For its part, the Council recommended, on 7 April 1995, the adoption of common criteria for security evaluation in information technology and the negotiation by the Member States of bilateral European or international mutual recognition of security evaluation certificates[7].

Other industrial sectors

In addition to the sectors we have just examined, the European Union is incidentally interested in certain sectors such as the motor vehicle industry or the chemicals industry, in particular as regards the functioning of the internal market, the encouragement of intangible investment in research and development and the coordinated approach of their problems vis-à-vis the outside.

Thus, in the **motor industry**, the European type-approval system for vehicles is designed to help to lower makers' costs, while maintaining identical technical specifications and a high level of protection throughout the European Union[8]. The Regulation on the exemption of certain categories of motor vehicle distribution and servicing agreements sets out to boost competition in motor vehicle distribution by changing the balance between the various interests involved[9]. In the field of research, a task-force on the car of tomorrow coordinates efforts in Europe to speed up the development of cars with very low emissions. As regards social measures, a transnational network disseminates vocational training programmes to help workers adapt to the structural changes in the industry. Finally, as

1   OJ C321, 01.01.1995.
2   OJ L269, 11.11.1995.
3   OJ C264, 11.10.1995.
4   COM (94) 248.
5   OJ L208, 30.07.1991.
6   OJ L338, 28.12.1994.
7   OJ L93, 26.04.1995.
8   OJ L225,10.08.1992.
9   OJ L145, 29.06.1995. See the chapter on competition.

part of the common commercial policy, the Commission has negotiated an agreement moderating exports of Japanese cars in the single market[1] and is currently negotiating a series of bilateral and multilateral trade agreements opening up access to the motor vehicle markets in third countries.

In the **pharmaceutical industry**, the free movement of its products in the common market has long been pursued by the harmonization of legislations and regulations monitoring their marketing[2]. Nowadays this is done by the Community authorization system for medicinal products for human and veterinary use. The authorization can be given either by a centralized or a decentralized procedure[3]. Under the centralized procedure, applications for marketing authorizations are submitted to the European Agency for the Evaluation of Medicinal Products, which conducts the scientific evaluation of the application and gives its opinion to the Commission, which adopts a decision, subject to endorsement by a committee of representatives of the Member States. The marketing authorization obtained at the end of this procedure is valid throughout the Community. Under the decentralized procedure, the pharmaceuticals company concerned asks one or more Member States to recognize the marketing authorization issued by another Member State. The Member States may refer the application to the Agency for arbitration. In a Resolution designed to implement the outlines of an industrial policy in the pharmaceutical sector, the Council invites the Commission to take stock of the operation of the internal market in this sector, to promote greater transparency and increase competition on this market[4].

Biotechnology, i.e. genetic engineering, which makes it possible to obtain new chemical, pharmaceutical or food products and highly competitive processes in a large number of industrial and agricultural activities. Indeed, biotechnology can provide important energy (fuel) and industrial outlets for agricultural raw materials is mainly developed in the pharmaceutical industry. Indeed, two thirds of the new medicines undergoing clinical trials are derived from modern biotechnology. Also preponderant in enzyme production, biotechnology can provide important energy (fuel) and industrial outlets for agricultural raw materials. This is the reason why, a specific programme of Community research, mentioned in the next chapter, is devoted to biotechnology. It should be noted that, while reinforcing European competitiveness, Community legislation endeavours to ensure the protection of both human health by a contained use of genetically modified micro-organisms[5] and the environment by a deliberate release of genetically modified organisms[6].

---

1   See the heading on the sectoral measures of the commercial policy in the chapter on the EU in the world.
2   OJ 22, 09.02.1965, OJ L147, 09.06.1975 and OJ L214, 24.08.1993.
3   OJ L214, 24.08.1993.
4   OJ C136, 08.05.1996.
5   OJ C136, 08.05.1996.
6   OJ L117, 08.05.1990 and OJ L103, 22.04.1994.

Appraisal and outlook

In general the EU intervenes in the industrial sector only to create an environment conducive either to the expansion of undertakings throughout the internal market (enterprise policy) or to the activity of certain industrial branches which present problems, to enable them to cope better at European level (sectoral policy).

Although disparities remain between Member States' industrial structures, we are nonetheless in the presence of a parallel development of the various data in the secondary sector. Thus, since 1974, the high cost of energy and of raw materials, the deregulation of the international monetary system, the amendment of the rules governing international trade and the rise of new trade competitors have affected every Member State at the same time and to virtually the same degree. Every country has been party to the slowing down of growth and the drop in investment. Every country has experienced a significant increase in unemployment. In fact a general structural change is involved, requiring vigorous measures taken jointly by all States affected at the same time. It must not be forgotten that, thanks to customs union, the bulk of the production of Community industries is traded within the Community. The adequate market for a large number of industrial branches is the internal market. The problems therefore need to be tackled at that level if the real wish was to resolve them. That was the message that finally became clear to those with responsibility at European level towards the mid-'80s. They, thus, decided on the completion of the internal market in order to give a new base to European industry.

In the 90s, the completion of the internal market provided a fillip to the restructuring of European industry. The removal of the physical, technical and fiscal barriers to intra-Community trade gave rise to strengthened trade and therefore bolstered competition within the Community. Thanks to the removal of border controls and technical trade barriers, businesses can now supply a single product for the whole of the single market. Manufacturers no longer have to produce for fifteen separate markets. This situation increases competition enormously in the internal market. Greater competition results in the alignment of national suppliers' prices on those of foreign suppliers, who penetrate markets which had previously been protected. In the short term that squeezes the profit margins of undertakings which have been protected or in monopoly situations. Some of them are even forced to leave the market.

The elimination of the least competitive producers enables, however, those firms which survive to expand on the market. They are thus able: better to exploit and maximize their production capabilities, or even increase them (economies of scale); to strengthen their domestic efficiency by restructuring and concentrating their activities and by proceeding with an improved allocation of human, technical and financial resources; to improve their organization and the quality and variety of their products, and in particular to innovate both as regards the production process and the products offered. This competitive pressure has already caused the wind of change to sweep the Union's industrial fabric. In addition to this, for mainly technological reasons, the pace of change is accelerating as regards production methods and the products themselves.

Generally speaking, the large undertakings are best equipped to conquer new markets, restructure their production, rationalize their organization; but they often do all this by using less labour and more natural resources. On the contrary, small undertakings are labour-intensive and more concerned with the preservation of the environment, because they are closer to the populations surrounding their plants. The European Union must therefore strengthen its policy towards small and medium-sized enterprises (SMEs) to ensure that they are better informed about European facts (regulations, directives, standards, invitations to tender, research projects) and about the opportunities offered by the large market (exportation, cooperation, concentration). In addition, the EU must, by the implementation of a European reference framework and the coordinated use of the various horizontal instruments, prepare a process of positive adjustment by its industry to the conditions of the single market and economic and monetary union.

Creation of a favourable business environment also implies the elimination of superfluous and niggling regulation. Community policies must also fulfill this requirement. The internal market must be made as unbureaucratic as possible. This involves especially a horizontal approach to harmonization, avoiding as much as possible sector specific rules. Both the Union and the Member States must therefore undertake actions specifically aimed at ensuring that in the development of regulation and procedures account is taken of the need not to impose undue burdens on industry, particularly on SMEs.

Of course, the macro-economic context of the EU has improved greatly over the recent period, thanks to the completion of the internal market and the conclusion of the GATT agreements. Nevertheless, its sensitivity to external shocks, in the fields of exchange rates and of oil prices, remains high. An open but vigilant policy, based on the rigorous enforcement of international rules agreed in the framework of the World Trade Organization, is a necessary complement to internal market opening. Identification of precise problems and specific action to remove them can make a significant contribution to improving the outlets for the European industries.

The Treaty on European Union emphasizes the need for competitiveness, making it a priority for the European Union in the 90s. In fact, there has been a substantial improvement in industrial competitiveness in recent years, due to the combined effect of the completion of the internal market and of the efforts made on restructuring, investment and productivity. But, European companies have yet to overcome the handicaps with which they are having to contend as a result of insufficient penetration of fast-growing markets, lower manufacturing productivity than their American or Japanese competitors and an inadequate research effort. In order to overcome the handicaps which have contributed to erosion of its competitiveness within the Triad, the EU must promote intangible investment, develop industrial cooperation, reinforce competition and modernize the role of the public authorities.

Last but not least, the European Union must move towards the "information society" of the 21st century by creating a common information area. This consists of several indivisible elements: trans-European infrastructure (terrestrial cable infrastructure, radio communications networks and satellites); the basic telecommunications services, particularly electronic mail, file transfer and interactive access to databases; the information itself, converted and collated in electronic, i.e. digital form (databases, CD-ROM, CDI, etc.); the hardware, components and software available to the user to process this information; and training of the users, that is of the general public to optimal use of information and communication technologies. This common information area is not only an indispensable requirement of the productivity and competitiveness of European industry, but is also an important factor for economic and social cohesion.

Bibliography on industrial policy

◻ BANGEMANN Martin, "La politique industrielle européenne: ce qu'elle est, ce qu'elle veut", in *Revue du Marché commun et de l'Union européenne*, N° 396, mars 1996, pp. 154-157.

◻ BUIGUES Pierre, JACQUEMIN Alexis, SAPIR André (ed.), *European Policies on Competition, Trade and Industry. Conflict and Complementarities*, Edward Elgar Publ. Co. Cheltenham, Glos, 1995.

◻ CEDEFOP, *La création d'entreprise dans l'Europe des Douze: Les programmes d'appui*, OPOCE, Luxembourg, 1994.

◻ COMMISSION EUROPÉENNE, *GEIE; L'émergence d'une nouvelle coopération européenne*, OPOCE, Luxembourg, 1993.

  - *Conditions propres à faciliter la coopération entre entreprises*, OPOCE, Luxembourg, 1993.

  - "Une politique de compétitivité industrielle pour l'Union européenne", *Bulletin de l'Union européenne*, Supplément 3/94.

  - *Droit des sociétés: Actes coordonnés*, OPOCE, Luxembourg, 1995.

  - *Panorama de l'industrie communautaire 1995/96*, OPOCE, Luxembourg, 1996.

◻ *Guide juridique de l'entreprise*, Kluwer, Éditions Juridiques Belgique, Bruxelles, 1993.

◻ EUROPEAN COMMISSION, *Enterprises in Europe: Third Report*, OOPEC, Luxembourg, 1994.

◻ GAVALDA Christian, PARLEANI Gilbert, *Droit des affaires de l'Union européenne*, LITEC, Paris, 1995.

◻ HIGHAM Nicholas, GORDON Leonie (ed.), *EC Telecommunications Law*, Chancery Law Publishing Ltd., Chichester, West Sussex, 1993.

- *Les autoroutes de l'information: enjeux sociaux et sociétaux*, Observatoire social européen, Bruxelles, 1995.

- MAILLET Pierre, "Politique industrielle et fonctionnement de l'Union européenne", in *Revue du Marché commun et de l'Union européenne*, N° 396, mars 1996, pp. 146-153.

- MARCHIPONT Jean-François, *Les nouveaux réseaux de l'information. Enjeux et maîtrise de la société de l'information*, Éditions Continent Europe, Paris, 1995.

- MICOSSI Stephano, "Nouvelle orientations de la politique industrielle dans l'Union européenne", in *Revue du Marché commun et de l'Union européenne*, N° 396, mars 1996, pp. 158-164.

- MOUSSIS Nicolas, "L'intérêt grandissant de l'Union européenne pour les petites et moyennes entreprises", in *Revue du Marché commun et de l'Union européenne*, N° 386, mars 1995, pp. 185-190.

    - "Une politique industrielle sous-jacente à d'autres politiques communautaires", in *Revue du Marché commun et de l'Union européenne*, N° 396, mars 1996, pp. 198-207.

- PETRELLA Riccardo (sous la dir. de), *Limites à la compétitivité. Pour un nouveau contrat mondial*, Éditions Labor, Bruxelles, 1995.

- PINON Arnaud, *Guide des affaires dans le marché unique européen*, SEFI, Boulogne, 1994.

- SCHAPIRA Jean, *Droit européen des affaires*, 4e édition, PUF, Paris, 1994.

- THE EUROPEAN OBSERVATORY FOR SMEs, *Third Annual Report*, European Network for SME Research, 1995.

- TOULEMON Robert, "Les malentendus autour de la politique industrielle", in *Revue du Marché commun et de l'Union européenne*, N° 396, mars 1996, pp. 165-169.

- TREGOUET René, *Préparer la libéralisation des télécommunications en Europe*, Rapport du Sénat N° 90, Paris, 1995/96.

- URBAN Sabine, VENDEMINI Serge, *Alliances stratégiques, coopératives européennes*, De Boeck-Wesmael, Bruxelles, 1994.

10. RESEARCH

Economic and social progress and the competitiveness of European States at world level come about through efficacious scientific research and technological development. European research, however, is handicapped in the international arena as a result of the fragmentation of research policies pursued in the Member States of the Union and the resulting dispersion of efforts. Community research and development policy is therefore essential for European construction. The aim of that policy is to co-ordinate national research policies and to define and implement research programmes of European interest, i.e. programmes geared to the large market, of interest to all Member States and necessitating technical and human resources which Member States cannot put together individually.

Research policy is closely linked to industrial policy, which we have just examined, and to energy policy, which we shall examine in the next chapter. Indeed, research is essential for the definition of industrial strategy, especially in high-technology sectors, by offering a common reference basis for technology forecasting. It is also necessary for the promotion of reliable energy sources which reduce Europe's dependence on imported oil, particularly for the development of thermonuclear fusion. At world level, only the coordinated research of the Member States can allow the European Union to play a leading role in vast international programmes such as the one on global change.

Although still insignificant in the European Coal and Steel Community, research policy got under way in the nuclear sector between 1958 and 1964, found itself in crisis at the same time as Euratom, between 1965 and 1973, and took off again in broader horizons in 1974. Since then it has been evolving continuously and extending to an ever-increasing number of areas.

Economic and legal framework

More than in any other field, priorities in the research field change very rapidly nowadays in line with the challenges facing European society. Those challenges were different in the '60s, in the '70s and in the '80s. They are still different today.

The challenges

Immediately after the Second World War the European countries which had been ravaged by the war, whose economic and technological development had been halted, had to devote several years to restoring their production plant and to catching up on their technological lag. During those years Europe stopped being the cockpit of technological innovation, yielding that role to the United States and, to some extent, to the Soviet Union. Europeans spoke resignedly of the "technological gap" separating them from the United States, which they saw increasing by the year and becoming ever-more difficult to fill.

Even the largest of the European countries did not have sufficient means to cope with competition from the United States. They had to adopt a selective policy and therefore relinquish many areas of research. As European undertakings were also suffering, as regards their own research, from an inferiority complex vis-à-vis their American competitors, significant gaps did not fail to emerge in the growth industries, i.e. aeronautics, electronics, information technology, etc. The consequences were the exodus of European scientists to the United States, the dependence of numerous European firms on their American competitors for the supply of patents, the purchase of European firms by American firms and, lastly, the creation of the Euro-dollar market, from which American multinational undertakings tapped European capital for their own expansion in Europe or elsewhere in the world. All these factors constituted a whole linked with the European technological gap, which was known in the 1960s as "the **American challenge**.

During the '70s although the gap was not yet filled, the conditions for the European economy to assimilate innovation were nevertheless met. The enlargement of markets by virtue of economic integration, the general modernization of the economy as a result of expansion, the presence of plentiful, skilled researchers and technicians brought about by the attention paid to higher education and the mobilization of funds for research at national and Community level had provided impetus for research and development in Europe. The Community's dependence on vital imports of raw materials and of energy and the aspirations of its peoples to better living and working conditions, however, presented European researchers with fresh challenges.

As we shall see in the next chapter, the energy problem had been growing so serious and costly since 1973 that only a common effort could make it possible to control it. What was needed was an overall strategy incorporating a vast range of projects to promote nuclear safety, which was required to ensure energy diversification in the short term, to seek the best use of the resources available and to develop new sources of energy in the longer term.

At the same time the quality of life had become an increasing preoccupation of Europeans. Research should not only ensure economic progress but also improve their living conditions. As pollution and nuisances do not recognize frontiers, all Community countries experienced similar problems, justifying wide-ranging cooperation. It was desirable to co-ordinate research at Community level in order to reduce its cost by sharing the work amongst highly-specialized laboratories and by eliminating futile duplication.

Although the major **challenges of the '80s** were economic revival and the guarantee of employment, signs were appearing in the background of a massive transformation of society. Traditional industrial structures were undergoing rapid change. The problems that were being observed in the structures of the traditional European industries, like textiles, shipbuilding and steel, were notably the result of the movement of production to countries with low wage levels induced by the internationalization of markets. That transfer of European industrial production to other countries could be offset only by new industries with a high level of technology.

Such new industries and technologies, which typify **post-industrial society**, the so-called "information society", are within the Europeans' reach, provided that they pool their efforts in the field of research. The research necessary for the advent of the post-industrial revolution is very onerous, and it will not bear fruit in practice until the twenty-first century. No European country could undertake it in isolation. Together, however, European countries have the dimension necessary to tackle with resolve the sectors for the future: thermonuclear fusion and other soft, diffuse and renewable sources of energy, which can resolve Europe's energy and environment problems; biotechnology and the massive exploitation of the oceans, which can resolve the problems of feeding mankind, and information technologies, which can provide the driving force for further growth and at the same time transform our life-styles and working methods. Its unique experience of economic integration, its political situation and its economic strength confer on the European Union major responsibility for the establishment of future international labour sharing. Such are the new challenges to European researchers.

Although the challenges facing the European nations change, and with them the scientific and technical research priorities, certain immutable reasons militate in favour of a **Community approach to research problems**. Owing to the high cost of research, to which we referred above, a European policy is necessary in order to define the economic, social, political and even military objectives of research, to draw up an inventory of the resources available in terms of manpower, laboratories and funds, to set the priorities and to apportion the work. In this way it can be ensured that no important sector is neglected, that duplication is avoided and that the Union's human, material and financial resources are put to best use. Labour distribution can also ensure that Europe's smallest countries, which would otherwise be excluded owing to a lack of resources, can participate in research and development.

European research would be poorly exploited without coordination and without common measures for the **dissemination of the knowledge** acquired. A wealth of accumulated knowledge in documents and proto-types and an industry capable of exploiting it are not, in fact, sufficient to ensure that such knowledge makes the transition to the industrial produc-tion stages. First, there needs to be a wide dissemination of that knowledge throughout the Member States to those capable of exploiting it. Moreover, with the inflow of knowledge, recourse to the traditional methods of collating and classifying scientific information is no longer sufficient; ever-greater use of information processing and international networks and databanks is needed, and such use can be efficient only at European level.

The linear model of **innovation**, with the innovative act being isolated, has in today's world been replaced by an interactive process, in which innovation requires constant and organized interdependence between the upstream phases linked to technology, and the downstream phases linked to the market. This means that, in order to have industrially efficient innovation, the needs of the market should be taken into account, particu-larly by modernizing the approaches and practices of marketing, and synergies in research and technological development (R&TD) should be facilitated by trans-European cooperation. These considerations are par-ticularly pertinent for SMEs, which are innovative by their nature, but which do not exploit efficiently their R&TD potential because of their structural and financial handicaps. As will be seen below, the fourth Community R&TD programme takes into account these considerations. Nevertheless, in a Green Paper on innovation, the Commission takes stock of the many obstacle to innovation which represent a serious handicap for European businesses and employment[1]. Among the most significant ob-stacles, it identifies in particular inadequate and disperse research and development input, and the difficulty of translating the results of this input into new products and services. The Commission therefore invites all the players concerned to take part in a wide-ranging debate on the priorities and lines of action of a genuine European strategy to promote innovation.

Legal provisions of the sectoral Treaties

Whilst we now see clearly the need for and objectives of Community research policy, that was probably not the case when the **EEC Treaty** was framed. That is why the Treaty, apart from a rather vague reference to the coordination of research and the dissemination of agricultural knowledge (Article 41), did not give the Community Institutions any powers to finance or even co-ordinate Member States' research in the other sectors of the economy. That was not, however, the case for the two sectoral Treaties, i.e. the ECSC Treaty and the Euratom Treaty.

---

1   COM (95) 688, 20 December 1995.

Under Article 55 of the **ECSC Treaty**, the Commission "shall promote technical and economic research relating to the production and increased use of coal and steel and to occupational safety in the coal and steel industries." It may, for that purpose, allot ECSC funds and funds received as gifts or induce joint financing by the undertakings concerned. In the first two instances the results of research is to be made available to all concerned in the Community. The multiannual research programmes in the steel industry and in the coal sector are also based on that Article of the ECSC Treaty, even although they now form part of the Community framework programmes for research[1]. In March 1994, the Commission redefined the medium-term guidelines for technical coal research (1994-99) covering mining engineering and coal utilization[2]. In November 1995 it drew up guidelines of the ECSC "steel" R&TD programme for the period up to 2002 when the ECSC Treaty expires[3].

The **Euratom Treaty** gives an even more important place to the development of (nuclear) research, devoting its first Chapter to it. Article 4 makes the Commission responsible for promoting and facilitating nuclear research in the Member States and for complementing it by carrying out a Community research and training programme. For purposes of coordinating and complementing research undertaken in Member States, the Commission calls upon Member States, persons or undertakings to **communicate to it their programmes** relating to the research which it specifies in the request. By its opinions the Commission should discourage unnecessary duplication and should direct research towards sectors which are insufficiently explored, of which it should publish at regular intervals a list. (Article 5).

To **encourage the carrying out of research programmes** communicated to it the Commission may : provide financial assistance within the framework of research contracts; supply, either free of charge or against payment source materials or special fissile materials; place installations, equipment or expert assistance at the disposal of Member States, persons or undertakings, either free of charge or against payment; promote joint financing by the Member States, persons or undertakings concerned (Article 6).

Community research and training programmes are determined by the Council, acting unanimously on a proposal from the Commission, which consults the Scientific and Technical Committee. The funds required for carrying out these programmes are included each year in the research and investment budget of the Community. (Article 7). After consulting the Scientific and Technical Committee, the Commission establishes a joint Nuclear Research Centre which should ensure that the research programmes and other tasks assigned to it by the Commission are carried out. (Article 8). The Commission may, by contract, entrust the carrying out of certain parts of the Community research programme to Member States, persons or undertakings, or to third countries, international organizations or nationals of third countries. (Article 10).

The second Chapter of the Euratom Treaty is given over to the **dissemination of information.** As regards information which is owned by the Community, Member States, persons or undertakings shall have the right, on application to the Commission, subject to suitable remuneration, to obtain non-exclusive licences under patents, rights, etc., which belong to the Community (Article 12). The Commission must communicate free of charge to the Member States, persons and undertakings any non-patentable information acquired by the Community (Article 13). As regards information which the Community does not own, the Commission must endeavour, by amicable agreement, to secure both the communication of information which is of use to the Community in the attainment of its objectives and the granting of licences under patents, rights etc., covering such information (Article 14). To that end it shall establish a procedure by which Member States, persons and undertakings may use as an intermediary for exchanging the results of their research. This procedure must be such as to ensure the confidential nature of the exchange (Article 15).

The Euratom crisis

Strengthened by all that legal armoury and optimistic, in the euphoric early years of European integration, the Euratom Commission had hoped

---

1   OJ C252, 06.10.1992.

2   OJ C67, 04.03.1994.

3   OJ C294, 09.11.1995.

to have all nuclear research in the Community enter directly or indirectly into the joint programme. It had thus left aside work on the coordination of Member States' research. It has to be said in the Commission's defence that its intentions seemed realistic at the outset, because of the six original Community countries only France pursued a genuine nuclear research programme. But they had not reckoned with General de Gaulle, who had other ideas for French nuclear research and no wish to allow it to be controlled by a supranational authority.

The first important crisis arose in 1965, when France, after succeeding, by virtue of the unanimity rule, in blocking a very promising project for the joint development of a heavy-water reactor ("ORGEL"), at the same time, albeit for other reasons, relinquished its seat on the Council of Ministers of the Communities. That "ORGEL" failure resulted in the Community countries, instead of developing an original and common family of nuclear fission reactors, having recourse to national - or American - families. In fact, as early as the mid-'60s, the other Community countries one by one sided with France, taking the view that the stage of development of nuclear energy had already reached the level of industrial applications and that it was therefore for industry, rather than a supranational authority, to choose the types of reactor to construct.

At any event, during virtually the whole of the '60s the Joint Research Centre (JRC) was at a standstill and could not pursue the objective laid down by Article 4 of the Euratom Treaty. At the same time, the Commission, which was too concerned to save the joint research programme, was not actively pursuing the objective set out in Article 5 of the Treaty, i.e. the coordination of research undertaken in the Member States. It has to be added that the Euratom Commission, which was the executive body of that Community, had neither the competence nor the power of delegation needed to release nuclear research from that impasse.

It was the single Commission, which was the issue of the merger of the executive bodies of the three Communities which was effected in 1967, which understood that Euratom's difficulties arose partly from the relative isolation and sectoral nature of that Community and that the situation could be redressed only if nuclear policy were incorporated into an overall Community policy on scientific and technical research.

Joint Research Centre

The Commission accordingly decided, on 13 January 1971, to reorganize the Joint Research Centre to confer on it the autonomy of administration and the structure necessary for the enlargement of its activities to non-nuclear fields[1]. An unofficial start was given to the implementation of an overall Community research and development policy on 14 January 1974. Giving effect to the political will expressed by the Heads of State and of Government in October 1972 and on the basis of the Commission's preparatory work, the Council adopted two very important Resolutions: one on the coordination of national policies and the definition of projects of interest to the Community, and the other on an initial outline programme in the field of science and technology, encompassing the specific programme of the JRC.

The future of the Joint Research Centre was thus guaranteed at the expense of the development of a Community nuclear fission family. That abandonment was offset by new activities which were incorporated in the framework of the Community's science and technology policy. Nowadays the JRC pursues two types of activity: institutional research and scientific and technical support for Union policies; and activities carried out on a competitive basis, including participation in shared-cost research projects,

---

1   OJ L16, 20.01.1971.

support for Commission departments and work performed under contract for public and private sector outside bodies.

Research programmes of the European Union

At first, Community research and development action out of the nuclear field could be based only on Article 235 of the EEC Treaty, which required unanimity for specific R&D programmes. Later on, in 1987, the Single European Act institutionalized the **framework programme** in research. The framework programme is a plan drawn up by the Commission in close cooperation with interested parties from the worlds of science, industry and politics. It lays the basis for a medium-term strategy by defining all its main elements for a period of five years: the legal and administrative framework, the scientific and technical content and objectives and, most importantly, the level of funding. By laying down the objectives, the priorities and the overall funds for Community action and their apportionment in broad terms, it constitutes a "guide" for decisions on specific programmes to be taken during the five years covered. In addition, the framework programme has the desired characteristic of making visible, for scientific establishments, undertakings or Member States, the medium-term research possibilities afforded by the Community. By providing clear indications of the specific measures which the Community intends to undertake, it allows the various European research operators better to programme their efforts and Community research to take its proper place in the concert of European cooperation actions.

The Maastricht Treaty further improves the position enjoyed by research in the process of European construction. First of all, Article 130f (EC) consecrates research and technological development as a policy of the Community, stating that the latter shall aim to strengthen the scientific and technological foundations of Community industry and boost its competitiveness at international level and shall promote the research activities deemed necessary by virtue of other Community policies. To this end, it adds, the Community shall in all the Member States encourage undertakings, including small and medium-sized undertakings, research centres and universities, in their research and technological development activities of high quality. Through its support for their cooperation efforts, the Community aims to enable undertakings to draw full benefit from the potential of the internal market, in particular through the opening up of national public contracts, the definition of common standards and the removal of legal and fiscal obstacles to cooperation.

The Maastricht Treaty then fine-tunes the **decision-making process** for research programmes. It in fact introduces a two-part mechanism: on the one hand adoption under the procedure referred to in Article 189b (co-decision of the Council and the European Parliament), after consulting the Economic and Social Committee, of multiannual research and technological development **framework programmes** which lay down the major scientific and technical objectives of the Community, define their respective priorities and establish the maximum overall amount for all the activities envisaged and its breakdown between the various activities[1]; and on the other implementation of these framework programmes through specific programmes adopted by the Council acting by a qualified majority after consultation of the European Parliament and the Economic and Social Committee (Article 130i). This two-phase mechanism facilitates the adoption of specific research and development programmes, especially of the framework programme. Similarly, the harmonized presentation of the new **specific programmes** facilitates their approval process and subsequently their management and access to them by interested parties, notably small and medium-sized enterprises.

In pursuit of the objectives detailed in Article 130f, the Community conducts the following **priority activities**, complementing the activities in the Member States: (a) implementation of research, technological development and demonstration programmes, by promoting cooperation with and between undertakings, research centres and universities; (b) promotion of cooperation in the field of Community research, technological development and demonstration with third countries and international organizations; (c) dissemination and optimization of the results of activities in Community research, technological development and demonstration; (d) stimulation of the training and mobility of researchers in the Community (130g).

The **fourth framework programme** (1994-1998), endowed with budget of ECU 13.1 million, is structured around the four priority activities defined by the Maastricht Treaty[2]. This programme aims at improving the management and efficiency of research financed by the Community in order to increase its economic efficiency. It thus gives priority to ensuring: greater integration between national and Community R&D activities, in particular through improved coordination of Member States' participation in major international projects; improved dissemination of research findings, in particular to SMEs; closer links between research and education/training; greater exploitation of possible synergies between research policy and economic and social cohesion policy; and greater flexibility as regards the framework programme, the specific programmes and the work programmes, to ensure that the European Union can respond rapidly to new scientific and technological challenges.

In order to implement Article 130h of the EC Treaty, which requires the Community and the Member States to coordinate their research and technological development activities, the Commission proposed a three-pronged approach: formulation of research policies, international scientific and technological cooperation, and implementation of research activities[3]. Agreeing with the Commission, the Council, in conclusions of 9 June 1995, advocated certain ways of facilitating the coordination of national and Community policies, based as far as possible on existing structures, notably CREST, which is mentioned below. One of the main purposes of this cooperation should be to help determine the priorities for future Community R&TD activities bringing Community added-value in compliance with subsidiarity, and help improve the use made of the resources available in the European Union.

Several scientific bodies assist the Commission in its tasks of conceiving and managing the Community policy of research and technological development. The Scientific and Tech-

---

1   See, for example, OJ L117, 08.05.1990.
2   OJ L115, 06.05.1994, OJ L126, 18.05.1994 and OJ L86, 04.04.1996.
3   COM (94) 438, 19 October 1994.

nical Research Committee (CREST) is an advisory body which assists the Commission and the Council in the R&TD field by identifying strategic priorities, establishing mutual consistency between national and Community policies, and helping to formulate Community strategy with regard to international cooperation[1]. An Industrial Research and Development Advisory Committee (IRDAC) advises the Commission on industrial research, to ensure a good balance between research expertise and industrial strategy and between the various industries represented, including SMEs.

By a decision founded on the Euratom Treaty, the Commission created a **European Science and Technology Assembly (ESTA)**[2]. Consisting of some one hundred eminent persons, the Assembly has the task essentially of helping the Commission to prepare, implement and monitor the research and technological development policy of the European Union. Thanks to its members' exceptional expertise, the Assembly may perform, on behalf of the Commission, the vital function of guaranteeing the relevance of scientific and technological options, the quality of research and the taking into consideration of the latest developments in knowledge and technologies as well as of the needs of the economy and society. At the Commission's request, the Assembly gives its views on such matters as the framework programme, the specific programmes and the related work programmes. It can also deliver own-initiative opinions on various subjects which are of importance to science and technology in Europe. In general, it assists the Commission in its efforts to promote a scientific and technical culture in Europe and stimulate debate on science and technology at European level.

In order to develop joint projects of industrial interest, improve the long-term coordination of industrial research in the Union and produce results of immediate relevance to the general public, the Commission set up in June 1995 six special "research/industry" task forces with subjects likely to ensure the widespread diffusion of research in all EU countries: the car of tomorrow; the new-generation aircraft; the train of the future; transport intermodality; multimedia educational software; vaccines and viral diseases. The aim of this coordination action is to bring about the convergence of research efforts in Europe in those areas which are closest to the needs of society and the daily concerns of citizens.

The forms of Community research

Community research policy does not necessarily mean the "communitarization" of all programmes or the joint financing of all research and technological development (R&TD) activities in the Member States. In application of the subsidiarity principle, a distinction has to be made between, on the one hand, fundamental research and the development of high technologies and, on the other, straight industrial development. With regard to **fundamental research and basic research**, which necessitate very large investment and highly specialized researchers and whose results can be expected only in the fairly distant future, it is in the interest of the EU countries to pool their efforts in laboratories financed entirely by the European Union and bringing together researchers of several nationalities.

For the development of leading-edge, nuclear, information, aeronautical and aerospace technology, the market dictates justify European coordination of the activities carried out in the Member States in order to ensure industrial success, the transnational restructuring of undertakings, the opening up of public contracts, and even the grouping of purchases by public electricity, telecommunications and transport services. For **indus-**

---

1   OJ C264, 11.10.1995.
2   OJ L98, 16.04.1994.

trial development, on the other hand, ample scope can be left to competition and the specialization of national laboratories, depending on the
relative advantages and industrial objectives of each country. European
R&TD therefore appears in three forms or three types of actions: direct
actions, indirect actions and concerted actions.

Direct actions are research activities proper pursued by the Commission in its research establishments and paid for entirely from the Community budget. They are divided amongst the four establishments of the Joint
Research Centre (JRC), the largest of which is at Ispra (Italy) and the three
others, of almost equal size, are at Geel (Belgium), Petten (Netherlands)
and Karlsruhe (Federal Republic of Germany). The activities of the JRC,
which were initially limited to the field of nuclear fission research, are
nowadays considerably diversified: controlled thermonuclear fusion, nuclear safety and safeguards, information and telecommunication technologies, industrial technologies, environment protection, life sciences and
technologies... The European dimension of its research is one of the fundamental strengths of the JRC. Its activities are characterized by a multidisciplinary approach based on the broad span of its capabilities. This
multidisciplinarity is reflected in the diversity of subjects covered by its
institutes and helps it meet Europe's scientific challenges as they rise.

The JRC carries out two research programmes: one for the European
Community and the other for the European Atomic Energy Community
(Euratom). For the EC, in the framework of the fourth R&TD programme
(1994-1998) and in line with the priorities defined in the White Paper on
"Growth, competitiveness and employment", the activities carried out by
the JRC pursue the following objectives: helping to strengthen the scientific and technological basis of European industry and to develop its
international competitiveness; providing the independent scientific expertise necessary for the implementation of Community policies and the tasks
which the Treaty assigns to the Commission; providing scientific and
technical services to Community institutions and making JRC capabilities
and installations available to public and private bodies; contributing to the
improvement of public safety aspects of new and applied technologies;
contributing to the improvement of environmental impact assessment and
protection; contributing to the reduction of scientific and technological
disparities between the Member States[1]. Thus, the JRC's specific programme for the European Atomic Energy Community (1995-1998) covers
the safety of nuclear fission, reactor safety, fuel cycle safety, safeguards
and fissile materials management and controlled nuclear fusion[2].

Related to direct research, **thermonuclear fusion research** is pursued
at Culham (United Kingdom) in an establishment which does not form
part of the Joint Research Centre, but which is administered by a joint
undertaking (JET) within the meaning of Article 45 of the Euratom Treaty
and whose Board of Governors is made up of representatives of the
participating States and of the Commission, with a budget 80% of which

---

1   OJ L361, 31.12.1994.
2   Ibid.

is financed by the Community[1].

The second form taken by Community R&TD is **indirect research**, that is, contractual or "shared cost" research. This form of research, which absorbs more than 80% of the financial resources of Community R&TD, is conducted in research centres, universities or undertakings, with financial assistance from the Commission and on conditions laid down by the rules governing participation in the various programmes, notably the participation of at least two partners from different Member States. Community financial assistance is as a general rule for 50% of the total cost of research work. The Commission, with the assistance of the Advisory Committees on Management and Coordination (ACMC)[2], prepares the research programmes on indirect action which are adopted by the Council. The Commission then publishes in the Official Journal of the European Communities calls for tenders for researchers from the Member States, specifying the research objectives written into the European programme. The tenders are appraised by the Commission and the Committees on the basis of criteria determined in advance and aimed at ensuring the best possible results. There are no national quotas for research assistance. The main criteria for selecting projects are, firstly, their scientific and technical quality and, secondly, their effects on growth and competitiveness. Only projects involving fundamental research at the pre-competitive stage are eligible, which means that the closer a project is to the market, the less chance it has to be assisted by the European Union. EU financial assistance plays a role in encouraging and guiding research activities conducted in the Member States. Shared-cost research found its most advanced expression in the "second generation" programmes for which ESPRIT served as a model (RACE, BRITE, Euram, etc.), which are programmes with highly integrated projects, but ones which necessitate international cooperation.

The third form of Community R&TD is that of **concerted action**. In that particular instance the Community quite simply defines the framework for action within which researchers from the Member States operate totally freely. As was seen above, Article 130h of the Treaty confers on the Commission the task of coordinating national research policies and activities. Coordination makes it possible to define jointly the major objectives to be attained, to avoid duplication, to bring teams of researchers of different nationalities into contact and to ensure the broad dissemination of research results. Closer coordination of the research activities of the Union and of the Member States is pursued, in particular, through integrated networks such as the European Network for Research in Global Change (ENRICH) and the European Technology Assessment Network (ETAN).

But European research is also coordinated on a broader level than that of the Fifteen. In fact **scientific and technical cooperation (Cost)** has existed since 1971 between the Community countries and several other western European countries. That operation, which now covers the coun-

---

1   OJ L117, 14.05.1996.
2   OJ L177, 04.07.1984.

tries of Central and Eastern Europe, is managed by a Committee of Senior Officials (Cost) and by specialized committees. It takes the form of memoranda of understanding by the Cost States on the execution of Cost activities in the most varied fields, such as medicine, transport or materials. The Council concludes concertation agreements between the Community and the Cost countries relating to concerted actions forming part of the Community research programme[1].

In addition to Cost, closer scientific and technical cooperation was established between the Community and the **EFTA countries** following the Luxembourg statement of 9 April 1984. Following the entry into force of the Agreement on a European Economic Area, on 1st January 1994, and the accession to the EU of three former EFTA countries, on 1st January 1995, Norway, Iceland and Liechtenstein participate in the non-nuclear Community R&TD specific programmes.

The specific programmes under the fourth framework programme are also open to the participation of the countries of Central and Eastern Europe and the new independent States of the former Soviet Union[2]. The Community, through the Commission participates in the financing and in the research activities of the International Association for the Promotion of Cooperation with Scientists from the New Independent States (INTAS)[3]. In 1992, the Community, the United States of America, Japan and Russia concluded an Agreement setting up an **International Science and Technology Centre (ISTC)**[4]. Established in Moscow, the ISTC is to channel the know-how of military research scientists and technicians of the former Soviet Union into non-military projects. Moreover, the Commission finances an International Association for the promotion of cooperation with scientists from the independent States of the former Soviet Union.

The EU's scientific cooperation with the **countries of the Third World** forms part of the RDT framework programme. The research programme in the field of sciences and technologies for development covers the areas of tropical agriculture (improving food plant production using systems suited to local conditions, restoring the environment, etc.) and medicine, health and nutrition (new methods for diagnosing and treating diseases, improving the nutrition of the population)[5].

However, the Community has also for a number of years been developing its cooperation with non-European **industrialized countries**, such as the United States, Canada and Australia, notably in the fields of energy, biotechnology and the environment. In 1995, the EAEC (Euratom) and the United States signed an R&TD cooperation agreement on the monitoring of nuclear safety and a general Nuclear Energy Cooperation Agreement. Euratom signed, also in 1995, a memorandum of understanding for cooperation in the field of controlled thermonuclear fusion[6]. On its part, the European Community concluded Agreements on scientific and technical cooperation with Canada[7], South Africa and Israel.

In 1988 the EAEC (Euratom) concluded a quadripartite Agreement (Community, Soviet Union, United States and Japan) for the execution of a conceptual design project for an International Thermonuclear Experimental Reactor (ITER), with the four parties providing equal contributions on an equal footing[8]. In 1992, the four parties - Russia having replaced the Soviet Union - signed a Cooperation Agreement for the detailed study of ITER which it is hoped will demonstrate the scientific and technological feasibility of using fusion energy for peaceful purposes[9].

Lastly, mention must be made of the technological cooperation programme **EUREKA**, which was launched in 1985 on the initiative of the French President, F. Mitterrand. That major R&TD programme, which combines the efforts of nineteen countries and major

---

1   OJ L344, 13.12.1988 and OJ L85, 31.03.1992.
2   OJ C271, 17.10.1995.
3   COM (95) 539, 13 November 1995.
4   OJ L409, 31.12.1992 and OJ L64, 08.03.1994.
5   OJ L196, 19.07.1991.
6   COM (94) 343.
7   OJ L74, 22.03.1996.
8   OJ L222, 12.08.1988.
9   OJ L244, 26.08.1992 and OJ L114, 05.05.1994.

European undertakings, notably in the fields of data-processing, telematics, biotechnology and the environment, is not part of the Community research framework programme. The Commission, however, which participates in the programmes, provides an essential contribution in terms of expertise and ensures coordination with Community programmes proper, such as ESPRIT or JOULE. Following its reform, in 1988, the JRC participates directly in some EUREKA projects.

A Community specific R&TD programme finances the various activities of cooperation with third countries and international organizations[1]. It covers scientific and technological cooperation in Europe and with international organizations, cooperation with other European R&TD fora (Cost and Eureka), cooperation with the countries of Central and Eastern Europe and with the independent States of the former Soviet Union, cooperation with non-European industrialized third countries and scientific and technological cooperation with the developing countries. The Commission has set out as priority courses of action for this programme, notably: increasing industrial involvement in international R&TD cooperation; strengthening the external dimension of European R&TD policy; achieving a better awareness of scientific achievements in third countries; and making use of other funds to support European R&TD[2]. Endorsing the overall objectives for Community scientific cooperation, the Council emphasized that this should be based on the principles of subsidiarity, mutual benefit and consistency with other Community policies, in particular the Union's external policies[3].

The fields of Community research

Having its origins in the ECSC Treaty and especially in the Euratom Treaty, Community research for a long time remained solidly anchored in the **energy sector**. This is no longer the case. The research subjects of the fourth framework programme of research and technological development (1994-1998) are categorized into two main fields: science and technology at the service of industrial innovation and science and technology for society and for Europe (health, the struggle against social exclusion, climatic change, etc.).

In the field of nuclear fission, Community research no longer deals with the direct development of reactors, but of a field which is by definition international, viz. **nuclear safety**, which is a problem that has increasingly preoccupied public opinion in particular since the Chernobyl nuclear power station disaster in April 1986. The specific Euratom programme in the field of **nuclear fission safety** (1994-1998) aims at stimulating collaboration at European and world level with the objective to develop a global and dynamic approach to nuclear safety in the broadest sense[4]. More specifically, it aims at exploring innovative approaches, reactor safety, radioactive waste management and disposal as well as decommissioning, radiological impact on man and the environment and mastering events of the past, including the consequences of the Chernobyl accident. Several specialized JRC institutes carry out research on nuclear safety.

The reason for the Community's paying such close attention to the safety of nuclear fission is that the latter involves certain hazards to the

---

1   OJ L334, 22.12.1994.
2   COM (95) 489, 18 October 1995.
3   OJ C110, 16.04.1996.
4   OJ L361, 31.12.1994.

environment and human health. This is not true of thermonuclear fusion, for the advent of which Community research is actively paving the way. Whereas fission splits the atoms of radioactive materials, fusion unites the atoms of non-radioactive materials and therefore represents no danger of radioactivity.

Thermonuclear fusion is a process which occurs on the surface of the Sun, releasing prodigious energy. In the Sun's core at temperatures of 10 to 15 million degrees Celsius, hydrogen is converted to helium providing enough energy to sustain life on Earth. Man has conceived of reproducing on earth, in a controlled fashion, what happens on the Sun. In fact, by heating gases such as deuterium (abundant in all forms of water) and lithium (plentiful in the Earth's crust) or tritium (manufactured from lithium) to a temperature of 100 million degrees Celsius, their electrons are completely separated from the atomic nuclei, atoms fuse and a fantastic release of energy within that "plasma" ensues. However, one must first obtain that extraordinary temperature, which is feasible, and the plasma must thereafter be confined within a magnetic space known as a "torus", which is more difficult. The objective of Community research is to produce and contain plasma which has the properties required for the reactors of the future in a magnetic field known as "tokamak".

It is towards that goal that the joint undertaking called the **Joint European Torus (JET)** set up at Culham in the United Kingdom[1] has been working since 1978. Thanks to the controlled thermonuclear fusion programme, remarkable results have been achieved on the JET, such as the first-ever production of 2 megawatts of fusion power in November 1991, enabling the European Union to hold a place in the forefront of world research in the field of fusion by magnetic confinement. The top priority of the specific R&TD programme in the field of fusion (1994-1998) is to lay the scientific and technical foundations and prepare industry for the construction of a "Next Step" (NET) experimental fusion reactor[2]. Work to this end involves not only the NET team at Garching, but also several JRC's institutes like the Institute for Systems Engineering and the Institute for Advanced Materials. A tokamak called ITER (International Thermonuclear Experimental Reactor) is also under preparation in the framework of the quadripartite agreement (Euratom, United States, Japan, Russia) mentioned above.

In the field of **non-nuclear energy**, three shared-cost research programmes succeeded one another between 1975 and 1988. They concerned the development of renewable sources of energy (solar energy, biomass, wind power, geothermal energy) and the rational use of energy (energy saving, solid fuels, new energy vectors, etc.). The new research and technological development programme in the field of non-nuclear energies **(JOULE-Thermie)** strives to develop new, economically viable energy options which have reduced or zero impact on the environment (and particularly on the climate)[3]. It distinguishes itself in two parts: research and technological development (JOULE) and technological demonstration (Thermie II). It covers three main areas: rational use of energy (energy efficiency in buildings, energy efficiency in industry, energy industry, energy storage, transport and urban infrastructure); renewable energies (solar, wind, hydroelectric, geothermal, energy from

1 OJ L151, 07.06.1978 and OJ L222 of 12.08.1988, see also the chapter on energy policy.

2 OJ L361, 31.12.1994.

3 OJ L334, 22.12.1994.

biomasse and waste); and solid fuels (clean technologies for solid fossil fuels, generic combustion, exploration and production of hydrocarbons).

It can be seen that energy research is still present in the Community's general research programme, but does not dominate it. Now, only about 18% of the budget of **action line 1**, which covers research, technological development and demonstration programmes (almost 87% of the total budget), goes to nuclear and non-nuclear energy, whereas some 28% of this budget is consecrated to information and communication technologies in programmes referred to in the chapter on industry because they are of great interest to industrial policy. **Action line 2** covers cooperation with third countries and international organizations (4.4% of the total budget). **Action line 3** concerns the dissemination and exploitation of the results of Community R&TD activities (2.7%) of the budget) and **action line 4**, the stimulation of training and mobility of researchers (6% of the budget).

The specific programme in the field of **industrial and materials technologies (BRITE-EURAM III)**, with some 14% of the budget of action line 1, covers three areas: production technologies for tomorrow's industry (incorporation of new technologies into production systems, development of clean production technologies, rational management of raw materials, safety and reliability of production systems, human and organizational factors within production systems); materials and technologies for product innovation, stimulating job creation (materials engineering, new methodologies for product design and manufacture, reliability and quality of materials and products, technologies for recovering products at the end of their lifecycle); and technologies for next-generation transportation means (vehicle design, production, efficiency, safety, operation and environmental considerations)[1]. The Brite-Euram programme is geared towards an approach based on "total quality" which integrates technological, economic and environmental considerations into the innovation process. Selected projects are, therefore, required to enhance industrial competitiveness and improve the quality of the environment. This programme also provides a framework for cooperative research projects (CRAFT projects) in which groups of SMEs without their own research facilities can form an association to contract out research to an outside partner (university institute or laboratory), in which case the Community covers up to 50% of the research cost. Thanks to the CRAFT method the participation of SMEs in the Brite-Euram programme has passed from 18% in 1985 to 32% in 1993.

A programme intended to provide technical support for the harmonization measures necessary for the smooth functioning of the internal market is that relating to **standards, measurements and testing**[2]. Indeed, without sound, reliable measurements, industries, particularly high technology ones, cannot operate, trade is impaired by disputes, health care becomes empirical and Community legislation, ranging from environmental and worker protection to the operation of the single market and the common agricultural policy, cannot be successfully implemented. The specific R&TD programme in the field of standards, measurements and testing (1994-1998) concerns three themes, namely: measurements for quality European products and reference data; research related to written standards and technical support to trade (support to Community legislation, concerning in particular "New Approach" directives, to standards for industry, to a European measurement infrastructure, to mutual recognition and accreditation and to the protection against the importation of illegal substances); and measurements related to the needs of society (health and safety of workers and the population, monitoring of the environment, forensic science and control, in particular, of narcotics, support of Europe's cultural heritage). The Institute for Reference

---

1   OJ L222, 26.08.1994.
2   OJ L334, 22.12.1994.

Materials and Measurements of the Joint Research Centre contributes to the implementation of the JRC's measurement and testing programme, its activities shifting from the nuclear to the non-nuclear field, and from basic research to more applied research.

The R&TD programme in the field of **environment and climate** disposes of almost 9% of the budget of line 1 and covers four areas: study of the natural environment, environment quality and global change; environmental technologies; space technologies for environmental monitoring; and the human dimension of environmental change[1]. Priority is given to studying the fundamental mechanisms of the climate and natural systems, understanding and reducing the impact of human activities on the environment and the effect of pollution on the cultural heritage. The Community's research in this field is carried out within the framework of the European Network for Research into Global Change (ENRICH). The JRC's Institute for the Environment and the Institute for Remote Sensing Applications participate in research into global change.

Old and new fields of Community research are to be found under the heading of the **exploitation of biological resources.** The first fields of research, which were engaged upon as early as the '70s on the basis of Article 41 of the EEC Treaty, concern, on the one hand, the competitiveness of agriculture and fisheries (including agro-industry, food technologies, forestry, aquaculture and rural development)[2] and, on the other, marine science and technology development (MAST III)[3]. May be regarded as new, although undertaken since as early as 1982, research programmes in the field of **biotechnology**, i.e. genetic engineering, which makes it possible to obtain new chemical, pharmaceutical or food products and highly competitive processes in a large number of industrial and agricultural activities. Indeed, biotechnology can provide important energy (fuel) and industrial outlets for agricultural raw materials. The specific research and technological development programme in the field of biotechnology (1994-1998) covers areas such as cell factories, genome analysis, plant and animal biotechnology, and cell communication in the neurosciences[4]. This specific programme is designed in particular to ensure a strong and innovative science base as well as a multidisciplinary approach to biotechnology-based processes. The "European biotechnology information service" is a network of teachers and researchers designed to make the public more aware of the issues at stake in biotechnology and increase its knowledge in this area. In 1996 Community research marked an international success by decoding the entire genome of a complex living organism, yeast, which has many similarities with human genes. This should help us understand the origin and development of some forty diseases, including many forms of cancer.

Community research is also directed towards the quality of life. The R&TD programme in the field of **biomedicine and health** covers: pharmaceuticals research; brain research; research into diseases with a major socio-economic impact (cancer, AIDS, tuberculosis...); human genome research; public health; and biomedical ethics[5].

The research and technological development programme in the **field of transport** aims at helping establish a genuine trans-European network as well as making the various modes of transport more efficient, inexpensive, safer and compatible with the quality of life and with the environment. In addition to overall optimization of the European transport system, Community research aims at the internal optimization of each mode (rail transport, integrated transport chains, air transport, urban transport, road transport, maritime and waterborne transport)[6].

The economy and the society are not neglected by Community research. The R&TD programme in the field of **target socio-economic research** is designed to help clarify decision-taking in order to lay the foundations for the sustainable development of Europe's economies to enable them to withstand international competition and create jobs[7]. It covers evaluation of science policy options, research into education and training, research into social integration and social exclusion.

In more general terms, the Community conducts programmes to stimulate the international cooperation and interchange needed by European research scientists. A specific R&TD

---

1   OJ L361, 31.12.1994.
2   OJ L334, 22.12.1994.
3   Ibid.
4   OJ L361, 31.12.1994.
5   Ibid.
6   Ibid.
7   Ibid.

programme encourages training and mobility of researchers[1]. It is divided into three inter-dependent areas: the establishment and functioning of research networks constituted from five or more research teams in at least three countries; access to large-scale facilities (particle accelerators, astronomic observatories, oceanographic vessels, etc.); and training through research by means of research periods of between three months and three years.

Knowledge is disseminated and optimized both in the framework of the specific R&TD programmes and by centralized action focusing on optimization of the results of R&TD activities and encouraging their dissemination particularly towards SMEs[2]. By virtue of its aims and content, this specific programme helps the least favoured regions of the Union and contributes to economic and social cohesion. In the context of this programme, the "VALUE" network of consultant services has been established to prepare and follow R&TD projects presented by SMEs and to promote transfer of technology to them. This network furnishes information on programmes and procedures, it facilitates contacts between potential partners and helps in the exploitation of the results of their research. In practical terms, the knowledge generated by Community R&TD programmes is disseminated via publications (around 600 per year) and via an on-line information service (**CORDIS**)[3].

Three Council Decisions establish the rules for the dissemination of research findings from the specific R&TD programmes as well as the rules for the participation of undertakings, research centres and universities in specific programmes dealing, on the one hand, with the European Community R&TD and, on the other, with research and training for the European Atomic Energy Community (Euratom)[4]. These rules guarantee, in particular, the protection of legitimate interests of the contracting parties and of rights linked to obtaining and exploiting the R&TD results, as well as their exploitation in conformity with the interests of the Community. They also specify that the Community financial participation must normally de paid to participants on the basis of the justification of actual costs, but that other methods, including fixed rates, may be agreed, where appropriate.

Appraisal and outlook

European research has made remarkable progress in five major fields, viz. energy, and in particular thermonuclear fusion, information and tele-communications technologies, technologies and materials which can be used in the manufacturing industry, biotechnology and environmental protection. The EU makes a constant effort to curb the dissipation of research and to promote collaboration through increased concertation and coordination as well as the dissemination of scientific and technological

1   Ibid.
2   Ibid.
3   OJ C202, 03.08.1988.
4   OJ L306, 30.11.1994.

knowledge in all Member States. However, on the whole, efforts are still unbalanced and fragmented. Three Member States (the Federal Republic of Germany, France and the United Kingdom) account for three quarters of total R&D expenditure in the European Union, and regional differences are very marked.

The research and technological development powers vested in the Community by the Single Act have provided a basis for raising the competitiveness of European undertakings. This has been reflected by growth in the funding allocated to research under the Community budget. Whilst Community research expenditure was of the order of ECU 300 million per annum at the beginning of the '80s and the bulk of the work was on energy research, in the '90s the Community is devoting more than ECU 2,500 million on research and is targeting it more on diffusing technologies relating to telecommunications, microelectronics and new products. The most important aspect is not so much the volume of expenditure - which represents only some 4% of the total research expenditure of the Member States - as the pooling by the EEC countries of their financial and human efforts to carry out research that would be out of the reach of any one country.

However, the EU's overall research and development effort (2.1% of GNP in 1991) is inferior to that of its main competitors, the United States (2.8% of GNP) and Japan (3.5% of GNP). Worse still, the financing of R&TD activities by European industry is lower than the same financing in the United States and far lower than that of Japanese industry. Thus, European R&TD is devoted in particular to fundamental research, whilst that of its main competitors is targeted on subsequent industrial uses. Technologies targeted on major industrial priorities reflecting the needs of industry as it endeavours to innovate must be developed alongside the traditional research programmes.

Certainly, the fourth framework programme on R&TD is part of the plan for the promotion of growth, competitiveness and employment in the Community. It tries to better coordinate the European rtesearch effort, to focus Community R&TD on the major problems of society, to strengthen the scientific and technological bases of Community industry and to promote its international competitiveness. Nevertheless, innovation is still handicapped in Europe by the dispersion of research efforts and by the difficulty of translating the results of these efforts into new products and services. To promote innovation and, therefore, the competitiviness of European business, the legal and regulatory as well as the tax environment should be improved. Research efforts should also be better directed towards innovation, technology watch and prospective studies. The financing of innovation should be improved, in particular by Community instruments, and innovation in enterprises, especially SMEs, should be encouraged, notably by simplifying administrative procedures.

Bibliography on research policy

□ ALBERT, M. B., NARIN F., *Assessment of Critical Technologies in Europe in Selected Fields Covered by EC Research Programmes*, OOPEC, Luxembourg, 1994.

□ ANDREASEN L. E., CORIAT B., DEN HERTOG F., KAPLINSKY R. (ed.), *Europe's Next Step. Organisational Innovation, Competition and Employment*, Frank Cass, Ilford, Essex, 1995.

□ BARKER K. E., KUHLMANN S., MARCIANO da SILVA C. (et al.), *Analysis of Experience in the Use of Verifiable Objectives*, OOPEC, Luxembourg, 1994.

□ BERNARD V., CHAPUIS M, KAVANAGH M., *COST: General Activity Report 1991-1992*, OOPEC, Luxembourg, 1994.

□ COLOMBO M. G., MULDUR U., PETRELLA R., *The European Community and the Globalization of Technology and the Economy*, OOPEC, Luxembourg, 1994.

□ COMMISSION EUROPÉENNE, *Regard sur la recherche européenne: Une sélection des résultats*, OPOCE, Luxembourg, 1995.

   – *Les programmes-cadres de recherche (1994-1998) et leur mise en oeuvre*, OPOCE, Luxembourg, 1995.

□ EUROPEAN COMMISSION, *Preparing a Technology Business Plan*, OOPEC, Luxembourg, 1994.

   – *Communication Concerning the Mid-Term Review of the Action on the Dissemination and Exploitation of Knowledge Resulting from the Specific Programmes of RDT of the Community (VALUE II)*, COM (94) 548 Final of 5 December 1994.

   – *Europe's Science and Technology - Towards the 21st Century*, "Europe on the Move", OOPEC, Brussels, Luxembourg, 1994.

□ *Management of Collaboration in EC R&D Programmes*, OOPEC, Brussels, Luxembourg, 1995.

□ *The Impact of EC Programmes on R&D Decision Making: Survey of a Sample of Industrial Participants*, OOPEC, Brussels, Luxembourg, 1995.

□ *Applying Information Technology. 101 Success Stories from Esprit*, OOPEC, Brussels, Luxembourg, 1996.

□ GRÜNEWALD W., SMITH K., *The Community Innovation Survey: Status and Perspectives*, OOPEC, Luxembourg, 1994.

□ KASTRINOS N., *The EC Framework Programme and the Technology Strategies of European Firms*, OOPEC, Luxembourg, 1994.

□ KRULL W., SENSI D., SOTIRIOU D., *Evaluation of Research & Development. Current Practice and Guidelines: Synthesis Reports*, Luxembourg, EC Commission, OPOCE, Luxembourg, 1991.

□ "La mondialisation de la recherche et de l'économie: Implications et conséquences pour la R&D communautaire" in *Nouvelles de la science et des technologies*, numéro spécial 09/02, 1991.

□ RUBERTI Antonio, ANDRÉ Michel, *Un espace européen de la science*, PUF, Paris, 1995.

□ SHARP Margaret, "Europe - A Renaissance? European Technology", in *Science and Public Policy*, Vol. 18, N° 6, December 1991, pp. 393-400.

□ SILVESTRO Massimo, "Le quatrième programme-cadre communautaire de recherche, de développement technologique et de démonstration", in *Revue du Marché commun et de l'Union européenne*, Paris, N° 378, mai 1994.

□ THIARD Antoine, PFAU Wilhelm, *Research and Development and Standardization: A Guide*, EC Commission, EFTA, Luxembourg, 1992.

□ TOSCHI Romano (e. a.), *NET. Next European Torus. Predesign Report*, Commission EC, North-Holland, Amsterdam, 1993.

11. ENERGY

Successive oil shocks, their impact on the economic and monetary system at international and EEC level and Community efforts to reduce its dependence on imported oil are the closely interrelated problems which topped the economic agenda in the seventies. The Community was ill-prepared to cope with these problems, for when the founding Treaties were signed in the fifties, it was almost self-sufficient in energy and hoped that a new source - atomic energy would soon take over from coal, the traditional source. Time proved otherwise and it was oil which made a spectacular entry onto the Community market in the sixties.

In that two Community Treaties dealt, often in some depth, uniquely with the energy of the past (coal - ECSC) and the perceived one of the future (nuclear - Euratom), the Commission did not have the legal instruments at its disposal to assume responsibilities in the energy sector (oil - EEC) which had since become the dominant player. The Community's eyes were only opened to the risks of this situation by the October 1973 energy crisis. From 1974 onwards, Community objectives began to be defined and steps taken to reduce dependency on imported petroleum products. It was from this point that Community energy policy began to take shape.

Energy is at the core of economic and social activity in industrialized countries. Energy costs affect not only industries with large energy consumption but also industry as a whole and even the cost of life of citizens, notably because of the impact of energy prices on transport cost and heating. While respecting the subsidiarity principle and environmental requirements, European energy policy aims, therefore, at influencing energy production and consumption with the objective of securing economic growth and safeguarding the well-being of the citizens of the Union. It must, on the one hand, ensure the smooth functioning of the single market in energy products and services and, on the other, guarantee the supply of relatively cheap and secure (from the strategic and environmental viewpoints) energy resources to the States of the Union. European energy policy thus revolves around two axes: the functioning of the internal energy market and the security of energy supplies.

Economic and legal framework

Community energy policy was not forgotten by the "founding fathers", who devoted two Community Treaties to this sector: the ECSC
Treaty, which deals with coal and Euratom, which covers nuclear energy.
Once the policy to be pursued in these two sectors had been defined,
occasionally in some detail, the matter was felt to be closed. The institutions of the European Economic Community were thus not given any clear
responsibility for the other sources of energy. Although with hindsight this
may be disputed, in the fifties coal was in abundant supply, was relatively
inexpensive and met 65% of the energy requirements of the six founding
countries. It was therefore seen as the energy which would fuel the creation
of the common market. Furthermore, impressed by the recent demonstration at Hiroshima of the force of atomic energy, experts were predicting a
bright future for its peaceful use.

No clear need for a Community or even national oil policy was
perceived in the years when oil was cheap and supply certain, which was
the case throughout the after-war years up to the beginning of the seventies. This golden era was anchored in major oil discoveries by Western oil
companies in the Middle East and Africa and in the legal system governing
the exploitation of oil reserves. The central principle of this system was the
granting of a prospecting and working monopoly over a given area by the
producer country to one or several foreign companies (licence). The activity spectrum of these companies covered all of the petroleum industry
activities (prospecting, production, transport, refining, storage and distribution) and they enjoyed a strong position enabling them, in the vast
majority of exporting countries and in relation to most of the importing
countries, to regulate petroleum output and marketing terms.

Although the Governments of the then six Member States showed a
clear tendency towards an "every man for himself" policy, they nevertheless approved a "Protocol of Agreement on Energy Problems"[1] in April
1964. In this Protocol, they stated their commitment to the development
and implementation of a Community energy policy, without considering
it necessary to set a time limit for its definition.

Time was however running against them, for world oil demand grew
more rapidly than supply and around 1970 the market changed from a
buyer's to a seller's one. Oil-producing countries became aware of the
power which they wielded and changed their attitude towards consumer
countries and oil companies. The calm which had reigned in the oil sector
during most of the post-war period was suddenly shattered in 1970 and
replaced by an incessant stream of demands by producing countries, by
agreements concluded and broken and finally by a mad rush for self-sur-
vival among consumer countries.

It is quite remarkable that even during the period of energy abundance, the Commission had already given thought to what steps should be taken in the event of a shortage. In
fact, in the "**Initial Guidelines** for a Community Energy Policy", dating back to December

---

1   OJ L69, 30.04.1964.

1968, the Commission had stressed the need for a policy of inexpensive and reliable supply and therefore for Community action in the areas of trade policy, investment guidance, structural policy and investment financing. The Council itself, in approving the "Initial Guidelines" on November 13, 1969, acknowledged the need for a Community energy policy pursuing two main goals: the creation of a common market in energy products through the removal of obstacles to trade and the harmonization of the various national pricing and intervention systems; and a common energy supply strategy ensuring sufficient deliveries at reasonable prices to all the Member States.

However, very few specific measures were adopted to turn the Community energy policy from a stated aim into a reality. Among the rare few was one on the obligation of the Member States to maintain minimum stocks of petroleum products as a security measure[1] and one on the notifying of the Commission of investments and imports of crude oil and natural gas[2]. Special mention must be made of a Directive adopted by the Council in July 1973, just a few months before the October 1973 crisis, urging the Member States to take measures, appoint bodies and prepare intervention plans to mitigate the effects of possible supply restrictions[3].

The 1973 crisis

The Member States had therefore already sensed which way the wind was blowing. The first occasion for a showdown between producer countries on the one hand and consumer countries and their oil companies on the other came with the Kippur war between Israel and the Arab countries from October 6 to 16, 1973. During this war and in the following months, the Arab countries successfully wielded the weapon represented by their oil resources. They notably placed an embargo, for a certain amount of time, on exports to countries which were branded "enemies of the Arab cause" - including practically all the countries of Western Europe - while reducing their overall oil output level. They decided to overturn the principle of price setting for crude oil through agreements with the oil companies and hiked up prices on a unilateral basis. Finally, they stepped up their claims to holdings in the companies producing crude oil. Under the combined impact of these measures, oil prices quadrupled in just a few months and uncertainty clouded the quantity and price situation which the world's biggest importer, the European Community, would have to face.

In the Member States, the first effect of the crisis was a **shortage of oil**, which led to a number of measures to restrict consumption (no use of cars on Sundays, speed limits, heating restrictions and so on). As shortage fears diminished, prices and their financial consequences became the uppermost concern. Although supply difficulties tailed off after December 1973, **higher prices for crude oil** persisted. The Community Member States, accustomed to trade surpluses, saw these frittered away into a deficit situation. Recession began to bite in nearly all the European countries and gave rise to what was termed "Euro-stagnation".

Aside from these economic consequences, the 1973 crisis created a **sense of insecurity** among the European countries, and rightly so, for it revealed the vulnerability of their economies due to their dependence on

1   OJ L308, 23.12.1968.
2   OJ L120, 25.02.1972.
3   OJ L228, 16.08.1973.

available quantities and price levels of oil, the economic lubricant. The cartel of producer countries inspired much less confidence than its predecessor, the "seven sisters" cartel (Exxon, Shell, B.P., Mobil, Texaco, Chevron and Gulf). The concept of everyone settling their own affairs and entrusting multinational oil companies with the common good took a serious blow when the seven sisters and their poorer relations such as Total, Elf and Agip lost ownership of their crude oil resources and were therefore unable to continue guaranteeing the supply security of Europe. This awareness of the Community's energy vulnerability led to the need for a coherent system of external relations to guarantee supply security. A common trade policy for oil could have considerably boosted the negotiating leverage of the EEC Member States, if only it had existed.

At the beginning of 1979, the Iran-Iraq war sparked off fresh tension on the oil market. The Organization of Petroleum-Exporting Countries (OPEC) took advantage of this situation to raise the official price for crude oil once again. The average barrel price consequently doubled in 1980 compared with its December 1978 level. Crude oil, following the two oil shocks, rocketed from barely 3 dollars in 1972 to 36 dollars in 1980. This twelvefold increase in crude oil prices in the space of ten years dealt a devastating blow to economies in several regions of the world, including the Community.

International energy cooperation

After the October 1973 oil crisis, the United States took the initiative of organizing an international conference in Washington in February 1974, whose work culminated in the conclusion of the International Energy Agreement and in the creation of the International Energy Agency under the auspices of the OECD. The **Agreement on an International Energy Programme**, signed on November 18, 1974, by the twenty-one OECD member countries, entered into force on January 19, 1976. It is a wide-ranging cooperation programme which seeks: to ensure, in the event of crisis, a common level of oil supply autonomy and common measures to restrict demand and share out the available oil; to establish an information system on the international oil market; to implement a long-term cooperation programme to reduce dependence on oil imports and to promote cooperation relations with producer countries and with other consumer countries.

The **International Energy Agency (IEA)** was set up on November 15, 1974 by the OECD's Council. Its main tasks are to: draw up and implement a long-term cooperation programme on the development of resources and energy savings; analyze national programmes for energy conservation and the development of new energy resources; improve the information system on oil and natural gas markets; create a statistics centre for energy; introduce a mechanism to restrict demand and share out oil resources in the event of supply difficulties. The European Commission has observer status within the Agency and coordinates, on the one hand, the positions of the EU Member States and, on the other, the action of the IEA with that of the EU, particularly in the areas where there is Community competence such as that of the commercial policy. The introduction of a contingency scheme by the IEA, on 17 January 1991, together with the commencement of Allied hostilities against Iraq - in compliance with UN Resolutions and under US command - after Kuwait's invasion, was instrumental in calming the oil markets, which remained stable until the end of the conflict.

The 1973 crisis gave rise to several initiatives seeking to establish "dialogue" between oil producer and consumer countries. These have not borne much fruit. There was first talk of a "North-South dialogue" and then, after December 1975, of "global negotiations". All that now remains of these initiatives are the occasional meetings between the European Commission and the secretariats of the Organization of Petroleum Exporting Countries (OPEC) and the Organization of Arab Petroleum Exporting Countries (OAPEC), which discuss oil trade, the situation on the international energy market and the interest of all, consumers and producers alike, in avoiding too large price fluctuations. This dialogue is certainly useful, but cannot in itself lay the foundation for cooperation between the European Union and energy producing countries, notably the Gulf countries where the World's most important hydrocarbon reserves are located.

The **European Energy Charter** laying down the principles, the objectives and ways of achieving pan-European cooperation in the field of energy would appear to be more promising. Signed in the Hague on December 17, 1991 by almost all European countries as well as by the Community, Canada, the United States, and Japan, the Charter is in fact a code of good practice. Its interest is to give the first tangible demonstration of a consensus based upon solidarity and complementarity, in particular between the countries of Western Europe - with their know-how and advanced technologies - and those of Central and Eastern Europe, including the countries of the former Soviet Union, which have relatively abundant energy resources.

The Charter pursues the following operational objectives: expansion of trade, especially through free market operation, free access to resources and the development of infrastructure; cooperation and coordination of energy policies; and the optimal use of energy and protection of the environment. These objectives should be attained through the implementation of joint measures by the signatory countries in six specific priority fields: access to resources; use of resources; investment arrangements; liberalization of trade; harmonization of technical specifications and safety rules; research and technological development and innovation. Given these aims, the implementation of the Charter should mark a turning point in the Community's energy policy. Such an implementation procedure is provided by the **European Energy Charter Treaty**, signed in Lisbon on 17 December 1994[1]. This Treaty is designed to develop new relations between the main European countries, most of the independent States of the former Soviet Union and Central and Eastern Europe, Canada, the United States and Japan concerning trade, investment and energy cooperation. The European Commission assists the Secretariat of the Conference, which is established in Brussels.

The pan-European cooperation in the energy field sought by the Charter is assisted by the Community's **PHARE Programme,** targeted on the countries of Central and Eastern Europe and by the **TACIS** programme concerning the independent States of the former Soviet Union. Technical assistance programmes in the energy field cover the drafting and planning of energy policy in these countries, energy supply and demand, tariff system and pricing, energy savings, the interconnection of East-West networks, training, environmental protection, the reshaping of the energy

---

1   OJ L380, 31.12.1994 and COM (95) 440, 20 September 1995.

industry and nuclear safety. Energy and nuclear safety appear also in the Europe Agreements concluded with CEECs in preparation to their accession to the EU. Several energy centres, created in the CEECs thanks to Community programmes, serve as contact points between economic operators of those countries and of the European Union.

From the financial point of view, cooperation with third countries is pursued under the **Synergy programme**, which provides support upstream of the technical activities implemented under other specific programmes such as PHARE and Thermie. It helps promote sustainable development, notably by reducing emissions of green-house gases and of pollutants linked to energy consumption, to enhance security of supply, and to improve energy efficiency[1]. Its main activities are providing assistance in the setting-up of energy institutions capable of defining the requirements of the countries concerned and channeling resources, advising national authorities, supporting the design of energy policy instruments, training, and providing information to the public authorities and economic operators, with special attention being given to transnational projects.

Internal energy market

The full **application of Community internal market law** - and in particular of provisions relating to the free movement of goods and services, to monopolies, to undertakings and to State aids - is the main path to a better integrated energy market. By the removal of barriers, whether of public or private origin, and the establishment of common rules, the opening up of energy markets may ensure the availability of energy on the most economic conditions for the end-user whether it be high energy consuming industries or just private individuals. Indeed, an open market on which energy users are free to choose the fuel they wish and the most efficient suppliers can generate competitive pricing. The integration of the energy market is therefore fundamental for the competitiveness of the industry of the EU and for the well-being of its citizens. But the energy sector does not benefit from this integration because the Member States use the security of supply and the diversity of their energy situation as excuse for the preservation of their national monopolies and of their different regulatory frameworks.

Different national rules and technical norms, which affect both the manufacture of equipment used by the energy industry and that for energy users, should be harmonized under the "new approach" adopted by the Council in 1985[2]. The energy sector, a source of high value contracts, also finds itself in the front-line of the general public procurement policy. Fiscal alignment by the convergence of the real rates of excise taxes is crucially important for the completion of the internal market for oil products. Last

---

1   COM (95)197, 23 May 1995.
2   OJ C136, 04.06.1985, see the chapter on the Common Market.

but not least, the introduction of competition in those sectors in which monopolies persist could play a prime role for the integration of the markets and the competitiveness of the economy of the EU.

The establishment of a real internal market for energy depends on the development of energy trans-European networks, which could irrigate the whole territory of the European Union with cheap, diversified from the supply point of view and environment-friendly energy. This development is particularly important for the less favoured regions, which have no access to the big interconnected networks for gas and electricity, this being a cause but also a consequence of their underdevelopment. In the meantime, the Regulation on notifying the Commission of investment projects of interest to the Community in the petroleum, natural gas and electricity sectors aims at a certain coordination of energy investments[1].

Following wide-ranging consultation on a Green Paper "For a European Union energy policy", the Commission set out in a **White Paper** of December 1995 guidelines for the energy policy of the Union in the years ahead[2]. It puts forward an indicative five-year action programme built around mutually agreed strategic goals towards which Community and national energy policies should converge. Security of supply remains a constant concern, but the general thrust of energy policy is to ensure the proper functioning of the internal energy market. This should take account not only of the supply and demand situation in the Member States, but also of concerns for environmental protection, industrial competitiveness and the development of new energy sources. Consideration for all these factors calls for a balanced approach based on the internalization of external energy costs and on new economic instruments, including fiscal measures.

Electricity and gas markets

The prime objective in the field of the internal energy market is to **liberalize and integrate electricity and natural gas markets**. The most important challenge here is to apply the competition rules of the Treaty to the monopolies for transmission and distribution of gas and electricity, even although these are entrusted with the operation of services of general economic interest. Another issue is the reconciliation of the objectives of the prevention of trade barriers and of energy efficiency by way of adoption of European standards established by the European Standardization Bodies (CEN/CENELEC)[3]. A last problem is the monitoring of the markets and the cooperation on interconnected systems between national regulatory authorities in both the gas and electricity sectors.

During the 1990s, some concrete steps have been taken in the direction of the electricity and gas markets integration. Thus, a Directive relating to the **transit of electricity** through the major European networks, the aim of which is to contribute to better integration of the internal market in electricity, through removing the obstacles to electricity trade between

---

1   OJ L120, 25.04.1996.

2   COM (94) 659, 11 January 1995 and COM (95) 682, 13 December 1995.

3   See on these subjects the chapters on competition and on the common market.

major networks[1]. Similarly, a Directive on the **transit of natural gas** through major networks aims at facilitating trade in natural gas[2]. Contracts on the transit of electricity and natural gas between major networks are negotiated between the entities with responsibility for these networks and the relevant bodies in the Member States. Transit conditions must be non-discriminatory and impartial as regards all the parties involved, must not contain unfair clauses or unjustified restrictions and must not place in danger either supply security or the quality of the service provided. Should a disagreement arise, parties concerned by transit contracts have the right to take their case to a conciliation body set up and presided by the Commission.

Another 1990 Directive, on the transparency of gas and electricity prices charged to industrial end-users, makes it compulsory for gas and electricity distribution concerns to communicate price data twice a year covering all the main categories of gas and electricity consumers[3].

Work on the liberalization of the gas and electricity sectors culminated in November 1994 in a Council agreement on four key aspects concerning electricity: the opening-up of electricity production to competition, the separation of the accounts relating to the activities of integrated undertakings, the transparency of public service obligations, and the role of the system operator[4]. Agreement was also reached on the principle of opening up the markets in areas other than production. To this end, work should continue concerning the possibility of having, at one and the same time, a third party access system and a single buyer system under comparable conditions concerning access to opening up of the market.

Concerning **trans-European energy networks** in the electricity and gas sectors, the Commission communicated to the European Parliament and the Council guidelines and propositions designed to create a favourable environment for their development[5]. The guidelines set the following objectives: strengthening the security of the EU's energy supplies by improving the efficiency and reliability of all European electricity and gas systems; ensuring effective operation of the internal market by providing an infrastructure which allows supply to respond to the demand for natural gas and electricity throughout the EU; promoting economic and social cohesion by facilitating the development and reducing the isolation of the less-favoured, peripheral and island regions.

In order to attain these objectives, the Commission proposes, on the one hand, broad lines of action to identify projects of common interest and, on the other, technical, administrative, legal and financial measures, concerning in particular authorization procedures. Indeed, unlike transport networks, the realization of trans-European energy networks is not in the first instance a financing problem, because investments in these networks are generally lucrative. The problem in this sector is that investments are often hampered by administrative constraints for the construction and operation of oil and gas pipelines, by exclusive import and export rights and by transport monopolies. Moreover, natural gas pipelines have to be built from gas fields, which are often located at great distances from the markets in Western Europe. Trans-European networks have therefore to

1   OJ L313, 13.11.1990.
2   OJ L147, 12.06.1991.
3   OJ L185, 17.07.1990.
4   OJ C123, 04.05.1995.
5   OJ C72, 10.03.1994.

be developed on all the countries of Europe and the basin of the Mediterranean. The priority for the European Union in this sector is therefore to
remove or bypass these obstacles.

Solid fuel market

The process of integration in the coal sector, which is regulated by the
ECSC Treaty, began on February 10, 1953. This was the date set by the High
Authority for the start of the transitional period for ECSC products. The
Treaty's basic rules are contained in Article 4, which notably forbids entry
or exit taxes, taxes having equivalent effect, and quantitative restrictions
on product movement. The Paris Treaty, which is based on the principle
of regulated competition, lays down rules for agreements, company concentrations and dominant positions and forbids price-based discrimination and notably unfair competitive practices and discriminatory practices,
i.e. the application by a seller of dissimilar conditions to comparable
transactions and especially on the grounds of the nationality of the buyer
(Article 60). It thus aims to ensure that users have equal access to sources
of production and to promote the development of international trade.

The industrial policy of the ECSC revolves around **continuous study
of market** and price trends which if need be can be regulated, and around
programmes indicating foreseeable developments in production, consumption, export and import (Article 46). The High Authority (Commission) has the power to collect the information it requires and to carry out
any checks necessary for the accomplishment of its tasks (Article 47). It can
require companies to inform it of their investment programmes and can
issue a reasoned opinion on such programmes. If its opinion is favourable,
the Commission can facilitate the implementation of investment programmes through borrowing funds at the international capital markets
and granting loans to the undertakings involved or through acting as a
guarantor for the loans which they take out[1]. If, on the other hand, it adopts
an adverse opinion, the undertaking in question can only use its own
equity capital for the implementation of the programme (Article 54). It
cannot therefore apply for an ECSC loan or State aid. State aid to the coal
industry is still possible but must respect the "Community regime" for such
aid introduced in 1965 by various Commission Decisions based on Article
95 ECSC, the most recent of which, adopted on 28 December 1993, stipulates that aid granted to the coal industry may be considered to be compatible with the proper functioning of the common market if it helps to
achieve at least one of the following objectives: progress towards economic
viability of the sector; solution to social and regional problems created by
reductions in the activity of production units; adjustment of the coal
industry to environmental protection standards[2].

These highly limited measures were evidently not sufficient to prevent coal from being swept aside by oil, which is a more flexible, easier to
handle and a less expensive product. Preservation of coal's supremacy

---

1   OJ C79, 29.03.1980.
2   OJ L329, 30.12.1993.

would have required measures much more drastic and expensive, in the form of a coal policy modelled on the Common Agricultural Policy. Europe of the sixties, awash with oil supply, was not prepared to pay the price of its energy independence.

The coal industry has not had luck on its side. When the common market was taking its first steps, Community coal undertakings only partially benefitted from soaring demand because extraction conditions and limited financing possibilities made sizeable short-term production rises impossible. Then, from 1958 onwards, the decisive entry of oil dealt the coal industry a hard blow sending it reeling into recession with the closure of 400 mines in the then six Member States. The remaining coal mines were faced with such large cost rises that even after the quadrupling of oil prices in 1973-74, they only managed to stabilize production after a struggle. In addition, demand had swung away from coal, prompting the Council to attempt through Recommendations to encourage investments in the use of solid fuel in industry, public buildings and district heating systems[1].

Despite its problems, **the common coal market has several achievements**, such as the gradual switch from a regulated management system conditioned by the war to a free market governed by competition; the abolition of agreements, concerted practices, dominant positions and other monopoly structures which were characteristic of this market; the impact of integration on intra-Community trade; and last but not least, the orderly retreat of the coal industry, which has meant that 700,000 workers have been laid off in this sector during the 70s and the 80s without social upheaval thanks to Community measures providing aid, and that none of the Member States gave in to the temptation to pass on its difficulties to its neighbours, which could have been catastrophic. Efforts to rationalize the coal industry were pursued during the 90s, because the contraction of the market for solid fuels was more important than expected[2]. In the mid-nineties, the total labour force in the coal sector of the Twelve hardly attained 200,000 workers.

Nuclear energy market

The economic factors pertaining to the nuclear energy market have not evolved in the manner predicted at the time of signature of the Euratom Treaty. In the fifties, the arrival on the industrial scene of nuclear energy was thought to be just around the corner and the drop in energy prices which caused this event to be postponed could not have been foreseen. Nuclear energy in fact only attained economic competitiveness after the 1973 crisis and the quadrupling of oil prices. In the period prior to this, the absence of a genuine nuclear energy market forced each Member State to create an artificial one through vast government research programmes targeted more on the acquisition of basic knowledge than on encouragement for industrial projects. This pushed the Member States off the straight and narrow path defined by the EAEC (Euratom) Treaty onto parallel technological roads, such as uranium enrichment systems, and sparked off a serious crisis in Euratom between 1965 and 1972[3].

The Euratom Treaty gives priority to the research and development of nuclear energy. As a sideline to this main concern, it defines, in Chapter IX, an outline for a **common nuclear energy market:** abolition of customs duties, charges having equivalent effect and all quantitative restrictions on imports and exports of natural and enriched uranium and other nuclear

---

1   OJ L140, 31.05.1983.
2   COM (93) 589, 26 November 1993.
3   See the relevant title in the Chapter on Research.

materials (Article 93); free movement and free establishment of individuals in the common nuclear energy market (Articles 96 and 97); free movement of capital for the financing of nuclear activities (Articles 99 and 100); free determination of prices as a result of balancing supply and demand within the Supply Agency (Article 67) and the forbidding of discriminatory pricing practices designed to secure a privileged position for certain users (Article 68).

The Commission periodically publishes **illustrative programmes** for the nuclear energy sector which encompass industrial and economic aspects of the future development of nuclear energy within the Community and seek to inform governments and economic operators in the Member States of the aims and prospects for nuclear energy production in the Community (Article 40). Economic operators have to inform the Commission of major investment projects prior to their implementation. Although the Commission's Opinion is not binding, it can point out the risk that over-capacities will emerge or that a particular project would duplicate the work carried out in an existing or planned plant in the Community.

One interesting feature of the Euratom Treaty is that it offers special status and certain advantages to **joint undertakings**, which are of primordial importance to the development of the Community's nuclear industry (Article 45). The Council, acting unanimously on a Commission proposal, can grant each joint undertaking all or some of the advantages listed in Annexe III to the Euratom Treaty, such as recognition that public interest status applies to the acquisition of immovable property required for the establishment of the joint undertakings or the exemption from all duties and charges when a venture is established (Article 48). In 1978, this status was granted to an undertaking of vital importance for the growth of the Community nuclear industry, namely the joint venture which, as seen in the previous chapter, builds the **Joint European Torus (JET)**, a thermonuclear fusion prototype[1].

Safety, a major feature of the common nuclear energy market, is perhaps the most important joint achievement in this field. This achievement is, however, of fundamental importance, because it determines the acceptance of the nuclear energy by the public. **Nuclear safety** is moreover approached from various different angles. Chapter VII of the Euratom Treaty provides for "safeguards". The Commission must be informed of the basic technical specifications of any nuclear plant. The Commission also has to approve procedures for the chemical processing of irradiated materials (Article 78). It must check that all ores, source materials and special fissile materials are not diverted from their intended uses as declared by the users (Article 77) and that the latter respect international safeguards and non-proliferation arrangements laid down by a Community Regulation[2]. The Commission can send inspectors to the Member States who must be given access at any time to all premises, all information and all individuals to the extent necessary to check the ores, source materials and special fissile materials used by the 800 or so nuclear installations, including 132 reactors, in the Community (Article 81). In fact, during the early 90s the Euratom Safeguards Directorate was called several times to take action in relation to cases of trafficking in nuclear materials from Eastern Europe.

Should individuals or undertakings be found to have infringed their safety obligations, the Commission can impose penalties, which can in serious cases take the form of the total

---

1   OJ L51, 07.06.1978 and OJ L375, 31.12.1991.

2   OJ L363, 31.12.1976 and OJ L191, 31.07.1993.

or partial removal of source materials or special fissile materials[1]. Member States are obliged to ensure that the penalties are implemented and, if necessary, that the infringements are corrected by those responsible for them (Article 83). In April 1992, the Agreement in force since 1975 between Euratom and the International Atomic Energy Agency (IAEA) was modified in order, in particular, to allow a number of joint inspections of Community installations enabling the IAEA to rationalize its inspection activities and reduce their cost by relying on the Euratom infrastructure (New Partnership Approach). The European Atomic Energy Community has signed the International Convention on Nuclear Safety concluded in September 1994 in the context of the IAEA. Its aim is to promote a high level of safety in nuclear power stations, to prevent accidents and to reduce their consequences by defining statutory obligations[2]. With the United States the EAEC has signed an Agreement for cooperation in the peaceful uses of nuclear energy[3].

In addition to this, there is a Community programme on **protection against radiation**, namely health protection measures for the population in general and workers in particular against the dangers of ionizing radiation (Chapter III, Euratom). Community Directives set basic standards for the protection of public health and worker health against the dangers inherent in ionizing radiation[4] and organize the monitoring of transfers of radioactive waste between the Member States and on entrance to and exit from the Community[5]. Finally, the Community is active in the field of research on reactor safety which, as seen in the previous chapter, is conducted in the Joint Research Centre and in specialized national research centres. The harmonization of safety criteria and practices in the Member States produced significant results, particularly with regard to the seismic re-evaluation of nuclear power stations and to highly-automated safeguards systems.

These various nuclear safeguards were reinforced after the Chernobyl accident in April 1986. Furthermore, since 1990, the Commission has initiated an inter-European cooperation for the exploitation of nuclear installations. The cooperation notably relates to nuclear safeguards in the countries of Central and Eastern Europe and in the Commonwealth of Independent States (CIS). This cooperation has allowed the Euratom Safeguards Directorate to become better acquainted with specific features of the nuclear capacity of the former Soviet Union, chiefly with regard to the mixed (civil/military) nature of the installations. The Euratom Safeguards Directorate offers the services of its specialists to assist in training CIS inspectors and thus provide a sufficiently high level of materials safeguards. The PHARE and TACIS programmes help the countries of Central and Eastern Europe and those of the former Soviet Union improve the safety of their nuclear installations. Moreover, the Commission is empowered to use Euratom borrowings to finance projects which increase the safety of nuclear power stations in many of these countries[6].

In 1995, the resumption by France of underground nuclear testing in Polynesia sparked off a serious controversy between the Member States of the EU as well as a debate about the role of the Union institutions in relation to the measures to protect the populations and the environment against such testing. A verification mission of the Euratom Safeguards Directorate in French Polynesia confirmed that the facilities established by the French authorities to carry out continuous monitoring of the level of radioactivity in the environment pursuant to Article 35 of the Euratom Treaty were operating efficiently. After evaluating the information provided by the French authorities, the Commission decided that Article 34 of the Euratom Treaty, concerning a "particularly dangerous" situation, did not apply in this case; but it asked France to give more substantial undertakings concerning the monitoring of the level of radioactivity at the sites. On its part, the European Parliament reiterated in several Resolutions its strong opposition to French and Chinese nuclear tests[7].

---

1   See, e.g., OJ L88, 03.04.1992
2   COM (94)362, 8 September 1994.
3   OJ L120, 20.05.1996.
4   OJ L159, 29.06.1996.
5   OJ L35, 12.02.1992.
6   OJ L84, 29.03.1994.
7   OJ C166, 03.07.1995 and OJ C269, 16.10.1995.

Oil market

The EEC Treaty governing oil stipulated that at the end of the transitional period, all quantitative restrictions to trade between Member States
and all measures having equivalent effect should be abolished. Tariff
obstacles to trade in petroleum products were phased out in July 1968. On
the external market, the Common Customs Tariff has set a zero rate for oil
and very low rates for refined products. The latter were further reduced
in the framework of the General Agreement on Tariffs and Trade (GATT).
All the freedoms written into the Treaty of Rome, such as freedom of
establishment and the freedom to provide services, are applicable in the
oil sector.

Although the **common oil market** is not yet perfect, petroleum products can move freely from Member State to Member State. The big oil
companies have been able to build refineries at certain nerve centres in the
common market to supply refined products to networks covering neighbouring regions in two or more Member States. When unexpected demand
for a particular product arises on a regional or national market, which
cannot be covered by local refineries, companies call on the services of
refineries situated elsewhere in the Community. This means that refinery
production and distribution activities can be rationalized to meet supply
in surrounding regions without regard for the dividing lines represented
by national frontiers. Oil and gas pipelines consequently start their journey
from the major ports of the Mediterranean and the North Sea, cut across
one or several Member States and supply crude oil to the refineries of
different oil companies situated in another Member State. Before the
creation of the common market, it would have been unthinkable for a
European state to entrust the supply of as vital a product as oil to the
benevolence of one or several neighbouring countries. The European
Community has rendered self-evident certain situations which would
have been inconceivable just after the war.

It must be said, however, that in an internal market organized in the same manner as
a national market, **price differences** for oil products, other than those due to transport costs,
should logically only have been marginal and temporary, as they should have been corrected
by the transfer of products from low-price to high-price regions in a short period of time.
This is not yet the case in the internal market of the European Union where the pre-tax price
differences for petroleum products are still important. Thus, for example, in 1993, 1000 liters
of premium gasoline without taxes were priced at ECU 179 in France and 258 in Denmark,
1000 liters of automotive diesel were costing ECU 186 in France and 271 in Ireland, the price
of these products in the other EU countries varying between these extremes. The specificities
of the oil market account in part for these price differences. In most cases, oil products are
transported at prices which do not make allowance for market conditions in the country of
destination. This may be due to the **oligopolistic structure of the oil industry** and in
particular to the sales policy of the large companies which have a near 80% market share.
While the oil multinationals are capable of trading petroleum products on a large scale, they
do so at subsidiary-to-subsidiary transfer prices which do not upset the conditions on each
specific market.

The levelling out of petroleum product prices in the internal common market has also
come to grief on different **price regulations** existing in the Member States. In the majority of
countries, these regulations set the maximum prices at which the main petroleum products
can be sold and are powerful economic and energy policy instruments. The problem is that
there is no one simple formula for setting petroleum product prices and energy policy

priorities vary from Member State to Member State. As a consequence, there is considerable variation in maximum price systems. The system which exists in a particular country influences the market policy of large oil companies and particularly the production cut in the refineries. Since the production cut is relatively flexible, it is in the interests of oil companies to produce larger quantities of the products which they can sell at a high price on any market at a given moment, while keeping prices within the ceilings stipulated by regulations.

Prior to the substantial fiscal harmonization made necessary by the completion of the internal market, differences in the prices of petroleum products were due primarily to the **different rates and structures of taxes**, notably excise duties collected on petroleum products. Excise duties represented a large fixed sum in the sales price of car fuel and domestic heating oil. A company seeking a larger market share would have had to slash cost prices of these products to achieve a small difference in tax-inclusive sales price. This was difficult to achieve for small and medium-sized oil companies, which might otherwise have attempted to exercise price pressure to obtain a stronger market presence. With the harmonization of rates of VAT and excise duties on mineral oils, the situation is certainly improved, concerning in particular the free movement of these products[1]; but the actual rates applied to mineral oils in the Member States still vary considerably and create distortions of competition at the level of consumer prices. There is therefore a need for a greater approximation of the rates of excise duties on petroleum products.

Energy supply

At the beginning of the fifties, the Community's energy economy revolved around indigenous resources, chiefly coal. In 1955, coal met 64% of gross internal energy consumption in the then Community; but little by little, demand switched from primary energy to processed energy, chiefly electricity and petroleum products. Due to strong growth in demand for light petroleum products, heavy fuels became residual products which refiners wanted to get rid of at any price, often below that of crude oil. Unfortunately for coal, these heavy, industrial use fuels were its main competitor.

From around 1960, oil became the decisive energy source in the Community. By 1966, it represented more than half of energy consumption in the then six Member States. By 1970, it had risen to more than 60% compared with 23% for coal. In that oil was almost exclusively imported from third countries, the consequences on the Community's energy independence were plain to see. Energy independence was sacrificed on the alter of rapid industrial growth, stimulated by low energy prices.

The crisis at the end of 1973 brutally highlighted the Community's energy problem and the soaring prices resulting from it aggravated the situation. The problem was structural and not short term. By 1973, in fact, the Community was 63% **dependent on third countries for energy supplies.** The energy crisis clearly illustrated the extent to which the economies of the Community countries and even their political decision-making independence could be jeopardized by a group of countries who held in their grip the bulk of energy supply. Even after the crisis had begun to attenuate, the problem of energy dependence remained.

Security of energy supply is defined as the possibility to ensure the continued satisfaction of essential energy needs by means of, on the one hand, sufficient internal resources exploited under acceptable economic conditions and, on the other, of accessible, stable and diversified external sources. With this definition, the security of supply of the Union is still not satisfactory. Despite its indisputable efforts during two decades, the improvement of its energy efficiency and the important reduction of its dependence from oil and oil products, the EU still depends from external sources for around 50% of its total energy supply. If supply conditions are

---

1   See the chapter on Taxation.

to be improved, the proportion of imported energy has to be reduced, energy use rationalized as much as possible and turned more and more towards renewable energy sources. These developments would not only increase the security of energy supply, but would also reduce the general cost of energy, if the external costs of traditional energy sources, associated with environment pollution, acidification, climate change and health risks, were taken into account. These issues are examined in the following pages.

Energy objectives and rational energy use

Following a number of Communications and proposals made by the Commission with the aim of easing the impact of the crisis, the Council adopted, in December 17, 1974, a Resolution on Community energy policy objectives. The Resolution set the aim of reduction to 50% and if possible to 40% of the Community's dependence on imported energy by 1985, from the level of 63% in 1973[1]. In order to achieve this, the Council adopted on the same day a Resolution on a **Community action programme** in the area of rational energy use[2].

In the framework of this Programme, the Council then adopted provisions on summer-time arrangements[3], which it was felt could save electricity, and numerous Recommendations on the rational use of energy consumed: by road vehicles, in urban passenger transport or for electrical household appliances[4]; in industrial undertakings[5] and in the building sector[6]. Referring to the new framework energy-saving programme implemented in 1980[7], the Council recommended that the Member States improve energy-saving programmes[8] and adopted a Directive on crude-oil savings through the use of substitute fuel components in petrol[9]. On its part, the PACE programme aims at promoting the efficient utilization of electricity[10].

The **harmonization of measures** taken by the Member States sought to ensure that standards for rational energy use did not become new technical barriers to the free movement of goods and did not distort competition within the common market. Such harmonization was achieved, for example, through a 1978 Directive on the performance of heat generators for space heating and the production of hot water in new or existing non-industrial buildings[11], and through a 1980 Directive on the alignment of legislation covering the fuel consumption of motor vehicles[12].

In 1991, the Community launched a legislative programme on the **promotion of energy efficiency (SAVE)**[13]. The aim is to reduce energy intensity per unit of GNP by 20% over the next five years and thus save energy while protecting the environment against carbon dioxide emissions. The Community also provides financial support for measures of the Member States aiming to extend or create energy efficiency infrastructure and those designed to change consumer behaviour. As part of the SAVE programme, the Council has already adopted: a Directive on the stand-

1   OJ C153, 09.07.1975.
2   Ibid.
3   OJ L205, 07.08.1980 and OJ L164, 30.06.1994.
4   OJ L140, 28.05.1980.
5   OJ L239, 12.09.1980.
6   OJ C78, 26.03.1985.
7   OJ C149, 18.06.1980.
8   OJ C20, 22.01.1985.
9   OJ L334, 12.12.1985.
10   OJ L157, 09.06.1989 and COM (95)225, 31 May 1995.
11   OJ L52, 23.02.1978.
12   OJ L375, 31.12.1980.
13   OJ L307, 08.11.1991 and OJ C346, 23.12.1995.

ardization of efficiency requirements for new hot-water boilers fired with liquid or gaseous fuels[1]; a Directive allowing consumers to choose the most energy-efficient domestic appliances, thanks to a label indicating their consumption of energy and other resources[2]; a Directive aiming to limit carbon dioxide emissions by improving energy efficiency[3]; and a Directive on energy efficiency requirements for household electric refrigerators, freezers and combinations thereof[4]. In this context, the Commission has adopted a Directive concerning the energy labeling of refrigerators and freezers[5].

Thanks in part to these various measures and in part to the reduction of energy demand, the increase of internal production - notably in the North Sea - and the diversification of the Community's suppliers, energy supply in the 90s registers considerable improvements. The EU imports about half of its total energy needs compared with two thirds twenty years ago. However, despite these improvements, the problems have not gone away. The European Union still has to cope with a massive oil bill, vast amounts of investment, the implications for environmental protection and energy dependence which cannot be reduced in any significant manner in the medium term.

This is why, the Commission is proposing more drastic measures. Since 1992 it has proposed a strategy for reducing carbon dioxide (CO_2) emissions by the introduction of a tax based on the consumption of carbon dioxide[6]. Such a tax would increase the prices of energy, except for renewable source, and contribute to saving energy. It would thus set in motion dynamic changes, which would have beneficial consequences for the environment and major impacts on the Union's energy sector. This proposal is still under discussion within the Council, because it presents obvious difficulties, particularly due to its effects on the competitiveness of European industries compared to that of their competitors in the world. Other energy consuming countries should be persuaded to follow the Community's policies in this area; but this would not be easy.

Coal supply

Regular supply of the common market is the prime objective of the **ECSC Treaty**, defined in its Article 3. Chapter IV of the Treaty outlines measures to be taken in the event of shortage, notably through the sharing out of ECSC resources among the industries covered by its jurisdiction. Coal supply was imperative for European reconstruction and economic growth at the time of creation of the European Coal and Steel Community. Community coal, which played the lead role on the energy stage in the fifties, was relegated by the

1   OJ L167, 22.06.1992.
2   OJ L297, 13.10.1992.
3   OJ L237, 22.09.1993.
4   OJ C120, 24.04.1996.
5   OJ L45, 17.02.1994.
6   COM (92)226, 27.05.1992.

beginning of the sixties to the support one by the newcomer to the scene, oil. Three phases can be identified in the evolution of the common coal market: growth period (1953-1957), a period of retreat (1958-1973) and a period of stabilization, which began with the October 1973 oil crisis and with the fivefold increase in the price of all energies in the space of a few months. Many German and British coal mines have since got back onto a competitive footing. But the cost prices of the majority of Community mines are still too high, and they still require support under a Community system of aid from the Member States in favour of the coal industry[1].

The Council's Recommendations of May 24, 1983 on promoting investments in the use of solid fuels in industry, public buildings and urban heating systems[2] have perhaps given a boost to coal, but the main determinant factor concerning its use is the price of heating oil. Thus, in the early 90s, a new contraction of the Community market for solid fuels was registered owing to the decline in internal hard coal deliveries and imports from third countries.

On the basis of Article 55 of the ECSC Treaty the Commission grants aid to technical coal research projects. In March 1994, the Commission has redefined the medium-term (1994-1999) guidelines for technical research covering mining engineering and coal utilization[3].

Coal is the most abundant non-renewable energy source available and will continue to play a very important role as a regulator of the Union's energy market, particularly in the generation of energy. In any case, the European Union does not face a problem in coal supply, both as far as indigenous resources are concerned, which are abundant, and imports from several third countries, which are more competitive. In this connection, it should be noted that Article 71 of the ECSC Treaty excludes Community competence in the trade of coal since it stipulates that "the competence of the governments of Member States on commercial policy is not affected by the application of the Treaty...". This provision is, today, without practical consequence, since there is not more restriction in the Member States on coal imports and any imported coal released for free movement in a Member State circulates freely in all the Community. In any case, after the expiration of the ECSC Treaty, the common commercial policy of the EC will also cover the coal products.

Oil and natural gas supply

If the ECSC Treaty expressly rules out a common trade policy for coal, the EEC Treaty does the same by omission for oil and natural gas. The general clauses under the title "trade policy" clearly could not form the basis of a supply policy for products as important as oil and natural gas. The **EEC Treaty** did not even give the Community institutions the possibility of collecting and publishing information of vital importance for the common oil market, such as those covering investments, production or imports, as is done by the ECSC and Euratom Treaties for their respective

1   OJ L329, 30.12.1993.
2   OJ L140, 31.05.1983.
3   OJ C67, 04.03.1994.

areas. In light of the growing importance of oil in the sixties, this vacuum had to be filled.

A Directive introducing an information and consultation procedure on the prices of crude oil and petroleum products in the Community was adopted in 1976[1]. On the basis of the information thus collected, the Commission draws up and passes on to the Member States every quarter **summary data on prices** of crude oil and petroleum products and on the comparison of oil supply costs and ex-refinery revenue. The Council adopted in 1979 a Regulation introducing the **registration of crude oil imports and petroleum products** in the Community[2]. On the basis of this Regulation and one specifying the rules under which registration of crude oil imports into the Community is carried out[3], the Member States notify the Commission of information revealing the terms at which imports have taken place. This information system was improved in the 1980s in the framework of the International Energy Agency, and it contributes to the transparency of the Community's oil market.

The collection and dissemination of all this information by the Commission would be pointless if not accompanied by joint measures to be taken by the Member States in the event of oil and gas supply difficulties. These measures take the shape notably of the **strategic storage of petroleum products**. A Council Directive of December 1972 obliges the Member States to maintain a minimum stock level of 90 days' consumption for crude oil and/or petroleum products, as a buffer against the effects of accidental or deliberate interruption in supplies and against the economic and political leverage enjoyed by suppliers[4].

Fresh measures designed to cope with supply difficulties were introduced in 1977: a Council Decision relating to the **export of crude oil and petroleum products** from one Member State to another was adopted, establishing a Community procedure to check that these exports were compatible with the parallel mechanism of the International Energy Agency[5]; and a Council Decision was taken setting a Community target for the reduction of primary energy consumption in the event of supply difficulties of crude oil and petroleum products in order to ensure that these difficulties were spread fairly among all consumers[6].

Thanks to these various measures, to the massive exploitation of British oil in the eighties and to crude oil savings achieved by the use of substitute fuels in the framework of a 1985 Council Directive[7], at the end of the eighties, net oil imports represented around 40% of gross energy consumption in the Community and 80% of its crude oil consumption. Thanks to the reduced dependency and the diversification of supply sources, Community supply of oil and natural gas was undoubtedly better guaranteed at the beginning of the nineties than at the beginning of the seventies, as demonstrated by the lack of panic in response to the Gulf crisis at the end of 1990, sparked by Iraq's invasion of Kuwait. However, the Community is still vulnerable as regards its oil and natural gas supply and lacks a genuine policy in this field. National governments continue to guard their prerogatives jealously, thanks, notably, to the subsidiarity principle. This is why, on 29 October 1991, the Council stated the need for a new approach to the management of oil crises in the context of the IEA, in which the Community would speak with one voice.

In the context of the completion of the internal market, a Directive on the conditions for granting and using **authorizations for oil and gas**

---

1   OJ L140, 28.05.1976.
2   OJ L220, 30.08.1979 and OJ L133, 24.05.1990.
3   OJ L297, 24.11.1979.
4   OJ L291, 28.12.1972.
5   OJ L61, 05.03.1977.
6   OJ L292, 16.11.1977.
7   OJ L334, 12.12.1985.

prospecting, exploration and extraction is designed to ensure non-discriminatory access to and pursuit of these activities under conditions which encourage greater competition in this sector[1]. However, Member States have sovereign rights over oil and gas resources on their territories. They therefore retain the right to determine the areas within their territory to be made available for oil and gas prospecting, exploration and production.

Supply of nuclear fuels

Supply of nuclear fuels is a matter dealt with in some depth in the **Euratom Treaty**. Article 52 of this Treaty stipulates that supply of ores, source materials and special fissile materials is accomplished with respect of the principle of equal access to resources and through a common supply policy. For this purpose, all practices which seek to provide certain users with a privileged position are forbidden. The Treaty set up a **Supply Agency,** the organization of which is explained in Articles 53 and 54. The Agency, which has legal status and is financially independent, is governed by Statutes adopted by the Council on the basis of a Commission proposal. The Euratom Supply Agency is under the control of the Commission, which issues it with policy guidelines, has a right of veto on its decisions and appoints its Director General[2]. In contrast with the coal and oil sectors, a common supply policy in the nuclear sector is exercised by the Agency, under the control of the Commission. In fact, the option right of the Agency, described in Article 57 EAEC, gives it de jure a monopoly on the trade of ores, raw materials and special fissile materials intended for peaceful nuclear use in the Community. In 1995, the Court of First Instance stressed that the Agency has the discretion to refuse to conclude supply contracts which could run counter to attainment of the objectives of the Euratom Treaty[3].

Article 52 grants the Agency two fundamental rights: (a) an option right on ores, source material and special fissile materials produced in the Member States and (b) the exclusive right to conclude contracts for the supply of ores, source materials and special fissile materials originating inside or outside the Community. The Agency's main role is to act as an **intermediary between producers and users.** Under Article 60, possible users inform the Agency periodically of their supply needs, specifying quantities, nature, places of origin, uses, price terms and so on, which would form the clauses of a contract which they would like to conclude. Producers inform the Agency of the supplies which they can put on the market, with all their specifications and notably the duration of the contracts. The Agency informs all potential users of supplies and of the demand volume brought to its attention, and invites them to order. Once it has all the orders, it makes known the terms at which they can be satisfied.

The Agency, acting in the framework of agreements concluded between the Community and a third country or international organization, has the exclusive right **to conclude agreements** whose main object is the supply of ores, source materials or special fissile materials originating outside the Community (Article 64). In 1962, the Agency set this in motion by concluding a framework contract with the United States Atomic Energy Commis-

---

1   OJ L164, 30.06.1994.

2   OJ 32 11.05.1960 and OJ L193, 25.07.1975.

3   Judgment of 15 September 1995, cases T-458/93 and T-523/93, Empresa Nacional de Uranio v Commission.

sion (USAEC) enabling Community undertakings to obtain enriched uranium at good price, regularity and safety terms. Since then the contract has been renewed and simplified as regards administrative formalities for the purchase of special fissile materials and other contracts have been concluded, notably with Canada and Australia, enabling the Community to diversify its supply sources in nuclear materials.

The bulk of Community supply continues to come via multiannual contracts, but due to the fact that the requirements of electricity companies for natural uranium and short- and medium-term enrichment services are now by and large met, very few long-term contracts are now concluded. The Agency rather concludes on spot purchases and swap transactions. The Community's level of dependence on imports of natural uranium is over 70% and its main supplier is the former Soviet Union, but there are eight external supplier countries and none accounts for more than 25% of total supplies.

The producers in the Community (natural uranium producers, converters and enrichers) express, however, their concern about the willingness of the independent States of the former Soviet Union to increase their share of the market in natural uranium and in conversion and enrichment services, particularly through swap transactions. They feel that their future viability is under threat from these low-cost supplies eroding their market shares. The Euratom Supply Agency is, therefore, encouraging users to revert to the practice of concluding long-term contracts at prices covering production costs and limiting specific contracts to the coverage of unexpected needs. Following a flexible and pragmatic approach, the Agency particularly encourages electricity companies to diversify their sources of supply in order to avoid excessive dependence on any one particular source.

New technologies and new energy sources

New energy technologies offer an alternative route to supply security. Since the middle of the seventies, the Commission has been providing financial support for technological development in the oil and natural gas sectors and for demonstration projects in the fields of energy savings and new energy sources. These various measures are now integrated in the **JOULE/THERMIE programme**, which has the double aim of promoting the use of indigenous energy sources and of reducing the environmental emissions, notably carbon dioxide (CO_2) emissions. Under this specific programme in the field of non-nuclear energy of the fourth RTD framework programme (1994-1998), projects that promote energy technology in the fields of the rational use of energy, renewable energies, solid fuels (clean technologies) and hydrocarbons (exploration and development) can be granted Community financial support[1]. This can be provided to projects focusing upon the development, application and/or promotion of energy technologies of an advanced innovative nature and whose high technical and economic risks would render their implementation improbable without Community financial support. A network of organizations for the promotion of energy technologies (OPET) covering almost all the Community's regions helps the Commission to implement the programme.

The security of the energy supplies of the Community can also be increased through the promotion of **new and renewable energies** (solar, wind, hydroelectric, geothermal, biomass). In addition, these energies can generate economic activity, thereby creating added value and employment in Europe, they both improve the quality of the environment and standards of living, and they are particularly important for the less developed regions of the EU, which have considerable potential for the development

---

1   OJ L334, 22.12.1994. See the chapter on research.

of renewable energy resources. For these reasons, in 1988, the Council adopted a Recommendation to the Member States on the exploitation of renewable energies in the Community. It seeks to clear the main obstacles to their use which, aside from technical progress still to be made in the framework of technological programmes, relate chiefly to the simplification and acceleration of procedures, the dissemination of information on their potential and technical possibilities for working resources, the extending of markets and possibilities for selling the electricity produced by renewable energies via the public sector network[1].

The promotion of renewable energies is the objective of the **ALTENER programme**, which focuses among other things on legislation and standardization to accelerate the maturity of the market for renewable energies such as hydroelectric power, biofuels and biomass[2]. The objectives of this programme, are to increase the share of renewable energies from the present 4% to 8% of the final demand and to achieve a reduction in carbon dioxide emissions of 150 million tons in 2005. To this end, the programme aims to increase the contribution of renewable energy resources to the coverage of total energy demand, to treble the production of electricity from renewable energy sources other than large hydro-electric power stations, and to increase biofuels' share of the market (cereals, oil seeds, pulses, beets and biomass energy).

Appraisal and Outlook

There is a general impression that Community energy policy is nonexistent or at best inefficient. This impression arises chiefly from confusion between energy policy and oil supply policy. The latter is clearly of vital importance and is still lacking. But it is only a part of energy policy. It cannot be denied that the common coal, oil and nuclear energy markets has been largely achieved thanks to Community policy. But their existence tends to be taken for granted and similarly significant achievements are expected in the area of supply, notably oil supply. The fact that the EEC Treaty did not provide for such a policy is often forgotten. The Treaty rarely set objectives in areas not viewed as vital for the completion of the common market and at the time oil did not swing the economic weight which it acquired in the coming years. Another fact often overlooked is that in the sixties, all the Member States chose to boost industrial growth through low energy prices rather than promoting indigenous energy production by high prices. This preference for the industrial rather than energy sector culminated, at Community level, in a system diametrically opposed to that existing for agriculture. It was a political decision, the advantages of which cannot be denied, even with hindsight of the post-1973 events.

---

1   OJ L160, 28.06.1988.
2   OJ L235, 18.09.1993.

It must also be acknowledged that the system of production licences for international oil companies lulled everyone into the idea that energy supply security was not a problem as such, and despite the Commission's warnings to the contrary, the threat of crisis passed unnoticed until 1973. But even after the illusion was shattered, at the end of 1973, the policies conducted by the Member States separately and by the Community as a whole were for many years fragmented, reflecting different national energy situations. The Member States, and this is their main failing, have proven unable to conduct a coherent policy towards their main oil suppliers.

Nonetheless, after 1974 supply security moved to the top of priorities in the Council's Resolutions on energy policy and targets were set for the reduction of dependence on imported oil. The Community adopted measures to give it a clearer insight into the oil market, tightened up compulsory storage provisions, set up mechanisms to defuse crisis both before and after the horse had bolted, financed technological development projects to work the oil resources in the North Sea and rationalized energy consumption. This policy has been a considerable success, with the Community attaining its main objective of reducing to around 40% dependence on imported oil. As a consequence, at the peak of the Gulf crisis in January 1991, the Community had at its disposal oil reserves representing more than 100 days of consumption and therefore enjoyed a breathing space of several weeks before it would have been obliged to take the binding measures provided for in the crisis mechanism of the International Energy Agency. This fact helped to prevent any upsurge of panic in the Community.

Thanks to the reduction of dependence from imported oil and to the diversification of fuels, the Union is now in a much more comfortable situation than the one the Community has experienced in the mid-seventies. But this situation could possibly change by the increasing use of imported fuels. Given the different energy situations and energy policies of the Member States, a sharp shift away from the present favourable world energy situation could have a catastrophic impact on the internal market and on the economies of the Union. This is why, a Community energy policy framework is needed in which Member States are working towards agreed common objectives, notably the development of nuclear, renewable sources and clean technologies, assisted by Community financial and fiscal measures.

Energy is certainly an important factor determining the economic performance of a country or of a group of countries such as the EU. However, economic performance is not measured only by industrial competitiveness, but also by the welfare of citizens taking account of the employment situation and the state of the environment. Therefore, the Community's Fifth Action Programme for Sustainable Development takes the view that the best and most efficient way of integrating environmental concerns would be the internalization of external costs and benefits, which still charge the society at large with a large part of the cost of polluting activities. The internalization of external costs could be achieved through fiscal measures such as the CO_2/energy tax proposed by the Commission, but since such a tax would risk to penalize the European industry alone, whereas all polluting industries of developed countries should be equally concerned, the EU should use its international weight to persuade other major industrial competitors to follow suit.

Bibliography on energy policy

◻ BOUTTES Jean-Paul, HAAG Denis, "L'électricité: l'intégration européenne d'une industrie de réseau", *Économie et statistique*, INSEE, Paris, N 266, 1993, pp. 21-30.

◻ COMMISSION EUROPÉENNE, *Le marché intérieur de l'énergie*, série "Marché intérieur", Volume 3, 1993.

- *Orientations communautaires en matière de réseaux transeuropéens d'énergie*, COM (93) 685, 19.01.1994.

- *Le premier traité de la Charte européenne de l'énergie: De nouvelles perspectives d'investissement*, OPOCE, Luxembourg, 1994.

- *Pour une politique énergétique de l'union européenne: Livre vert*, OPOCE, Luxembourg 1995.

◻ DUMOULIN M., GUILLEN P., VAISSE M., *L'énergie nucléaire en Europe. Des origines à Euratom*, Peter Lang, Berne, 1994.

◻ EUROPEAN COMMISSION, *Energy in Europe: Energy Policies and Trends in the European Union*, Bi-annual publication.

- *Energy in Europe: Community Assistance in the Energy Sector to the Countries of Central and Eastern Europe and the Former Soviet Union*, OOPEC, Luxembourg, August 1993.

- *Energy Prices 1973-1993. A Survey of Consumer Prices for Gas, Electricity and Oil in the Community up to July 1993*, OOPEC, Luxembourg, 1994.

- *The European Renewable Energy Study: Prospects for Renewable Energy in the European Community and Eastern Europe up to 2010*, 4 Volumes, OOPEC, Luxembourg, 1994.

- *An Energy Policy for the European Union: White Paper*, COM (95) 682, 13. 12. 1995.

◻ GALLEGO Martin, JONES David, *The Internal Market for Energy*, Brussels, Centre for European Policy Studies, 1992.

◻ HANCHER Leigh (ed.), *The European Energy Market: Reconciling Competition and Security of Supply*, Academy of European Law, Trier, 1995.

◻ HELM Dieter, *Major Economic Issues Raised by the Creation of the Internal Energy Market*, Oxford Economic Research Associates Ltd, Oxford, 1992.

◻ HOUSE OF LORDS, *Structure of the Single Market for Energy, with Evidence*, HMSO, London, 1993.

□   KNOX Richard, *New Renewable Energy Sources - Technical Realities and Commercial Opportunities*, MDIS Publ., Chichester, 1993.

□   McGOWAN Francis, *The Struggle for Power in Europe: Competition and Regulation in the EC Electricity Industry*, The Royal Institute of International Affairs, London, 1993.

□   MONNIER Lionel, "L'organisation du secteur électrique dans la Communauté européenne", in *Annales de l'économie publique sociale et coopérative*, Liège, Vol. 64, N 4, 1993, pp. 531-573.

□   PADGETT Stephen, "The Single European Energy Market: the Policies of Realization", in *Journal of Common Market Studies*, Oxford, Vol. 30, N 1, March 1992, pp. 53-75.

□   ROMIEU Michel, "L'Europe du gaz: vers la maturité", *Défense nationale*, 52e année, février 1996, pp. 43-53.

12. TRANSPORT

The Treaty of Rome set the objective of a common policy for the transport sector, but what has emerged is a Community policy, i.e. a policy restricted to the harmonization and integration of national policies. This is the crux of the problem in the transport sector: because the official texts speak of a "common transport policy", its achievements as a "Community" policy are not fully appreciated.

This said, it must be emphasized that the EEC Treaty only sought a common policy for inland transport, namely roads, rail and inland waterways. The concept of a common transport market was consequently limited from the outset to inland transport and more specifically, in light of the highly specific situation of railway and inland waterway undertakings, to road transport. However road haulage services represent by far the bulk of goods carriage in the European Community. They clearly have a strategic role to play in enabling the free movement of goods and persons in the single market. As will be seen below, the Council has finally recognized this simple truth and has accomplished the internal market for road transport.

In addition to the integration of inland transport markets, Community policy in this area seeks to organize the various means of transport in accordance with "Community rules", in other words measures tending towards the approximation of the economic conditions and the structures of each mode of transport in the Member States. For many years, the Community institutions concentrated upon road haulage rates, but achievements are thin on the ground. The aim in the railway sector was to improve the financial situation, but the many provisions adopted with this aim in mind have, thus far, had little impact. By way of contrast, sea and air transport which only made their entrance onto the Community stage in the middle of the seventies, have seen spectacular progress recently, not only in the completion of the internal market in these sectors, but also of their Community organization.

Nowadays, the priority in the transport sector is moving towards infrastructures and, in particular, trans-European networks, which will help complete the internal market by reinforcing the links between the Member States. These networks will also permit: better, safer travel at lower cost, thus improving both industrial competitiveness and quality of life; effective planning in Europe, thus avoiding a concentration of wealth and population; and bridge-building towards Eastern Europe, which is essential in order to promote trade and prepare their accession to the Union.

Legal and economic framework

The **EEC Treaty** stipulated that, in all, three common policies should be established: agricultural policy, trade policy and transport policy (Article 3). Title IV of its second part entitled "Foundations of the Community" was devoted to transport policy. It stated that common policy in the transport sector would be implemented via common rules applicable to international transport, through the admission of non-resident transport operators to the national transport market and through all other appropriate provisions (Article 75). According to the Treaty, aid which responded to the need for the coordination of transport services or for the reimbursement for the discharge of certain obligations inherent in the concept of public service would be compatible with the common market. It ordered the gradual abolition of discrimination which took the form of carriers charging different rates and imposing different conditions for the carriage of the same goods over the same transport links on grounds of the country of origin or destination of the country in question (Article 79). Finally, it banned the imposition by a Member State of rates and conditions involving any element of support or protection in the interest of one or more particular undertaking or industry, unless authorized by the Commission (Article 80).

The Treaty of Rome showed special interest in the transport sector for three reasons. First of all, economic integration was expected to lead to growth in trade and consequently in transport flows. The Treaty therefore saw the transport sector as one of the major motors of economic integration. Secondly, transport costs, which put a serious strain on the cost price of certain goods, could act as a barrier to trade or a source of discrimination between European undertakings. Last but not least, the transport sector involves 40% of public investment in the Member States. Routing choices for means of communication, their construction and use have considerable impact on regional development, the environment, town and country planning, traffic safety and energy consumption. Coordination of investment decisions can eliminate the risk of works whose socio-economic profitability is not sufficient and can open the way to the economies of scale offered by the wider internal market.

It is worth bearing in mind that transport and communications are in themselves a major economic sector, employing 6 million people in the European Union and representing around 7% of its GNP (compared with 5% for agriculture, for example). In as much, it merits the attention which can encourage its deployment at European level. The healthy operation of the transport sector depends to a large extent on healthy trade and business in the EU. Investments, whether they originate from the public sector (construction of transport infrastructure) or from the private one (all kinds of means of transport), indisputably affect employment in the industrial sector. Finally, the testing of technological innovations in the transport sector (aircraft, high speed trains, underwater tunnels, etc.) stimulates innovation in industry in general. It is not a coincidence that apart from the specific programme of research and technological development in the transport sector, four of the six research/industry task forces, constituted in the framework of the Community policy on R&TD concern transport (car of tomorrow, new-generation aircraft, train of the future and transport intermodality)[1].

Transport is an industry of the future whose main growth factors are: structural changes in the manufacturing industry, which is transferring its production sites from urban areas to new industrial sites; the evolution of production methods, which encourages stock reduction and more flexible, more varied and more rapid delivery systems; the increasing importance of the services sector and the dispersion of its activities to multiple sites, which stimulates professional mobility; the increase in income levels and the evolution of demographic structures, which boosts demand for leisure, tourism and family reunions.

Special aspects of the transport sector

Although the authors of the EEC Treaty felt that a common transport sector was necessary, they restricted its scope from two angles. First of all, Article 83 excluded sea and air transport from the provisions of Title IV (transport), which thus became applicable solely to the three modes of inland transport: rail, road and waterways. However, Article 84 stipulated that the Council, acting unanimously, could extend the appropriate provisions to sea and air transport.

Article 61 furthermore excluded transport from the general provisions governing the free movement of services. Article 75 stipulates that the common policy should make allowance for the **"special aspects of the transport sector"**. These special aspects were that (a) transport undertakings were dependent upon infrastructure voted and built by the States; (b) that in general, competition was between large state controlled railway monopolies and a multitude of small road haulage and inland waterway transport operators; (c) that the State required certain undertakings, notably the railways, to fulfil public service obligations, which distort competition conditions; and (d) that supply and demand were extremely rigid in this sector.

The situation was most complex in the **road transport sector,** which represents 80% of goods carriage between the Member States. Depending on the routes, international road traffic was either restriction free or subject to prior authorization or to the granting of authorizations in the framework of a quota. Authorization issuing provisions (length of validity, possibility of return trip loaded) varied from one route to the next. The

---

1   OJ L361, 31.12.1994. See the chapter on research.

conditions governing Community transit differed from one State to the next and provisions relating to combined rail/road transport were practically nonexistent.

Although the Treaty excluded transport from the general liberalization of services, it was not with the aim of ruling out liberalization in this sector but rather of recommending its **specific liberalization** in the framework of the common policy. The question was then whether the Treaty rules defined elsewhere than in Title IV were applicable to the transport sector. France and the Commission clashed on this point. The matter was settled by a Court of Justice ruling in 1974 which established that, in the absence of specific rules drawn up in the framework of the common transport policy, general rules on the right of establishment, the free movement of goods, labour and capital, tax provisions and so on were well and truly applicable to the transport sector. As regards more specifically the sea and air transport sectors, the Court stated that even if, in the absence of a Decision taken by virtue of Article 84, paragraph 2, these sectors were excluded from the rules of Title IV in the second part of Treaty which deal with transport, they were subject to the general rules of the Treaty, namely those governing freedom of movement, competition, aid, social policy and taxation[1].

Belated departure after Parliament's instigation

Fifteen years and the helping hand of the Court's rulings were needed to shed some light on certain fundamental areas of transport policy which the Treaty either deliberately or accidentally left vague. This gave enough excuse for those against change to dig in their heels and reject measures which, they maintained, would upset **competition conditions** between the various modes of transport and inside each one of them.

The Commission was aiming precisely at a level playing field for competition among transporters. Since 1961, the Commission had been attempting, in the absence of precise instructions in the Treaty, to define an overall and consistent concept for the organization of the transport market at Community level. Certainly, the Council had adopted between 1968 and 1970 some vital provisions to harmonize competition conditions. But it had failed to resolve the pivotal issue for economic integration of this sector, namely **free access to the market** of one Member State for road haulage operators from other Member States, access which would stimulate competition and improve market conditions. Transport Ministers had in fact spent some twenty years trying to resolve the philosophical question of whether market liberalization or harmonization of competition conditions should come first.

The clear lack of political commitment to creating a "common" transport policy eventually exasperated the European Parliament. With the support of the European Commission, it adopted a Resolution relating **to proceedings for failure to act** (Article 175 of the EEC Treaty) against the Council on September 16, 1982. The Parliament stated, indeed, that only minimum provisions had been adopted in the area of transport policy, falling well short of the objectives set in the Treaty, particularly in Articles 3 and 74. The judgment delivered by the Court of Justice on May 22, 1985 was a partial success for the Parliament and the Commission[2]. The Court established that the Council had, in violation of the Treaty, failed to ensure the free provision of services in the area of international transport and to define conditions for the admission of non-resident transport operators to the national transport market of a Member State. The Court nevertheless found it impossible to go any further in its criticism of the Council. It pointed out that the EEC Treaty-contrary to the provisions on agricultural policy - did not contain any precise indications of the implementation time scale or the content of the common transport policy upon which it could have ruled that the Council had failed to act.

---

1   Judgment of 4 April 1974, case 167/73, ECR 1974, p. 367.
2   Case 13/83, European Parliament v Council, OJ C144, 13.06.1985.

The Parliament's proceedings for failure to act and the Court of Justice ruling nevertheless had significant political consequences. The grievances of the Parliament, aired for the scrutiny of public opinion, could no longer be ignored by the governments of the Member States, nor the Council's prevarications be hidden in the skilful technical language of experts. This political pressure combined with the legal pressure exercised by the **Single European Act** to give fresh impetus to transport policy. In 1986, the Council adopted important measures in the area of sea transport. In 1987, it took even more major steps in the air transport sector. In 1988, it finally agreed to liberalize the weighty road haulage sector for 1992. Thus the internal transport market was completed twenty years behind the provisions of the Treaty in parallel with the internal markets for products and services.

With the completion of the single market in the transport sector, the common transport policy has not, however, attained all its objectives. In fact, the continuing integration of the economies of the Member States, necessarily entails increased transport movements across frontiers and places new challenges for the European transport policy. Thus, in addition to the consolidation of the internal market in transport, three new objectives of the **Treaty on European Union** concern transport policy: transport safety, trans-European networks and environment protection.

Thanks to a modification of Article 75 EC, brought at Maastricht, **transport safety** is now one of the objectives to be attained by the transport policy. Safety requirements may fall within the area of the Community's exclusive powers, for example, because they affect the free circulation of vehicles or transport services. In other cases, in application of the subsidiarity principle, transport safety is a matter which should be addressed by the Community when it is in a position to act usefully.

The provisions of the TEU on trans-European networks and economic and social cohesion provide a new basis for the Community to devise a strategy for the development of transport infrastructure. This strategy should allow, amongst other things, the less favoured peripheral regions of the Union to take full advantage of the opportunities which stem from the completion of the internal market. It should also aim at increased security for users, improved environmental protection and interconnection of the transport networks of the Member States with those of Central and Eastern European countries, thus facilitating their future integration in the EU.

All power-driven transport means consume energy and cause air, soil, water or marine pollution. Most polluting for the environment is road transport, which consumes over 80% of the total final energy used in the transport sector and contributes over 75% to its total CO_2 emissions. To **reduce pollution caused by the transport sector**, it is essential in this sector, as in that of energy, to: set progressively higher standards for gaseous emissions; incorporate into the transport prices the cost of transport, namely road, infrastructure; and internalize the external costs of pollution by means of financial and fiscal instruments, such as the tax on CO_2. Those measures which, in addition to environmental protection, would facilitate road decongestion and increase transport safety, would, however, have a direct impact on the competitive position of transport systems and operators. For this reason, measures of this kind could best be taken within the Community framework.

Those various measures were proposed by the Commission in its 1992 White Paper and in its 1995 action programme[1]. The guidelines adopted cover the following areas: improving quality by developing integrated transport systems based on advanced technologies which also contribute to environmental and safety objectives; improving the functioning of the single market in order to promote efficiency, choice and the user-friendly provision of transport services while safeguarding social standards; and broadening the external dimension by improving transport links between the European Union and third countries and the access of Community businesses to transport markets in other parts of the world. Likewise, the Commission adopted in 1995: a Green Paper on efficient pricing in transport, i.e. on the real costs of transport, including external costs[2]; and a Green Paper on public passenger transport ("The citizens' network"), whose aim is to provoke broad discussion on the use of public transport as an alternative to cars[3].

The internal market for inland transport

The first Community measures adopted in the inland transport sector sought to integrate national transport markets while at the same time creating a common market for goods and services. In this sector, it was necessary to create a genuine internal market to which transport operators from all the Member States would have access under the same conditions as those prevalent on their national markets. This implied freedom of establishment, the removal of barriers to freedom of movement and the harmonization of competition conditions.

No special problems were encountered in the free movement of individuals and the right of establishment in the transport sector. The Regulation of 1968 on the **free movement of workers** within the Community had been applied to the inland transport sector in the same way as to other economic sectors[4]. The **right of establishment** formed part of the general programme to remove restrictions to the freedom of establishment adopted by the Council in December 1961[5], but was also the subject of a specific Directive on mutual recognition of diplomas and certificates of road carriers[6]. It was the **free movement of services** in the transport sector which was the source of complex problems, due to restrictive national regulations in the Member States, particularly for road haulage services. Awareness of these problems had caused the authors of the Treaty to

1   COM (92) 494 and COM (95) 302, 12 July 1995.
2   COM (95) 691, 20 December 1995.
3   COM (95) 601, 29 November 1995.
4   OJ L257, 19.10.1968 and OJ L245, 26.08.1992.
5   OJ 2, 15.01.1962. See the chapter on the common market.
6   OJ L334, 24.12.1977 and OJ L212, 22.07.1989.

exclude, by Article 61, transport services from the general process of liberalizing services and to subject them to special provisions in the Title on transport.

Article 79 of this same title stated that in the case of transport within the Community, **discrimination** which took the form of carriers charging different rates and imposing different conditions for the carriage of the same goods over the same transport links on grounds of the country of origin or of destination were to be abolished, at the latest by the end of the second stage. In fact, a 1960 Regulation on the abolition of discrimination in transport rates and conditions, adopted in implementation of Article 79, prohibited such discrimination, including the setting of rates or prices, regardless of their form, or of transport conditions whose application amounted to discrimination[1].

Pursuing a similar line of thought, Article 80 prohibited from the second stage onwards the application by a Member State to transport services within the Community of rates and conditions involving an **element of support or protection** in the interest of one or several specific undertakings or industries, except in cases where Commission authorization had been granted, notably for reasons of regional development. The abolition of these subsidized rates did not pose any problems. As an illustration, however, of the scope of these provisions, 622 rates were abolished and 322 special rates amended in Member States of service origin.

The removal of discrimination and abolition of subsidies is however only the negative side of the process of liberalizing the Community's transport market. For a genuine common market to exist in the transport sector, common rules were required to guarantee: (a) free access to the market for all Community transport operators; (b) harmonization of competition conditions; (c) coordination of transport infrastructure. These are the points which are examined below.

Access to the Community transport market

Article 75 stipulated that, in order to open up access to the Community transport market, the Council should draw up common rules applying to international transport services from or to a destination in another Member State (intra-Community traffic) or crossing the territory of one or several Member States (Community transit). Considerable legislative harmonization was necessary for the attainment of the Treaty's objectives in this area, naturally requiring a great deal of time and effort. From the access viewpoint, the carriage of goods by road was the hardest nut to crack. International road haulage required the authorization of the State to be crossed, usually granted on a bilateral basis by the States in question. This authorization system sought to protect national railways and hauliers and naturally acted as a brake on the opening up of the Community transport market.

Work began fairly early on to break down the defences of this protectionist system by liberalizing certain special transport services such as frontier transport, mail carriage and, notably, combined road/rail carriage[2]. However, these specific measures only concerned a minute proportion of carriage by road between the Member States, the bulk of which was subject to a **system of quotas and bilateral authorizations.** As soon as the starter's gun of the Community policy was fired in 1961, the Commission proposed the gradual replacement of bilateral quotas, or in other words carriage authorizations negotiated between the Member States, by a Community quota negotiated at Community level and under which authorized holders would be able to transport goods throughout the Community. This request fell on deaf ears. In 1968, the Council merely created a small Community quota representing less

1   OJ 52, 16.08.1960 and OJ L1, 03.01.1994.
2   OJ L48, 22.02.1975 and OJ L368, 17.12.1992.

than 10% of the bilateral quotas. It was this situation, flying in the face of the concept of a common transport market, which pushed the Parliament to the end of its tether and prompted it to launch, in 1983, proceedings for failure to act against the Council in the Court of Justice.

Acting on the Court ruling of May 22, 1985, which went against it in this respect, and on the entry into force of the Single European Act, the Council finally made the move expected of it for twenty years, namely the **liberalization of the internal goods carriage market**[1]. This liberalization is established by a Regulation on access to the market in the carriage of goods by road within the Community and departing from or en route to a Member State, or crossing the territory of one or several Member States[2]. It replaces the quantitative restrictions by qualitative conditions (fiscal, technical and safety) with which a carrier must conform in order to obtain the Community road haulage operator licence and which are specified in the directives on access to the transport profession, examined below. The licence is valid for six years, but the criteria for holding it have to be controlled every three years. Should economic crisis hit the road haulage market, the Commission can take measures to prevent any further capacity increases on the market affected[3].

The Regulation laying down the conditions under which non-resident carriers may operate **national road haulage services within a Member State (cabotage)** is the culmination of many years of work towards the liberalization of the road haulage sector[4]. The Regulation allows the gradual introduction of the freedom to provide services by 30 June 1998 when the internal market will have been completed in this sector. During the transitional period each Member State may allow, temporarily, non-resident carriers to undertake road haulage operations without making them subject to quantitative national market access restrictions, provided that they are covered by a Community authorization and quota system, which will be increased annually.

More specifically as regards five-axle lorries with **trailers or semi-trailers**, free intra-Community movement was hampered by varying national regulations as to **maximum weights and dimensions** (50 tons in the Netherlands, 32 in the United Kingdom...). In 1971, the Commission proposed harmonization at the maximum weight of 44 tons. Thirteen years later, on December 19, 1984, the Council finally adopted the first Directive on the weight, dimensions and certain other technical characteristics of certain road vehicles[5]. This Directive stipulates, among other things, the maximum dimensions of goods vehicles and the maximum weights of trailers, road trains and articulated vehicles with 5 or 6 axles and the maximum weight of the axles themselves. In practice, freedom of movement was guaranteed for combined vehicles of up to 40 tons (or 44 tons for articulated combined vehicles carrying large 150 containers in combined transport), with a temporary derogation granted to the United Kingdom and Ireland. The maximum authorized length for road trains is 18.35 m[6].

---

1   OJ L163, 30.06.1988.
2   OJ L95, 09.04.1992.
3   OJ L375, 31.12.1990.
4   OJ L279, 12.11.1993 and OJ L350, 31.12.1994.
5   OJ L2, 03.01.1985 and OJ L226, 03.08.1989.
6   OJ L37, 09.02.1991.

Contrasting sharply with the market access situation for goods carriage by road, where progress has been so painstaking, the market in passenger carriage by road was rapidly and smoothly opened to competition. As far back as 1966, common rules were introduced for the international carriage of passengers by coach and bus, standardizing issuing procedures for authorizations covering: occasional passenger services, vital for the development of intra-Community tourism[1]; shuttle services between Member States; scheduled services provided on a specific route and with specified frequency; and special scheduled services, carrying specific categories of individuals, such as workers, from their home to place of work[2].

The **freedom to provide passenger transport services by road** for hire or reward or on one's own account is guaranteed by a Council Regulation of March 16, 1992[3]. It notably provides for the liberalization of shuttle services with sleeping accommodation, along with nearly all occasional services, and simplifies authorization procedures. The detailed rules with regard to documentation covering the international carriage of passengers are laid out in a Commission Regulation[4]. Another 1992 Regulation lays down the conditions under which non-resident carriers may operate national road passenger transport services within a Member State (cabotage in road passenger transport)[5].

The **admission to the occupation** of road haulage operator and road passenger transport operator and the mutual recognition of diplomas, certificates and other evidence of qualifications intended to facilitate for these operators the right to freedom of establishment in national and international transport operations were originally pursued by several Directives, which are now consolidated in one[6]. It stipulates that individuals or undertakings wishing to exercise the occupation of road haulier or road passenger transport operator must satisfy certain conditions relating to good repute (no insolvency), sufficient financial capacity for correct management of the undertaking and professional skills acquired through attendance of a training course or through practical experience.

The controls carried out by Member States in relation to means of transport by road or by inland waterway are no longer performed at the Community's internal frontiers but as part of the normal procedures performed throughout Community territory[7]. These controls concern not only the means of transport registered or put into circulation in the Member States but also those registered in third countries. Agreements on transit traffic between the Community and certain third countries strengthen cooperation between the contracting parties in certain areas, in particular the distribution of rights of transit (**ecopoints**)[8].

A 1995 Directive on the licensing of railway undertakings establishes common conditions of **access to the Community rail market**, in particular by requiring that undertakings

---

1   OJ L147, 09.08.1966.
2   OJ L67, 20.03.1972.
3   OJ L74, 20.03.1992.
4   OJ L187, 07.07.1992 and OJ L266, 27.10.1993.
5   OJ L251, 29.08.1992.
6   OJ L124, 23.05.1996.
7   OJ L395, 31.12.1992.
8   OJ L373, 21.12.1992.

applying for a licence meet specified standards of financial capacity and professional competence[1].

International waterway transport has enjoyed freedom of navigation embodied in international treaties, such as that for navigation on the Rhine since before the creation of the Community. However, a 1976 Directive ensures reciprocal recognition of navigability licences for inland waterway vessels[2] and a 1987 Directive lays down conditions for access to the profession of waterway transport operator[3]. Since January 1, 1993, non-resident carriers can provide goods and passenger services by inland waterway within a Member State for hire or reward, provided that they have an established business in another Member State in accordance with the legislation of the latter[4].

Competition conditions

For there to be effective freedom to provide services, all transport operators in the Member States had to be placed on an equal footing from the viewpoint of competition conditions, a really difficult requirement. In effect, transport systems based on the exploitation of single networks constituted monopolies or oligopolies. Service obligations in the public interest tended to involve the granting of correlative special or exclusive rights. Rail and air transport operators frequently relied on public finance, including subsidies not compatible with the functioning of the common market.

After the achievement of customs union, a 1968 Regulation sanctioned the application of **competition rules** to the rail, road and inland waterway transport sectors[5]. This Regulation in principle forbids, for all three modes of transport, agreements between companies, decisions of association and concerted practices, along with abuse of a dominant position in the common market. However, an exemption is granted to agreements which contribute to productivity, along with certain types of agreements, decisions and concerted practices in the field of transport which have as sole object and impact the application of technical improvements or technical cooperation. A Commission Regulation of August 1969 facilitates the presentation of complaints, applications and notifications by natural or legal persons who claim a legitimate interest[6]. By a Decision of 25 July 1995 pursuant to Article 85(3) of the EC Treaty, the Commission granted a three-year exemption to two cooperation agreements concluded between the national railway companies, which, although they restrict competition between the parties, particularly in international combined services, may promote economic progress.

However, competition rules alone do not suffice to guarantee free competition in the transport sector. Competition conditions for different modes of transport and for the undertakings of different Member States running the same type of transport services must also be harmonized. The first step in this direction was taken by the Council Decision of May 13,

---

1   OJ L143, 27.06.1995.
2   OJ L21, 29.01.1976.
3   OJ L322, 12.11.1987.
4   OJ L373, 31.12.1991.
5   OJ L175, 23.07.1968 and OJ L1, 03.01.1994.
6   OJ L209, 21.08.1969 and OJ L336, 31.12.1993.

1965 on the harmonization of **certain provisions affecting competition** in transport by rail, road and inland waterway[1]. Under this Decision, the Council agreed to take action in three fields: taxation, State intervention in the transport sector and social regimes. It therefore represented both a commitment and a clearly defined framework for the Community's work to eliminate imbalances which could distort competition between modes of transport and between undertakings operating the same mode of transport; but, it needed application provisions in order to work.

Thus, a 1970 Regulation, amended in 1992, provides arrangements on the **granting of aids** for transport by rail, road and inland waterways[2]. Although it allows aids relating to the costs of running combined transport services in transit across the territory of certain third countries (Switzerland and the States of former Yugoslavia), it defines rules for the non distortion of competition between the transport operators of the various Member States. Through another Regulation the Member States undertook to abolish and no longer to impose public service obligations upon railway, road and inland waterway undertakings, unless a satisfactory level of transport services cannot otherwise be guaranteed[3]. An amendment to this Regulation, adopted in 1991, introduces the principle of abolishing public service obligations and replacing them, when public interest justifies the preservation of transport services of no commercial viability for the operator, by **public service contracts** negotiated between governments and undertakings. It also provides for separate accounting of public service activities and commercial activities in transport undertakings[4].

In the area of **fiscal harmonization**, a common VAT system was introduced in the transport sector by the two first Directives of April 1967 and by the sixth Directive of May 17, 1977[5]. A 1968 Directive introduced standardizing provisions regarding the duty-free admission of fuel contained in the fuel tanks of commercial motor vehicles[6] and a 1970 Regulation established an accounting system for expenditure on infrastructure in respect of transport by rail, road and inland waterway[7]. But the real harmonization of taxation on road haulage is pursued by means of the Directive on the application by Member States of taxes on certain types of infrastructure requiring heavy goods vehicles to contribute towards the costs they engender through an excise duty on diesel oil, vehicle taxes or tolls and charges for the use of road infrastructure[8]. Member States are required to apply, from 1 January 1995 at the latest, a vehicle tax based on a minimum rate to which special and limited in time derogations may be granted. Member States may also maintain or introduce tolls or user charges provided they do not discriminate on the basis of carrier nationality or consignment origin or destination. All these provisions will apply until a road charging system based on common state-of-the-art technical standards is adopted.

Finally, the Council Decision of May 13, 1965 stipulated that there should be coordination "in a manner tending towards progress" of specific provisions concerning work conditions which affect competition in the three inland transport sectors. Action has only been taken in the harmonization of certain **social legislation relating to road transport**. Thus, a Council Regulation concerns journeys or parts of journeys within the Community using vehicles registered in a Member State or third country[9]. It lays down minimum driver age, total number of hours which can be spent behind the wheel between two rest periods and weekly rest periods. To prove that they are actually respecting the social provisions, road hauliers must, in accordance with a Regulation adopted on the same date as the one above, install and regularly use approved **recording equipment in vehicles** for passenger or goods

1   OJ 88, 24.05.1965.
2   OJ L130, 15.06.1970 and OJ L364, 12.12.1992.
3   OJ L156, 28.06.1969 and OJ L1, 03.01.1994.
4   OJ L169, 29.06.1991.
5   See the chapter on taxation.
6   OJ L175, 23.07.1968.
7   OJ L130, 15.06.1970 and OJ L353, 17.12.1990.
8   OJ L279, 12.11.1993.
9   OJ L370, 31.12.1985.

carriage which are registered in a Member State[1]. The Member States must organize an adequate and regular inspection system for road transport undertakings[2].

The aim of all of these rules is not simply to harmonize social conditions for those working in the road transport sector; harmonization of competition conditions between undertakings and improved **road safety** are two further objectives. The latter has been a source of increasing concern for the Community. In 1986, it organized a number of events on this theme. One Community Directive relating as much to road safety as to competition conditions between transport undertakings in different Member States deals with the approximation of the laws of Member States relating to **roadworthiness tests** for vehicles and their trailers[3]. The growing density of road traffic has meant that all the Member States are up against the same safety problems on the same scale. At the same time, the immobilization of vehicles for periodic checks and the costs resulting from these could affect competition conditions in the road haulage sector from Member State to Member State, giving rise to a need for harmonization of their frequency and standardization of checking methods. A 1991 Directive extended the application scope of the earlier Directive to private cars[4].

With a view to evening out competition between carriers and improving road safety, a Council Directive provides for the generalized installation and compulsory use of **speed limiters** on heavy vehicles for the carriage of goods and passengers[5]. For heavy vehicles, speed is limited to 90 km/h and for coaches with a maximum weight in excess of 10 tons, the limit will be set at 100 km/h.

Transport infrastructure

Infrastructure plays a determinant role in the competition conditions enjoyed by the various modes of transport. Through its choice of means of communication, the State determines the expansion and link up possibilities of the various modes of transport. Transport undertakings are dependent upon the infrastructure which they use in as much as decisions on its construction and maintenance are taken by governments. Coordination at European level is in the interests of the latter. However, transport users have not been obliged to pay the full cost of the infrastructures that they use. This is particularly true of road infrastructures and has contributed to the phenomenal expansion of road transport. In other respects, transport networks having been designed largely from a national point of view, there is in Europe frequent absence of adequate interconnections between national networks, missing links, bottlenecks and obstacles to interoperability. Moreover, whereas the central regions of the EU suffer from a growing congestion and have to bear a disproportionate burden of the

1   OJ L370, 31.12.1985 and OJ L256, 26.10.1995.
2   OJ L325, 29.11.1988.
3   OJ L47, 18.02.1977 and OJ L147, 14.06.1994.
4   OJ L178, 06.07.1991.
5   OJ L57, 02.03.1992.

costs of cross-frontier traffic, there is an underinvestment in peripheral areas, which contributes to their economic underdevelopment.

The EEC Treaty did not give the Community institutions any powers in this field. However, the Council of Ministers, acting on a proposal from the Commission, established a **consultation procedure** and set up a Transport Infrastructure Committee[1]. This procedure considerably improved cooperation between the Commission and Member States, keeping the former informed about national plans and programmes. This enabled better planning at national level both as regards time scale and geographical aspects. In 1982 a specific budget line was created and, in 1984, specific measures of Community interest were initiated in the field of transport infrastructures[2]. Moreover, the European Investment Bank and the Structural Funds have much helped the financing of infrastructures. But the overall infrastructure deficit of the Community has increased with the accession of peripheral States. This is why, it is very important that the development of transport infrastructures was provided for in the Treaty under the heading of trans-European networks.

Indeed, the new Article 129c of the Treaty calls for a series of guidelines covering the objectives, priorities and broad lines of measures envisaged in the sphere of **trans-European networks**. These networks are not only necessary in order to complete the internal market, improve the links between the European regions, avoid traffic congestions, reduce environment pollution and improve the competitiveness of European industries, but they can also enliven the European economy through the realization of very big projects and thus contribute to its growth. Community financial assistance is granted under certain rules to projects of common interest[3]. Concerning transport networks the goal is not so much the improvement of transport infrastructure in general but the integration of the Community's transport system through the completion and combination of its networks, taking particular account of its more geographically isolated regions.

The Council has already adopted the master plans on the high speed rail, the combined transport, the road and inland waterway networks. These master plans, which are indicative in nature and do not entail any financial commitments on the part of any Member State or the Community, aim at supplying the missing links between national networks, making them technically compatible and opening up the Community's isolated regions. The Commission has proposed guidelines aimed at the intermodal integration of all transport infrastructures in order to ensure by 2010 optimum and environmentally sound exploitation of all modes of transport[4]. These guidelines set out a precise but flexible framework for action for the national and regional authorities and will serve as a reference for Community intervention. Concerning, in particular, the high-speed train network, the Commission proposes the establishment of a regulatory framework comprising mandatory technical specifications for interopera-

1   OJ L54, 25.02.1978.
2   OJ L376, 31.12.1982 and OJ L177, 04.07.1984.
3   OJ L228, 23.09.1995. See the heading on trans-European networks in the chapter on the common market.
4   OJ C220, 08.08.1994 and COM (95) 298, 16 June 1995.

bility (TSIs) applicable to the various network subsystems (infrastructures, energy, transport material, etc.)[1].

Sector-by-sector organization of the transport industry

In addition to the proper functioning of the internal market for transport, the transport policy of the EU also tackles the sector-by-sector organization of the various modes of transport. This requires measures to align the economic conditions and the structures of each mode of transport in the Member States. The Treaty of Rome did not call for specific action in this field, but nevertheless stated that there should be common rules applicable to international transport to or from the territory of a Member State, or passing across the territory of one or more Member States (Article 75,1,a). The European institutions slowly put in place common rules, first for road transport rates and for improving the financial situation of the railways and, then in reaction to the Court of Justice ruling of April 4, 1974 on the interpretation of Article 84 of the Treaty, on the organization of activities and the establishment of the internal market for the sea and air transport sectors. For concision's sake, all measures adopted in those two sectors are examined in this part of the chapter, since they often pursue simultaneously the two objectives of the common transport policy mentioned above.

Road transport

The part of road haulage in the total freight transport of the Community increased from aound 50% in 1970 to almost 70% in 1990. This increase was partly due to the choice of the Member States not to charge the prices of road transport with the cost of infrastructures. In 1968, the Council, acting on a proposal by the Commission, had introduced bracket tariffs only for the carriage of goods by road between the Member States. This experimental system was replaced, since 1990, by a single system providing a **free price setting** applicable to all carriage of goods by road between the Member States[2]. This new tariff regime allowed for the introduction of cost indexes, i.e. indicators of the various cost elements which a haulier should take into account when drawing up a transport price to be negotiated with the client, but the real cost of infrastructures was not among those indicators.

However, the Commission in a Green Paper entitled "Towards fair and efficient pricing in transport", suggests introducing a system of fair and efficient pricing that takes account of the **development of the real costs** with a view to reducing the problems related to the use of road transport[3]. To this effect it identifies a number of steps that could be taken, such as: adjusting existing Community legislation on road charges for heavy goods vehicles; initiating electronically measured kilometre charges based on infrastructure damage; introducing road tolls in urban, congested or sensitive areas; instituting differentiated fuel taxes reflecting differences in fuel quality and differentiated vehicle taxes reflecting the environmental and noise characteristics of the vehicles.

---

1   OJ C134, 17.05.1994 and COM (95) 271, 15 June 1995.
2   OJ L390, 30.12.1989 and OJ L1, 03.01.1994.
3   COM (95) 691, 20 December 1995.

These proposals aim not only at the decongestion of roads and the protection of the environment but also at **road safety**, which becomes an ever more important problem of the EU. The principal actions taken so far in the area of road safety have been concerned with the harmonization of rules relating to: vehicle construction, through the adoption of over 100 Directives on: minimum tyre tread depth[1]; the periodic inspection of vehicles[2]; speed limiters for heavy vehicles[3]; the mandatory wearing of seat belts[4]; maximum driver's hours[5]; and the general standards for obtaining a Community model driving licence[6]. Nevertheless, even with the advances that have been made in technical and behavioural standards, the road safety record of Member States varies significantly and, in general, the average risk on Community roads is nearly twice that in the United States.

Moreover, the completion of the internal market entails a growth of transport flows and highlights the necessity of appropriate action on **road safety**. In its conclusions of 30 November 1993, the Council declared that attention should focus first of all on the causes of the most serious accidents, the categories of users most frequently involved in road accidents and the most vulnerable categories of users. To this effect the Council approved the creation of a Community database on road accidents (CARE)[7] and adopted a Resolution concerning young drivers of cars and two-wheeled vehicles[8]. By a Resolution of 1994, the Council encouraged the use of telematics in the transport sector and particularly the harmonized deployment of road traffic information and warning services[9].

Another Directive harmonizes the rules applicable to the national and intra-Community **transport of dangerous goods** so as to ensure, on the one hand, a high level of safety compatible with the European Agreement concerning the international carriage of dangerous goods by road (ADR), and on the other, the creation of a single market for such transport services within the EU[10]. Another Directive establishes uniform procedures for checks on the transport of dangerous goods by road[11].

Railways

Railways, once the dominant means of transport, were relegated by the car in the sixties. In the early 1990s, railway transport represented around 15% of freight transport in the Community, whereas twenty years before it represented practically the double. The bulky organization of the railways has not given them sufficient flexibility to structure their service to new transport requirements, to the "European dimension" and to competition from other modes of transport. The Member States must shoulder part of the blame for the unfortunate situation in which their railways find themselves. They oblige the railways to bend to the requirements of public service and regional development, which is not required of their private competitors, while not raising the capital endowment of railways undertakings in line with this obligation. This forces the railways into the red, hampers their modernization and therefore causes constant growth in total State expenditure on railway transport.

---

1   OJ L226, 03.08.1989 and OJ L1, 03.01.1994.
2   OJ L47, 18.02.1977 and OJ L147, 14.06.1994.
3   OJ L129, 14.05.1992.
4   OJ L373, 31.12.1991.
5   OJ L370, 31.12.1985.
6   OJ L237, 24.08.1991 and OJ L337, 24.12.1994.
7   OJ L329, 30.12.1993.
8   OJ C351, 30.12.1993.
9   OJ C309, 05.11.1994.
10   OJ L319, 12.12.1994.
11   OJ L249, 17.10.1995.

Good intentions towards the railways have abounded. In 1969 the Council adopted two major Regulations in principle concerning the economic situation of the railways: one on action by the Member States concerning the obligations inherent in the concept of a public service, which affects first and foremost the railways, and the other on common rules for the normalization of the accounts of railway undertakings[1]. The latter Regulation sought to iron out the disparities resulting from the responsibilities laid on the shoulders of the railways by the Member States, or from the granting of advantages to railway undertakings. It would involve a financial balancing of these responsibilities and advantages. However, to no avail. This is why, the Council adopted in 1977 a Regulation on the measures necessary to achieve comparability between the accounting systems and annual accounts of railway undertakings[2], followed, in 1978 by a Regulation laying down uniform costing principles for railway undertakings[3]. In 1981, the Council again adopted a Resolution on Community railway policy[4], in 1982, it reached an agreement on the fixing of rates for the international carriage of goods by rail[5] and, in 1983, it proclaimed the commercial independence of the railways in the management of their international passenger and luggage traffic[6]. None of this had much impact. Until the early nineties, railways failed to break out of the vicious circle created by the shrinking of their market, rising expenditure, insufficient revenue and greater State intervention.

Suddenly, however, there was light at the end of the tunnel in the shape of the **high speed trains**, which have given a new lease of life to European railways and imposed the liberalization of the market. Thus, a Directive on the **development of the Community's railways** purports to make relations between the railways and the public authorities more transparent and to ensure the financial, administrative, economic and accounting independence of the railway undertakings[7]. It also allows access of new railway operators into the combined transport market, which should stimulate a higher quality of service from all concerned. However, as mentioned above, a Directive requires that undertakings applying for a licence to the Community railway market meet specified standards of financial fitness and professional competence[8]. Another Directive establishes the general framework for a uniform, non-discriminatory Community system regarding access to railway infrastructure, so that railway undertakings and their customers can reap the full benefits of the internal market in this sector[9]. With a view to a gradual opening of the market in rail transport, a Directive establishes a uniform set of national safety rules which avoid distorting competition between modes for the transport of dangerous goods[10].

Inland waterway transport

Inland waterways, which accounted for almost 14% of freight transport in the Community, in the early 1970s, represented only 9% of that transport twenty years later. Yet,

1   OJ L156, 28.06.1969 and OJ L169, 29.06.1991.
2   OJ L334, 24.12.1977 and OJ L353, 17.12.1990.
3   OJ L258, 21.09.1978 and OJ L353, 17.12.1990.
4   OJ C157, 22.06.1982.
5   OJ L234, 09.08.1982 and OJ L353, 17.12.1990.
6   J L237, 26.08.1983 and OJ L353, 17.12.1990.
7   OJ L237, 24.08.1991 and COM (95) 337, 19 July 1995.
8   OJ L143, 27.06.1995.
9   Ibid.
10   OJ C313, 24.11.1995.

well-equipped waterways, such as the Rhine and the Rhone, are particularly efficient for bulk traffic and are capable of handling much more than the current traffic, provided investment is made in maintenance and works to improve the existing network.

The Community institutions reacted late in the day to the need for structural improvements in inland waterway transport in order to fight over-capacities[1] and the bulk of over-capacity reductions in this sector were carried out at national level. In May 1995, the Commission presented an overall strategy for the organization of the inland waterway transport market and scrapping, which should allow more flexibility, create a better balance between supply and demand and enable prices to move in line with market rules[2]. The Council approved the Commission's approach and created a legal basis to allow for a Community financial contribution to the national scrapping funds of the Member States[3].

Maritime transport

Maritime transport has steamed well out in front of the railways as regards common market organization. There are four main strands to this market organization: market monitoring, international routes, the alignment of structures and the operation of the internal market.

Market monitoring was rendered necessary at the end of the seventies by the problem of unfair competition from the fleets of certain State-trading countries and certain Far East countries. This competition had to be countered by shared information and possibly by common action. A 1978 Council Decision introduced an information system to keep the Community institutions abreast of the activities of the fleets of third countries[4]. On the basis of this system, the decision was taken to monitor the activities of carriers operating regular merchant shipping services between the Community, Eastern Africa and Central America[5] and between the Community and the Far East[6].

International shipping relations are clearly of vital importance in the maritime transport sector. This is why one of the first measures taken in this area was the introduction of a consultation procedure on international links and on action relating to such matters within international organizations[7]. Most of the rules and requirements for seagoing vessels are negotiated in the International Maritime Organization (IMO), a specialized agency of the United Nations, of which all Member States are members. The Community can make an important contribution by developing common approaches to the implementation of IMO rules and to the even application by States of the rules that have been agreed. In view of the liberalization of cabotage, mentioned below, the Community can complement IMO requirements, which do not apply to passenger vessels on national voyages. In a move designed to satisfy the developing nations, which are seeking a stronger role in shipping trade, and to thwart the rise of the fleets from State-trading countries, the Council asked the Member States in 1979 to ratify the United Nations Convention on a Code of

---

1   OJ L116, 28.04.1989 and OJ L350, 31.12.1994.
2   COM (95) 199, 23 May 1995.
3   OJ L292, 07.12.1995.
4   OJ L258, 21.09.1978.
5   OJ L5, 09.01.1979.
6   OJ L88, 02.04.1981.
7   OJ L239, 17.09.1977.

Conduct for **Liner Conferences**[1] , namely agreements between shipping companies of several nationalities on the orderly servicing of various shipping routes.

A 1983 Council Decision provided for the possibility of counter-measures in the event of unfair competition in international merchant shipping[2]. A Council Regulation of 1986 stipulates that the Member States will take coordinated action when a measure introduced by a third country or by its agents restricts or threatens to restrict the free access of shipping from a Member State to ocean trade[3]. Another Regulation on the same date draws up the procedure to be followed to counteract unfair pricing practices by certain shipowners who are nationals of third countries and are servicing international cargo shipping routes, when these practices seriously upset the structure of trade on a route to, from or within the Community[4]. In January 1989, the Council applied this Regulation for the first time with the introduction of corrective duty on containerized cargo to be transported in liner service between the Community and Australia by a South Korean company[5]. Important progress on the promotion of the principles of freedom to provide services and of freedom of access to ocean trade for Community operators was achieved, however, in 1992, in relations with Japan, Korea and China.

Matters of **shipping safety** became a major concern in Europe towards the end of the seventies. With the Amoco Cadiz catastrophe fresh in people's minds, the Council recommended to the Member States in June 1978 that they ratify international conventions on shipping safety[6]. This was followed by the adoption in December 1978 of two Directives: one urging the Member States to take all necessary steps to ensure that tankers carrying oil, gas and chemicals and docking in the Community's sea ports be obliged to respect certain conditions; and the other requesting that Member States with a North Sea or Channel coastline take steps to ensure that ships in these areas are piloted by properly qualified sea pilots[7]. In order to ensure a coherent and complete coverage of the European maritime area and to compensate for the lack of radionavigation aids in certain areas, the Member States can participate in agreements on the establishment of Loran-C terrestrial radionavigation chains[8]. Ships using Community ports and sailing in the waters under the jurisdiction of the Member States must respect the international standards for ship safety, pollution prevention and shipboard living and working conditions[9]. Clear and efficient safety procedures are also applied to ro/ro (transfer) passenger vessels[10].

In conclusions adopted on 25 January 1993, following the casualties of La Coruña and the Shetland Islands, the Council ("Environment and Transport") urged the Community and its Member States to support the work carried out by the International Maritime Organization (IMO), particularly as regards the implementation of the following measures: limitation of the misuse of flags of convenience; improved surveys of oil tankers; reduction of accidents caused by human error; and improved routeing of vessels carrying hazardous cargoes. This

1   OJ L121, 17.05.1979.
2   OJ L332, 28.11.1983.
3   OJ L378, 31.12.1986.
4   Ibid.
5   OJ L4, 06.01.1989.
6   OJ L194, 19.07.1978.
7   OJ L33, 08.02.1979.
8   OJ L59, 04.03.1992.
9   OJ L157, 07.07.1995.
10   OJ C297, 10.11.1995.

conclusions were reiterated and reinforced in a Council Resolution on a **common shipping safety policy**[1].

In order to implement this Resolution the Council adopted a Directive concerning minimum requirements for vessels bound for or leaving Community ports and carrying **dangerous or polluting goods**. Its aim is to ensure that Member States are kept informed about the movements of such vessels[2]. On its side, the Commission declared applicable to the Member States - and therefore to ships flying their flags - amendments to the International Conventions for the Safety of Life at Sea (SOLAS) and for the prevention of pollution by ships (MARPOL)[3]. A Council Directive of 22 November 1994 sets up common rules and standards for ship inspection and survey organizations in order to ensure a high level of competence and independence of these organizations[4]. A Regulation of the same date aims at obtaining substantial reductions in port fees for environment friendly oil tankers with segregated ballast[5].

The most recent wing of the Community's maritime transport policy concerns the operation of the **internal market**. In 1986, the Council applied the principle of freedom to provide services, (Articles 55, 58 and 62 of the Treaty) to shipping services between the Member States and third countries[6]. The freedom to provide services to maritime transport within Member States is established by a Council Regulation of 7 December 1992[7]. This Regulation provides for the liberalization of **maritime cabotage** for Community shipowners who have their ships registered in and flying the flag of a Member State, provided that these ships comply with all the conditions for cabotage in that Member State. For vessels carrying out mainland cabotage and for cruise liners, all matters relating to manning are the responsibility of the State in which the vessel is registered. However, for ships smaller than 650 Gt. and for vessels carrying out island cabotage, all matters relating to manning are the responsibility of the host State. The ability to transfer ships from one register to another within the Community can improve the operating conditions and competitiveness of the Community merchant fleet[8]. In a Resolution of December 1995, the Council approved the action programme contained in Commission communication on the development of short sea shipping, including cabotage, in the intermodal transport chain[9].

In 1986, the Council also laid down detailed rules for the application of Articles 85 and 86 of the EEC Treaty to maritime transport in order to ensure that competition is not unduly distorted within the common market, but, in 1992, it has provided for a block exemption for certain concerted practices between liner shipping companies (**maritime conferences and consortia**), which generally contribute to ensure regular, sufficient and efficient maritime transport services[10]. A second Regulation grants a block exemption for the carriage of cargo, to liner shipping consortia, which

1   OJ C271, 07.10.1993.
2   OJ L247, 05.10.1993.
3   OJ L194, 03.08.1993.
4   OJ L319, 12.12.1994.
5   Ibid.
6   OJ L378, 31.12.1986.
7   OJ L364, 12.12.1992.
8   OJ L68, 15.03.1991.
9   COM (95) 317, 5 July 1995.
10   OJ L378, 31.12.1986, OJ L376, 31.12.1988, OJ L55, 29.02.1992 and OJ L336, 31.12.1993.

provide international liner shipping services from or to one or more Community ports[1]. On the basis of the agreements covered by the exemption, shipowners may jointly organize services, thus rationalizing their activities as maritime carriers and obtaining economies of scale and cost reductions, while at the same time providing users with a better-quality service. The exemption relates notably to the coordination and joint fixing of sailing timetables, the determination of ports of call, the exchange, sale or cross-chartering of space or "slots" on vessels, the pooling of vessels, port installations and operation offices.

In a communication on a **new maritime strategy**, the Commission stresses that this sector has undergone far-reaching changes in recent years: increasing internationalization, globalization of services, increasing numbers of "open" registers, greater use of flagging-out, ageing of the fleet and shortage of manpower[2]. It ascertains that in spite of the undeniable know-how in the sector and major efforts to improve its competitivity, it has not been able to arrest the trend towards flagging out and job losses. It therefore proposes a new threefold strategy: to ensure a high level of maritime safety and fair competition founded, in particular, on rules of safety and environmental protection enforced by the port state and respected both by EC flagged ships and ships flying the flag of non-EC States under penalty of refusal of access to Community ports; to promote greater opening up of the markets, including free access to world markets and fair competition; and to reinforce the competitiveness of the Community maritime transport sector.

Air transport

For air transport, in the same way as for maritime transport, the April 4, 1974 Court of Justice ruling heralded the application of the Treaty's general rules, notably those relating to competition and right of establishment. This was no simple matter for the air transport sector for, unlike shipping companies, the major airlines are state-owned and have a near monopoly at national level. Each State, anxious to fly the national airline colours around the world and exploit certain advantages arising for example from its geographical situation or special relationship with certain parts of the world, jealously guards its airline or airlines. This has practical consequences on flight routes and fares.

At the time of the Court ruling, air services between the Member States were regulated by **bilateral agreements.** These official agreements were often supplemented by confidential memoranda exchanged between aviation authorities which interpreted, filled in or even modified the provisions of the agreements and which occasionally depended upon commercial arrangements between airlines. Fares for scheduled air services were by and large negotiated by airlines on a multilateral basis, but in the final analysis were set by the States. As a rule of thumb, the States took on board the international fares and carriage conditions set in the framework of the International Air Transport Association (IATA). The IATA gave the airline operating a scheduled service the option of filing a set of fares with it. But since each of these fares had to be approved by at least two governments, innovative fares were

---

1   OJ L89, 21.04.1995.
2   COM (96) 81, 13 March 1996.

not possible on a national level. The States were in favour of consultation on fares and did not wish any far-reaching competition. Covered by the governmental decisions which they were simply implementing, the airlines escaped Articles 85 and 86 of the EEC Treaty and disposed of a captive market. The need for a Community policy and also the difficulties which it was up against were manifest.

The first Council measures did not tackle the crux of the problem, namely the lack of competition. Duplicating the procedure applied to shipping, the Council set up in 1979 a **consultation procedure** for relations between Member States and third countries in the field of air transport and on action relating to such matters within international organizations, such as the International Civil Aviation Organization (ICAO), the European Civil Aviation Conference (ECAC) and Eurocontrol[1]. At the same time, the Council adopted a Directive rendering it compulsory for the Member States to check that civil subsonic aircraft registered on their territory had a noise limitation certificate, a measure of interest both from an ecological viewpoint and from that of the harmonization of structures in the Member States[2]. In the field of **air safety**, the Council adopted in 1980 a Directive on cooperation and mutual assistance between the Member States in the field of air accident investigation[3]. This Directive was completed, in 1994, by a Directive establishing fundamental principles governing the investigation of civil aviation accidents and incidents[4]. A couple of measures, adopted in December 1991, concerned both air safety and market organization: the Directive on the mutual recognition of crew licences and the Regulation on the harmonization of the technical requirements and administrative procedures in the field of civil aviation[5].

The Commission, on the other hand, wanted to get down to the heart of the matter, namely **market operation**. It attempted to do so in a Memorandum in February 1984, which sought to reply to the growing criticism of a system viewed by users as excessively rigid, against their interests and running counter to certain aspects of the Treaty. It was only after three years of hard-hitting negotiations in the Council that a first set of measures proposed by the Commission on fares, capacities, market access and competition rules was adopted on December 14, 1987[6]. This first set of measures was replaced on July 24, 1990 by a second package, forming the second phase in the liberalization of air transport within the Community[7]. The third air transport package, adopted by the Council on 22 June 1992, constituted the final stage in the liberalization of Community air transport[8]. Its main objectives were the freedom to provide services within the Community, technical and economic harmonization and free price setting.

The Regulation on the **licensing of air carriers** defines the technical and economic requirements which airlines must meet in order to obtain national licences authorizing them to operate on Community territory without restrictions on the grounds of nationality[9]. The licences in question are: the air operator's certificate (AOC), which affirms the technical quality and competence of the airline concerned; and the operating licence, granted to undertakings which comply with certain conditions regarding nationality and which meet certain economic criteria and are covered by a suitable insurance scheme. This Regulation guarantees, then, that only

1   OJ L18, 24.01.1980.
2   OJ L18, 20.01.1980.
3   OJ L375, 31.12.1980 and OJ C172 of 24.06.1994.
4   OJ L319, 12.12.1994.
5   OJ L373, 31.12.1991.
6   OJ L374, 31.12.1987, OJ L376, 31.12.1988 and OJ L336, 31.12.1993.
7   OJ L217, 11.08.1990.
8   OJ L240, 24.08.1992.
9   Ibid.

airlines under Community control, and with adequate technical and economic capacity, are able to take advantage of the opening up of the European market.

The Regulation on **access for air carriers** to intra-Community air routes opens up all airports on the territory of the Community to all those who are registered according to the above-mentioned Regulation[1]. It provides, in particular, for: the abolition of the previously existing sharing of passenger capacity between airlines; the unrestricted exercise of the **'fifth freedom'** (the right to pick up passengers in a Member State other than that in which the airline is registered and disembark them in a third Member State); and the authorization to undertake **cabotage operations** (to pick up passengers in a Member State other than that in which the airline is registered and disembark them in that same Member State). Concerning cabotage services, however, certain restrictions remain until 1 April 1997.

Finally, the Regulation on **fares and rates for air services** guarantees the unrestricted setting of new passenger fares and cargo rates for scheduled air services and charter flights under certain conditions safeguarding the interests of both the industry and of consumers[2]. It defines, in particular, the arrangements for the examination of new fares and rates by the Member States and the system of 'double disapproval' (whereby a new fare or rate may not be turned down unless both Member States concerned disapprove of it). If this is not the case, Community air carriers may freely fix passenger fares. Charter fares and air cargo rates are freely fixed by the parties to the air transport contract.

As regards, more particularly, the operation of air **freight services,** a Council Regulation seeks to open up access to the market, liberalize fares and boost the operating flexibility of these services[3]. A Member State approves air freight carriers whose licence has been issued by another Member State and which has been authorized by the State of registration to exercise third-, fourth- and fifth-freedom traffic rights. Fifth freedom traffic rights are exercised on a service which is the extension of a service on departure from the State where the carrier is registered or a preliminary to a service whose end destination is this State. The prices applied by Community air carriers for freight transport are set freely by mutual agreement of the parties to the transport contract. Air carriers operating services within the Community must place all their standard freight rates at the disposal of the general public on request.

The Commission, acting in close and regular contact with the relevant authorities in the Member States, can take measures to ensure the application of Articles 85 and 86 of the Treaty to international air services between Community airports[4]. A Regulation adopted in 1987, in application of Article 85, paragraph 3 of the Treaty, enables the Commission to approve certain categories of **agreements** and concerted practices in the air transport sector[5]. The Commission put this possibility into practice with a Regulation on the application of Article 85(3) of the Treaty to certain categories of agreements and concerted practices concerning joint planning and coordination of schedules, joint operations, consultations on passenger and cargo tariffs on scheduled air services and slot allocation at airports[6]. These exemptions pursue two aims: encourage airlines to cooperate with a view to improving the

---

1   Ibid.
2   Ibid.
3   OJ L36, 08.02.1991 and OJ L240 of 24.08.1992.
4   OJ L374, 31.12.1987 and OJ L240, 24.08.1992.
5   Ibid.
6   OJ L155, 26.06.1993.

service on offer to passengers, particularly in the exploitation of new or low density lines, while remaining competitive from the viewpoint of fares and service quality. In addition there exists a block exemption for agreements subject to the code of conduct for computerized reservation systems, the purpose of which is to ensure that there is fair competition between air carriers and that users are well informed[1].

As part of the third liberalization package for air transport, the Council has established a code of conduct guaranteeing the transparent, efficient and non-discriminatory allocation of **slots for civil aviation**[2]. The code is based on the 'use it or lose it' principle. It lays down conditions of access for new entrants to the market, for free exchange of slots and for safeguard mechanisms where there is a clear imbalance between air carriers. In the same context, a Directive on access to the groundhandling market at Community airports is designed to enable European airlines to control their operating costs more effectively and to adapt their services more closely to their customers needs[3].

A Council Regulation drawing up common rules for the compensation of passengers refused the right to board due to over-booking[4] is of particular importance to the ordinary citizen. It stipulates that should a passenger be refused the right to board, he has the right to choose between full reimbursement of the price of the ticket for the part of the journey which he was unable to carry out or rescheduling on a later date of his choice. Regardless of the choice made by the passenger, the air carrier must pay, immediately after the boarding refusal, compensation which varies in line with the distance of the flight and the rescheduling delay. The carrier must moreover offer passengers refused the right to board meals, hotel accommodation if necessary and the cost of a telephone call and/or telefax message to the place of destination.

Strong growth rates in air traffic inside and to and from Europe have placed severe strain on some parts of the air transport infrastructure and have worsened air traffic delays. In its conclusions on **air traffic control** in the Community, adopted on 7 December 1992, the Council noted the importance of the development of an effective Air Traffic Management system for the future of civil aviation in Europe. In a 1995 Resolution, it invited the Member States and the Commission to coordinate their actions in the framework of the European Organization for the Safety of Air Navigation (Eurocontrol), the independent organization responsible for coordinating the Member States' air traffic management systems, in order to combat congestion and better manage crises situations in the European airspace[5]. As a matter of fact, the Directive of 19 July 1993, which is designed to achieve the gradual harmonization and integration of national air-traffic systems, makes mandatory the technical specifications drawn up by Eurocontrol[6]. However, the Commission finds that the existing arrangements between the Member States are inadequate in terms of meeting the growth in demand, satisfying user requirements and achieving high safety objectives[7]. It therefore recommends giving Eurocontrol greater political legitimacy and decision taking, monitoring and support

---

1   OJ L278, 11.11.1993 and OJ L333, 31.12.1993.
2   OJ L14, 22.01.1993.
3   OJ C142, 08.06.1995.
4   OJ L36, 08.02.1991.
5   OJ C323, 04.12.1995.
6   OJ L187, 29.07.1993.
7   COM (95) 318, 5 July 1995.

powers, conferring on it responsibility for airspace management and technical specifications[1].

A particularly thorny problem in the field of air transport is that of Community competence in foreign relations. Member States have resisted the exercise of this competence and have continued to negotiate agreements with third countries, concerning, for example, access of the Community internal market by third-country operators. In the future, the Community should be granted the authority to act in **external matters** touching upon civil aviation, a sector which is by and large regulated at international level by bilateral agreements between States. The Community should gradually take responsibility for this process and defend the interests of the Member States, particularly in the area of service provisions, including the granting of the "fifth freedom" to third countries. Although existing bilateral agreements should be respected, the Community as such should, whenever this proves possible, conduct negotiations with third countries on market access, capacity, fares and related matters[2]. In conclusions on relations with the United States in the air transport sector, the Council asked the Commission to define more clearly the economic implications of comprehensive negotiations with this country, in order to reinforce the competitiveness of European operators.

Appraisal and outlook

Until the end of the eighties, the Community achievements in the transport sector did not correspond to the energy invested in it or to the clear need for progress on a policy expressly mentioned in the Treaty of Rome as a crucial cornerstone of the common market. It is true that in the first thirty years of its existence, the Community policy succeeded in harmonizing admission conditions to the profession of transport operator, in abolishing fare, fiscal and other such discrimination, while harmonizing to a certain extent competition conditions for inland transport. Viewed from this angle, Community social regulations in the area of road transport represent considerable progress, both as regards the alignment of competition conditions and as regards social policy and traffic safety, with notably the introduction of compulsory maximum driving periods per day and per week.

However, the market for goods carriage by road remained boxed in by a quota system, the railways were undermined by State intervention, transport infrastructure was not planned at Community level and sea and air transport remained outside the Community's action scope. Thus at the beginning of the eighties, transport policy did not correspond to the evolution in the economic integration of Europe. This point was forcefully made by the European Parliament's proceedings against the Council for

---

1   COM (96) 57, 6 March 1996.
2   COM (92) 434.

failure to act. Its case was at least partially upheld by the Court of Justice in its ruling of May 22, 1985.

The Council's failure to act was chiefly due to an absence of political commitment to pushing economic integration in this field. However, the experts agree that the matter is extremely complex, a point admitted by the Treaty itself in Article 75 when it speaks of the "special aspects" of the transport sector. The diversity of structures in the five modes of transport is further heightened by the variety of situations in which they operate in each of the Member States. These difficulties were further complicated by the often very technical nature of the questions discussed. As a consequence, national experts, who prepared the Council meetings, played a very important role in examining the Commission's proposals. Since these proposals, by their very nature, were likely to upset the apple cart in transport systems and the economic policy concepts of the Member States, very often there was exaggerated defence of national interest and sectoral perception of the problems which did not make sufficient allowance for the requirements of Community integration.

Whether under pressure of the European Parliament and public opinion or the need to integrate transport into the post-1992 Single Market, transport policy stepped on the accelerator in the middle of the eighties, particularly in three fields: maritime transport, air transport and road haulage.

In the area of maritime transport, which is the carrier for 85% of the EEC's external trade, the Member States undertook to apply the rules of free competition and the principle of free provision of services to this sector. They also agreed to fight unfair tariff practices and guarantee free access to ocean trades and progressively to cabotage.

As regards air transport, the liberalization measures completed in 1992 will have a major impact on competition between air carriers and consequently on the fares practised, which are still high if compared to those in other regions of the world, especially the United States. Provisions on market access will moreover stimulate the creation of new services and the opening of new routes, giving a better service to the Community's regions. Finally, in the area of capacity, airlines will be able to respond more rapidly and with greater flexibility to the evolution in traffic, which is expanding every year. The main fear for the future is even greater saturation of the Community's airports and air corridors.

The greatest breakthrough for Community transport policy has undoubtedly been in the area of liberalizing international road haulage services. At the beginning of the eighties, no-one would have dared hope that in ten years at the most all the quotas applicable to cross-border transport within the Community would be replaced by a system of Community licences issued on the basis of qualitative criteria. Following the completion of the internal market, this is viewed as something totally normal, which is perhaps all the better, for road transport is one of the essential cogwheels of the Single Market.

However, the Community must find the answer to several challenges in the field of transport. In particular, it must face the problems caused by the saturation of existing networks, the uneven modal split and increasing pollution caused by means of transport. At the same time, transport liberalization involving the arrival of new entrants and greater competition between operators, engenders important structural changes, technical innovations and new investments; all, certainly, good developments, but which need to be coordinated at Community level. To answer these challenges the Community should adopt an overall approach combining: improvements to infrastructure and means of transport and their more rational use; enhancing the safety of users; achieving more equitable working conditions and better environmental protection.

In the near future, the common transport policy must adopt a global approach consisting of going beyond the internal market and promoting an integrated transport system which should be environmentally and socially acceptable and should provide a high of safety for users and transport workers. To give a fair chance of success to this new approach, the external costs, which are now largely paid by society, should be internalized. This internalization of external costs would ensure the development of an environment-friendly and therefore sustainable transport system. On the external front, the Community should have competence to negotiate and act in areas which concern the internal market, such as access to this market of third-country operators and rules applicable to international transport, including safety and environmental protection.

Bibliography on transport policy

▫ BAVOUX Jean-Jacques, CHARRIER Jean-Bernard, *Transports et structuration de l'espace dans l'Union européenne*, Masson, Paris, 1994.

▫ BRAUN-MOSER Ursula, *European Transport Policy: Prospects and Objectives*, Libertas, Sindelfingen, 1992.

▫ BUTTON Kenneth J. (ed.), *Transport Policy - Ways into Europe's Future*, Bertelsmann Foundation Publishers, Gütersloch, 1994.

▫ COMMISSION EUROPÉENNE, *Concurrence et coopération dans le transport aérien en Europe*, OPOCE, Luxembourg, 1992.

  – *Réseaux transeuropéens: vers un schéma directeur du réseau routier et de la circulation routière*, OPOCE, Luxembourg, 1993.

  – *L'Europe à grande vitesse: Groupe à haut niveau "réseau européen de trains à grande vitesse"*, OPOCE, Luxembourg, 1995.

▫ DIEKMANN Achim, *Towards more Rational Transport Policies in Europe*, Deutscher Instituts-Verlag, Köln, 1995.

▫ DEHOUSSE Franklin, BARTHELEMY Brigitte, "Le marché unique des transports aériens", in *Journal des Tribunaux*, Bruxelles, année 112, N° 5669, 27 mars 1993, pp 237-242.

□   EUROPEAN COMMISSION, *The Future Development of the Common Transport Policy*, Bulletin of the European Communities, Supplement 3/93.

-   *The Trans-European Transport Network*, OOPEC, 1995.

□   FOURNIER Patrick, "Perspectives du réseau autoroutier communautaire, Horizon 2010", in *Transports*, Paris, année 37, N° 353, mai-juin 1992, pp. 150-158.

□   HART Paul, LEDGER Gillian, ROE Michael, SMITH Brian, *Shipping Policy in the European Community*, Ashgate Publishing Group, Aldershot, Avebury, 1992.

□   HEDDEBAUT Odile, JOIGNAUX Guy, "Le réseau européen de transports à l'horizon 2010. 'Maillons manquants' et intégration térritoriale", in *Futuribles, Analyse - Prévision - Prospective*, Paris N° 195, février 1995, pp. 31-51.

□   POWER Vincent, *EC Shipping Law*, Lloyd's of London, London, 1994.

□   STOFFAËS Christian, BERTHOD Jean-Claude, FEVE Michel, *L'Europe: avenir du ferroviaire*, ASPE Europe Éditions, Paris, 1995.

□   VINOIS Jean Arnold, "Les réseaux transeuropéens: une nouvelle dimension donnée au marché unique" in *Revue du marché unique européen*, Paris, N° 1, 1993, pp. 93-125.

□   VOUGIAS S., "Transport and Environmental Policies in the EC", in *Transport Reviews*, London, Vol. 12, N° 3, July-September 1992, pp. 219-236.

13. AGRICULTURE

The share of agriculture in the Union's GDP is just under 3%; but the sector accounts for over 6% of the employed civilian working population of the Fifteen and is the principal source of income in many rural communities. Moreover, food, beverages and tobacco account for about 20% of average EC household consumer expenditure and form a substantial proportion of internal trade and exportations of the EU. The economic, social and political importance of agriculture is, therefore, much greater than its share in the GDP of the Union.

Without a shadow of a doubt, agriculture is the economic sector where the process of European integration is furthest advanced. This achievement is all the more significant in that prior to the common market, the Member States were actively interventionist in agriculture. National interventionism had to be corrected to enable free trade and free play of competition in the agricultural sector. But the high degree of state interventionism and the conflicts of national interests complicated the task of creating a common policy in this sector. The creation of the Common Agricultural Policy (CAP) is therefore an exemplary achievement of the economic integration process.

The common agricultural policy is also extremely difficult to manage, for it implies the use of common prices, common price management instruments, joint financing of support measures and common external protection. Complications are heightened by monetary fluctuations which hinder the setting of common prices in ECU and have made it necessary to use "green currencies".

All these cumbersome but unavoidable mechanisms form part of the CAP's market organization. The latter is one of the CAP's two wings, the other being structures. Although the common market in agricultural products has ensured supply security of foodstuffs at reasonable prices for consumers, it would not have been sufficient in itself to attain the other objectives of the Treaty, namely increased agricultural productivity and a higher standard of living for farmers. The latter has required an active socio-structural policy which works hand in hand with other Community policies, such as the regional and social policies, to guarantee the Community's rural areas a place in the forthcoming Single Market.

Economic and legal framework

The founding fathers of the European Economic Community were well aware of the need to include the agricultural markets of the Member States in the future common market. But they were also aware that the common agricultural market could not simply be achieved by abolishing the barriers to free movement and introducing common competition rules, as in the sectors of industry, craft industry and services. This is why Article 38 of the Treaty of Rome states in its first paragraph that the common market includes agriculture and trade in agricultural products, while specifying in paragraph 4 that the operation and growth of the common market in agricultural products must be accompanied by the introduction of a common agricultural policy.

There are several reasons why agriculture was afforded "special treatment". The primary one is the **very nature of agriculture**, which is at the mercy of weather conditions, crop and livestock diseases and many other factors which often elude human control. As a consequence, it is very difficult to ensure a perfect balance between agricultural output and demand for foodstuffs. In addition, demand has very pronounced social and political characteristics. Governments are obliged to ensure that demand for basic commodities be satisfied at all times and at reasonable prices. The original Community was far from self-sufficient in foodstuffs and conditions on the world market provided no justification for the unilateral opening up of markets. Consequently, if food security was to be guaranteed at stable prices, the Community had to organize its own agriculture. This appeared all the more reasonable in that output of the different Member States was complementary. Northern Europe could supply cereals, dairy products and meat, whereas Southern Europe could specialize in fruit and vegetables, citrus fruit and wines.

The agricultural diversity of the six founding Member States, which increased with each enlargement of the Community, generated difficulties for the unification of their agricultural markets, providing further justification for an **interventionist agricultural policy**. Different natural, structural, social and trade conditions, the prominence of agriculture in the national economy and different farming traditions led to the use in each European State of agricultural policy instruments which diverged considerably as to their application scope and magnitude. The common market therefore had not only to align structurally different agricultural systems, but also to iron out tenaciously held privileges resulting from the interplay of national political institutions: State monopolies or similar regulations, price guarantees, farm income aid, export subsidies, direct or indirect import restrictions, customs protection and so on. A new agricultural policy stepping in the shoes of the national ones had to be defined. The complexity of the latter created the need for their blending into one common agricultural policy.

In the negotiations for the last enlargement of the Union to Austria, Finland and Sweden agriculture was a key issue, because of the use of agricultural policy by the applicant countries as an instrument of regional policy for strategic, environmental, social and cultural reasons. Eventually, it was agreed that the applicant countries would adopt the basic machinery of the common agricultural policy and would align their farm prices from the start on those in the rest of the Union. Acceptance of the immediate alignment of farm prices was linked to financial assistance from the Community in the form of an agro-budgetary package agreed between the applicants and the EU. Provision was also made for several transitional measures relating to market organization and veterinary and plant health legislation. Sweden was integrated fully into the CAP from the first day of accession, which is keen on preserving its traditional alpine farming, and Finland, whose agriculture is also highly protected, have been authorized to make special income support payments to farmers for a maximum period of five years. The two Nordic countries were also allowed, subject to certain conditions, to grant State aids to farmers in certain regions to compensate for the handicaps peculiar to farming in an arctic or sub-arctic environment[1].

Rules of the Treaty

The **objectives** of the common agricultural policy are specified in Article 39 of the Treaty: higher agricultural productivity; guarantee of a fair standard of living to farmers; market stabilization; supply security and reasonable prices for consumers. In order to attain these objectives, Article 40 called for the **common organization of agricultural markets** which, depending on the product, could take one of three forms: common coordination rules, compulsory coordination of the various national market organizations or European market organization. It is interesting to note that it is always this last and most stringent concept that has been applied to the common organization of agricultural markets.

The Treaty was also prudent as regards the applicability of **competition rules** to the agricultural sector, a sector where State intervention was rife. According to Article 42, the applicability of the general Articles on competition was subordinated to specific provisions of the common agricultural policy. As early as 1962, however, the Council decided that the Treaty competition rules applicable to undertakings (Articles 85 to 91) should also be applied to agricultural undertakings. Only cooperatives and farming associations could be granted a special regime; as it turned out, certain common market organizations assigned specific functions to producers' groups, thus involving them in the common policy[2].

Competition rules for **State intervention** (Articles 92 to 94) became applicable to agricultural markets as and when common market organizations were established. Many of the market organizations consequently incorporate specific provisions on national or Community aid. The Member States became obliged to notify the Commission of all aid granted to agriculture as early as 1962. Since this date, aid to agriculture has been treated by the Commission in the same way as all other national aid.

The other Articles of the Treaty devoted to agriculture were chiefly transitional provisions. Article 43, however, was of special importance. It stipulated that a conference of the Member States was to be called by the Commission as soon as the Treaty had entered into force to enable the Member States to compare their agricultural policies and consequently come to an agreement on an outline of the common agricultural policy. This conference was called by the Commission in **Stresa** in July 1958. Agricultural officials from the six signatory States, despite their different points of view and different situations as importers or exporters

1   OJ L328, 20.12.1994 and OJ L43, 25.02.1995.
2   OJ 30, 20.04.1962 and OJ L215, 30.07.1992.

of agricultural produce, succeeded in reaching a general agreement on the protection of the common agricultural market against distorted external competition, on the need for a structural policy and a farm price policy and on the principle that farmers should be paid in a manner comparable to workers in other sectors. The Stresa Conference clarified the agricultural objectives of the Treaty, stipulating that for European agriculture to be internationally competitive, its structures must be overhauled, but that the family nature of European farms should be preserved; that for common farm prices to offer a decent standard of living, they must be set above world prices but not at a level encouraging over-production[1].

The first common market organizations

The Commission's first drafts of the common agricultural policy, submitted to the Council at the end of 1959, and its first proposals for common market organizations in June 1960 were built on the foundations laid at Stresa. The Commission's proposals fired the starting gun for the hard-hitting negotiations in the Council, which became known as "**agricultural marathons**". Each of these negotiating rounds produced a common market organization for the various agricultural products: at the beginning of 1962, those for cereals, pigmeat and poultry meat, eggs, fruit and vegetables and wine were in place; they were followed at the end of 1963 by those for rice, beef and veal and dairy products. By this date, a common market organization existed for almost 85% of the agricultural output of the then six Member States.

However, the completion of the common agricultural policy required the Community to take control of the Member States' expenditure under the common market organizations. The Council was scheduled to take a decision on this point before June 30, 1965. The Commission suggested in March 1965 that the common agricultural market be completed on July 1, 1968, thus coinciding with the customs union for industrial products. However, the Council failed to meet its deadlines and the Community lived through the most serious crisis in its history. For seven months, France practiced an **"empty chair"** policy in the Council and thus blocked any new Community initiative.

Work on the common agricultural policy only got back on track after the Luxembourg compromise of January 28, 1966. It culminated, in May 1966, in a Council agreement on Commission proposals for the financing of the agricultural policy[2]. This agreement under its belt, the Council was able to make fresh progress on the common market organization for sugar and oils and fats, on tightening up that for fruit and vegetables and on the setting of common prices for milk, beef and veal, sugar, rice, oilseeds and olive oil. Thanks to these decisions, the common agricultural market was able to be an integral part of the customs union created on July 1, 1968.

CAP reforms

With most of the major decisions on the common market organization thus taken, the Commission turned its attention to structures. In December 1968 it submitted to the Council a "Memorandum on the reform of agriculture in the European Economic Community: Agriculture 1980", otherwise known as the **Mansholt Plan** after the Commissioner who had inspired it. The main aims set by the memorandum were as follows: help elderly farmers to cease farming and thus leave their land free for the younger ones: encourage structural modernization and larger farm size to enable optimal combination of factors of production; encourage vocational training and socio-economic information for farmers; guide production in accordance with demand and discourage a build-up of surpluses by appropriate

1   OJ 11, 01.08.1958.
2   OJ 165, 21.09.1966.

pricing policy. Two and a half years after the submission by the Commission of its memorandum, the Council, in a "marathon" session from March 22 to 25, 1971, agreed to a Resolution containing several options for a structural policy for agriculture[1]. On the basis of this Resolution, the Commission drew up proposals and the Council adopted in April 1972 the Directives of the **first reform of the CAP** dealing respectively: with the modernization of farms; measures to encourage the cessation of farming and the reallocation of utilized agricultural area for the purposes of structural improvement and the provision of socio-economic guidance for and the acquisition of occupational skills by persons engaged in agriculture[2].

The other structural measures which were adopted later on covered mountain and hill farming and farming in certain less-favoured areas, the processing and marketing of agricultural produce and producer groups and associations thereof. But other problems also emerged, such as permanent surpluses of the main agricultural products and continuing imbalances in the Community. These problems too had to be tackled, not simply for the benefit of the common agricultural policy, but also for that of the entire process of European construction, which would otherwise have been placed in jeopardy. Twenty-five years after its creation, the difficulties which the common agricultural policy had accumulated along the way justified a reform of its mechanisms, both structural - as was accomplished on March 12, 1985[3] - and those pertaining to the common market organizations.

It was with this aim in mind that the Commission transmitted a "**Green Paper**" to the Council and Parliament on July 23, 1985. This Paper contained the fruits of its reflection on the outlook for the common agricultural policy. The **second CAP reform** thus recommended by the Commission was approved by the Brussels European Council on February 11-13, 1988, which gave the green light to the "**Delors package**". This package covered, in addition to reform of the common agricultural policy, the level of agricultural expenditure, budgetary discipline, the system of own resources and support policies, including the reform of the structural funds of which the EAGGF Guidance section. Acting on this European Council agreement, the Council of Ministers adopted the measures necessary for a new reform of the common agricultural policy, in April 1988[4].

As a consequence, market related measures, such as dairy quotas, the system of stabilizers (maximum guaranteed quantities) and the co-responsibility levies were adopted. These were paralleled by structural measures in favour of afforestation, the protection of certain environmentally fragile areas, the diversification of agriculture and incentives for the set-aside of farmland. But since the impact of this set of measures proved to be too small, the Commission, through a 1991 discussion document, stated its intention to carry out much more radical reform of the market mechanisms.

After several agricultural "marathons", the Council, on May 21, 1992, reached a political agreement on the Commission's proposals for the **third reform** of the CAP. The Council upheld the three guidelines proposed by the Commission: a substantial cut in the target prices of agricultural products in order to make them more competitive on internal and external markets; full and sustained compensation of this drop in farmers' income by compensatory amounts or premiums not linked to the quantities produced; and recourse to measures limiting the use of means of production (set-aside of arable land, withdrawal of part of the land for major crops, limits on livestock numbers per hectare of fodder area) accompanied by the preservation of more stringent regulations such as quotas. In this context, a major event was the start, in 1993, of a three-year programme of phased reductions in cereal prices with compensation per hectare being

---

1   OJ C52, 27.05.1971.
2   OJ L96, 23.04.1972.
3   OJ L93, 30.03.1985.
4   OJ L106, 27.04.1988 and OJ L108, 29.04.1988.

paid directly to farmers provided production is cut back by means of set-aside[1].

At the same time, the Council has decided to increase measures to conserve the environment and landscapes, encourage the early retirement of certain categories of farmers with the transfer of their land to other uses and facilitate the use of farmland for other purposes, such as afforestation or leisure. These support measures are analyzed under the structural policy heading.

These decisions incorporate major changes. First of all, the Community is self-sufficient as regards the main products required to feed its population. It is consequently seeking only to increase production in areas where the extra quantities can find an outlet either within the Member States or in third countries. Secondly, farm income support is no longer solely or chiefly through price support; it also includes aid to farmers in the form of compensation or premiums. Finally, the Community, which is the world's biggest trading entity, has through the profound revision of its regulations clearly demonstrated its commitment to the liberalization of international trade through the GATT, while conserving the principles and basic instruments of the CAP[2].

The latest reform, like its predecessors, does not call into question the principles adopted in 1962 as the basis for the common agricultural policy: price unity, Community preference, financial solidarity and farmer responsibility. These principles, which are examined in the next part of this chapter, have given good overall results insofar as they have ensured the maintenance of a sufficient number of farmers on the land and have guaranteed the supply security of consumers at stable and reasonable prices. Reform is necessary precisely because the CAP and Community agriculture have performed well, because agricultural productivity has increased and because markets - both inside and outside the Community - are unable to absorb production surpluses.

CAP management and financing

The unity of the European Union's agricultural market requires common prices, common support instruments for these prices, common external protection, joint financing and, in general, **joint management**, for which the European Commission has responsibility. The Commission, as for other areas of Community activity, is also invested with the power of initiative, i.e. the power to make proposals. The genesis of any agricultural policy measure is a Commission proposal. Once a Commission proposal for a Regulation in the area of common agricultural policy has been put before it, the Council entrusts the preparation of its proceedings to a committee of senior officials known as the **Special Committee on Agricul-**

---

1   OJ L154, 25.06.1993.
2   OJ L349, 31.12.1994. See the heading on sectoral measures of the commercial policy in the chapter on the European Union in the world.

ture (SCA). In the area of agriculture, the SCA assumes the role normally fulfilled by the Committee of Permanent Representatives (Coreper)[1].

Consultations of interested parties

A vast number of experts are involved in drafting and implementing the common agricultural policy. The Commission, acting in accordance with the Treaty, naturally consults the European Parliament and the Economic and Social Committee. The ESC is made up of representatives of the various socio-professional categories and farmers are therefore also in its midst. In addition, the Commission expressed from the outset its wish to cooperate closely with **farmers' professional bodies** to ensure that allowance is made for their interests in the drafting of common policy and the management of the common market organizations. This is why a large number of professional farming bodies have emerged at European level, the most important of which are. the Committee of Agricultural Organizations in the European Community (COPA), an umbrella body for farmers; the General Committee for Agricultural Cooperation in the EEC (COGECA), which represents farm cooperatives; and the Commission of the Agriculture and Food Industries (CIAA), representing these industrial sectors.

However, consultation of these large general organizations tends to be on the mainstream policies of the CAP. The Commission rapidly felt a need to be better informed on specific problems in each agricultural sector. As a consequence, as part of the process of implementing the common market organizations, it has set up an **advisory committee** for each product or product group falling under a common market organization. Half of their members consist of representatives of producers and their cooperatives and the other half of representatives of trade, industry, workers and consumers. The Committees give an opinion on the proposals of measures put before them during the drafting phase within the Commission. No vote is taken for the advisory committee opinion, which is in no way binding for the Commission[2].

Management

After adoption of the basic regulations by the Council comes management of the common organizations. Management is either the joint responsibility of the Commission and Council or that of the Commission alone. This is the case for general policy decisions such as the annual setting of farm prices, undertaken in application of the basic regulations. In this instance, the full procedure is used: the Commission after consulting professional organizations submits a proposal to the Council, which takes a decision after consultation of the European Parliament and very often of the Economic and Social Committee. For long-application management provisions, such as adjustments of market mechanisms or of basic criteria, a medium-length procedure is used: the Commission proposes measures to the Council, which takes a decision without consulting either the European Parliament or the Economic and Social Committee.

On the other hand, the application provisions for basic regulations and management measures in the strict sense of the term, such as the setting of export refunds, which are applicable on average for a few weeks or a few months, are adopted by the Commission using a procedure known as the "Management Committee" procedure, whereby the Commission acts after having received the opinion of the relevant **management committee**[3]. Under the basic regulations, a management committee is set up for each common organiza-

---

1   OJ L45, 14.02.1987. See the heading on the Council in the Introduction.
2   Ibid.
3   OJ L324, 27.12.1969.

tion of market or product. Beside them exist regulatory committees, such as the Standing Veterinary Committee, the Committee on Plant Health and the Standing Forestry Committee. They are made up of representatives of the Member States and chaired by a representative of the Commission and give their opinion on proposals for measures submitted to them by the Commission. The committees vote by qualified majority. In cases where the Commission is empowered by the Council to take decisions after consultation of a management committee, it must submit a draft of the measures which it intends adopting to the relevant committee in good time. If the committee issues a favourable opinion or no opinion at all, the Commission can proceed with the adoption of the planned measures. Should a negative opinion be given, the Commission can adopt the measures but must notify them to the Council, which has one month to adopt a different decision by a qualified majority[1].

There are also some market management mechanisms which operate almost automatically. This is the case of the common market organization in cereals, which stipulates that levies applying to cereals imported into the Community should be set on a daily basis. The Commission sets these levies daily, basing itself on data received from national intervention bodies and on information received directly from major world cereals markets. The management committee procedure would be too slow in this case[2]. The Commission also acts alone to introduce emergency measures when a market is seriously upset by an unforeseeable event, such as, for example, a massive influx of low-price products onto the world market. Given the urgent nature of the measures to be taken, the Commission is empowered by the Council to decide on the necessary protective clauses. It must, however, report to the Council that such a decision has been taken.

Every day, a large number of measures are introduced in the framework of the common market organizations as part of the process of CAP management. In the following pages, two general problems which dominate the management of the CAP - financing and agrimonetary matters - are analyzed.

Financing of the CAP

Article 40 of the Treaty of Rome - devoted to the gradual development of the common agricultural policy - declared that one or several agricultural guidance and guarantee funds should be created to enable the common organization of agricultural markets to fulfil its goals. On January 14, 1962 during the first agricultural marathon, the Council opted for the creation of one single fund to finance all Community market and structural expenditure in the various agricultural sectors: the **European Agricultural Guidance and Guarantee Fund (EAGGF)**[3].

EAGGF management falls to the Commission, which is assisted by the EAGGF Committee, made up of representatives of the Member States and chaired by the Commission. The Committee is consulted on either an obligatory or optional basis on all matters affecting the EAGGF in the framework of the so-called "management committee" procedure, described above. Although the Commission has sole responsibility for EAGGF management, it nevertheless passes through the channel of state organizations in the Member States for the payment of intervention expenditure on the Community's agricultural markets. The Commission would in fact be unable directly to carry out all the payments resulting daily from

---

1   OJ L197, 18.07.1987.
2   OJ L281, 01.11.1975.
3   OJ 30, 20.04.1962 and OJ P258, 25.10.1967.

the implementation of the common agricultural policy. The national organizations however give the Commission an activity report and the payments carried out by them are considered as EAGGF payments[1].

The EAGGF's "**Guarantee Section**" has full responsibility for expenditure resulting from the implementation of the common organization of agricultural markets, namely: refunds for exports to third countries; operations on the internal market, such as purchases, aid and premiums for production or processing and storage or withdrawal costs; the monetary compensatory measures and part of the expenditure resulting from food aid for Third World countries[2].

Management of expenditure in the EAGGF's Guarantee Section is anchored in a system of **advance payments to the Member States**, with annual clearing of accounts. The Commission places at the disposal of the Member States the funds necessary so that the organizations appointed by them can, in accordance with Community rules, pay the expenditure required under the EAGGF Guarantee Section. These advance payments take the form of a lump sum for each Member State and are paid into a special "EAGGF Guarantee" account opened by each Member State with its Treasury or another financial institution. The funds are finally acquired by the Member States after an audit of compliance of their expenditure with Community rules[3].

The expenditure charged to the EAGGF's Guarantee Section has a number of specific features: it is compulsory expenditure, being the result of existing market regulations; it is difficult to forecast, because it depends on factors such as weather conditions and market management (quantities produced, price difference between world market and Community market); Guarantee expenditure can consequently overstep available funding, in which case a supplementary budget must be adopted during the financial year, as was the case on several occasions in the eighties. However, following an agreement reached by the Brussels European Council on February 11 to 13, 1988, the annual rate of growth of EAGGF-Guarantee expenditure should not be more than 74% of the annual growth rate of the Community's GDP. This restriction on expenditure growth is known as a "guideline". The Edinburgh European Council concluded that if agricultural expenditure should exceed the guideline, thereby compromising the financing of the reformed CAP, the Council would take appropriate steps to fund the EAGGF Guarantee Section. Thus, any increase in costs will have to be covered from the EAGGF budget until the guideline is reached, then by calling on the monetary reserve, and finally by means of 'ad hoc' measures once that has been exhausted.

The expenditure financed by the EAGGF's **Guidance Section** is not at all similar to that under the Guarantee Section. The latter is the consequence of market policy, the former of structural policy. Whereas the Guarantee Section finances totally the Member States' expenditure, the Guidance Section only part finances outlays. Aid granted by the EAGGF Guidance Section complements national aid; furthermore, to be eligible, projects have to meet certain criteria.

The provisions for financial contribution from the EAGGF Guidance Section vary in accordance with the aims of each of the joint socio-structural activities, but generally speaking the Member States have responsibility for implementing the measures and granting the aid by virtue of national legal, regulatory or administrative provisions. For the Community's financial contribution to be awarded, the national criteria must be approved by the Community bodies and must win a favourable decision

---

1   OJ L94, 28.04.1970 and OJ L125, 08.06.1995.
2   OJ L154, 25.06.1993.
3   OJ L125, 08.06.1995 and OJ L158, 08.07.1995.

from the Commission. Once this is the case, the Fund reimburses the Member States for part of the expenditure which the latter assume to implement joint actions. The Community's financial contribution generally runs at 25% of eligible expenditure, but can rise as high as 50% for investment aid in underprivileged regions and areas.

In order to verify the expenditure carried out by the Member States on behalf of the Community, be it for the Guarantee Section or for structural activities, the Commission carries out checks on documents and often on the spot in the relevant departments. **Fraud prevention and policing** is the responsibility of the Member States, which must take steps against any irregular operations and inform the Commission of them. The financial consequences of irregularities are, however, borne by the Community, unless government departments of the Member States are responsible for the irregularities or incorrect payment of sums[1]. Fraud often hits the headlines in the Member States and fuels the criticism of the CAP's opponents. A response to the problem has been given by a Council Regulation which requires the Member States to scrutinize themselves the transactions forming part of the system of financing by the Guarantee Section of the EAGGF[2]. Another Regulation tightens up measures to combat fraud and irregularities relating to the financing of the common agricultural policy[3]. In this context, the Council established a control system using satellite pictures and air photographs of agricultural land benefiting from EAGGF subsidies, it has reinforced physical checks at the export of agricultural products having obtained a refund[4] and provided for customs checks to be targeted on high-risk sectors, notably export refunds[5]. The Council has also established a legal framework making it possible to identify unreliable economic operators in the field of export refunds and of sales at reduced prices of products held in public storage ("black list") and to make them known to the national authorities concerned[6].

This is a good beginning, but the effort has to be intensified in order to save the CAP from those who want to dismantle it by using fraud as an arm against it. Fraudsters must be tracked and brought to justice, be they large international companies playing on export refunds or small farmers inventing non-existent milking cows or multiplying the amount of olive oil or cotton produced. According to the rulings of the Court of Justice, the Community has the power to establish the penalties needed for the effective application of agricultural regulations, provided they are necessary for the attainment of the objectives of the CAP[7].

Agrimonetary problems

Another management problem, which is a subsidiary issue for the CAP, is agrimonetary in nature. As will become clear below, one of the cornerstones of the common agricultural market is the possibility for all producers in the sectors under a common market organization to be able to sell their products to an intervention body, at a guaranteed price which is the same for all the Member States and set each year by the Council. For this to be possible, the common agricultural policy requires a denominator common to the different currencies in which guaranteed prices are expressed. This requirement provided the impetus for the creation in 1962 of the Unit of Account (UA) a fictive currency or rather measuring standard whose value corresponded to the gold parity of the US Dollar registered with the International Monetary Fund (IMF). Since each of the currencies of the EC Member States also had a parity registered with the IMF, it was possible to set common prices in Units of Account and to reimburse the expenditure of each Member State for the support of these prices in national currency. After 1979, the UA was replaced by the ecu.

---

1   OJ L158, 08.07.1995.
2   OJ L388, 30.12.1989 and OJ L328, 20.12.1994.
3   OJ L67 14.03.1991.
4   OJ L42, 16.02.1990 and OJ L224, 21.09.1995.
5   OJ L355, 05.12.1992 and OJ L24, 29.01.1994.
6   OJ L145, 29.06.1995.
7   Judgment given on 27 October 1992, Case C-240/90, Germany v Commission.

Since the ecu consists of the weighted value of the Member States' currencies, the revaluation or devaluation of an individual currency led to a change in the value of the ecu and in the relative position of each currency towards it. As a consequence, every time there was a change in the central rate of a national currency, all the conversion rates (green rates) used to express agricultural prices in national currencies were changed in turn and all the monetary gaps must be closed by **"Monetary Compensatory Amounts"** (MCAs)[1]. The application of the MCA regime naturally engendered technical and administrative difficulties complicating the normal process of marketing agricultural produce within and outside the Community and distorting competition.

In view of the completion of the internal market, in order to eliminate the need for border controls related to the MCA and, at the same time, to preserve the unity and stability of the common agricultural market, the Council adopted, in December 1992, a Regulation on the unit of account and the conversion rates to be applied for the purposes of the CAP[2]. Thus, the MCA mechanism has been discontinued, but the specific agricultural conversion rates ("**green rates**") have been retained. In the absence of a unique currency which would solve agrimonetary problems, the agricultural conversion rates are necessary but complicated expedients, because they result from compromises between the interests of strong-currency countries, which reject cuts in their farmers' earnings after revaluations of their currencies, and those of weak-currency countries, which refuse to support the revenues of the farmers of the most prosperous countries of the Union.

In view of the risks entailed since August 1993 by the widening of the margin of fluctuation to 15% under the EMS, the gaps authorized between the green rates and the market rates have been increased to a maximum of 5%. However, following the deterioration of the monetary situation and the reduction of the green rates for certain currencies, the Council has allowed that degressive national aid be granted, in 1995, to compensate for income losses, with the Commission's approval[3].

Common market organization

The common agricultural market is underpinned by **common market organizations (CMO)** which remove obstacles to intra-Community trade and create common protection at frontiers. At present, almost all the Community's agricultural production is regulated by common organizations. Article 38 of the Treaty defines agricultural products as products of the soil, livestock products and fishery products, along with products of first-stage processing which are directly related to these products. Foodstuffs are considered as products of second-stage processing and are therefore not included in agricultural products. To make matters as clear as possible, products covered by the provisions under the heading "agriculture" are listed in Annexe II of the Treaty. This is why, in Community

---

1   OJ L164, 24.06.1985 and OJ L310, 21.11.1985.

2   OJ L387, 31.12.1992 and OJ L22, 31.01.1995.

3   OJ L148, 30.06.1995 and OJ L312, 23.12.1995.

terminology, agricultural arrangements are often stated as being applicable to "Annexe II products".

One could ask why organize agricultural markets at all? The answer is that the agricultural markets of the Member States were already organized in various ways at national level. Indeed, almost all States intervene in one way or another to ensure the income of their farmers and stable supply for their consumers. The only difference is that the system of intervention varies from one to the other. They can however be divided into two main categories: direct income aid systems for farmers, which existed in the United Kingdom before its entry to the Community and was called deficiency payments; and the system of price support on the internal market combined with external protection, the system representing 80% of the total public support to agriculture in the OECD countries. This system was recommended by the Stresa Conference and chosen for the bulk of the EEC's agricultural production[1].

The Community had no choice but to opt for a system of support for agricultural prices. In effect, under the **direct income aid** system, agricultural products are imported at world prices, generally low when they are in ample supply, and the income of national farmers topped up by a subsidy from the budget. This system can be integrally applied in a few countries in the world which are almost self-sufficient in agricultural products and/or where farmers are not very numerous. If a large group of countries such as the EU which is the world's biggest trading power and has a large number of farmers were to begin purchasing openly on the world market, world prices would escalate and cause important price increases and, sometimes, shortages of foodstuffs.

The **system of price support**, on the other hand, was better adapted to the conditions in the Community. Under such a system, to provide national farmers with sufficient income, internal prices which are higher than world prices of agricultural products are practiced and the difference is compensated by import levies or customs duties and by export refunds (subsidies)[2]. The higher prices stimulate agricultural output and productivity. They also tend to guarantee self-sufficiency in basic agricultural products and foodstuffs, which is another point in their favour. If they are set too high they can naturally lead to production surpluses, which is a negative point but which results more from the manner in which the system is applied than from the system itself. Inasmuch, however, as agricultural prices determine farmer income, it is socio-politically very difficult for Agricultural Ministers within the Council to cut these prices, even if the Commission, in its pricing proposals, provides them with arguments in favour of reducing surplus production through prices.

In view of these problems, the last reform of the CAP introduced a mixed system: price support was reduced, but the farmers' revenue was maintained at its previous level by subsidies. In other words, the reduction of price support was compensated by the support of the revenue of the farmers, so as that these may still live decently, entertain Europe's farm-

---

1   OJ 11, 01.08.1958.

2   OJ L351, 14.12.1987 and OJ L205, 31.08.1995.

lands and landscapes and produce the goods necessary for the foodstuffs independence of Europe. Thus, the 1992 CAP reform and the 1993 GATT Agreement, based on it, have not much affected the fundamental principles of the CAP.

The principles of the CAP

Three basic principles defined in 1962 characterize the common agricultural market and consequently the common market organizations: market unity, Community preference and financial solidarity. Since the end of the seventies, the principle of co-responsibility of producers has been added.

Market unity means that agricultural products move throughout the European Union under conditions similar to those in an internal market, thanks to the abolition of quantitative restrictions to trade (quotas, import monopolies,...) and the removal of duties, taxes and measures having equivalent effect. Market unity supposes common agricultural prices throughout the EU. The Council, acting on a proposal from the Commission, thus, early in each marketing year, sets common agricultural prices expressed in ECU[1]. In principle, the common agricultural prices should be attained through the free play of supply and demand so that the only variations in the prices paid to farmers in all regions of the Union are the outcome of natural production conditions and distance from main centres of consumption. But in reality, as will be seen below, the common market organizations incorporate intervention measures, the force of which varies according to product, in order to support common prices should there be insufficient demand or external supply at low price.

Community preference, the second bulwark of the common agricultural market, signifies that products of Community origin are bought in preference to imported products, in order to protect the common market against low-price imports and fluctuations in world prices. This principle, spread throughout the world, is enacted through import and export measures. The European Union usually does not impose any quantitative restrictions on imports, but only tries to bring the prices of imports into the EU at the prices practised on the common market. The price gap between the world market and the minimum guaranteed price in the EU was traditionally covered by import levies, which after the GATT Uruguay Round are progressively replaced by customs duties[2]. To the extent that external prices taxed with import duties are at the same level as internal prices, it is not to the advantage of European traders to buy supplies from outside the EU and they therefore give preference to Community products. But whereas this was practically always the case with the import levies, it is much less certain with the customs duties, which are about to replace them. And yet, Community preference is also in the interest of consumers. Thus, in the event of shortage or when supply on the world market dwindles, the Union's internal prices are lower than world prices and an

---

1   See, for example, OJ L148, 30.06.1995.
2   See below, "The external wing of the CAP".

export levy raises the export price to keep the products within the European Union and ensure its supply at stable prices.

The third basic principle of the common agricultural market is that of **financial solidarity**. It is implemented through the intermediary of the European Agricultural Guidance and Guarantee Fund (EAGGF) and signifies that the Member States are jointly liable as regards the financial consequences of the common agricultural markets policy. Since the European Union organizes agricultural markets and defines and applies the intervention measures on them, it is logical that it is responsible for the financial consequences of these measures. The EAGGF Guarantee Section therefore covers all the expenditure rendered necessary by the common market organizations. The other side of the coin is that the customs duties (which have replaced levies) collected at the Union's frontiers on imports from third countries do not go into the coffers of the Member States but are a source of revenue for the Community budget.

These basic principles which steered the launch of the common agricultural market were joined at the end of the seventies by the **principle of co-responsibility**, namely the contribution of farmers to the financial costs engendered by growing Community agricultural production. This means that in sectors where surpluses constantly or frequently exist (milk, cereals, olive oil...), the disposal guarantee is not limitless. Mechanisms to control agricultural production and expenditure known as **stabilizers** exist. They basically set, often for a period spanning several years, maximum guaranteed quantities as regards production or intervention buying in. The European Union has thus attempted to reconcile budgetary constraints with the need to maintain farm income.

Common market organizations cover almost all of production in the Member States and therefore revolve around these principles. The market organization of each product uses different mechanisms defined by its basic regulation and adopted by the Council using the full-blown procedure, but all of them are underpinned by, on the one hand, internal market measures, more often than not relating to price setting and support, and on the other by a trade regime with third countries, which is in conformity with the Agreement on agriculture concluded in the context of the GATT Uruguay Round.

Agricultural prices and product quality

Prices are a central component of the common market policy and the terminology surrounding them is very complicated. This is due to the various different roles which agricultural prices play and to the need for them to be adapted to specific conditions on different markets. Generally speaking, prices play three roles in the common agricultural market: they guide production, trigger intervention mechanisms and secure common external protection. Each of these three functions will be analyzed in turn.

The **guide price** (beef and veal, wine), which is also known as the **target price** (cereals, sugar) or the **norm price** (tobacco) is the price that the common market organization seeks to guarantee to producers. It is set each year by the Council in accordance with both evolution in the cost of living and that of supply and demand on each market. It therefore guides the production of each of the agricultural sectors for which such a price exists.

The **intervention price** (cereals, sugar, butter, beef and veal, tobacco) or the **basic price** (pigmeat), which is a certain percentage lower than the guide price, is the price at which intervention organizations in each Member State must buy products of Community origin which farmers put in for storage. For fruit and vegetables, which cannot be stored, there are **withdrawal prices** below which producers' groups, in their role of intervention organizations[1], stop selling and send surplus quantities for distillation, to charities or for destruction until such time as more sluggish supply triggers a recover in the market prices[2].

Thus, in order to face the consequences of the **mad cow disease** (Bovine spongiform encephalopathy -BSE), in addition to veterinary measures, exceptional support measures for the beef market in the United Kingdom as well as in Belgium, France and the Netherlands were adopted[3]. Other measures were taken in order to limit the negative consequences of banning beef exports from the United Kingdom to third countries[4].

The intervention arrangements are very often tied into a **storage system**, which varies according to the product and helps attenuate the impact of cyclical production variations on prices and guarantee supply continuity[5]. The stocks in the system are often necessary for normal regulation of the market. It is only when stock levels remain abnormally high that structural surpluses and consequently serious imbalance between supply and demand exist, which must in principle be corrected by lowering of the intervention price. In the context of various **food aid programmes**, large quantities of food from intervention stocks are supplied both to designated organizations for distribution to the most deprived persons in the Community[6] and to the undernourished populations of numerous countries in the world[7].

Connected with the question of agricultural prices is the question of the **quality of agricultural products** and foodstuffs. This question will gain in importance in an internal market characterized by the over-abundance of most agricultural products. The quality and characteristics of these products are often linked to their geographical origin. Two Council Regulations are designed to raise consumer awareness of the producers' efforts to improve the quality of their products. The first establishes a Community system for the protection of **geographical indications and designations of origin** for agricultural products and foodstuffs[8]. It spells out with what requirements a product or foodstuff should comply in order to qualify for a protected designation of origin (PDO) or for a protected geographical indication (PGI). The other Regulation introduces an instrument for registering the names of products, thus enabling producers who so wish to obtain **certificates of the 'specific**

1   OJ L166, 23.06.1978 and OJ L338, 31.12.1993.
2   OJ L205, 03.08.1985.
3   OJ L99, 20.04.1996 and OJ L112, 07.05.1996. See also "Veterinary and plant health legislation" in the chapter on customs union.
4   OJ L104, 27.04.1996 and OJ L130, 31.05.1996.
5   OJ L327, 14.11.1981.
6   OJ L352, 15.12.1987 and OJ L260, 31.10.1995.
7   OJ L370, 30.12.1986 and OJ L174, 07.07.1990. See the heading on "Fight against hunger" in the chapter on the EU in the world.
8   OJ L208, 24.07.1992 and OJ L275, 26.10.1994.

character' of a traditional product (or foodstuff), the specific character being defined as the feature which distinguishes the product or foodstuff clearly from other similar products or foodstuffs belonging to the same category[1]. Another Regulation concerns **organic production** of agricultural products and indications referring thereto (labelling) on agricultural products and foodstuffs[2].

External wing of the CAP

The external wing of the common market organizations seeks to protect European agricultural prices against low price imports. In the same way as intervention on the internal market attempts to prevent the market prices falling too far below the intervention prices, intervention at the external frontiers tries to prevent that imports at low prices upset the European market. The **threshold price** (cereals, sugar, dairy products, olive oil) or the **sluice-gate price** (pigmeat, eggs and poultry) is a minimum price above which imports from third countries enjoy free access. For products for which a target price or guide price exists, the threshold price is determined in such a manner that the sales price of the imported product, allowance made for transport costs, is on a par with this price. For products for which there is no guide price (fruit and vegetables, table wine), the **reference price** is the minimum price at which a third country product can be imported and a tax is collected if the reference price is not respected.

The gap between the world price and the threshold price was originally bridged by an import levy. In accordance with the GATT agreements of December 1993, this gap is now partially closed by **customs duties**. However, for certain product groups such as cereals, rice, wine and fruit and vegetables, certain supplementary mechanisms that do not involve the collection of fixed customs duties are introduced in the basic regulations of the CAP by a Regulation, which lays down the adaptations and transitional measures required in order to implement the agreements concluded in the GATT framework[3]. The granting of **export subsidies** is limited henceforward to certain groups of agricultural products. In addition, such refunds are subject to limits in terms of quantity and value. The developed countries, including those of the EU, have committed themselves to reduce export subsidies by 36% and the actual volume of subsidized exports by 21% over a six-year period. Moreover, the Community has undertook to cut the global level of internal support by 20% over a period of six years, in line with the reform of the CAP. The basic principles of the CAP have been safeguarded, but Community preference will henceforward be ensured by customs duties instead of import levies, and these will risk to be not sufficient in some cases.

In fact, although customs duties on imports are a marketing bonus for Community products, the European Union is nevertheless very liberal in its agricultural external relations. The good will of the EU in the world arena was demonstrated by the reform of the common agricultural policy which permitted the Blair House pre-agreement with the United

---

1   Ibid.
2   OJ L198, 22.07.1991 and OJ, L159, 28.06.1994.
3   OJ L349, 31.12.1994.

States, on 20 November 1992[1], and the conclusion of the GATT Uruguay Round negotiations, on 15 December 1993.

The across-the-board **tariff concessions** which result from multilateral trade negotiations, such as those of GATT, are only part of the commitments weighing upon the EU's agricultural relationships. There are in addition preferential bilateral agreements with the majority of Mediterranean countries, in the form of association agreements or cooperation agreements which provide for concessions in the agricultural sector. Similarly, the Lomé Convention, concluded between the Community and 70 developing countries, grants free access to the EU for the products of these countries. Tariff reductions have, finally, been granted by the Community under the Generalized System of Preferences (GSP) to almost all the developing countries, notably in the framework of the United Nations Conference on Trade and Development (UNCTAD) and in the framework of the Europe Agreements with the countries of Central and Eastern Europe[2].

Structural policy

"Agricultural structures" are taken as meaning all production and work conditions in the sphere of agriculture, i.e. the number or age spread of people working in agriculture, the number and size of farms, the technical equipment on farms, the qualificational level of farmers, producers' groups, marketing and processing of agricultural products and so on. In December 1968, twelve years after the signature of the EEC Treaty, the Commission stated in its Memorandum on the reform of agriculture in the European Economic Community that in no other sector of the economy had traditional production structures clung on so tenaciously. As a consequence, the socio-economic situation of people working in agriculture was lagging far behind that of other economic groups.

A Community socio-structural policy was required to rectify this situation. Since the Community had initially turned all of its attention to establishing a common agricultural market, it had barely given a thought to structural policy. Although the Commission had been given the task in 1962 of coordinating national structural measures one with the other and with the Community policy on agricultural markets, it did not have sufficient powers to carry out this task correctly[3]. It is true also that, unlike market and pricing policy which, by its nature, required uniform provisions and centralized management, socio-structural policy could remain more in the realm of the Member States in that it had to be adjusted to the specificities of the different regions. But policy blueprinting and supervision had to be brought under the wing of the Community to promote economic and social cohesion and prevent uneven competition conditions for Community producers.

Agricultural information

Before embarking on a structural policy in the full sense of the term, the Community Institutions required exact information on farm income and the other parameters of agricul-

---

1   OJ L147, 18.06.1993.
2   On all these subjects see the chapter on the European Union in the world.
3   OJ 136, 17.12.1962.

tural economy in the Community. As a consequence, the **Farm accountancy data network** (FADN) was created in 1965[1]. The FADN relies on the services of farm accountancy offices in the Member States and on the participation of specially selected agricultural holdings, now numbering over 60,000, to produce objective and practical data on the economic situation of the various categories of agricultural holdings, including those upon which a close watch needs to be kept at European level. Thanks to the use of individual data, the FADN can carry out detailed analyses which make allowance for the variety of European agriculture. The FADN's conclusions form part of the prior study to any major Commission proposal. Parallel to the FADN is the European forestry information and communication system (EFICS)[2].

The other side of the equation, that of information on the activities of the European institutions for agricultural holdings, has been fulfilled by the European Centre for Promotion and Training in Agricultural and Rural Areas (**CEPFAR**), created in 1972 under the joint impetus of the Commission and professional agricultural organizations at European level. CEPFAR seeks to promote information and the basic and advanced vocational training of training staff, while contributing to the groundwork which goes into Community measures and decisions in the socio-structural field and in that of vocational training.

EAGGF-Guidance and socio-structural measures

The principle of partial financing of agricultural structures policy by Community funds won early recognition. When the European Agricultural Guidance and Guarantee Fund (EAGGF) was set up in 1962, it was stipulated that the "Guidance" Section would fund structures policy and should, in as much as this were feasible, enjoy one-third of the Fund's available resources[3]. The Fund Regulation stipulated that after a short transitional period, the EEC's financial contribution would be effected through financing programmes tackling major structural problems in Community agriculture. As things turned out, for more than ten years the Guidance Section chiefly funded individual projects in the Member States, such as farm roads, electrification and the construction of abattoirs.

The Commission felt that such an approach led to a dispersal of funds and recommended in its December 1968 Memorandum on the reform of agriculture that the Community opt for **common measures**, based on common criteria. These common measures, it suggested, would be defined in Community Directives but implemented from a legislative, regulatory and administrative viewpoint by the Member States. Following the proposals of the Commission, the Council adopted in 1972, the first three socio-structural Directives[4]. These three Directives sought to encourage older farmers to cease farming so that the area thus freed could be reallocated for the purposes of structural improvement, to provide an acceptable income level to those remaining in agriculture and to improve their socio-economic guidance and occupational skills. They were followed in 1975, by a special Directive on mountain and hill farming and farming in less favoured areas[5]; in 1977, by a Regulation on the development and rationalization of undertakings treating, processing or marketing agricultural products[6]; and in 1978, by a Regulation to encourage the formation of producers' groups and unions[7].

While these first common measures in the area of agricultural structures made an undeniable contribution to better socio-structural conditions, the results were not as spectacular as had been hoped, particularly since the Directive on the cessation of farming was a flop. Its failure can be attributed to the meagre nature of resources at its disposal and more importantly to the fact that it coincided with the recession of 1974 onwards, which hampered the professional mobility of the agricultural workforce. This in turn prevented people giving up farming and leaving the land free for modernization of holdings. Modernization consequently led not to changes in the structure of the holdings, but rather to an intensification of

1   OJ 109, 23.06.1965 and OJ L291, 06.12.1995.
2   OJ L165, 15.06.1989 and OJ L54, 25.02.1994.
3   OJ 30, 20.04.1962.
4   OJ L96, 23.04.1972 and OJ L362, 31.12.1985.
5   OJ L128, 19.05.1975 and OJ L327, 24.11.1982.
6   OJ L51, 23.02.1977 and OJ L91, 06.04.1990.
7   OJ L166, 23.06.1978 and OJ L338, 31.12.1993.

production having unfavourable effect on surplus levels of certain products. This was due, among other things, to the fact that access to modernization aid was simpler for agricultural holdings which were already the high performers. In the least favoured regions of the Community, farmers did not have the financial leeway or the professional, administrative and economic environment to be able to modernize their holdings.

The need to re-balance output against available outlets while helping farmers adapt to the new market and pricing policies led to more radical measures being introduced in 1988, their aim being to promote the set-aside of arable land and the extensification of certain types of production[1], to encourage the cessation of farming[2] and to provide farm income aid[3]. These measures have expired in 1993.

In implementing the **structural fund reform**, dealt with in the Chapter on Regional Development, the financing of the EAGGF's Guidance Section falls into the general framework of the Community's structural policy. The EAGGF's attention is focused on the objectives 5a (adaptation of farm structures), 5b (development of rural areas), for which it is the only source of aid, and 1 (development of regions whose development is lagging behind), where it operates jointly with other funds while taking special responsibility for aspects relating to rural development[4]. As a consequence of the revision of the Structural Funds in July 1993, the procedures were simplified and the financial monitoring and assessment systems were strengthened[5]. Financing from the EAGGF Guidance Section, like that from the other Structural Funds, is granted under the Community support frameworks (CSFs) and the single programming documents (SPDs) drawn up for the 1994-99 programming period.

The Guidance Section of the EAGGF may finance measures for speeding up the **adjustment of agricultural structures** in the framework of the reform of the CAP **(Objective 5a)** and in particular:

— market policy accompanying measures which help re-establish the balance between production and market capacity, where the financing of such measures is not provided for under the EAGGF Guarantee Section;

— measures to support farm incomes and to maintain viable agricultural communities in mountain, hill or less-favoured areas;

— concrete measures to encourage the installation of young farmers of either sex;

— measures to improve the efficiency of the structures of holdings, especially investments aimed at reducing production costs, promoting quality, improving the living and working conditions and promoting the diversification of production, including the production of non-food agricultural produce;

— measures to improve the marketing and processing of agricultural and forestry products, and to encourage the establishment of producers' associations.

Financial assistance by the EAGGF for the promotion of rural development and for the structural adjustment of regions whose development

1   OJ L106, 27.04.1988.
2   OJ L110, 29.04.1988.
3   OJ L84, 29.03.1989 and OJ L371, 20.12.1989.
4   OJ L185, 15.07.1988.
5   OJ L193, 31.07.1993.

is lagging behind (Objective 1) may, in addition to the above-mentioned measures, relate in particular to the following measures:
— the conversion, diversification, reorientation and adjustment of production potential;
— the promotion, quality labelling and investment for quality of local or regional agricultural and forestry products;
— individual or collective land or pasture improvement;
— irrigation and improvement of drainage systems;
— encouragement for tourist and craft investment;
— development and exploitation of woodlands, protection of the environment and maintenance of the countryside, where their financing is not provided for under the accompanying measures adopted under the reform of the CAP;
— development of agricultural and forestry advisory services and improvement of agricultural and forestry vocational training;
— financial engineering measures for agricultural and forestry businesses and for businesses for the processing and marketing of agricultural and forestry products.

Development of rural areas (Objective 5b) concerns rural areas in difficult circumstances which are not located in Objective 1 regions and involves approximately 9% of the population of the Fifteen. These areas have many weaknesses in the fields of infrastructures, social and other services, education and training. But they also have environmental assets which should be preserved and developed. The promotion of rural development in these areas is pursued through an integrated approach. Measures co-financed by the EAGGF concern not only the production, marketing and processing of agricultural products, but also the modernization of SMEs, the development of tourism and the crafts, reafforestation and environmental protection.

In the framework of socio-structural measures, a Regulation aims at improving the efficiency of agricultural structures[1] and another one at improving processing and marketing conditions for agricultural products[2]. Agri-environmental measures and those concerning afforestation and early retirement adopted in 1992 under the reform of the CAP are now financed by the EAGGF Guarantee Section[3].

Support measures for CAP reform

Alongside the market measures introduced by the 1992 reform, three types of "support measures" were adopted to ensure that farmers enjoy a fair income level, to increase the viability of farms and to protect the environment. These measures pursue three objectives: favour the introduction of early retirement schemes for farmers and farm labourers; promote the use of land for forestry, ecological or leisure purposes; and introduce or maintain protection schemes which favour the protection of the environment, the landscape and natural resources.

---

1   OJ L218, 06.08.1991 and OJ L244, 12.10.1995.
2   OJ L91, 06.04.1990 and OJ L302, 25.11.1994.
3   OJ L193, 31.07.1993 and OJ L338, 31.12.1993. See also the chapter on regional development.

The early retirement scheme enables Member States to grant aid to farmers and farm labourers aged at least 55 who wish to cease farming before the normal retirement age[1]. This aid can take the form of a premium upon cessation of farming, of annual compensation not linked to area, of an annual premium per hectare or a supplementary pension when the amount of this is too low to act as a retirement incentive. Early retirement is also offered to salaried staff if justified by sufficient professional capacity. Member States' expenditure on the establishment of early retirement schemes is 50% financed by the Community budget, a proportion rising to 75% for Objective 1 regions of the Structural Funds. Member States enjoy a certain degree of latitude for the adjustment of the early retirement scheme to their own social security regulations. Nevertheless, a Regulation sets out a common framework for introducing an integrated administration and control of direct aids under the reformed common agricultural policy[2].

The land thus released can either be farmed with respect of environmental requirements by new operators, who thus develop the structures and economic viability of their farm, or handed over to organizations which later transfer it back to new operators fulfilling the same conditions, or used by non-agricultural operators under environmentally compatible conditions. Community **support is granted to producers of certain arable crops** (cereals, oilseeds and protein plants) who agree to a fixed set-aside or to a rotational set-aside of part of their lands. Taking account of cereal stock trends in the Community and in the world, the Council reduced the compulsory set-aside rate to 10% for the 1996 harvest[3]. Arable land withdrawn from production for environmental purposes or for afforestation can be counted towards compulsory set-aside.

Afforestation aid is designed to offer an alternative use of agricultural land and contribute to the development of forestry[4]. It can cover: aid to meet the cost of afforestation; a premium per wooded hectare for its upkeep in the first five years; an annual per hectare premium to compensate for income losses due to the ceasing of agricultural activities; or aid for investments to improve the lay-out of wooded areas. The Member States implement these aid schemes by drawing up national or regional afforestation programmes. Community financing rises to 75% in regions falling under Objective 1 and to 50% in other areas.

The **agri-environmental arrangements** are designed to accompany the changes in the common market organizations and contribute to the attainment of the Community's agricultural and environmental policy objectives, such as: recourse to less polluting farming methods; the extensification of crop and livestock production in an environmentally favourable manner; the use of farmland in a manner allowing for protection of the environment, nature, landscapes and soil; the upkeep of abandoned agricultural and forestry land; the long-term set-aside of agricultural land for environment-related purposes; awareness raising and training of farm-

1   OJ L215, 30.07.1993.
2   OJ L355, 05.12.1992.
3   OJ L181, 01.07.1992 and OJ L312, 23.12.1995.
4   OJ L215, 30.07.1992.

ers in production methods which meet environmental protection require-ments[1]. Farmers agreeing to respect the defined requirements for at least five years receive an annual premium per hectare of farmland or per livestock unit. For set-aside, farmers must sign up for twenty years.

Agri-environmental measures and those concerning afforestation and early retirement adopted under the reform of the CAP are financed by the **EAGGF Guarantee Section**. Expenditure relating to set-aside arrangements is henceforth fully borne by the Guarantee Section, as opposed to just 50%[2].

Appraisal and outlook

The Common agricultural policy intrigues those who take an interest in European integration, both because of its advance on the Community's other policies and because of its complexity. The resources in its grasp represent nearly three-quarters of the Community Budget; the instruments which it applies are extremely varied and the terms which it uses to describe them would appear to be chosen precisely to prevent outsiders from understanding what they are. A close look, however, reveals that the complexity of the agricultural policy is due first and foremost to the variety of natural and economic situations which exist, the first relating to production and marketing conditions for different products, the second to the fact that the fifteen Member States have different structures and different currencies.

Despite their complexity and their separation according to product, the common market organizations are the kingpins behind the creation and operation of the common agricultural market. Customs duties, quantitative restrictions and measures having equivalent effect have been relegated to the dustbin of history and trade between the Member States has been fully liberalized. The **single agricultural market** signifies that a good originating in one Member State can be stored in another and marketed in a third. It can also be exported to third countries from any Member State. The merchandise of third countries gains entry to the common market by crossing just one of the Member States' borders. This has led to considerable growth in the agricultural and foodstuffs product range available to consumers.

The common market organization has buffered the European agricultural market against major fluctuations on the world market. In normal times, it has provided **market stability** through a policy of staggering supply (storage, monthly increases), of surplus disposal (refunds, denaturing) or through one of diversifying supply (imports from third countries, export levies). In times of crisis, it has resorted to drastic measures

---

1   Ibid. See also the heading on the protection of the flora and the fauna in the chapter on the environment.
2   OJ L182, 24.07.1993.

ranging from import or export bans to the withdrawal from the market of part of production or even the reduction of production factors.

Market stabilization is not an end in itself. It is a path to the other objectives of the common agricultural policy, notably that of food supply security. Europe has been spared any serious food shortages, which would have jeopardized both the common agricultural policy and European economic integration. Comparison of the abundance of foodstuffs in Western Europe with the shortages in Eastern Europe, before and after the fall of communist regimes, is a sufficient gauge of the CAP's success. The price of the Community's independence in foodstuffs has not been too high to pay. It goes without saying that the level of common prices corresponds to Europe's industrial and social development level. These prices are naturally enough not below those of the world market. Farmers have often had to be granted prices above world rates to encourage them to keep production at a level sufficient to guarantee internal demand in periods of world shortage. It is a mistake to think that European consumers could have enjoyed sustained abundance demand at low and stable world prices. These prices are often only for small quantities and minor products. If the European Union, which is the world's biggest importer, were to turn its attention to these products, European consumers would be the first victims of the resultant soaring prices. In the future, the EU must maintain its food-sufficiency and must convince its citizens that food-supply independence is in their own interests.

It must be said, however, that the common market organization has been a victim of its own success. Thanks to it, the Community which originally had a food supply deficit has reached a point of full self-supply for almost all agricultural products. It was in the seventies and even more so in the eighties that structural surpluses began to appear in several sectors: milk, wine, cereals, beef and veal. The press tarred these surpluses "butter mountains" and "wine lakes". It is true that in these sectors the price levels set by the Council were higher than that which the market would have reached itself by balancing out supply and demand. As a consequence, production outstripped both internal and external demand. A cut in the guarantee level would force many farmers out of agriculture. The number of farmers in Europe is, however, already so low that a further decrease would be catastrophic for cultivations, rural areas, landscapes and even European traditions that farmers preserve. Moreover, in a Europe that is after its economic and social cohesion it is unthinkable to live a part of its population without means of subsistence.

In response to this situation and to the hostility shown by the United States and other agricultural exporting countries towards the CAP during the GATT Uruguay Round negotiations, the Commission stated its commitment to in-depth revision of the market organization mechanisms. Proposals pursuing this aim were tabled and accepted by the Council, after several "agricultural marathons", in May 1992. The most radical change relates to the introduction of an agricultural income support system alongside the price support system, which has been the hallmark of the CAP since the 1958 Stresa conference. This basic adjustment should ensure better matching of production to internal and external market needs while preserving farmers' income level and along with it the rural economy and the environment.

These objectives are pursued through the accompanying of market measures - such as price cuts, production controls and set-aside - by structural measures. Early retirement and land release measures, the use of marginal land for purposes other than agriculture, the search for less intensive, and therefore less costly, farming methods, may contribute to the restructuring of farms, their conservation and, to a certain extent, better farm economics without any increase in production. In effect, since the 1992 reform, production has been brought under control, public stocks have gone down, the use of fertilizers and plant-health products has been reduced and the level of farm incomes overall has improved.

Finally, it should be emphasized that the agri-environmental arrangements introduced by the latest reform of the CAP open up a new future for farmers alongside their traditional role, as guardians of the environment and of Europe's rural heritage. In a Europe where urbanization is proceeding apace, this new role may be as vital for city-dwellers in need of calm and a breath of fresh air as the food produced by farmers. City-dwellers should acknowledge that rural areas, with their products, their traditions, their landscapes and their calm, are preserving their own standards of life. It is therefore only just that these city-dwellers, as tax-payers, also contribute to the upkeep of the green areas which surround their cities.

Bibliography on the common agricultural policy

□ BARAGIOLA Patrick, CHEVENIER Alain, SIMON Xavier, *DICOPAC; diction-naire de la politique agricole commune, le guide de la nouvelle Europe verte*, Agra-Europe, Bruxelles, 1994.

□ BAUDIN Pierre, *L'Europe face à ses marchés agricoles. De la naissance de la politique agricole commune à sa réforme*, Paris, Economica, 1993.

□ BLANCHET Jacques, LEFÈVRE Denis, *PAC, GATT, OMC: Le grand chambarde-ment*, Éd. France agricole, 1995.

□ BLUMANN Claude, *Politique agricole commune: Droit communautaire agricole et agro-alimentaire*, Litec, Paris, 1996.

□ BRINBAUM Dominique, "Un premier bilan de la réforme de la politique agricole commune", in *Problèmes économiques*, Paris, N° 2454, 10 janvier 1996, pp. 20-25.

□ CASPARIT Conrad, "Enlargement and CAP Reform", in *European Trends*, The Economist Intelligence Unit, London, 1996, pp. 76-81.

□ COMMISSION EUROPÉENNE, *Les négociations agricoles dans le cadre de l'Uruguay Round du GATT*, OPOCE, Luxembourg, 1995.

□ EUROPEAN COMMISSION, "EC Agricultural Policy for the 21st Century", *European Economy - Reports and Studies*, N° 4/1994.

   - *The Agricultural Income Situation in Less Favoured Areas of the EC*, OOPEC, Luxembourg, 1994.

   - *The Economics of the Common Agricultural Policy (CAP)*, OOPEC, Luxembourg, 1995.

□ FOLMER C. (et al.), *The Common Agricultural Policy beyond the MacSharry Reform*, Elsevier, Amsterdam, 1995.

□ GRANT Wyn, "Is Agricultural Policy still Exceptional?", in *Political Quarterly*, Oxford, Vol. 66, N° 3, July-September 1995.

□ GUYOMARD Hervé, MAHÉ Louis-Pascal, "Le GATT et la nouvelle politique agricole commune. Une réforme inachevée", in *Revue économique*, Paris, Vol. 46, N° 3, mai 1995, pp. 657-666.

□ LAUDE Yannick (ed.), *The Enlargement of the Common Agricultural Policy to the Ten Central and Eastern European Countries*, Club de Bruxelles, Brussels, 1996.

□ MAHÉ Louis-Pascal, CORDIER Jean, GUYOMARD Hervé, ROÉ Terry, "L'agriculture et l'élargissement", in *Économie internationale*, la Revue du CEPII, Paris, N° 62, 1995, pp. 233-254.

□ OCKENDEN Jonathan, FRANKLIN Michael, *European Agriculture: Making the CAP Fit the Future*, Royal Institute of International Affairs, London 1995.

□ PARLEMENT EUROPÉEN, *L'Europe et la forêt*, tome 1, tome 2, Série Agriculture - Pêche - Forêts, N° E-3, Luxembourg, 1994.

□ PETIT Yves, "La révision du système agrimonétaire: bis repetita placent" in *Revue du Marché commun et de l'Union européenne*, Paris, N° 391, octobre 1995, pp. 510-516.

□ TABARY Philippe, *Entre tracteurs et détracteurs. Les chocs de la PAC*, Le Cherche Midi éditeur, Paris, 1995.

□ TANGERMANN Stefan, "Eastward Enlargement of the EU: Will Agricultural Policy be an Obstacle?", *Intereconomics*, Hamburg, Vol. 30, N° 6, November-December 1995, pp. 277-284.

□ TROTMAN Charles, "Agricultural Policy Management: A Lesson in Unaccountability", in *Common Market Law Review*, Dordrecht, Vol. 32, N° 6, December 1995, pp. 1385-1406.

14. FISHERIES

Fisheries policy, which the Treaty of Rome initially made part of the Common Agricultural Policy by placing fishery products, products of the soil and stock-farming products in the same basket, became a fully-fledged common policy in 1983. It no longer has much in common with the CAP, apart from the fact that it makes use of instruments of market organization comparable to those of the CAP. Although the fishery sector does not carry the same weight in the Gross Domestic Product and does not employ as many people as agriculture, the establishment of a common policy required just as much effort as the Common Agricultural Policy.

The fishery resources policy, which embraces both internal and external policy, was the most troublesome to put into practice. It is the forum for such thorny questions as total allowable catch (TAC), the sharing out of TAC between the Member States (quotas) and access of the vessels from one Member State to the territorial waters of the others. Resources policy also has to cope with difficult negotiations with third countries to settle questions of access for Community vessels to their waters and vice versa. Although this kingpin of the common fisheries policy is analyzed first, it was the last arrival on the fisheries scene.

The origins of the two other pillars of the common fisheries policy date back to 1970. The common organization of markets has clearly covered a great deal of ground since then and its reform, in 1981, opened the door to the final compromise on fisheries. Structural policy, for its part, has been torn by national differences on the question of resource conservation. For many years it was restricted to interim measures and was only firmly established with the agreement on resources, reached in January 1983.

Economic and legal framework

The market in fishery products is similar to that in agricultural products. This is why the EEC Treaty stipulates that by agricultural products is meant products of the soil, stock-farming products and fishery products and that the operation and establishment of a common market for all of these products must be accompanied by the introduction of a Common Agricultural Policy (Articles 38 and 39). This is therefore the fundamental reason for and legal basis of a common policy in the fisheries sector.

The Treaty consequently placed fisheries policy and the Common Agricultural Policy in the same basket and the two were initially one and the same. More precisely, the organization of the market and structural policy covering fisheries formed part of the Common Agricultural Policy. There is however a basic difference between products of the soil and stock-farming on the one hand and fisheries products on the other. Whereas the first two remain within the boundaries laid down by man, fish have no respect for frontiers! Migratory fish, such as herring and tuna, do not have to show their passports when they enter the economic zone of a Member State! There are therefore problems relating to fisheries resources which simply do not exist for products of the soil and stock-farming. This is the first reason why a specific common policy was required for fisheries products. This specificity is now acknowledged by the EEC Treaty in Article 3, as amended in Maastricht, which speaks of a common policy in the fields of agriculture and fisheries.

The second justification for a common fisheries policy is specific to this sector. Between 1956 and 1965, world fish production rose by 50%. Investments over this period of economic growth, vessel modernization and higher productivity pushed up catches to such a high level that stock replenishment was threatened and the commoner species, such as herring, began to be exhausted. In times of surplus, storage aid, export subsidies and import restrictions were required. In times of shortage, on the other hand, it was necessary to regulate and monitor fishing to ensure that the seas fished by the Member States did not become empty of fish. All of this had to be achieved at Community level, if the aim was a common fisheries market.

The 200 mile rule

The development which revolutionized fishing in Community waters and beyond was the adoption of the 200 mile rule. Since the end of the Second World War, certain coastal states had begun to eat into the "mare liberum" to reserve for themselves the riches which they held, particularly fish. National bagging of coastal waters, traditionally held at canon range - taken to be three nautical miles - was unilaterally extended by several States to 12 miles after the failure of the 1958 and 1960 United Nations Conferences to uphold their demands.

But certain Latin American countries were already calling for a reserved fishing zone of 200 miles. They sought thus to protect themselves against the dynamism of North America vessels, 200 miles being the distance from the coasts of Chile to the Humboldt Current, a warm current which stimulates fish spawning and marks the boundary of a zone rich in fishery resources. The North Americans, for their part, were not adverse to the idea of keeping their own waters, also rich in fish, for their own vessels. The vote in the US Congress at the beginning of 1976 in favour of the extension of a fishery conservation zone to 200 miles from March 1, 1977 stepped up the pace of the so-called "creeping jurisdiction" movement. Mexico and Iceland had already adopted similar measures in the North Atlantic. They were to be followed by Canada and Norway.

Over the same period, the Commission became increasingly conscious of the fact that the movement to extend fishery limits to 200 miles would create special problems for the EEC, notably as regards access to the fishing zones of the Member States and the conservation of resources. But at the same time it was aware that the movement in this direction was unstoppable. It proposed negotiating briefs moving with the tide which were accepted by the Council on July 27, 1976. The Community was therefore ready to accept the 200 mile limit introduced by the fifth session of the third United Nations Conference on the law of the sea.

Free access to fishing zones

The implementation of the 200 mile rule provided a striking illustration of the need for a common conservation policy for these new Community resources. The principle of free access to the fishing zones of Member States was incorporated into the Regulation establishing the fisheries structural policy, adopted as far back as 1970[1], the year in which accession negotiations were opened with four countries - the United Kingdom, Ireland, Denmark and Norway - all major fishing nations, the total catch of which amounted to double that of the six founding Member States.

The principle of equal access to fishing zones therefore formed part of the "acquis communautaire" (existing Community legislation) which applicants had to accept. Although they attempted to abolish the rule of equal access during accession negotiations, they only succeeded in postponing its full application. Articles 100 to 103 of the **Act of Accession** granted a temporary derogation to the 1970 Community Regulation, authorizing the Member States to maintain until December 31, 1982 exclusive fishing rights for their vessels in waters up to six nautical miles from their coasts (stretched to twelve miles for certain regions of the acceding States and of France), provided that the historic fishing rights of vessels from other Member States were respected in these waters. Despite this temporary derogation, the principle of equal access to economic zones was one of the main causes for the negative votes of the Norwegian people on Community membership, in 1973 as in 1994.

Basic principles of the common policy

The Accession Act further stipulated that at the latest six years after accession, the Community would set fishing conditions in such a manner as to guarantee the protection of fishing grounds and the conservation of the sea's biological resources. But fishing conditions were turned on their head in September 1976 by the adoption of the 200 mile limit by the United Nations Conference.

In October 1976, the Commission put forward proposals for the establishment of a Community system for the management and conservation

---

1   OJ L236, 27.10.1970.

of fishery resources. This system was based upon three main ideas: selective conservation measures, catch quotas and fishing licences. Selective conservation measures include, for example, measures to stop or restrict fishing at certain periods, to define types of fishing vessels, to set norms for the mesh sizes of fishing nets or to define the minimum size and weight for each species fished. Catch quotas represent the sharing out between the Member States of the Total Allowable Catch (TAC). Fishing licences are the manner in which national quotas are shared out at national level, with the registration and the granting of a licence to each fishing vessel and/or skipper.

There could be grounds for viewing these quotas as measures having equivalent effect to quantitative restrictions, forbidden by Articles 30 et seq. of the Treaty of Rome. This point was made at the Court of Justice which rejected this argument, concluding that catch quotas were applicable at production stage, whereas Articles 30 et seq. concern distribution. The Court further declared that although the quotas sought to restrict short-term production, their aim was to avoid the depletion of fishery resources which would jeopardize consumer supply in the long term[1]. The main significance, however, of this ruling was that it acted as a forerunner to the Community decision-making process by clarifying the **Community's powers** in the fisheries sector. The Court noted that in the internal framework, the Community had the power to take all measures concerning the conservation of fishery resources and that on the external front, the Community had the power to enter into international stock conservation commitments. The Court ruled that the powers of the Member States in the area of the conservation of fishery resources were of a temporary nature and, in accordance with the provisions of Article 102 of the Act of Accession, should cease at the latest from the sixth year after accession.

In another ruling the Court confirmed that, in matters concerning the high seas which fall under its jurisdiction, the Community has the same legislative powers as are enjoyed under international law by the flag State, namely the power to introduce measures for the conservation of marine stocks applying to vessels flying the flag of a Member State or registered in a Member State[2].

The Commission felt that **the total allowable catch** should be shared out in accordance with the golden rule of the common market, namely freedom from all form of discrimination. This amounted to equality of access for the vessels of the Member States to Community waters. However, the very uneven spread of fishery resources between the waters of the Member States and the fact that fishermen consider it their exclusive right to fish in the strip of coastal water under the jurisdiction of their State and to continue to fish in areas where they have traditionally fished, even if these areas are no longer covered by open access but fall into the economic zone of another Member State, give a measure of the difficulties faced by a Community policy of fishery resources management and conservation. As will be seen in the next section of this Chapter, six years of hard-hitting discussions were required on these points, before a policy finally emerged in January 1983.

Three years later, the **entry of Spain and Portugal** to the Community had considerable impact on the common fisheries policy, due to the size of the fishing fleets of the two new Member States and the volume of their production which made the Community the third biggest producer of fishery products in the world. In the process of adapting to this new

---

1   Judgment of 14 July 1976, joined cases 3/76, 4/76 and 6/76, Kramer, ECR 1976.
2   Judgment of 24 November 1993, Case C-405/92, ECR 1993.

situation, the Community had to consolidate or obtain new fishery resources in the waters of third countries and certain international waters (Atlantic Ocean, Indian Ocean) and to bolster its structural policy in an attempt to modernize the fishing fleet and adapt it to catch possibilities. New guidelines were accepted by all and the principles of the common policy launched in 1983 were not called into question; only some temporary exemptions were granted to the two new Member States, which expired on 1 January 1996[1]. Identical arrangements for access for the vessels of all the Member States exist since that date. These arrangements take into account, however, the special needs of the regions whose socio-economic development is especially dependent on fisheries[2].

Conservation and management of resources

The need for a policy to conserve fishery resources became evident towards the middle of the sixties, when, after long years of overfishing, production began to stagnate and the Community's levels of self-supply began to fall for certain popular species, notably herring and tuna. Since a similar situation prevailed in the rest of the world, the concept of a **total allowable catch (TAC)** was adopted by the United Nations Conferences on the law of the sea, culminating in the extension of fishing zones to 200 miles. Under the TAC rule, each coastal state uses scientific data to set a catch level which enables sufficient reproduction of fishery stocks, then it determines the amount which can be fished by its own vessels and that which can be granted to third countries in exchange for or through sale of catch rights. The central aim of the TAC is to conserve and enhance existing fishing zones in the interests of both the fishing industry and consumers.

In a Resolution of November 3, 1976 made public on May 7, 1981[3], the Council agreed that the Member States would extend, by concerted action, the limits of the fishing zones to 200 miles from January 1, 1977 for North Sea and North Atlantic coasts, without prejudice to action of a similar nature for other fishing zones under their jurisdiction, notably the Mediterranean. From January 1, 1977, the Community's exclusive economic zone therefore embraced numerous and potentially rich fishing grounds, the conservation and correct management of which was the responsibility of the Community.

While the extension of **the economic zones** to a distance of 200 miles off coasts - or to the median line when the distance between coasts did not permit a limit of 200 miles - extends the rights of coastal States in these zones, it also means greater obligations for them. The most significant of these obligations is that of conserving biological resources which, given the interdependence of fishery stocks, is a matter of some importance to fishermen and consumers both of the coastal state and of neighbouring states.

The conservation of fisheries resources and the preservation of marine biodiversity are common objectives of the fisheries policy and of the **environment policy**. The environmental

---

1   OJ L140, 03.06.1994.
2   OJ L71, 31.03.1995.
3   OJ C105, 07.05.1981.

impact of fisheries and the sustainable development of resources are taken into account, in particular, by the systematic consultation of scientific experts when legislative measures on the exploitation of resources are drafted by the Commission. But the proposals of the Commission, which are based on scientific opinion are generally revised upwards by the Ministers responsible for fisheries, who at the annual fixing of TAC often yield to the pressures exercised by the influential fishing lobbies.

Fisheries research is essential for both the decision-making process and the implementation of the common fisheries policy, particularly the conservation and management of resources. Following a Commission communication on European fisheries research[1], the specific RTD programme in the field of marine science and technology (MAST III) gives priority, in fundamental research, to the ecology and economics of fisheries[2]. As regards applied research, priority is given to the conservation and replenishment of stocks and new fishing methods.

Allocation of resources

The question of equal access conditions and that of the allocation of resources between Member States formed the crux of the design and implementation of the common fisheries policy. In this field as in many others, the diverging interests of the Member States proved to be a formidable obstacle. Many of them, pushed by the 200-mile rule out of the waters in which they had traditionally fished, had to fall back on the North Sea, where overfishing had already frittered away available resources. Since the three Member States which had acceded to the Community in 1973 (United Kingdom, Ireland, Denmark) had much vaster and richer fishery zones than the founding members, their resources were jealously coveted by the latter. Founding members, to shore up their claims, called upon the Community principle of equal access to and working of fishing grounds in the sea waters under the sovereignty of the Member States by boats flying the flag of one of the Member States. This principle, embodied in the 1970 Regulation establishing the policy of fishery structures, was fiercely fought by applicant States, who succeeded in winning a temporary derogation running to December 31, 1982.

Against this backdrop, the Commission put together in October 1976 its first proposals for a Community system to conserve fishery resources, revolving around three main principles: restriction of catches by the setting of an annual total allowable catch (TAC); the allocation of available resources between the vessels of the Member States, allowance made for the interests of coastal fishermen; and technical measures to manage resources and monitor the system. These proposals sparked off six years of "marathon" negotiations which would not have been out of place in the Common Agricultural Policy. Although the Member States hammered out agreements on many points, such as interim measures and the external aspects of the resource conservation policy, the stumbling block was Community regulations on access to fishing grounds and diverging national interests in this area. France and other continental Member States claimed "**historic rights**" in fishing grounds situated in British waters. The United Kingdom, which held nearly 60% of the Community's fishery resources in its waters, called for a preferential system for its fishing industry within a strip of 12 miles off the coast.

Discussions continued as the deadline of 1982, the last year under which the derogation to the principle of equal access granted by Article 100 of the 1972 Act of Accession, drew closer. During this year at the latest, the Council, in accordance with Article 101 of the Act of Accession, had to examine the provisions which could replace the derogations running to

---

1   COM (93) 95, 16.03.1993.
2   OJ L334, 22.12.1994. See the chapter on research.

December 21, 1982. If it failed to do so, freedom of access would normally have become applicable in the fishery sector, as provided for by the Regulation on fishery structures. Either the risk of this, the Commission's tireless efforts or the pressure of public opinion, which had come to see the negotiations as somewhat of a red herring, pushed France and the United Kingdom in June 1981 into a compromise maintaining the status quo. The system in force was to be extended for ten years, possibly renewable, during which the United Kingdom would keep an exclusive 12-mile zone off its coast, but would respect the historic rights of fishermen from other Community Member States.

The Commission took the Franco-British arrangement on board in its proposals and all seemed set for the Community system of resource management and conservation to be in place well before December 1982. But in October 1982, Denmark put a spoke in the wheels, demanding that the catch quotas for its fleet be increased in the agreement. The Council had to buckle down to talks on a number of occasions and several strange incidents took place (including the departure in January 1983 of a flotilla of Danish fishing vessels to conquer British waters!) before Denmark was brought back into line and a group of Regulations implementing the Community policy to conserve fishery resources adopted on January 25, 1983[1]. This policy covered both internal and external aspects that we examine successively.

Internal aspects

The new **Community system for fisheries and aquaculture,** approved in December 1992, replaced the system established on 25 January 1983 keeping, however, some of its features: reserved access within the 12-mile band; special arrangements for the 'Shetland box'; the principle of relative stability in the allocation of fishing possibilities with limited exploitation rates[2]. It covers all activities relating to the exploitation of living aquatic resources, and also to the processing and marketing of fishery and aquaculture products. Its basic objective is to tackle the depletion of stocks and ensure responsible and sustainable exploitation of aquatic resources by means of, in particular, the establishment of an appropriate framework for the conservation and protection of these resources.

To that end a series of measures are provided for: the establishment of a Community system of fishing licences, administered by the Member States and applicable to all Community fishing vessels, both in its waters as in those of third countries[3]; the issuing and management by the Member States of special fishing permits (authorization of exploitation of specific fisheries)[4]; the setting , on a multiannual basis, of multiannual guidance programmes (MGPs)[5] as well as of the objectives and detailed rules for restructuring the Community fisheries sector with a view to achieving a

---

1   OJ L24, 27.01.1983.
2   OJ L388, 31.12.1992 and OJ L350, 31.12.1994.
3   OJ L341, 31.12.1993.
4   OJ L171, 06.07.1994.
5   OJ L401, 21.12.1992.

balance on a sustainable basis between resources and their exploitation[1]; and the establishment of systems for the management of fishing effort and for control of the CFP, examined below.

When, for a particular species or related species, restriction of catch volume is necessary, the total allowable catch (TAC) for the stock or group of stocks, the share available to the Community, the allocation of this share between Member States, total catch allocated to third countries and the specific conditions under which it must take place are drawn up every year[2]. The same is true of the setting of prices for fishery products[3]. The **annual allocation of catch quotas** between the Member States is a process almost as difficult as the annual setting of agricultural prices. In both cases, a delicate balance must be struck between the aspirations of the different Member States.

The annual setting of TACs and their allocation between the Member States are, naturally enough, based on certain criteria. **TAC setting** takes into account scientific opinions on the need to protect fishing grounds and fish stocks, balancing them against the interests of Community consumers and fishermen. It was mentioned above that quite often the latter interests weigh more than the scientific opinions. However, TAC setting also takes into consideration the agreements which the Community has with third countries, such as Norway and Canada. The allocation of the TACs between Member States (catch quotas) is also carried out in light of traditional fishing activities, possible loss of fishing potential in the waters of third countries and the specific needs of regions which are particularly dependent on fishing and its related industries. In order to improve the conditions for exploiting resources, **special fishing permits** may be issued to Community fishing vessels and to vessels flying third-country flags operating in the Community fishing area[4], or, inversely, to Community vessels operating in the waters of a third country in the context of a fisheries agreement[5].

The policy of resource management, which was traditionally based on quantitative limitation of catches, was complemented in 1995 by a **system for the management of the fishing effort**. It establishes the criteria and procedures for bringing fleet capacities and efforts under control in the Community waters of the Atlantic and aims at a spatial distribution of fishing effort which preserves the existing balances between different areas[6]. On this basis another Regulation establishes a system for the management of fishing effort relating to certain Community fishing areas and resources by fixing the annual maximum fishing effort for each Member State and each fishery, defined by the fleet capacity deployed and by the fleet's activity in terms of days at sea[7]. This system is designed to guarantee no increase in overall fishing effort, full use of the fishing

---

1   OJ L10, 14.01.1994.
2   See, for example, OJ L330, 30.12.1995 and OJ L115, 09.05.1996.
3   See, for example, OJ L292, 07.12.1995.
4   OJ L171, 06.07.1994.
5   OJ L350, 31.12.1994.
6   OJ L71, 31.03.1995.
7   OJ L199, 24.08.1995.

opportunities of the Member State, observance of the principle of relative stability and the preservation of the balance of resources in highly sensitive areas.

Technical conservation measures are defined to protect marine biological resources. They concern, for example, mesh sizes, levels of by-catches, minimum marketing sizes and catch restrictions in certain zones, during certain periods or with certain gear[1]. Nets with a mesh below that authorized can only be kept aboard ship if they are correctly stowed and kept in such a manner that they cannot easily be used. The use of drift-nets for fishing certain species in certain waters is banned. The use of explosives, poison, sleep-inducing substances or fire arms for fishing is forbidden. Fish which do not reach the minimum size cannot be kept aboard, transferred at sea, unloaded, transported, sold or stored, but must be immediately thrown back into the sea. Purse seines may be used only for catching the target species without endangering marine mammals.

All the catches of a stock or group of stocks subject to a quota and landed by fishing vessels of a Member State are counted against the quota of the Member State in question. When the quota has been exhausted, the Member State sets a date from which the fishing of this stock is forbidden. The final decision in this matter rests however with the Commission, who informs the Member States of its decision. In 1995, for example, the Commission closed 67 fishing grounds following the exhaustion of a TAC or a quota. The Commission informs the Member States that fishing is soon to be halted due to the exhausting of the TAC, the quota, allocation or part available to the Community, it is possible that some Member States have overstepped their quota, whereas others may still have some slack to take up. In such a case, quotas can be exchanged after notification of the Commission. Rules also exist for remedying the injury caused by the halting of certain fishery activities[2].

If resources are to be fished in an optimal manner, there must be **permanent monitoring of fishing** by surveillance ships. This is a somewhat complicated matter for the Community, which does not have its own powers or means of coercion and has to rely on those of the Member States. Member States authorities are obliged to inspect fishing vessels in accordance with certain common rules to ensure that these restrictions on fishing possibilities are respected[3]. Fishing vessel captains must keep a log book listing the quantities of each species caught and kept and must submit a declaration listing the quantities unloaded after each trip to the authorities in the place of unloading. A **Community fishing vessel register** establishes rules on the collection by Member States of the data necessary to determine their vessels fishing effort exerted on fish stocks, so as to ensure balanced exploitation of them[4]. The characteristics for fishing vessels are defined by Regulation[5].

The inspectors of the Member States are, however, themselves monitored by the Commission. It exercises its power to monitor the observance by Member States of TAC, quotas and technical conservation measures by sending inspectors to fishing ports in the Member States and on board surveillance ships in Community waters and in certain international waters. In this framework, it opens infringement proceedings against Member States which overstep their catch quotas or fail to respect their obligations in the area of surveillance or fishery resource conservation and management. The Community makes a financial contribution to national expenditure for the modernization and development of surveillance and monitoring facilities rendered necessary by the application of the Community arrangements for the conservation of fishery resources[6].

The Community arrangements for the conservation and management of fishery resources set up in 1983 did not include the Mediterranean. The fishery resources of this sea, under major threat from pollution and over-working, had to be protected by specific arrangements. The first such arrangements were set up by a Council Regulation of November 28, 1991, establishing a Community framework for specific measures to conserve and manage **fishery resources in the Mediterranean**[7]. Projects which can be financed by the

1   OJ L288, 11.10.1986 and OJ L329, 30.12.1995.
2   OJ L50, 19.02.1987.
3   OJ L261, 20.10.1993 and OJ L301, 14.12.1995.
4   OJ L19, 22.01.1994.
5   OJ L288, 11.10. 1986 and OJ L339, 29.12.1994.
6   OJ L301, 14.12.1995.
7   OJ L331, 03.12.1991.

Community notably include the restructuring of traditional fisheries, the adaptation of specialized fisheries (sponges, coral, sea urchin), the monitoring of fishing activities, the development of a statistical network and the coordination of research and the use of scientific data. Another Regulation lays down certain technical measures for the conservation of fishery resources in the Mediterranean[1].

External aspects

The external aspects of the resource policy are governed by the Council Resolution of November 3, 1976, known as **The Hague Agreements** and made public on May 7, 1981[2]. In this Resolution, the Council agreed that from January 1, 1977, fishing by third country vessels within the economic zone of the Community would be governed by agreements between the Community and the third countries in question. It also agreed that there was a need to ensure, through **Community agreements**, that the Community's fishing industry was granted or kept rights in the waters of third countries. With this aim in mind, the Council charged the Commission with opening negotiations with third countries to conclude framework agreements on general conditions for access to fishery resources in the fishing zones of these third countries and in the fishing zones of the Member States.

As a consequence, although the Community had not yet settled its internal fishery problems, by the end of 1976 it presented itself to the outside world as a single coastal state, obliging third countries which wished to fish in the fishing zones of the different Member States to conclude an agreement with the Community as such. The framework agreements negotiated by the Commission in the Community's name implied recognition of the Community's jurisdiction over the **Community 200 mile zone**, its right to set TACs within this zone and to give third countries access to the surplus part of TACs while obtaining access for the Member States to the surplus of co-signatory third countries.

Since this date, numerous fishery agreements have been concluded between the Community and countries with rich fishing grounds such as Madagascar, Angola, Mauritania, Morocco, Mozambique, the Seychelles and Senegal. These agreements and their renewal are negotiated by the Commission and concluded after a Council Decision, often in the form of an exchange of letters, defining the fishing rights of the Community and the financial compensation to be paid by it to the government of the country in question[3].

On the multilateral front, the Community is either a member or an observer of several international fishery organizations, such as the North-West Atlantic Fisheries Organization (NAFO)[4], the North East Atlantic Fisheries Commission (NEAFC), the International Council for the Exploration of the Sea (ICES)[5]; and International Baltic Sea Fishery Commission[6]. The Community is also a signatory of the Agreement relating to the implementation of Part XI of the United Nations Convention on the Law of the Sea, which concerns the exploitation of the seabed[7]. It had a major influence on the text of the Agreement, concluded in 1955 in the

---

1   OJ L171, 06.07.1994.
2   OJ C105, 07.05.1981.
3   See, for example, OJ L193, 16.08.1995 and OJ L76, 26.03.1996.
4   OJ L389, 30.12.1989.
5   OJ L149, 10.06.1987.
6   OJ L237, 26.08.1983 and OJ L59, 08.03.1996.
7   OJ L215, 20.08.1994.

framework of that Convention, on the conservation and management of straddling stocks and highly migratory species such as tuna and swordfish.

Following clashes between Canadian authorities and Spanish fishing vessels, an agreement was concluded between the Community and Canada on fisheries in the context of the NAFO Convention, that allocates the total allowable catches of Greenland halibut and provides for new controls on fishing activities in that area[1]. To the latter end the Council adopted various measures: the establishment of an observer scheme applicable to Community fishing vessels operating in the NAFO regulatory area; a pilot project on satellite tracking in that area; new provisions for the application of the scheme of joint international inspection; and conservation and management measures for fishery resources in the NAFO regulatory area[2].

Common organization of the market

Contrasting sharply with the gestation of the policy for the management and conservation of fishery resources, the creation of a **common market for fishery products** did not come up against major difficulties. Such a market organization was moreover expressly provided for by the Treaty, with Articles 38 and 40 stipulating that the operation and development of the common market for agricultural products (including fishery products) should be accompanied by the establishment of a common (agricultural) policy and that the latter should incorporate common organization of the market. Common organization of the market in the fishery sector was born in October 1970 and amended several times at later stages. The most recent Regulation in this field aims at adapting the common organization of markets and the support mechanisms to developments in production and marketing conditions[3].

One of the measures necessary to implement the common organization of markets is the application of **common standards for the marketing** of the products in question, to ensure that products which do not meet a sufficient quality level are not marketed and to stimulate trade on the basis of fair competition. A Regulation adopted on January 19, 1976 sets common marketing standards for certain fresh or chilled fish for human consumption and representing around 60% of Community production and 80% of imports[4]. In accordance with this Regulation, fish freshness plays a determinant role in assessment of its quality. The common marketing standards therefore take the form of a breaking down into freshness grading on the one hand and size grading on the other, the latter necessary due to differences in consumers' buying habits.

The application of these standards means that there must be inspection of the products subject to them. Member States must therefore submit products to a **conformity check**, which can take place at all the marketing stages and also during transport. The Member States must also take all appropriate steps to penalize infringements of marketing standards.

The adjustment of supply to market requirements is left in the hands of producers' organizations, but they must not hold a dominant position on the common market. A

---

1   OJ L317, 30.12.1995.
2   OJ L329, 30.12.1995 and OJ L330, 30.12.1995.
3   OJ L388, 31.12.1992 and OJ L350, 31.12.1994.
4   OJ L20, 28.01.1976 and OJ L176, 20.07.1993.

producers' organization is taken as being any recognized organization or association of such organizations, set up on the initiative of producers in order to take measures ensuring that fishing is carried out in a rational manner, to improve sales conditions for their production and to stabilize prices. The Member States officially recognize producers' organizations which so request provided that they meet certain conditions[1]. They can be granted national aid in the three years following their recognition, to help with their operation and with the investments engendered by the application of common rules.

A **guide price** is set at the beginning of the fish marketing year for the main fresh or chilled products[2]. This price is based on the average of the prices recorded on wholesale markets or in representative ports during the three previous fish marketing years. It makes allowance for possible evolution in production and demand and for the need to ensure stable market prices and to contribute to supporting the income of producers, without forgetting consumers' interests. A **Community withdrawal price** is set in line with the freshness, size or weight and presentation of the product, which must be equal to at least 70% while not exceeding 90% of the guide price.

Within this range, producers' organizations can **set a withdrawal price** below which they no longer sell the products supplied by their members. Should this situation arise, the organizations must grant compensation to member producers in line with the quantities of the main fresh or chilled products withdrawn from the market. The organizations set up intervention funds formed by contributions based on the quantities put on sale or run a compensation system to finance these withdrawal measures.

As part of their support for the organizations' activities, the Member States grant **financial compensation** to organizations operating in accordance with Community regulations. Financial compensation is only granted for products which, once put up for sale under normal conditions, do not find a buyer at the Community withdrawal price. Products for which financial compensation has been paid must be disposed off for use other than human consumption. Some products withdrawn from the market at the withdrawal price can, however, be granted a **carry-over premium**, provided that certain conditions are satisfied. This premium seeks to limit sporadic withdrawals and to create the economic conditions enabling later use for human consumption[3].

The common organization of the market in fishery products entails a system governing trade in these products with third countries[4]. For the main fishery products, a **free-at-frontier price** is set on the basis of the prices recorded by the Member States. Depending on the products, various measures can be taken should the free-at-frontier price remain below the reference price during at least three successive market days and if large quantities of products are imported from third countries[5]. However, the fishing vessels of third countries may land directly and market their catches at Community ports, subject to special conditions concerning health checks, declaration and prices[6]. Inasmuch as is necessary to enable

---

1   OJ L331, 26.11.1982.
2   See, for example, OJ L292, 07.12.1995.
3   OJ L392, 31.12.1992 and OJ L129, 14.06.1995.
4   OJ L388, 31.12.1992 and OJ L350, 31.12.1994.
5   OJ L48, 26.02.1993 and OJ L73, 26.03.1993.
6   OJ L121, 12.05.1994.

economic export on a large scale of fishery products on the basis of the prices for these products on the world market, the difference between the latter and Community prices can be made up by an **export refund**[1].

Structural policy

The fishery sector is at least as vulnerable as agriculture. Production depends on several factors which cannot be controlled by producers: weather, water pollution, delimitation of fishing zones. The sea fishing sector, which makes up the bulk of the fishing industry, has a highly specific social structure and arduous living and working conditions. Fishing is moreover often economically vital in certain coastal regions without other economic resources and it is a major breadwinner for the people living in these regions. This is why the common organization of the fishery market must be accompanied by a common structural policy. This fact was recognized in 1970, which saw the combined adoption of the Regulation establishing a common structural policy and that of the Regulation creating a common organization of the market for the fishery products sector.

Despite the structural measures that were thus implemented during the seventies and the eighties, the fisheries sector was confronted in the early nineties by a very serious structural crisis, characterized notably by: the widespread chronic overcapacity of the fleets; the over-capitalization and high debt levels of the companies; the restrictions brought to certain fishing techniques in respect of the conservation of resources; the setting of Community standards with regard to hygiene, health, product quality as well as safety on board. Moreover, many coastal regions suffered from a fragile socio-economic fabric, in particular the areas dependent on fishing, for many of which - if one took account of the induced activities - fishing was the principal or even the only activity.

On account of the aggravation of the structural problems of the fisheries sector, when the Community revised the Regulations of the Structural Funds, in July 1993, it decided to establish a **Financial Instrument for Fisheries Guidance (FIFG)**[2]. Designed to group together the financial resources allocated to structural measures in the fisheries sector which had hitherto come under the common fisheries or agricultural policies, the FIFG has the following tasks: to contribute to achieving a sustainable balance between resources and their exploitation; to strengthen the competitiveness of structures and the development of economically viable undertakings in the sector; and to improve the market supply and the value added to fisheries and aquaculture products.

The FIFG may contribute towards the funding of investments and measures which contribute to the accomplishment of one or more of its tasks in the following fields:
— restructuring and renewal of the fishing fleet;
— modernization of the fishing fleet;

---

1   OJ L93, 07.04.1978.
2   OJ L193, 31.07.1993.

— improvement of the conditions under which fishery and aquaculture products are processed and marketed;
— development of aquaculture and of structural works in coastal waters;
— facilities at fishing ports;
— search for new markets;
— specific measures.

A Council Regulation has fully integrated from 1 January 1994 the structural aspects of the common fisheries policy into Structural Fund legislation[1]. The Regulation sets rules for the granting of assistance from the FIFG for: implementation of multiannual guidance programmes for fishing fleets, covering in particular adjustment of fishing effort, reorientation of fishing activities, fleet renewal and vessel modernization; investment in aquaculture, resource development in coastal waters, fishing port facilities and processing and marketing of production; other activities such as promotion campaigns, searching for new outlets and temporary cessation of fishing. It also defines socio-economic measures linked to the restructuring of the fisheries sector to assist the oldest fishermen (early retirement, individual compensatory payments to fishermen whose vessel ceases fishing).

Of course, most fishing-dependent coastal communities are located in **areas assisted by the Structural Funds** (areas covered by objectives 1, 2 or 5b of the structural policy[2]); but one eighth of all the fishermen of the Twelve are located out of such zones. Moreover, it is the zone as a whole which usually benefits from the Structural Funds. The fishing industry and the fishermen themselves are not generally in a position to take advantage of most of the facilities. Indeed, owing to its extreme localized nature, the fisheries sector often experiences difficulties in benefiting from Community structural interventions, with the exception of Objective 5a (assistance to the restructuring and modernization of undertakings in the fisheries sector). Even this objective is only able to intervene in the area of major structural issues within the industry, but can provide no socio-economic assistance.

For all these reasons the Commission, in its communication on the future of Community initiatives under the Structural Funds for the period 1994-99, proposed the creation of a **Community initiative concerning the restructuring of the fisheries sector, named PESCA**, complementary to structural aid available through the Community Support Frameworks[3]. The aim of PESCA is to put the fisheries sector in a position enabling it to adapt to change, to help it to bear the resulting social and economic consequences, and to contribute to the diversification of the regions concerned by the development of creative employment activities.

To this end, **eligible measures to PESCA support** are the following:
— diversification of activities in the eligible areas, including the development of fishing ports, with a view to attracting new activities, such as tourist activities, and the development of new craft undertakings and SMEs;
— services to companies, such as the creation or development of companies or organizations involved in management advice, aid for technology transfer and training in marketing;
— maintenance or job creation through, for example, retraining and vocational training of fishermen, aid for geographical mobility and aid for entry to the labour market;
— financial engineering, notably the facilitation of access by SMEs and craft enterprises to the capital market and the financing of interest rebate schemes;

---

1   OJ L346, 31.12.1993 and OJ L283, 25.11.1995.
2   See the chapter on regional development.
3   OJ C180, 01.07.1994.

— concrete projects of a general and/or transnational nature in the fisheries sector, such as common management of shared fisheries, rationalization of distribution chains and promotion of fishery products;
— productive investment in the sector, including aid for the improvement of productivity and employment rationalization, diversification and reconversion of companies in the sector, in particular towards maritime tourism.

Appraisal and outlook

The Treaty of Rome did not provide for a fully fledged fisheries policy, for it included fishery products in the products to be covered by the Common Agricultural Policy. Little by little, however, the specific charac-teristics of the fisheries sector pushed for a separate common policy. Towards the end of the sixties, therefore, the Community began to turn its attention to the need to protect its resources in the Atlantic and the North Sea, under serious threat from overfishing. Its concern was heightened by the creation of exclusive economic zones, decided upon within the United Nations Conference on the law of the sea. A Community policy to conserve fishery resources was necessary to protect the most threatened species in Community waters. Its main manifestations have been the setting of total allowable catches (TACs), the allocation of catch quotas between the Member States and technical management and surveillance measures. Through an external fisheries policy, the Community has sought to guar-antee its own fleet access to the waters of countries with surplus resources and to restrict access to Community waters for foreign vessels, notably Soviet, Polish and Japanese factory ships.

Curiously enough, third countries made no difficulties about accept-ing the Community as sole negotiator for the EEC Member States, even if internal problems hindered these negotiations and held up agreements. These internal problems took many years to iron out. The Community had declared equal access to the fishery zones of the Member States (12 miles) when there were six states which had begun to turn a jealous eye towards the rich waters of applicant countries. The latter, unwilling to share the bounty, succeeded in writing into their Act of Accession a ten-year dero-gation to the rule of equal access, which was to remain at the crux of discussions on the common fisheries policy and brought the United King-dom to blows with the other Member States, particularly France. The United Kingdom wanted to exclude vessels from the other Member States within a 12-mile zone around its coasts. France maintained that its fisher-men had "historic rights" to fish in certain British fishing grounds, even if these rights were relatively recent.

Six years of negotiations were required before, on January 25, 1983, the Community reached one of its "historic compromises". On this date, a Community system of resource conservation, endeavouring to protect the biological resources of the sea under severe threat from modern fishing methods, was added to the common fisheries policy. This system intro-duced measures to restrict fishing and set conditions under which it could take place, along with measures governing access to the waters of the

Member States. Measures to conserve and manage fishery resources thus came to join the "common organization of the market", which sets common marketing standards for fisheries and aquaculture products, dividing them up into a freshness grading and seeking to ensure that products which do not reach a satisfactory quality level are not marketed. It obliges the Member States to carry out conformity control checks on these products and to apply sanctions to any infringements. This policy therefore helps protect consumer interests. Producers' interests are not neglected either in the common fisheries policy. Structural policy, inaugurated in 1970, makes use of common measures to restructure, modernize and develop the fishery sector, to develop aquaculture, encourage experimental fishing and adapt Community fishing capacities to disposal possibilities.

This does not mean that the Community fisheries sector is riding on the crest of a wave. The depletion of resources, due notably to the over-fishing of juveniles combined with fleet over-capacity, make the entire European fisheries sector extremely vulnerable from the economic and social viewpoint. In order to redress this situation, there must be more balanced and rational exploitation of resources and consequently a reduction in both fishing and fishing capacity through more stringent regulation of access to resources and closer monitoring of vessel movements in order to respect the general interest.

In light of the lasting nature of restrictions on authorized catches, fishery concerns should seek to raise the qualitative value of their production, an objective which is consistent both with the common fisheries policy and with consumer protection policy. Due to the fall in prices for the majority of species, to the imperatives of freshness and hence of conservation and to operating constraints, many firms in the sector are, however, facing a shortage of financial resources and a lack of profitability. This crisis situation is tending to become entrenched because of the growing share of imports, upon which the Community market is already dependent for over 50% of its supply.

To remedy the crisis, actions should be taken to improve resource management and restructure the industry within the framework of the new structural rules. The new monitoring arrangements for fishing activities, the establishment of the fishing licence scheme and the integration of the structural aspects of the common fisheries policy into the revised Structural Fund arrangements may settle a number of matters of importance for European fisheries. If socio-economic upheaval in the fisheries sector is to be minimized, social support measures must, indeed, be taken, combining Community means and instruments in favour of the least developed regions and those most heavily dependent on the fishing industry.

Bibliography on the common fisheries policy

□ ALEXANDRE Roger, "Pêche: les quatre défauts du filet", in *Expansion*, Paris, N° 474, 7 avril-20 avril 1994, pp. 110-113.

□ CHURCHILL Robin, OEREBECH Peter, "The European Economic Area and Fisheries", in *International Journal of Marine and Coastal Law*, 08/04, 1993, pp. 453-469.

□ COMMISSION EUROPÉENNE, *Mise en oeuvre des nouveaux éléments de la politique commune de la pêche*, COM (93) 664.

   - *La nouvelle politique de la pêche*, OPOCE, 1994.

   - *Ressources côtières et développement littoral intégré*, OPOCE, Luxembourg, 1995.

□ CREAN Kevin, SYMES David, "The Discards Problem: Towards a European Solution", in *Marine Policy*, Vol. 18, 1994, n. 5, pp. 422-434.

□ CROCI Osvaldo, "Le Canada et l'Europe: de l'indifférence à la friction?", in *Europe en Formation. Les cahiers du fédéralisme*, Nice, N° 298, 1995, pp. 41-52.

□ DEL VECCHIO, Angela, "La politique commune de la pêche: axes de développement", in *Revue du Marché unique européen*, Paris, N° 2, 1995, pp. 27-36.

□ GWILLIAM H., LUGTEN G., "Norway and the European Union. Fishing for Compliments", in *Environmental Policy and Law*, Bonn, Vol. 24, N° 5, September 1994, pp. 254-260.

□ HOLDEN Mike, *The Common Fisheries Policy: Origin, Evaluation and Future*, Fishing News Books, Oxford, 1994.

□ KATSOUFROS Théodoros, *Questions de droit international de délimitation maritime dans la jurisprudence de la Cour de justice des Communautés européennes: les lignes de base*, Institut européen d'administration publique, Maastricht, 1994.

□ LLOYD-EVANS, L. P. M., *The Aquaculture Market*, PJB Publ., Richmond, 1993.

□ MUNK Knud Joergen and MOTZFELDT Malene, *Definition and Measurement of Trade Distortion for the Fishing Industry*, Luxembourg, OPOCE, 1993.

□ OECD, *The Use of Individual Quotas in Fisheries Management*, OECD Documents, Paris, 1993.

□ PARLEMENT EUROPEEN, *Manuel de la politique commune de la pêche*, Luxembourg, OPOCE, 1994.

□ PILLAY T. V. R., *Aquaculture. Principles and Practices*, Fishing News Books, Oxford, 1993.

□ PROUTIERE-MAULION Gwenaele, "De la gestion des stocks à l'aménagement des pêcheries: la licence de pêche communautaire instaurée par le règlement 3690/93 du 20 décembre 1993", in *Revue du Marché commun et de l'Union européenne*, Paris, N° 388, mai 1995, pp. 314-319.

□ TROADEC Jean-Paul, "Le nouvel enjeu de la pêche: l'ajustement des institutions aux nouvelles conditions de rareté des ressources", *Problèmes économiques*, Paris, N° 2407, 18 janvier 1995, pp. 12-20.

▫ WILLIAMS Caroline, "Fisheries in the Future: Sustainability or Extinction?", in *Marine Policy*, Guildford, Vol. 20, N° 1, January 1996, pp. 91-95.

▫ YOUNG James, SMITH Andrew, MUIR James, "Representing the Individual Fishermen: An Attitudinal Perspective on One PO's Membership", in *Marine Policy*, Guildford, Vol. 20, N° 2, March 1966, pp. 157-169.

15. THE EUROPEAN UNION

AND ITS CITIZENS

In the introduction to this work, it was demonstrated that while individuals have an active role to play in the process of European construction, they are practically not aware of this role. Both their professional and private lives are influenced by the process of European construction and they unconsciously influence it in turn through their ardent desire for peace and economic and political freedom which are the Community's main tenets. On the conscious level, however, the average citizen has a very vague idea of what European construction means and of the role which he or she is called upon to play in it. The main illustration of this is given by the European elections, to which a large number of citizens in the Member States are largely indifferent.

Concern about this indifference prompted the Fontainebleau European Council in June 1984 to set up an ad hoc "People's Europe" Committee to identify fields in which an effort could usefully be made to give the process of European construction a more human dimension and bring it closer to ordinary people. This Committee, also known as the **Adonnino Committee** after its chairman, was made up of representatives of Heads of State and Government and of the Commission's President. In March and in June 1985 it submitted two reports to the European Council. The Commission, influenced by the reports of the Adonnino Committee but taking its ideas much further in certain fields, adopted in November 1985 a Work Programme for the creation of a People's Europe.

These **symbols** of the Community's existence were the easiest part of the package to put into practice. In 1986, the Ode to Joy of Beethoven's ninth symphony was proclaimed to be **the Community's anthem** and has since this date been played at official ceremonies where the Community is represented. At the same time, the twelve star flag, already used by the Council of Europe, was adopted as **the Community's flag**. The number of stars is symbolic and will not change with the entry of new Member States to the Union. The European Union's flag and the flag of Europe, which one day will be united, are one. The European flag is already flown alongside the national flag outside public buildings in many Member States and, even more importantly, **the Community's emblem** is used in a range of manners by citizens who want to proclaim there adherence to the European idea. Still in the area of symbols, the Council and representatives of the Member States' governments meeting within the Council decided in November 1986 to abolish the customs signs at the internal borders of the twelve Member States with effect from January 1, 1988[1]. They have been replaced by signs bearing the symbol of the Community (twelve stars in a circle on a blue background) and giving the name of the Member State in question.

The Treaty on European Union establishes the **citizenship of the Union.** Every person holding the nationality of a Member State is a citizen of the Union. Citizens of the Union, thus defined, enjoy the rights conferred by the Treaty and are subject to the duties imposed thereby (Art. 8). Every citizen of the Union is, in the territory of a third country in which the Member State of which he is a national is not represented, entitled to protection by the diplomatic or consular authorities of any Member State, on the same conditions as the nationals of that State (Art. 8c). Two Decisions specify the **right to diplomatic protection**[2]. This right is not negligible, as there are many cases where one Member State is not represented in a third country. It includes assistance in the event of death, illness or serious accident, arrest, detention or assault as well as help and repatriation in the event of difficulty.

In addition, every citizen of the Union residing in a Member State of which he is not a national has the right to vote and to stand as a candidate at European and municipal elections in the Member State in which he resides, under the same conditions as nationals of that State (Art. 8b). In order to implement Article 8b(2) of the Treaty, the Council adopted in December 1993 a Directive laying down arrangements for the exercise of the right to vote and to stand as a candidate **in elections to the European Parliament** in the Member State of residence[3]. While including provisions to ensure freedom of choice and to prevent individuals from voting or standing for election in two constituencies at once, the Directive is based on the principles of equality and non-discrimination and is designed to facilitate the exercise by the citizens of the Union of their right to vote and to stand for election in the Member State where they reside.

The Directive laying down detailed arrangements for the exercise of the **right to vote and stand as candidates in municipal elections** ensures the same rights to Union citizens in elections by direct universal suffrage at local government level[4]. Member States may, however, reserve for their own nationals the posts of mayor and deputy mayor, which involve participation in an official authority or in the election of a parliamentary assembly. The Directive also allows Member States where the proportion of nationals of other Union countries exceeds 20% to restrict the right to vote and stand as candidate to those who meet certain criteria regarding length of residence.

Measures of great importance to the individual in areas such as employment, social protection, the fight against poverty and health care are part of social policy and are dealt with in the Chapter on social progress. This Chapter also tackles the major issues of public health, security at work and the education of young people. The following pages

---

1   OJ C303, 27.11.1986.
2   OJ L314, 28.12.1995.
3   OJ L329, 30.12.1993.
4   OJ L368, 31.12.1994 and OJ L122, 22.05.1996.

look at measures of interest to the individual and not touched upon in other parts of this book, notably information, training and cultural activities; protection of consumers' health, safety and economic interests; the rights of citizens to enter and reside in the Member States; and internal and judicial matters.

Information, audiovisual, culture

Brussels shares with Washington and New York the honour of being one of the world's major press centres. Interest in Community affairs has been reflected by regular growth in the number of correspondents in Brussels. The number of **journalists accredited** to the Commission, which stood at less than 20 in 1960, now amounts to 770 from 61 countries, of whom 616 are from the press and 154 from radio and television. These journalists represent between them 75 international and national press agencies. The **Stendhal Prize** is awarded annually to the press and television throughout Europe for articles, reports, programmes or illustrations which contribute most to explaining and clarifying the process of European integration.

Nevertheless, the referendums organized in the course of the ratification procedures of the Maastricht Treaty in Denmark and France have demonstrated the lack of information for the general public on Community procedures and its concerns for transparency, subsidiarity and democracy. Even more disquieting is the fact revealed by the debates on ratification of the Treaty on European Union - often conducted with demagogic overtones - that part of public opinion unjustly attributes the depressed economic situation of the early nineties and the growing unemployment to the Community and doubts as to whether further European integration is necessary or indeed advisable. Aware that the European Union cannot progress unless its citizens are convinced of the values on which it is based and the importance of its achievements, the European institutions developed projects designed to bring the Union closer to its people.

In a Declaration adopted by the European Council in Birmingham on 16 October 1992, called the Birmingham Declaration, the Heads of State and Government stressed their determination to respond to public concern by demonstrating more clearly the benefits of Community integration, notably by increasing the visibility of institutional proceedings and the benefits of European integration. At the Edinburgh European Council of December 1992, they committed themselves to opening up the work of the Council, encouraging the rapid transmission of material, making new Community legislation clearer and simpler and making existing Community legislation more accessible, notably through its consolidation or codification, i.e., the publication of new legal acts integrating the basic act and the acts modifying it without changing the substance.

Answering the call of the European Council, the Commission defined, on 30 June 1993, a new approach for its information and communication policy outlined in the next heading. At the same time, the Commission decided to publish more documents of interest to the public in the Official Journal, indicating in the legislative programme those proposals which would appear to be suitable for preliminary broad discussion and publishing more **Green Papers** (reflection documents inviting a debate on the options of a policy before the preparation of proposals) and **White Papers** (general documents announcing a programme of actions). As well as making better use of the tools it has for putting its message across to the public and receiving feedback, the Commission is trying to improve public access to the documents of the European institutions. In December 1993 the Council and the Commission approved a code of conduct laying down general rules on such right of access[1]. The underlying principle is to give the public the widest possible access to documents held by the Commission and the Council. The institutions may, however, refuse access to any document where disclosure could undermine the protection of the public or private interest, commercial and industrial secrecy or the Community's financial interests[2]. On the basis of this code the Commission introduced practical procedures which enable the public to have simple, rapid and decentralized access to the documents of the EU institutions[3]. A Council Resolution is aimed at promoting the electronic dissemination of Community laws and at improving access conditions[4].

Transparency, as regards the legislative texts of the European Union, their application and their implications for individuals and firms, is a key to bringing the Union closer to its citizens. In order both to appreciate the possibilities offered by the internal market and to be able to make use of those possibilities, the citizens of the Union need information about the laws that apply to them. They also need the assurance that new laws are introduced only where they are needed, that they minimize compliance costs, and that they are coherent, both in themselves and vis-à-vis existing laws. To those ends, the Commission pledged itself on "doing less but doing it better", by being more selective in making proposals and by establishing ongoing and open dialogue with the public at large, the Member States and all relevant circles[5].

Information for the general public

The new **information policy** of the Commission is designed to contribute to the objectives of transparency and accessibility of Community legislation. The aim is to inform citizens of the nature and the scale of the challenges facing the European Union, to demonstrate the comparative benefits of European integration and to show people in concrete terms, at local level, the effect of European policies on their daily lives. To attain these objectives the Commission has taken a series of initiatives such as: setting up a Users' Advisory Council to canvass representatives of the various social groups on the Commission's information policy; increasing the role of the Commission offices in the Member States as discussion and

---

1   OJ L340, 31.12.1993.
2   See judgment of the Court of First Instance of 19 October 1995, case T-194/94.
3   OJ L46, 18.02.1994.
4   OJ C179, 01.07.1994.
5   COM (95) 580, 22 November 1995.

information fora and as centres for coordinating national relays; the administration of the server "Europa" on the global Internet network; and the launching of a major information campaign aimed at providing citizens with detailed information on their rights in the single market and on how to exercise them.

Various other activities of the Commission are designed to improve the dissemination of available information. They include the activities of the Office for Official Publications and of the Statistical Office, the management of the historical archives of the Communities and the provision of information to universities.

The Community's **Office for Official Publications** publishes and distributes, on behalf of all the institutions, the **Official Journal of the European Communities** and other publications. The Official Journal is published every day in eleven languages and every year contains more than a million pages, giving a measure of the work volume of the Office for Official Publications and its importance for citizens who want to keep abreast of European affairs. The distribution network of the OPOCE or EUR-OP is built on an increasing number of bookshops in the Member States and in several third countries.

As regards the Official Journal, a special effort has been made to improve access to Community legislation. All of the legislation in force (Treaties, external relations, secondary legislation and other instruments) as well as Court of Justice decisions is stored in the interinstitutional computerized documentation system on Community law (CELEX). The public has access to this optic memory, from which the desired texts can be extracted and transferred, either electronically or by post. For example, this system can supply without supplementary research the text of a Basic Regulation and all its subsequent amendments. Similarly, on the morning of publication, summaries of Official Journal issues can be accessed on-line. Combined with the optic memory, this service enables selected and near instantaneous access by users to the relevant legislative texts. Those interested can become direct subscribers to the following data bases: TED (electronic version of the Supplement to the Official Journal), SCAD (documentary base on selected publications, documents and articles on European integration) EUDOR (the European Union's electronic document library) CATEL (the Publications Office's electronic cataloguing system) and Pabli (electronic version of the blue pages of the ACP Courrier - EDF and Commission development projects). The Office has also set up and markets a computerized administrative directory for all EU institutions, which is regularly updated and thus offers to the interested public actual information on the administration and the "Who's Who" of the Union.

The use of telecommunications and computer technology has made it possible to diversify the traditional methods of distribution via publications and microfiches, adding to them direct on-line access to the **Community statistics** contained in the data banks. Comparable, reliable and relevant statistics throughout the Community are a source of growing interest to the general public. The **Statistical Office of the European Communities (Eurostat)**, which works alongside national statistical offices, draws up statistics which attempt to meet the needs of the general public arising from the various Community activities: economic, industrial, agricultural, social, regional and so on. The **general statistical classification** of economic activities within the European Communities (NACE), adopted in 1990, is one of the cornerstones of the Community's statistical system and is often adopted by the countries of the EFTA and of Central and Eastern Europe for their own statistical purposes[1]. The Member States have agreed to pass on data subject to statistical confidentiality to the Statistical Office, on condition that all the necessary steps are taken to ensure confidentiality[2].

Researchers into European integration now enjoy access to the **European Community's historical archives**. Under the 30-year rule, the archives of the ECSC have been open to public

---

1   OJ L293, 24.10.1990.
2   OJ L151, 15.06.1990.

consultation since 1952 and those of the EEC and Euratom since 1958[1]. The Archis data base lists the files stored in the archives of the Florence European University Institute.

The **Commission's Information Offices** in the Member States normally act as discussion and information forums and as centres for coordinating national relays and networks to reach both the public at large and specialized audiences in the Member States. The Commission also promotes teaching on European integration at university level, notably by granting financial support for the setting-up of "**Jean Monnet chairs**", a symbolic term for full-time teaching posts devoted to European integration. This initiative is designed to encourage the development of centres of excellence on European issues at universities (some 260 in 1996).

But what the Community has not tackled yet is the **education of citizens in schools**. History lessons, in particular, taught from the national angle, accentuate the divisions, the wars and the hatreds among European nations rather than their common cultural heritage. The Ministers of Education should one day agree on a handbook of European history and culture, which could make young Europeans understand that the national cultural particularities, which make up Europe's wealth, are all parts of a great European civilization.

Audiovisual Sector

The audiovisual sector, which covers programme production and distribution ("software") and equipment manufacturing ("hardware"), was identified by the Commission in its White Paper on growth, competitiveness and employment as having great potential for growth and job creation. The European film and television programme industry, which plays a strategic role in the development of the audiovisual sector, is, in addition, a prime vector of European culture and a living testimony to the traditions and identity of each country. It must, therefore, illustrate the creative genius and the personality of the people of Europe; but, to do this, it must be competitive in an open, worldwide market[2].

The audiovisual sector in Europe took on a totally new face at the end of the eighties, with the rapid growth in broadcasting by cable and telecommunications satellite and the emergence of the first European direct broadcasting satellites. European television viewers should have won access to an extraordinary choice of television programmes. However, national markets in the Member States were too narrow to be able to offer at competitive rates the equipment and programmes required by the new technologies and the proliferation of channels. This was a handicap for the European audiovisual sector which was expected to be one of the principal service sectors in the 21st century. The demand for audiovisual products would double in Europe, the number of TV channels would be multiplied by ten and that of cable connected households would be multiplied by three during the nineties. It was imperative that the growth of this market

---

1   OJ L43, 15.02.1983.
2   COM (94) 96, 6 April 1994.

led to the creation of numerous jobs in Europe and did not jeopardize its cultural identity.

In the eighties the Community was consequently faced with a dilemma: it either had to step up intra-European trade so that European manufacturers were able to participate profitably in this technological revolution; or it had to let the opportunity for joint action slip through its fingers and capitulate to its powerful American and Japanese competitors, capable of meeting the requirements of national and international markets without much difficulty. American serials and Japanese cartoons are indeed cheap, because they are amortized on a world scale. Scattered and confined in their smallish national markets, European producers found themselves in conditions of uneven competition as far as the costs were concerned.

At the same time a "technological revolution" was underway with the introduction of **high definition television (HDTV)**. Firstly, this gives to the image an almost perfect quality. TV pictures being constituted by small dots invisible to the eye, that of the HDTV is made up of a very large number of such dots and allows therefore a faithful reproduction of reality, notably as regards colours. Secondly, the HDTV screen is very large with a ratio of 16 (length) over 9 (height), as against 4/3 of the traditional television set. This ratio corresponds better to the normal vision angle and to the format of cinema films, theatre scenes and football fields. Thirdly, the use of digital sound technology, apart from the quality and hearing comfort, make it possible for the image to be accompanied by four sound channels, which permits, for example, a stereophonic sound and the simultaneous transmission of dialogues in two languages at the choice of the spectator.

To prepare this revolution, the **Community's strategy** on the introduction of new technologies in the audiovisual sector has been strengthened by two Decisions on cooperation between the Member States to promote the European standard for high definition television[1]. The strategy covers three interrelated areas: the establishment of standards for satellite television; aid for technological development, which should enable European industrialists to produce equipment compatible with the standards; and aid to audiovisual operators for launching services and producing programmes utilizing the new technology. In a memorandum of understanding approved on 15 June 1992, the representatives of interested organizations (broadcasters, cable distribution companies, manufacturers of television equipment and producers) agreed to assist the Community strategy on the synchronized provision of advanced television services to consumers.

In the context of this strategy, the Council adopted, on 22 July 1993, an **action plan** for the introduction of advanced television services in Europe, with a budget of ECU 228 million over a period of four years, of which at least half is to be spent on programme production[2]. This financial support is intended to create favourable conditions for the emergence of

---

1   OJ L142, 25.05.1989 and OJ L363, 13.12.1989.
2   OJ L196, 05.08.1993.

advanced television services in Europe by compensating for the extra costs incurred by the introduction of the new 16:9 format for television, both for new programmes and for reformatting old material. The plan is directed solely at promoting the 16:9 format, irrespective of either the European television standard used or the broadcasting mode (terrestrial, satellite or cable).

In view of developments on the market and technological progress, a Directive on the use of transmission standards for television established the Community **regulatory framework** for advanced television services, including digital television[1]. It provides for transition from the PAL and SECAM standards to the high-definition standard via the D2-MAC and HD-MAC systems for satellite broadcasting and cable transmission. To promote the accelerated development of advanced television services it lays down technical requirements to be met by all television services and a set of rules governing access to digital pay-television rules.

A regulatory framework is also necessary to permit the free provision of audiovisual services in the European space. To this end, a Directive concerning the exercise of television broadcasting activities (**"television without frontiers"**) aims at the free movement of television programmes within the Community through the freedom to pick up and re-transmit programmes from another Member State which meet the national law of the broadcasting country as harmonized by the Directive[2]. It consequently lays down the principle that compliance with the rules is to be enforced by the broadcasting State, without interference from the country of retransmission of the programme. The Directive introduces minimum harmonization of advertising (breaks, duration, advertising for certain products, ethical rules), sponsorship, protection of minors and right of reply, while promoting the production and distribution of European audiovisual works. The Directive stipulates that the Member States must ensure, "where practicable" and by appropriate means, that broadcasters reserve a majority proportion of their transmission time, excluding certain types of programme, for European works. The Directive also stipulates that at least 10% of air time or of the programming budgets should be earmarked for European works by independent producers. These conditions, which are still non-obligatory, are subject to controversy, as some Member States as well as the Commission and the European Parliament want to render them binding in order to promote the European programme industry.

The Directive on "television without frontiers" is completed by a Directive on harmonization of the protection of **copyright and certain related rights** in the cases of satellite transmission and cable distribution[3]. It should notably provide high protection standards for authors, creative artists, phonogramme producers and broadcasters, as well as collective and obligatory management of the rights for cable retransmission through collective societies representing the various categories of rightholders.

---

1   OJ L281, 23.11.1995.
2   OJ L298, 17.10.1989 and OJ C185, 19.07.1995.
3   OJ L248, 06.10.1993.

Since 1987, a programme of **measures to encourage the development of the audiovisual industry (MEDIA)**, stimulates audiovisual production of all kinds (films, cartoons, documentaries, etc.) and encourages the cross-border distribution of films[1]. It intervenes upstream and downstream of production without interfering with it. As a rule, its financial assistance consists of reimbursable advances on receipts, the returns of which are immediately reinvested in the programme. As part of this programme, the Media Business School, in Madrid contributes to the development of training activities in the Member States designed better to equip audiovisual professionals to cope with the requirements of a large European market. These activities have included the European Film Distribution Office, creative independent production talent (SCRIPT) and promotion of independent productions (GRECO). MEDIA II (1996-2000) consists of two parts: a training programme which aims to provide professionals in the audiovisual industry with the skills they need to exploit the European dimension of the market to the full and make use of new technologies, notably with the assistance of the Media Business School of Madrid; and a programme to promote the development and distribution of European audiovisual works, particularly by encouraging independent European producers to work with European distributors on the production of programmes likely to appeal to a vast audience[2]. To supplement the MEDIA II programmes, the Commission proposes the establishment of a European Guarantee Fund, administered as part of the structures of the European Investment Fund (EIF), to promote European cinema and television production[3].

Cultural activities

The European Union's activities in the cultural sphere are relatively recent. It operates on two fronts: at the level of European cultural heritage, particularly architectural, and to help those working in the cultural sector, for whom better social protection is desirable. In July 1984, the Council and Ministers with responsibility for cultural affairs meeting within the Council (formula used to cover the numerous cultural activities that remained outside the Community context) adopted three Resolutions on measures to combat audiovisual piracy, the rational distribution of cinema works throughout the audiovisual media and measures to ensure that audiovisual programmes of European origin are given sufficient air time[4]. Other Resolutions followed in 1985: the annual naming of a European **"cultural capital"**[5], showing of European audiovisual productions in third countries[6], a European sculpture competition[7], cooperation between libraries in the area of computer technology[8] and special entry conditions to museums and cultural events for young people[9] .

In 1986, the Ministers decided to foster effective cooperation between the Member States to preserve **Europe's architectural heritage,** by supporting pilot projects, and to look at the possibility of promoting and monitoring the work of the Member States in the area of

---

1   OJ L380, 31.12.1990 and COM (93) 364 of 23.07.1993.
2   OJ L321, 30.12.1995.
3   COM (95) 546, 14 November 1995.
4   OJ C204, 03.08.1984.
5   OJ C153, 22.06.1985.
6   Ibid.
7   Ibid.
8   OJ C271, 23.10.1985.
9   OJ C348, 31.12.1985.

conserving art objects and works and in promoting patronage of cultural activities by companies[1]. They also decided to create transnational cultural routes[2]. In 1988, the Council and Ministers of Culture meeting within the Council adopted conclusions[3] on a **multiannual programme of priority actions** (audiovisual, printed works, cultural training, patronage) for cultural cooperation within the Community. They also adopted a Resolution for the creation of a **cultural affairs committee** which could coordinate cultural activities conducted either in the framework of the Community system or under the banner of intergovernmental cooperation.

In the more specific world of **books**, the Ministers adopted in 1989 a Resolution on **promoting books and reading**[4]. In this Resolution, the Ministers approved what they felt to be eight priority measures: the production of an author's and translator's guide and of a book statistics programme, the creation of a European literary prize and prize for the best translation of a literary work, a pilot project under which financial aid is granted for the translation of contemporary literary works, the provision of grants for translators, the conservation of books on acid paper and the use of "permanent paper", research into measures to promote book exports and finally a campaign to raise awareness of books and reading among the European general public. In response to the Council Resolution, the Commission launched in 1989 a pilot project providing financial aid for the translation of contemporary literary works to ensure that translation costs are covered for around thirty works per year. Priority is given to the translation of works written in one of the Community's minority languages[5]. Each year, the Commission also awards a European literature prize and a European translation prize (the **Aristeion prizes**).

Other permanent cultural activities of the Commission concern: encouragement of the cooperation between foundations promoting art and culture (patronage); support for a growing number of **training grants** and for cultural and artistic projects throughout the European Union; an annual operation under which financial aid is granted to projects for the preservation and promotion of Europe's **architectural heritage** selected by a European jury. The Athens Parthenon, the cathedral of Aix-la-Chapelle and the Forum Romanum in Rome are among those already granted aid. In addition, through its annual **Kaleidoscope programme**, the Commission encourages European artistic and cultural creation, cultural events, cultural exchanges and other projects involving all artistic disciplines. It also supports a number of high-profile activities of which the best known are the Youth Orchestra and the Baroque Orchestra of the European Community.

Culture was brought fully into the action scope of the Community through the Treaty on European Union. Its Article 128 EC states that the Community should contribute to the flowering of the cultures of the Member States, while respecting their national and regional diversity and at the same time bringing the common cultural heritage to the fore. Its action aims at encouraging cooperation between Member States and, if necessary, supporting and supplementing their action in the following areas: improvement of the knowledge and dissemination of the culture and history of the European peoples; conservation and safeguarding of cultural heritage of European significance; non-commercial cultural exchanges; artistic and literary creation, including in the audiovisual sector. In order to achieve these objectives, **four means are employed**: cooperation between Member States; consideration for cultural aspects under other Community policies, including competition policy, concerning in particular aid to promote culture and heritage conservation (Art. 92); cooperation between the Community and its Member States with third

1   OJ C320, 13.12.1986.
2   OJ C44, 26.02.1986.
3   OJ C197, 27.07.1988.
4   OJ C183, 20.07.1989.
5   OJ C56, 03.03.1992.

countries and the competent international organizations; specific measures to support action taken by Member States which may take two forms: incentive measures, excluding any harmonization of the laws and regulations of the Member States, adopted unanimously by the Council under the co-decision procedure after consultation of the Committee of the Regions; and recommendations unanimously adopted by the Council.

The European Union must strike a balance between the objectives arising from the completion of the internal market and those relating to the **protection of the national heritage**. In fact, a Council Regulation subjects the **export outside the Community of cultural goods** of artistic, historical or archaeological value to an export licence issued by the Member State on whose territory it is lawfully located[1]. In the same vein, a Directive provides for the return of cultural objects unlawfully removed from the territory of a Member State[2]. It notably establishes a judicial procedure for the return of cultural objects and cooperation between the competent authorities of the Member States.

Copyright is also protected at European Union level. In fact, a 1993 Directive harmonizes the term of copyright at 70 years after the death of the author in the case of literary, artistic, cinematographic or audiovisual works[3]. For the last two categories, calculation of the term of protection begins after the death of the last of the persons to survive from among the principal director, the author of the screenplay, the author of the dialogue and the composer of the music. The same Directive harmonizes at 50 years the term of protection of the main **related rights** (those of performers, producers of phonograms or of films and broadcasting organizations). Another Directive provides protection for both paper-based and electronic databases for a period of 15 years from their completion, so as to create an attractive environment for investment in them while preserving the interests of users[4].

In a communication of 27 July 1994, the Commission seeks to establish a **reference framework for cultural action** with a view to bringing the action already agreed by the Community closer to the provisions of the new Article 128 of the Treaty, restructuring existing support measures while making them more effective, exploring the possibilities for achieving the cultural objectives set out in the Treaty which are not already covered by specific measures, integrating culture into other Community activities and taking into account the implications of the burgeoning information society[5]. The Commission defines three priority areas of action in support of culture: the cultural heritage, including the movable heritage and museums; promotion of artistic activities with a e dimension; and establishment of a multiannual programme for the promotion of books and reading (Ariane).

In this framework the Commission published a Green Paper on **copyright and related rights in the information society**, in which most works will be disseminated in digital format making it possible to produce an unlimited number of copies of the same quality as the original[6]. The Commission endeavours in particular to identify the challenges arising from the development of new technologies, such as digitization, on copyright and related rights, an insufficient protection of which could hinder the creation, viability or free movement of

---

1   OJ L395, 31.12.1992.
2   OJ L74, 27.03.1993.
3   OJ L290, 24.11.1993.
4   OJ L77, 27.03.1996.
5   COM (94)356 and OJ C235, 23.08.1994.
6   COM (95) 382, 19 July 1995.

information services. It points out that digitization itself offers new ways of identifying and protecting works, thus facilitating the administration of rights. In a resolution on **culture and the multimedia**, the Council, on its part, stresses the importance of giving thought to the development of multimedia as a means of promoting and conserving Europe's heritage and cultures[1].

Consumer policy

An overall Community policy to protect consumers and users of products and services is vital if there is to be a proper balance in the way in which the Single Market operates. The aim of consumer policy is to ensure that the European Union's 370 million consumers draw maximum benefit from the completion of the internal market and play an active role in it. The Single Market must be put in place by and for consumers. In other words, it must serve their maximum well-being and give them a free choice of goods and services of the best possible quality and at the best possible price, without consideration for their origin or for the nationality of their supplier. Furthermore, within the single Community market consumers must enjoy a similar level of protection to that provided within the national market.

Since 1975, pilot actions have been organized to provide an all-round approach to the physical dangers inherent in certain consumer products. Initiatives have also been launched with a view to establishing regular dialogue between representatives of producers and of consumers in certain trade and industry sectors, so that both sides can understand the interests of the other and reach, when necessary, voluntary agreements. On the more specific issue of making allowance for consumers' interests in **other Community policies**, a Council Resolution provides notably for the examination of a periodical progress report in this field, strengthened procedures for the consultation of consumers and analysis of the impact of certain common policies on consumers' interests[2].

The **Treaty on European Union** gives the Community, for the first time, the task of contributing to a high level of protection for consumers. This goal can be pursued through: (a) measures adopted pursuant to Article 100a (approximation of legislations) in the context of the completion of the internal market; and (b) specific action which supports and supplements the policy pursued by the Member States to protect the health, safety and economic interests of consumers and to provide adequate information to consumers. These actions may be adopted by a qualified majority in the Council acting in co-decision with the Parliament and after consulting the Economic and Social Committee (Art. 129a EEC).

The third three-year action plan in respect of consumer policy (1996-98) reflects the fact that consumer activity impinges on the daily life of all citizens of the European Union and endeavours to anticipate the changes generated by technological developments and the opening up of markets[3]. The plan is focused on ten priority areas for consumers: improve their

---

1   OJ C247, 23.09.1995.
2   OJ C3, 07.01.1987.
3   COM (95) 519, 31 October 1995.

education and information; strengthen their representation; ensure that their interests are fully taken into account in the internal market; facilitate their access to financial services; protect their interests in the supply of essential public utility services; enable them to benefit from the opportunities presented by the information society; improve their confidence in foodstuffs; encourage a practical approach to environment-friendly consumption; and assist Central and Eastern European countries as well as developing countries to develop consumer policies.

Representation, information, education

In 1995 the Commission replaced the Consumers' Consultative Council by a Consumer Committee, in the interest of a more effective **representation of consumers** through a more flexible structure attuned to national realities[1]. The 20 members of the Committee are appointed by the Commission and comprise 15 representatives of national consumer organizations and 5 representatives of European and regional consumer organizations. Its main task is to advise the Commission so as to ensure that the requirements of consumers are taken into account in the formulation of Community policies.

Consumer information seeks to ensure that consumers are able to compare the prices for the same product within a country and are as well informed as possible on price differences between the Member States. Since 1990, the Commission has been encouraging the creation of consumer information centres for consumers who have problems with or are seeking to inform themselves about the operation of the Single Market. These centres are concentrated in cross-border regions to provide better information for consumers who make cross-border purchases. The Commission encourages the development of these centres by covering a part of the costs of organizations which are willing to assume this information task and appear capable of doing so efficiently. The **Coline** European network creates a computerized link between several national consumer information services. In addition, the Commission gives financial aid to radio and TV stations to encourage them to give a European dimension to broadcasts on consumer problems. It publishes the "European consumer guide to the single market" and organizes the "European Young Consumer Competition" to encourage young people to become aware of consumer issues.

The **indication of the prices** of the products represents an important means of information and protection of consumers. Two Directives concern the indication of the prices, one of foodstuffs and the other of non-food products[2]. They establish a general obligation to indicate the unit price for products pre-packaged in pre-established quantities, but they provide exceptions which may be either obligatory or optional for specific ranges of products. However, the existing mechanism has proved to be extremely difficult to implement and the Commission proposes to replace it by a

---

1   OJ L162, 13.07.1995.
2   OJ L158, 26.06.1979, OJ L142, 09.06.1988 and OJ L299, 12.12.1995.

simplified system governing the indication of the price of all products sold in the shops[1].

Labelling of products is an important way of achieving better information and transparency for the consumer and ensuring the smooth operation of the internal market[2]. To that effect, the Commission adopted in November 1993 a communication on language use in the information of consumers and a communication on the use of languages in the marketing of foodstuffs[3]. Although they serve specific purposes, the two communications are designed to encourage multilingual information and to improve cooperation between producers, distributors and consumers on the subject of labelling of products in the internal market.

Protection of health and physical safety

The Community turned its attention to the physical safety of consumers in the seventies. A Scientific Committee for Food was set up in 1974[4]. But for many years, efforts in this field were overshadowed by other Community policies, notably the agricultural one and that of removing technical barriers to trade. This was particularly true of the Directive on the alignment of legislation on cosmetics[5] and that on the classification, packaging and labelling of dangerous preparations[6]. This was also the case of the Directive concerning the prohibition of certain substances having a hormonal action and of any substances having a thyrostatic action[7]. These Directives, however, adapted over the years to technical progress, have gradually become more protective of human health.

The accident at the Chernobyl nuclear power plant in April 1986 gave the Community an opportunity to complete its legislation on **radioactive contamination**. In addition to ad hoc measures adopted in order to coordinate national measures covering agricultural produce[8] and definition of conditions under which agricultural produce originating in third countries could be imported[9], the Council adopted in December 1987 a Regulation setting maximum permitted levels of radioactive contamination of foodstuffs and of feeding stuffs following a nuclear accident or any other case of radiological emergency[10].

In 1984, the Council introduced a Community system of **rapid information exchange** on dangers arising from the use of consumer products[11]. Thanks to this system of exchange of information between the Member States and the Commission, the former can take the necessary urgent steps when it becomes known that a particular consumer product is a source of immediate and serious danger for consumer health and physical safety. Managed by the Commission since 1985, the system has permitted the withdrawal from the market of several dangerous products, particularly foodstuffs. Since July 1994, the system of rapid information exchange has been included in the instruments set up by the Directive on the general safety of products, discussed below.

Another information network, the Community system of information and monitoring of **accidents in the home and during leisure (EHLASS)** is geared to the collection of data from the casualty departments of 65

---

1   OJ C260, 05.10.1995.
2   OJ C186, 23.07.1992 and OJ C110, 20.04.1993.
3   COM (93) 456 and OJ C345, 23.12.1993.
4   OJ L136, 20.05.1974.
5   OJ L262, 27.09.1976 and OJ L181, 15.07.1994.
6   OJ L187, 16.07.1988 and OJ L104, 29.04.1993.
7   OJ L191, 23.07.1985 and OJ L151, 03.06.1989.
8   OJ L118, 07.05.1986.
9   OJ L371, 30.12.1986.
10 OJ L371, 30.12.1987 and OJ L211, 22.07.1989.
11 OJ L70, 13.03.1984 and OJ L278, 11.11.1993.

hospitals in the fifteen Member States and from household surveys covering the nature and origin of home and leisure accidents[1]. Analysis of the data enables Member States and the Commission to take appropriate measures to reduce the number of accidents and victims by means of information campaigns, negotiation with industry and introduction of standards of regulations.

Once again, however, it was the effort to complete the internal market which proved the effective trigger of a genuine policy to protect the health and physical safety of consumers. If the Community's end objective was to be an advanced society which placed the well-being of its citizens high on its list of priorities, the completion of the internal market had to be preceded by the adoption of **general legislation guaranteeing the safety of individuals** in their capacity as users of products, regardless of the origin of the latter. A great deal of work was first of all accomplished to integrate matters relating to the physical safety and health of consumers in other policies, particularly the agricultural policy (definition of dairy products and imitation dairy products, regulation of organic products, veterinary problems, promotion of high quality products and, in general, food policy), the process of completing the internal market (machinery, foodstuffs, construction materials) and health policy (measures to combat smoking). Quality promotion has become a central aspect of the response to better protection of consumer physical safety and better provision of information. Then the Council adopted a Directive on the approximation of the laws of the Member States concerning products which, appearing to be other than they are, endanger the health or safety of consumers[2]. This Directive attempts to ban the marketing, import and either manufacture or export of dangerous imitations of foodstuffs. Under the Directive, such products can be withdrawn from the market and the Commission and the Member States are informed of their existence.

A major Directive in the context of the Single Market was adopted in 1988 dealing with **toy safety**[3]. It is the first instance of application to a consumer product of the new approach to standardization which the Council opted for in a May 7, 1985 Resolution[4]. The Directive sets the basic safety requirements which must be met by all toys manufactured in the Community or imported from third countries. The European standardization committees then adopt harmonized standards and manufacturers respecting these are covered by a presumption that their toys meet the basic safety requirements defined in the Directive. This Directive consequently promotes the free movement of goods while encouraging the manufacture of high-quality danger-free toys for the Union's children.

A general legal instrument in the area of product safety was needed, however, in order to convince consumers and economic operators that the internal market is working correctly and contributing to the elaboration of a consistent general safety policy and mechanisms giving a suitable response to safety concerns. This instrument is provided by a Directive on

---

1   OJ L331, 21.12.1994 and OJ L120, 31.05.1995.
2   OJ L192, 11.07.1987.
3   OJ L187, 16.07.1988.
4   OJ C136, 04.06.1985. See chapter on the common market.

general product safety[1]. It introduces a general safety requirement for all products, not simply for consumer products. It defines the obligations of economic operators and those of government authorities. Its scope is basically of a subsidiary nature, in that it does not take over from national legislation but that its implementation will harmonize on a high level the protection offered to the consumer throughout the internal market. On the level of Community law, it encompasses sectors which are not yet the subject of specific regulations and closes any gaps in existing regulations. The Member States must set up the legislative, regulatory and administrative mechanisms enabling them to check that products meet the safety obligation. Under this obligation, producers are required: only to place on the market products which are safe under normal and reasonable conditions; inform consumers of any possible risks inherent in their use; and inform consumers of the dangers inherent in the use of these products. The Directive also sets up a special instrument providing a Community response to situations of extreme urgency of particular Community interest. By virtue of this instrument, the Member States must in urgent cases ensure smooth operation of the Community system of rapid information exchange (mentioned above) and, should the danger be serious and immediate, restrict and possibly suspend marketing of the product in question.

Protection of economic and legal interests

Many of the Directives adopted under this banner kill two birds with one stone, in that they protect consumers while also helping remove obstacles to trade in goods and services. This is true notably of the Directives on the making-up by volume of certain prepackaged liquids[2]; on the ranges of nominal quantities and nominal capacities permitted for certain prepackaged products[3]; on the indication of alcoholic strength by volume in the labelling of alcoholic beverages for sale to the end consumer[4]; and on the organic production of agricultural products and indications referring thereto on agricultural products and foodstuffs[5].

A 1984 Directive seeks to protect consumers, traders and the public in general against **misleading advertising** and its unfair consequences[6]. It has the merit of defining a Community concept of "misleading advertising", namely advertising which in some way misleads the people to whom it is addressed, a concept which is very useful at a time when evolution in communications techniques, particularly television, mean that advertising has become a transnational phenomenon. When a user considers that he has been misled by an advertising text or presentation, he can launch proceedings against the manufacturer. Community institutions are close

---

1   OJ L228, 11.08.1992.
2   OJ L42, 15.02.1975 and OJ L1, 03.01.1994.
3   OJ L51, 25.02.1980 and OJ L1, 03.01.1994.
4   OJ L113, 30.04.1987 and OJ L1, 03.01.1995.
5   OJ L198, 22.07.1991 and OJ L186, 05.08.1995.
6   OJ L250, 19.09.1984.

to agreeing to an amendment of this Directive, which would authorize **comparative advertising** at Community level on certain conditions with a view to stimulating competition in the internal market[1]. Comparative advertising is defined as being any advertising which explicitly or implicitly identifies a competitor or goods or services offered by a competitor.

Another Directive on **liability for defective products** introduces the concept of "responsibility for the risk" inherent in defective products[2]. The manufacturer can consequently be liable regardless of whether or not it has been guilty of misconduct. The 'proof burden' is on the shoulders of the manufacturer. Liability is jointly extended to suppliers and to people acting as such (e.g., distribution chains). While this Directive has reinforced the rights of consumers in case of accidents due to defective products, it has not led to an important increase of lawsuits or an increase of insurance premiums, as maintained by some at the time of its adoption.

A number of Directives concern contractual relations. The Community dealt first with the protection of consumers in respect of contracts negotiated away from business premises (**door-to-door sales**). A Directive grants consumers seven days in which to reconsider and renounce any agreement on a door-to-door sale[3]. The trader must inform the consumer in writing of the right of renunciation at his disposal. In the same spirit, a Directive lays down minimum consumer protection rules concerning distance selling regardless of the technology used (e.g. mail-order sales by pots, telephone, minitel, television, etc.)[4].

Another Directive concerns **unfair terms** in contracts concluded between a consumer and a professional[5]. It establishes, in particular, a distinction between contractual terms negotiated among the parties and terms which the consumer has not negotiated expressly. A non-negotiated clause is to be regarded as unfair where, in spite of the requirements of good faith, it creates a significant imbalance, to the detriment of the consumer, between the rights and obligations of the parties to the contract. The Directive establishes the principle that consumers are not bound by unfair terms in contracts, and makes Member States responsible for implementing appropriate and effective means of ensuring that professionals cease to use such terms.

A uniform protection in the European Union is ensured to consumers who resort to credit to finance their purchases. The Directive on **consumer credit** obliges the Member States to apply common rules to all forms of credit, thus avoiding the distortion of competition among suppliers and protecting consumers on the basis of certain prescribed guarantees. It seeks to bring into the calculation of the effective annual rate of interest all the cost factors which the consumer must pay in order to obtain the credit, excepting certain expenses listed in a precise manner[6].

---

1   OJ C136, 19.05.1994.
2   OJ L210, 07.08.1985.
3   OJ L372, 31.12.1985 and OJ L1, 03.01.1994.
4   OJ C288, 30.10.1995.
5   OJ L95, 21.04.1993.
6   OJ L42, 12.02.1987 and OJ L61, 10.03.1990.

The Commission has encouraged the inter-operability of all **payment cards** throughout the Community through the harmonization of electronic payment systems. It has also monitored the relationship between card holders and issuers, with a view to establishing uniform contract terms, notably as regards who is liable in the event of loss, theft, poor operation or counterfeiting, as part of the process of obtaining the inter-operability of payment cards throughout the Community[1].

Payments abroad are particularly relevant to tourism, an area where a uniform protection of consumers in the EU is needed. In fact, a Council Directive on **package travel, including package holidays and package tours**, protects millions of tourists against possible corrupt practices by the organizers of these popular holidays[2]. Contract clauses must be recorded in writing and the consumer must receive a copy of them. The information supplied cannot be misleading: brochures placed at the disposal of the consumer must contain clear and precise information on prices, means of transport, type of accommodation, its situation, category and so on. In principle, prices cannot be revised, unless express provision is made for this in the contract. Even when surcharges are possible, they are subject to certain conditions. If the organizer cancels the package, the consumer has the right either to another package of equivalent or higher quality, or to reimbursement of all sums already paid, without prejudice to any compensation. The consumer also has the right to compensation if the organizer does not supply a large part of the service agreed upon. Finally, the organizer or the travel agency must give proof of sufficient guarantees to ensure repayment of the sums paid or the repatriation of the consumer in the event of insolvency or bankruptcy.

Still in the field of tourism and of cross-border vacations a Directive protects purchasers of a right to utilize one or more immovable properties on a **timeshare** basis[3]. The purchaser must be provided with a description relating, in particular, to the property itself, its situation, details of any communal services to which the purchaser will have access and the conditions governing such access, the period of enjoyment, the price and an estimate of the charges payable. The contract and the document describing the property covered by the contract must be drawn up in the official Community language (or one of the languages) of the Member State in which the purchaser resides or, if he or she so wishes, in the language (or one of the languages) of the Member State of which he or she is a resident. In addition, the vendor must provide the purchaser with a certified translation of the contract in the official Community language (or one of the languages) of the Member State in which the property is situated. In any case, the purchaser is entitled to withdraw within 10 days without giving any reason. Any advance payment by the purchaser before the end of that cooling-off period is prohibited.

With the emergence of information systems spanning the entire internal market, the European Union has increasingly to concentrate on the

---

1   OJ L365, 24.12.1987 and L317, 24.11.1988.
2   OJ L158, 23.06.1990.
3   OJ L280, 29.10.1994.

protection of the personal data of its citizens. Thus a Directive aims at the development of the information society and the service sector in the EU, while guaranteeing individuals a high level of protection with regard to the processing of personal data[1]. Accordingly, it imposes obligations on data controllers such as public authorities, companies and associations, and establishes rights for data subjects, such as the right to be informed of processing carried out, the right of access to data and the right to ask for data to be corrected. In any event, the Directive prohibits the processing of sensitive data, such as data revealing racial or ethnic origin, political opinions, religious or philosophical beliefs, or state of health, except in certain circumstances that are exhaustively listed, in particular when the data subject has given his explicit consent or where a substantial public interest requires such processing (e.g. medical or scientific research).

All this offers a clear demonstration that citizens' interests are increasingly taken into consideration in the Single Market. However, consumers must also have the means to exercise and defend their rights in the Community legal context, where traditional - and often costly - legal proceedings are ill-adapted to transfrontier conflicts and put off would be complainants. This is why, a Council resolution accords considerable attention to **consumer access to justice**, in the widest sense of the term, embracing mechanisms for out-of-court settlement of disputes in a transnational setting, when consumers residing in one Member State are involved in a dispute in another Member State[2]. In a Green Paper on consumer access to justice and the settlement of consumer disputes in the single market, the Commission highlights the problem of the absence of a "European legal space" and develops a number of arguments designed to launch a debate on initiatives to be envisaged at Community level in regard to the settlement of consumer disputes and, in particular, transfrontier disputes[3].

Citizens' rights

The citizens of the European Union have many rights, some of which they are not even aware of because they appear obvious. Their self-evident nature is a consequence of the existence of the Union and the membership of their State of origin to it. The Court of Justice has established that Community law, independent from the legislation of the Member States, can create obligations and rights for individuals[4]. These rights are so numerous that it would be tedious to list them all here. Almost all the provisions of Community law examined thus far create rights and obligations for the citizens of the EU's Member States, particularly as regards professional activities. Some examples suffice to illustrate this point.

---

1   OJ L281, 23.11.1995.
2   OJ C176, 04.07.1987.
3   COM (93) 576, 17 November 1993.
4   Judgment of 5 February 1963, case 26/62, van Gend en Loos, ECR 1963, p. 1.

The citizens have the right to purchase goods and services, e.g. insurance, in anyone country of the Union without paying customs duties or any tax supplements; they have the right to transfer money from one country to another, e.g. to pay for their dealings or their investments; they have the right borrow from a financial institution established in another country of the Union at the conditions prevalent in that country. Farmers have the right to guaranteed prices for their produce and therefore to a certain guarantee of income; sea fishermen also enjoy this right. Traders have the right to consider the entire European Union as a potential market and therefore to purchase in any of the Member States and sell anywhere in the Union without any quantitative restrictions or import taxes. Industrialists have the right to set up subsidiaries or branches anywhere in the EU where they feel that favourable growth conditions for their company exist and to transfer capital to and from these subsidiaries without restriction. Members of the professions - lawyers, architects, doctors and so on - have the right to set up practice and to exercise their profession in any Member State. Workers have the right to seek employment anywhere they wish in the Union, set up home with their family in the country where they are working and remain there even after they have lost their job; they have the right to exactly the same social benefits as the citizens of the Member State in which they are residing; this is a natural consequence of Article 6 of the EC Treaty, which forbids discrimination on the grounds of nationality.

These are just a few examples of the very long list of rights created by all kinds of Community provisions. Citizens must be conscious of their rights to be able to defend themselves when they think that a Member State is not respecting these; for, very importantly, they are entitled to **defend their rights** acquired through Community law. They can do so by taking their case to the national courts, which can either issue a ruling or turn to the Court of Justice of the EU, or by simply lodging a complaint with the Commission or a petition with the European Parliament (Art. 8d and 138d). The Parliament has a Committee on Petitions which examines the complaints of citizens, for example in the areas of social security, the environment or diploma recognition[1]. If the complaint concerns instances of maladministration in the activities of the Community institutions or bodies, the citizen may address himself to the Ombudsman appointed by the European Parliament (Art. 8d and 138e)[2].

Regardless of whether they are lodged with it or with the Parliament, the Commission is obliged to examine the **grievances of citizens,** which number around one thousand per year. Often they are not justified and the Commission must explain to the citizen why this is the case. Often, too, they are justified and the Commission must address the Member State in question and ask it for explanations; if it does not get a good answer it must formally ask the Member State to correct its legislation or administrative practices which are causing injury to one or several citizens either of the State in question or of another Member State. If the Member State does not

---

1   OJ C175, 16.07.1990.
2   OJ L113, 04.05.1994; See the heading on the European Parliament in the introduction.

come into step with Community law as requested by the Commission, the latter must take the State to the Court of Justice, which will give a final ruling on the obligations of the Member State. According to the Court, the Member States are obliged to compensate for damage caused to individuals by violations of Community law attributable to them[1]. The citizens of the European Union therefore have powerful means at their disposal to obtain justice under Community law. They are more favoured than if they were just citizens of an individual State, for they can go beyond national judicial bodies to international ones in order to defend their rights and interests.

It goes without saying that if they are to defend these rights, they must be aware of them. The vast majority of citizens are not **aware of their rights as citizens** of the European Union. The task of informing them therefore falls to the Union, which as seen above strives to do so through information and education. But citizens should also know European as well as national law. Ignorance of either is not something of which to be proud. Nor can they hide behind the complexity of European law. While European law may be abundant and complex, it is no different in this from any other body of law. The average citizen does not have to know every intricate detail; that is a job for his or her professional adviser. The main features of European law suffice and citizens can acquaint themselves with them by reading a book such as this one.

Citizens cannot either claim that they have no influence over the **shaping of European law**. They indirectly influence it through the choice of political party or parties which makes up the national government and which are consequently involved in any European decision adopted by the Council of Ministers. Citizens have direct influence over the choice of Members of the European Parliament which, as seen in the introduction to this book, has growing influence over the process of European construction. Some people - in large number in certain Member States - do not bother to vote in European elections and in so doing deprive themselves of the right to have a say in the shaping of European law.

The weight of this law is growing as European construction marches forward. It is superimposed on national law and in many cases simply replaces it. It therefore has growing influence over the professional and day-to-day lives of European citizens. Some of the rights acquired by citizens in the professional arena thanks to European law were mentioned above. In the following pages, some of the rights which influence people's day-to-day lives are discussed, although it must not be forgotten that professional rights have an impact on private life and vice versa.

One of the most important rights of European Union citizens is that of being able to **travel freely** throughout the Community. By virtue of Article 8a of the Treaty, every citizen of the Union has the right to move and reside freely within the territory of the Member States, subject to the conditions laid down in the Treaty and to the measures adopted to give them effect. This right has become such standard practice for the European citizen that it is forgotten that it did not exist as recently as the fifties and

---

1   Judgment of November 19, 1991 in the joint cases C-6/90 and C-9/90.

still does not exist for citizens of many of the world's countries. To ensure its effective exercise, this right has to be shored up by a range of secondary rights, guarantees of safety, simplifications of all kinds and removal of all administrative red tape. All of these conditions, particularly the last one, were not yet satisfied at the end of the eighties, particularly in a number of Central and Eastern European countries.

Tourism or business travel in the EU is much facilitated by European law. Travellers can buy goods without any limits in the Member State visited at the same conditions as the nationals of that State. Checks on the car insurance green card were abolished; those of disembarkment cards also. Citizens of the Member States can carry a near limitless sum of currency on their intra-Community trips. On package tours, they have won protection against the unfair practices of tour operators under a Community Directive[1]. On air trips, they are also protected against the over-reservation practices of airlines[2]. In the event of illness or accident in a Member State other than that of residence they are covered by the social security system on presentation of an E111 which proves their entitlement to social security cover in the country of residence. Eurocheques, accepted throughout the Community, make payments in local currency simpler and the cash dispensers in the Member States can be used by holders of cards issued by banks in other Member States. In the ports and airports of the Member States, special channels exist for citizens of the European Union who possess a uniform passport[3].

In what way, then, is the **crossing of a border** between two Member States different from passage from one region to the next in a nation State or from that of state to state in a federal State? The sole difference is simply the existence of police checks at borders which, as seen above, no longer serve any purpose, since criminals and traffickers have no problems crossing frontiers, notably by car. These checks only annoy the citizens of the Union, who can not understand why the internal market is completed for goods and not for them. Free movement of persons already exists in the EU and consists in the right of every citizen of the Fifteen to move freely from one Member State to another, to settle wherever he or she wants and take up a job in the country of his or her choice. What some countries do not want to abolish is the identity checks at their frontiers, citing internal security, whereas a "common market" exists already for criminals, drug dealers, and clandestine immigrants - who can cross quite easily land and maritime frontiers - and only a close cooperation between police and judicial authorities of the Member States can hinder their illicit enterprises.

Many EU countries accepted this fact on June 19, 1990, when they signed the **Schengen agreement** for the abolition of border checks at the frontiers between them, the reinforcement of controls at external frontiers and the cooperation among their administrations. This agreement, signed now by the countries of Benelux, Germany, France, Italy, Spain, Portugal and Greece, will demonstrate to the other Member States that they can and

---

1   OJ L158, 23.06.1990. See the preceding subtitle.
2   OJ L36, 08.02.1991. See the heading on air transport in the chapter on transports.
3   OJ C241, 19.09.1981, OJ C185, 24.07.1986 and OJ C200, 04.08.1995.

must, as provided for by article 7a of the EC Treaty calling for a frontier-free space, abolish all checks at internal borders. In order to do this, police checks must be tightened up at the Community's external frontiers and cooperation between national police forces must be strengthened, on the basis, in particular, of the Schengen Information System (SIS), a computerized data bank containing all search warrants issued by the Member States in the system.

The entry into force of the Schengen agreement, on 26 March 1995, may, despite its initial problems, serve as a model that will provide the Commission with a basis for making proposals to achieve further progress, both in Community matters and in justice and home affairs, examined under the next subtitle. In order to show its impatience at the delay in completing a People's Europe, the European Parliament, on 18 November 1993, brought an action against the Commission for failure to present the proposals necessary for the establishment of the free movement of persons in accordance with Article 7a of the Treaty[1]. It should be noted that the problem is both political and legal because it creates a breach between the Schengen States and the Member States of the EU and a discrimination against the citizens of the latter due to the behaviour of their own authorities. The Court of Justice has already condemned the discriminations against their own citizens perpetrated by Member States which do not apply Community rules[2]. But in this case a Community rule has still to be adopted by the Council, acting with a qualified majority, in cooperation with the Parliament. In July 1995, the Commission adopted the proposals, claimed by the Parliament, concerning the elimination of controls by 31 December 1996 on all persons, whatever their nationality, crossing any internal frontier (by air, land and sea)[3].

At the internal frontiers of the Member States, on the other hand, police and customs officers must be replaced by tourism officers ready to welcome the millions of tourists who move around the Community every year. **Tourism** is also one of the paths to a united Europe. The European Parliament, which was behind the declaration of 1990 as European Tourism Year, was well aware of this point[4]. Two years from the deadline for completion of the internal market, European Tourism Year served as a reminder that Europe will not only be built for goods, but also for the good of its citizens. In April 1995, the Commission presented a Green Paper on the role of the European Union in the field of tourism[5].

The EU citizens must feel at home in all the Member States of the Union. As a consequence, the right to travel freely throughout the Union is backed up by the **right to reside** where they choose in the EU. The section on the free movement of workers mentioned the right of workers to keep their **residence** in the country where they are living at the time of ceasing their professional activity and the right for members of their family to

---

1   Case C-445/93, OJ C1, 04.01.1994.
2   Judgment of 7 February 1973, case 39/72, Commission/Italy, ECR 1973, p. 115.
3   OJ C289, 31.10.1995.
4   OJ L17, 21.01.1989.
5   COM (95) 97, 4 April 1995.

remain in this country even after the death of the worker[1]. This basic right is given tangible form by a number of Community Regulations abolishing work permits and guaranteeing migrant workers and members of their families entitlement to social security and trade union rights, vocational training, the free education of their children and, in general, the same treatment as national workers.

The right of residence in any Member State has been teamed up with a number of practical measures such as the mutual recognition of driving licences. This measure, taken in 1981, will cease to be applicable from January 1, 1996, for holders of a Community driving licence will no longer be obliged when they change their residence to another Member State to exchange their licence for a licence issued by the host Member State[2]. As mentioned at the beginning of this chapter, the citizen residing in a Member State of which he is not a national has the right to vote and to stand as candidate at municipal and European elections, under the same conditions as nationals of that State.

Three Council Directives establish the **right of residence** of, respectively, students, salaried workers and non-salaried workers who have ceased working and other Community nationals not yet covered by a Community right of residence[3]. By virtue of these Directives, nationals from the Member States enjoy right of residence provided that they satisfy certain conditions, notably if they themselves and the members of their families have sickness insurance covering all the risks in the host Member State.

Justice and home affairs

Within the vast area created by the Single Market and later consolidated by European Union, equality of treatment applies not only to all the nationals of the Member States but also to the nationals of third countries. The abolition of checks at internal borders of the Community is effective both for the citizens of the Community and for third country nationals, once they have crossed the external frontiers of a Member State. In other words, freedom of movement applies to all those within the territory of the Community. This is why the Member States must have common rules for the crossing of their borders by foreigners and for the treatment of foreigners within their territory. These are new concerns for the Community which emerged with the completion of the internal market and which are taken into account for the first time by the Treaty on European Union. Justice and home affairs are, however, dealt with in part in the Community framework governed by the Treaty establishing the European Community and in part in the framework of the intergovernmental cooperation covered by Title VI of the Treaty on European Union, which excludes the

---

1   OJ L257, 19.10.1968.
2   OJ L375, 31.12.1980 and OJ L237, 24.08.1991.
3   OJ L180, 13.07.1990 and OJ L317, 18.12.1993.

Court of Justice from affairs that may affect vital personal rights and freedoms. Despite this dichotomy, Title VI of the Treaty marks an important step forward in that, for the first time, it imposes an obligation on Member States of the Union to cooperate in fields which, in the past, have generally been covered by "ad hoc" arrangements outside the Treaty.

Article K.1 of the Treaty on European Union defines a number of areas of common interest, which fall into the sphere of intergovernmental cooperation. These are: the crossing of external borders; conditions of entry and movement by nationals of third countries; conditions of residence for these people on the territory of Member States; asylum policy; immigration policy; the combatting of unauthorized immigration, residence and work; the combatting of drug addiction; the combatting of fraud on an international scale; judicial cooperation in civil matters; judicial cooperation in criminal matters; customs cooperation; and police cooperation.

The latter is focused in particular on the prevention and combatting of terrorism, unlawful drug trafficking and other serious forms of international crime. If necessary, it can include certain aspects of customs cooperation and the organization of a Union-wide system for exchanging information within a European Police Office (**Europol**). According to the Declaration on Police Cooperation, annexed to the Maastricht Treaty, exchanges of information relate notably to: support for national criminal investigation and security authorities; the creation of data banks; the central analysis and assessment of information; the collection and analysis of national prevention programmes; and measures relating to training, research, forensic matters and criminal records departments. In March 1995, the Council adopted on the basis of Article K.3 of the Treaty a Joint Action establishing the Europol Drugs Unit (EDU), which, in addition to illicit drug-trafficking, is charged with the fight against illicit trafficking in radioactive and nuclear substances, illicit vehicle trafficking, crimes involving clandestine immigration networks as well as the criminal organizations involved and associated money-laundering activities[1]. On 26 June 1995, the Council formally adopted the Act drawing up the Europol Convention, which was signed the same day[2]. And on 25 September 1995 the Council adopted a Joint Action defining the detailed arrangements for the Community financing of cooperation activities in the fields of JHA, a major element for the functioning of Europol[3].

In the fields referred to in Article K.1, the Member States must inform and consult one another within the Council with a view to coordinating their action (Article K.3). A Coordinating Committee consisting of senior officials contributes, without prejudice to the provisions on the COREPER, to the preparation of the Council's decisions. The Council can, on the initiative of any Member State or of the Commission, adopt **joint positions, joint action** or draw up conventions which it recommends to the Member States for adoption in accordance with their respective constitutional requirements. The Commission cannot take the initiative in fields of judicial cooperation in criminal matters or in customs and police cooperation (Article K.3). However, the Commission is fully associated in the work in all areas of justice and internal affairs (Article K.4). The conventions adopted by the Council can stipulate that the Court of Justice has jurisdiction to interpret their provisions (Article K.3).

---

1   OJ L62, 20.03.1995.
2   OJ C316, 27.11.1995.
3   OJ L238, 06.10.1995.

The Council acts unanimously, except on matters of procedure. It can, however, decide that measures implementing a joint action can be adopted by a qualified majority (Articles K.3 and K4). In any event, any measures applying the conventions adopted, unless otherwise provided by these conventions, are adopted by a two-thirds majority (Article K.3). The European Parliament is regularly kept informed by the Presidency of the Council and by the Commission of the main aspects of activities in the field of justice and home affairs. It can ask questions of the Council or make recommendations to it. Every year, it holds a debate on the progress made in these fields (Article K.6).

It appears that the institutional and legal arrangements for cooperation on justice and home affairs lie somewhere between the classical Community model and simple intergovernmental cooperation. The Commission and the European Parliament have some part to play, though less so than in the Community field. However, the interpretation and application of Treaty provisions in this area are beyond the jurisdiction of the Court of Justice (Article L). This means that neither the Member States nor the institutions (Commission, European Parliament) can act to secure compliance with obligations imposed by decisions that have been taken. It is true that conventions concluded on the basis of Article K.3c may be made subject to the jurisdiction of the Court of Justice in an optional and limited way; but there is no monitoring whatsoever concerning the interpretation or the implementation joint actions and common positions. Moreover, the fact that unanimity is required for all areas covered by Title VI is a major source of paralysis. For all these reasons, the Commission, in agreement with the Parliament, defends at the Intergovernmental Conference the principle of bringing all fields covered by Article K.1, with the exception of police cooperation and judicial cooperation in criminal matters, within the Community system as such[1].

A "gateway" between the Community procedure and intergovernmental cooperation is provided for in Article K.9, which authorizes the Council, acting unanimously on the initiative of the Commission or a Member State, to decide to apply Article 100c of the EC Treaty to action in areas referred to in Article K.1, with the exception of judicial cooperation in criminal matters and customs and police cooperation. In cases where it decides to apply the Community procedure, the Council determines the related voting conditions. Council decisions in this area must, however, be adopted by the Member States in accordance with their respective constitutional requirements, which means that they may not be adopted at all, if a national parliament does not agree to this.

It will not always be easy to make the distinction between the internal and judicial affairs falling under the Community procedure and those subject to intergovernmental cooperation. The Council has already taken decisions under the Community procedure on the illegal manufacture of narcotic drugs and psychotropic substances[2], on the manufacture and the placing on the market of certain substances used in the illicit manufacture of narcotic drugs and psychotropic substances[3], on the monitoring system for "precursor" chemicals, namely substances which can be misused for the manufacture of narcotic drugs and psychotropic substances[4] and on control of the acquisition and possession of weapons[5]. Such provisions, which are vital for the removal of intra-Community frontiers and therefore are based on Community law, will inevitably influence the rules governing the crossing of external borders, in principle covered by intergovernmental cooperation. The same is true of the European Drug Monitoring Centre and the European Information Network on Drugs and Drug Addiction (Reitox) which are founded on a Community instrument[6], whereas the combatting of drug abuse in principle falls under intergovernmental cooperation.

It will be interesting to see in the future how many of the subjects covered by Article K.1 will in fact be dealt with under the Community procedure. If all the Member States agree that one of these subjects is of primordial interest to the European Community as a whole, it will probably not even be necessary to use the "gateway" mentioned above. On the other hand, if one Member State does not agree on a proposal regarding one of these subjects, it will be able to block - through unanimity voting - both the switch over to the Community procedure and the adopting of a joint position or joint action as provided for in Article K.3. Thus, the dispute between Spain and the United Kingdom over Gilbraltar prevents the

---

1   COM (95) 566, 22 November 1995.
2   OJ L357, 20.12.1990.
3   OJ L370, 19.12.1992.
4   OJ L96, 10.04.1992 and OJ L267, 28.10.1993.
5   OJ L256, 13.09.1991.
6   OJ L36, 12.02.1993 and OJ L341, 30.12.1994.

signature of the convention on the crossing of external borders which would encourage the harmonization of immigration and asylum policies, since it stipulates that foreigners with a residence permit for one of the Member States are exempted from the visa requirement for movement throughout the rest of the EC.

Visa policy offers a good example of the complications arising from the existence of various "pillars". In fact, in May 1995 the Council adopted by Regulation based on Article 100c (EC) the provisions laying down a uniform format for visas for nationals of third countries[1]. This single, clearly identifiable visa is issued by the Member States and includes all the necessary information. It meets the highest technical standards, notably as regards safeguards against counterfeiting and falsification. It guarantees, however, protection of the personal data involved. Also by an EC Regulation the Council laid down a common list of 101 countries and territorial entities whose nationals must be in possession of visa when crossing the external borders of the Member States[2]. On the other hand, it is in the context of cooperation in the field of JHA that the Council adopted, in March 1996, a Joint Action on airport transit arrangements[3] and a recommendation on consular cooperation regarding visas[4].

Immigration policy, clearly stipulated in Article K.1 to be a matter for intergovernmental cooperation, has also entered the Community arena through the prior consultation procedure on migratory policies towards third countries in place since June 8, 1988[5]. The Maastricht European Council, after referring to the declaration on racism and xenophobia adopted by the European Parliament, the Council and the Commission on June 11, 1986[6], expressed its conviction that the fight against all forms of discrimination was crucial for the European Community as a community of States governed by a State of law. In the Community framework were adopted the Council Resolutions on the fight against racism and xenophobia in the fields of employment and social affairs and on the response of educational systems to the problems of racism and xenophobia[7]. On the contrary, in the framework of cooperation in the fields JHA were adopted: the Council recommendations on harmonizing means of combating illegal immigration and illegal employment and on concerted action in carrying out expulsion measures[8]; and the Council resolution on the status of third-country nationals residing on a long-term basis in the territory of the Member States[9].

A particularly difficult area, in view of different traditions, but essential for the smooth operation of the internal market is that of the **right of asylum**. Of course, the asylum Convention, signed on 14 June 1990 in Dublin by the Member States (with the exception of Denmark, which may

---

1   OJ L164, 14.07.1995.
2   OJ L234, 03.10.1995.
3   OJ L63, 13.03.1996.
4   OJ C80, 18.03.1996.
5   OJ L183, 14.07.1988.
6   OJ C158, 25.06.1986.
7   OJ C312, 23.11.1995.
8   OJ C5, 10.01.1996.
9   OJ C80, 18.03.1996.

accede after the solution of certain political and legal problems), commits all signatories to examining all asylum demands deposited by a citizen of a third country at the frontier or on the territory of Member States and exchanging individualized information on all such demands. But this Convention does not harmonize national legislations on asylum and, therefore, it does not create a Community refugee status. Nevertheless, the Community set up, in June 1992, a Centre for Information, Research and Exchange on Asylum matters (CIREA). In the context of cooperation in the fields of JHA, the Council adopted on 21 June 1995 a Resolution on minimum guarantees that asylum procedures must present to ensure that they comply with the Geneva Convention of 28 July 1951 on the Status of Refugees. In the same context it adopted in March 1995 a joint position concerning harmonized application of the term "refugee" in Article 1 of the Geneva Convention and it established an alert and emergency procedure for burden-sharing with regard to the admission and residence of displaced persons on a temporary basis[1].

As regards **extradition,** the Fifteen adopted, in March 1995, the Convention on the simplified extradition procedure between the Member States of the European Union of persons whose extradition is requested and who consent to this. It aims to facilitate the application, between Member States of the EU, of the European Convention on Extradition adopted by the Council of Europe in 1957. This Convention, which is the first to be adopted under Article K.3 of the Treaty, sets down the conditions under which the simplified procedures are implemented, notably concerning the consent of the interested person[2].

In the context of **judicial and police cooperation** the Council adopted: a resolution on the protection of witnesses in the fight against international organized crime[3]; a Joint Action concerning a framework for the exchange of liaison magistrates[4]; and a recommendation on guidelines for preventing and restraining disorder connected with football matches[5].

Bibliography on citizens' Europe

◻   BARENDT Eric, *Broadcasting Law: A Comparative Study*, Clarendon Press, Oxford, 1993.

◻   BEKEMANS Leonce (ed.), *Culture: Building Stone for Europe 2002*, Presses Interuniversitaires européennes, Bruxelles, 1994.

---

1   OJ L63, 13.03.1996.
2   OJ C78, 30.03.1995.
3   OJ C327, 07.12.1995.
4   OJ L105, 27.04.1996.
5   OJ C131, 03.05.1996.

▫ BIEBER Roland, MONAR Joerg (ed.), *Justice and Home Affairs in the European Union. The Development of the Third Pillar*, Presses Interuniversitaires Européennes, Brussels, 1995.

▫ BUNYAN Tony, *The Europol Convention*, Statewatch, London, 1995.

▫ *Code européen des personnes*, Éditions Dalloz, Paris, 1994.

▫ COMMISSION EUROPÉENNE, *Communication de la Commission au Conseil, au Parlement européen et au Comité économique et social sur le deuxième plan d'action triennal (1993-1995) en matière de politique des consommateurs*, COM (93) 378 du 28 juillet 1993.

  - *Communication au Conseil et au Parlement européen sur les politiques d'immigration et d'asile*, COM (94) 23, 23.02.1994.

  - Guide du consommateur européen dans le marché unique, OPOCE, Luxembourg, 1994.

  - *Vers la société de l'information en Europe: un plan d'action*, COM (94) 347, 19.07.1994.

▫ CORNU Marie, *Compétences culturelles en Europe et principe de subsidiarité*, Éditions Bruylant, Bruxelles, 1993.

▫ DEJEMEPPE Pierre (sous la dir. de), *Les consommateurs et l'Europe des services financiers*, Éditions Bruylant, Bruxelles, 1992.

▫ DEHOUSSE Franklin, VINCENT Philippe, "Le marché unique des personnes", in *Journal des Tribunaux*, Bruxelles, N° 5755, 8 avril 1995, pp. 273-277.

▫ EUROPEAN COMMISSION, *Strategy Options to Strengthen the European Programme Industry in the Context of the Audiovisual Policy of the European Union*, Green Paper, April, 1994.

  - *EUROBAROMETER, Public Opinion in the European Union*, N° 44, Spring 1996.

▫ GIRAUDEL Catherine, "Produits alimentaires naturels et protection des consommateurs", in *Revue juridique de l'environnement*, N 3/1993, pp. 437-452.

▫ HANDOLL John, *Free Movement of Persons in the EU*, John Wiley & Sons, Chichester, 1995.

▫ HREBLAY Vendelin, *La libre circulation des personnes: Les accords de Schengen*, PUF, Paris, 1994.

▫ HYLAND N., LOFTUS C., WHELAN A., *Citizenship of the European Union*, Institute of European Affairs, Dublin, 1995.

▫ KENDALL Vivienne, *EC Consumer Law*, Wiley Chancery Law Publ., Chichester, West Sussex, 1994.

▫ LAGER Carol, *L'Europe en quête de ses symboles*, Peter Lang, Berne, 1995.

▫ LAWLOR Eamonn, *Individual Choice And Higher Growth. The Aim Of Consumer Policy in the Single Market*, 2nd edition, OOPEC, Luxembourg, 1992.

▫ LOMAN A., MORTELMANS K., POST H., WATSON S., *Culture and Community Law, Before and after Maastricht*, Kluwer Law and Taxation Publishers, Deventer, 1992.

▫ MAZZAFERRO Francesco, "European Citizenship and New Rights for Union Citizens", in *The Federalist, a Political Review*, Year XXXV, 1993, N 2, pp. 63-79.

□   MONAR Joerg, MORGAN Roger (ed.), *The Third Pillar of the European Union - Cooperation in the Fields of Justice and Home Affairs*, Presses Interuniversitaires européennes, Bruxelles, 1994.

□   OBSERVATOIRE SOCIAL EUROPEEN, *La coopération des polices en Europe*, Actes du séminaire organisé par l'OSE, Bruxelles, 1993.

□   O'KEEFFE David, "The Emergence of a European Immigration Policy", in *European Law Review*, Vol. 20, N° 1, February 1995, pp. 20-36.

□   PINAULT Agnès, "Premiers pas des accords de Schengen", in *Regards sur l'actualité*, N° 218, février 1996, pp 3-10.

□   POULOT D., "Le patrimoine culturel, valeur commune de l'Europe", in *Relations internationales*, N 73, printemps 1993, pp. 43-62.

16. THE EUROPEAN UNION

IN THE WORLD

The European Union is present on the world stage in three main roles, examined in turn in this Chapter: development aid, common commercial policy and external relations. In the first two areas it is a central player - as it is the world's largest trading entity and one of the largest providers of funds for the developing countries - and in the third it is rapidly becoming one. The three often overlap; development aid is tied in with commercial policy and commercial policy with the Union's foreign policy.

The first two roles of the European Union as a world power form part of the central pillar or edifice of the Union, which is that of the European Community. Nearly all of the policies examined thus far, with the exception of justice and home affairs, fall into the domain of the European Community. Justice and home affairs form the third pillar of the Union. According to Article 3 of the Treaty on the European Community, as amended in Maastricht, the activities of the Community include, among other things, a common commercial policy, a policy in the sphere of development cooperation and association of overseas countries and territories. Article 110 confirms that in establishing a customs union, the Member States seek to contribute, in accordance with the common interest, to the harmonious development of world trade, the gradual removal of restrictions on international trade and the lowering of customs barriers. Under Article 130x, the Community and the Member States coordinate their policies on development cooperation and consult each other on aid programmes, including in international organizations and during international conferences. They can undertake joint action. The Member States contribute, if necessary, to the implementation of Community aid programmes.

The third international role of the European Union, which is often called its second pillar, is constituted by the provisions on a common foreign and security policy, provided for in Title V of the Maastricht

Treaty. The new Treaty in its first pages consecrates this role, declaring in the common provisions (Article B) that the Union has the objective of asserting its identity on the international scene, in particular through the implementation of a common foreign and security policy, which might in time lead to common defence. The external activities of the European Union now form a coherent whole which embraces foreign policy, including all aspects of security, and also commercial policy, development policy and even cooperation in the fields of justice and home affairs. This comprehensive approach has a single institutional framework, with the Council and the Commission both taking responsibility for coordination.

The European Union, through one or other of its international roles, has diplomatic relations with 162 countries, which for their part have representations in Brussels. The EU has its own representations, organized by the Commission, in most of these countries and in international organizations. The Maastricht Treaty calls for closer collaboration between the diplomatic and consular missions of the Member States and the Commission Delegations in third countries. In organizations such as the General Agreement on Tariffs and Trade (GATT) and in international fishery organizations, the Community speaks in the name of and in place of the Member States, through the mouthpiece of the Commission. It participates in the work of the OECD and has observer status in the United Nations and in some of its specialized organizations. It has relations with other international organizations, such as the Council of Europe. It is represented, by the President of the Commission, at the economic summits of the most industrialized countries, called G7, between four of its Member States - France, Germany, the United Kingdom and Italy - and the United States, Canada and Japan. It signs and manages association or cooperation agreements with more than 120 countries and is also responsible for numerous multilateral agreements. When these agreements cover an area for which it has exclusive responsibility, such as international trade or fisheries, the European Union is the sole party to them on behalf of its Member States. In other cases (some agreements on the environment, transport and so on), the Union is a party in addition to its Member States.

Development aid

Development aid reflects both the search for solidarity between the developed countries and the disadvantaged countries of the world and the economic necessity for the Community of guaranteeing its raw material supply and creating outlets for its products. At the outset the Community, under the influence of France in particular, opted for a selective policy, placing the emphasis on African countries which had a "special relationship" with the Member States. Little by little, however, nudged by the United Kingdom and anxious to develop trade with the world as a whole, the Community fanned out its action in favour of developing countries. Aware that advantages granted at world level diminished the attractiveness of regional preferences, the Community has been caught up in a process of continually expanding the instruments on offer to developing countries.

Article 130u of the Treaty on European Union specifies that Community policy in the sphere of development cooperation is complementary to the policies pursued by the Member States and must foster: the sustainable economic and social development of the developing countries; the smooth and gradual integration of the developing countries in the world economy; and the campaign against poverty in the developing countries. Community policy, which must take account of the objectives agreed within the context of the United Nations and other competent international organizations, must contribute to the general objective of consolidating democracy and the rule of law, the respect of human rights and fundamental freedoms.

Although the political neutrality of the Lomé Convention enables development cooperation to take place between the Union and ACP governments of every political hue, the EU strives to link development cooperation with the **respect of human rights**. In effect, Article 228a EC allows the EU to apply politically motivated economic sanctions. In a declaration of 25 May 1993, the Community and its Member States reserved the right to take measures which might even involve suspending aid if the democratization process was halted or if serious violations of human rights occurred. Since then the EU took measures such as altering the content of aid programmes, withholding the signatures necessary for the implementation of aid, or even suspending it altogether, while taking care to avoid harming the people of the country concerned. In two 1995 communications on democratic principles and human rights, the Commission defines the main thrust of Community policy on those subjects[1]. In particular it proposes enhancing the legal force of the wording to be inserted into new draft negotiating directives for agreements with third countries, namely the clause first introduced in 1992 stipulating that respect for democratic principles and human rights is an "essential element" of contractual relations, by means of a provision suspending implementation if this key element in the agreement is flouted.

The European Union currently has an impressive store of development aid instruments, spanning the Convention with the ACP countries, special relations with the Overseas Countries and Territories, aid for non-associated countries, the Generalized System of Tariff Preferences (GSP), participation in world commodity agreements and aid provided through non-government organizations fighting world problems such as hunger. This variety of forms which development aid takes clearly demonstrates the EU's commitment to an outward-looking approach. In fact, in the early nineties, the EU and its Member States provided 43% of official development assistance, whereas the United States provided 18%.

The European Union also has a wide range of **development policy resources**, from industrial and technological cooperation to trade promotion, food aid and financial aid. Financial aid takes the form of European Investment Bank (EIB) loans and risk capital or European Development

---

1   COM (95) 216, 23 May 1995 and COM (95) 567, 22 November 1995.

Fund (EDF) subsidies or is granted under other Articles of the Community Budget, concerning notably food aid. The EDF, is funded by a five-year specific contribution of the Member States but is an integral part of the Community Budget.

ACP-EC Association

In the first years following the entry into force of the EEC Treaty, the Community's development aid policy was more or less restricted to the association provided for in the fourth part of the Treaty and covering the former colonies of France, Italy, Belgium and the Netherlands. After most of these countries were granted independence, a first Convention was signed in Yaoundé (Cameroon) on July 20, 1963 between the EEC and an association of 17 African countries and Madagascar, the EAMA. In addition to better structuring of the aid granted to these countries, this Convention lowered the external tariffs of EEC Member States for tropical products and created joint institutions between the Community and the EAMA for the implementation of the agreement. The second Yaoundé Convention, signed on July 29, 1969, increased European Development Fund (EDF) and EIB aid, made their provisions more flexible and targeted aid on manufacturing. In addition, a special Reserve Fund was set up to intervene should world prices of a commodity of vital economic interest to an associated country plummet. This was the starting point of attempts to stabilize the export revenue of the associated countries.

The enlargement of the Community in 1973 substantially boosted the ranks of the associated countries, drawing in the former British colonies. This prompted an overhaul of the content of the agreement. The Convention signed in Lomé (Togo) on February 28, 1975 between the then nine Member States of the EEC and the 46 States of **Africa, the Caribbean and the Pacific (ACP)** signalled a fresh start for the Community's development aid policy. This Convention embodied several principles, such as that of free access to the Community market for almost all products of ACP origin on a basis of non-reciprocity, and introduced new mechanisms, such as that to stabilize export revenue (Stabex) and others relating to the development of industrial infrastructure. The second Lomé Convention, signed on October 31, 1979[1] between the then nine Member States and 57 ACP States, substantially increased the range of agricultural products covered by the Stabex mechanism, created a similar mechanism for ores (Sysmin) and introduced a significant chapter on agricultural coopera-tion. The third Lomé Convention, signed on December 8, 1984[2] between the ten Member States and 66 ACP States, placed the emphasis on aid programming.

The fourth EEC-ACP Convention, also signed in Lomé on December 15, 1989, firmly cemented cooperation between the EC Member States and 70 ACP States, including the whole of sub-Saharan Africa and, in the near future, South Africa. This cooperation is based on solidarity, mutual interest and respect of the sovereignty of each of the participating countries[3]. The Convention has a number of innovative features, such as aid for the processing and local marketing of commodities, the promotion of the service sector, environmental protection measures and a support mechanism for structural adjustment policies in the ACP countries. Before giving its aid to ACP States, the Community approves their national indicative programmes (NIP), which describe the objectives and measures of national development, as well as the financial aid available for the purpose.

A **mid-term review of Lomé IV** has strengthened the political and institutional facets of the Convention, defined the development of trade as

---

1   OJ L347, 22.12.1980.
2   OJ L61, 01.03.1985.
3   OJ L229, 17.08.1991 and OJ L317, 30.12.1995.

the engine of ACP-EC cooperation and streamlined implementation of financial and technical cooperation. The revamped Lomé IV contains a clause allowing for the total or partial suspension of the Convention in the event of any breach of human rights or democratic principles. The renewal of the financial protocol for the period 1995-2000 sets total funding for the ACP countries at ECU 14.6 billion (of which ECU 13 billion comes from the eighth EDF and ECU 1.6 billion from EIB operations) and represents an increase of almost 22% in the EU's financial contribution compared with the previous five years.

As was mentioned above, the financial assistance of the Union passes by the **European Development Fund (EDF)**. The import of the EDF evolves naturally and gradually as each Convention generates new development projects and increases Community aid. A number is given to the EDF corresponding to each Convention, and thus EDF 7 corresponds to Lomé IV and EDF 8 to revised Lomé IV. Because an EDF programming and implementation cycle is far longer than the five-year periods covered by successive Lomé Conventions, the European Commission simultaneously manages several EDFs that are at different stages of maturity. Funding is programmed in two instalments, with the second payment only being released if a mid-term assessment shows that resources have been used properly during the first.

Over the years, specific institutions governing the ACP-EEC association have come into being: there is a joint assembly which meets twice a year, a Council of Ministers meeting once a year and a Committee of Ambassadors which prepares the ministers' work. But the association's main achievement has been to build cooperation in a range of fields, examined below.

Under the wing of **trade cooperation**, which strives to promote the diversification of exports and the research into new markets, manufactures and agricultural products which do not directly compete with the products coming under the common agricultural policy enter the Community at zero customs duty and free of quantitative restrictions. These concessions are not reciprocal. The ACP States can preserve their customs barriers and undertake simply to treat the Community Member States in an identical manner and as well as the most favoured industrial nation. Special attention is devoted to trade policy in national and regional programmes, notably as concerns the support which the Community grants to: professional trade promotion and development bodies, the creation of ACP Chambers of Commerce and ACP participation in international trade and tourism fairs and exhibitions. The emphasis is placed on the establishment of coherent commercial strategies, the optimization of human resources and the improvement of product quality and competitiveness.

The Community's most original contribution to problem-solving in the under-developed countries is through a mechanism to stabilize their export earnings, thus cushioning the disastrous blows dealt by large fluctuations in the world market prices for certain raw materials (coffee, tea, cotton, groundnuts, bananas, wood and leather). The development plans of these countries cannot be efficiently implemented if their export earnings are not guaranteed against the sudden falls in agricultural prices

occasionally experienced on the world market, for example after over-production.

The **System of Stabilization of Export Earnings (Stabex)** set up by
the Lomé Conventions is relatively simple. If, in relation to a reference
level consisting of average exports in the four previous years, the value of
exports to the Community by an ACP country of a product vital for this
country's economy falls by more than 6% (trigger threshold), stabilizing
transfers are made to correct the drop in earnings. Stabex covers around
fifty agricultural products, but coffee, tea and cocoa make up more than
two-thirds of total transfers. Transfers take place under a special EDF
chapter, set up for this purpose. Until the end of Lomé III, the resources of
this Fund had to be reconstituted by the beneficiary States in later years if
their revenue recovered to a sufficient degree. The reconstitution obligation has been abolished under the fourth Convention and the debts accumulated by the ACP States under the first three Conventions have been
written off. The Commission receives all the applications for transfers
under Stabex and examines them for admissibility with the management
rules of the system, which are specified in the Convention. It can also
request that the ACP-EC Council of Ministers release additional resources
if it sees a major gap opening up between available resources and total
eligible transfers. Such was the case in 1991/1992 following the sustained
and unprecedented drop in coffee and cocoa prices.

The **Sugar Protocol** grants sugar more favourable treatment than that
afforded under Stabex. It incorporates a mutual purchase and delivery
commitment for a certain quantity at a price which is negotiated on an
annual basis and is set within the range of prices for that particular
Community marketing year[1]. This price represents a minimum guaranteed income level, which may be improved if suppliers obtain better terms
on the Community market.

A **Special Financial System for Mining Products (Sysmin)** was introduced under Lomé II. It seeks to preserve the mining potential of the ACP
States. Prevention or correction of mining investment shortfalls through
the Lomé Convention is both in the interest of the ACP States, in that it
promotes their economic and social development through optimizing their
natural resources, and in that of the EU countries, who thus have a vital
guarantee of supply continuity for mineral raw materials. Under Sysmin,
an ACP State can apply to the Commission for support to fund projects
which will maintain or recover its production capacity if, for an ore which
represented at least 15% (10% for the poorest countries) of its total exports,
production or export capacity to the EU risk being cut by more than 10%
following a drop in world market prices or other negative factors. Through
cooperation in the energy and mining sectors, the Community thus contributes to the evaluation of ACP resources and helps adapt their infrastructure to the attainment of self-sufficiency in energy production.

Industrialization of the developing countries has come up against two major obstacles:
a lack of sufficient return on investments, due to numerous difficulties relating to the
country's under-development (absence of external savings, of infrastructure or specialized

---

1   OJ L179, 09.07.1988.

staff); and low security for foreign investments, given the risk of nationalization or expropriation. The ACP-EC Convention has sought to promote stability of the investment climate through encouraging and protecting Community investments in the ACP States. **Industrial cooperation** is confined chiefly to the agri-industrial sectors (abattoirs-refrigerators, nut factories, textiles...) and to construction (cement works, marble works, quarries...). The Commission is striving to play an active role in the emergence of a climate which promotes the development of private enterprise, in particular through the drawing up and implementation of projects which will further the development of enterprises and the flow of investments. The Centre for the Development of Industry (CDI) supports the organization of various industrial promotion events, such as the Community-Central Africa Forum.

Community action under the banner of **agricultural cooperation** spans such fields as integrated rural development, the promotion of food crops and cash crops, stock rearing, fisheries and, more generally, the protection and upgrading of natural resources. The Technical Centre for Agricultural and Rural Cooperation concentrates upon vocational training, research, technical meetings and the dissemination of information. The food self-sufficiency which is one of the goals of this cooperation is primordial for the ACPs, for it would kill several birds with one stone, such as rural development, the population flood from the countryside to the cities and the desertification of the countryside. Community import arrangements applicable to agricultural products originating in the ACP States and to certain goods resulting from their processing are established by a Council Regulation[1]. A special system of financial and technical assistance for traditional ACP banana suppliers helps them adapt to the new market conditions created by the introduction of a common organization of the market for bananas[2].

The **financial and technical cooperation** is organized around three basic principles: focusing of aid on a limited number of sectors, dialogue between the Commission and each ACP State on aid programming and coordination with other donors. Funding is concentrated in indicative programmes which are structured and on a large scale. They notably involve the use of sectoral import programmes (rapid disbursement aid) which, through the injection of hard currency which they give, are particularly well suited to revitalizing the development process in certain ACP States. The main thrusts of Community support are rural development which respects the environment, road and socio-economic infrastructure and the development of human resources, particularly women.

The Community also supports structural adjustment efforts in ACP States facing debt problems (transformation of special loans, Stabex transfers and Sysmin funding into subsidies). **Structural adjustment support (SAS)**, for which specific resources have been earmarked under Lomé IV, focuses on a number of key points such as the social aspects of adjustment, the choice of long-term development objectives and a pace of macroeconomic reforms suited to each State's capabilities. In December 1987, the Council adopted a special programme in favour of certain poor and heavily indebted countries in Sub-Saharan Africa[3]. Drawn up in conjunction with the World Bank and other donors, this programme supposes that effective coordination exists between all the parties making it possible for the Commission to ensure that the reforms supported are not only economically efficient but also politically and socially acceptable. In this connection, since Lomé III, the EDF has been able to grant financial aid to ACP States providing reception facilities for refugees or repatriated persons. This objective is to meet acute needs or to support longer-term projects aiming at self-sufficiency and the integration of the population groups in question. The European institutions also focus their attention on aid for reconstruction and rehabilitation in the aftermath of war, civil strife or natural disaster.

The **ecological dimension** of development is also given consideration in the definition of objectives and of main intervention sectors (ban on movements of toxic and radioactive waste), and in implementation provisions for financial and technical assistance. In the framework of this assistance, allowance is also made for the **cultural and social dimension** of development, to ensure that the identity and dignity of the population groups concerned by it are respected. The emphasis is placed on human resources, including the contribution of women to the economic and social development of the ACP States. The situation of ACP migrant workers and students in the EU can moreover be discussed in the framework of the joint institutions.

1   OJ L84, 30.03.1990 and OJ L265, 15.10.1994.
2   OJ L286, 05.11.1994.
3   OJ C348, 23.12.1987.

Under the heading of **regional cooperation**, the Community supports the fight against problems affecting several ACP States and requiring long-term solutions, such as natural disasters, endemic diseases and, more significantly, drought and desertification. Given that regional projects normally take more time to prepare, since they often involve co-financing with other donors and since in principle several governments must agree on the joint presentation of a regional project, the emphasis is placed on **regional programming** with the aim of favouring the creation of viable and coherent economic areas. In Western Africa, thus, resources are to be channelled as a priority towards the Community cooperation effort to combat desertification and develop transport. In Central Africa, top priority will be given to transport and means of communication and to rural development and the optimization of forestry and fishery resources. Regional cooperation for East Africa takes a pragmatic approach - given the extreme variety found in this region - tailored to priorities and to the possibilities for cooperation. Under the regional indicative programmes (RIP), financial and technical support is also given to ambitious regional integration initiatives, such as the setting-up of an economic union of the countries of the West African Economic and Monetary Union (UEMOA), a customs union of the Central African countries (UDEAC), and reforms designed to reduce barriers to trade, investment and intra-regional payments in East and southern Africa and the Indian Ocean.

Having supported the process of democratic and multiracial transition in **South Africa**, with a coordinated programme of assistance in the preparation of elections and with the setting-up of a cooperation framework aiming at consolidating the economic and social bases for transition[1], the European Union tends to develop relations with this country that resemble those of an ACP associate. In 1994, the generalized system of preferences (GSP) scheme, which gives developing countries preferential tariff treatment for their exports to the European Union, has been extended to South Africa and, since 1995, it covers the agricultural products of this country[2]. A draft framework cooperation agreement between the European Union and South Africa lays the foundations for a trade and cooperation agreement, which could lead to a free trade area, as well as the conditions for an accession of South Africa to the Lomé IV bis Convention[3]. The cooperation agreement would govern all financial, technical as well as trade and economic relations and should lead to a free trade area between the EU and South Africa.

While much clearly remains to be done, given an international backdrop of economic crisis in the developing countries and the fratricidal conflicts and political instability in many of them, the ACP-EC association is a remarkable contribution to solidarity between the North and South of the planet. However, aid cannot make up for a lack of sound domestic policies or trade outlets, but is much more effective when used as a lever for the implementation of economic and political reforms. What is therefore needed is an approach which encourages internal reforms in the developing countries, on the basis of the four main themes expounded in the Treaty on European Union: consolidation and development of democracy, sustainable economic and social development, integration into the world economy and a battle against poverty.

Overseas countries and territories

Article 131 of the EC Treaty associates to the Community the non-European countries and territories which have special relationships with certain Member States. The aim of this association is promotion of the economic and social development of the **Overseas Countries and Territories (OCTs)** and the establishment of close economic relations between them and the Community. In accordance with the principles set out in the Preamble of the Treaty, the

---

1   OJ L316, 17.12.1993.
2   OJ L225, 31.08.1994 and OJ L273, 16.11.1995.
3   OJ L341, 30.12.1994 and OJ C134, 06.05.1996.

association must encourage trade in the interest of the inhabitants of these countries and territories, in a manner leading to the economic, social and cultural development to which they aspire.

The list of OCTs annexed to the EC Treaty has changed considerably first of all with the winning of independence by the majority of these countries and secondly with the accession to the Community of the United Kingdom, whose OCTs have swollen the original ranks. The majority of these ex-OCTs which are now independent have become ACPs and the regulations relating to the association of OCTs to the Community have evolved in line with the arrangements applicable to the ACP States in the framework of the Lomé Conventions.

The regulations currently in force relating to the association of overseas countries and territories to the EC apply to twenty-five OCTs dependent on France, the Netherlands, the United Kingdom and Denmark (Greenland)[1]. While they come under the wing of Member States and their nationals are recognized since 1996 as EU citizens, the OCTs do not form part of the Union, but they are associated with it and thus benefit from the EDF and the same types of development cooperation measures as ACP States. Community solidarity in their connection is reflected chiefly by the near free access to the Community market for products originating in the OCTs, by the implementation of export stabilization systems similar to Stabex and Sysmin and by financial and technical cooperation drawing on the resources of the EDF and the EIB. The fields covered by this financial and technical cooperation are agricultural and rural development, fisheries, industrial development, the exploitation of mining and energy potential, transport and communications, the development of trade and services, regional cooperation and cultural and social cooperation. Depending on the development level and situation of the OCTs, an attempt is also made to establish firm cooperation between them and the ACP States. The new arrangements in favour of OCTs, introduced on July 25, 1991, include many elements contained in the fourth Lomé Convention and establish a three-way Commission - Member State - OCT partnership[2]. The programming of EDF resources in favour of the OCTs is based on the resources allocated by each of the three Member States concerned (France, the Netherlands and the UK.) within the overall amounts laid down by the Council.

Aid for non-associated countries

Under the impetus of the United Kingdom, the Community adopted in 1976 a programme of financial and technical aid for the developing countries of **Latin America and Asia,** complementing its aid to associated countries. The EU's relations with these countries are less structured than those with the ACP countries and take the form of cooperation agreements. These agreements are limited in scope. They do not provide for preferential access to EC markets for exports from Asian and Latin American countries, except under the Generalized System of Preferences, which is explained below. Nor do they contain provisions for financial aid to the

1   OJ L175, 01.07.1986.
2   OJ L263, 19.09.1991 and OJ L26, 02.02.1996.

partner countries, but such aid is provided under special inscriptions in the Community budget and, therefore, must be decided every year by the budgetary authorities.

Funding - which always takes the form of subsidies - goes directly to the beneficiary countries or to regional organizations. The Commission must request the opinion on the proposed projects of a financing committee which it chairs and which is made up of representatives of the Member States. Most of the funding is earmarked for the agricultural sector (agriculture in general, irrigation, fisheries) or for agriculture-related activities (agricultural and food research, rural credit). A certain proportion of the funding is set aside for emergency operations in response notably to disasters. The Council moreover set up in 1987 a system of compensation for loss of export earnings, similar to Stabex, for least-developed countries which are not signatories of the ACP-EC Convention. This chiefly concerns Latin American and Asian countries[1]. Since 1988, aid for the developing countries of Latin America and Asia is split on the basis of 65% for Asia and 35% for Latin America[2].

Cooperation with the countries of Asia and Latin America is now focused on the poorest population groups and on economic cooperation with high growth potential countries and regions. Since 1992, the Community's cooperation with these countries includes both financial and technical aid and new priorities such as the environment, the human dimension of development and the promotion of human rights[3]. The framework programme of industrial cooperation and investment promotion (AL-Invest) allows the use of the services of outside consultants.

The financial instrument **"EC Investment Partners"(ECIP)** is designed to promote investments of mutual interest to Community and local operators, notably in the form of joint ventures, in some 60 countries of Asia, Latin America and the Mediterranean as well as in South Africa[4]. The scheme provides support for private sector investments of mutual interest to businesses in the Community and in eligible countries by means of four financing facilities covering all stages of the establishment of a joint venture: identification of projects and partners; feasibility studies and pilot project; financing capital requirements of a joint venture or a local company; training of managers and assistance in managing joint ventures. The management of funds is decentralized, thanks to a network of financial institutions and investment promotion bodies.

Generalized System of Preferences

The Community provided the initiative behind the Generalized System of Preferences (**GSP**), the principle of which was taken on board by the other industrialized countries at the 2nd Session of the United Nations Conference on Trade and Development (UNCTAD) in 1968. Although it has traditionally come under Article 113 (EC) and, therefore, in theory, under the common commercial policy, the GSP is in practice a tool of development. It offers some 130 developing countries tariff reductions or

---

1   OJ L43, 13.02.1987.
2   OJ L226, 06.08.1988.
3   OJ L52, 27.02.1992.
4   OJ L28, 06.02.1996.

in some cases duty-free access for their manufactured exports and certain agricultural exports as well. Being a tariff instrument, it operates purely at the level of tariffs which, with a few sectoral exceptions, are now far from being the main barrier to trade. Being an autonomous instrument, its preferences are granted (not negotiated) by the Community under a special GATT enabling clause designed to ensure the system is non-discriminatory. Indeed, the GSP is complementary to GATT and not an alternative to the multilateral liberalization of trade within the GATT.

The GSP covers more the industrial products of developing countries than agricultural products. In principle, the EU imports industrial goods from developing countries free of customs duty, within certain limits (ceilings or quotas). The severity of this limit increases with the sensitivity of the product in question. For non-sensitive products, duty may be re-introduced on a Commission Decision when the ceiling is reached. For highly sensitive products, the re-introduction of customs duties is automatic once the limits have been reached. Top of the list of sensitive products come **textiles**, for which for many years an attempt was made to encourage the orderly growth of trade while not disrupting the markets of the industrialized countries[1]. The product/country differentiation policy, which means the exclusion from the GSP of some sensitive products originating in competitive countries, has worked in favour of Asian countries, which account for almost 70% of the preferential advantage. Within the region the lion's share goes to China, which takes nearly 25% of total GSP benefits. From 1990, the GSP was extended to the countries of Central and Eastern Europe[2] and from 1993 it was extended to Georgia and the independent States of the former Soviet Union[3]. As mentioned above, the GSP was extended to South Africa in 1994 and covers the agricultural products of this country[4].

After the conclusion of the Uruguay Round, the European Union needs to update the GSP by taking account of the new international situation and institutional changes within the EU itself. In addition to the standard scheme, there now exist special incentive arrangements granting additional tariff reductions when more enlightened social and environmental practices are introduced. A "graduation mechanism" will make the most competitive developing countries lose little by little the GSP advantages for the production sectors that do not need them anymore. The differentiated schemes now cover a three-year period. Thus, in December 1994, the Council adopted the multiannual scheme of generalized preferences for industrial products for the period 1995-1997[5].

Cooperation at world level

Many developing countries are heavily dependent on the export of just one or two **commodities**. As a consequence, an attempt has been made in recent years in the framework of the United Nations Conference on Trade and Development (UNCTAD) to conclude agreements which support or stabilize the production of commodities. These agreements generally cover three aspects: prices, quantities and mechanisms (production

---

1   OJ L370, 31.12.1990 and OJ L338, 31.12.1993. See the heading "Sectoral commercial policy measures" in
      the following part of this chapter.
2   OJ L370, 31.12.1990 and OJ L362, 31.12.1991.
3   OJ L396, 31.12.1992 and OJ L108, 01.05.1993.
4   OJ L225, 31.08.1994 and OJ L273, 16.11.1995.
5   OJ L348, 31.12.1994 and OJ L326, 30.12.1995.

quotas, buffer stocks and so on). The producer countries see these agreements on commodities chiefly as a way of guaranteeing export earnings and ensuring a certain level of income for their producers, whereas importers view them as a way of guaranteeing supply of a given quantity of a product at a price set in advance. The agreements differ from one product to the next, some aiming at better marketing and heightened competitiveness, other involving attempts to intervene in the free play of market mechanisms at world level.

The Member States of the Community are importers of most of the commodities covered by **world agreements**. During the seventies, they tended to negotiate the terms of these agreements individually rather than as members of the Community. However, during the fourth UNCTAD Conference in Nairobi in 1976, at which a draft "integrated programme" for commodities was outlined, external pressure was put on the Community to define a common policy in negotiating such agreements. As a consequence, from 1980 the Community has taken an active part in negotiating and managing many world agreements, including those on jute and jute articles[1]; coffee[2]; cocoa[3]; rubber[4]; tropical wood[5]; wheat[6]; olive oil and olives[7]; and sugar[8].

During the Nairobi Conference of 1976, the decision was also taken to set up a United Nations **Common Fund for Commodities**. The agreement establishing this Fund was concluded in 1980 and signed by the Community on October 21, 1981. But for it to become operational, the agreement had to be ratified by at least 90 states representing two-thirds of its capital. This condition was only fulfilled in 1989. The Fund consequently became operational on June 19, 1989. It reinforced the operation of agreements on certain commodities which are regulated by organizations with specific responsibility for them. To this effect, the Fund has two "windows", one contributing to the financing of buffer stocks and national stocks coordinated at international level and managed by international organizations with specific responsibility for certain commodities; the other supporting measures other than storage (for example research and other measures seeking to improve productivity and marketing). The Community is a member of the Fund on the same footing as its Member States.

In January 1986, the **United Nations Industrial Development Organization (UNIDO)** was transformed into a specialized United Nations institution and its activities retargeted upon both sectoral and regional priorities. This transformation brought to the fore the UNIDO's dual role as a forum for the exchange of views on industrial development policies in Third World countries and on cooperation with the more developed countries, on the one hand, and as the inspiration for and implementor of cooperation programmes revolving around the marketplace and enterprises. The Community, which has observer status in the UNIDO, negotiated in 1989 the relationship between the two institutions in order to be able

1   OJ L185, 08.07.1983 and OJ L293, 09.10.1992.
2   OJ L22, 26.08.1994.
3   OJ L52, 23.02.1994.
4   OJ L219, 04.08.1992.
5   OJ L236, 03.09.1985.
6   OJ L195, 17.07.1986.
7   OJ L214, 04.08.1987.
8   OJ L379, 23.12.1992.

to play an effective role in all the Organization's work. The Commission, which represents the Community in UNIDO, shows strong interest in the activities of this organization in the restructuring of the formerly centrally planned economies.

The Community also participates in the work of the **United Nations Food and Agriculture Organization (FAO)**. The activities of this organization have been hindered for several years now due to late payments by its main contributor, the United States. Its main tasks are to re-establish order in international trade in agricultural produce, the replenishment of food stocks following the droughts of recent years and the fight against hunger in the world. In November 1991, the ministerial Conference of the FAO recognized the Community as a member "sui generis", stating its views through the Commission on all matters coming within its sphere of competence, such as forestry or development, and alternately with the Member States. In addition the Community can now accede to any convention or agreement concluded under the aegis of the FAO, although the arrangements for its participation have to be negotiated on a case-by-case basis.

Fight against hunger and other afflictions

The Community is the third biggest contributor to the **World Food Programme** (WFP). It supplies food and financial support to cover the transport of food products in the framework of "food for work" projects or free distribution projects managed by the WFP or the International Emergency Food Reserve. It also contributes to aid programmes for refugees. Community food aid policy, since its reform in 1987[1] is a fully-fledged development instrument totally separate from the Common Agricultural Policy. It is naturally paradoxical when developed countries, such as the those of the Community, have to take measures to reduce surplus production which cannot find either an internal or external outlet by slowing the growth of their agriculture when many developing countries are experiencing serious food supply problems. The response to this paradox is being sought by the **World Food Council** (WFC), to which the Community is giving its active support.

Alongside this international activity and to the individual activity of its members, the Community develops its own initiatives to combat hunger in the world. A framework Regulation of December 22, 1986 defined the Community's **food aid** policy and management[2]. This Regulation, which is the legal basis for the Community's food aid action, stipulates that the Council sets a general outline for the activities to be undertaken - including notably the list and quality of products to be supplied, list of eligible countries and organizations[3] - and the Commission sets, after consultation of a management committee, the quantities of food products to be granted to the different countries and beneficiary organizations[4]. It also provides for "triangular operations", whereby the European Union purchases foodstuffs in one developing country in order to grant them as food aid to another. Food aid policy is thus integrated in the EU's development policy.

---

1   OJ L370, 30.12.1986 and OJ L174, 07.07.1990.
2   Ibid.
3   See OJ L174, 07.07.1990.
4   See OJ L138, 21.05.1992.

The bulk of food aid is allocated by the Commission under the "normal procedure" whereby each allocation of aid is submitted for the prior opinion of the Member States. Community food aid is granted either directly to the governments of beneficiary countries, which distribute the produce free of charge or put it up for sale on the local market, or indirectly through the intermediary of inter-governmental international organizations (UNHCR, WFP, ICRC, LICROSS) or of non-governmental organizations (NGOs), which re-distribute it to refugees and to the most vulnerable categories in the framework of special nutritional programmes. Aid is granted as a priority to low-income countries with a food supply shortfall. Part of food aid is set aside for emergency action.

The framework Regulation gives the Commission overall control of all the aid mobilization and delivery operations. Its control ends when the aid is in the hands of the beneficiary country. Furthermore, the successful tenderer is responsible for the aid until its delivery to the location stipulated in the agreement concluded with the beneficiary countries. Finally, the Regulation stipulates that aid is to be monitored by professionals appointed by the Commission to ensure that the operation is correctly followed through. When, due to evolution in the crop or stock situation of a given country - for example should the harvest be exceptionally good - the supply of food aid would serve no purpose or would damage the local economy, it can be replaced by financial assistance[1]. The Community encourages the developing countries to strengthen their food security through the provision of financial support[2]. Thus the Community focuses its attention on **food strategies** where food security tops the list of priorities. An attempt is made to ensure that all Community and bilateral aid observes this priority, is committed for a long period and is organized in a coherent manner.

A significant proportion of funding is earmarked every year for development cooperation with **non-governmental organizations (NGOs)**. Funds go chiefly to integrated rural development projects, vocational training and health care. The Commission seeks to trigger cooperation in the various cooperation fora with European NGOs, who have a liaison committee and hold their annual assembly in Brussels[3]. The co-financing of purchases of food products or seeds by international bodies and non-governmental organizations is covered by a Regulation adopted on August 4, 1988[4]. The approach introduced in Lomé IV, now applicable to other areas of the world entitled to financial and technical assistance under specific protocols or conventions, consists of giving direct financial and institutional support to partners other than the national authorities (local authorities, NGOs, trade and vocational bodies and unions), with the aim of strengthening local management capabilities and initiative.

In addition to normal food aid, the Community earmarks considerable quantities of agricultural products (cereals, sugar, vegetable oils) every year for **emergency food aid** to help the victims of disasters. It also grants considerable amounts of funding for **emergency aid** to the ACP States and the OCTs on the one hand, through the European Development Fund, and to all other countries on the other, through the general Budget of the Community. Emergency aid is granted in response to difficulties created by political events or natural disasters such as cyclones, floods, droughts or epidemics. Emergency aid funding is used for foodstuffs, medical material, medical assistance, clothes, shelter, seeds and means of transport. Governments, specialized international and non-governmental organizations and the Commission take charge of the use of these credits.

In April 1992, the Commission set up a **European Office for Emergency Humanitarian Aid (ECHO)**, with the role of enhancing the Community's presence on the ground, of grouping together all its emergency humanitarian actions and improving coordination with the Member

---

1   OJ L165, 23.06.1984.
2   OJ L220, 11.08.1988 and OJ L174, 07.07.1990.
3   COM (94)468.
4   OJ L220, 11.08.1988 and COM (91) 52.

States, other donors, NGOs and specialized international agencies. ECHO is wholly responsible for administering humanitarian and emergency food aid, and disaster preparedness. By improving the arrangements for mobilizing Community relief, ECHO provides both an efficient service and a higher profile. It gives, indeed, public opinion tangible evidence of the Community's role as an active contributor in the field of humanitarian aid. At present, the humanitarian aid of the EU exceeds ECU 1 billion a year and its scope has been broadened to cover the violent ethnic conflicts in Africa, the aftermaths of the war in former Yugoslavia and the consequences of the collapse of the Soviet Union[1]. In fact, more than 95% of ECHO's activities cover man-made disasters. By its humanitarian aid the Community tries to calm tensions and reduce sufferings so as to encourage the opening of negotiations and limit the scale of the disaster

Since 1987, the Commission, on the basis of Council conclusions, has been implementing a programme **to combat AIDS** in the ACP States. In 1988, a special budget heading was created to broaden the geographical scope of the programme to other developing countries. The programme seeks to contribute to improving health services in beneficiary countries and to provide technical, financial and scientific assistance to those fighting the disease (prevention of transmission through sexual contact, blood transfusion centres, epidemiological research, conferences, training)[2].

In the framework of North-South cooperation, the Community has been active, also since 1987, in fighting **drug abuse**. Its action focuses mainly on prevention, treatment and rehabilitation and on the provision of alternatives to drug-growing in the developing countries. By referring explicitly to the drug issue, the fourth Lomé Convention created new opportunities for cooperation, although the ACP partners have yet to take full advantage of them. The cooperation agreements between the Community and the countries of Asia and Latin America also contain clauses on the fight against drugs. The same is true for the association agreements with Central and Eastern European countries, which contain clauses on drug trafficking and money laundering. In October 1990, the Council adopted the Decision relating to the conclusion of the International Convention against Illicit Traffic in Narcotic Drugs and Psychotropic Substances, concluded in Vienna on December 20, 1988[3]. The Community is already a major contributor to the United Nations Fund for Drug Abuse Control. The European Committee to Combat Drugs (ECCD) plays a catalyzing and coordinating role in the action of the Member States at international level.

---

1   OJ C180, 14.07.1995.
2   COM (93) 479.
3   OJ L326, 24.11.1990.

Common Commercial Policy

The creation of a customs union in the Community in 1968 was implemented internally through the abolition of customs duties, quantitative restrictions and measures having equivalent effect between Member States and, on the external front, through the introduction of a common customs tariff and a common commercial policy. In fact, goods imported from third countries had to be treated in the same way by all Member States in order to circulate freely in the customs union. But the customs union itself had to be integrated into the existing international economic order, regulated by the 1948 General Agreement on Tariffs and Trade (GATT). This is why, in Article 110 of the EC Treaty, the Member States declared that in creating a customs union, they intended to contribute, in accordance with the common interest, to the harmonious development of world trade, the gradual removal of restrictions to international trade and the lowering of customs barriers. They have kept their word. The creation of the customs union has led to strong growth in intra-Community trade, but the Community has not become introspective. Instead, it has developed into the world's biggest importer and exporter. In addition, the rules of the GATT, and the various international agreements drawn up under its aegis, formed the legal basis for the Community's own commercial policy instruments and action, notably in the field of tariffs, the application of safeguard measures, anti-dumping and anti-subsidies actions.

The common commercial policy was founded on uniform principles, notably as regards tariff charges, the conclusion of tariff and commercial agreements and the harmonization of liberalization measures, export policies and trade defence measures, including those to be taken in cases of dumping and subsidies (Art. 113 EC). The implementation of the common commercial policy therefore falls into the Community's sphere of competence. If agreements have to be negotiated with third countries, the Commission submits recommendations to the Council which then authorizes it to open negotiations. The Commission is the Community's negotiator and consults a special committee appointed by the Council to assist it in this task (113 Committee). It works within the framework of guidelines issued by the Council. In exercising the powers granted to it by Article 113, including the conclusion of agreements, the Council acts by a qualified majority.

In international agreements, the Community as such, represented by the Commission, is more often than not a party alongside the Member States, which means that it takes part in the negotiations, signs the agreement and if necessary participates in their management as a member of the organization in question. In areas for which the Community has exclusive responsibility (agriculture, fisheries), the Member States are not at the forefront; the Commission negotiates and manages the agreements on the basis of a negotiating brief delivered by the Council (world commodity agreements, traditional trade agreements, preferential agreements, association agreements)[1]. According to Article 234 EC, rights and obligations arising from agreements concluded by the Member States before their accession to the Community are not affected by the provisions of the EC Treaty; but to the extent that such agreements are not compatible with this Treaty, the Member States concerned must take all appropriate steps to eliminate the incompatibilities established[2].

Given the complexity of international relations and of external policy instruments in the broad sense of the term, the Community powers occasionally spill out of the framework defined in Article 113. In such cases, the Community Institutions cannot act alone. They must draw in the Member States, which considerably complicates the negotiating process and the conclusion of international agreements. However, the Court of Justice has stated that Article 113 of the EEC Treaty cannot be interpreted in a manner which would have the effect of restricting the common commercial policy to the use of instruments designed to influence only the traditional aspects of external trade, excluding more developed mechanisms[3]. The Court has formulated the limits of the action of the Member States in areas where powers are shared with the Community: measures must be "common", must involve close cooperation "both in the process of negotiation and conclusion and in the fulfilment of the obligations entered into", and must ensure "unity in the international representation of the Community"[4]. On the dispute between the Community and the Member States regarding jurisdiction for concluding the Uruguay Round, the Court ruled in an opinion that the Community has exclusive powers in relation to trade in goods and in the cross-border supply of services. However, with respect to the other issues relating to the agreements on services and intellectual property, the Court ruled that powers are shared between the Community and the Member States[5].

The **Common Customs Tariff (CCT)** is the key to the Community's commercial policy. As seen in the Chapter on customs union and as will be seen later in this Chapter, the blueprinting and evolution of the CCT have taken place against the backdrop of the General Agreement on Tariffs and Trade (GATT). CCT tariffs were low at the outset, responding to the central objective of liberalization of international trade. They have been cut even further in the framework of successive GATT negotiations. It should be borne in mind that the Commission, acting on a negotiating brief issued by the Council, and not the Member States individually, is the Community's negotiator in the GATT arena.

The rare **bilateral agreements** which still exist between the Member States and third countries, notably state-trading nations, are subject to Community vetting. Every year the Council, acting on a Commission proposal, authorizes the extension or the tacit renewal for a year of certain trade agreements concluded by the Member States with third countries, insofar as they do not constitute a barrier to the implementation of the common commercial

---

1   See: judgment of 31 March 1971, case 22/70, AETR, ECR 1971, p.263; and opinion of 26 April 1977, ECR 1977, p. 741.
2   See judgment of 14 October 1980, case 812/79, Burgoa, ECR 1980, p.2787.
3   Opinion 1/78 of the Court of Justice of 14 November 1978, ECR 1978.
4   Opinion 2/91 of the Court of Justice of 19 March 1993, ECR I-1064.
5   Opinion 1/94 of the Court of Justice of 15 November 1994.

policy[1]. Under similar conditions, the automatic renewal or maintenance in force of certain friendship, trade and navigation treaties concluded between the Member States and third countries is authorized[2].

The Member States can continue to have recourse to the **safeguard clause** provided for in Article 115 of the EC Treaty. This Article stipulates that in order to ensure that the execution of commercial policy measures taken by any Member State is not obstructed by a deflection of trade, or where disparities between such measures lead to economic difficulties in one or several States, the Commission can recommend ways of bringing about the requisite cooperation between Member States. Failing this, it authorizes the Member States to take the necessary protective measures, the conditions and details of which it determines. In urgent cases, however, the Member States can themselves take the necessary steps and notify the other Member States and the Commission of them. The Commission then decides if these measures should be changed or abolished altogether[3]. The completion of the Single Market has smoothed out the remaining differences between export and import arrangements. Thus, no safeguard measures nor any measure based on Article 115 was adopted in 1994. However, for certain sensitive sectors, the Community could envisage the introduction of Community measures taking over from the safeguard clause.

The EU, which is the world's biggest exporter, is highly dependent on international trade and therefore it is in its vital interests to keep trade open and free. Indeed, in 1992, the imports of the EU (twelve) accounted for 17% of world imports and for 10% of its GNP. Its exports accounted for 9% of its GNP and for 16% of world exports, compared with 12% for the United States and 9% for Japan. The level of protection in the Community did not rise with the advent of the internal market. On the contrary, exporters from third countries, as the firms of the Member States, need to comply to only one set of standards in order to market their products anywhere in the Single Market. As Community operators they thus enjoy scale economies and easier market access. The Commission and the European Council have stated on a number of occasions that the Community has no intention of becoming a "**Fortress Europe**", as feared by some of its trade partners. This was proved by the concessions made by the Community to allow the conclusion of the GATT Uruguay Round. However, one of the central principles of the GATT is that of balance of mutual advantages (global reciprocity). This means, for the European Union, that it can establish linkage between access for third country economic operators to the benefits of the Single Market and the existence of similar opportunities for European undertakings in the country in question, or at the least to the absence of any discrimination. This implies a case-by-case approach for third countries, but a common approach by the Member States. The Single Market obliges the latter to show a united face to third countries. At the same time, the globalization of the economy is creating a state of interdependence and a growing realization that trade problems need to be solved wherever possible in a multilateral framework.

---

1   OJ L89, 21.04.1995.
2   OJ L326, 29.12.1969 and OJ L89, 21.04.1995.
3   OJ L238, 21.08.1987.

Common import arrangements

The Common Customs Tariff, analyzed in the Chapter on Customs Union, is one of the kingpins of the common commercial policy. The other main elements are the common import arrangements and the protective measures. Together they contribute to ensuring an even competition playing field for Community undertakings, for they give them access to equal prices for imported raw materials and level the quantities and prices of competitor products.

The new **common rules for imports** were established by Council Regulation of 22 December 1994[1]. They apply to imports of products originating in third countries, with the exception, on the one hand, of textiles subject to specific import arrangements, discussed under the heading of sectoral measures of the commercial policy, and, on the other, products originating from certain third countries, including Russia, North Korea and the People's Republic of China, mentioned below. Apart from those exceptions, imports into the Community are free and not subject to any quantitative restrictions. The new Regulation strives to establish a balance between a Community market normally open to the world following the conclusion of the Uruguay Round and more rapid and simplified procedures in case of a risk of serious injury caused by imports of a product to Community producers

The Regulation establishes a **Community information and consultation procedure**. When trends in imports appear to call for surveillance or protective measures, the Commission must be informed of this fact by the Member States. This information must contain all available evidence, drawn from certain specific criteria. The Commission then passes on forthwith this information to all the Member States. Consultations may be held either at the request of a Member State or on the initiative of the Commission. These consultations must take place within eight working days of the Commission receiving the information. They take place within an advisory committee consisting of representatives of each Member State and chaired by a representative of the Commission (113 Committee). These consultations concern notably: a) the terms and conditions of import, import trends and the various aspects of the economic and commercial situation as regards the product in question; and b) the measures, if any, to be taken.

When, after consultations have taken place, it is apparent to the Commission that there is sufficient evidence, it initiates an **investigation** within one month of receipt of information from a Member State and publishes a notice in the Official Journal of the European Communities, giving a summary of the information received and asking for any relevant information, including the views of the interested parties. The Commission seeks all information it deems to be necessary and, where it considers it appropriate, after consulting the Committee, endeavours to check the information with importers, traders, agents, producers, trade associations and organizations. The Member States supply the Commission at its

---

1   OJ L349, 31.12.1994 and OJ L21, 27.01.1996.

request and following procedures laid down by it with all information at their disposal on developments in the market of the product being investigated.

The examination of the trend of imports, of the conditions under which they take place and of serious injury or threat of serious injury to Community producers resulting from such imports covers the following factors in practice: a) the volume of imports; b) the price of imports; and c) the consequent impact on the Community producers of similar or directly competitive products as indicated by trends in certain economic factors such as production, capacity utilization, stocks, sales, market share, prices and so on.

Where the trend in imports of a product originating in a third country threatens to cause injury to Community producers, import of that product may be subject, as appropriate, to prior or retrospective **Community surveillance**. Products under prior Community surveillance may be put into free circulation only on production of an import document endorsed by the competent authority designated by Member States and valid throughout the EU, regardless of the Member State of issue. The surveillance may be confined to imports into one or more regions of the Community (regional surveillance). The decision to impose Community or regional, prior or retrospective surveillance is taken by the Commission. In the case of retrospective surveillance, however, any Member State may refer the Commission's decision to the Council, which, acting by a qualified majority, may confirm, amend or revoke it. The imposition of surveillance measures implies a monthly communication by the Member States to Commission of certain information on the imports in question. Surveillance measures are of limited duration. Failing provisions to the contrary, they cease to be valid at the end of the second half calendar year following that in which they were introduced. In any case, the Community surveillance measures are few and far between. The most recent concerned certain steel cables originating in any third country[1] and certain steel products originating in third countries[2].

Where a product is imported into the Community in such increased quantities and/or on such terms as to cause, or threaten to cause, serious injury to Community producers, the Commission may, acting at the request of a Member State or on its own initiative take **safeguard measures**, i.e.: limit the period of validity of import documents required in compliance with surveillance measures; alter the import rules for the product in question by making its release for free circulation conditional on production of an import authorization granted under certain provisions and in certain limits laid down by the Commission. As regards Members of the World Trade Organization (WTO), safeguard measures are taken only when the two conditions indicated above (quantities and terms of imports) are met. No safeguard measure may be applied to a product originating in a developing country Member of the WTO as long as that country's share of Community imports of the product concerned does not exceed 3% and

---

1   OJ L242, 17.09.1994.
2   OJ L68, 19.03.1996.

that the import share of all developing countries does not account for more than 9% of such imports.

Any Member State may refer to the Council the Commission's decision on safeguard measures. The Council, acting by a qualified majority, may confirm, amend or revoke the decision of the Commission. The Council, acting by a qualified majority on a proposal by the Commission, may also transform the Community surveillance measures into safeguard measures. The duration of safeguard measures must be limited to the period of time necessary to prevent or remedy serious injury and to facilitate adjustment on the part of Community producers. The period should not exceed four years.

In addition to the general common rules for imports, there still exist some specific rules. The most important of such rules apply to imports from certain third countries, notably Russia and the other countries of the Commonwealth of Independent States, Albania, the People's Republic of China, North Korea and Vietnam[1]. These rules establish the liberalization of imports, namely the absence of any quantitative restrictions on the part of EU Member States. However, for a limited number of products originating in the People's Republic of China (notably footwear, tableware, kitchenware of porcelain or china and certain toys), owing to the sensitivity of the Community industry, they set out quantitative quotas and special surveillance measures. Apart from these special rules, the Community procedures on information and investigation, as well as the safeguard measures concerning imports from these countries are quite similar to those set out by the general common rules applicable to imports in the EU. Community importers can now use a uniform import licence, valid throughout the EU. Other specific import regimes concern textile products and the agricultural sector and are examines under the heading of "Sectoral commercial policy measures".

Trade protection

As seen above, the Community can introduce surveillance and protection measures in the framework of the common rules for imports when imports at prices viewed as normal are causing or risk causing serious injury to Community producers. In cases where the export price is lower than the normal value of a like product (**dumping**), the Community can take trade protection measures, notably through the application of **anti-dumping duties**. Since 1979, Community rules in this area are broadly inspired by the provisions of the Anti-Dumping Code and the Code on Subsidies and Countervailing Duties of the General Agreement on Tariffs and Trade (GATT). Community rules being compatible with those of the GATT, economic operators must now comply to only one set of rules. On the jurisdictional level, anti-dumping and anti-subsidy cases must be brought before the Court of First Instance[2].

According to the Regulation on **protection against dumped imports** from countries not members of the EC, anti-dumping duty may be applied to any dumped product whose release for free circulation in the Community causes injury[3]. A product is considered as having been dumped if its export price to the Community is less than a comparable price for the like product, in the ordinary course of trade, as established for the exporting country. The term like product means a product which is identical in all respects or has characteristics closely resembling those of the product under consideration. In order to determine the dumping the normal price

---

1   OJ L67, 10.03.1994 and OJ L103, 24.04.1996.
2   OJ L66, 10.03.1994.
3   OJ L56, 06.03.1996.

and the dumped price must be defined and these two values must than be compared. It should be noted that these definitions as well as the anti-dumping procedures are, after the Uruguay Round, similar in the EU and in other GATT Member States.

Normal value is generally based on the prices paid or payable, in the ordinary course of trade, by independent customers in the exporting country. Where there are no or insufficient sales of the like product in the ordinary course of trade, or where such sales do not permit a proper comparison, the normal value of the like is calculated on the basis of the cost of production in the country of origin plus a reasonable amount for selling, general and administrative costs and for profits. In the case of imports from non-market economy countries, normal value is determined on the basis of the price or constructed value in a market economy third country, or the price from such a third country to other countries, including the Community, or where these are not possible, on any other reasonable basis.

The **export price** is the price actually paid or payable for the product sold for export to the Community. Where there is no export price or where it appears that the export price is unreliable because of association or a compensatory arrangement between the exporter and the importer or a third party, the export price may be constructed on the basis of the price at which the imported product is first resold to an independent buyer or on any reasonable basis. In such cases, allowance must be made for all costs incurred between import and resale (transport, insurance, general expenses), including duties and taxes, and for a reasonable profit margin.

A **fair comparison** must then be made between the export price and the normal price. This comparison must be made at the same level of trade and in respect of sales made at as nearly as possible the same time and with due account taken of other differences which affect price comparability. Where the normal value and the export price as established are not taken on such a comparable basis due allowance, in the form of adjustments, must be made in each case for differences in factors which are claimed, and demonstrated to affect prices and, therefore, price comparability, notably: the physical characteristics of the product concerned; import charges and indirect taxes; discounts, rebates and quantities; transport, insurance, handling and ancillary costs; and the cost of any credit granted.

The **dumping margin** is the amount by which the normal value exceeds the export price. Where dumping margins vary, a weighted average margin may be established. The determination of the **serious injury** caused to the Community industry or the threat of such injury must be based on positive evidence and involve an objective examination of both (a) the volume of the dumped imports and the effect of the dumped imports on prices in the Community market for like products, and (b) the consequent impact of these imports on the Community industry, i.e. the Community producers as a whole or as major proportion of the like products.

An **investigation** to determine the existence, degree and effect of any alleged dumping is initiated upon a written **complaint** submitted to the Commission or to a Member State by any natural or legal person, or any association acting on behalf of the Community industry.

Where, in the absence of any complaint, a Member State is in possession of sufficient evidence of dumping and of injury resulting therefrom for the Community industry, it must immediately communicate such evidence to the Commission. The investigation is conducted by the Commission in cooperation with the Member States. It covers both dumping and injury. **Provisional measures** may be taken by the Commission, after consultation with the Member States, no sooner than 60 days but not later than nine months from the initiation of the proceedings. The final conclusions of the investigation must be adopted within a further six months. The amount of the **provisional anti-dumping duty** must not exceed the margin of dumping as provisionally established. Investigation may be terminated without the imposition of provisional or definitive duties upon receipt of satisfactory voluntary undertakings from the exporter to revise his prices or to cease exports to the area in question at dumped prices.

Where a provisional duty has been applied and the facts established show that there is dumping and injury, the Council decides, irrespective of whether a definitive anti-dumping duty is to be imposed, what proportion of the provisional duty is to be definitively collected. If the **definitive anti-dumping** duty is higher than the provisional duty, the difference must not be collected. If the definitive duty is lower than the provisional duty, the duty must be recalculated. Provisional or definitive anti-dumping duties must be imposed by Regulation, and collected by Member States in the form, at the rate specified and according to the other criteria laid down in the Regulation imposing such duties.

Another Regulation of December 1994 establishes the rules on **protection against subsidized imports** from countries not members of the European Community[1]. Here again the Community legislation is compatible with GATT rules and, therefore, business must comply with only one set of rules. A **countervailing duty** may be imposed for the purpose of offsetting any subsidy granted, directly or indirectly, for the manufacture, production, export or transport of any product whose release for free circulation in the Community causes injury. A subsidy is deemed to exist if: 1) there is a financial contribution by a government or by a private body entrusted by it (direct transfer of funds, loan guarantees, fiscal incentives, provision of goods or services other than general infrastructure, payments to a funding mechanism); and 2) a benefit is thereby conferred.

Subsidies which are not specific to an enterprise or industry or group of enterprises or industries cannot be subjected to countervailing measures. Even when they are specific, subsidies cannot be subjected to countervailing duties, if they are given: for research activities; pursuant to a general framework of regional development; to promote adaptation of existing facilities to new environmental requirements. The amount of subsidies to be subjected to countervailing duties is calculated in terms of the benefit conferred to the recipient which is found to exist during the investigation period. Where all conditions are met, a provisional or definitive **countervailing duty** is imposed following procedures similar to the ones described above concerning the imposition of anti-dumping duties.

Reports on the Community's anti-dumping and anti-subsidy activities supplied by the Commission every year to the Council and Parliament suggest that less than 1% of Community imports are affected by such activities. A very wide range of products and countries are

---

1   OJ L349, 31.12.1994I and OJ L122, 02.06.1995.

cited in European complaints, but the countries most involved are the People's Republic of China, in a number of measures, and Japan, in market value of the products concerned. The cases range from anti-dumping measures on imports of disodium carbonate originating in the United States and on photocopiers originating in Japan[1] to measures on imports of unwrought magnesium originating in Russia and Ukraine[2] and on imports of microwave ovens originating in the People's Republic of China, the Republic of Korea, Malaysia and Thailand[3].

In 1984, the Community had adopted procedures allowing it to respond to illicit commercial practices of third countries with a view to removing the injury resulting therefrom. These procedures have not proved to be entirely effective. This is why, in December 1994, the Council adopted a new Regulation destined to improve Community procedures on **commercial defense** and to ensure the exercise of the Community's rights under international trade rules, in particular those established under the auspices of the World Trade Organization (WTO)[4]. This Regulation allows the Community to respond to obstacles to trade, i.e. to any trade practice adopted or maintained by a third country in respect of which international trade rules establish a right of action. Thus, following the Community examination procedures and after consultation with the Member States, the Commission may take any commercial policy measures which are compatible with existing international obligations and procedures, notably: (a) suspension or withdrawal of any concession resulting from commercial policy negotiations; (b) the raising of existing customs duties or the introduction of any other charge on imports; (c) the introduction of quantitative restrictions or any other measures modifying import or export conditions or otherwise affecting trade with the third country concerned.

Common export arrangements

By virtue of a Council Regulation of December 20, 1969, Community exports to third countries are free or, in other words, are not subject to quantitative restrictions, with the exception of a few products for certain Member States and of petroleum oil and gases for all the Member States[5]. However, when exceptional market trends, which cause scarcity of an essential product, justify protective measures in the opinion of a Member State, it can set in motion the **Community information and consultation procedure**. Consultations take place within an Advisory Committee and cover notably the conditions and terms of exports and, if necessary, the measures which should be adopted.

Should the Community market be in a critical situation due to a lack of essential products and should the interests of the Community demand immediate action, the Commission, at the request of a Member State or acting on its own initiative, can make exports subject to the granting of an

---

1   OJ L244, 12.10.1995.
2   OJ L312, 23.12.1995.
3   OJ L2, 04.01.1996.
4   OJ L349, 31.12.1994 and OJ L41, 23.02.1995.
5   OJ L324, 27.12.1969 and OJ L372, 31.12.1991.

export authorization, issued if certain provisions and restrictions defined by it, while waiting for a Council Decision, are satisfied. The Council can uphold or invalidate the Commission's Decision, in light of the international commitments of the Community or of all its Member States, notably as regards trade in primary products. **Quantitative export restrictions** can be limited to specific destinations or to the exports of certain regions of the Community. They must give due consideration to the volume of contracts concluded at normal terms, before bringing in a protective measure.

Article 112 of the EC Treaty stipulates that the **aid arrangements** applied to exports by the Member States should be gradually harmonized to ensure that there is a level competition playing field for the Community's exporting undertakings. A great deal of effort has been invested in evening out conditions in the area of credit insurance and financial export credits. The senseless competition between the Member States and other industrialized countries at the beginning of the seventies to see who could grant the biggest credits, with the most favourable repayment and cost terms, to state-trading countries - a process which pushed several of these countries into alarming levels of debt - had to be halted. The 1978 Community Arrangement on guidelines in the field of officially supported export credits has been extended for an indefinite period[1].

As regards **export credits**, the Community has applied since 1983 the arrangement concluded in the framework of the OECD and providing guidelines for officially supported export credits ("consensus"). The new rules, which entered into force on 15 February 1992, confine official support to the interest rates for export credits to certain countries. The Community should express a common position on decisions taken within the OECD[2]. Thus, substantial progress has been made on the formula for calculating the differentiated discount rate (DDR). This means that long-term market rates are reflected more accurately and that interest rates based on special drawing rights (SDR), which bear no relation to the rates for the various currencies, need no longer to be used.

Exports as well as imports of certain chemicals are subject to prior authorization by the relevant authorities in the Member States[3]. Authorization must be refused if there are grounds for believing that the products in question could be used to develop or manufacture chemical weapons or could be delivered directly or indirectly to belligerent nations in areas of high international tension.

The Commission contributes from the Community Budget to **export promotion** and notably to closer cooperation at Community level and to research for joint action in favour of European exports (international exhibitions, trade forums, conferences, seminars) in coordination with Community programmes and with Member States' export promotion programmes. The cooperation with trade federations and with national export promotion organizations pursues two aims: first of all, to ensure that any activities on a particular market strengthen the Community dimension and secondly, to focus activities on a number of target countries, the list of which is topped by China, Japan, the countries of ASEAN (Association of South East Asian Nations) and the countries of Central and Eastern Europe. In 1993 the programme was expanded to cover the Gulf

---

1   OJ L44, 22.02.1993.

2   Ibid.

3   OJ L251, 29.08.1992 and OJ L332, 22.12.1994.

countries, which provide ready outlets for an extensive range of products and are close enough to Europe to attract small and medium-sized enterprises from many Member States.

However, whereas customs tariffs diminish thanks to the Uruguay Round and the rules of the World Trade Organization impose in principle the freedom of international exchanges, European companies are still faced with obstacles to trade and investment in a large number of countries. Thus, the "Buy American" clause still excludes European firms from public works and supply contracts in the United States, and an environment propitious and legally sure for international exchanges and investments is still lacking in many Asian and South American countries. The European Community has the necessary power to redress these situations; but its Member States must render a supporting hand. In a communication of February 1996 the Commission sets out a two-pronged strategy to eliminate trade barriers confronting European firms through a bilateral approach (action vis-à-vis the countries concerned) and a multilateral approach (actions within the World Trade Organization)[1].

GATT and WTO

The General Agreement on Tariffs and Trade (**GATT**) came into being in 1947. Along with the International Monetary Fund and the World Bank it was one of the institutions set up in the post-war period to help regulate the international economy and prevent a recurrence of the disastrous policies undertaken between the two World Wars. The GATT was charged with overseeing international trade in goods and, in particular, the liberalization of this trade by means of a negotiated reduction in tariff barriers. The scope of the GATT was, therefore, somewhat limited initially, but the conclusion of the Uruguay Round negotiations enlarged its field of activities and placed them under the auspices of the World Trade Organization. It is the Member States which are the contracting parties to the GATT, although because of the common commercial policy, they participate as the Community in the GATT's work. The Commission is the single negotiator and spokesman of the European Community. The latter is signatory to a number of international GATT agreements.

As stated in the Chapter on Customs Union, the EC Member States and other industrial countries made major tariff concessions - particularly in favour of the developing countries - during the successive negotiating rounds between 1960 and 1979 under the aegis of the General Agreement on Tariffs and Trade. Thanks to the Dillon (1960-1962) and Kennedy Rounds (1965-1967), the customs tariffs of the States participating in the General Agreement were slashed by nearly 50%[2]. Following the Tokyo Round (1973-1979), a fresh one-third reduction in customs tariffs was agreed upon, to be implemented in eight stages the last of which was timed for January 1, 1987[3]. These tariff reductions made a considerable contribu-

---

1   COM (96) 53, 14 February 1996.
2   OJ L305, 19.12.1968.
3   OJ L71, 17.03.1980.

tion to keeping the international trade system open, despite the fact that in the first years of the eighties, the world economy went through the worst period in its post-war history causing protectionist pressures to flare up. Since 1985, the Community has committed itself wholeheartedly to the process of launching a new cycle of multilateral trade negotiations under the GATT. The round got underway at the Punta del Este (Uruguay) Conference in September 1986.

The **Uruguay Round** negotiations involved 117 countries from all over the world and covered a large range of subjects. In addition to the issues traditionally covered by trade talks, generally confined to tariff questions, the Uruguay Round encompassed the revision of GATT rules and disciplines, plus the adoption of disciplines for "new" areas: the trade-related aspects of intellectual property rights, trade-related investment measures and international trade in services. Also on the agenda were the sensitive issues of agriculture and textiles, areas in which trade was traditionally subject to special rules and for which the participants were to devise an agreement for their gradual incorporation into the GATT framework. Unprecedented in scope, the Uruguay Round's main achievement, obtained in December 1993, was to improve market access to a significant degree.

Market access for **industrial products** has been considerably improved by a reduction of one third or more in the customs duties imposed by the industrialized countries and many developing countries on the following sectors: building materials, agricultural machinery, medical equipment, steel, beer, spirits, pharmaceutical products, paper, toys and furniture[1]. The average level of tariffs for industrialized countries fell from 5% to about 3.5%, whereas it stood at 40% or more prior to the various rounds of GATT negotiations. In total close to 40% of the EU' industrial imports are to be duty free. On their part, developing countries are to apply substantial reductions of their customs duties on these products, whereas prior to the Uruguay Round they had taken very few such commitments.

Concerning **agricultural products**, the European Union succeeded, on the one hand, in achieving a better balance between supply and demand on world agricultural markets and, on the other, in ensuring that the results of the Uruguay Round were compatible with the mechanisms of the reformed common agricultural policy[2]. The Agreement provides for the first time for the liberalization of trade in agricultural products and the commitments cover market access, the gradual reduction of production support and also the observance of export disciplines. The lowering of customs duties will be spread over a period of six years for industrialized countries, including the European Union (36% reduction) and ten years for the developing countries (24% reduction).

A first step was taken towards the liberalization of world trade in services. It should be noted that trade is not limited to exchange of goods but also increasingly involves services, a sector which contributes nearly half of the EU's GDP. The **General Agreement on Trade in Services (GATS)** includes general rules for trade in this area, specific provisions for given

---

1   About the textile sector, see the following title.
2   See the chapter on agriculture.

service sectors and national schedules showing the services and activities which each country agrees to open up to competition, with possible limitations. The GATS establishes notably the principles: of the most favoured nation provisions, i.e. the principle that all third countries must be treated equally; of transparency on market access; and of national treatment, meaning that a company from a third country cannot be placed at a competitive disadvantage in relation to a domestic country. Although it has still to be completed in a number of sectors, such as financial services and maritime transport, the Agreement establishes for the first time a multilateral framework based on satisfactory rules and comprising sufficient commitments to trigger the liberalization process. The audiovisual sector was included in the GATS, which means that the rules relating to transparency and of progressive liberalization apply to it. However, the EU has made no market access commitment nor, as a result, any commitments on national treatment. It also took an exemption from the principle of most favoured nation conditions and is, therefore, not bound to give equal treatment to all third countries. On their part, the United States do not guarantee access to the US market on a most-favoured-nation basis in the interim agreement providing better market access to financial services concluded in the framework of the WTO on 28 July 1995. The United States also prevent the completion of the WTO negotiations on market access and national treatment for basic telecommunications services (local, long-distance and international).

The Uruguay Round negotiations included also the protection of **trade-related intellectual property (TRIPs)**. Intellectual property concerns an ever-increasing of world trade, be it related to pharmaceuticals, computer software, books or records. As trade has increased so too have cheating, counterfeiting and copying. A further problem has been the appropriation of brand names and, in the case of wines and foodstuffs, certain geographical appellations. The conclusions of the Uruguay Round have reinforced existing international conventions, for example the Bern and Paris Conventions for the protection of literary and artistic works, by bringing them within the ambit of the GATT dispute settlement procedures. In addition, there has been a strengthening of intellectual property rights concerning the protection of trade marks, industrial designs, patents and geographical appellations. A clear set of principles has been established for the enforcement through the national courts of intellectual property rights, any breaches being subject to sanctions under the dispute settlement procedure. The Community has amended the Regulation on the Community trade mark, notably in order to comply with the national treatment obligation established by the TRIPs Agreement[1].

The Uruguay Round resulted also on an Agreement on **trade-related investment measures (TRIMs)**. An illustrative list of non-permissible measures is included in the agreement, covering such things as local content rules, trade balancing and local sales requirements. Such measures must be phased out over a two- to seven-year period, depending upon whether the country is developed or developing. The TRIMs Agreement is particularly important for the EU, which is responsible for 36% of direct foreign investment in the world and receives 19% of such investments on its territory.

Very substantial results were achieved in the field of rules and disciplines thanks to the reform of the provisions on safeguards, subsidies, anti-dumping measures, the balance of payments, the "standards" and "public procurement" codes. The Agreement on **Government Procurement**, of which are part the EU, the United States, Japan and a limited number of other countries on a reciprocal basis, is open to all and is largely based on the Community rules on public procurement concerning, in particular, the procedures, the thresholds which apply and the recourse mechanisms if firms believe that they have been denied equal treatment. Under this Agreement which is founded on "national treatment", in accordance with which foreign suppliers of goods and services must be dealt with in the same way as national suppliers, public procurement contracts of over ECU 300 billion will be open to international competition for the first time. The Agreement includes, in principle, water, ports, airports,

---

1   OJ L349, 31.12.1994. See also the chapter on the common market.

electricity and urban transport, although not every country has made a commitment in each sector.

The **World Trade Organization (WTO)**, established in 1995, is gradually to replace the GATT, taking all the agreements concluded under its auspices, and settle trade disputes on a multilateral basis. In fact, the WTO brings together under a single decision-making and administrative body the three agreements resulting from the Uruguay Round: the General Agreement on Tariffs and Trade (GATT), the General Agreement on Trade in Services (GATS) and the Agreement on trade-related aspects of intellectual property rights (TRIPs). The WTO operates on the basis of a ministerial conference, which must meet at least once every two years, and of a General Council made up of representatives of all the member countries. The European Community as well as all its Member States are members of WTO, a code of conduct defining the participation of the Community and its Member States in areas of shared power.

Thus, the GATT continues to exist, while frozen in its pre-Uruguay Round situation, for those countries which are not in a position to accept the entire package of its conclusions. On the contrary, the WTO is open to those who agree to abide by the entire Uruguay Round package of rules. This increases the certainty of the world exchange system, since all the members of the WTO are perfectly aware of their own rights and obligations and of those of their partners. The national law of each contracting party must be in conformity with the rules of the WTO, thus precluding unilateral action.

The unique structure of the WTO allows an integrated system of **dispute settlement**. The parties must refrain from making rulings themselves regarding violations and must abide completely by the provisions of the dispute settlement procedure in dealing with all matters, including the determination of "cross-retaliation". The Agreement establishes an appeals procedure providing for a review of the conclusions of the "panels" of first instance. A Dispute Settlement Board (DSB) oversees the proceedings. Safeguard measures are authorized, but their scope is limited both in terms of the measures taken and of their duration. A Safeguards Committee monitors all measures taken and ensures that they are in conformity with the agreement.

Sectoral commercial policy measures

In the framework of the General Agreement on Tariffs and Trade, several agreements or arrangements had been concluded in particularly sensitive sectors. The agreements to which the Community and/or its Member States were signatories sought to ensure the orderly growth of international trade in textiles, beef and veal, dairy products and civil aircraft. The most important of these arrangements was that on international trade in textiles, better known as the **Multifibre Arrangement (MFA)**, signed in 1974, in the framework of the GATT and owing its name to the fact that it covers most textile products, spanning artificial and synthetic fibres, cotton and wool. Under the terms of the Arrangement, signatories undertake not to introduce new unilateral or bilateral restrictions on trade in textiles and to regulate their trade relations by bilateral agreements The Community has based its textiles policy on this clause of the MFA, concluding with supplier countries bilateral agreements revolving chiefly around the principle of voluntary restraint of export quantities by signatory countries for a limited number of products, with gradual growth of the authorized quantities. The existing bilateral agreements seek to promote, through cooperation between the Contracting Parties, the orderly and equitable development of trade in textiles between the Community and supplier countries and to defuse the real risk that international trade in textile products be disrupted[1].

All these bilateral agreements and the Multifibre Arrangement itself need, however, to be revised in order to progressively liberalize the international trade in textiles as provided in the GATT Agreement of 15 December 1993. In fact, the WTO **Agreement on Textiles and Clothing (ATC)** will govern trade between all Members of the WTO until such time as they have been integrated into normal WTO rules and disciplines. This integration will be phased in three stages and will be completed in January 2005. The Agreement provides in particular for the strengthening of the GATT rules and disciplines, notably as regards market access, dumping, subsidies and counterfeiting. It contains a transitional safeguard clause in order to prevent any serious market disturbance in the importing countries.

A CommunityRegulation modifying the common rules for imports of certain textile products from third countries lays down a clear Community procedure for the selection of products to be integrated and notified to the WTO at each stage[2]. This Regulation also establishes the annual growth rates which will be applied automatically to remaining Community quantitative limits on imports from WTO members at each ATC stage. Another Regulation lays down common rules for imports of textile products from certain third countries not covered by bilateral agreements, protocols or other agreements, notably the countries of the Commonwealth of Independent States and the People's Republic of China[3]. It eliminates the exceptions and derogations resulting from the remaining national commercial policy measures and establishes quantitative restrictions and surveillance measures applicable at Community level for a limited number of products originating from these countries. New bilateral agreements have been concluded in 1995 with China - which is the European Union's main supplier of textiles and clothing, with twelve countries of the former Soviet Union, with a number of countries of the Mediterranean and the Middle East and with Taiwan[4].

The specific nature of ship-purchase transactions make it impossible to apply to **shipbuilding** the general anti-dumping and anti-subsidy measures in force. A Community Regulation, based on the OECD Shipbuilding Agreement, accordingly institutes a procedure specific to this sector[5]. It lays down detailed rules for determining the existence of an injurious pricing and of an injury to Community industry, initiating proceedings, undertaking an investigation, imposing and levying an injurious pricing charge, counter-measures, etc.

---

1   OJ L94, 26.04.1995.
2   OJ L349, 31.12.1994.
3   OJ L67, 10.03.1994 and OJ L128, 13.06.1995.
4   OJ L326, 30.12.1995.
5   OJ L56, 06.03.1996. See also the heading on shipbuilding in the chapter on industry.

Commercial policy measures have also existed for **steel products**. In the framework of the steel crisis plan[1], the Commission had introduced " **an external wing**" in 1978[2] with the aim of boosting the efficiency of internal measures to restructure the Community steel market. The voluntary-restraint arrangements concluded in this framework with the main exporting countries were ended in 1992. Imports are no longer subject to restrictions, with the exception of residual national quotas, but ECSC contact groups, whose task is limited to exchanging commercial and technical information, have been set up in conjunction with the Central European countries and also with Brazil, Korea and Russia. The 'autonomous ECSC quotas' maintained by five Member States (Germany, Benelux, Italy) were progressively replaced by the Europe Agreements concluded with Central and Eastern European countries and by the cooperation Agreements concluded with the independent States of the former Soviet Union[3].

Since 1990, exploratory discussions have been underway in the context of the GATT with a view to an international agreement establishing liberalized conditions for trade in steel products, inspired notably by the strict disciplines negotiated between the Community and the United States in the framework of the bilateral consensus signed in 1989[4]. Following the failure to conclude a multilateral steel arrangement in the context of the Uruguay Round, the participants had agreed to resume negotiations in 1994. However, their differences were not settled. The EU is determined to see the establishment of strict rules for granting subsidies, elimination of tariff and non-tariff barriers to trade and prevention of the misuse of legitimate commercial instruments for protectionist purposes.

In the **automobile sector**, Japanese car imports was a key sectoral problem to be settled. In 1991, the Community has reached an agreement with Japan on trade in motor vehicles in the Single Market. In accordance with the joint declaration between the Community and Japan adopted in The Hague on July 18, 1991[5], the agreement on motor cars provides for close cooperation between the interested parties during a transitional period which will run until the end of 1999. During this period, steps will be taken to contribute to the necessary adaptation of Community production to attain adequate levels of international competitiveness. The Community market will be harmonized - thus replacing the national reception procedures by a single Community reception - and imports gradually liberalized in the five protected markets (France, Italy, Portugal, Spain and United Kingdom). For its part, Japan will "moderate" exports in line with the market hypotheses on which negotiations were based, namely the evolution of supply and demand, including production within the Community. At the end of the period, Japanese exports should not exceed a total amount of 1,230,000 vehicles on a market of 15,000,000. Japan must also remove technical barriers to imports of Community vehicles. Joint half-yearly monitoring provides a bilateral check on the application of this arrangement.

Among the various agreements concluded at the Uruguay Round, several concern the **agricultural sector**, notably the Agreement on Agriculture. In order to reduce the trade-restricting effects of national policies, including the common agricultural policy, whilst ensuring that domestic objectives could be pursued, it was agreed to convert the various forms of protection into customs duties. The Agreement on Agriculture requires, in particular, the abolition of variable import levies provided for under the common market organizations and

---

1   See chapter on Industry.
2   OJ L196, 13.05.1978.
3   OJ L396, 31.12.1992 and OJ L17, 20.01.1994.
4   OJ L368, 18.12.1989.
5   See below section on relations between the Community and Japan.

the fixing of customs duties in the Common Customs Tariff. However, for certain product groups, such as cereals, rice, wine and fruit and vegetables, certain supplementary mechanisms not involving the collection of fixed customs duties are inserted into the basic Regulations of the CAP by a Regulation which sets out the adjustments and transitional arrangements required in the agricultural sector in order to implement the agreements concluded during the Uruguay Round[1]. The granting of export subsidies is limited henceforward to certain groups of agricultural products. In addition, such subsidies are limited in terms of quantity and value. Developed countries, including all the Member States of the EU, committed themselves to reduce export subsidies by 36% and the actual volume of subsidized exports by 21% over a six-year period. Moreover, the Community undertook to cut the global level of internal support by 20% over a period of six years, this being in line with the figures agreed in the CAP reform. The result is a better compatibility of the CAP and the GATT but also a Community agriculture more market-oriented and competitive. The access into the Community market is certainly facilitated, but the principle of Community preference is maintained.

External relations

The external relations of the European Community, which date back to its first years of existence, should not be confused with the foreign policy of the European Union, introduced by the Treaty of Maastricht but which still has to be defined. However, the Community's external relations, tied in as they are with common commercial policy and the Community's development aid policy, give a foretaste of this policy and an indication of the scope which it will assume. Common foreign policy has already taken its first steps thanks, notably, to **European political cooperation**.

Political cooperation, which got off the ground in 1970 with the "Davignon report" which provided for reciprocal information procedures and regular contacts in order to harmonize the viewpoints of the Member States in the field of international policy, for a long time remained on an informal footing. Its main manifestation was the occasional adoption of political positions by the Heads of State and Government first of all during the "summit" meetings and then during the European Councils. At the Paris Summit in October 1972, it was agreed that the objectives of the Community's external activities and of political cooperation with a view to European union would be examined and determined during regular meetings between the Heads of State and Government of the member countries, meeting within a "European Council". This was the birth of "political cooperation" between the Member States.

Foreign Affairs Ministers have also consulted one another for many years on the sidelines of the General Affairs Councils on all major issues: Cold War, Middle East conflict, relations with major trading partners. It was at their meeting in London on October 13, 1981 that the Ministers of Foreign Affairs approved a report on European political cooperation, restating their political commitment and endorsing better consultation mechanisms, in the shape of a small team of officials from the past and future Presidencies (**Troika**), given the task of assisting the current Presidency and of a procedure enabling meetings to be called within 48 hours if three Member States so request. The Commission was also made a fully-fledged partner in political cooperation at all levels.

---

1   OJ L349, 31.12.1994. See also the chapter on agriculture.

However, it was the **Single European Act**, which entered into force on July 1, 1987, which gave a legal framework to European political cooperation[1]. In Title III of the Single Act, the Member States undertook to strive towards the joint definition and implementation of a European foreign policy and, more specifically, to inform one another and consult one another on any question of foreign policy which is of general interest, to ensure that their combined influence is exercised in the most efficient manner through consultation, alignment of positions and the fulfilment of joint actions. It is thus that the Member States have, since 1987, monitored major developments on the international stage and have adopted positions on them. Positions have related to such matters as the evolution in South Africa, the upheaval in Central and Eastern Europe, the Gulf crisis and subsequent war, and violence in the former Yugoslav Republics. It was also in this framework that Member States pursued their policy of promoting human rights and fundamental freedoms in the world at large. Continuing serious violations of human rights in many countries prompted the Community and its Member States to react either by making behind-the-scenes representations or by issuing hundreds of statements.

Towards a common foreign and security policy

The Treaty on European Union takes a further step forward on the Single Act. Whereas under the latter, the Member States undertook to strive to draw up and implement in common a European foreign policy, in Title V of the new Treaty they undertake to "define" and implement a common foreign and security policy (CFSP). This policy, called the second pillar of the European Union, remains, however, an intergovernmental process distinct from the supranational structures of the Community and removed from the jurisdiction of the Court of Justice. The Member States are advancing with caution into this new ground which, in the long term, will imply major transfers of national sovereignty. However, they are aware that this new policy must evolve relatively rapidly, for they provide for its revision by the 1996 intergovernmental conference on the basis of evaluation of progress made and experience gained in the meantime (Article J.4 and N.2).

The objectives of CFSP are: to safeguard the common values, fundamental interests and independence of the Union; to strengthen the security of the Union and its Member States; to preserve peace and strengthen international security; to promote international cooperation; to develop and consolidate democracy and the rule of law, and respect for human rights and fundamental freedoms. The general nature of these objectives reflects the fact that the common policy covers nearly all the fields of foreign and security policy.

The Union pursues these objectives in **two ways**: through systematic cooperation between Member States in conduct of policy; and through the gradual implementation of joint action in the areas in which the Member States have important interests in common. The Member States undertake to actively and unreservedly support the Union's external and security policy and to refrain from any action which is contrary to the interests of the Union or likely to impair its effectiveness (Article J.1).

In the framework of their **systematic cooperation**, which is in actual fact a follow on from their previous political cooperation, the Member States inform and consult one another within the Council on any matter of

---

1   OJ L169, 29.06.1987.

foreign and security policy of general interest in order to ensure that their combined influence is exerted as effectively as possible by means of combined and convergent action. When it deems it necessary, the Council defines a **common position** and the Member States must ensure that their national policies conform to common positions. They must coordinate their action in international organizations and at international conferences and uphold the common positions in these fora if necessary (Article J.2), where compliance with this undertaking is of particular importance in terms of effectiveness and credibility. This process, which need not take place in the public domain, can however lead to the issuing of a statement where issues of special political significance are involved. Article C of the Union Treaty contains an obligation to ensure the consistency of the Union's activities. Therefore, a common position adopted on the basis of Article J.2, while respecting the division of responsibilities set out in the Treaty, has to be compatible with the guidelines governing the EU's economic relations with a third country and with the objectives and priorities of its external policies, although it is the European Community that is responsible for adopting practical measures. The Union has already adopted a number of common positions expressed in statements concerning, notably, the Independent States of the former Soviet Union, the former Yugoslavia, the Mediterranean and the Middle East.

The new concept of **joint action** is more interesting, for it implies consistent foreign policy measures by the Union and by its Member States. It could pave the way to the establishment of a genuine foreign policy. This new instrument represents a qualitative change in that greater discipline is required of the Member States and all the resources necessary for attaining the objectives of the Union are to be pooled. On the basis of general guidelines from the European Council, the Council (Foreign Affairs Ministers) decides that a matter should be the subject of joint action and lays down its specific scope, objectives and the means, procedures, conditions and if necessary duration of its implementation. If necessary, the Council can review the principles and objectives of the joint action. Joint actions commit the Member States in the positions they adopt and in the conduct of their activity. Any plans to adopt a national position or take national action pursuant to a joint action must be the subject of information provision to the Council allowing time, if necessary, for prior consultations within the Council. In cases of imperative need, however, a Member State can take the necessary measures and immediately inform the Council of these (Article J.3). The practical implementation of joint actions is the responsibility of the presidency, assisted if need be by representatives of the previous and next Member States to hold the presidency (the Troika), in association with the Commission (Article J.5).

For the CFSP, Article C of the Union Treaty establishes the principle of a **single institutional framework** designed to ensure the consistency and continuity of the activities carried out, while respecting the "acquis communautaire" and the Union's external relations, security, economic and development policies. It should be noted, however, that in general the common foreign and security policy provisions do not fully respect Community procedures. In this area, the European Council defines general principles and guidelines. On the basis of these guidelines, the Council takes the decisions required for the definition and implementation of the common foreign and security policy. It acts unanimously, except for procedural questions and questions which it has decided to deal with by a qualified majority on the basis of Article J.3. In a declaration annexed to the Treaty, the Member States agreed that for decisions requiring unanimity, the Member States will, to the extent possible, avoid preventing a unanimous decision where a qualified majority exists in favour of this decision. In fact, the effectiveness of the CFSP decision-making process could only be ensured by applying to this new policy the traditional working methods of the Council, and notably the possibility of acting by a qualified majority. However, questions relating to the security of the European Union and its common defence policy are not subject to the procedures defined in Article J.3 of the Treaty, which means, in particular, that there can be no question of qualified majority vote on these matters.

Although it is fully associated in the work carried out in the common foreign and security policy field, the Commission does not have exclusive right of initiative. Both it and any Member State can refer to the Council any question relating to the common foreign and security policy and can submit proposals to the Council (Articles J.8 and J.9). The Council can decide unanimously that operating expenditure arising from the common foreign and security policy can be charged either to the Community budget or to the Member States, in accordance with a scale to be decided. Administrative expenditure is, in any case, charged to the Community budget (Article J.11). On 13 June 1994, the Council defined the categories of expenditure regarded as administrative, to be financed from the "Council" section of the general budget. Concerning operational expenditure to be financed by the Member States, the Council agreed on sharing out on the basis of the gross national product.

For matters relating to the common foreign and security policy, the Presidency of the Council represents the European Union. It is responsible for the implementation of common measures and expresses the position of the Union in international organizations and international conferences (Article J.5). It consults the European Parliament on the main aspects and the basic choices of the common foreign and security policy and ensures that its views are duly taken into consideration and that it is kept regularly informed of the evolution of the situation (Article J.7). In cases requiring a rapid decision, the Presidency, of its own motion or at the request of the Commission or a Member State, convenes an extraordinary Council meeting within forty-eight hours or, in an emergency, within a shorter period (Article 8). The Presidency is assisted, if necessary, by the Member State which previously held the Presidency and by the future Presidency. The Commission is fully associated in the tasks of the Presidency and contributes to the debate on the CFJH proposals that the Presidency submits to the European Council.

A Political Committee consisting of Political Directors of the Member States monitors the international situation in the areas covered by common foreign and security policy and contributes to the definition of policies by delivering opinions to the Council at the latter's request or on its own initiative. It also monitors the implementation of agreed policies, without prejudice to the responsibilities of the Presidency, Commission and COREPER (Article J.8). The diplomatic and consular missions of the Member States and Commission delegations in third countries and international conferences and their representatives to international organizations are stepping up their cooperation by exchanging information and carrying out joint assessments. They also cooperate to ensure that the common positions and common measures adopted by the Council are complied with and implemented (Article J.6).

Common foreign and security policy includes all questions related to the security of the European Union, including the **eventual framing of a common defence policy**, which might in time lead to a common defence (Article J.4). The language used here gives an indication of Member States' extreme caution in venturing into the field of common defence involving, in the long term, the integration of their Armed Forces. However, the objectives of the security policy were clearly defined at the Brussels European Council in October 1993. This must be aimed in particular at reducing risks and uncertainties which could impair the territorial integrity and political independence of the Union and of its Member States, their democratic nature, their economic stability and the stability of the neighbouring regions.

In this field, a very important role is attributed to the **Western Euro-pean Union (WEU)**, the political and military alliance set up in May 6, 1955 and binding its member countries by a clause of automatic military en-gagement in the event of aggression against one of its signatories. The Maastricht Treaty stipulates that the WEU is an integral part of the devel-opment of the European Union and elaborates and implements decisions and action of the Union which have defence implications. To this end, the nine original member countries of the WEU have invited the other Member States of the European Union (Greece, Ireland, Denmark) to accede to WEU or become observers and have invited other European Member States of NATO to become associate members of the WEU in a way giving them the possibility of full participation in its activities. In fact, in 1993, Greece became the tenth member of WEU, whereas Ireland, Denmark, Sweden and Finland opted for the "observer" status. The other European members of NATO, Norway, Turkey and Iceland are considered as "associate mem-bers", while Hungary, Poland, the Czech Republic, Slovakia, Romania, Bulgaria, Lithuania, Latvia and Estonia are considered as "associate part-ners". The institutions of the WEU (Council, General Secretariat and Par-liamentary Assembly) remain separate from those of the European Union, but must work in close cooperation with the latter and harmonize their work methods. Relations between the European Union and the WEU will evolve and will have to be reviewed in the framework of the 1996 inter-governmental conference.

In a Declaration annexed to the Maastricht Treaty, the Member States of the WEU agree on the need to develop a European security and defence identity and to assume greater responsibility for defence. They declare that the WEU should be developed as the defence component of the European Union and as the means to strengthen the European pillar of the Atlantic Alliance. The WEU, to this end, will frame a common European defence policy and ensure its tangible implementation by strengthening its opera-tional role. This will be achieved through defining appropriate missions, structures and means, covering in particular: a WEU planning cell; closer military cooperation complementary to the Alliance, particularly in the fields of logistics, transport, training and strategic surveillance; meetings of WEU Chiefs of Defence Staff; military units answerable to the WEU.

Article J.4 of the Treaty does not rule out the development of closer cooperation between two or more Member States on a bilateral level, in the framework of the WEU and the Atlantic Alliance, provided such cooperation does not run counter to or impede multilateral cooperation. Thus, on 5 November 1993, France, Germany and Belgium took the impor-tant initiative of placing under common command certain units of their armies. The **Eurocorps**, which is placed under the authority of a "Joint Committee" made up of the Heads of Staff and political directors of the three countries, could be used autonomously by these three countries, or else placed at the disposal of NATO and the WEU.

Article J.4 also underlines that the policy of the Union does not prejudice the specific character of the security and defence policy of certain Member States, respects the obligations of certain Member States under the **North Atlantic Treaty** and is compatible with the common security and defence policy established in that framework. With a view to strengthening the European pillar of the Atlantic Alliance, the Member States of the WEU state their readiness to develop further the close working links between the WEU and the Alliance and to strengthen the role, responsibilities and contributions of the WEU Member States in the Alliance. This will be undertaken on the basis of the necessary transparency and complementarity between the emerging European security and defence identity and the Alliance. The WEU will act in conformity with the positions adopted in the Atlantic Alliance. However, WEU Member States will intensify their coordination on Alliance issues which represent an important common interest, with the aim of introducing joint positions agreed in the WEU into the process of consultation in the Alliance, which will remain the essential forum for consultation among its members.

The **Organization for Security and Cooperation in Europe (OSCE)** is also called upon to play a key role in pan-European security and cooperation. It has begun functioning as the Conference on Security and Cooperation in Europe (CSCE) with the signature of the Helsinki Final Act on August 1, 1975. The Helsinki text adopts in three baskets the principles which the signatories undertake to respect in the fields of security, economic cooperation and human rights. 52 States participate in the CSCE: all the EU Member States, the countries of Central and Eastern Europe, the members of the Commonwealth of Independent States (CIS), the United States and Canada. The Helsinki II document, entitled 'The challenges of change', issued at the close of the Helsinki Summit meeting of 9 and 10 July 1992, introduces new provisions for conflict prevention and crisis management. It also provides for the establishment of a security forum.

The **Stability Pact in Europe**, signed the 21 March 1995 in Paris, is European Union initiative launched by the Brussels European Council of October 1993[1]. First exercise in preventive diplomacy, this Pact is designed to foster peace and stability in Europe, by resolving the problem of minorities, reinforcing the inviolability of frontiers, strengthening the development of democracy and regional cooperation in Central and Eastern Europe. The OSCE was entrusted with the follow-up and the implementation of the Pact.

Several joint actions were adopted since 1993, in particular: support for the delivery of humanitarian aid in Bosnia-Hercegovina[2], support for the process of democratic and non-racial change in South Africa and support for the peace process in the Middle East[3]; EU's involvement in the structures implementing the peace agreement for Bosnia-Herzegovina[4]; and the EU's participation in the administration of the city of Mostar[5]. In the field of common security policy, the Council adopted a first joint action on the preparation of the 1995 Conference on the Treaty on the non-proliferation of Nuclear Weapons (NTP) designed to encourage the indefinite and unconditional prorogation of NTP[6]. In December 1994, the Council adopted simultaneously a Community Regulation and a Decision concerning a joint action to control exports of dual-use military/civilian goods[7]. In April 1995, the Council adopted a joint action on anti-personnel mines, comprising notably a moratorium on the export of such mines and a major Union contribution to international mine clearance[8].

The following pages will examine the relations which the European Community as a body has already established with many countries throughout the world. Although these relations are of economic or commercial origin, they have on more than one occasion stepped out of this setting into the purely political arena. This is notably the case of relations with the countries of Central and Eastern Europe. In the future it will be interesting to see how many foreign affairs decisions will be taken under the common foreign and security policy procedure and how many under the Community procedure. In other words, it will be interesting to see just where the European Community's external domain ends and that of the European Union begins. In the following brief description of the Community's external relations, we will see that the latter has already been listened to, commanded the respect of, been sought out and rebuked by countries large and small throughout the world, which have seen it as a European Union in all but name.

---

1   OJ L339, 31.12.1993 and OJ L165, 01.07.1994.
2   OJ L286, 20.11.1993 and OJ L326, 17.12.1994.
3   OJ L119, 07.05.1994.
4   OJ L309, 21.12.1995.
5   OJ L313, 27.12.1995.
6   OJ L205, 08.08.1994.
7   OJ L367, 31.12.1994 and OJ L52, 01.03.1996.
8   OJ L115, 22.05.1995.

European Free Trade Association and European Economic Area

As stated in the introduction to this work, the European Free Trade Association (EFTA) was set up in 1959 on the initiative of the United Kingdom, which thought that the Community was going too fast and too far along the path of European integration. When the United Kingdom and Denmark switched allegiances from EFTA to the EEC in 1973, the scale of their commercial relations with the other EFTA countries made it impossible to preserve customs barriers between the two groups of countries. As a consequence, free trade agreements were signed in 1972 and 1973 between the Community and Austria, Sweden and Switzerland, Iceland, Norway, Finland and Portugal, which joined the Community in 1986. These agreements abolished customs duties and restrictions on trade in industrial products. Furthermore, the Community agreed to certain compromises on the Common Agricultural Policy, which were matched by reciprocal EFTA concessions in the agricultural field. EEC-EFTA free trade has operated in a satisfactory manner and has brought about sustained growth in trade between the two groups of countries. This trade, by the end of the eighties, represented 25% of total Community trade and between 40% and 65% of that of the EFTA countries.

In a speech to the European Parliament on the policy guidelines of the new Commission in January 1989, President Delors invited the EFTA countries to consider different ways of further strengthening relations with the Community, notably through "a new form of association which is more structured on the institutional level". The Heads of Government of both the EFTA countries, in a meeting of March 15, 1989, and of the European Community, during the European Council of December 8 and 9, 1989, responded favourably to this initiative. The negotiations got underway in 1990 and were completed in October 1991 between the Community and EFTA as a body on the basic, legal and institutional aspects of such a global agreement.

The Treaty on the **European Economic Area (EEA)** was signed in 1992 by the governments of twelve EU countries and six EFTA countries. As a result of the negative Swiss referendum on 6 December 1992, however, and the accession to the European Union since 1 January 1995 of Austria, Sweden and Finland, the EEE Treaty associates to the EU only Norway, Iceland and Liechtenstein[1]. The institutional framework of the EEA comprises: the EEA Council, which is made up of members of the Council of the EU and the Commission plus one member for each signatory EFTA government, and which provides political impetus for the implementation of the Agreement and lays down general guidelines; the EEA Joint Committee, comprising representatives of the contracting parties and responsible for the implementation of the Agreement; the EEA Joint Parliamentary Committee; and the EEA Consultative Committee, which provides a forum for representatives of the social partners.

The aim of the EEA Treaty is to establish a dynamic and homogeneous integrated economic entity based on common rules and equal conditions of competition. The EFTA States, minus Switzerland, undertook to take on board existing Community legislation concerning the free movement of goods, persons, services and capital, subject to a few exceptions and transitional periods in certain sectors. Apart from the implementation of the 'four freedoms', the EEA Agreement also provides for relations between the Community and the EFTA countries to be reinforced and extended in areas which have an impact on business activity. These are the 'horizontal policies', notably social policy, consumer protection, environment, statistics and company law, and the 'flanking policies' covering

---

1   OJ L346, 31.12.1993 and OJ L1, 03.01.1994, OJ L160, 28.06.1994 and OJ L1, 01.01.1995.

fields such as research and development, information, education, the audiovisual sector, SMEs and tourism. Special arrangements on agriculture, fisheries and transport are provided in bilateral Agreements which accompany the EEA Agreement. This contains provisions designed to iron out economic, social and regional disparities under the cohesion principle. The EFTA countries contribute to the financing of the Cohesion Fund in favour of Spain, Portugal, Greece and Ireland.

Central and Eastern Europe and Commonwealth of Independent States

Until the end of the eighties, this part of Europe known as the Eastern bloc was cut off from the rest of the continent by the "Iron Curtain" which closed off frontiers and by the planned economy system which prevented normal economic relations with market economy countries. Quite apart from the political and ideological problems, trade with planned economy countries was hindered by the fact that their external trade was run by the State and trading relations therefore had to be established between States.

When, at the end of 1989, the pace of history suddenly accelerated with the rapid and successive collapse of the Communist regimes in Central and Eastern Europe, the Community rushed to help the people of these countries, working to promote political reform and develop a private sector in their economies. At the Arche summit of June 14-16, 1989, the Heads of State and Government of the seven main industrial nations (G7) asked the President of the Commission to coordinate the provision of aid for **economic restructuring in Poland and Hungary**, the first two Eastern bloc countries to launch themselves into the process of democratization. Through this request, the Summit implicitly recognized the Commission's international role. As part of this task, the Commission convened in Brussels the first consultation meeting between representatives of twenty-four OECD member countries, the International Monetary Fund, the World Bank and the Club of Paris, the latter consisting of the credit countries of any debtor state. All the participants declared their willingness to participate in the consultation and coordination process and identified priorities for an aid programme covering the two countries. These are: improvement of export opportunities, vocational training assistance (including that for managerial executives), promotion of investment and of joint ventures and cooperation on the environment.

Acting on these guidelines, the Commission unveiled to the group of 24 countries meeting in Brussels on September 26, 1989 an action plan for the **operation PHARE** (Poland and Hungary: aid for economic restructuring). This plan was designed as a framework for action by the Community and as an incentive for similar initiatives pursuing the same aims by other members of the group of 24. The latter welcomed the general policy slant and the blueprint of the plan and confirmed their support for action in the fields in question. After this meeting, the Commission got down to preparing the transformation of this plan into specific Community measures: the regulation on economic aid for Poland and Hungary[1]. The PHARE programme was extended, in 1990, to practically all the **Central and East European countries (CEEC)**[2], in 1991, to Albania and the Baltic countries[3], in 1992, to Slovenia[4] and, in 1996, to the Former Yugoslav Republic of Macedonia[5].

The central aim of **PHARE** for the years 1993 to 1997 is to provide assistance for economic reform, structural adjustment and sustainable development in Central and Eastern Europe, and more particularly to help to convert centralized economies into economies based on market-oriented mechanisms. The partner countries are free to set their own priorities

---

1   OJ L375, 23.12.1989 and OJ L162, 03.07.1993.
2   OJ L257, 21.09.1990.
3   OJ L357, 28.12.1991.
4   OJ L227, 11.08.1992.
5   OJ L65, 15.03.1996.

for PHARE financing within the framework of indicative programmes agreed with the European Union. Under these programmes, PHARE and the partner countries together decide how best to achieve the priorities targeted. Programmes are implemented and run by programme management units (PMUs), which are the driving force behind PHARE in the field.

The technical and financial assistance programmes agreed with the recipient countries in the framework of the PHARE programme place the emphasis on breaking up monopolies, privatization, the restructuring of nationalized firms, the fostering of small and medium-sized enterprises and the development of the financial sector, the private-sector company and the labour market. Attention is also devoted to the modernization of infrastructure in sectors such as telecommunications and transport, structural reform in agriculture, energy and the environment. In 1991, regional cooperation programmes bringing together several countries of Central and Eastern Europe in the fields of statistics, standards, customs, government and environmental protection were launched. In 1992, these programmes were extended to transports, telecommunications, energy and nuclear safety. PHARE's **JOPP** programme helps small and medium enterprises in Central and Eastern Europe to set up joint ventures with similar firms in the European Union. A cross-border cooperation programme, adopted in July 1994, is designed to promote structural initiatives and economic, social and technical measures to foster cooperation between border regions of EU Member States and adjacent PHARE countries[1].

In parallel with PHARE and in relation with it three specific but large-scale instruments are designed for assistance to CEECs: the European Bank for Reconstruction and Development, the European Training Foundation and the programme of trans-European mobility for university students.

On April 9, 1990 in Paris the text defining the operating provisions for the **European Bank for Reconstruction and Development (EBRD)** was signed[2]. It was inaugurated on April 14, 1991. The Bank's purpose is to support the transition to open market economies and promote private and individual enterprise in the countries of Central and Eastern Europe adopting and implementing the principles of multi-party democracy, pluralism and market economics. The EBRD has two member institutions, the European Commission and the European Investment Bank (EIB) and forty member countries: the EC and EFTA countries, the countries of Central and Eastern Europe, the independent States of the former USSR, the Baltic States, Albania, Turkey, Cyprus, Malta, the United States, Japan, Canada, Australia, New Zealand, Israel, Morocco, Egypt, South Korea and Mexico. It has a capital of 10 billion ECU, 51% of which is held by the EU Member States, reflecting the predominant role which the latter wish to play in the reconstruction of their Eastern neighbours. This influence is even more marked in the area of the educational and training assistance offered to the countries of Central and Eastern Europe. The two instruments existing in this area are essentially Community although they are

---

1   OJ L171, 06.07.1994.
2   OJ L372, 31.12.1990.

open to operations by non-Community countries which are members of the Group of 24.

The **European Training Foundation** is constituted in the form of an independent body which is cooperating closely with the European Centre for the Development of Vocational Training (**CEDEFOP**)[1]. The Foundation is open to public or private sector participation by non-Community countries and focuses its action on vocational training, continuing training and training in certain specific sectors. Its role is to ensure efficient cooperation in the provision of aid to the countries in question, to help identify their training and refresher training needs and to define a strategy which can help meet these needs. It acts as a kind of clearing house, matching up information on aid offers and requests and encouraging and helping multilateral assistance.

The **programme of trans-European mobility for university students (TEMPUS)** is cast in the same mould as existing Community exchange programmes, but is adapted to the specific needs of the countries in question[2]. In addition to various complementary activities, it makes provision for joint training projects between universities and companies in Eastern European countries and their counterparts in at least two Member States. It also seeks to encourage the mobility of teachers, students and administrative officials. Its priority action fields are management, business administration and language learning.

On the bilateral level, **"Europe Agreements"** creating specific links and reflecting the growing interdependence between the Community and the Central and Eastern European countries (CEECs) take over from the commercial and economic cooperation agreements. The first Europe Agreements establishing an association between the European Communities and their Member States and Hungary and Poland respectively came into force on 1 January 1994[3]. In 1994, identical Agreements were signed with Bulgaria and Rumania as well as with the Czech Republic and the Slovak Republic after the dissolution of their federation[4]. In 1995, Europe Agreements were also concluded with the three Baltic States of Estonia, Latvia and Lithuania as well as with Slovenia. The agreements, which have a common framework adapted to the specific situation of each partner, incorporate provisions on the political dialogue and provide for the gradual introduction of free trade arrangements on industrial products and trade in agricultural and fishery products subject to specific provisions. In a few years' time the Community market will be entirely open to all products imported from these countries, with the exception of agricultural produce, for which considerable concessions have nevertheless been granted. The associated countries will introduce reciprocal arrangements, although over a longer period of time. Provisions based on Community law are included for free competition, the freedom of establishment and

---

1   See the chapter on Social Progress.

2   OJ L131, 23.05.1990 and OJ L122, 07.05.1992, see also the sub-heading on programmes for the training of young persons in the chapter on social progress.

3   OJ L319, 21.12.1993.

4   OJ L357, L358, L359 and L360, 31.12.1994.

the gradual liberalization of the movement of workers, services and capital.

On the more specific question of political dialogue, the agreements
institutionalize regular high level political meetings on subjects of common interest, notably as regards external policy. The associated countries
can coordinate their position with joint positions of the European Union
and associate themselves in its joint action. The final provisions provide
for an association Council, which will meet at ministerial level at least once
a year. A transitional period of ten years is planned and is broken down,
except for the commercial arrangements, into two five-year periods. Concluded for an indefinite period, the Europe Agreements are designed
eventually to pave the way for the integration of the countries concerned
in the European Union.

In fact, the Essen European Council, in July 1994, confirmed the
conclusions of the Copenhagen and Corfu European Council meetings
stating that any associated country which so wished could become member of the European Union once it was able to fulfil the obligations
associated with membership and meet the economic and political requirements. A White Paper of the Commission aims at the preparation of the
associated countries of Central and Eastern Europe for integration into the
internal market of the Union[1]. It concerns the six countries mentioned
above, which have already concluded association agreements with the
Union, and the Baltic States and Slovenia, which are negotiating Europe
Agreements with it. The White Paper presents the essential legislative
measures in the sphere of the internal market and in other spheres such as
competition and social and environmental policy, which are of vital importance for the operation of this market. It also stresses the need to create
the necessary administrative and organizational context to ensure that this
legislation can be implemented effectively. In December 1995, the Commission adopted reports on the pre-accession strategy, on alternative
strategies for the development of relations in the agricultural field and on
the effects of enlargement on the policies of the Union[2].

The Community is not ready to establish as close relations with the republics of the
former Soviet Union as it has with its ex-satellites. For many years non-existent, the diplomatic relations between the Community and the USSR were gradually established during
the period of President Gorbatchev's "perestroika" and resulted in the signature in December
1989 of a trade and commercial and economic cooperation agreement[3]. The Rome European
Council of December 1990 decided to support the efforts of the USSR government to reform
and revive its economy, through the granting of technical assistance, decided upon by the
Council on July 15, 1991[4]. In the meanwhile, the Council had decided to grant emergency
food aid and set up a credit guarantee to ensure the export of Community food and
agricultural products to the Soviet Union[5]. After the failed coup d'Etat in the Soviet Union
in August 1991, the Community granted it a medium-term loan worth 1.25 billion ECU for
the import of foodstuffs and agricultural products and for medical supplies. 50% of this
amount was earmarked for triangular operations with the countries of Central and Eastern
Europe. In the wake of the break-up of the Soviet-Union, on 10 February 1992, the Council

---

1   COM (95)163, 10 May 1995.
2   COM (95) 605, 606 and 607.
3   OJ L68, 15.03.1990.
4   OJ L201, 24.07.1991.
5   OJ L67, 14.03.1991.

decided to extend the credit guarantee to Russia only. As far as the loan is concerned, the Council noted on 13 July 1992, that nine independent States of the former Soviet Union had met the conditions making them eligible for it. Moreover, the Council decided to lift all specific quantitative restrictions from these countries[1].

The scale of needs in the new republics of the **Commonwealth of Independent States (CIS)** calls for a major international assistance effort which the Community cannot assume alone. However, in light of the scale of financial decisions which it has taken in their favour, the Community plays a decisive role in the provision of technical assistance and food aid to these countries. The EC technical assistance to the Commonwealth of Independent States and Georgia **(TACIS programme)** aims to create in a number of key sectors the right environment for a market economy and a democratic society[2]. It closely involves the recipients of the aid in the preparation and implementation of the projects that concern them in order to thus improve local skills and know-how. The level and intensity of assistance depend on the population and the GNP but also on the extent and progress of reform in the recipient countries. The European Union and its partner countries work closely to assess reform objectives and the needs for Tacis support. This joint assessment produces an indicative programme for each country which establishes the priority sectors for Tacis funding, notably restructuring of State enterprises and private sector development, human resources development, food production and distribution, agriculture, energy, transport, telecommunications and nuclear safety. The Community is also heavily involved in the creation and operation of the International Centre for Science and Technology which will provide employment for certain of the nuclear experts of the ex-USSR, who could otherwise be tempted to emigrate to countries wishing to acquire or build up nuclear weapons capacity[3].

Designed to replace the Agreement concluded in 1989 with the Soviet Union, **partnership and cooperation agreements** laying the foundations for a qualitative change in economic ties based on the market economy and respect for democratic principles have been negotiated with Russia and Ukraine[4] as well as with several Independent States of the former Soviet Union. Implementation of these agreements, which combine areas of Member State and EU responsibility and have an initial validity of ten years, will depend on political and economic developments in each of the countries in question and on the closeness of their relations with the European Union.

Mediterranean, Middle East

The countries of the Mediterranean are of considerable economic significance for the European Union, constituting as a group one of its largest trading partners and having close historic and cultural ties with some of its Member States. Relations between the Community

---

1   OJ L89, 14.04.1992.
2   OJ L187, 29.07.1993.
3   OJ L409, 31.12.1992 and OJ L64, 08.03.1994. See the chapter on research.
4   See the interim agreements covering trade aspects in OJ L247, 13.10.1995 and OJ L311, 23.12.1995.

and the Mediterranean countries have become ever closer in three phases, during a period extending from the sixties to the eighties. A new phase of close cooperation began in 1995.

Acting on the conclusions of the Corfu European Council, the Commission in a communication of October 1994 proposed the establishment of a Euro-Mediterranean partnership, chiefly with the Maghreb and Mashreq countries and Israel, whose process would begin with a gradual liberalization of trade, supported by a substantial financial aid package, before moving on to closer political and economic cooperation and finally to close association[1]. In another communication the Commission proposed three areas of priority assistance: for economic transition, for a better socioeconomic balance and for regional integration[2]. In future, the EU's Mediterranean policy should become multi-faceted, encompassing all those areas where interdependence exists such as economic development and trade, immigration and the environment.

An important Euro-Mediterranean ministerial conference took place on 27 and 28 November 1995 in Barcelona between the European Union and its twelve Mediterranean partners (Algeria, Cyprus, Egypt, Israel, Jordan, Lebanon, Syria, Tunisia, Turkey and the Palestinian Authority). At the end of the proceedings, the ministers adopted a Declaration and a work programme instituting a regular political dialogue and enhanced cooperation fostering peace, security, stability and prosperity in the region. The three key components of the **Euro-Mediterranean partnership** are: a reinforced and regular political dialogue; an enhanced economic and financial cooperation aiming at the creation of a free trade area; and a further strengthening of the social, cultural and human dimension. A new budget heading called **MEDA** constitutes the single financial instrument for the implementation of all cooperation activities with the countries concerned. The long-term objective is the creation of a Euro-Mediterranean economic area with more than 800 million inhabitants from some 40 countries.

The Mediterranean policy has not only been staggered in time but has differed from country to country. The Community always took an open line towards the European Mediterranean countries, with a view to a possible customs union or even accession. This policy has paid off, for it helped establish strong democracy in three Mediterranean countries: Greece, Spain and Portugal, which are now fully-fledged members of the European Community. The others have close relations with it.

Malta has thus been associated to the Community since March 1971[3]. An association agreement with **Cyprus** was concluded in May 1973[4]. Their agreements provide for a customs union with the Community. In July 1990, the two republics applied for Community membership. The latter keeps a close watch on the conflict in Cyprus, has never recognized the so-called autonomous Turkish Cypriot State and on several occasions has declared, in the framework of political cooperation, that the parties to the conflict should cooperate with the Secretary General of the United Nations to find a peaceful solution. The Corfu European Council of June 1994 stressed that any solution to the Cyprus problem should respect the country's sovereignty, independence, territorial integrity and unity. The European Council meeting in Madrid in December 1995 confirmed that accession talks would start six months after the Intergovernmental Conference of 1996 in the light of its outcome. A structured dialogue between the EU, on the one hand, and Cyprus and Malta, on the other, should prepare the two republics for their accession to the Union. Concerning Cyprus the sole interlocutor in this dialogue will be the recognized Government of this country.

---

1   COM (94)427, 19 October 1994.
2   COM (95)72, 8 March 1995.
3   OJ L61, 14.03.1971 and OJ L278, 21.11.1995.
4   OJ L133, 21.05.1973 and OJ L278, 21.11.1995.

More recently, the Community concluded agreements for the creation of a customs union between it and the principality of **Andorra**[1] and the republic of **San Marino**[2] respectively.

Despite the regime in **Yugoslavia**, the Community had concluded with this country in 1983 an economic and technical cooperation agreement spanning science and technology and incorporating trade preferences and financial aid[3]. In 1990, the Community had stated that it would support the reforms under way in Yugoslavia, with measures falling into the framework of the action plan of the Group of 24 for the countries of Central and Eastern Europe, and that it was willing to transform the cooperation agreement into an association agreement if the right economic and political conditions existed in this country. However, the break-up of the Federal State and the civil war between its republics have made it impossible for the Community to continue its relations with Yugoslavia. On November 25, 1991, the Council terminated the 1983 agreements[4]. As a consequence of United Nations Security Council Resolutions, the Community adopted in 1992 and strengthened in 1993 embargo measures against Serbia and Montenegro[5]. On the other hand, the Community strove to maintain normal economic and trade relations with the republics that cooperated with the peace process and re-established for them the preferential arrangements provided for under the old EEC-Yugoslavia Cooperation Agreement[6]. Thus, Croatia is still eligible for the preferential trade arrangements granted to the former Yugoslavia. With the Republic of Slovenia, the European Union has concluded an Agreement on economic, commercial and financial cooperation[7]. After the signature in Paris on 14 December 1995 of the Dayton peace agreement, the European Union reiterated its resolve, in the Madrid European Council, to contribute to the reconstruction of ex-Yugoslavia. In terms of the aid effort in this region, the EU is in fact the world's foremost donor. On the other hand, the Council decided to suspend the restrictions on trade with the Federal Republic of Yugoslavia (Serbia and Montenegro) and with the Bosnian Serbs[8].

Relations between the Community and **Turkey** have been subject to a number of ups and downs, reflecting the political situation in the latter. The association agreement[9] has occasionally operated normally and occasionally been put on the back burner. This was especially true between 1980 and 1986, when the Community pointed out to the Turkish authorities several times that it attached a great deal of importance to the re-introduction of democracy and the full respect of human rights. The Community's attitude has paid off and its influence acknowledged by the Turkish Government after a return to democracy, for one of the first acts of the new government was, on April 4, 1987, to request the accession of Turkey to the Community.

It was on December 17, 1989 that the Commission adopted an Opinion on this application in accordance with Article 237 of the Treaty. After in-depth study of the economic and social situation in Turkey, the Commission concluded that it would have difficulty coping with the adjustment requirements which it would face in the medium term were it to join the Community. Furthermore, certain major political problems, such as the extension of political pluralism, continued positive progress in the area of the respect of human rights and of minorities, the persisting differences of opinion with an EC Member State, Greece, and the absence of a solution to the situation in Cyprus, should be taken into consideration. Despite these problems the EC-Turkey Association Council reached agreement in March 1995 on the completion of the customs union between the EU and Turkey, an agreement which the Parliament endorsed in December 1995, thereby paving the way for entry into force of the customs union on 1 January 1996[10]. This has not prevented new conflicts between Turkey and Greece, in February 1996, over their respective sovereignty in the Aegean Sea and therefore the blocking by the latter of all decisions on EU financial aid to Turkey, until

---

1   OJ L374, 31.12.1990.
2   OJ C302, 22.11.1991.
3   OJ L41, 14.02.1983 and OJ L389, 31.12.1987.
4   OJ L325, 27.11.1991.
5   OJ L102, 28.04.1993.
6   OJ L63, 07.03.1992, OJ L312, 29.10.1992 and OJ L406 of 31.12.1992.
7   OJ L189, 29.07.1993.
8   OJ L297, 09.12.1995.
9   OJ L217, 29.12.1964 and OJ L53, 27.02.1988.
10 OJ L35, 13.02.1996.

its government renounced on aggressions band accepted to submit its eventual claims to the International Court of the Hague.

The preferential arrangements for **Israel**, introduced by the 1975 agreement, are operating reasonably well and have resulted in steady growth in trade between the Community and this country. In the framework of the common foreign policy, the EU brought its support to the peace process between Israel and the Palestinian Territories[1]. In November 1995 a new Association Agreement was concluded between the EU and Israel within the framework of the Euro-Mediterranean partnership[2]. This Agreement introduces the principle of a permanent political dialogue, provides for further concessions on agricultural trade and extends the scope of economic cooperation. A Euro-Mediterranean Association Agreement is also negotiated between the Commission and the Palestinian Authority.

Under the Euro-Mediterranean partnership Association Agreements are also to be concluded with three **Maghreb countries, Tunisia, Morocco and Algeria** as well as with three **Mashreq countries, Egypt, Jordan and Lebanon**. As indicated above, these Euro-Mediterranean Agreements provide for a regular political dialogue, the step-by-step establishment of a free trade area, provisions on the right of establishment, services, competition rules and free movement of capital, strengthening of economic cooperation on the broadest possible front complemented by social, cultural and financial cooperation.

In the Middle East, progress and dialogue are inexorably slow, despite the major efforts of the Community to conduct and expand dialogue with the Arab countries. In September 1981, the EEC's Foreign Affairs Ministers expressed their wish to establish relations with the **Gulf Cooperation Council (GCC)**, then a new body set up by the United Arab Emirates, Saudi Arabia, Bahrain, Oman, Qatar and Kuwait. After exploratory high-level talks lasting several years, the agreement was reached at a Ministerial level meeting between the Community and the GCC in October 1985 that the two parties would open discussions on the conclusion of a cooperation agreement. This agreement was finally signed on June 15, 1988 in Luxembourg[3].It formalizes relations between the two parties and provides for the implementation of all-round cooperation in the sectors traditionally covered by this type of agreement, namely industry, trade promotion, agriculture, science and technology and energy. Special attention was given in the agreement to environment-related questions. The agreement set up a joint council, responsible for its management. As regards trade, the two parties granted one another most favoured nation treatment.

After the **invasion of Kuwait by Iraq** at the beginning of August 1990, the Community as a body took the decisions required for the imposition of a complete embargo on trade with the two countries. This embargo was lifted as concerns Kuwait after its liberation[4]. On September 27, 1990, the Community and its Member States on the one hand and the Gulf Cooperation Council and its States on the other condemned the invasion of Kuwait by Iraq and agreed actively to implement their cooperation agreement and to open negotiations on a free trade agreement. At the Joint GCC-European Union Cooperation Council of 20 July 1995, the two parties reiterated yet again their commitment to the speedy conclusion of the ongoing free trade negotiations.

The two parties see the EEC-GCC agreement as a complement to and not a substitute for the **Euro-Arab dialogue**, but progress is even slower in this last area. It was in February 1974, in the heat of the oil crisis sparked off by the Arab countries[5], that the Council accepted the principle of the dialogue proposed by the Commission. This dialogue was to be built not on the burning issue of energy, but on themes such as technology transfer, encouragement of investment, commercial cooperation, agriculture, labour force problems and cultural exchanges. The Community saw it as an original attempt at establishing closer relations with a group of developing countries. The States deliberately took second fiddle to the two regional organizations, the European Community and the Arab League.

Over the years, different specialized groups and working commissions covering economic, technical, social and cultural matters have met in the framework of the Euro-Arab dialogue, but without making a great deal of headway. Political headway has been even less forthcoming. The French Presidency called a Euro-Arab Ministerial Conference on December 22, 1989 in Paris. This meeting was outside the formal framework of the Euro-Arab dialogue,

---

1   OJ L119, 07.05.1994 and OJ L130, 14.06.1995.

2   OJ C78, 18.03.1996.

3   OJ L54, 25.02.1989.

4   OJ L213, 09.08.1990 and OJ L60, 07.03.1991.

5   See the chapter on Energy.

but its main purpose was to set the dialogue off on a fresh track. The informal nature of the debates proved to be a winning formula. The Ministers published two texts on the restructuring of the Euro-Arab dialogue with a view to making it more efficient. The political side of the dialogue is henceforth to be implemented through an annual "troika" Ministerial meeting, which can decide to convene Euro-Arab plenary Ministerial conferences. The economic, technical, social and cultural aspects of the dialogue remain in the hands of the General Committee, which is the central body and guides and monitors the activities of the three working commissions on economic, technical and social and cultural questions. The General Committee meets annually prior to the "troika" Ministerial meeting, to which it submits a report and recommendations.

Asia, Oceania

In 1994 the Commission launched a **new Strategy for Asia**, founded on a development partnership and on political dialogue[1], which was approved by the Essen European Council in December 1995. These priorities include notably: backing cooperation schemes aimed at safeguarding peace and security; improving Europe's image in Asia and creating a climate conducive to the development of trade and investment; and improving coordination in the management of development aid so that the region's less prosperous countries experience economic growth and poverty is reduced. This new policy was solemnly launched at the Euro-Asia summit of 1 and 2 March 1996, which brought together the Heads of State or Government of the European Union, of the seven ASEAN member countries, of China, Japan and South Korea. The summit was concluded by statement which underlines in particular the desire of all parties to build a new partnership between the two continents, step up political dialogue and expand relations and cooperation in several areas.

The Asian countries were covered by a declaration of intent by the Community on their behalf annexed to the Act of Accession of the United Kingdom. The countries of **Southern Asia (India, Pakistan, Bangladesh, Sri Lanka)** were dealt a severe blow by the accession of the United Kingdom to the Community, for they lost the preferential links which existed within the Commonwealth. The Community attempted to compensate for this loss, without however watering down the privileged relationship which it had with the countries of Africa, the Caribbean and the Pacific (ACP), dealt with in the part of this Chapter on development aid.

The Community thus signed commercial and economic cooperation agreements with Sri Lanka[2], Pakistan[3], Bangladesh[4] and India[5]. In the framework of these agreements, the Commission has implemented cooperation activities relating to rural development, food aid, trade promotion and scientific and industrial cooperation. The Commission furthermore applied the system of compensation of export earnings to the least advanced countries in the region, notably Bangladesh and Nepal. Despite this action, combined with food aid and preferential agreements for trade in textiles[6], the Community's efforts have fallen far short of pulling these countries out of their state of under-development. The new agreement concluded with India is an advanced framework cooperation agreement emphasizing economic cooperation and private sector investment, intellectual property rights, technology

---

1   COM (94) 314.
2   OJ L247, 23.09.1975.
3   OJ L168, 28.06.1976 and OJ L108, 25.04.1986.
4   OJ L319, 19.11.1976.
5   OJ L328, 16.11.1981.
6   OJ L255, 05.09.1987 and OJ L410, 31.12.1992.

transfer and diversification of economic and trade relations[1]. Similar **non-preferential agreements, called "third generation"**, comprising three areas of cooperation, namely trade, economic and development cooperation, and making respect for human rights a key condition for the development of dialogue and partnership have been concluded with Mongolia[2], Sri Lanka[3], Vietnam[4] and Nepal[5].

Community aid has had a more positive impact in the countries belonging to the **Association of South-East Asian Nations (ASEAN)**, which comprises **Brunei, Indonesia, Malaysia, the Philippines, Singapore, Thailand and Vietnam**. The cooperation agreement between the Community and most of these countries dates back to 1980[6]. It is completed by trade agreements on manioc from Thailand and Indonesia[7] and on textiles from the five countries[8] granting better access for their products to the Community markets without major commercial problems. The Community supports the strengthening of cooperation between these countries in the context of ASEAN, provided that it is integrated into an open multilateral exchange system.

The Community clearly would not wish the forthcoming industrialization of these countries to create similar competition problems to those which it has been experiencing for a number of years with the **Republic of Korea**. After the war and the domestic difficulties of this country, the beginning of the eighties saw a return to normal relations between the Community and South Korea. The Community welcomed the stated intentions of this country to diversify its trade geographically and took it at its word with a voluntary-restraint agreement for its textile exports[9]. The rapid industrialization of this country in the second half of the eighties, however, gave several causes for Community concern: the degree of openness of the Korean market, the abolition of restrictive legislation on foreign investment and equal treatment for foreign and Korean investors; non-discrimination, particularly in the areas of the protection of intellectual property and the problem of diversifying Korean foreign trade; industrial policy and competition problems in the shipbuilding sector. These problems could be better faced in the context of the trade and cooperation agreement that the EU is negotiating with the Republic of Korea. The aim of this non-preferential agreement is to provide a framework for trade, economic and industrial cooperation, scientific and technological cooperation and cultural and environmental cooperation. The agreement would be based on respect for democratic principles and human rights.

Relations between the Community and **China**, after the retrogression that followed the events of Tiananmen Square on June 4, 1989, are marking a steady improvement. A 1978 framework trade agreement evolved into the 1985 trade and economic cooperation agreement covering industrial and technical fields[10] and trade in textiles[11]. Imports of products not liberalized at Community level from China and the other Asean countries with State trade (North Korea and Viet Nam) continue to be subject to arrangements differing substantially from one Member State. However, the import quotas to be opened by the Member States are set up each year by the Council[12]. In a communication of July 1995, which forms part of the new strategy for Asia, the Commission underlines China's importance for Europe

---

1   OJ L223, 27.08.1994.
2   OJ L41, 18.02.1993.
3   OJ L85, 19.04.1995.
4   OJ L136, 07.06. 1996.
5   OJ L137, 08.06.1996.
6   OJ L144, 10.06.1980.
7   OJ L219, 28.07.1982 and OJ L347, 12.12.1990.
8   OJ L233, 19.08.1987 and OJ L255, 05.09.1987.
9   OJ L263, 14.09.1987.
10   OJ L250, 19.09.1985.
11   OJ L380, 31.12.1988 and OJ L104, 06.05.1995.
12   See, for example, OJ L66, 10.03.1994.

and the many areas of joint interest where closer relations are required in the future[1]. It calls for dialogue in various areas to promote mutual understanding and identify common interests, and for a closer cooperation programme focusing on human resources, continuing economic reform, measures to alleviate poverty, environmental protection, business coop-eration and closer links of research. These guidelines were approved by the Madrid Euro-pean Council of December 1995.

Japan poses problems of a completely different nature for the Euro-pean Union. Japan has a huge trade surplus with the Community, with its exports to the EU running at three times its imports from it. Japan is at an advantage compared with the other industrialized countries due to such specificities as a limited social security budget, low military expenditure and low aid level to the developing countries. But the success of Japanese policy is chiefly due to certain basic economic factors: strong competitive-ness and productivity, rigid organization of the domestic market, inte-grated industrial and trade strategy working towards precise and planned objectives. As regards more specifically trade relations with the EU, the determinant factors in the disequilibrium are: the concentration of Japa-nese exports on a limited number of sectors, high quality, leading-edge products, marketed with highly effective marketing methods supported by a favourable financing system; and, on the other side of the equation, the closing of the Japanese market by various technical and administrative barriers as well as by prevalent Japanese national habits and attitudes. Nevertheless, the Community is becoming an increasingly important trad-ing partner for Japan because of the size of the single European market and the efforts made to develop trade and cooperation.

Closer relations between the Community and Japan culminated in the adoption, on July 18, 1991, of a joint declaration similar to those defining the Community's relations with the United States and Canada. It sets out the general principles and objectives of cooperation between the two parties, notably stipulating that access to respective markets must be equitable and offer comparable opportunities through the removal of obstacles to trade and investments. It also stipulates the framework for dialogue, with annual summits and other meetings. As regards more especially trade in motor vehicles, the Community and Japan agreed on July 31, 1991 on a solution aiming at gradual liberalization of the Commu-nity market as part of the completion of the Single Market, while avoiding market distortion caused by exports from Japan[2].

The first joint initiative between the Community and Japan is the consolidation of the EC-Japan industrial cooperation centre[3]. Situated in Tokyo, this Centre seeks to contribute to industrial cooperation between the Community and Japan, notably through organizing management training programmes for the executives of European companies, supply-ing information on the Japanese industrial environment and its possibili-ties, and running programmes for European specialists in alternative energies. In 1993 a new method of analysis of trade relations between the European Union and Japan was devised, the Trade Assessment Mecha-

1   COM (95) 279, 5 July 1995.
2   See the heading above on sectoral commercial policy measures.
3   OJ L144, 26.05.1992.

nism (TAM), through which both parties cooperate to reach an objective picture of how European products are faring on the Japanese market.

In November 1994, the European Union obtained, on the one hand, the establishment of an EU-Japan equal-treatment arrangement, comparable to that which exists between the US and Japan, to ensure the equal treatment of American and European products in Japan, and on the other, the invitation of European industry representatives to Japanese Government discussions on public procurement. In addition, the elimination of certain specific obstacles which prevented European goods from penetrating the Japanese market was also achieved. In a communication entitled "Europe and Japan: the next steps", the Commission defines its new strategy for securing greater access to the Japanese market, by emphasizing economic cooperation and political dialogue, in order to reduce the EU's trade deficit and, in the longer term, to promote structural changes[1].

Australia and **New Zealand** have also been at odds with the European Community since the entry into force of the Common Agricultural Policy and more especially since the entry of the United Kingdom to the Community. The UK had in fact always been the main outlet for the agricultural produce of these two countries and although it tried to protect their interests on its accession, the integration of the United Kingdom into the Community seriously upset trading relations with Australia and New Zealand, relations largely due to the cultural, social and political affinities of these two countries with the European Union, which is their major economic partner, if account is taken of trade in goods and services and investments as a whole. The agricultural problems that had dominated relations until the early 1990s having at last disappeared from the forestage following the entry into force of the WTO agreement on agriculture, the EU's relations with both Australia and New Zealand are in the process of being strengthened.

The Community and Australia in fact have a similar viewpoint on many of the international political problems. On the economic front, both parties are, however, satisfied with their 1982 agreement, relating to transfers of nuclear material from Australia to the European Atomic Energy Community[2] and their cooperation, since 1986, on research, technology and, since 1991, the environment. The completion of the Single Market, the reform of the Common Agricultural Policy and Australia's new industrial policy are pushing for closer trade links between this country and the Community. Indeed, in 1994, the EU and Australia signed agreements on trade in wine[3], on sheepmeat and goatmeat[4] as well as on cooperation in science and technology[5].

The trade problems between the Community and New Zealand are also in principle settled thanks to arrangements between the two parties entered into force applying to imports of cheese[6] and sheepmeat and goatmeat[7]. In addition to the amount of imports permitted every year, these arrangements introduced a price surveillance system to ensure balance between imported and home-produced products and suspending the levy at zero,

---

1   COM (95)73, 8 March 1995.
2   OJ L281, 04.10.1982.
3   OJ L86, 31.03.1994.
4   OJ L308, 27.11.1984.
5   OJ L188, 22.07.1994.
6   OJ L308, 27.11.1984.
7   OJ L47, 18.02.1994.

on the proviso that the conditions laid down in the framework of the price surveillance system are satisfied.

North America

The European Union is the biggest trading partner of the **United States** (the bilateral exchanges totalling US$ 200 billion, in 1993, and the direct investments between the two parties amounting to US$ 460 billion) and is linked to this country by culture, tradition and a sense of fellow feeling and by common economic and political interests embodied within international organizations such as the OECD and NATO. From the political viewpoint, the United States has always supported European integration. This has not prevented strong economic antagonism between the two richest regions of the planet.

The rapid historical changes in Europe at the beginning of the 1990s breathed fresh life into relations between the United States and the Community. The United States grasped the fact that the completion of the internal market was irreversible and that the Community, heavily dependent on international trade, could not become a closed "fortress Europe". Furthermore, it understood that a strong and united Western Europe was more necessary than ever given the political and economic upheaval in Eastern Europe. The changing nature of the relationship led to the adoption on November 22, 1990 by the United States on the one hand and by the Community and its Member States on the other of a joint **transatlantic declaration**. Considering that their relationship is a vital factor for political stability in a changing world, the two parties confirmed their commitment to continuing and developing cooperation on an equal footing and, for this purpose, they agreed to consult one another on important subjects of common interest and to intensify their dialogue in a formal contact structure.

The EU-US summit on 3 December 1995 approved a **new transatlantic agenda** and joint action plan completing the Transatlantic Declaration of 1990 and heralding new areas of cooperation between the two partners. The cooperation is now organized around four pillars: promoting peace, stability, democracy and development throughout the world, responding to global challenges, contributing to the expansion of world trade and closer economic relations, and establishing closer ties between the partners. In addition, an agreement between the Community and the United States established a cooperation programme in the field of higher education and vocational training[1].

The transatlantic dialogue has already permitted a better coordination of respective policies concerning aid to Central and Eastern European countries, Russia and the Independent States, the conflict and the management of peace in former Yugoslavia and the Middle East peace process. In the Uruguay Round, the Blair-House pre-agreement, concluded on 28 November 1992 between the United States and the EU, was a pre-condition for the conclusion of the GATT multilateral trade negotiations. Moreover, a number of trade differences have been settled, notably the ones on trade in large civil aircraft[2] on veterinary

---

1   OJ L279, 22.11.1995.
2   OJ L301, 17.10.1992.

matters concerning beef and pigmeat[1] and on openness in the field of public procurement of the two parties[2].

However, other disputes persist, particularly on American retaliatory measures connected with the Community hormones Directive and on the anti-dumping duties imposed on Community steel products. Moreover, although the dialogue is intended to encourage convergence between regulations with an impact on the economy in the Community and the United States, a new unilateral action by the United States, in 1996, has again troubled the relations between the two parties. It is the Helms-Burton law, under which the United States threaten lawsuits against third country companies maintaining trade relations with former American companies expropriated since 1959 in Cuba. Since a large number of European companies have relations with nationalized companies in Cuba and neither they or their governments can accept the interference of a third country in their affairs, this legislation risks to envenom transatlantic relations. Moreover, the United States prepare similar laws against Iran and Libya and complain about the opening-up of the EU vis-à-vis China. On 22 April 1996 the Council expressed its deep concern about the extra-territorial implications of new and prospective US legislation and invited the relevant experts to draw up all WTO and other options regarding EU action in defence of its rights and interests, including the possibility of countermeasures.

The Community's relations with **Canada** have been just as tumultuous, despite the cooperation agreement between Euratom and Canada on the peaceful use of atomic energy, which dates back to 1959 and was renewed in 1991[3], that between the Community and Canada on commercial and economic cooperation adopted in 1976[4] and the 1981 fisheries agreement[5]. Canadian development policy for the country's most difficult regions, combined with various controls on economic activity and investment, have culminated in extreme trade protectionism, based on restrictions and import quotas and on the recourse, and occasionally misuse, of the safeguard rules provided for in the GATT agreements.

High-level meetings were however launched in 1988, giving renewed momentum to EEC-Canadian relations. This culminated in the adoption on November 22, 1990 of a joint declaration based on the preferential relations introduced by the 1976 framework cooperation agreement which reinforces the institutional framework for consultations in order to give them a long-term horizon. The new propensity to cooperate is manifest in sensible fields such as animal-health regulations and trade in alcoholic beverages[6].

While the relations between the EU and Canada are generally good, some specific problems persist. Thus, despite the existence of the 1993 fisheries agreement between the EU and Canada, this country's legislation allows action to be taken against foreign vessels outside the Canadian 200-mile fishing limit, in contravention of the United Nations Convention on the Law of the Sea, thus leading to small "fisheries battles" with the Union or some of its members. The new fisheries agreement between the EU and Canada, concluded in the framework of the North-West Atlantic Fisheries Organization (NAFO) after the strong protest of the EU for the

---

1   OJ L68, 19.03.1993.
2   OJ L125, 20.05.1993 and OJ L146, 17.06.1993. See this heading in the chapter on the common market.
3   OJ 60, 24.11.1959 and OJ C215, 17.08.1991.
4   OJ L260, 24.09.1976.
5   OJ L379, 31.12.1981 and OJ L340, 31.12.1993.
6   OJ L71, 15.03.1989.

Canadian authorities stopping of a Spanish fishing vessel in March 1995, is designed to put an end to such situations[1].

Latin America

As seen in the section of this Chapter devoted to development aid, the Community has been granting aid to Latin America as a group of non-associated countries for many years. The Community is aware of its responsibility for development in these countries, home to some of the poorest people in the world. This awareness has been further accentuated since the entry of Spain and Portugal to the Community, two countries which share the same cultural heritage with Latin America

In 1982, the Argentinean invasion of the Falkland Islands, a territory dependent on the United Kingdom and associated to the Community, led the latter to suspend imports from Argentina for several months, until after the Argentinean military defeat. It was in 1990 that a framework trade and economic cooperation agreement was concluded between the Community and **Argentina**, introducing several innovations and notably a clause referring to respect of democratic principles and of human rights as a prerequisite for any cooperation between the two parties[2]. Similar framework cooperation agreements, termed third generation agreements, have been concluded between the Community and **Chile**[3], **Mexico**[4], **Paraguay**[5], **Uruguay**[6] and **Brazil**[7]. A new economic partnership and political consultation agreement between the EU and Mexico is to be concluded soon[8].

Efforts have been stepped up in the area of industrial cooperation and a systematic strategy incorporating training activities has been developed for use in promoting European technologies and investments in SMEs, with the aim of boosting local output and export capacities. Financial and technical cooperation with the Latin American countries, mentioned in the part of this chapter on development aid, is targeted on the poorest developing countries. The Community's solidarity with the Andean countries which are fighting to combat drug abuse has been given tangible demonstration with the extension to Colombia, Bolivia, Peru and Ecuador of the generalized tariff preferences applied to certain of the least advanced developing countries[9]. In 1991, these arrangements were extended to Costa Rica, El Salvador, Guatemala, Honduras, Nicaragua and Panama.

Alongside these bilateral relations and financial and technical cooperation, the Community has established relations with regional groupings in Latin America. It is thus that, in 1984, the Community concluded a cooperation agreement with the countries of the **Andean Pact (Bolivia, Colombia, Ecuador, Peru and Venezuela)**[10]. This was followed in 1986 by a framework agreement for commercial and economic cooperation and development with the countries of the **Central American common market (Costa Rica, El Salvador, Guatemala, Honduras, Nicaragua)** and with

1	OJ L327, 30.12.1995.
2	OJ L295, 26.10.1990.
3	OJ L79, 26.03.1991.
4	OJ L340, 11.12.1991.
5	OJ L313, 30.10.1992.
6	OJ L94, 08.04.1992.
7	OJ C163, 30.06.1992.
8	COM (95) 3, 8 February 1995.
9	OJ L308, 08.11.1990.
10	OJ L153, 08.06.1984.

Panama[1]. The new cooperation agreements signed in 1993 between the Community and the Andean Pact countries, on the one hand, and Central American countries and Panama, on the other, place particular emphasis on the consolidation of the regional integration systems and on the respect of democratic principles and human rights[2]. The main aims of the agreement are: to stimulate, diversify and improve trade; to encourage cooperation between industrialists; and to stimulate scientific and technical cooperation.

The European Union is also providing technical assistance to the common market between the **Mercosur** countries (**Argentina, Brazil, Paraguay and Uruguay**). In the wake of the conclusions of the Corfu and Essen European Councils and the Solemn Joint Declaration between the European Union and Mercosur[3], an interregional framework commercial and economic cooperation Agreement between the EU and Mercosur was signed in Madrid on 15 December 1995. Aimed at strengthening existing ties and preparing for eventual association, this Agreement provides: regular, institutionalized political dialogue; trade cooperation leading to trade liberalization; economic cooperation geared to promoting reciprocal investment; cooperation on regional integration, intended to allow Mercosur to draw upon the experience of the European Union; and a wider cooperation in fields of mutual interest, such as culture, information and communication, training on integration and the prevention of drug abuse.

A political declaration, adopted in Rome on 20 December 1990 between the Community and the Latin American countries belonging to the **Rio Group (Argentina, Bolivia, Brazil, Chile, Colombia, Ecuador, Mexico, Paraguay, Peru, Uruguay and Venezuela)** aims at strengthening links between the two groups of countries. In this document, the parties defined several general objectives relating to the principles of democracy, human rights, the right to self-determination and the specific common objectives such as reducing armament levels, economic development and the protection of the environment. The declaration also stipulates the focal areas for cooperation between the two groups of countries: trade, economic cooperation, investment, reduction of debt levels, the environment, the fight against drug abuse and terrorism.

The new opening provided by the Uruguay Round Agreements and the developments in the various integration processes in Latin America are the two vital elements for intensifying cooperation between the EU and Latin American countries. In giving its support to the development efforts of the latter (at bilateral level) and to their integration efforts (at multilateral level) the European Union hopes to contribute to the political stability and economic and social development of a region of the world which, despite its current economic and social difficulties, is rich in raw materials and is a vast potential market.

1   OJ L172, 30.06.1986.
2   OJ C255, 20.09.1993.
3   OJ C377, 31.12.1994.

Bibliography on the EU in the world

▫ BACOT-DECRIAUD Michele, PLANTIN Marie-Claude, *L'Union européenne: une contribution communautaire à la sécurité et à la défense de l'Europe*, CERIEP, Lyon, 1994.

▫ BATTIAU Michel (sous la dir. de), *Le commerce international de marchandises de l'Europe occidentale*, Éditions Nathan, Paris, 1994.

▫ BLANCHET Therese, PIIPPONEN Risto, WESTMAN-CLEMENT, *The Agreement on the European Economic Area (EEA)*, Clarendon Press, Oxford, 1994.

▫ BOURGEOIS Jacques, BERROD Frédérique, GIPPINI FOURNIER Eric, (ed.), *The Uruguay Round Results. Presses Interuniversitaires Européennes*, Bruxelles, 1995.

▫ BREUSS Fritz (ed.), *The World Economy after the Uruguay Round*, Fachverlag, Wien, 1995.

▫ COFFEY Peter, *The EC and the United States*, Pinter Publishers, London, 1993.

▫ COMMISSION EUROPÉENNE, *Le courrier ACP-CEE*, revue mensuelle.

  - *L'Uruguay Round: un accord global au bénéfice de l'économie mondiale*, OPOCE, Luxembourg, 1994.

  - *Conventions ACP-CE de Lomé: Recueil de textes XVIII*, OPOCE, Luxembourg, 1995.

  - *GATS: Accord général sur le commerce des services. Un guide pour les entreprises*, OPOCE, Luxembourg, 1995.

▫ CONSEIL DES MINISTRES ACP-CEE, Secrétariat, *Rapport annuel*, Bruxelles.

▫ EECKHOUT Piet, *The European Internal Market and International Trade. A Legal Analysis*, Clarendon Press, Oxford University Press, Oxford, 1994.

▫ EUROPEAN COMMISSION, "EU - ACP Cooperation", *the ACP - EU Courier*, special issue, May 1994.

  - *AL-INVEST: A European Programme for Business Cooperation and Partnership with Latin America: Institutional Operator's Handbook*, OOPEC, Luxembourg, 1994.

▫ HOLLAND Martin, *European Union Common Foreign Policy. From EPC to CFSP Joint Action and South Africa*, St. Martin's Press, 1995.

▫ HOWELL John, *Understanding Eastern Europe. The Context of Change*, Kogan Page, London, 1994.

▫ JOPP Mathias, *The Strategic Implications of European Integration*, Brasseys and The International Institute for Strategic Studies, London, 1994.

▫ KHAVAND Fereydoun, *Le nouvel ordre commercial mondial. Du GATT à l'OMC*, Nathan éditions, Paris, 1995.

▫ KUPERUS Tom, *Expanding the European Peace Zone Eastward. Reducing the Importance of Geopolitics in Russia's Foreign Policy*, CEPS Document N° 99, Brussels, 1996.

▫ LIPPERT Barbara, SCHNEIDER Heinrich (ed.), *Monitoring Association and Beyond: The European Union and the Visegrad States*, Europa Union Verlag, Bonn, 1995.

□ MESSERLIN Patrick, *La nouvelle organisation mondiale du commerce,* Institut Français des relations internationales (IFRI) et Bordas/Dunod, Paris, 1995.

□ NDOUNG Jean-Pierre, *L'évolution du Fonds européen de développement prévu par les Conventions de Yaoundé et de Lomé,* Éditions Bruylant, 1994.

□ PAEMEN Hugo, BENSCH Alexandra, *Du GATT à l'OMC. La Communauté européenne dans l'Uruguay Round,* Leuven University Press, Leuven, 1995.

□ RAHMANI Tahar, BEKKOUCHE Adda, *Coopération décentralisée. L'Union européenne en Méditerranée occidentale,* Éditions Continent Europe, Paris, 1995.

□ RUPNIK J., HASSNER P., TATU M., BRANDS M., HAVENAAR R., *Challenges in the East,* SDU Servicecentrum Uitgeverij, The Hague, 1995.

□ TELO', Mario (sous la dir. de), *L'Union Européenne et les défis de l'élargissement,* Université Libre de Bruxelles, Bruxelles, 1994.

□ THUROW Lester, *Head to Head. The Coming Economic Battle among Japan, Europe and America,* Nicholas Brealey Publ., London, 1994.

□ VAN EEKELEN Willem, *The Security Agenda for 1996. Background and Proposals,* CEPS Paper n° 64, Bruxelles, 1995.

APPRAISAL AND OUTLOOK

Since the first stone was laid on July 25, 1952, the date when the ECSC Treaty entered into force, the process of European construction has never halted. Naturally enough, work accelerates at some points and slows at others. It also gets more complicated as the construction becomes more advanced. Clearly, it became more difficult to reach agreement when the team expanded from six to nine, then ten, then twelve and now fifteen. But work has never really been suspended, even when de Gaulle put into effect France's 1965 "empty chair" policy. At no point has it been necessary to take a step backwards or dismantle part of the construction already completed, which is exceptional for an experimental venture on such a scale, without precedent in human history. How is it that such an ambitious and audacious venture has been so successful that it can consolidate, progress and extend day by day into new fields and that it is so attractive to those not participating in it? It can only be that the construction method is sound and has been resolutely observed. Brick by brick, provision by provision, the edifice has been built up and is still expanding; every new provision fits so well into the existing ones that it fills a gap while consolidating the surrounding provisions. A new surge forward such as the one decided in December 1991 at Maastricht does not imply that the old method has been abandoned. It simply implies the new use of the progressive method for the construction of a new floor, the EMU, on the existing edifice and of two new edifices next to it, the CFSP and the JHA, all three joined under the roof of the European Union.

European construction can be just as sound a process in the future, if the method is conserved, if not too many gaps are left in the construction, if solidarity can enable it to negotiate the difficulties and if the latecomers are swept along by the tide of progress. Provided that these conditions are satisfied, economic and monetary union on the one hand and political union on the other are not hazardous ventures, but the logical continuation of the construction of the big market. The outlook for them will be examined after an appraisal of the European construction venture.

Appraisal of Community policies

The fifties and sixties were the glorious years of **customs union**, first of all in the coal and steel sector within the ECSC and then for all industrial and agricultural products within the EEC. The removal of customs duties and of quantitative restrictions on imports and exports, followed by the introduction of a common customs tariff on July 1, 1968, one and a half years before scheduled in the EEC Treaty, filled the apprentices of European construction with enthusiasm. These measures moreover formed the foundations of the edifice and considerably boosted intra-Community trade.

And yet customs union was not complete at the end of the sixties. It was not even complete by the end of the eighties, as demonstrated by the continued presence of customs officers at the borders between Member States. But these "customs officers" were no longer collecting customs duties, since these had been abolished by customs union. They checked that the charges had been removed on products for export or transit and collected the consumption taxes of the country of destination of the goods.

In any case, the **common market** was not a single or internal market as sought by the EEC Treaty. This Treaty stipulated that in addition to customs duties and quantitative restrictions, all measures having equivalent effect should be removed. However, although a precise timetable was set for the abolition of barriers to trade falling into the first two categories, no such provision was made for the third category. It was thanks to this loophole that national administrations were able to keep old technical, fiscal and administrative obstacles to trade and were even able to introduce new ones, believing that they thus protected their national industry and indirectly their own existence. Despite progress made in the area of the free movement of goods, individuals, services and capital, the common market, at the end of the eighties, still stopped well short of a single internal market. It was this shortfall between the Treaty aims and reality which gave Jacques Delors the simple yet brilliant idea of completing the Treaty of Rome by setting a deadline for the completion of the Single Market, an act accomplished by the Single European Act.

This said, it should be stressed that contrary to what is thought by some, the seventies and the eighties were not the lost years of European construction; on the contrary. They were the years which saw the development of support policies for the common market. These are not only policies expressly provided for in the Treaty in areas such as agriculture, fisheries and competition, but also those mentioned more vaguely, such as regional and social policy, or not at all, such as environment and consumer affairs policy.

In other words, the Member States adopted the majority of the provisions making up the policies examined in this book without being under any contractual obligation to do so. They acted rather because, on each occasion, they found it both useful and necessary to make progress towards integration in new fields. Very wisely, the founding fathers of the Community did not require that the Member States give up part of their sovereignty in return for the implementation of Community policies in the first stages of economic integration. They left that for later. It was, in fact, only little by little, after weighing up the pros and cons of each of the measures proposed by the Commission, that the Member States were able to adopt hundreds of Regulations and Directives underpinning Community policies, each time removing a chink of their national sovereignty.

It was thus that the internal market was completed on January 1, 1993, twenty-three years after the completion of customs union. More precisely, this signifies the full achievement of the four freedoms: freedom of movement within the European economic area for goods, persons, services and capital. From this date, a lorry loaded in Barcelona and headed for Amsterdam and a coach full of tourists from Berlin and making for Rimini can cross the borders of the Member States without being stopped for fiscal or police controls. Students can study in the country of their choice, employees and self-employed workers can search out the best working conditions in the Community, individuals can take out insurance and negotiate loans with an insurance company or bank in any of the Member States, choosing the one offering the best terms, and so on.

Is the completion of the internal market as simple as that? From the angle of what is visible and striking to the individual, it is that simple, but this eye-catching outcome requires the adoption of a range of Community Directives, tax provisions and joint police measures to prevent fraud and illegal trafficking. The effort is worthwhile. For exporting and importing companies, the absence of controls at the European Union's internal frontiers will signify the end of many costs: internal administrative costs, such as general, staff and computer expenses rendered necessary by the need to complete forms in order to cross borders; external costs directly related to the crossing of frontiers, such as those of customs agents and other advice services; costs arising from a backlog of customs procedures, such as storage and transport costs for goods stuck at customs posts. In addition to these costs directly arising from border formalities and related administrative expenses, the Community industry will save a great deal of money due to the fact that it will no longer have to bring its products into line with diverging technical and administrative regulations.

Despite this, the Community's Single Market, in place since January 1, 1993, does not resemble exactly a State's domestic market. It lacks first and foremost the monetary stability provided by the irrevocable setting of exchange parities for the currencies of the Member States or, even better, the replacement of these currencies by a single currency. This fact was grasped as early as the beginning of the seventies. The original Member States of the Community, anticipating its enlargement and the difficulties to which this could give rise, felt that the simple coordination of their economic and monetary policies provided for by Article 104 was insufficient. On March 22, 1971 they declared their political commitment to an **economic and monetary union** meaning, among other things, the total and irreversible convertibility of their currencies, the elimination of fluctuation margins around exchange rates, the irrevocable setting of exchange parities and the full liberalization of capital movements. Although this bold venture was premature, given the international monetary environment and the level of the Community's economic integration, it has nevertheless proved very useful. It enabled the introduction and testing out of many accompanying policies and of monetary instruments which were passed on, on April 13, 1979, from the monetary snake system to the European Monetary System. Improved and reinforced versions of these instruments - a monetary fluctuation band, the European Monetary Cooperation Fund, the ECU - will continue to be used during the first two stages of the economic and monetary union decided upon in Maastricht.

Economic policy follows a step behind monetary policy. Vaguely provided for in the Treaty of Rome, which called on the Member States to consider their economic policy as a matter of common interest, to consult one another in this area and coordinate their economic policies, it swelled in importance with the decision of the Member States to pursue the goal of economic and monetary union. Already by the early years of the seventies, all the requirements of the Treaty concerning notably the short-term coordination of economic policies, had been satisfied. Community financial solidarity, reflected through medium-term financial support, the New Community Instrument, EIB loans and aid from the various Community funds, have been developed to an extent not provided for in the Treaty of Rome. However, if further progress is to be made down the road to economic and monetary union, there must be compensation of the constraints on the system, implying greater coordination of national economic policies, as stipulated by the Maastricht Treaty, leading to the gradual removal of structural and regional disparities between the Member States. A step in this direction was taken by the Edinburgh European Council of December 1992 with the adoption of the "Delors II Package" relating to the revision of the Structural Funds and to the European growth initiative.

The Community's **regional policy** is one of the features of economic and monetary union. Its beginnings date back to the above-mentioned Resolution of March 22, 1971 and to the declaration of the October 1972 Paris Summit. The latter mapped out the path of the Community's regional action: the coordination of the Member States' regional policies and the creation of a Regional Development Fund. It is thus only since the middle of the seventies that the Community has had a regional policy worthy of the name and it is only since the beginning of the eighties that this policy has had relatively large sums at its disposal. But, with each enlargement of the Community, regional disparities worsen. The effort required of the weakest Member States to attain the increasingly more ambitious goals set in common must be compensated by a transfer of resources from the richer Member States to attenuate these regional disparities. This principle is in the interests of both the poorer and richer partners since the economic development of the former represents market growth for the latter. It has been followed to date, notably on the enlargement of Spain and Portugal, when IMPs were adopted for the Mediterranean regions; and in the process of completing the internal market, with the doubling of the structural fund resources between 1987 and 1993. The fresh financial effort decided upon in Edinburgh (160 billion ECU over five years, or three times the amount of the Marshall plan, which permitted the reconstruction of

Europe after the world war) will enable the weaker Member States to keep up the pace of economic and monetary union.

The regional imbalances are matched by social imbalances which must be corrected by the Community's **social policy**. In the preamble to the Treaty of Rome, the Member States declare that they resolutely intend to tackle these disparities through the continual improvement of the working and living conditions of their populations. However, given the lack of specific provisions in the Treaty, this ambitious objective was, in the first fifteen years of the Community's existence, pursued chiefly through economic and technological progress which was boosted by the process of economic integration. It is certain that the closer economies become, the more social problems are similar and the more common solutions must be found. Thus, the acceleration in the process of European integration since the middle of the eighties has resulted in major progress in Community social policy, spanning fields such as vocational training, social protection and worker health and safety. This process will have to be stepped up in the economic and monetary union, which will take out of governments' hands many economic and monetary instruments and hence their ability to tackle their social problems alone. The Community Charter of fundamental social rights adopted by eleven Heads of State and Government at Strasbourg in December 1989 and reaffirmed at Maastricht in December 1991 is not therefore a theoretical or ideological device. The improvement of living and working conditions of workers that it implies is the social bedrock on which the EMU will be built. The agreement on social policy concluded in Maastricht between the United Kingdom and its eleven partners illustrates both the determination of the latter to forge forward in the social arena and the end of the era where one Member State could veto progress despite the commitment of its partners to a given policy.

Another Community policy which has also gone beyond the requirements of the EEC Treaty is the one on **taxation**. The Treaty simply stipulated that the rule of fiscal neutrality must be respected in intra-Community trade. The Member States, however, in the first decade of the Community's existence, succeeded in replacing their cumulative multi-stage turnover taxes with value added tax, the structures of which have been closely harmonized. Although the aims of the Treaty in the fiscal field had been attained and even overshot since the end of the sixties, fiscal harmonization could not be restricted to the harmonization of the structure of turnover taxes given the Community's aim of completing its internal market and progressing towards economic and monetary union. The abolition of tax frontiers, made possible by the approximation of VAT rates and excise duties and by increased cooperation between national tax authorities, makes a vital contribution to final completion of the internal market. It has rendered obsolete 60 million documents per year and has thus lightened the procedural burden for undertakings and considerably facilitated intra-Community trade. As economic and monetary union advances, company and savings taxes must also be harmonized; other forms of direct taxation will come later. These make up large chunks of national sovereignty which have to be snatched out of the hands of the governments and parliaments of the Member States. The harmonization of direct taxation can thus only further greater integration and real convergence between the Member States' economies.

Tax harmonization also provides a level playing field for competition, to which the EEC Treaty confers the role of economic regulator in the common market. Indeed, **competition policy** is essential for the achievement and maintenance of the common market. While not hindering the freedom of undertakings to engage in international business, it prevents market compartmentalization from being restored by means of international agreements. While not prohibiting cooperation and concentration between small and medium enterprises, it prevents multinational undertakings from securing windfall profits through exploitation of their dominant position or through monopolization of a market by acquisition of independent economic operators. As regards State initiatives, the role of the Community competition policy is not only to prevent national aid schemes that are harmful to intra-Community trade or to the economic activity of the other Member States, but also to limit State intervention to aid which fits in with the prospect of adjusting the structures of the European Union's production mechanism to changes in demand and to the international division of labour. The Community competition policy is thus not only a necessary instrument for completion of the internal market and achievement of the economic and monetary union, but also a complement to Community sectoral policies - industrial, agricultural, energy, transport - aimed at improving production structures.

At the crossroads between the European Union's horizontal and vertical policies, **environment policy**, unheard of in the sixties, was launched by the Paris Summit of October 1972. The first environmental protection programme was adopted as a result in November 1973. On the basis of this programme and its offshoots, an impressive number of Community environmental protection provisions have been adopted in what is record time for a Community policy. It is certainly difficult to evaluate the specific results of the Community measures in this area because the quality objectives that they lay down are incessantly thrust aside by economic development and urbanization. But if Europeans want to preserve their quality of life in the 21st century, the effort must continue and increase. In a European economy which undergoes structural change, the challenge of policy-makers is to take measures which will make it possible painlessly to achieve the objective of growth which is compatible with the essential requirements of the environment. This involves foreseeing the ecological problems of technological development and limiting them from the outset, for example by encouraging the selection of environment friendly products before market launch, the application of stringent safety standards to potentially dangerous manufacturing procedures, the disposal of waste without danger to the environment or to human health and the systematic evaluation of the foreseeable environmental impact of any new economic activity. Moreover the Community cannot work in isolation in this field. Water and air pollution do not respect frontiers. Thus, the fresh economic start of the countries of Central and Eastern Europe, assisted by the West, must go hand in hand with increased consideration of environmental constraints, which have been tragically neglected in the past. This is vital for the survival of Europe and the planet itself and is also a prerequisite for even-handed competition between economies respecting both market laws and human values.

The Single Market forces give rise to a need for the restructuring of Community industry against the backdrop of economic and monetary union. The Treaty signed in Maastricht consequently provides a legal basis for an **industrial policy**. Here too, the Community is not starting from scratch. The Treaties establishing the European Coal and Steel Community and the European Atomic Energy Community constituted sectoral industrial policies in the relevant industrial sectors. Whilst it made no call for an industrial policy, the EEC Treaty itself chiefly regulated the common market in industrial products (rules of competition, approximation of laws, tax provisions...). It assumed that the abolition of protectionist measures and the opening-up of the markets would provide sufficient impetus for the restructuring of sectors and undertakings. In fact, thanks to customs union, the bulk of the production of the Member States industries is traded within the Community. The Community market is the one the best suited to the output of a large number of industrial branches. But since, by means of the technical barriers to trade and the selectivity of public procurement, national protectionism persisted until the early '90s, a limited industrial restructuring and rationalization of production took place at national rather than at Community level. Now that the Single Market has become a reality, small and, above all medium-sized enterprises must adjust to the new conditions of heightened competition. They certainly must, first and foremost, rely on their own efforts to achieve success in the single market. However, the new **enterprise policy** of the Community shores up their efforts. It has three main objectives: to provide a legal framework which lends itself to the setting up and development of European firms; to create an economic environment which helps undertakings to develop fully in the single market; and to encourage cross-border cooperation between SMEs in the Community.

A **research policy** is a vital rung on the ladder of the European Union's industrial development. It is essential for the definition of industrial strategy, for technical progress in high-technology sectors, for the mastery of the Community's energy problems and, finally, for the passage to a post-industrial society. The aims of the Community research policy are to co-ordinate national research policies and to define and implement research programmes of Community interest, i.e. programmes geared to the large market, of interest to all Member States and necessitating technical and human resources which Member States cannot put together individually. Community research and the Joint Research Centre got under way in the nuclear sector with the Euratom Treaty. A large proportion of European research is still related to the energy sector: nuclear safety, energy savings and the development of new energy sources, including thermonuclear fusion. But the failure in the sixties of the joint development of a nuclear reactor family led to a diversification of the projects funded, whether entirely (direct actions) or partially (indirect actions) by the Community Budget. Community research has thus branched out into other fields: information technology and telecommunications, materials technology, biotechnology, environmental problems... The Community must keep up with the rapid progress at world level in science and technology and must step up its own activities alongside those of the Member States. The latter are aware of the challenge. In the Single Act, and then in the Maastricht Treaty, they undertook to strengthen the scientific and technological foundations of European industry and boost its international competitiveness. Increased concertation and coordination in research and development, the emergence of new "European" enterprises in high technology sectors, a more innovative spirit and, last but not least, a firmer grip on Europe's technological future should logically be the fruits of the completed internal market.

Research is a key feature of European **energy policy**, the aim of which is to reduce Europe's dependence and raise the competitiveness of European industry through the development of cheap, safe and clean energies. While the founding fathers did not neglect energy, they could not foresee the manner in which the sector would develop. The ECSC and Euratom Treaties provided the Community with legal instruments for the energy of the past (coal) and that of the future (nuclear). But no provisions were made for what became the dominant energy source in the sixties (oil). When the oil crisis broke out, in 1973, the Community was without means to respond to it, a failing which it paid dear. The crisis was instructive for the Member States, which have since attempted to reduce energy dependence through a common strategy. The Member States now accept the existence, in addition to national energy policies, of a Community structure responsible for coordinating national measures, setting basic energy objectives and implementing independent Community programmes in the energy sector. The European Energy Charter which they have signed provides a strategic framework defining the main political, economic, energy and environmental principles to be respected by countries of both Western Europe and those of Central and Eastern Europe. Cooperation between them in the energy sector is essential since the latter possess abundant energy resources which can be developed through the technical and financial resources of Western countries.

Unlike most other Community policies, **transport policy** was specifically mentioned in the EEC Treaty, even with the specification that it should be a common policy. The founding fathers did not therefore underestimate the impact of transport, notably inland transport, on the free movement of goods within the common market. But they did not predict the major splits which would emerge in this sector because of diverging national interests. The persistence of these splits within the Council blocked for many years several Commission proposals to remove restrictions on transport operations, abolish discrimination and introduce the common rules necessary for the correct operation of the transport market. While during the first thirty years of the Community's existence, progress was made in such matters as social security regulations governing road haulage, the harmonization of access conditions to the profession of haulier, the abolition of tariff discrimination and the harmonization of competition conditions, the vital market of goods carriage by road remained boxed in by a quota system, transport infrastructure was not planned at Community level and air and sea transport remained outside the application scope of the Treaty. It was the 1982 Parliament's proceedings against the Council for failure to act in road haulage liberalization, as well as the prospect of completion of the internal market in 1992, which finally caused the Member States to step on the accelerator in the transport arena. It was thus that the beginning of the 90s saw large-scale liberalization in the areas of road haulage, sea and air transport. This is most fortunate, since the completed internal market is expected to witness strong growth in demand for transport services. Furthermore, the links between the outlying regions and the centre of the EU need to be improved. Transport services and infrastructure adapted to the requirements of the Single Market are in fact essential cogwheels in the process of European integration.

One common policy which has covered a great deal of ground is the **common agricultural policy**. Before the implementation of the Treaty of Rome, agriculture was the sector where there was the greatest State interventionism and where there was the greatest divergence between the interests of the Member States. Competition conditions were so distorted that it was certain that, without a common policy taking over from national policies, agricultural products would not be able to move freely around the fledgling common market. Sustained political commitment was required for the introduction of the first common market organizations, in 1962, their gradual extension to almost all agricultural products and the adoption every year of common prices for these products. The effort was certainly worthwhile, for the common agricultural market thus created provided a guarantee of the Community's supply in foodstuffs at reasonable prices for consumers and stable prices compared with world rates. However, of all the Community's policies, the CAP has been the most controversial. Its critics maintained that it was too expensive for the Community Budget and therefore for the tax-payer, that it produced surpluses in certain areas (the infamous "butter mountains" and "wine lakes") and that it favoured the products of Northern Europe to the detriment of those from the South, leaving the poor farmers poor and making the rich ones richer. These problems culminated in the reform of the CAP at the end of the eighties and at the beginning of the nineties. The latter reform abolished the link between agricultural support and the quantities produced, a link which acted as an incentive to intensify production and push up yield as much as possible, without consideration for the market's ability to absorb this production. Community action in the internal agricultural market will be better balanced and better spread between market and income support. It will respond to the requirements of economic efficiency, Community solidarity and rural development.

The **fisheries policy**, initially a part of the common agricultural policy, gives a good illustration of how a Community policy can develop. It starts out with a few isolated measures reacting to a particular situation or shared problems in a sector and, little by little there is a realization that if the Community achievements are to be safeguarded, other measures are required. The fishing sector having a highly specific social structure and arduous living and working conditions, structural measures were needed to keep fishermen at sea. In 1970, these two wings of the fisheries policy were set up and, at the same time, the freedom of access of fishing vessels from one Member State to the territorial waters of another Member State was proclaimed. This simple principle was, however, very difficult to apply when it became necessary to preserve fishing stocks threatened with exhaustion, when the fishery areas were extended from 3 to 200 nautical miles, when the grounds of certain Member States were much better stocked than those of the others and when the vessels of these other Member States had traditionally fished in grounds which were previously open to all but which had been brought under the sovereignty of their neighbours. Ten years were required to fit the various pieces of the jigsaw puzzle together and thus complete the third wing of the common fisheries policy, that dealing with fishery resources. Once this had been achieved, the Community had in 1983 an additional common policy for which no special provision had been made in the Treaty of Rome. Thanks to this policy, the fishery sector was ensured relatively smooth sailing conditions into the Community's internal market.

The appraisal of the Community policies is, without a shadow of a doubt, positive. The Community has come far since the middle of the fifties. It has brought to a successful conclusion the bulk of the integration programme stipulated in the original Treaties and has gone beyond it in many fields. It is true that the numerous measures that we have examined in this book do not constitute yet a complete policy for the European society of the 21st century; they may even be considered as the prelude of what is still to come; but the distance covered since the mid-fifties is enormous. The **common policies** already have the upper hand over national policies in several vital economic fields: trade, competition, agriculture and fisheries. **Community policies** provide a framework for national policies in many other fields: monetary, economic, social, regional, environmental, research.

Common or Community policies are not rigid. They are constantly evolving, as is normal, to adapt to national and international realities and problems. The constant evolution in Community policies implies that several of them are tending to become common policies, i.e. policies gradually substituting national policies. This is notably true of the monetary, regional, environmental and research policies. The symbiosis between national legal systems and cooperation between national government administrations in the European Union have already reached a level never before seen within an international organization. New European provisions are adopted every day, harmonizing a little more the living and working conditions in the EU and establishing firmer relations between the States and between the citizens of the Union. This is a demonstration of the success of the Community method of making and implementing decisions, an original method founded on the interaction of three institutions, that each defends different but complementary interests: the Commission the common interest, the Council the interests of the Member States, the Parliament the interests of the peoples of the Union.

Given that the economic activities of the Member States are guided by European law, the activities of individual **citizens** are influenced and governed to a large extent by the European policies which dictate that law. Regulations on the right of entry and residence in the Member States, vocational training, major regional infrastructure, protection of the environment and of the consumer and the prices of foodstuffs, to mention but a few, are all the outcome of the various European policies. Citizens are aware that the Community has provided a guarantee of peace and prosperity in Western Europe for the last forty years and therefore support the idea of the Community in principle. But this Community - confounded with the European Union - is perceived as something distant, formless, cumbersome and incomprehensible. They are totally unaware of the extent to which they are surrounded by the workings of the Union in their daily and professional life. We examine the reasons and the remedies of this lack of awareness in the next part, because citizens' assent is very important for the outlook of the European construction.

Curiously enough, the European Union is better perceived by those outside than those inside it. Through its development aid policy, its common commercial policy and external relations, the EU has a **strong presence on the world stage**. Whereas at the outset the Community was viewed with indifference, scepticism or even hostility by third countries, it is now recognized as being a major economic, commercial and increasingly political power. The Third World countries more and more frequently turn to the Community to seek help with their development, the industrial nations negotiate their trade agreements directly with the Community and its neighbours are, with different degrees of insistence, seeking membership. "Objective '92" has fired the imaginations not only of the citizens of the Member States but also of those of third countries. The prospect of a united, democratic, free and prosperous Western Europe precipitated the fall of the Communist regimes in Eastern Europe just as much as perestroika did. More generally, Europe's experiment with economic and political integration is being watched with close attention throughout the world and countries in other regions of the globe are trying to imitate it.

European outlook

When at the end of the eighties and more exactly at the end of 1989 European history suddenly gathered pace with the collapse of the Communist regimes in Eastern Europe, the sceptics thought that the 1992 venture would be called into question or placed on the back burner. Ignorant of the continent's economic imperatives, some saw the collapse of the Iron Curtain and the end of the Cold War as the end of the raison d'être of the Community which they perceived as a simple emanation of this Cold War. Impressed by the economic power of Germany, others thought that the latter would henceforth lose interest in the process of

European construction and buckle down to its own reunification. Some, still living in the past, saw this reunification as a danger to peace in Europe.

The European Union has disproved them all. **Its presence in Europe is central** and irrefutable. As the reader of this book has certainly found out, the European Union monitors the free exchange of industrial and agricultural goods between its members. It stimulates and supports the development of its poorer regions. It guarantees the rights of the workers of its members. It imposes the same rules for the protection of the environment to all of them. It encourages the competitiveness of their industries by imposing uniform rules of competition and by supporting their efforts for research and development. It ensures the respect of the rights of its citizens to travel, to live and to work wherever they choose on its territory. It makes possible the access of all citizens to the universal services of banks, insurances, telecommunications and audiovisual offered in the large European area. It prepares the future by setting the bases of transport, energy and telecommunications trans-European networks, as well as those of the information society.

The Union contributes also to the elevation of the standard of living of its citizens. There are certainly still important differences of prosperity between regions, that the Union endeavours to iron out. However, a **European social model** exists already and guarantees, not only the fundamental human rights and the democratic and pluralistic principles, but also the fundamental rights of workers: training adapted to the technical progress, fair pay allowing decent living conditions and social protection covering the hazards of life, illness, unemployment, old age. This social model, which is attacked by those who would like to dispose in Europe, as elsewhere in the world, of a cheap labour force, but which is defended by the immense majority of labour unions and political parties in Europe, places the European Union in the van of social progress in the world.

Why then do opinion polls reveal that these citizens are not satisfied with its realizations and convinced of its benefits? For two principal reasons. First, because they ignore them. The governments, when they propose innovating laws to national parliaments or when they change their administrative practices rarely, because of their "electoral strategy", take the trouble to explain to the general public that they are thus transposing Community Directives and Regulations into national law or administrative practices. The media rarely report the realizations of the Union because they are too technical, too detailed and often quite difficult to understand. They extensively report, instead, the problems, the failures and the disagreements within the Union because these are easier to understand by the large public and more liable to be analyzed and criticized in an objective or subjective manner. The result is a deep frustration of the public, which quite sincerely believes that the European Union is rather a "disunion" of European people, unable to solve their problems and even responsible of increasing some of them, such as unemployment. Second, the disenchantment of Europeans, and particularly the younger among them, for their Union arises from the fact that they expect ever more important results from it. The preservation of peace among peoples, that just half a century ago were still killing each-other, the unprecedented affluence of goods and services on the Old Continent, the possibilities to travel, to live and to work anywhere as at home, have become matters of course to Europeans, and more particularly to the young who have not suffered the inconveniences of their non-existence.

The conclusion is simple. To survive, **the European Union needs to advance perpetually while drawing closer to its citizens**. The two postulates go together. Every time it takes a step forward - and it takes hundreds of such steps every year in all fields - the Union must take pains to explain to the large public, through the mass media, in a simple language, the reasons of its movement, the consequences of inertia and the benefits of its action for the interests of everyone and of the whole. This would not be propaganda, but information necessary in any democratic community, concerned for the participation of all its members into the communal life through an exact information allowing a correct judgment. Community legislation, that guarantees peace and prosperity in the old Continent is too precious to be left at the mercy of demagogues, who kindle old nationalisms in order to divide and rule. Likewise, the European Union, through its institutions - the Commission, the Council, the Parliament - should insist that its Member States introduce the teaching of European integration in the high schools. This, again, would not be an indoctrination dangerous for the democracy, but, on the contrary, a socialization of the young, necessary for the right functioning of the democratic institutions which will concern them later in their life.

The perpetual movement of the Union is provided for in Article 235 EC, which authorizes the Community institutions to take the appropriate measures concerning actions not provided for by the Treaty but necessary to attain one of its objectives. The very fact that the States, which signed the Maastricht Treaty, provided in its Article N the revision of this Treaty in 1996, just three years after its coming into force, is remarkable. It shows that the authors of this Treaty did not consider it as an end in itself but as the legal basis of a stage of European integration. It also shows that they followed the construction method taught by Schuman and Monnet, which is that of a step by step advance after careful evaluation of the previous experience. Indeed, European integration could not and should not be brought to an end one day. It is a continuous process which aims at the ever closer union of European peoples. The 1996 **Intergovernmental Conference (IGC)** should, thus, treat the next stage of the European construction, endeavouring to clarify certain points that were voluntarily left in half-darkness in Maastricht, simplify the texts of the Treaty and, at the same time, improve the mechanisms of the second and third pillars of the Union. The conclusions of the IGC will condition the success of two on-going processes, the completion of the economic and monetary union and the future enlargement of the Union.

To a large extent, the next stage of the overall integration process, pivotal for the well-being of Europeans, can be mapped out. As soon as the common market was completed, work began on the next stage, **economic and monetary union**, following the directions set at Maastricht. The scaffolding is already there, since the second stage of this union began on January 1, 1994. The vital instruments also exist and are used by the

Member States in the framework of the European Monetary System, despite the fact that they are enfeebled by international speculation. Instead of questioning the EMU, monetary instability justifies, indeed, its realization. The European Monetary Institute is already managing the EMS and preparing the passage to the third stage of EMU. The majority of central banks are already completely independent of their governments and the others will be very soon. The treasuries no longer have privileged access to the financial markets and they can no longer draw on credit lines in the central banks. Both central banks and governments act already in terms of economic rather than political criteria. When governments are tempted, in view of impending elections, to depart from the economic orthodoxy established in Maastricht and confirmed by them all at several occasions, they are soon called to order, not only by the European institutions but by their own Finance Ministers responsible for the respect of the Maastricht criteria. These criteria are not contested by any big political party in the countries of continental Europe.

The fact is that the Member States of the Union have already lost a large part of their economic sovereignty. The ability of their governments and of their central banks to operate independent national monetary policies is greatly reduced and the common institutions are not yet able to conduct a really common policy. The Member States are thus forced to speed up the progress towards economic and monetary union, which should solve this problem. Indeed, in the final stage of EMU, the European Central Bank (ECB) will control the money supply of participating countries and will be largely responsible for the stability of the single currency. The European System of Central Banks (ESCB), made up of independent national central banks, will manage the official currency reserves of the participating Member States. It will define and implement the monetary policy of the Union, including exchange-rate policy in relation to currencies of non-member countries, notably the American dollar and the Japanese yen.

Within the economic and monetary union, the major indicator of importance would be **the Union's global balance of payments** with the rest of the world. Equilibrium within the Community would already exist at this stage, as within a nation state, thanks to the mobility of production factors and financial transfers from the public and private sector. Under such circumstances, homogeneous price evolution throughout the Community would be vital. In as much as government, budgetary or monetary measures have an impact on the general level of prices, these actions in the various Member States would have to be perfectly consistent one with the other. In order to achieve this, all the essential data on government budgets, particularly the variation in the volume, outstanding balances, methods of funding and of use of the latter would be coordinated at Community level. The creation of money for the entire area and monetary and credit policy would be centralized. The broad lines of Member States' and the Union's economic policies will be determined by the Council acting by qualified majority on a recommendation of the Commission and in line with the opinion of the European Council. Regional and structural policies would no longer be in the exclusive sphere of competence of the Member States.

The single currency will complement the single market by facilitating transfrontier exchanges and investments. It will, thus, promote the competitiveness of the European economy and consequently job creation. Although it is true that the single currency by itself will not create new jobs and that active employment policies will be needed to that end, it is false to say that the single currency will engender unemployment; as if the existence of fifteen different currencies had prevented unemployment to grow these last years! On the other hand, it is certain that the passage to the single currency will imply considerable transfers of national sovereignty and major constraints on the governments of the Member States. Although the possibility of autonomous monetary policy is already greatly reduced because of the interdependence of their economies and of the free movement of capital, it is not to be excluded that some of them might refuse to accept these new obligations; and others might not be able to fulfill the necessary conditions for participation in the third phase of the EMU. What would happen in such a case? Those Member States which were willing and able to move to the third stage of EMU, would press ahead with European construction. The others would remain at a lower stage in the process of European construction, namely that of the common market, until the time that they would be able and willing to join the first ones. This is the model of organized flexibility (envisioned by the Treaty for the changeover to the single currency), which consists in the pursuit of a common objective at various paces and differs radically from the model of "pick-and choose Europe" (e.g. the social protocol), which disowns the common objectives and the links and bonds that it engenders and which is, therefore, rejected by the vast majority of the Member States.

The phases for the changeover to the single currency, the criteria allowing its adoption and the mechanisms which will determine the relations between the countries which will have adopted this currency among themselves and with the others are provided in their broad lines in the Treaty on the Union and their details have been specified by the European Council. After the meeting of the latter in Madrid in December 1995 it is known that: the decision to launch EMU, with the designation of the participating countries, will be taken early in 1998; the irrevocable fixing of the conversion rates among the participating currencies and against the Euro will take place on 1 January 1999; Euro banknotes and coins will start to circulate alongside national notes and coins by 1 January 2002 and will replace the latter, at most, six months later. It is also known that the vast majority of the governments of the Member States take hard measures in order to reorganize their public finances and thus meet the Maastricht criteria, which themselves have established and confirmed on several occasions. What is not known yet is the number of Member States which will satisfy these criteria at the beginning of 1998 and will thus be the first to adopt the single currency. The problem is not so much the relations between those first of the class and those who will strive to join them soon after and who will certainly benefit from the experience of the first. The problem consists rather in the relations between the Member

States, which would have set as objective the adoption of the single currency and those that would reject this objective.

The second knot of questions, which in contrast to the first must be resolved by the Intergovernmental Conference, concerns **justice and home affairs**, and thus the free movement of persons. In order to translate into practice this fundamental freedom, some Member States have had to resort to an ad hoc agreement (the Schengen Agreement), which does not how- ever offer the same guarantees as Community law. These Member States as well as the Commission and the Parliament advocate the "communita- rization" of practically all fields covered by Article K.1. The Treaty itself in Article B invites the Member States to examine whether the policies and forms of cooperation introduced by it, including those under Article K, need to be revised so as to ensure the effectiveness of the mechanisms and the institutions of the Community. Indeed, if common policies for visas, for the asylum and for immigration are to be implemented and if the fight against drug-trafficking and organized crime are to be effective, there should be adopted for these issues, which now depend partly on the intergovernmental method and partly on the Community method, always and only the latter. This method implies decision-making by qualified majority and full implication in these affairs of the Commission and of the Court of Justice to ensure the respect of the decisions taken. There is a paradox in the fact that the adversaries of the Community method, those who refuse the resolution of these problems by common effort, are the same who evoke them as proofs of the incapacity of the Fifteen to manage in common their justice and home affairs. If this paradox persists after the conclusion of the work of the IGC, would the Member States which believe in the Community method not be forced to go ahead alone in the frame- work of a Schengen-type agreement or of a more vast arrangement cover- ing monetary affairs, justice and home affairs as well as common foreign and security policy?

The situation is similar in this last area. The Treaty on the EU invites the Union to "assert its identity on the international scene", but it does not give it the means to do so. For the time-being the external activities of the Union are conducted through two parallel channels: the Community method in the fields of foreign trade and of aid to development; and the loose mechanisms of the common foreign and security policy. This dual- ism does not allow the Union to exercise all its influence in international affairs. Developing an effective **common foreign and security policy** is a time-consuming process, for it involves the development of concerted practice, the ability to analyze situations jointly, and systematic searching for the common interest, all particularly sensitive elements, relying upon the traditional modes of expression of national sovereignty much more than economic affairs. Time is not in favour of the slow apprenticeship of foreign policy by the European Union, however, for the public expects its effective involvement in the solution of international conflicts and non- member countries have difficulties in distinguishing clearly the responsi- bilities of the different parts of the Union, and the legal status and powers of each. Indeed, for third countries, which were accustomed to consider the Community as a single entity, the functional duplication of the Community and the Union puts into doubt the ability of the one or the other to commit itself effectively at the international level. The loss in terms of identity and impact in the international sphere is considerable and the cost in terms of public affection is exorbitant. This is why, in order to reinforce the coherence and rapidity of foreign policy, several Member States, backed by the Commission and the European Parliament, advocate bringing together the various strands comprising foreign relations into a single effective whole, with structures integrating WEU with EU, enabling the latter to speak with one voice by having recourse to procedures based on qualified majority.

In any case, even if no fundamental change were envisaged concerning the two non-Community pillars of the EU, the European **institutions** should be prepared to function in the context of a Union composed of some twenty-six members. These institutions - which were imagined in order to manage the customs union and the common market between six Member States and which were adjusted in order to manage an ever growing number of Community policies and serve successively, nine, twelve, fifteen Member States - could not function effectively when the EU would count four times the number of the original members and would have advanced towards the stage of economic and monetary union and, possibly, that of political union as well. The Commission could not still function effectively as a collegial organ if its members were not reduced to one by Member State or even to one for two or three small Member States. A Council composed of nearly thirty members would be condemned to inertia, if its decisions were not taken by qualified majority, possibly redefined in order to give more weight to the more populous States. So as to simplify and at the same time democratize the decion-making process, the European Parliament should be involved in all decisions of the Union through one and only procedure instead of the three or four actual ones which differentiate its responsibility. In a few words, the deepening of the Union should precede its widening, to avoid its dilution into a vast and soulless free trade area.

The big question is to what extent the new or, rather, the refurbished institutions would have a federal character. It should be easily understood that the States, which would have united their currencies and closely coordinated their economic policies, which in addition would want to create a common home and judicial area, place under common command certain units of their armies and have a common strong voice in the international scene, would be led to create federal institutions able to compensate the losses of national sovereignty that all these changes would entail. No one ignores that some Member States are firmly opposed to those changes. In a group of democratic States, it is out of the question that some would impose their will to the others. It is not possible that those that would want to march forward carry along those that do not want or cannot follow them, but these should neither block the progress of the first.

In view of the unanimity requirement for the modification of the Treaty on the Union, every effort should be brought about by the Member States to agree on common objectives and on the terms and conditions for attaining them, including the differentiation in time. But the Member

States should not try to arrive to a strained compromise, which would not really satisfy anyone. If at the end of the work of the Intergovernmental Conference they should ascertain a net division as to the objectives of integration, they should rather decide to ask their citizens by referendum some simple questions on their choice of a model of European construction. The first model could be based on a Maastricht II Treaty, integrating the amendments accepted by the majority of the Member States after the conclusion of the work of the IGC, simplifying the Community Treaties, communitarizing the JHA and CFSP and arranging definitely and positively the problems of the opt outs in the social and monetary fields. For the States which have ratified the Treaty without any opt-outs the question of the passage to the single currency would not be posed and this would follow its course. The second model could comprise all the reforms of the first and provide, in addition, new institutions of a federal type, able to manage effectively the single currency, the single internal area and the common foreign and security policy, while preserving the national and cultural identity of the peoples of Europe.

Given the existing model of the European Economic Area, which preserves at maximum national sovereignty inside a vast free trade area, every European nation would in fact have a choice of participation to one of three concentric circles of European cooperation and/or integration: a vast free trade area; an economic and monetary union comprising a single market and a single currency; and a nucleus of States having federal institutions and a really common foreign and security policy.

All governments should describe in the same clear and correct way the three possible models of cooperation/integration. In each country a large debate should take place, after the conclusion of the work of the IGC, culminating, after the passage to the single currency, i.e. at the end of 2002, with a popular consultation by referendum on the model of integration preferred by each nation. Only then should governments sign and Parliaments ratify the treaty preferred by their people. The States which are candidates to accession and their people should also have the choice of participation to the European Economic Area alone or to the economic and monetary union or to the federation. Thus, there would no longer exist doubts as to the model of integration or cooperation wanted by each European nation. All of them would participate to the vast free trade area. Some would in addition participate to a common market, comprising a customs union and common and/or Community policies. Finally, some others would go farther in their economic, monetary and political integration establishing among themselves a federation. All of them would thus have with each other more or less strong ties of cooperation. Of course, the doors between the three circles should stay open so that the nations which would initially opt for a a free trade area or a common market, could join the federation later on.

The advantages of the latter should normally become felt very soon and it could become a pole of attraction for the nations which, at first, would have legitimate hesitations. On the basis of past experience it can, in any event, be surmised how the European Union could become, in the 21st century, a **world superpower**, the only vision that could excite the imagination of Europeans and give them confidence in themselves and in their common future.

By putting in place its customs union and its common commercial policy, the Community became a **commercial superpower**, which is respected and heeded in the context of the GATT and of the World Trade Organization. With the completion of its internal market, the European Union has in addition become an **economic superpower**, which can confer at equal terms with the other members of the triad, the United States and Japan, and, tomorrow, with the other superpowers in gestation, China and the Commonwealth of Independent States. In view of the globalization of production and economies, only the single market, completed by its accompanying policies, can provide European undertakings with a sufficient basis in order to face on equal terms the multinational companies of the other industrial powers. The single market, irrigated by trans-European networks, can allow the European States to access by their own means the information society and not stay irremediably behind in the race of world civilization. But the single market cannot compensate the dispersion of efforts which subsists in other fields and weakens the European States.

To become a real internal market the single market must be complemented by a single currency. Such a currency could protect the internal market from the international speculation, which perturbs intra-Community exchanges and capital movements. This currency could measure itself on equal terms against the dollar and the yen, serve as a reference currency in international exchanges and as a reserve currency for small and big investors throughout the world. The single currency could thus make the federation issuing it a **monetary superpower**. It is obvious that the more numerous were the Member States which would have adopted the single currency while satisfying the pre-established criteria, the stronger would this be and the more able to ensure the prosperity of Europeans.

Likewise, a European federation could become a **political superpower**. To that effect, it should have a real common foreign and security policy and institutions able to implement it: an executive and a legislative organ of federal nature and a common army or national armies under common command. Under those conditions, a European federation could make its voice heard in the international scene, take an effective part in the settlement of international conflicts and face the religious fundamentalisms which become ever more menacing. Each of its Member States should, of course, abandon an important part of its national sovereignty. This would be the price to be paid by a nation in order to be part of a political and military superpower, thus increasing its national security and its influence in world affairs. How many of the States of the actual European Union will be ready to pay this price in order to enter with a firm step into the 21st century? The answer to this question should be given before the end of this century.

The radical changes in both East and West have given Europe a new role on the international stage. After the collapse of the Soviet Empire, Europe can take its destiny into its own hands and become the political superpower to which its economic weight permits it to aspire. In a world which from bipolar has become unipolar, it is extremely useful for international balance that a free and pluralist Europe, with no expansionist ambitions, assume the international role endowed upon it by its cultural affinities and privileged relations with many different parts of the world. Its unique experiment of a peaceful and democratic integration of nations, which only yesterday were killing each other, can place Europe once again at the forefront of human progress. It must assume its world responsibilities by giving the nation-State a new meaning, serving better its interests within a strong, democratic, peaceful and prosperous entity. Europe has invented the model of democratic government, the model of the nation State and the model of economic integration. It can certainly invent a model of political integration preserving what constitutes its wealth, the cultural diversity of its peoples.

Bibliography on European outlook

□ BUZELAY Alain, *Intégration et désintégration européennes*, Economica, Paris, 1996.

□ *Challenge 96*, IGC Intelligence Service (Belmont group), Brussels, 1996.

□ CLUB DE FLORENCE, *Europe: l'impossible statu quo*, Éditions Stock, Paris, 1996.

□ COFFEY Peter, *The Future of Europe*, Edward Elgar Publishing Limited, Cheltenham, Glos, 1995.

□ COMMISSION EUROPÉENNE, *Conférence intergouvernementale 1996. Rapport de la Commission pour le groupe de réflexion*, OPOCE, Bruxelles, Luxembourg, 1995.

□ De BERRANGER, Thibaut, *Constitutions nationales et construction communautaire*, Librairie Générale de Droit et de Jurisprudence, Paris, 1995.

□ DEHOUSSE Renaud (ed.), *Europe after Maastricht. An Ever Closer Union?*, Verlag C. H. Beck, München, 1994.

□ DESCHEEMAEKERE François, *L'Union européenne: les grands défis*, Les Éditions d'Organisation, Paris, 1995.

□ DUFF Andrew, PINDER John, PRYCE Roy (ed.), *Maastricht and Beyond. Building the European Union*, The Federal Trust, London, 1994.

□ DUVERGER Maurice, *L'Europe dans tous ses États*, Presses Universitaires de France, Paris, 1995.

□ GUELLEC Jean, *Relations internationales. Naissance du troisième millénaire*, Ellipses, Paris, 1994.

□ HOLM Erik, *Europe, a Political Culture? Fundamental Issues for the 1996 IGC*, Royal Institute of International Affairs, London, 1994.

□ LUDLOW Peter (ed.), *Preparing for 1996 and a Larger European Union: Principles and Priorities*, CEPS Special Report N° 6, Bruxelles, 1995.

▫ MAILLET Pierre, VELO Dario, *L'Europe à géométrie variable. Transition vers l'intégration*, Éditions l'Harmattan, Paris, 1994.

▫ MASCLET Jean-Claude, *Où en est l'Europe politique?*, La Documentation Française, Paris, 1994.

▫ MATTERA Alfonso (ed.), "La Conférence intergouvernementale de 1996", *Revue du Marché unique européen*, N° 3/1995.

▫ MOUSSIS Nicolas, "Au-delà de la CIG de 1996: Les grands enjeux de l'Union européenne", in *Revue du Marché commun et de l'Union européenne*, n° 394, janvier 1996, pp. 15-20.

▫ SABOURIN Paul, *L'État-nation face aux Europes*, PUF, Collection "Perspectives internationales", Paris, 1994.

▫ TELO' Mario (sous la dir. de), *Démocratie et construction européenne*, Éditions de l'Université de Bruxelles, Bruxelles, 1995.

▫ VANDAMME Jacques, MOUTON Jean-Denis (sous la dir. de), *L'avenir de l'Union européenne: élargir et approfondir*, Presses Interuniversitaires européennes, Bruxelles, 1995.

▫ VAN TARTWIJK-NOVEY, *The European House of Cards. Towards a United States of Europe?*, Macmillan, Basingstoke, Hants, 1995.

ALPHABETICAL INDEX